Lecture Notes in Computer Science **16260**

The series Lecture Notes in Computer Science (LNCS), including its subseries Lecture Notes in Artificial Intelligence (LNAI) and Lecture Notes in Bioinformatics (LNBI), has established itself as a medium for the publication of new developments in computer science and information technology research, teaching, and education.

LNCS enjoys close cooperation with the computer science R & D community, the series counts many renowned academics among its volume editors and paper authors, and collaborates with prestigious societies. Its mission is to serve this international community by providing an invaluable service, mainly focused on the publication of conference and workshop proceedings and postproceedings. LNCS commenced publication in 1973.

Fabrice Kordon · Laure Petrucci · Jörg Desel ·
Jetty Kleijn · Maciej Koutny · Lukasz Mikulski
Editors

Transactions on Petri Nets and Other Models of Concurrency XVIII

Editors-in-Chief
Fabrice Kordon
Sorbonne University
Paris, France

Laure Petrucci
University Sorbonne Paris Nord
Villetaneuse, France

Editors
Jörg Desel
FernUniversität in Hagen
Hagen, Germany

Maciej Koutny
Newcastle University
Newcastle upon Tyne, UK

Jetty Kleijn
Leiden University
Leiden, The Netherlands

Lukasz Mikulski
Nicolaus Copernicus University in Toruń
Toruń, Poland

ISSN 0302-9743 ISSN 1611-3349 (electronic)
Lecture Notes in Computer Science
ISSN 1867-7193 ISSN 1867-7746 (electronic)
Transactions on Petri Nets and Other Models of Concurrency
ISBN 978-3-662-73304-2 ISBN 978-3-662-73305-9 (eBook)
https://doi.org/10.1007/978-3-662-73305-9

This Springer imprint is published by the registered company Springer-Verlag GmbH, DE,
part of Springer Nature.
The registered company address is: Heidelberger Platz 3, 14197 Berlin, Germany

Preface by Editors-in-Chief

The 18th issue of LNCS Transactions on Petri Nets and Other Models of Concurrency (ToPNoC) presents peer-reviewed articles based on the lectures delivered during the 6th Advanced Course on Petri Nets (ACPN2023, Toruń, Poland, 3–8 September 2023). We would like to thank the four guest editors of this special issue: Jörg Desel, Jetty Kleijn, Łukasz Mikulski, and Maciej Koutny. Moreover, we would like to thank all authors, reviewers, and organisers of the Advanced Course, without whom this issue of ToPNoC would not have been possible.

February 2026

Fabrice Kordon
Laure Petrucci

LNCS Transactions on Petri Nets and Other Models of Concurrency: Aims and Scope

ToPNoC aims to publish papers from all areas of Petri nets and other models of concurrency ranging from theoretical work to tool support and industrial applications. The foundations of Petri nets were laid by the pioneering work of Carl Adam Petri and his colleagues in the early 1960s. Since then, a huge volume of material has been developed and published in journals and books as well as presented at workshops and conferences.

The annual International Conference on Application and Theory of Petri Nets and Concurrency started in 1980. For more information on the international Petri net community, see: https://world.petrinet.net/.

All issues of ToPNoC are LNCS volumes. Hence they appear in all main libraries and are also accessible on SpringerLink (electronically).

ToPNoC contains:

- Revised versions of a selection of the best papers from workshops and tutorials concerned with Petri nets and concurrency
- Special issues related to particular subareas
- Other papers invited for publication in ToPNoC
- Papers submitted directly to ToPNoC by their authors

Like all other journals, ToPNoC has an Editorial Board, which is responsible for the quality of the journal. The members of the board assist in the reviewing of papers submitted or invited for publication in ToPNoC. Moreover, they may make recommendations concerning collections of papers for special issues. The Editorial Board consists of prominent researchers within the Petri net community and in related fields.

Topics

The topics covered include: system design and verification using nets; analysis and synthesis; structure and behavior of nets; relationships between net theory and other approaches; causality/partial order theory of concurrency; net-based semantical, logical and algebraic calculi; symbolic net representation (graphical or textual); computer tools for nets; experience with using nets, case studies; educational issues related to nets; higher-level net models; timed and stochastic nets; and standardization of nets.

Also included are applications of nets to: biological systems; security systems; e-commerce and trading; embedded systems; environmental systems; flexible manufacturing systems; hardware structures; health and medical systems; office automation; operations research; performance evaluation; programming languages; protocols and networks; railway networks; real-time systems; supervisory control; telecommunications; cyber physical systems; and workflow.

For more information about ToPNoC see: https://link.springer.com/series/8379.

Submission of Manuscripts

Manuscripts should follow LNCS formatting guidelines, and should be submitted as PDF or zipped PostScript files to topnoc-submission@petrinet.net. All queries should be addressed to the same e-mail address.

LNCS Transactions on Petri Nets and Other Models of Concurrency: Editorial Board

Preface by Guest Editors

This volume of ToPNoC contains articles based on the lectures delivered during the 6th Advanced Course on Petri Nets (ACPN 2023, 3–8 September 2023) hosted by the Faculty of Mathematics and Computer Science, Nicolaus Copernicus University, Toruń, Poland:

- **Modeling Distributed Systems and Processes with Petri Nets – the Big Picture**, by Jörg Desel and Julia Anna Fleischer, is an introduction to Petri nets focusing on modelling as a discipline and on distributed systems as the target of modelling. Based on Stachowiak's fundamental characterization of modelling, it discusses what Petri net models actually model, leading to a strict distinction between modelled systems and their models, and also between system behaviour and model behaviour.
- **Essentials of Petri Nets**, by Wolfgang Reisig and Peter Fettke, highlights some concepts and aspects of Petri nets that are often neglected, but that the authors consider important or interesting, or that Carl Adam Petri emphasized. In particular, it gives a historical overview of some aspects of the development of Petri nets, including distributed runs, schematic modelling, and composition.
- **Semantics of Concurrent Systems**, by Ryszard Janicki, Jetty Kleijn, Maciej Koutny, and Łukasz Mikulski, presents different classes of partial orders and relational structures which can specify sets of individual runs of concurrent systems, and are also able to capture intrinsic relationships between executed events, e.g., causality and independence. The paper also describes language-theoretic constructs corresponding to the different classes of partial orders and relational structures.
- **From Behaviour to Nets via Regions**, by Maciej Koutny, Łukasz Mikulski, and Marta Pietkiewicz-Koutny, provides an introduction to the theory of regions of transition systems which support a method for synthesising Petri net models from given transition systems. The paper then describes the recent application of regions to the synthesis of Petri nets where transitions have non-atomic duration, and the dynamic behaviour is captured using interval partial orders.
- **The Reachability Problem in Petri Nets: Decidability and Hardness**, by Sławomir Lasota, is concerned with the fundamental algorithmic and verification problem, where one asks whether from a given initial configuration there exists a sequence of valid execution steps reaching a given final configuration. This paper aims at an easy introduction to the problem and to some ideas underlying the complexity bounds developed in recent years.
- **Model Checking Timed and Strategic Properties**, by Étienne André, Wojciech Penczek, and Laure Petrucci, deals with the verification of real-time systems using temporal logic methods which have proven valuable, particularly in the context of finite abstract models that can be analysed using model checking techniques. Essentially, this approach involves determining whether a temporal formula holds true for a model that represents all possible system computations.

- **Analysis and Synthesis of Some Subclasses of Petri Nets**, by Raymond Devillers and Kamila Barylska, presents a range of results concerned with important theoretical aspects of Petri nets. The main issues discussed are synthesis algorithms designed for specific classes of Petri nets, enabling faster solution acquisition.
- **Design Decisions in Process Discovery and the Inductive Miner Framework**, by Dirk Fahland, presents several fundamental design decisions and heuristics used in process discovery for resolving the trade-off between fitness and the other quality criteria. It specifically studies discovery algorithms built on the "directly-follows abstraction" of an event log, showing how to create variations of existing process discovery techniques or design new ones that may be more suitable for a particular analysis task.
- **Extracting and Pre-processing Event Logs**, by Dirk Fahland and Xixi Lu, focuses on event log extraction considering it an act of modelling as the analyst has to consciously choose which features of the raw data are used for describing which behaviour of which entities. The paper provides fundamental concepts and formalizations and discusses design decisions in event log extraction from a raw event table and for event log pre-processing.
- **Application of Coloured Petri Nets for Modelling the Software Architecture of the SmartOcean Data Service Platform**, by Lars Michael Kristensen, presents the Coloured Petri Nets (CPNs) modelling of the SmartOcean software platform aimed at providing cloud-based services for data-driven systems and applications relying on marine data. This work exemplifies representative CPN modelling patterns for system-of-systems modelling, service provision and consumption, and service interaction.
- **A Gentle Tour Through a Petri Net Model Checking Tool**, by Karsten Wolf, surveys the main ingredients of a Petri net model checking tool. For each topic, it presents a selection of methods with emphasis on simplicity. The paper provides a comprehensive overview on what tool developers should take care of when designing their own competitive Petri net model checking tool.

We invited all ACPN 2023 lecturers to submit papers based on the material they delivered during the course, and we managed an anonymous review process where each paper was thoroughly reviewed by at least two reviewers, both to evaluate their intrinsic quality and to assess their overall contribution to the relevant sub-field. We are therefore extremely grateful to the reviewers, who helped us evaluate each article and provided valuable feedback to the respective authors. Most importantly, we would like to recognize the authors themselves, whose work is the reason for this special issue of ToPNoC.

November 2025

Jörg Desel
Jetty Kleijn
Maciej Koutny
Łukasz Mikulski

Organization

Program Committee

Jörg Desel	FernUniversität in Hagen, Germany
Jetty Kleijn	LIACS, Leiden University, The Netherlands
Fabrice Kordon	LIP6, Sorbonne Université & CNRS, France
Maciej Koutny	Newcastle University, UK
Łukasz Mikulski	Nicolaus Copernicus University in Toruń, Poland
Laure Petrucci	LIPN, Université Sorbonne Paris Nord & CNRS, France

Reviewers

Kamila Barylska	Nicolaus Copernicus University in Toruń
Robin Bergenthum	FernUniversität in Hagen
Jörg Desel	FernUniversität in Hagen
Raymond Devillers	Université Libre de Bruxelles
Mateusz Kamiński	Nicolaus Copernicus University in Toruń
Jetty Kleijn	LIACS, Leiden University
Maciej Koutny	Newcastle University
Damian Kurpiewski	Polish Academy of Sciences
Łukasz Mikulski	Nicolaus Copernicus University in Toruń
Laure Petrucci	LIPN, Université Sorbonne Paris Nord & CNRS
Piotr Przymus	Nicolaus Copernicus University in Toruń
Natalia Sidorova	Eindhoven University of Technology
Walter Vogler	Augsburg University
Karsten Wolf	University of Rostock
Alex Yakovlev	Newcastle University

Contents

Lectures

Modeling Distributed Systems and Processes with Petri Nets – The Big Picture

Jörg Desel(✉) and Julia Anna Fleischer

FernUniversität in Hagen, Hagen, Germany
{joerg.desel,julia-anna.fleischer}@fernuni-hagen.de

Abstract. This introduction to Petri nets focuses on modeling as a discipline and on distributed systems as the target of modeling. Based on Stachowiak's fundamental characterization of modeling, we discuss what Petri net models actually model. This leads to a strict distinction between modeled systems and their models, and also between system behavior and model behavior. In a "Big Picture" we locate the typical practices of Petri net modeling of systems. Furthermore, we consider typical Petri net properties and add the concept of process in this terminology.

1 Introduction

This contribution is not an introduction to Petri nets per se, but rather an introduction to Petri net modeling. We will approach Petri nets not merely as a formal language but as a modeling tool for complex dynamic systems and their behavior. Furthermore, we ask not only how systems are modeled, but also why. We will provide one big picture that includes the roles of systems in the real world, Petri net models of systems, behavior of systems and of Petri nets, properties of systems and of models, as well as their analysis. We will identify processes (in the sense of business processes) as specific systems that are embedded in larger systems but have their own behavioral properties. This overall picture will prove very helpful in defining various practices in the field, such as modeling itself (to better understand a system and its behavior), model validation, model synthesis, and the different variants of system and process mining.

In the following section, we review the state of the art in Petri net modeling with a special emphasis on different paradigms for behavior modeling, and also present our perspective. Section three applies Herbert Stachowiak's modeling theory to Petri net modeling in detail and provides precise terminology to distinguish important aspects of Petri net modeling. The most important application area for Petri nets is distributed systems; in fact, they were invented precisely for this purpose. Of course, there are also applications in areas where distributedness plays a less significant role. However, to understand the principles of Petri net theory and the description of behavior, one must consider examples of systems that actually consist of many distributed components. This is the aim of Section four.

F. Kordon et al. (Eds.): *Transactions on Petri Nets and Other Models of Concurrency XVIII*, LNCTPN 16260, pp. 3–28, 2026.
https://doi.org/10.1007/978-3-662-73305-9_1

The Big Picture announced in the title of this work will be presented in Section five. It places all the prepared ingredients in relation to each other. This image can be used to clarify and differentiate between different Petri net modeling practices. Section six provides a closer look at the modeling process itself. Finally, Section seven is devoted to properties of systems and of business processes and their respective Petri net models. Processes will be interpreted as systems, and thus process models as particular system models, which, however, differ crucially from other models.

Key aspects of this work have already been presented in [9]; the present contribution elaborates and expands upon them.

Related work

This article is complementary to introductory texts on Petri nets, which contain a careful mathematical description of the syntax, semantics, analysis, and synthesis of Petri nets. Of the many recommended textbooks on Petri nets in general, we would like to highlight the recent book by Eike Best and Raymond Devillers [3]. More focused on verification techniques is the book [15] by Guanjun Liu.

The textbook of Wolfgang Reisig [18] is more aligned with our objective because it relates Petri net models to reality, but not as explicitly as we do in this article. Although it focuses on the composition of Petri nets, the book [12] is also suitable as an introduction to Petri net modeling.

Other Petri net textbooks concentrate on particular application areas and their special requirements in modeling. Although somewhat older, the textbook [13] should be mentioned here as it deals with larger development cycles of software and hardware. One of many introductions to Petri nets for business process modeling is [2].

The field can also be approached via different Petri net classes which can either restrict the general Petri net definition, such as free-choice Petri nets [6] or extend it, e.g. by considering duration times [16].

The field can also be accessed via tools such as GreatSPN or CPN, or WoPeD for beginners. There are older publications on these tools, but current versions and current reports can be easily found online.

Finally, traditionally the proceedings of the regularly held Advanced Courses on Petri Nets represent the state of the art in the field. In fact, this volume (in which this article is found) contains contributions to the Advanced Course 2023 on Petri Nets in Toruń, Poland.

2 Petri Net Models

Most introductions to Petri net theory begin by emphasizing that Petri nets are particularly well-suited for modeling distributed systems, though not exclusively. These introductions typically proceed with the formal definition of Petri nets and the token game, which can be formalized in a seductively simple way in the form of transition sequences. The modeled system, together with its behavior, is not considered further and is often even identified with its model. Such definitions often overlook several essential facts:

1. Considering a model without its original may be useful for theoretical considerations, but it makes little sense for modeling. The model itself, as well as its behavior and properties, is only valuable if it can be related to what is being modeled.
2. A modeled system is, in most cases, distributed. This means that it consists of components that operate independently of each other, except when they communicate. Furthermore, each modeled system communicates with components that have not been modeled. Therefore, a system model – or, better yet, a model of each system component – must explicitly provide interfaces through which this communication can take place.
3. The core of Carl Adam Petri's original idea was not limited to places, transitions, edges, and tokens, but fundamentally included concurrency as a central assumption. This focus on concurrency is the foundation of the theory that Petri developed. Concurrency is not primarily a property of the behavior of a system model, but of the behavior of the system itself, resulting from the assumption that the system is distributed. Therefore, it is unavoidable to explicitly distinguish and relate the behavior of the modeled system and the behavior of its model with a particular focus on concurrency.
4. Like any model, a Petri net model of a system is the result of a modeling process and is by no means unique. Herbert Stachowiak's general model theory teaches us that the relationship between a model and its original follows certain rules, including a pragmatic perspective that states that modeling serves a specific purpose that we must make explicit.
5. Stachowiak's work also shows that modeling always abstracts, omitting aspects of the original (and, if possible, adding nothing that does not correspond to the original). The mere decision to model with Petri nets already implies that we will emphasize discrete dynamic aspects and abstract from other aspects. The selection of a section of the observed world, which we call a *system*, means abstraction from everything else. And finally, the chosen level of abstraction is one of the decisions made during modeling. Therefore, there is almost never a single correct unique model.

Our aim is to address and consider these aspects. In this paper, we particularly focus on the relationships between the system and the model, as well as between the system and its behavior, which of course should have a strong connection with the model's behavior. As mentioned above, we postulate that the behavior of a distributed system is concurrent. This includes cases where it happens to be sequential, namely, when each two actions (i.e. each two occurrences of activities) depend on each other in either direction. This dependency is often referred to as *causality*. However, dependency simply means that one activity cannot occur unless the other activity has occurred beforehand.

A Petri net model, on the other hand, is not itself distributed but is a graph or an algebraic structure. It just models a distributed system. The occurrence rule immediately tempts one to define sequences of transitions (*occurrence sequences*) of Petri nets, which describe sequential model behavior. Since the quality of a model can be measured by the extent to which the behavior of the model matches the behavior of the modeled system, the respective behavioral concepts must match. However, the natural behavior of distributed systems is concurrent and hence not sequential in general. We are therefore faced with a discrepancy between the behavioral concepts of systems and their Petri net models.

To solve this problem, it is often assumed that, also in system runs, the set of all actions is totally ordered. This is justified by a supposed global timeline: every activity occurs at a specific point in time. Therefore, according to the assumption, if scaled precisely enough, any two actions can be objectively sequenced.

This approach is questionable for several reasons: first, there is no publicly accessible and infinitely precise global clock, and it would moreover be of little use for distributed systems. Ultimately, it contradicts modern physics, even though the systems under consideration are usually not based on such phenomena. The assumption that such a clock can be safely assumed, even if it does not exist, contradicts the modeling principle that one may only abstract, not add. Furthermore, it only creates new problems that would not otherwise exist. For example, one must then ask in which order independent activities are carried out and treat this formally like a selection from various alternatives.

Other groups of scientists, including Carl Adam Petri himself, are attempting the desired alignment of behavioral concepts on the model side. They do not represent model behavior by occurrence sequences, but rather by partially ordered structures. Their elements represent actions together with pre- and post-conditions. Their dependencies represent the causal structure in the system's behavior. In particular, concurrency at the system level is expressed by the lack of order between these model elements. These partially ordered structures are often nicely formulated as Petri nets (called *occurrence nets* or *process nets*), so that this approach can also be used as an example for Petri net morphisms. However, this approach has not been widely adopted because the definition of partially ordered Petri net runs is already too complicated. Moreover, these partially ordered model runs are actually constructed sequentially, so that an implicit occurrence sequence is secretly considered beforehand. Finally, the arguments for distributed, partially ordered runs that apply at the system level are not transferable to the model level, because a model is just a model, usually not actually physically distributed, but rather only a piece of mathematics or a suitable syntactical representation of it.

Our current approach combines both perspectives on behavior modeling: the behavior of a system is given by partially ordered runs (we intentionally avoid the term *process* here, as it will later refer to a specific subset of systems, each of which has its own runs). However, it is fine to consider occurrence sequences as the primary behavioral concept of a Petri net. But what about the relationship between these concepts? There are two possible answers, both described in detail in the literature (albeit in different contexts). First, we can consider linearizations of partially ordered runs at the system level, i.e., ordered sets of activity occurrences that do not contradict the partial order. These sequences are often considered observed *action logs* (*event logs* for business processes), since an assumed – naturally non-distributed – observer of all system activities could note and log these actions in such an order. Another observer might detect a different linearization of the same run. We can then relate these observed sequences to the occurrence sequences of the model.

Second, as already mentioned, from the occurrence sequences of a Petri net one can construct according partially ordered representations of runs, provided information about mutual dependency of transitions is known. This is done either step by step, by adding the next transition occurrence to an already existing partial order and placing this new element only "after" those transition occurrences that generated tokens that are now consumed [17]. Alternatively, concepts from *trace theory* [11] are applied that transfer an *independence relation* between transitions of a Petri net to their occurrences in sequential runs.

As a small digression, let us mention *stratified orders* of transition occurrences at this place (see [14]). Their core idea is that transitions can also occur simultaneously. This either models a possible observation of concurrent transition occurrences where the observer does not perceive any time difference between two actions, or the approach presupposes a concept of parallelism in which activities are carried out in a clocked way. Simultaneously occurring transitions are named *steps*. Sequences of steps clearly generalize occurrence sequences. A variant of this *step* semantics is *maximal step semantics* where only maximal steps (w.r.t. set inclusion) are allowed to occur. Maximal steps correspond to clocked systems without any delay.

Occurrence sequences can be considered total orders. *Step sequences* can be considered partial orders, where only transition occurrences in the same step are not ordered. Another use of partial orders "between" step sequences and arbitrary partial orders is given by *interval orders*, also discussed in detail in [14]. In an interval order, each transition occurrence is considered to take some time and thus has a starting time and an ending time ($\text{start}(x)$ and $\text{end}(x)$ for a transition occurrence x). A transition occurrence x occurs before another transition occurrence y ($x \prec y$) if x ends before y begins, i.e., if $\text{end}(x) < \text{start}(y)$. Since transition occurrences can overlap in time, they can be unordered. So $\prec$ is a partial order. However, not every partial order can be interpreted this way. If $x \prec y$ and $z \prec w$ then either $x \prec w$ or $y \prec z$ (otherwise $\text{end}(x) > \text{start}(w) > \text{end}(z) > \text{start}(y)$ which is impossible because $x \prec y$). Partial orders with the above property are called *interval orders*. The above interpretation of interval orders implicitly assumes notions of time and duration of transition occurrences.

Now we return to explicit notions of time. As already mentioned, the assumption of a generally available global clock, which leads to a linearization of all actions of a system run, is neither helpful nor realistic. However, there are other dependencies related to time in many systems. Here are some examples:

- At a railway barrier, one expects that a train can pass safely one minute after it is closed.
- An airbag opens in time after a collision to save lives.

- A processor with a known clock speed will make the result of a multiplication available in a timely manner if this value is subsequently used by other processors.

In all of these cases, we see a dependency related to time, which is not related to causality, i.e., the train does not wait for crossing cars, the driver's head does not wait for the airbag, etc. One is tempted to express these relationships in terms of numbers that represent time. In Petri nets, however, such dependencies are strictly distinguished from causal dependencies because their validity depends on the functioning of cars, airbags, or processors. If they do not function properly, there will be another behavior, usually an undesirable one. However, this behavior is not excluded by the definition of the model and is intentionally made still visible. Instead, it is possible to express such dependencies through additional assumptions and to distinguish behavior that satisfies these assumptions from general behavior. This is admittedly somewhat cumbersome, but it is a consequence of the fundamentals of Petri nets in their original form. Some authors have proposed alternative approaches to integrating time into Petri nets and their semantics, but usually at the cost of raising more questions than they answer.

3 Modeling Theory

A Petri net can be thought of as a graph, a mathematical element, or a syntactic unit that can be entered into an analysis tool [10]. However, this view does not take into account that a Petri net is a model, and therefore something is modeled by the Petri net. Since this work is about modeling systems and processes with Petri nets, we will take a closer look at models and the relationship between a model and its corresponding original, i.e. the thing modeled by the Petri net.

The General Model Theory (translated from German "Allgemeine Modelltheorie"), introduced by the philosopher and mathematician Herbert Stachowiak about 50 years ago (see [19], unfortunately only available in German), provides us with the following basic model properties that properly characterize models in computer science and related disciplines:

Fundamental Model Properties

- **Mapping.** A model is always a model of something, i.e. an image or a representation of an original, which can be natural or artificial. The original can be constructed using syntactic means, can be an idea or something from the physical world. It can be naturally occurring, engineered, or given in some other way. When models and originals are interpreted based on their attributes, the model attributes are mapped to the attributes of the original.
- **Reduction.** A model does not capture all attributes of the original but only those relevant to the model creator and/or model user. In this sense, something is reduced. In particular, an original is usually not a model of

itself. Stachowiak's did not use the word *abstraction*, which is one of the computer scientist's favorite terms. When we abstract from something of the original, we intentionally do not include it in the model.

- **Pragmatism.** A model is not per se uniquely assigned to its original. It fulfills its replacement function for a specific (human or artificial) user for a specific purpose and does so within a certain time interval.

Let us try to instantiate these rules for Petri net modeling. For illustration, we will use an example, the well-known vending machine [8]:

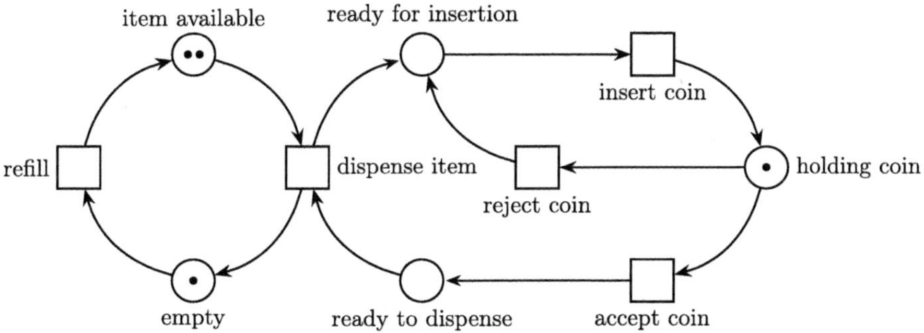

Fig. 1. A model of a vending machine

Mapping: What do we model with Petri nets?

Each Petri net model has an original, and there are several examples for this original. In particular, a Petri net model can refer to something that exists, or it is used as a blueprint for something that will exist (or at least could exist). The original can be physical, just an idea, a piece of mathematics, or something formulated syntactically, like an algorithm. All these originals have in common that they have a behavior. Therefore, there are runs (or executions) and at least local conditions whose values change during a run. Notice that behavior is not only given by a set of possible runs; for example, points of decisions also play a role for behavior specification. However, in this contribution we restrict ourselves to the view that behavior is defined by the possible runs.

Each original is embedded in a bigger original, say the real world. It is essential to identify the interfaces between the modeled and the unmodeled. The modeled segment will be called *system* in the sequel (note that, in the Petri net world, this term was also used for Petri nets with initial marking, but here we need it for a better purpose). The concept of an interface directly enables the definition of subsystems of a system and interfaces between subsystems, as well as between a system and its subsystem, and between a system and its environment.

In the vending machine example, we model its physical unit (on the left hand side) and its control (on the right hand side). Both parts can be viewed as subsystems with respective interfaces "dispense item", see Fig. 2.

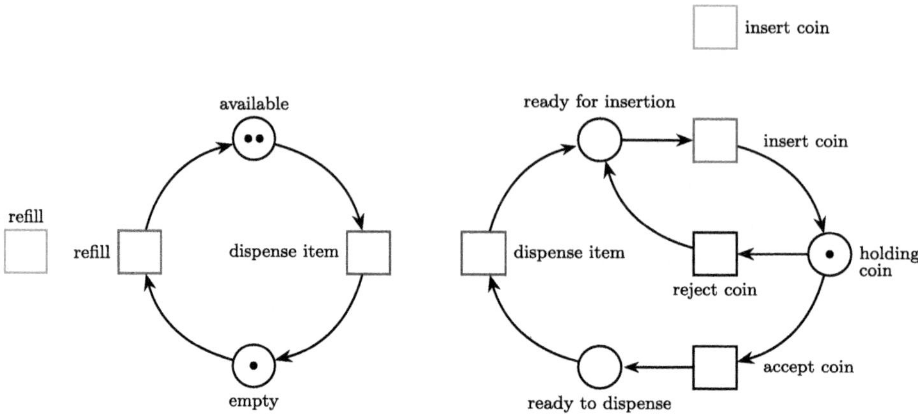

Fig. 2. Components of the vending machine model and their interfaces

It might be worth mentioning that the right model can be interpreted as an elementary net system because each place represents a condition that can either be fulfilled (marked) or not fulfilled (unmarked). Actually, in this model, always exactly one condition is fulfilled. At the same time, the right model can be viewed as a (place/transition) Petri net, as the left model. Both transitions "dispense item" can only occur when the respective transition of the other component can occur, too, as in the modeled system both activities of the physical unit and of the control can only occur together. Within each subsystem model, we call these transitions *external*, indicating that they only occur when the environment agrees. Possible users belong to the unmodeled real world, with interface "insert coin", whereas operating staff will interact via "refill". Both transitions should be considered external, too, because the modeled system will neither fire "insert coin" without a user inserting a coin nor "refill" without a corresponding physical partner.

One often encounters Petri nets whose elements have abstract names like a, b, c. These can be useful in theory and especially as examples in teaching, but they are not models in the true sense.

Reduction: What do Petri nets abstract from?

Since each Petri net models only a part of the real world, namely the system, one could argue that it abstracts from the rest. More importantly, like any modeling language, Petri net models abstract from everything that cannot (or can hardly) be expressed with Petri nets. For example, the vending machine model makes no mention of the color, weight, or price of the machine. Therefore, the choice of modeling language predetermines certain abstractions due to their representational bias.

Even when considering behavioral aspects, Petri nets typically abstract from all aspects of time. This does not apply to the global clock mentioned above, since it does not exist and is therefore not subject to abstraction. However, in Petri nets transitions model timeless state changes, which seldom refer to real changes. In particular, Petri nets abstract from continuous behavior, as expressed, for example, by differential equations. However, there are various extensions of Petri nets (e.g., *Time Petri Nets*, *Timed Petri Nets*, *Generalized stochastic Petri Nets* etc.) that take time explicitly into account. Most of these concepts also assume a global time axis.

A concrete Petri net model can also abstract from the data if it is not relevant to the behavior under consideration. And it always represents its original on a certain level of abstraction, thereby abstracting from irrelevant details.

Pragmatism: What is the purpose of a Petri net model?

Let us answer this question by an enumeration of possible purposes. A Petri net model might help to

- understand the behavior of the modeled system,
- understand the (relevant) structure of the modeled system,
- gain insights into the behavior of the modeled system by simulation,
- gain insights into the behavior of the modeled system by analysis,
- prove properties of the modeled system,
- specify a system,
- run a real system, if the model is an interpreted part of it,

and sometimes the purpose of a Petri net is purely didactic.

We will come back to the purpose of Petri net models together with Petri net-based practices in section five.

Terminology

For our further considerations, it is helpful to summarize the terminology which consistently distinguishes between systems and their models and between the respective structure of system and model and their behaviors, see Table 1.

4 Distributed Systems – Chameleons

The vending machine example shown in Fig. 1 is often used in this or in a similar form to introduce Petri nets. It has some very nice features such as choice (initially between "accept coin" and "reject coin") and concurrency (initially between "refill" and "accept coin"). It can be viewed as a composition of two smaller nets, and it is well suited to discuss the relation between a model and the modeled system, together with interfaces of the models and of the systems.

However, the example misses one of the most important aspects of Petri net models, which is a high degree of concurrency, and the related complexity,

Table 1. Terminology in system and Petri net model behavior

Level	Elements	Relation
system structure	activities and local states	dependencies between elements
system run	actions (occurring activities)	causal structure (partial order)
action/event log	observed actions	sequence (total order)
Petri net model	transitions and places	flow relation (arcs)
occurrence sequence	transition occurrences	sequence (total order)
Petri net run	transition occurrences	causal structure (partial order)

which is typical for highly distributed systems. Therefore, this example does not convincingly demonstrate that a sequential view at behavior leads to unnecessary complexity, or, in other words, that it makes sense to distinguish (partially ordered) runs of the net from their (sequential) observations.[1]

In the sequel, we will provide a distributed toy example which is very simple in most aspects, but can be huge. The difficulty lies in managing its size and distribution.

The "real world" of the example is given by the following story:

The Chameleons

> Many chameleons live happily in a large forest and can move freely within it. Each chameleon can take on exactly one of three colors: blue, red, and green. As is well known, chameleons can change their color. In our example, the color of a chameleon changes if and only if it meets another chameleon of a different color. In this case, both chameleons change the third color. So: if a blue and a red chameleon meet, they both turn green. If a blue and a green chameleon meet, they both turn red, and so on.

The chameleon game, originally found in [5] and [4], was modeled and analyzed with Petri nets in [7]. The question asked there was whether it is possible for all chameleons to have the same color at some point, i.e., whether at some state no further color change is possible. The answer depends on the original coloration of the chameleons, as was shown in [4], and with Petri nets analysis means in [7]: the dead constellation can be reached if and only if initially the number of chameleons of one color differs from the number of chameleons of another color by a multiple of 3 (including the case that the two numbers are equal).

[1] One of the major problems with education of system modeling – and especially modeling of complex distributed systems – is that the motivating examples for training purposes are too small to illustrate the complexity necessary to motivate appropriate means of handling complexity.

Here, we concentrate on modeling. We abstract from almost everything of a chameleon, except that it has a color out of the three colors, that it can meet other chameleons, and that chameleons change color according to the given rule. The possible behavior of a single chameleon is simply given by three possible states (colors) and six state transitions, from any color to any other color. A Petri net representation of this behavior is shown in Fig. 3.

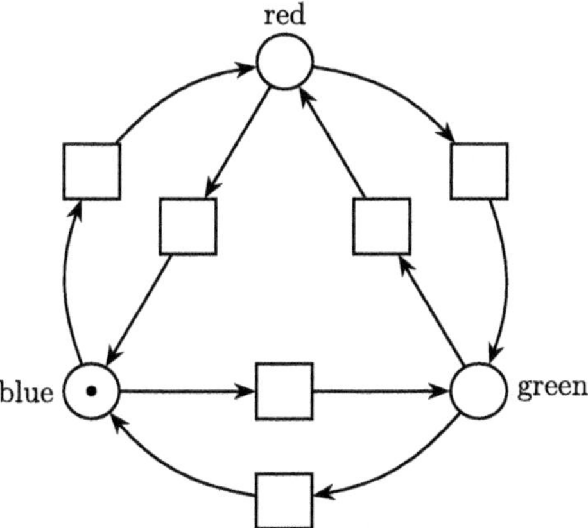

Fig. 3. Behavior of a single chameleon

The crucial aspect of chameleon behavior is that chameleons never change color alone, but that two chameleons must synchronize in a particular way. Therefore, all transitions of a single chameleon's behavior have to be considered external, just like the "insert coin" transition of the vending machine model.

Therefore, since a single chameleon can never change its color alone, let us continue with two chameleons, as shown in Fig. 4. This Petri net models the *closed system* of two chameleons, that are the only chameleons in the entire forest. Its behavior is a bit frustrating, because the chameleons either share the same color initially, in which case nothing can happen, or they have different colors (as depicted in the figure). But then, after the occurrence of the unique enabled transition, the system stops as well.

Next, we model two chameleons that can interact with each other but also with any other chameleon, as shown in Fig. 5. The additional transitions (drawn in red and blue) represent external activities that can only occur together with activities of further, non-modeled components.

We could continue by drawing closed Petri net models for three chameleons with 9 places and 18 transitions, for four chameleons with 12 places and 36 transitions, ..., for n chameleons with $3 \cdot n$ places and $3 \cdot n \cdot (n-1)$ transitions. Since this will yield confusing figures very soon, Petri net theory offers with *high-level Petri nets* the possibility to represent nets more compactly by summarizing sets of places and sets of transitions (technically, this is called *folding* of places and of

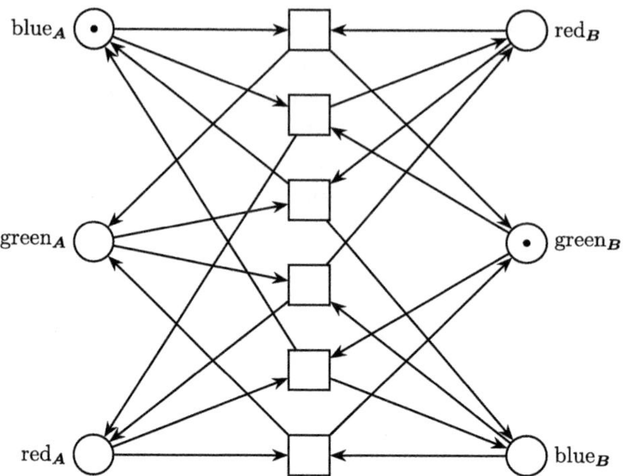

Fig. 4. Two chameleons (alone in the forest)

transitions). The idea is that several places are represented by a single *high-level place*, which carries all tokens of all places of the set. Different colors of tokens of the summarized place indicate to which original place a token belongs (hence the alternative name *colored Petri nets* for high-level Petri nets). Similarly, a summarized *high-level transition* can occur in more than one *mode*, where each mode represents the occurrence of an original transition and thus modeling a separate action.

Figure 6 shows such a colored Petri net for five chameleons A, B, C, D, E. Each high-level place can carry blue, red and green tokens. A red token on place A indicates that the place "red" for chameleon A of the original model is marked. Each high-level transition of the colored Petri net stands for the six transitions representing the possible interactions between two chameleons and can therefore occur in six different modes. Formally, possible colors and modes belong to the specification of a high-level Petri net. This specification can be done syntactically in various ways, but is omitted in the figure for clarity.

The specification given by the high-level Petri net must ensure, for each transition, that it consumes two different tokens (colors) via the two input arcs and produces two tokens of the unique third color via its output arcs. Figure 7 shows arc annotations which, together with $x \neq y \neq z \neq x$, syntactically express this specification.

This takes us one step further and allows us to model n chameleons with n places and $\frac{1}{2} \cdot n \cdot (n-1)$ transitions. However, this isn't much help for really large chameleon populations.

Instead of folding the three colors of single chameleons, we can fold all places representing blue chameleons, all places representing red chameleons and all places representing green chameleons, ending up with only three places, see Fig. 8. Each chameleon appears as a token on exactly one of the three places. So,

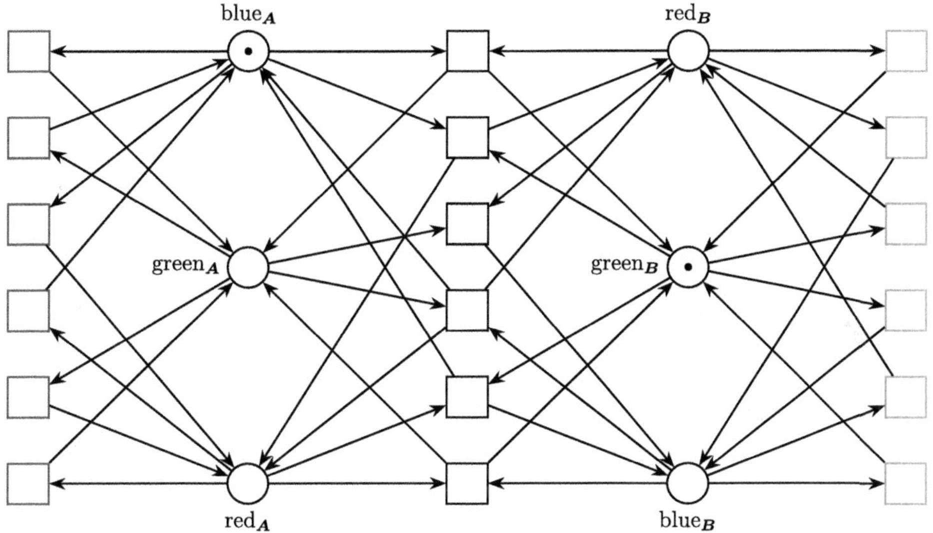

Fig. 5. Two chameleons with interfaces to other chameleons (Color figure online)

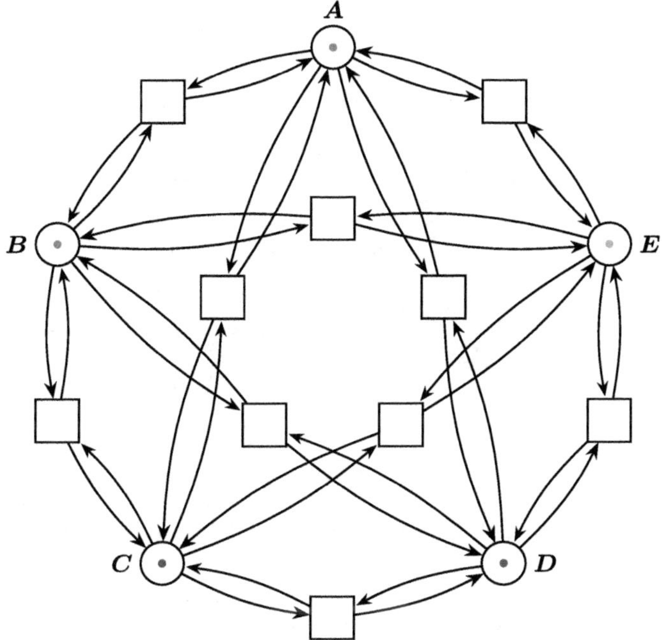

Fig. 6. Colored Petri net representing five chameleons A, B, C, D, E (Color figure online)

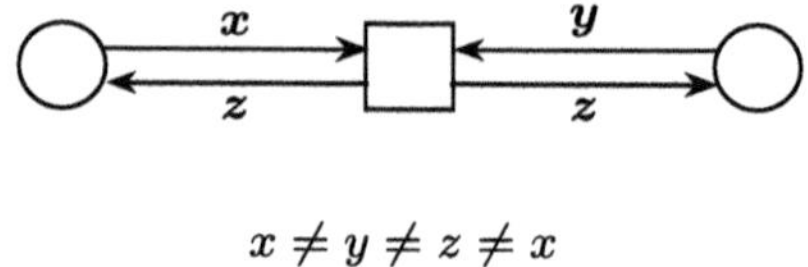

Fig. 7. Annotations of all arcs of the net in Fig. 6

in this net, a token does not represent a chameleon's color as before, but rather the identity of a chameleon. The location of a token indicates this chameleon's color. The folding results in one single net for an arbitrary number of chameleons. The net has three places – for the three colors – and three transitions, representing the three options in which two chameleons become blue, red, or green. Technically, for n chameleons, each of the three transitions has $n \cdot (n-1)$ modes, namely a mode for each pair of two different chameleons. Again, we did not formally specify domains of places and modes of transitions. A specification is given by the arc annotations: Each transition consumes tokens x and y from its two input places and adds both tokens x and y to its output place (x and y being variables for chameleons).

One could furthermore require that the two tokens consumed by a transition should be different, but this turns out to be a property of the model because each token occurs only once initially and no transition occurrence duplicates tokens.

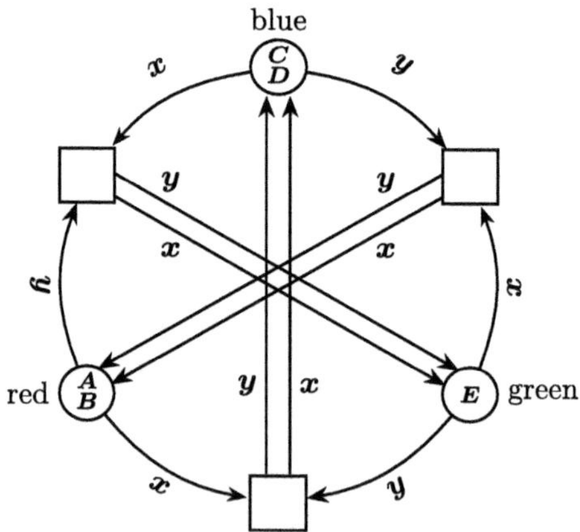

Fig. 8. High-level Petri net model of 5 chameleons

This folding has the advantage of being small and clear and independent of the number of chameleons. Its disadvantage compared to their earlier model is that the distributedness of the chameleons is no more visible in the net. In fact, two chameleons of the same color, located at different edges of the forest, are represented by two tokens on the same place.

Both high-level Petri nets are representations of the same Petri net with 15 places and 60 transitions, which we did not draw for obvious reasons.

Now let us consider the behavior of the five chameleons. Chameleons A and B are initially red, chameleons C and D are blue, chameleon E is green. In one possible run, B and C meet and both become green. Independently, D and E meet and both become red. After both actions, the green C meets the red D, so both become blue. Instead of continuing a textual description, Fig. 9 is intended to show what is happening. We use a Petri net style[2] to illustrate the run, where the horizontal lanes represent the lives of the five chameleons and the colored places the respective colors of chameleons. The system has 60 possible activities (as the colored net of Fig. 6 has 10 transitions, each of which can occur in 6 different modes). In Fig. 9, the transitions represent actions, and their annotations $a, b, c, \dots$ corresponding activities. We use this notation to express that 9 out of 60 activities occur, where one activity occurs twice (there are two actions annotated with activity d).

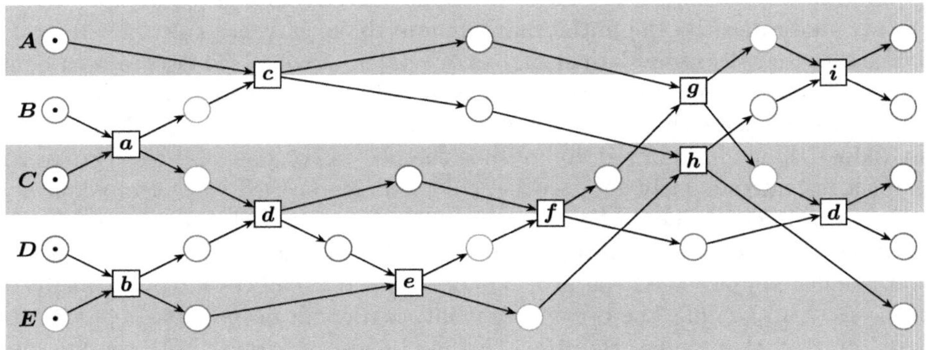

Fig. 9. Illustration of a run of five chameleons

A possible observation of the run is given by the sequence $a\ b\ c\ d\ e\ f\ g\ h\ i\ d$. Another observation is $b\ a\ d\ e\ f\ c\ h\ g\ d\ i$, and there are many more observations. Actually, any linearization of the partial order indicated in the figure is a possible observation. In reality, it might be difficult to observe a large number of chameleons in a vast forest along with their behavior. Therefore, the concept of observers is sometimes more of a metaphor than a realistic subject.

On the model side, the Petri net behaves according to its occurrence rule. It does not matter whether the undrawn huge low-level Petri net is considered or any of the two high-level representations. Assuming respective names of transitions, the two sequences above are such occurrence sequences. Generally, each occurrence sequence represents a possible observation of a run of the system.

[2] Here we face a didactic dilemma. The only way to illustrate a particular behavior of this system is to provide a figure that is inherently already a model. Therefore, please consider this figure merely as an illustration of the real behavior.

Conversely, when the structure of the net providing dependencies between transitions is known, one can construct partially ordered runs from occurrence sequences, for example in terms of occurrence nets. Actually, the illustration of Fig. 9 is an occurrence net and thus a partially ordered representation of one run of the Petri net model.

If we now consider possible runs of, say, 100 chameleons, then in general the number of reachable constellations is 3^{100}, and this is also the number of different markings reached by occurrence sequences of the Petri net model. It is quite obvious that considering that many global states does not help to understand the system's behavior. Instead, only the concurrent view describes the dependencies between color changes of chameleons, which are purely local: when a chameleon turns green and then red, then these two activities are ordered, and only one other chameleon is involved in each of the two color changes.

In the previous model, we distinguished the identities of chameleons carefully by representing them by distinguishable tokens. The transitions, however, take any differently colored chameleons and color them in the third color. One could require that no transition consumes the same token from two places, but this is already guaranteed by the initial marking and the occurrence rule. It will never be the case that the same chameleon has two different colors. Therefore, as a final simplification, we can ignore the token identities and the transition modes, but rather just count the chameleons of a particular color. A transition will then simply reduce the number of red and of blue chameleons by one, and add two green chameleons, and similarly for the other colors. This so-called *place/transition net* is shown in Fig. 10. The arc annotations "2" indicate that the occurrence of the adjacent transition will always produce two tokens along this arc. This abstraction is much simpler than the previous model, and it suffices for many analysis purposes. For example, the previously mentioned result on possible deadlocks is based only on this model. However, this model also abstracts from the life history of individual chameleons, so no conclusions can be drawn about individual chameleons from this model.

5 The Big Picture

The Big Picture, presented in Fig. 11, comprises a system within the real world with subsystems, models and their respective behaviors. It allows to illustrate and structure typical problem scenarios and corresponding modeling practices (see Fig. 12).

When we refer to behavior of systems or models in these practices, we always have to distinguish between sequential behavior (e.g., occurrence sequences of Petri nets) and partially ordered behavior (p.o. runs). As mentioned above, these two concepts are related by observation (from partially ordered behavior to occurrence sequences) and construction of partial orders from sequences.

1. **Improving the model (validation)**
   If discrepancies exist between expected system behavior and model behavior,

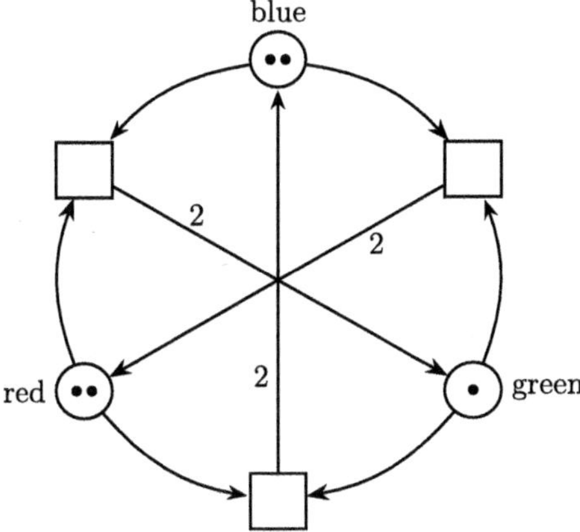

Fig. 10. Place/transition net model of the chameleon game

the model must be revised. This requires comparing both behaviors.
Imagine that we made the following modeling error in the vending machine model: Instead of the arc from "reject coin" to "ready for insertion" we have an arc from "reject coin" to "ready to dispense". Then, in this model it is possible to dispense an item without ever accepting a coin. This does not correspond to the system's behavior, whence the model is not usable for analysis or simulation of the system.

2. **Exploring system behavior (simulation)**
The system is known, but its behavior is unknown or cannot be observed directly. In this case, a model is used to simulate the behavior, which serves as a proxy for the actual system behavior.
Playing the token game for the vending machine model will show that after output of two items no further item can be dispensed unless the refill transition occurs. This result can be used to identify corresponding facts of the modeled system.
3. **Deciding system properties (analysis)**
If the model correctly reflects the system, properties like deadlock-freeness can be assessed by analyzing the model.
Assuming that the vending machine model is valid, analysis will show liveness and boundedness of the model. Thus the vending machine itself enjoys these properties.

4. **Discovering a model from behavior (mining)**
If the system itself is unknown, but behavioral data is available (e.g., action logs), a model can be derived from this behavior.
Imagine that we can play with the (real) vending machine without knowing its behavior precisely. This will yield a set of action logs. There are many sophisticated algorithms for mining the model from action logs. However, they can only achieve good results if a really large number of logs is available.

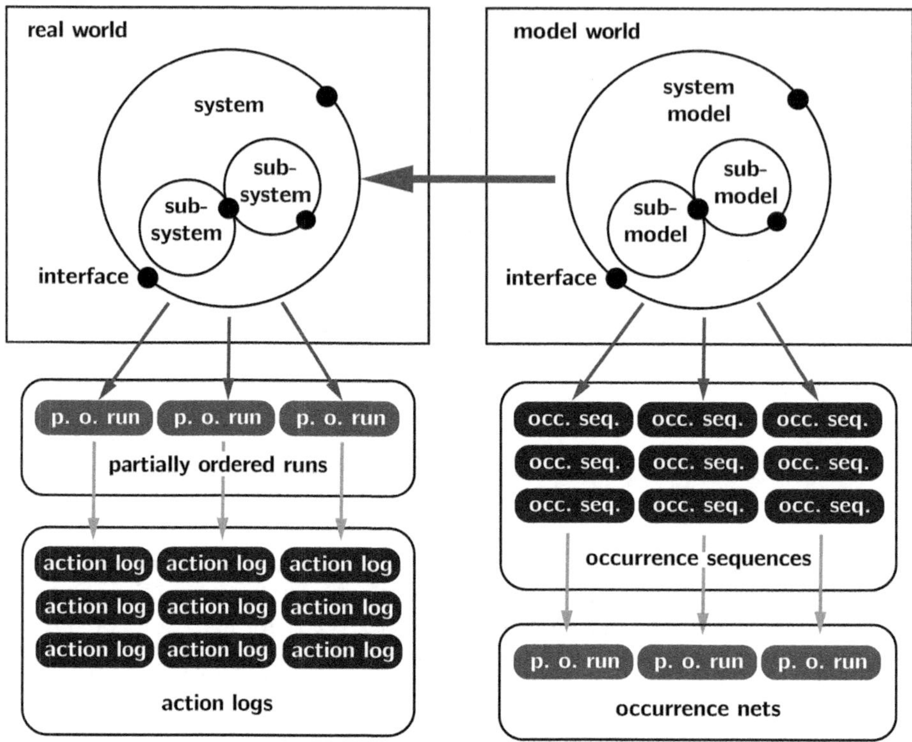

Fig. 11. The Big Picture

Often, even a small portion of the logs is allowed to be corrupted.

5. **Constructing a model from behavior (synthesis)**
   If the system does not yet exist, but the desired behavior is known, a model can be constructed to generate a system with that behavior.
   For the vending machine, this practice could be used to construct a machine with specified behavior. This specification is usually given in terms of a state automaton which is then interpreted as marking graph of a suitable model. For simplicity, we consider a specification in the form of sequential or partially ordered runs. As in mining, a model is created from the runs. Unlike in mining practice, however, this model must behave exactly as specified. The specification does not contain repetitions of runs, but rather a minimal and consistent set of runs required to define the desired behavior.

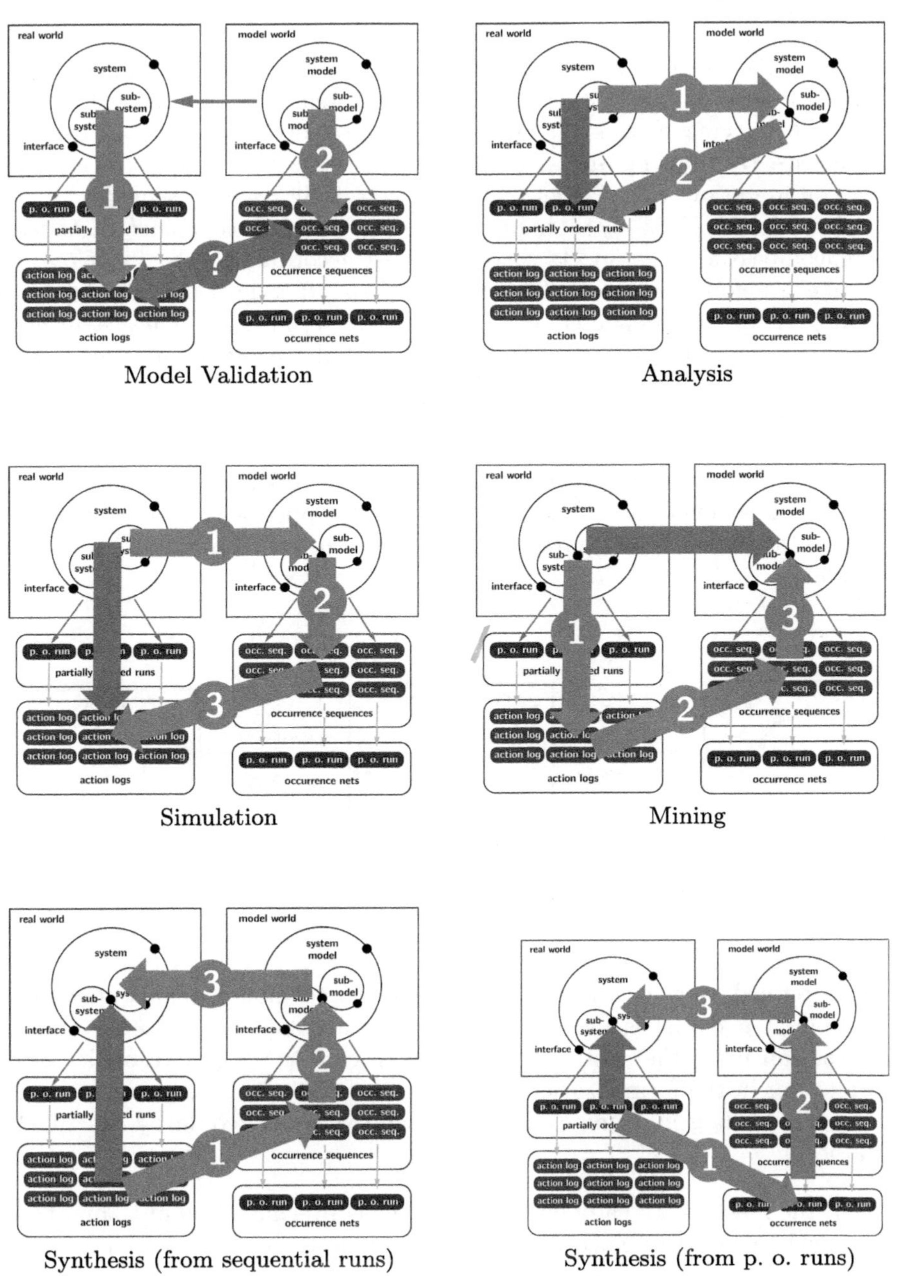

Fig. 12. Practices on Petri net models

6 Modeling

The reader might have noticed that the first mentioned practice was validation of models, instead of the practice of modeling (i.e., construction of a model) itself. The Big Picture contains a representation for "system", the original of the model considered. Of course, this system representation does not exist in modeling applications. By drawing any symbol that represents the original of the model under consideration, this system representation itself becomes a model.

For models created by a human modeler, a *cognitive model* of the system, encompassing the aspects to be modeled according to the *modeling purpose*, exists before a system *abstraction* is *formalized* in a suitable language. This cognitive model depends both on the *modeling purpose*, which determines the abstraction, and on the expressive power of the *modeling language*, which restricts the aspects that can be modeled. As shown in Fig. 13, meaning can also be assigned in the opposite direction: The cognitive model describes the *perception* of the system, and the *interpretation* of the formal model leads back only to the cognitive model and can only be compared with it. Therefore, a (formal) model is a deliberate twofold abstraction: it suppresses phenomena deemed irrelevant for the modeling purpose and codifies the remaining ones in a formal vocabulary.

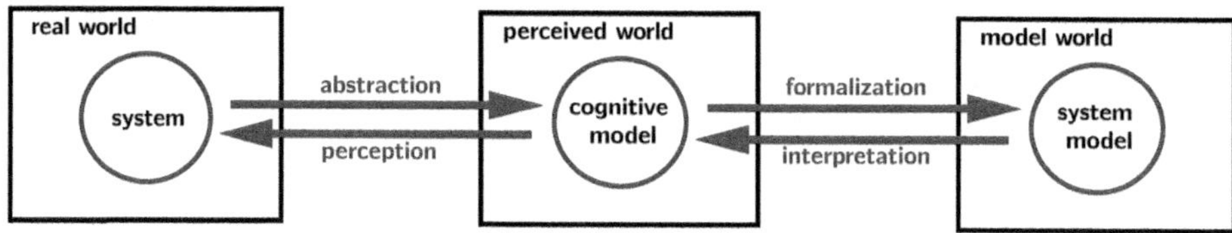

Fig. 13. The cognitive model

This refined view is relevant when it comes to model quality and model validation. If a model is incorrect with regard to the system to be modeled, the error can lie in the abstraction - in which case the cognitive model is also incorrect - or in the formalization - in which case the cognitive model is correct.

For the vending machine example, a cognitive model could be described in verbal form:

> If the machine is ready for insertion, then, after insertion of a coin, the machine decides to accept or reject the coin. If the coin is accepted ...

Let us now look at the modeling process itself. An engineer and an architect will first develop a model and then construct the modeled original, whereas an artist might be inspired by an original and then construct a model. Petri net models can also be prescriptive (model first) or descriptive (original first), depending on the respective application. However, with the exception of automatically generated models, modeling starts with some cognitive model. Either the cognitive model corresponds to the respective understanding of reality given by different views of the system, or it is the result of a creative process in which the basic principles of the system to be constructed are invented. In this first step, the modeler also determines what he actually wants to model and what he does not want to model, i.e. what the system boundaries are.

Everything written so far applies to any model. However, behavior plays a crucial role in Petri net models, as shown in the Big Picture. So how do we look at behavior of cognitive models in the context of Petri net modeling?

Do we first understand the basic principles of a system and then its runs, or is the understanding of these principles based on its runs? There is little research on these questions, but it is obvious that, especially with prescriptive models, the runs are developed first, while in descriptive models this often seems to be the other way around.

What is the natural behavioral concept for cognitive models: sequential or partially ordered? Humans are somewhat sequential individuals, although the functions of the body and brain are highly distributed. A human is used to observing the world sequentially, as he or she cannot perceive the concurrency of distributed actions, but only observe them. Petri nets support this sequential view of the world by their occurrence sequences, but Petri net theory also helps in understanding concurrency.

7 Properties of Systems and Processes and Their Models

In Petri net courses, one will sooner or later encounter properties of Petri nets that relate to behavior. These properties are often called "nice properties". In truth, this is not justified at the abstract level of Petri nets themselves. Rather, the beauty of the properties of Petri net models is that Petri nets that possess certain properties often enable elegant or efficient analyses with respect to other properties. Instead, these properties refer to respective properties of the systems modeled, and should be interpreted on that level. We will continue this distinction later, after introducing some of the properties.

The following definitions refer to occurrence sequences and to markings reached by occurrence sequences. For convenience, the empty sequence is considered an occurrence sequence, too. It leads from the initial marking to the initial marking. A marking is called reachable if it can be reached by some occurrence sequence. For more precise definitions, see e.g. [3].

Markings of Petri nets correspond to *global states* of systems, i.e., to combinations of local states represented by tokens on places of the model. In a distributed system one can argue whether these global states actually exist objectively, since they implicitly refer to a concept of simultaneity which contradicts concurrency. Actually, a global state might be observable by an observer during a concurrent run (sometimes the term "snapshot" is used). However, another observer, who records the actions of the run in a different order, might see different (sequences of) global states. Whereas the respective observations of action sequences are permutations of each other, the corresponding state sequences differ considerably. A state observed by one observer may not be observable by another observer.

The only global states on which all observers agree are the initial state and the final state, i.e., the state reached after a finite run. In Petri nets, every permissible permutation of a sequence of occurrences of an occurrence sequence results in the same overall change in the number of tokens in places. Therefore, reachable markings of Petri net models (defined via occurrence sequences) actually correspond to global states of systems reached by finite runs.

The properties defined below refer to distributed systems that are meant to run forever, such as operation systems, elevator control systems, vehicle traffic or the internet. In reality, none of these systems will run forever, but any reason to stop eventually (such as the demolition of a building with elevators) is outside the scope of the system.

- **Deadlock-freeness**
  A *deadlock* is a state that does not allow any action. The term is only used in a negative sense, when states enabling no action are not desirable. Typically, a deadlock appears in distributed systems when distributed components wait for each other circularly. For example, at an unregulated intersection with cars on all four sides, no car can proceed without violating the right-before-left rule. A system considering only this rule can run into a deadlock. For processes, however, final states enabling no action might be desirable end states.
  A Petri net is *deadlock-free* if no reachable marking represents a deadlock, i.e., if each reachable marking enables at least one transition.
- **Liveness**
  Deadlocks are an important topic in various disciplines of computer science, but they often just refer to a part of the considered system: Some activities block each other, whereas other activities can still occur. Since these "partial deadlocks" also represent irregular behavior, the stronger[3] concept of liveness was introduced: A system is *live* if, for each reachable state and each activity, there is a run starting with this state that contains an occurrence of this activity.
  The definition of a *live* Petri net can easily be transferred from above. A perhaps easier, equivalent definition reads as follows: Each occurrence sequence σ is a prefix of an occurrence sequence $\sigma\ \sigma'$ such that σ' contains all transitions (whereas deadlock-freeness is: Each occurrence sequence σ is a prefix of an occurrence sequence $\sigma\ t$ for some transition t).
- **Boundedness**
  A system is *bounded* if its set of reachable states is finite. One might argue that any system has a finite set of reachable states because everything in this world is finite. A digital counter cannot represent all natural numbers, no

[3] Liveness only implies deadlock-freeness if the system under consideration has at least one activity; otherwise by definition the system is live but in a deadlock state.

matter how many digits are available. Every buffer and every memory has a limited size. However, it is possible to ignore this inherent boundedness by choosing the system boundaries in such a way that the considered system in isolation could potentially have an unlimited number of reachable states. For example, if coins inserted into the vending machine (see Fig. 1) are considered part of the system under consideration, then the system will have any number of reachable states – as long as the emptying of the coin storage is not also part of the considered system.
A Petri net is *bounded* if its set of reachable markings is finite. If its set of places is finite (which is a usual assumption), then boundedness of a Petri net is equivalent to boundedness of all places, where a place is bounded if the number of tokens on that place will never exceed some bound.

- **Safeness**
  Safeness is somewhat complicated to motivate for systems. Roughly speaking, it means that the local states of a system can be broken down into binary logical elements (called conditions) that can only have the values "true" or "false" and can swap these values during system behavior.
  In Petri net models, *safeness* means that all places not only have some bound, but that this bound is one. In other words, in a safe Petri net, each reachable marking assigns to each place either no token or one token. In this case, a reachable marking can also be characterized by the set of marked places. Usually, a marked place represents a true condition of the system, whereas an unmarked one represents a false condition.
- **Reversibility**
  A system is *reversible* if it can always return to its initial state. As a consequence, a reversible system can reach any reachable state from any other reachable state, if necessary via the initial state.
  For Petri nets, *reversibility* is defined by reachability of the initial marking from any other marking. A marking is called *home state* if it is reachable from all other reachable markings. So a net is reversible if its initial marking is a home state. It might be surprising that liveness and boundedness does not imply the existence of home states and that live and bounded nets with home states are not necessarily reversible.
- **Persistence**
  A system is *persistent* if, whenever two activities are enabled, they are enabled concurrently, i.e., the occurrence of one does not disable the other.
  Petri nets usually model persistent systems by nets without shared places, i.e., without places with more than one outgoing arc. This restriction suffices to guarantee persistence because, without shared places, two transitions can never compete for a token and thus never disable each other. However, this structural restriction is not necessary for persistence.

There are several other relevant properties of systems and of Petri net models of systems, such as the occurrence of *confusion*, which also relate to reachable states and markings as well as to enabled transitions. However, their explanation goes beyond this text.

As already mentioned, the notion of reachability is convenient for Petri nets, but it is somewhat inappropriate for distributed systems. In particular, the definition using finite sequences ending in a certain state is counter-intuitive when referring to live systems that should not actually end. A reachable state is not objectively reached during an infinite run of a distributed system, but is only a helpful concept for the definitions provided above. The same holds for the initial state, which is also not obvious in many examples. It might be worth mentioning that the original definition of elementary net systems given by Carl Adam Petri (formerly called Condition/Event-Systems, see e.g. [20]) did not consider a fixed initial marking but instead considered infinite runs with infinite future and infinite past.

Processes as Systems

One of the most important applications of Petri nets is the modeling of business processes. In particular, process mining has become a well-established field of research. How do the concepts developed specifically for process models fit into our Big Picture? We consider a process to be a specific subsystem, whose supersystem is typically an enterprise information system or something similar. Since business processes, by definition, have a start and an end, interfaces always exist, both for the system and for its model, because a process is started by its environment and its end is identified by the environment.

Whereas for other systems liveness and boundedness are desirable properties, in the case of processes, we aim for *soundness* [1] as a correctness criterion. A process is sound if every activity can occur and furthermore if the end state can be reached from all other reachable states. In terms of specific Petri net models of processes, called *Workflow nets*, every transition occurs in some occurrence sequence and every occurrence sequence is prefix of an occurrence sequence leading to the final state. The soundness property refers to the liveness and boundedness of the supersystem of a process. It can be analyzed by studying a system that includes the process, with the rest of the supersystem abstracted to a single transition.

Process mining is the most common practice in this context – very often, neither the process nor a corresponding model is initially known. The result of process mining is one or several process models. This indicates that the existence of a unique process original is debatable. In practical applications, when asked to define "the process itself" one is typically referred to descriptions, rules, or documents – all of which are models themselves. Therefore, the entire field is reminiscent of The Emperor's New Clothes—and the upper-left element in the Big Picture figure is, in a sense, fake for business processes.

In the world of processes, the observation of an action is often called an *event*, whence action logs are called *event logs* in process mining.

8 Conclusion

The main contribution of this paper is a figure that relates models to their original, which we call the system, as well as to system and model behavior. We discussed these relations in depth and showed how typical practices of Petri net modeling can be interpreted as paths within this figure.

We also discussed the process of modeling, i.e. the construction of the model, adding a cognitive model between the original and the formal model.

The approach could be refined in various directions. For example, we could explicitly mention places, transitions, and the flow relation together with their counterparts in systems, thereby reflecting the very nature of Petri nets. Another direction is to apply Stachowiak's modeling theory in greater depth. Finally, we shall study the cognitive model during the modeling process in detail. Open questions include the consideration of the potential role of its behavior including the relations to both the system's behavior and the Petri net's behavior.

References

1. van der Aalst, W.M.P., van Hee, K.M.: Workflow Management: Models, Methods, and Systems. Cooperative Information Systems, MIT Press (2002)
2. van der Aalst, W.M.P., Stahl, C.: Modeling Business Processes - A Petri Net-Oriented Approach. Cooperative Information Systems series, MIT Press (2011). http://mitpress.mit.edu/books/modeling-business-processes
3. Best, E., Devillers, R.: Petri Net Primer - A Compendium on the Core Model, Analysis, and Synthesis. Springer (2024). https://doi.org/10.1007/978-3-031-48278-6
4. Beutelspacher, A.: Das Geheimnis der zwölften Münze: Neue mathematische Knobeleien. C.H. Beck (2021)
5. Dambeck, H., Niestedt, M.: Verwirrspiel im Terrarium. https://www.spiegel.de/karriere/verwirrspiel-im-terrarium-raetsel-der-woche-a-404e0560-ca83-418c-a5f3-8acfa3167d3d (2021). Accessed 01 Mar 2022
6. Desel, J., Esparza, J.: Free Choice Petri Nets. Cambridge Tracts in Theoretical Computer Science, Cambridge University Press (2005). https://books.google.de/books?id=n5ipzgEACAAJ
7. Desel, J.: The chameleon game. In: Köhler-Bussmeier, M., Moldt, D., Rölke, H. (eds.) Petri Nets and Software Engineering 2022. CEUR Workshop Proceedings, vol. 3170, pp. 202–210 (2022)
8. Desel, J., Esparza, J.: Free Choice Petri Nets. Cambridge University Press, USA (1995)
9. Desel, J., Fleischer, J.: Modeling distributed systems and processes with Petri nets – the Big Picture. In: Köhler-Bußmeier, M., et al. (eds.) Joint Proceedings of the Workshops at the 46th International Conference on Application and Theory of Petri Nets and Concurrency (Petri Nets 2025), Paris, France, June 23-24, 2024. CEUR Workshop Proceedings, vol. 3998. CEUR-WS.org (2025). https://ceur-ws.org/Vol-3998/paper16.pdf
10. Desel, J., Juhás, G.: What is a Petri net? In: Ehrig, H., Juhás, G., Padberg, J., Rozenberg, G. (eds.) Unifying Petri Nets, Advances in Petri Nets. Lecture Notes in Computer Science, vol. 2128, pp. 1–25. Springer (2001)
11. Diekert, V., Rozenberg, G. (eds.): The Book of Traces. World Scientific (1995)

12. Fettke, P., Reisig, W.: Understanding the Digital World - Modeling with HERAKLIT. Springer (2024). https://doi.org/10.1007/978-3-031-61898-7
13. Girault, C., Valk, R.: Petri Nets for Systems Engineering - A Guide to Modeling, Verification, and Applications. Springer (2003). http://www.springer.com/computer/swe/book/978-3-540-41217-5
14. Janicki, R., Kleijn, J., Koutny, M., Mikulski, L.: Semantics of Concurrent Systems (2025). in this volume
15. Liu, G.: Petri Nets - Theoretical Models and Analysis Methods for Concurrent Systems. Springer, Cham (2022). https://doi.org/10.1007/978-981-19-6309-4
16. Popova-Zeugmann, L.: Time and Petri Nets. Springer, Heidelberg (2013). https://doi.org/10.1007/978-3-642-41115-1
17. Reisig, W.: A primer in Petri net design. Springer Compass International, Springer, Heidelberg (1992)
18. Reisig, W.: Understanding Petri Nets - Modeling Techniques, Analysis Methods, Case Studies. Springer, Heidelberg (2013). https://doi.org/10.1007/978-3-642-33278-4
19. Stachowiak, H.: Allgemeine Modelltheorie. Springer, Wien (1973). https://glossar.hs-augsburg.de/Stachowiak,_H._(1973):_Allgemeine_Modelltheorie
20. Thiagarajan, P.S.: Elementary net systems. In: Brauer, W., Reisig, W., Rozenberg, G. (eds.) ACPN 1986. LNCS, vol. 254, pp. 26–59. Springer, Heidelberg (1987). https://doi.org/10.1007/978-3-540-47919-2_3

Essentials of Petri Nets

Wolfgang Reisig[3] and Peter Fettke[1,2(✉)]

[1] German Research Center for Artificial Intelligence (DFKI), Saarbrücken, Germany
peter.fettke@dfki.de
[2] Saarland University, Saarbrücken, Germany
[3] Humboldt-Universität zu Berlin, Berlin, Germany
reisig@informatik.hu-berlin.de

Abstract. This contribution highlights some concepts and aspects of Petri nets that are often neglected, but that the authors consider important or interesting, or that Carl Adam Petri emphasized. In particular, we give a historical overview of some aspects of the development of Petri nets, in particular distributed runs, schematic modeling, composition, and other aspects.

Keywords: systems composition · data modeling · behavior modeling · composition calculus · algebraic specification · Petri nets

Introduction

This contribution presents a collection of concepts and aspects of Petri nets, that fundamentally differ from other models of computation, and in particular from other models of concurrency. As a previous staff member of Carl Adam Petri, the first author of this contribution, Wolfgang, tried to select topics that he assumes Petri would have liked to see in such a collection (among many others, not addressed here). Nevertheless, some views and aspects of this contribution are personal perception of today, looking back 40 years. In the early 1980s other themes would certainly have been chosen.

We start by trying to give an account of the technical circumstances of the emerging computer science in the late 1950s and early 1960s when Petri submitted his seminal PhD thesis. In seven temporal steps we present some highlights of concepts, as they developed until today.

The reader is assumed to be familiar with the standard notions and graphical conventions of Petri nets [14]. However, he or she must be prepared to accept slightly different views.

1 The Late 1950s

In the1950 s computing started to become scientifically and commercially interesting. In those times, computers weighted tons and costed millions of dollars. Theoretical Computer Science was emerging. Undisputedly, Turing machines were conceived as adequate abstract models for computers. First papers on automata theory and formal languages emerged.

F. Kordon et al. (Eds.): *Transactions on Petri Nets and Other Models of Concurrency XVIII*,
LNCTPN 16260, pp. 29–47, 2026.
https://doi.org/10.1007/978-3-662-73305-9_2

Fig. 1. Carl Adam Petri in the late 1950s

2 The Early 1960s

In this atmosphere, in 1962, Carl Adam Petri submitted a text, entitled "Communication with Automata", as his PhD thesis [10] (Fig. 1). This title deliberately has two readings: first, a person communicates with an automaton, or second, a group of persons communicates with the help of automata. With this thesis, Petri intended to strive towards a comprehensive theory for discrete dynamic systems, not just another theory for symbol processing automata. The thesis itself is a collection of ideas, a research agenda, towards this goal.

Particularly striking is a nice thought experiment in the thesis: How to implement a non-primitive recursive function f? One may write a corresponding program p, and for a given argument a, one may run the program p on a given computer C and hope that the computation will stop, returning $f(a)$. But one can not be sure that the computation will eventually stop. And even if it will eventually stop, beforehand one cannot estimate the amount of resources needed. So, the resources of C, in particular storage for intermediate results, may not suffice, and the computation may eventually fail due to lack of resources of C. In this case, one may engage a bigger computer C' with more resources, and start computation from scratch. Of course, also C' may fail. One may iterate this process until either the resources suffice, or one gives up.

Petri suggested to improve this procedure: Instead of replacing the computer C by C', just extend C by more storage, and continue computing! Iterate this procedure until either the resources suffice, or give up. This, however, requires an architecture that can be extended unboundedly often. Can such an architecture be physically achieved? Petri argues that this requires the absence of any global feature, in particular of a global clock. Generally, any construction element must do with a bounded fan out of wires, and with a maximal length of all wires, to guarantee a stable clock pulse. This in turn prevents unboundedly many extensions to be connected to one device. So, no device can directly be connected to all extensions. Summing up, this kind of architecture is feasible at the price of asynchronous components, and locally bounded causes and effects of events.

This thought experiment can be interpreted as the observation that asynchronous systems can do more or be more efficient than synchronous systems. A corresponding theory of asynchronous system should reflect and quantify this observation. But such a theory is still missing. It would contradict, to some extent, the popular version of the Church thesis that everything that can be done with computers, can be mimicked by Turing machines. Petri's arguments did not meet the spirit of the time, and Petri's PhD thesis did not find much attention.

3 The Late 1960s

As mentioned above, Petri intended to design a comprehensive theory for discrete dynamic systems in the real world, not just another theory for symbol processing automata. Therefore, Petri intended to base his theory on concepts of logic.

The most fundamental notion of logic is the notion of a proposition or an assertion. Already Aristotle suggested this concept. A proposition is either always true ("5 is a prime number") or always false ("The earth is flat"). Aristotle and his followers investigate special structures and combinations of propositions and their relation to aspects of the real world, until today (e.g. [17])

Petri suggested to parallel the "always true or always false" principle by "sometimes true and sometimes false". As an example, "the bakery offers freshly baked bread" may now be true; it turns false by the bakery selling the last bread. It becomes true again, by baking and offering a new load of freshly baked bread. Hence, the truth value of such a proposition can occasionally be updated. Such a proposition is denoted as a (local) state; the proposition is true in case the state has been reached, and the proposition is false in case the state has been abandoned.

The question arises as to how to organize proposition updates. Petri suggested steps and their composition, resulting in runs. A step may occur; in this case, some previously reached states are abandoned, and some previously abandoned states are reached. Figure 2 shows four steps: The leftmost, *bake*, can occur in case the local state *ready to bake* has been reached, and the local state *on counter* has been abandoned. Occurrence of *bake* then swaps the truth values of both

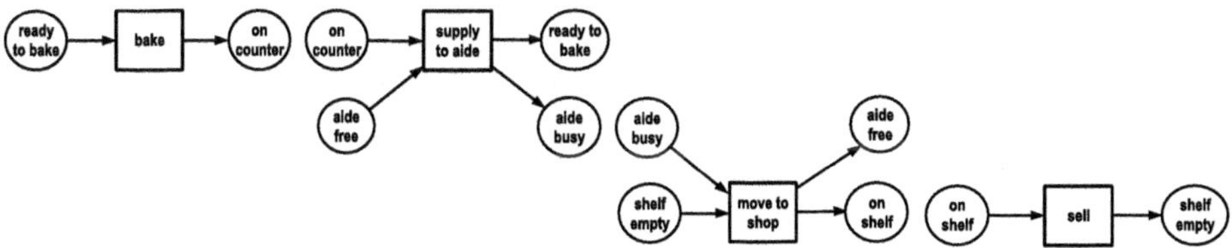

Fig. 2. Four steps of a bakery

local states. The step *supply to aide* apparently updates four states, in an obvious manner.

Figure 2 outlines the four steps in such a way that identical states are drawn side by side. It is intuitively obvious to merge them, as in Fig. 3, resulting in a distributed run. In such a run, an arc from an element a to an element b represents the causal dependency of b from a. So, this kind of runs present fine grained relationships between the elements of a run. However, such an idea did not receive much attention at the time. It was quickly replaced by the global notion of markings, and global steps replaced local steps. Figure 4 gives examples. We return to this issue later.

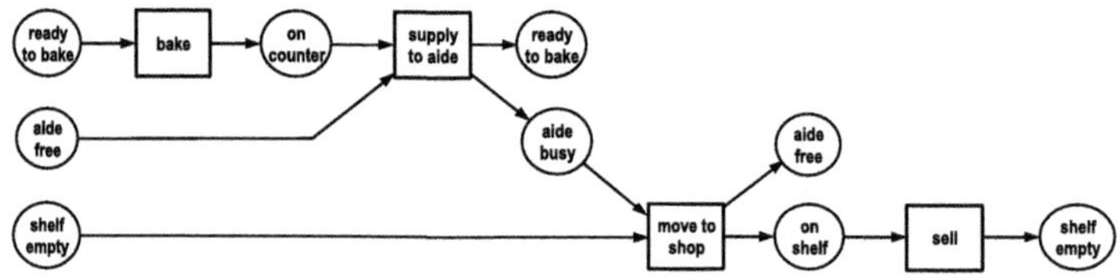

Fig. 3. A distributed run composed of four steps

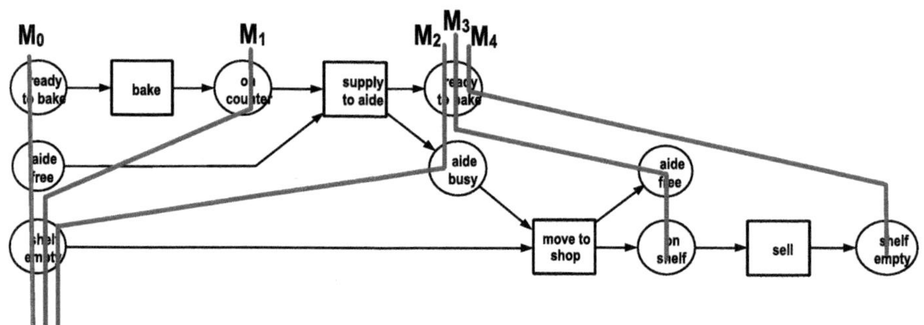

Fig. 4. Markings: global steps $M_0 \xrightarrow{\text{bake}} M_1 \xrightarrow{\text{supply to aide}} M_2 \xrightarrow{\text{move to shop}} M_3 \xrightarrow{\text{sell}} M_4$

4 The Early 1970s

In the early 1970s two contemporary trends in informatics were particularly unfavorable for Petri Nets: Firstly, with the emerging notion of software engineering, it became common to construct software directly from intuitive imaginations, without too much of intermediate modeling. Secondly, automata theory became a success story, with deep rooted, interesting mathematical problems such as $P = NP$, complexity theory, and its relation to logic. To some extent, Petri nets adjusted to this trend: Each Petri net was assigned an automaton, its marking graph; classes of Petri net languages were identified; the reachability problem gained much attention; etc. Much of this came from the area of notions and concepts that Petri envisaged as central for his theory. Nevertheless, in the early 1970s specific features for Petri nets were identified. This includes net classes such as free choice nets [6], and invariants [9]. In particular, place invariants exploit the observation that Petri net steps, in contrast to assignment statements of programming languages, are reversible, i.e., in the notation framework of vectors and matrices, with markings M and M' and a transition t, a step from M to M' can be written as:

$$M' = M + \underline{t}. \tag{1}$$

Equation 1 implies:

$$M = M' - \underline{t}. \tag{2}$$

In this era, Petri suggested the four seasons model as particularly interesting [12]. Figure 5 (a) shows this net. One may conceive it as intuitively impressive. But technically it is quite simple: it is just a sequence of four transitions, occurring repeatedly. It has no alternative and no concurrent transitions; so, central expressive means of Petri nets are missing. Furthermore, the four "inner" propositions, *days are short*, *days rise*, *days are long* and *days shrink* are redundant: without them, the behavior remains. In the sequel, we motivate why Petri found this net particularly interesting.

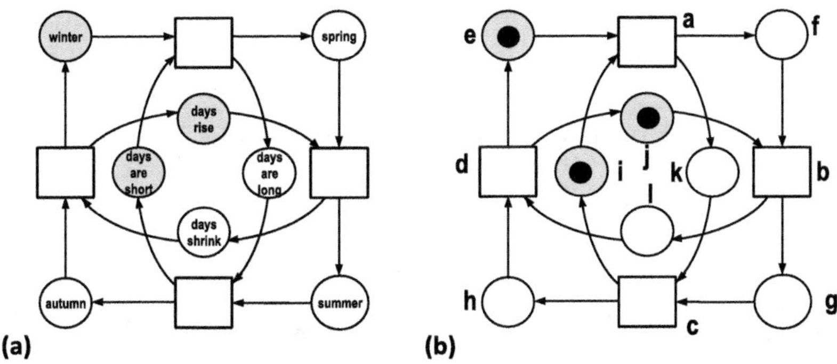

Fig. 5. Four seasons, intuitive model (a) and technical model (b)

Petri intended to define a notion of concurrency. Concurrency is intended to be a relation between system elements. The four seasons system is supposed to be the smallest system where each two elements are connected by a sequence of concurrent elements. Here we define concurrency as follows:

1. Two propositions p and q are concurrent, if and only if whenever p is reached, before p is abandoned, also q is reached, and whenever q is reached, before q is abandoned, also p is reached.

2. A proposition p and a transition t are concurrent, if and only if each time when t occurs, p is reached.

To exemplify this notion, as a technicality, Fig. 5 (b) renames the four season's elements. Figure 6 (a) shows a part of the distributed run of the four seasons system (as discussed in Sect. 3), albeit in confusing layout: the upper row includes the occurrences of the propositions of the "outer" circle, the middle row includes the occurrences of the propositions of the "inner" circle, and the lower row includes the occurrences of the transitions. This layout allows a quite symmetric representation of the concurrency structure of the distributed run, as in Fig. 6 (b): Concurrent pairs of elements are linked by a dotted line.

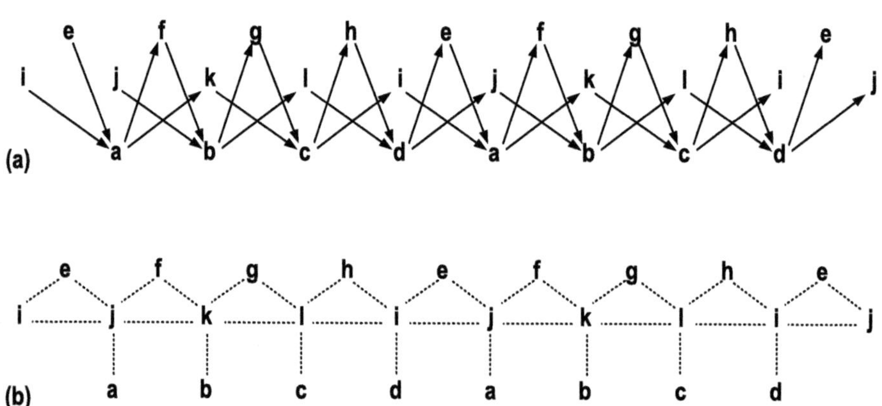

Fig. 6. Distributed run of the four seasons (a) and concurrency structure of the four season

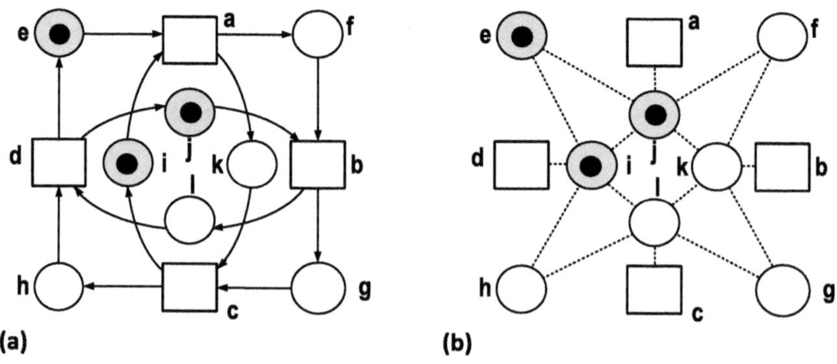

Fig. 7. Concurrency: (a) technical model, (b) concurrent model

Figure 7 (a) repeats the technical model of Fig. 6, and Fig. 7 (b) shows the concurrency structure of the four seasons model. It is easy to see that from each place and each transition, each other net element is reachable by a sequence of dotted lines. Furthermore, skipping one of the propositions, would either ruin the behavior, or leave one of the transitions isolated.

This concurrency relation is intuitively appealing. But so far, this notion has not made much impact in the world of concurrent systems.

5 The Late 1970s

In the late 1970s interest in topics of concurrency increased in the informatics community. In particular, process algebras such as calculus of communicating systems (CCS) and communicating sequential processes (CSP) emerged. However, semantics of such formalisms was undisputedly defined in terms of transition systems; viz., a single behavior (run) was – and is – conceived as a sequence of states and steps. Petri extended his concept of distributed runs as in Sect. 3 [11]. As an example, the above Figs. 3 and 4 show a run of Fig. 8. Its final marking, M_4, enables the transition *bake* a second time. Here the quest arises, where in the run of Fig. 3 this event is to be inserted (Fig. 9): before *move to shop*? Together with *move to shop*? After *move to shop* but before *sell*? Together with *sell*? After *sell*? Are there five alternatives, depending on a shared clock? Do we assume the existence of a notion of "time", in absolute precision, such that one of the five cases is "clearly taken"? Who decides this? What is assumed about "time" in Fig. 8 and Fig. 10 shows Petri's answer: the second *bake* event occurs after the first *bake* and the *supply to aide* event, but independent of *move to shop* and *sell*. In technical terms, the second *bake* event is not ordered with respect to *move to shop* and *sell*. Notice that this kind of unorder can not be interpreted as "at the same time". The events *move to shop*, *sell* and the second *bake*, cannot be totally ordered in any temporal sense. This is what the system in Fig. 8 expresses. Figure 11 extends Fig. 10: the second occurrences of *move to shop* and *sell* are inserted.

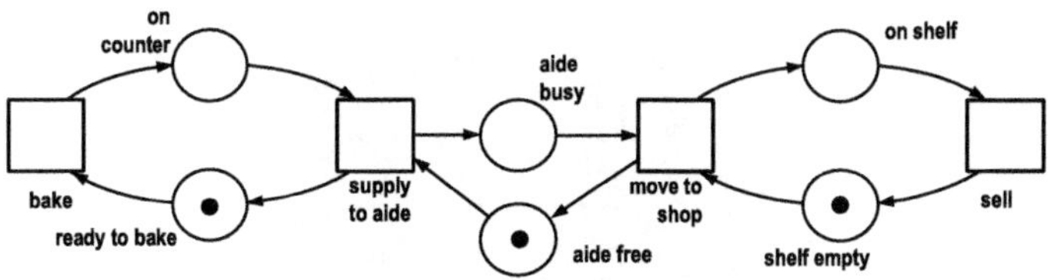

Fig. 8. Bakery

However, the idea of partially ordered runs never prevailed over interleaving sequences. They appeared intuitively odd, technically intricate, and overall not too beneficial. We return to these aspects later.

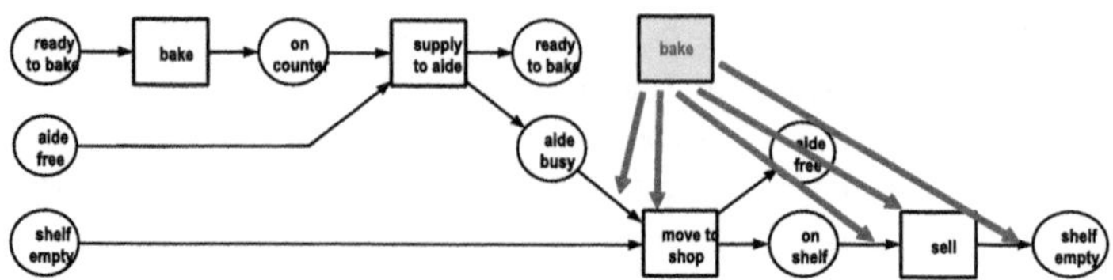

Fig. 9. Second bake

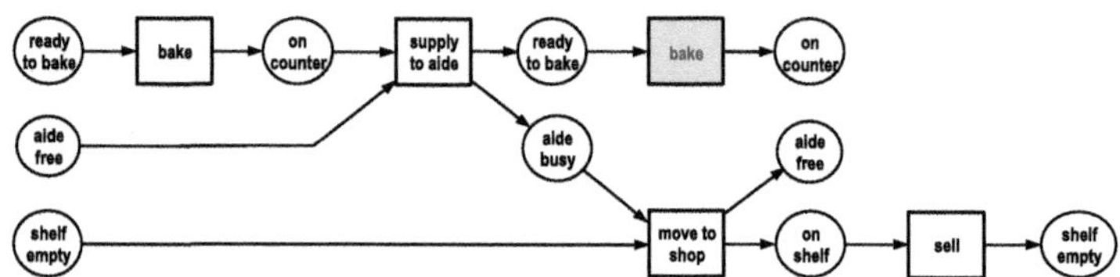

Fig. 10. Partial order

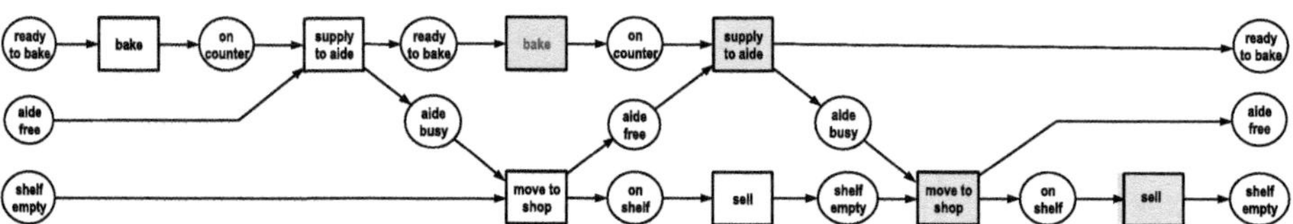

Fig. 11. 2nd round

Fig. 12. Carl Adam Petri in the 1980s

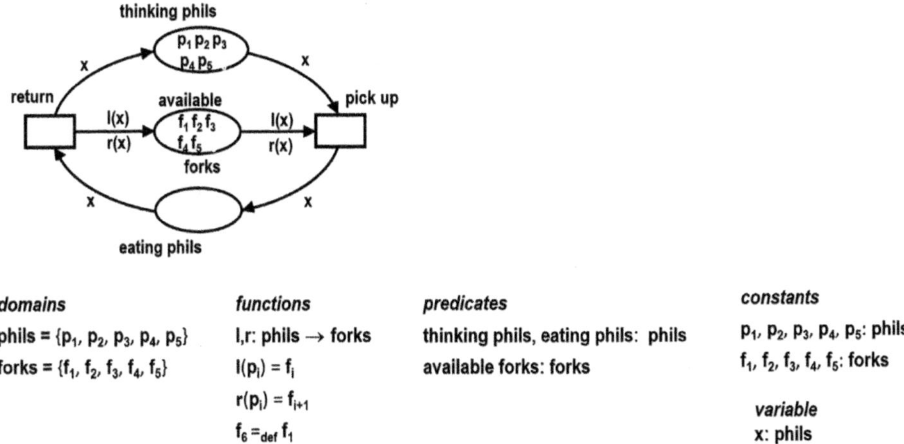

Fig. 13. Five thinking philosophers

6 The Early 1980s

Black token Petri nets are used to describe control and synchronization, and to count resources. In order to cope with data, it suggests itself to replace black dots by any kind of individual tokens, and to equip them with any kind of semantics. Various such versions of Petri nets have been suggested; essentially, two prevailed: colored Petri nets [7] and predicate transition nets [5]. Colored net essentially equip Petri nets with conventional data structures as well-known from programming languages. Additionally, each data set is canonically expanded to the corresponding multiset (Fig. 12).

Section 3 described the rise of Petri nets out of propositional logic. As the name suggests, predicate transition nets lifted this idea from propositional logic to predicate logic, extended by multisets. The basic idea is simple: Each place denotes a predicate p, and the place contains an element a, if p applies to a. Figure 13 shows an example: in the given situation, the predicate *thinking phils* applies to $p_1, \ldots, p_4$, the predicate *available forks* applies to $f_1, \ldots, f_5$, and the predicate *eating phils* applies to no element. Transition *pick up* is enabled for each valuation of the variable x by one of the philosophers. With $x = p_1$, occurrence of *pick up* yields the situation of Fig. 14. Finally, Fig. 15 shows the case of 100 philosophers in a circle.

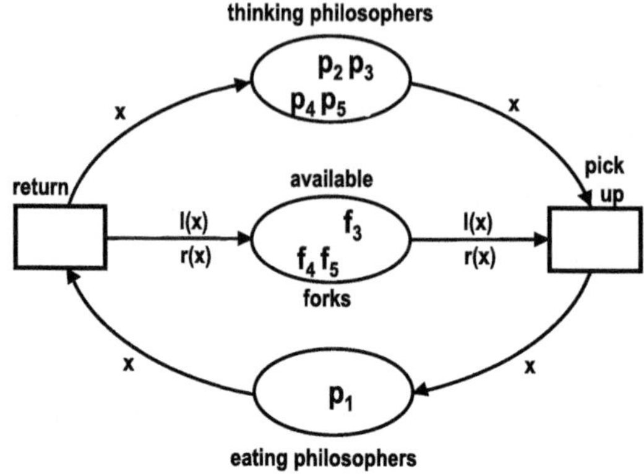

Fig. 14. Thinking philosophers: $x = p_1$

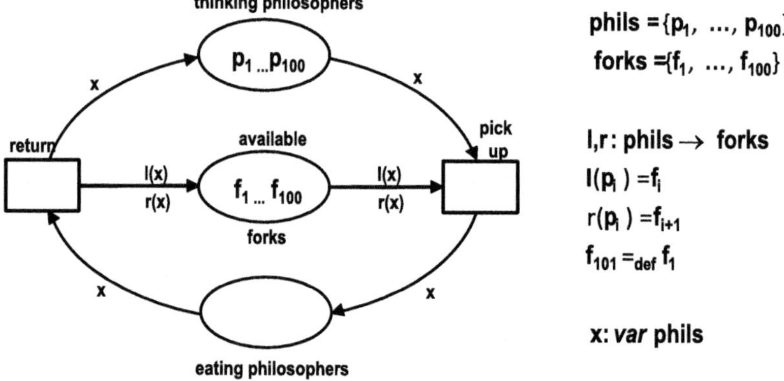

Fig. 15. 100 thinking philosophers

Predicate logic is about symbolic, schematic representations. Real world items are then conceived as interpretations of symbols. As a first example, in Fig. 16, the symbols P, F, l, and r are intended to be interpreted by sets of philosophers and forks, and by corresponding functions. One such intended interpretation yields the system in Fig. 13. Figure 15 gives a second intended interpretation. However, Fig. 16 is fundamentally flawed: according to the occurrence rule of Petri nets, P and F are two tokens, albeit interpreted as sets of philosophers. Occurrence of *pick up* would remove the entire sets. But this is not intended: rather, single elements of these sets are to be removed: the symbol P should not be interpreted as one set, but as "all single elements" of one set.

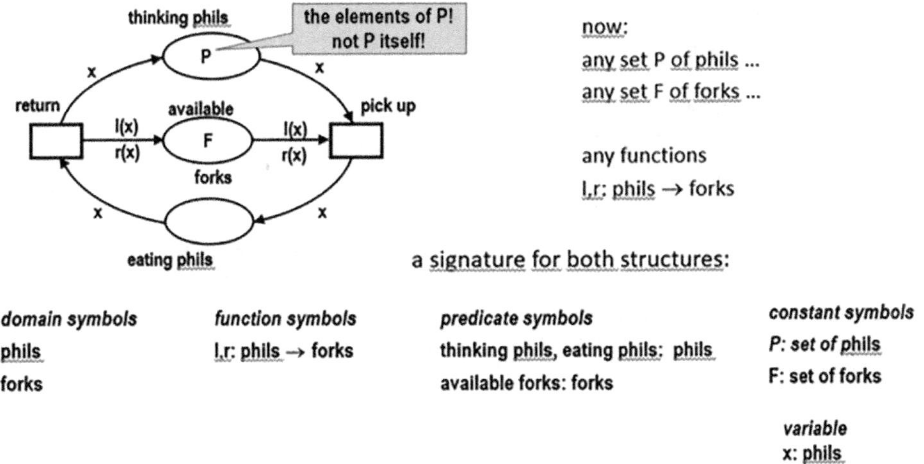

Fig. 16. Attempt

Historically, this kind of nets has been suggested in the early 1980s [5], called *predicate-transition nets*. However, predicate-transition nets cannot model the above problem, i.e. the initial marking on a symbolical, schematic level. This substantially weakens the expressive power of predicate-transition nets.

In the early 1980s this problem has not been addressed. Only recently, in [4], it was suggested to understand this feature in the framework of predicate logic: Remembering that *thinking phils* and *available forks* are predicates and that the symbols P and F are to be interpreted as a set of philosophers and of forks, respectively, we want to express

$$\text{“}\forall p \in P : thinking\ philosophers(p)\text{”}, \tag{3}$$

and

$$\text{“}\forall f \in F : available\ forks(f)\text{”}. \tag{4}$$

We express this by the inscriptions

$$elm(P) \text{ and } elm(F), \tag{5}$$

as in Fig. 17.

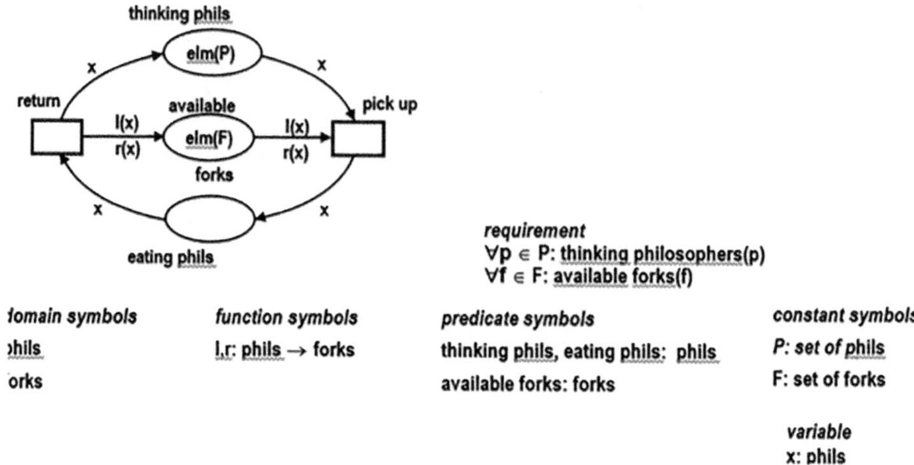

Fig. 17. Use of the *elm*-operator

For example, each philosopher p may be assigned its specific set $S(p)$ of forks, that p picks up and returns upon occurrence of the transitions *pick up* and *return* in the assignment $x = p$ (mode). Figure 18 represents this case. Finally, each time forks are picked up, the set of picked up forks may change. Figure 19 shows this case. More on the *elm* operator can be found in [4] (Fig. 20).

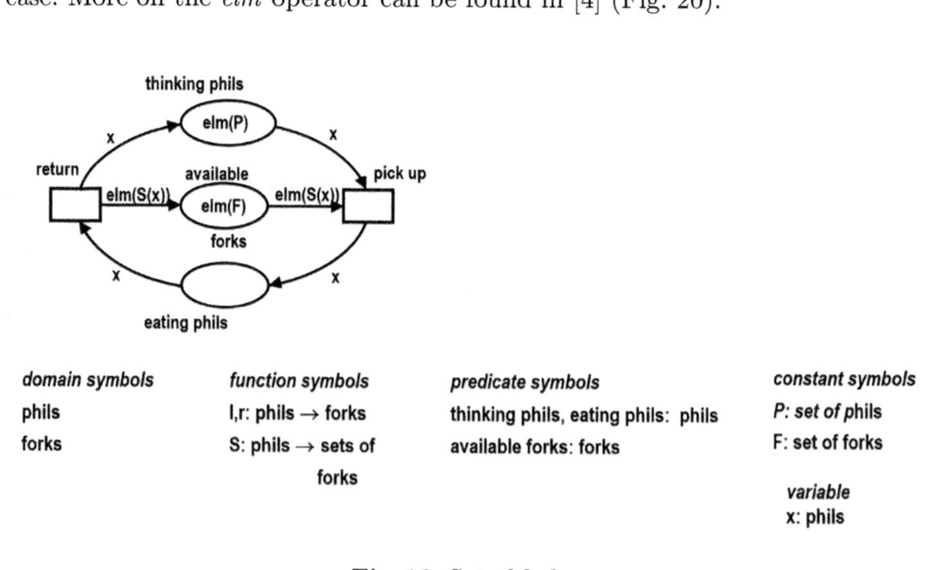

Fig. 18. Set of forks

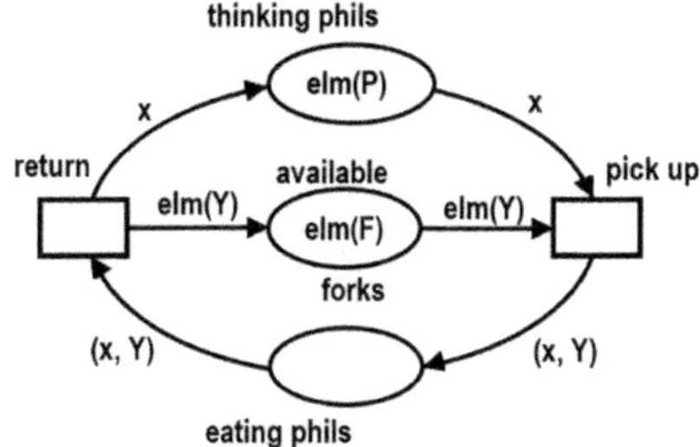

domain symbols
phils
forks

predicate symbols
thinking phils, eating phils: phils
available forks: forks

constant symbols
P: set of phils
F: set of forks

variables
x: phils
Y: sets of forks

Fig. 19. Most liberal

Fig. 20. Carl Adam Petri in the 1990s

7 Actual Contribution: the Composition Problem

Among long standing and contemporary problems and contributions to Petri nets, composition of nets certainly belongs to the most crucial ones. Composition of Petri nets has a long tradition, with many contributions. We just mention some relevant ideas of the last three decades: [3] composes many Petri net modules in one go, merging all equally labeled places as well as transitions. A long-standing initiative with many variants is algebraic calculi for Petri nets, such as the box calculus and Petri net algebras in various forms [2]. These calculi define classes of nets inductively along various composition operators, merging equally labeled transitions. [1] defines composition $A \bullet B$ of "composable" nets A and B

in a categorical framework, with A and B sharing a common net fragment, C. The effect of composition on distributed runs is studied. [8] suggests a general framework for "modular" Petri nets, i.e. nets with features to compose a net with its environment. A module may occur in many instances. Petri nets with two-faced interfaces are discussed in [13,16]. They suggest Petri nets with boundaries (PNB), with two composition operators.

All these approaches are technically quite intricate, even for intuitively simple cases such as the composition of distributed runs. The infrastructure HERAKLIT suggests a technically simple composition operator. Its expressive power covers all above mentioned operators. In particular, HERAKLIT allows mixed interfaces, i.e. two nets may be composed along places and transitions in one go. For technical details we refer to [4]. In the sequel, we present some intuitively obvious examples, that show the expressive power of the HERAKLIT composition operator.

7.1 A Producer/Consumer System

Figure 21 shows three modules. The producer and the broker negotiate an offer to the client. If the client rejects, they re-negotiate the offer. If the client accepts, the producer produces a corresponding product and ships it directly to the client. Each module has a left and a right interface, with the corresponding elements drawn on the margin of the module's surrounding box. Graphically, the interfaces of a module are depicted in different ways. The left interface of the producer, and the right interface of the client are empty. As a general rule, to compose two modules A and B, equally labeled elements of the right interface A^* of A and the left interface ${}^*B$ of B are merged. Figure 21 (b) shows the composed module *producer* • *broker* • *client*.

7.2 Claim Settlement

As a second example, Fig. 22 (a) shows six modules, A, B, C, D, E, F, representing single activities of a car driver and his insurance company, in case of a car accident. Figure 22 (b) shows the composition $A \bullet B \bullet C \bullet D \bullet E \bullet F$, i.e. the overall behavior: the driver reports the accident and hires one or more times a car, until he is informed about the insurer's decision. The insurance receives the driver's report, may solicit more information, and eventually decides and informs the driver.

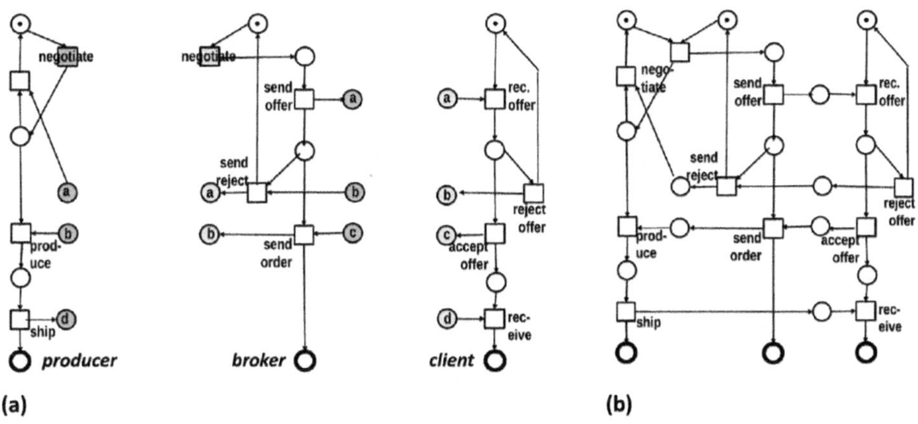

Fig. 21. (a) A producer, a consumer, and a client, and (b) the composition *producer* • *broker* • *client*

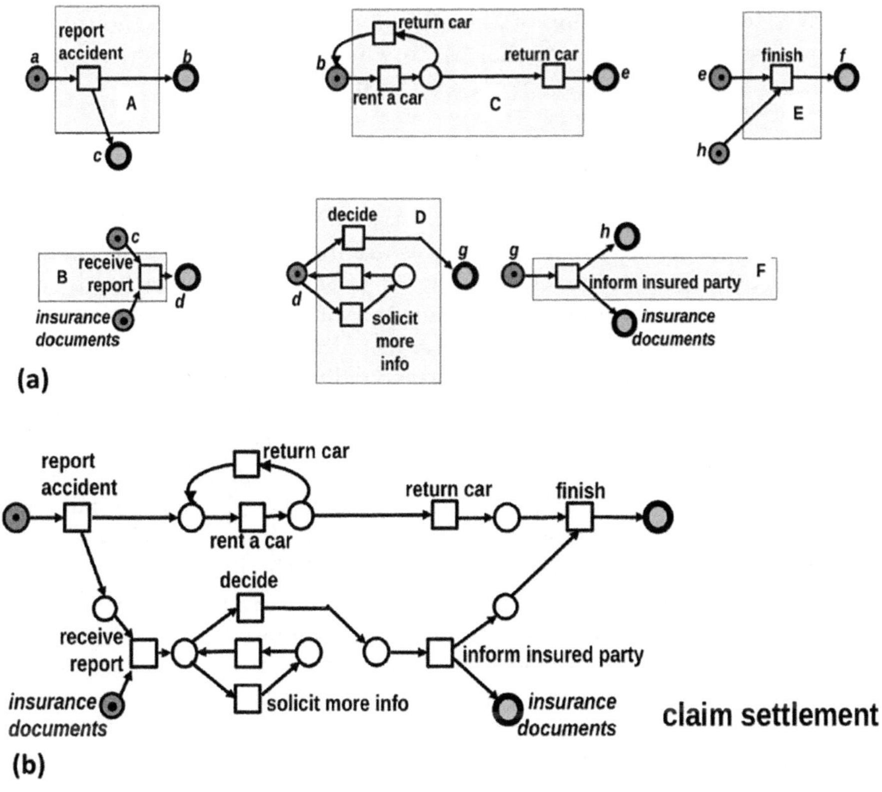

Fig. 22. (a) Six modules A, B, C, D, E, F, (b) their composition $A \bullet B \bullet C \bullet D \bullet E \bullet F$

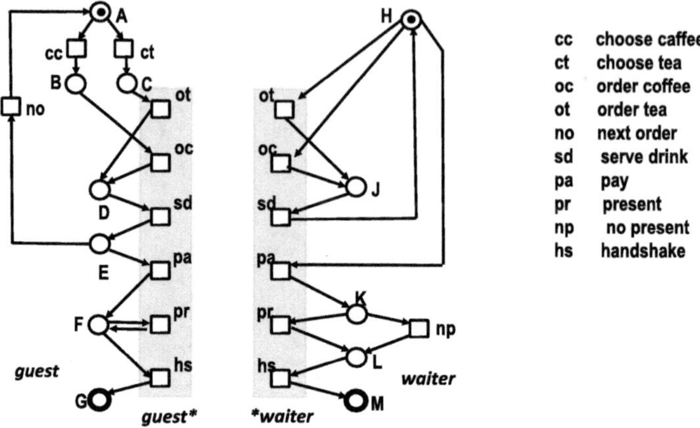

Fig. 23. Coffee house

7.3 Coffee House

Figure 23 shows the interaction of a guest and a waiter in a coffee house. Notice that the guest has a number of choices, to which the waiter reacts adequately. Composition *guest* • *waiter* is obvious; we skip it here.

7.4 The Light/Fan System

A fundamental feature of Petri nets is the strict distinction between passive and active elements. It is often convenient to start modeling by identifying typical propositions as places, and involved activities as transitions. Then, each activity is related to the involved propositions, thus generating a single step. These steps can be composed into typical distributed runs of the intended elementary system module. Furthermore, to construct a corresponding elementary system module N, all occurrences of a proposition in all steps are merged, generating a place of N. The transitions and arcs of N are inherited from the steps.

As an example of this procedure, we start with a colloquial description of a system containing a fan and a light, as they are standard in modern bathrooms: In the case of the fan is off, when you turn on the light, after some time, the fan will start running. In this situation, if you turn off the light, the fan continues running for some time. Hence, in the case of the fan is off, when you turn the light on and off quickly, the fan will not start running at all. And in the case of the fan on, when you turn the light off and on quickly, the fan will run continuously. To model this system, we first extract the involved propositions from the description: fan is off, fan is on, light is off, and light is on. Furthermore, we identify four activities: turn light on, turn light off, fan starts running, and fan stops running.

The effect of each activity on the propositions can be represented as a step, shown in Fig. 24. Starting in a situation with both light and fan off, the system

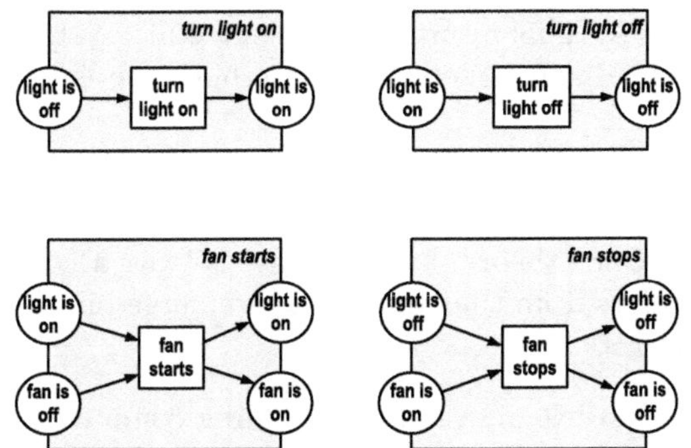

Fig. 24. Four steps

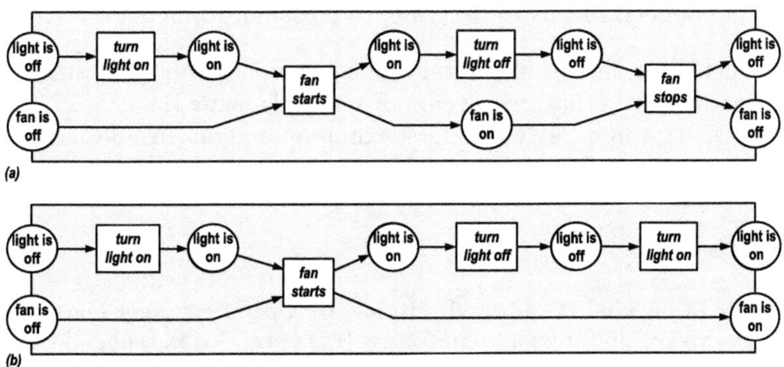

Fig. 25. Two runs: (a) *turn light on* • *fan starts* • *turn light off* • *fan stops*, (b) *turn light on* • *fan starts* • *turn light off* • *turn light on*

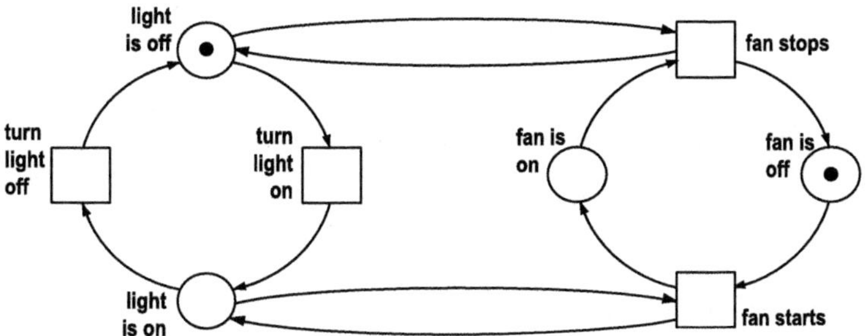

Fig. 26. The light/fan system

can evolve in different runs; it is non-deterministic. Figure 25 shows two such runs. The system itself permits infinitely many runs. It is now easy to derive an elementary system module N, such that the runs of N are exactly the runs of the system: for each proposition p in the steps of Fig. 24, merge all occurrences of p into one place of N. This results in the elementary system module of Fig. 26. As an initially assumed state one may choose both the light and the fan off.

Conclusion

The essence of Petri net theory, as Petri saw it, was a comprehensive look at informatics, that differs from that what in fact emerged in the 1960s In his view, a theory of informatics

- is about discrete models of systems (including computers);
- should base on a dynamization of logic (propositions and predicates with varying extensions);
- respects local causes and effects of events, hence considers distributed runs;
- avoids unbounded means to describe, to measure, to model systems.

Consequently, a theory of informatics must not be about abstract, symbol crunching automata – that per se cannot be implemented.

More on Carl Adam Petri as a person and more about his ideas can be found in [15].

References

1. Baldan, P., Corradini, A., Ehrig, H., König, B.: Open Petri Nets: non-deterministic processes and compositionality. In: Ehrig, H., Heckel, R., Rozenberg, G., Taentzer, G. (eds.) ICGT 2008. LNCS, vol. 5214, pp. 257–273. Springer, Heidelberg (2008). https://doi.org/10.1007/978-3-540-87405-8_18
2. Best, E., Devillers, R., Koutny, M.: Petri Net Algebra. Springer Science & Business Media (2001)
3. Christensen, S., Petrucci, L.: Towards a modular analysis of coloured Petri nets. In: Jensen, K. (ed.) ICATPN 1992. LNCS, vol. 616, pp. 113–133. Springer, Heidelberg (1992). https://doi.org/10.1007/3-540-55676-1_7
4. Fettke, P., Reisig, W.: Understanding the Digital World: Modeling with HERAKLIT. Springer (2024). https://doi.org/10.1007/978-3-031-61898-7
5. Genrich, H.J., Lautenbach, K.: System modelling with high-level Petri nets. Theoret. Comput. Sci. **13**(1), 109–135 (1981)
6. Hack, M.H.T.: Analysis of production schemata by Petri nets. Tech. rep, Massachusetts Institute of Technology (1972)
7. Jensen, K., Kristensen, L.M.: Coloured Petri Nets. Springer-Verlag, Berlin Heidelberg (2009)
8. Kindler, E., Petrucci, L.: Towards a standard for modular petri nets: a formalisation. In: Franceschinis, G., Wolf, K. (eds.) PETRI NETS 2009. LNCS, vol. 5606, pp. 43–62. Springer, Heidelberg (2009). https://doi.org/10.1007/978-3-642-02424-5_5
9. Lautenbach, K.: Exakte Bedingungen der Lebendigkeit für eine Klasse von Petri-Netzen. Ph.D. thesis, Universität Bonn, Math.-Naturwiss. Fak. (1973)
10. Petri, C.A.: Kommunikation mit Automaten. Ph.D. thesis, Universität Bonn (1962)
11. Petri, C.A.: Non-sequential processes, interner bericht isf-77-5. Gesellschaft für Mathematik und Datenverarbeitung (1977)

12. Petri, C.A.: Concurreny as a basis of systems thinking. In: Jensen, F.V., Mayoh, B., Moller, K.K. (eds.) Proc. from 5th Scandinavian Logic Symposium, Jan., 1979, Aalborg, Universitetsforlag, 1979, pp. 143–163 (1979)
13. Rathke, J., Sobociński, P., Stephens, O.: Compositional reachability in petri nets. In: Ouaknine, J., Potapov, I., Worrell, J. (eds.) RP 2014. LNCS, vol. 8762, pp. 230–243. Springer, Cham (2014). https://doi.org/10.1007/978-3-319-11439-2_18
14. Reisig, W.: Understanding Petri Nets. Springer (2013)
15. Smith, E.: Carl Adam Petri: Life and Science. Springer (2015)
16. Sobociński, P.: Representations of petri net interactions. In: Gastin, P., Laroussinie, F. (eds.) CONCUR 2010. LNCS, vol. 6269, pp. 554–568. Springer, Heidelberg (2010). https://doi.org/10.1007/978-3-642-15375-4_38
17. Suppes, P.: Introduction to Logic. Dover Publications, Mineola, N.Y. (1957)

Semantics of Concurrent Systems

Ryszard Janicki[1], Jetty Kleijn[2], Maciej Koutny[3(✉)], and Łukasz Mikulski[4]

[1] Department of Computing and Software, McMaster University, Hamilton, ON L8S 4K1, Canada
janicki@mcmaster.ca

[2] Leiden Institute of Advanced Computer Science, Leiden University, Einsteinweg 55, 2333 CC Leiden, The Netherlands
h.c.m.kleijn@liacs.leidenuniv.nl

[3] School of Computing, Newcastle University, 1 Science Square, Newcastle upon Tyne NE4 5TG, UK
maciej.koutny@ncl.ac.uk

[4] Faculty of Mathematics and Computer Science, Nicolaus Copernicus University in Toruń, Chopina 12/18, 87-100 Toruń, Poland
lukasz.mikulski@mat.umk.pl

Abstract. Discrete formal semantics of concurrent systems can be defined and investigated at different (consistent) levels of abstraction: from representations of non-branching individual runs, to structures specifying sets of related individual runs, to system models such as Petri nets. The choice of representation of individual runs leads to different semantical frameworks, and this paper considers three kinds of representations. In each case, a class of partial orders is chosen according to which events occurring in individual runs are arranged. The resulting semantical frameworks are: the sequential semantics (based on total orders), the step semantics (based on stratified orders), and the interval semantics (based on interval orders). The paper then presents different classes of relational structures which can specify sets of individual runs, and are also able to capture intrinsic relationships between executed events, e.g., causality and independence. The paper also describes language-theoretic constructs corresponding to the different classes of partial orders and relational structures. Finally, it is demonstrated how to develop a sequential semantical framework for a fundamental class of Petri nets.

Keywords: concurrency · total order · partial order · stratified order · interval order · relational structure · Petri net · elementary net system · causality · acyclicity

1 Introduction

Discrete formal semantics of concurrent systems can be defined and investigated at different (consistent) levels of abstraction: from representations of non-branching individual runs, to structures specifying sets of related individual runs, to system models such as Petri nets. The choice of representations of individual runs leads to different

F. Kordon et al. (Eds.): *Transactions on Petri Nets and Other Models of Concurrency XVIII*, LNCTPN 16260, pp. 48–92, 2026.
https://doi.org/10.1007/978-3-662-73305-9_3

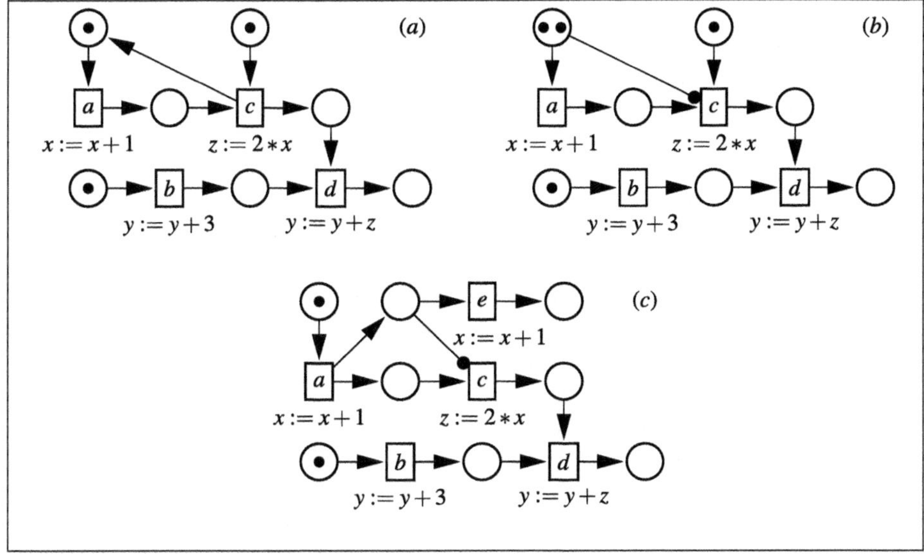

Fig. 1. Different Petri net models for an execution scenario.

semantical frameworks. Considering non-branching individual runs often amounts to choosing a class of partial orders (e.g., total, stratified, or interval) according to which event occurrences are arranged. Then, suitable relational structures which can cover sets of individual runs may also be able to capture intrinsic relationships between events, such as causality and independence.

1.1 A Concurrent Execution Scenario

As a running example, we will consider a fragment of program code shown in Table 1, where the first statement, $x = x + 1$, is the same as the last one. The first stage of defining an abstraction of this code is to assign labels to the five statements, and here a decision needs to be taken whether the first and fifth statements should be labelled differently or not. In fact, we will consider both options.

Table 1. Prog 1

```
x = x+1 ;
y = y+3 ;
z = 2*x ;
y = y+z ;
x = x+1 ;
```

Table 2. Prog 2

```
(a) x = x+1
(b) y = y+3
(c) z = 2*x
(d) y = y+z
(a) x = x+1
```

Suppose first that the first and last statements have the same label, as shown in Table 2. We then note that there are some clear independencies between pairs of assignment statements (e.g., between $x = x + 1$ and $z = 2 * x$, $y = y + 3$ and $y = y + z$, as well as $z = 2 * x$ and $y = y + z$), and clear data dependencies between pairs of assignment statements (e.g., between $x = x + 1$ and $y = y + 3$ as well as $y = y + 3$ and $z = 2 * x$). The Petri net in Fig. 1(a) captures the relations/dependencies between the events and has a (partially concurrent run) $abcda$. Also, e.g., $bacda$ and $acbda$ are runs of that net. However, if we want to support simultaneous executions of assignments, then more intricate situations arise.

For example, it is quite natural to assume that the data needed for performing the actions is broadcast first, then the computation is performed simultaneously, and finally the obtained results are shared. An example programming model that works according to the described scheme is Map-Reduce [40]. We can use the current values of some variables when they are modified simultaneously, i.e., we read (map) the old values before they are updated (reduced). In the discussed example we observe such a relationship between the two assignments, $x = x+1$ and $z = 2*x$. When considering their execution, the effect of executing them in the same step is the same as executing $z = 2*x$ first and after that $x = x+1$. However, executing $x = x+1$ first and then $z = 2*x$ produces a different outcome in terms of the value assigned to z. Hence, in the program fragment we are considering, the first instance of $x = x+1$ cannot be executed together with $z = 2*x$, but the second instance of $x = x+1$ and $z = 2*x$ can be executed together. To model the asymmetric data conflict that we have just described, we will use activator arcs (which check for the presence of tokens but neither use nor block tokens).

Table 3. Prog 3

$(a)\ x = x+1$
$(b)\ y = y+3$
$(c)\ z = 2*x$
$(d)\ y = y+z$
$(e)\ x = x+1$

One of the possible Petri net solutions is depicted in Fig. 1(b), where the activator arc ensures that the execution of the second instance of $x = x+1$ will occur not before (i.e., will be after or simultaneous with) the execution of $z = 2*x$. This Petri net also has *abcda*, *bacda*, and *acbda* as runs and in fact allows the same sequences of length 5 as the previous one, but it deadlocks after two occurrences of a in case c has not occurred by then, as intended. Thus it properly captures the relations between the two occurrences of a and that of c. Note furthermore that this net is not safe. If one insists on safe solutions, then we need to use the alternative assignment of labels and treat the two instances of the assignment statement $x = x+1$ differently, as shown in Table 3. This way we obtain the safe Petri net model shown in Fig. 1(c). Similar to the previous case, this net deadlocks after the occurrence of e in case c has not yet been executed.

1.2 About this Paper

Formal models of operational semantics of concurrent systems are often based on models for representing individual (non-branching) system runs, where two events (executed actions) can be observed as either happening one after another, or as being simultaneous. Such behaviours can be represented as partially ordered sets of events where execution precedence is transitive, and simultaneity or overlapping is captured by the lack of ordering. In this paper, we are interested in three kinds of partial orders modelling concurrent system executions: (i) total orders modelling sequential executions of individual (instantaneous) actions; (ii) stratified orders modelling sequential executions of sets of simultaneous (instantaneous) actions; and (iii) interval orders modelling behaviours where events can take time and the corresponding time intervals can overlap [62]. The use of interval orders in the area of concurrency theory can be traced back to [22,24,29,41,42,56,61]. It is important to emphasize Petri net theories in, e.g., [1,2,53,54], consider executions to be general partial orders, where ordering represents causality, and unorderedness represents event independence. In this paper, partial orders of this kind are considered as specifications of sets of individual executions (see below).

Dealing with the semantics of concurrent systems purely in terms of their individual runs, such as total orders (sequences), stratified orders (step sequences), or interval orders is far from being computationally efficient in terms both of behaviour modelling and of property validation. To address this shortcoming, more involved relational structures have been introduced, aiming at a succinct and faithful representation *rs* of (often exponentially large) sets *RS* of closely related individual runs. Examples include causal partial orders for sequences, and stratified order structures for step sequences. Succinctness is usually achieved by retaining in *rs* (through intersection) only those relationships which are common to all executions in *RS*. Faithfulness, on the other hand, requires that all potential executions which are extensions of *rs* belong to *RS*. Structures like *rs*, referred to as invariant (or closed) structures represent concurrent histories and both desired properties (succinctness and faithfulness) follow from generalisations of Szpilrajn's Theorem (i.e., a partial order is the intersection of all its total order extensions). Although *rs* provides a clean theoretical capture of the set *RS*, to turn them into a practical tool (as, e.g., in [47]) one needs to be able to derive them directly from single executions using the relevant structural properties of the concurrent system. This brings into focus relational structures with acyclic relations on events (e.g., dependence graphs introduced in [45] and analysed in detail in [15]), which yield invariant structures after applying a suitable closure operation (e.g., the transitive closure for acyclic relations). The approach sketched above has been introduced and investigated in [18, 19] as a generic model that provides general recipes for building semantical frameworks based on relational structures.

Using relational structures to model concurrent behaviours in the way presented in this paper was initiated in the late 1980s [11, 21, 22, 24, 42]. More recently, the approach has been substantially revised and generalised first in [17] and then in [18–20] on which this paper is to a large extent based.

We would like to stress that the aim of this paper is to present basic concepts and constructs of three different discrete semantical frameworks for concurrent systems. Issues related to algorithmic aspects, implementations, and applications are outside the scope.

2 Preliminaries

In this section, we present some basic notions and notations used later on.

To start with, $\subset$ denotes the strict set inclusion, and if $f : X \to Y$ is a mapping and $X' \subseteq X$ and $Y' \subseteq Y$ are such that $f(X') \subseteq Y'$, then $f|_{X' \to Y'}$ denotes the mapping $f' : X' \to Y'$ such that $f'(x) = f(x)$, for all $x \in X'$.

To handle the naming of various mappings, we use the mnemonic notation x2y to denote some (uniquely defined) mapping from X to Y. Moreover, if the mapping is from the subsets of X or to the subsets of Y, then the corresponding part of the notation will be denoted in uppercase. For example, a mapping converting integers *INT* into binary numbers *BIN* could be denoted by int2bin, and a mapping returning all prime factors of natural numbers in *NAT* by nat2NAT.

Actions and Events. Throughout this paper, we assume that $\mathbb{A}$ is a non-empty finite set of *actions* regarded as abstract representations of activities which a concurrent system may carry out. The set of all finite sequences of actions is denoted by $\mathsf{SQ} = \mathbb{A}^*$, and all finite sequences of sets of actions are denoted by $\mathsf{SSQ} = (2^{\mathbb{A}})^*$. The concatenation operation for sequences in SQ and SSQ is denoted by $\odot$.

An action $a \in \mathbb{A}$ may occur more than once in a concurrent system run. We will refer to these occurrences as *events*, and represent/index the i-th occurrence of a as $a^{(i)}$, where $i \geq 1$. We will also denote $\ell_{a^{(i)}} = a$ and $\iota_{a^{(i)}} = i$.

The number of *occurrences* of action $a \in \mathbb{A}$ in a sequence $\tau \in \mathsf{SQ} \cup \mathsf{SSQ}$ is denoted by $\#_\tau(a)$, and the *events* $\mathbb{E}_\tau$ of τ are all the events $a^{(i)}$ such that $i \leq \#_\tau(a)$. Then the *position* $\mathrm{pos}_\tau(a^{(i)})$ of an event $a^{(i)} \in \mathbb{E}_\tau$ within τ is the $k \leq n$ such that:

- a_k is the i-th occurrence of a within $\tau = a_1 \dots a_n \in \mathsf{SQ}$,
- A_k contains the i-th occurrence of a within $\tau = A_1 \dots A_n \in \mathsf{SSQ}$.

For example, $\mathbb{E}_{abbaa} = \{a^{(1)}, a^{(2)}, a^{(3)}, b^{(1)}, b^{(2)}\}$ and $\mathrm{pos}_{abbaa}(a^{(2)}) = 4$. A set of events Δ is *left-closed* if, for every $a^{(i)} \in \Delta$ with $i > 1$, we have $a^{(1)}, \dots, a^{(i-1)} \in \Delta$.

Relational Structures. In this paper, a *relational structure* is a pair $rs = \langle \Delta, \prec \rangle$ or a triple $rs = \langle \Delta, \prec, \sqsubset \rangle$, where $\prec$ and $\sqsubset$ are irreflexive binary relations over a left-closed finite set of events Δ (the *domain* of *rs*). We will use Δ_{rs}, $\prec_{rs}$, and $\sqsubset_{rs}$ to denote the components of *rs*, and call the relational structure *label-linear* if $x \prec y$, for all $x, y \in \Delta$ satisfying $\ell_x = \ell_y$ and $\iota_x < \iota_y$.

In the approach followed in this paper, relational structures are used to specify relationships between domain elements (events). Intuitively, $x \prec y$ will be interpreted as stating that event x *precedes* event y, whereas $x \sqsubset y$ will be interpreted as stating that event x *weakly precedes* event y which means that y does not precede x. Hence, it is never the case that x precedes y as well as y weakly precedes x, i.e., $x \prec y \sqsubset x$ never holds. It is, however, possible that x weakly precedes y as well as y weakly precedes x, i.e., $x \sqsubset y \sqsubset x$. An intuitive interpretation of such a situation differs depending on the nature of the two events: if x and y are instantaneous events then they are considered as *simultaneous*, and if x and y are events with non-zero duration then they are considered as *overlapping*.

Remark 1. The indexing scheme for events is meant to match the implicit order between different occurrences of the same action so that $a^{(i)}$ precedes $a^{(j)}$ whenever $i < j$. (Clearly, this holds for all label-linear relational structures.) This rules out *auto-concurrency* which allows simultaneous execution of different occurrences of the same action (note that this is in accordance with the theory of traces [44]). As a consequence, the approach presented in this paper is not directly applicable to non-safe Petri nets. $\diamond$

Let *rs* and *rs'* be relational structures with two relationships. Then *rs'* is an *extension* of *rs* if $\Delta_{rs} = \Delta_{rs'}$, $\prec_{rs} \subseteq \prec_{rs'}$, and $\sqsubset_{rs} \subseteq \sqsubset_{rs'}$. We denote this by $rs \trianglelefteq rs'$. Moreover, $rs \triangleleft rs'$ if, additionally, $rs \neq rs'$. Also, if R is a non-empty set of relational structures with same domain Δ and two relationships, then

$$\bigcap R = \langle \Delta, \bigcap_{rs \in R} \prec_{rs}, \bigcap_{rs \in R} \sqsubset_{rs} \rangle$$

is the *intersection* of the relational structures in R. For relational structures with one relationship, the above notions are re-stated by simply ignoring the second relationship.

We use the following notations for a set of relational structures $\mathscr{R}$ and $rs \in \mathscr{R}$:

$$\begin{aligned} \text{ext}_{\mathscr{R}}(rs) &= \{rs' \in \mathscr{R} \mid rs \trianglelefteq rs'\} \\ \mathscr{R}^{max} &= \{rs' \in \mathscr{R} \mid rs \in \text{ext}_{\mathscr{R}}(rs') \implies rs = rs'\} \\ \mathscr{R}^{min} &= \{rs' \in \mathscr{R} \mid rs' \in \text{ext}_{\mathscr{R}}(rs) \implies rs = rs'\} \\ \text{maxext}_{\mathscr{R}}(rs) &= \text{ext}_{\mathscr{R}}(rs) \cap \mathscr{R}^{max} . \end{aligned}$$

Their meaning is as follows: $\text{ext}_{\mathscr{R}}(rs)$ are the extensions of rs in $\mathscr{R}$; $\mathscr{R}^{max}$ are the maximal relational structures in $\mathscr{R}$; $\mathscr{R}^{min}$ are the minimal relational structures in $\mathscr{R}$; and $\text{maxext}_{\mathscr{R}}(rs)$ are the maximal extensions of rs in $\mathscr{R}$.

To easily capture notions related to cyclicity or transitivity in a relational structure $rs = \langle \Delta, \prec, \sqsubset \rangle$, it is convenient to refer to the *graph of rs*, defined as a directed graph $G_{rs} = (\Delta, \prec, \sqsubset)$ with the set of vertices Δ and two distinct kinds of arcs, $\prec$ and $\sqsubset$. In such a graph, the notions of paths and cycles are straightforward generalisations of paths and cycles in the standard directed graphs. For example, we will write $x \prec y \prec z \sqsubset w$ to denote a directed path in G_{rs} made up of three arcs $\langle x, y \rangle \in \prec$, $\langle y, z \rangle \in \prec$, and $\langle z, w \rangle \in \sqsubset$. As another example, the graph in Fig. 6 contains cycles $y \sqsubset z \sqsubset w \prec x \sqsubset y$ and $y \sqsubset z \prec w \prec x \sqsubset y$.

3 Semantical Frameworks Based on Relational Structures

At the centre of the approach adopted in this paper lies a set $\mathscr{R}$ of *finite* relational structures which are assumed to be valid *specifications* of possible individual runs of a class of concurrent systems (e.g., $\mathscr{R} = \mathscr{R}_{acyclic}$ comprises all relational structures $\langle \Delta, \prec \rangle$ such that $\prec$ is an acyclic relation). Each relational structure $rs \in \mathscr{R}$ describes relationships between pairs of events in the domain of rs. Different relational structures with common domains belonging to $\mathscr{R}$ can be compared w.r.t. the conveyed information about the relationships between pairs of events. In particular, we interpret $rs \triangleleft rs'$ as stating that $rs' \in \mathscr{R}$ carries *more information* than $rs \in \mathscr{R}$, or that rs' is more *concrete* than rs. We are primarily interested in two kinds of structures in $\mathscr{R}$, as described next.

Maximal Relational Structures. The *maximal* relational structures $\mathscr{R}^{max} \subseteq \mathscr{R}$ represent all the individual runs which are captured by the relational structures in $\mathscr{R}$ (e.g., $\mathscr{R}^{max}_{acyclic}$ comprises all total orders). Any relational structure $rs \in \mathscr{R}$ can be considered as an abstract specification of all the individual runs represented by its maximal extensions $\text{maxext}_{\mathscr{R}}(rs) \subseteq \mathscr{R}^{max}$.

Closed Relational Structures. The *closed* relational structures $\mathscr{R}^{clo} \subseteq \mathscr{R}$ are structures which convey maximal information about relationships between events which are common to all the individual runs they specify. That is, rs is closed if, for every $rs' \in \mathscr{R}$:

$$rs \triangleleft rs' \implies \text{maxext}_{\mathscr{R}}(rs') \subset \text{maxext}_{\mathscr{R}}(rs) , \tag{1}$$

i.e., no proper extension of *rs* carries information about relationships between events which is shared by all the maximal extensions of *rs*. In a way, closed structures are the most informative relational specifications of sets of individual runs, and so can also be regarded as the 'richest' specifications. It is therefore desirable, e.g., to be able to identify them for practical applications. Yet another way of looking at closed structures is to see them as 'invariant' relationships embedded in their maximal extensions (such an interpretation can often be found in the literature).

It turns out in the settings we consider that a relational structure $rs \in \mathscr{R}$ is closed if and only if

$$rs = \bigcap \text{maxext}_{\mathscr{R}}(rs) \ . \tag{2}$$

Such a property can be seen as a generalisation of Szpilrajn's theorem [60] which states that every partial order is the intersection of its total order extensions (e.g., $\mathscr{R}^{clo}_{acyclic}$ is the set of all partial orders). It is immediate to see that all maximal structured are closed, i.e., $\mathscr{R}^{max} \subseteq \mathscr{R}^{clo}$.

Moving on, for each $rs \in \mathscr{R}$ there exists a unique closed relational structure $rs' \in \mathscr{R}^{clo}$ extending *rs*. Moreover, such a closed structure is given by:

$$rs' = \bigcap \text{maxext}_{\mathscr{R}}(rs) \ . \tag{3}$$

This, in turn, means that there is a well-defined *structure closure* mapping $f : \mathscr{R} \to \mathscr{R}^{clo}$ which, for every specification *rs*, returns maximal information about the events which is common to all the individual runs conforming to *rs*.

Calculating $f(rs)$ using the formula given in Eq. (3) can be computationally expensive, e.g., the number of total order extensions of $rs = \langle \Delta, \prec \rangle \in \mathscr{R}_{acyclic}$ can be as high as $|\Delta|!$. It is therefore essential to find better ways of deriving $f(rs)$, and we will present examples of suitable formulas greatly improving on the worst case scenario. For example, if $rs = \langle \Delta, \prec \rangle \in \mathscr{R}_{acyclic}$, then $f(rs) = \langle \Delta, \prec^{+} \rangle$, and so the derivation of $f(rs)$ boils down to finding the transitive closure of $\prec$ which can be done in low-polynomial time.

Knowing $f(rs)$ may be crucial, e.g., to perform effective analyses of causal relationships between the events of an individual run. For example, one may be given such a run in the form of a firing sequence of a system modelled by an EN-system. Then, as explained in Sect. 7.1 one can derive a relational structure $rs \in \mathscr{R}_{acyclic}$ such that $x \prec y$ iff there is a directed path from x to y in the graph of *rs*. As establishing whether two events are causally related would then require finding potentially very long paths in *rs*, a naive approach could be very costly. A practical way of going about this would be to first construct the transitive closure of *rs*, i.e., to apply the closure mapping for $\mathscr{R}_{acyclic}$, as then all causally related events would be directly related.

4 Partial Order Models of System Runs

Individual runs of concurrent systems can be represented by partial orders (or be based on partial orders) as the acyclicity of runs is a very minimal requirement resulting from physical considerations, and event precedence is transitive. Moreover, the simultaneity of instantaneous events, or the overlapping of non-instantaneous events, can be represented by the lack of ordering.

In this paper, a *(strict) partial order* is a label-linear relational structure $po = \langle \Delta, \prec \rangle$ such that $\prec$ is an irreflexive and transitive (precedence) relation. The set of all partial orders is denoted by PO. Note that the last part of this definition ensures that all the occurrences of the same action are ordered according to the increasing order of their indices, as described in Remark 1.

Each partial order $po = \langle \Delta, \prec \rangle$ induces two further relationships. The first is *unorderedness*, denoted by $x \frown y$, which holds for all $x \neq y \in \Delta$ such that $x \not\prec y$ and $y \not\prec x$. The second is *direct precedence*, denoted by $x \prec^{dir} y$, which holds when $x \prec y$ and there is no z satisfying $x \prec z \prec y$. Note that $\langle \Delta, \prec^{dir} \rangle$ is usually referred to as the Hasse diagram of po.

Remark 2. The interpretation of unorderedness depends on the intended role of the partial order po. If po is meant to represent an individual run, then $x \frown y$ is interpreted as stating that x and y are simultaneous or overlapping. However, if po is meant to represent a specification of individual runs, then $x \frown y$ is interpreted as stating that x and y are independent (and po is regarded as a *causal partial order*). $\diamond$

There are different kinds of partial orders used to represent individual runs, e.g., reflecting key properties of the underlying hardware and/of software. In the literature, one can find at least three kinds of such models, namely the total, stratified, and interval orders. A partial order $po = \langle \Delta, \prec \rangle$ is:

- *total* if $x \prec y$ or $y \prec x$, for all $x \neq y \in \Delta$.
- *stratified* if $y \frown x \prec z \implies y \prec z$ and $z \prec x \frown y \implies z \prec y$, for all $x, y, z \in \Delta$.
- *interval* if $x \prec y \wedge z \prec w \implies x \prec w \vee z \prec y$, for all $x, y, z, w \in \Delta$.

The sets of total, stratified, and interval orders are denoted by TO, SO, and IPO, respectively.

Theorem 1. $\mathsf{TO} \subset \mathsf{SO} \subset \mathsf{IPO} \subset \mathsf{PO}$.

Example 1. Figure 2(a) depicts a total order, Fig. 2(b) depicts a stratified order which is not total, Fig. 2(c) depicts an interval order which is not stratified, and Fig. 2(d) depicts a partial order which is not interval. $\diamond$

Thinking about total, stratified, and interval orders as captures of individual runs, leads to alternative—more operational—definitions:

- $to = \langle \Delta, \prec \rangle$ is a total order if Δ can be enumerated (in a unique way) as $x_1, \dots, x_n$ in such a way that $\prec$ is equal to $\{\langle x_i, x_j \rangle \mid 1 \leq i < j \leq n\}$. We will denote $\mathrm{line}(to) = x_1 \dots x_n$.
- $so = \langle \Delta, \prec \rangle$ is a stratified order if there are (unique) sets $\Delta_1, \dots, \Delta_n$ forming a partition of Δ in such a way that $\prec$ is equal to $\bigcup_{1 \leq i < j \leq n} \Delta_i \times \Delta_j$. Intuitively, this means that events can be partitioned into totally ordered strata (or steps) such that within each stratum all the events are unordered. In this case, the unorderedness of events satisfies the following transitivity-like property: $x \frown y \frown z \wedge x \neq z \implies x \frown z$. We will denote $\mathrm{strata}(so) = \Delta_1 \dots \Delta_n$.

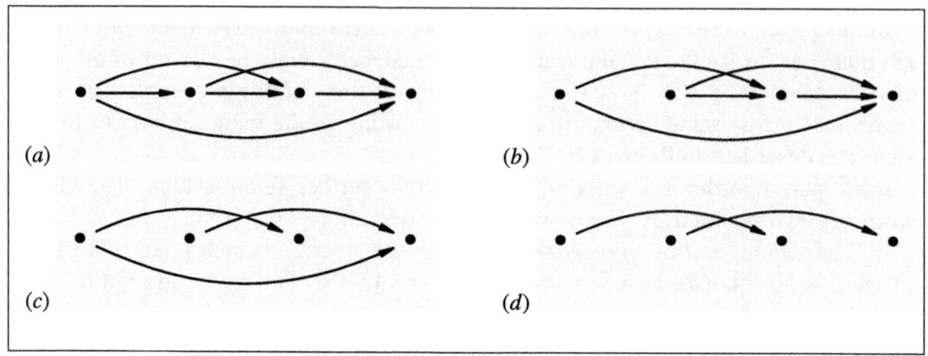

Fig. 2. The hierarchy of partial orders represented as directed graphs.

- $\langle \Delta, \prec \rangle$ is an interval order if there exist real-valued mappings, β and ε, such that $\beta(x) < \varepsilon(x)$ as well as $x \prec y \iff \varepsilon(x) < \beta(y)$, for all $x, y \in \Delta$. Intuitively, β and ε represent the 'beginnings' and 'endings' of time intervals corresponding to the events in Δ. In this case, the unorderedness of events satisfies the following property: $x \frown y \iff [\beta(x), \varepsilon(x)] \cap [\beta(y), \varepsilon(y)] \neq \varnothing$.

Orders and Sequences. Individual runs captured by the total and stratified orders can also be represented by language-theoretic notions. First, there is a close link between total orders and sequences in SQ. We can capture it using two mappings:

- to2sq : $\mathsf{TO} \to \mathsf{SQ}$ given by $to \mapsto \ell_{x_1} \ldots \ell_{x_n}$ assuming that $\mathrm{line}(to) = x_1 \ldots x_n$.
- sq2to : $\mathsf{SQ} \to \mathsf{TO}$ given by $a_1 \ldots a_n \mapsto to$ where $to \in \mathsf{TO}$ is such that $\mathrm{line}(to) = a_1^{(k_1)} \ldots a_n^{(k_n)}$ and $k_i = \#_{a_i}(a_1 \ldots a_i)$ for $1 \leq i \leq n$.

Second, there is a close link between stratified orders and sequences in SSQ which can be captured using the following two mappings:

- so2ssq : $\mathsf{SO} \to \mathsf{SSQ}$ given by $so \mapsto A_1 \ldots A_n$ assuming that $\mathrm{strata}(so) = \Delta_1 \ldots \Delta_n$ and $A_i = \{\ell_x \mid x \in \Delta_i\}$ for $1 \leq i \leq n$.
- ssq2so : $\mathsf{SSQ} \to \mathsf{SO}$ given by $A_1 \ldots A_n \mapsto so$ and $so \in \mathsf{SO}$ is such that $\mathrm{strata}(so) = \Delta_1 \ldots \Delta_n$ and $\Delta_i = \{a^{(\#_a(A_1 \ldots A_i))} \mid a \in A_i\}$ for $1 \leq i \leq n$.

Theorem 2. to2sq *and* so2ssq *are two bijections with the inverses* sq2to *and* ssq2so, *respectively.*

5 Relational Structures for Specifying Sets of Runs

We have already argued that sets of individual runs can be specified using suitable (abstract) relational structures. We will demonstrate this separately for the total, stratified, and interval orders assuming that the relations used in the specifications are the precedence and weak precedence of events.

Recall that by fixing a class $\mathscr{R}$ of relational structures which can specify individual runs, we have already determined all the individual runs $\mathscr{R}^{max} \subseteq \mathscr{R}$ and all the closed structures $\mathscr{R}^{clo} \subseteq \mathscr{R}$ of the framework being developed. However, the intrinsic properties of the maximal and closed structures, such as algorithmically effective methods for calculating the closure mappings, still need to be discussed.

The three subsections that now follow deal with the total, stratified, and interval runs of concurrent systems, each subsection being organised under the following headings:

- **Structures:** Here we introduce a precise definition of all those relational structures $\mathscr{R}$ which can serve as specifications for a given class of partial orders representing individual runs $\mathscr{P}$.
- **Maximal structures:** Here we argue that the maximal relational structures of $\mathscr{R}$ coincide with the partial orders in $\mathscr{P}$.
- **Closed structures:** Here we provide a capture of all closed structures of $\mathscr{R}$, i.e., those which can be seen as most informative relational structures in $\mathscr{R}$. We also state a variant of Szpilrajn's theorem for the closed structures in $\mathscr{R}$, and provide algorithmically effective definition of the closure mapping.

5.1 Relational Structures for Total Order Runs

The first question we face here is:

> *What relational structures $\mathscr{R}$ with single relationship provide a suitable specification model for* TO*?*

The answer is straightforward, namely all one needs to require is that $\mathscr{R}^{max} = \mathsf{TO}$. Note that, in such a case, $rs \in \mathscr{R}$ implies $\varnothing \neq \mathrm{maxext}_{\mathscr{R}}(rs) \subseteq \mathsf{TO}$, and so rs specifies a non-empty set of total order runs.

Structures. An *acyclic relation* is a relational structure $ao = \langle \Delta, \prec \rangle$ such that the graph of the relation $\prec$ does not contain any cycles, and $x \prec^{+} y$, for all $x, y \in \Delta$ satisfying $\ell_x = \ell_y$ and $\iota_x < \iota_y$. The set of all acyclic relations is denoted by AR.

Requiring the acyclicity of $\prec$ has a straightforward operational interpretation:

> *In a given run there should not be events $x_1, x_2, \ldots, x_n$ such that 'each x_i preceded x_{i+1}' and, in addition, 'x_n preceded x_1'.*

Moreover, the second part of the above definition ensures that all the occurrences of the same action are ordered according to the increasing order of their indices, as described in Remark 1.

Maximal Structures. As stated below, total orders are the maximal acyclic relations.

Theorem 3. $\mathsf{AR}^{max} = \mathsf{TO}$.

The mapping $\mathrm{ar2TO} : \mathsf{AR} \to 2^{\mathsf{TO}}$, given by $ar \mapsto \mathrm{maxext}_{\mathsf{AR}}(ar)$, yields all the total orders extending acyclic relations.

Closed Structures. Recall that, by Eq. (1), a closed acyclic relation is any $ar \in \mathsf{AR}$ such that, for every $ar' \in \mathsf{AR}$:

$$ar \lhd ar' \implies \text{ar2TO}(ar') \subset \text{ar2TO}(ar) .$$

The next result 'reveals' that partial orders are the closed acyclic relations, and that the transitive closure of a binary relation underpins the closure operation for acyclic relations.

Theorem 4. $\mathsf{AR}^{clo} = \mathsf{PO}$ *and the mapping* ar2po : $\mathsf{AR} \to \mathsf{PO}$, *given by the formula* $\langle \Delta, \prec \rangle \mapsto \langle \Delta, \prec^+ \rangle$, *is the closure mapping for acyclic relations.*

A version of Szpilrajn's theorem also holds.

Theorem 5. $\text{ar2TO}(po) \neq \varnothing$ *and* $po = \bigcap \text{ar2TO}(po)$, *for every* $po \in \mathsf{PO}$.

Note that for $po = \langle \Delta, \prec \rangle \in \mathsf{PO}$ understood as a specification of a set of total orders $\text{ar2TO}(po)$, we have the following:

- $x \prec y$ indicates the *precedence* of x over y in all the total orders of $\text{ar2TO}(po)$, and
- $x \frown y$ indicates that x and y are *concurrent* or *independent*.

The latter interpretation is further supported by the fact that if $x \frown y$ then there is at least one total order $to \in \text{ar2TO}(po)$ such that $x \prec_{to} y$, and at least one total order $to' \in \text{ar2TO}(po)$ such that $y \prec_{to'} x$.

Consider again the program fragment in Table 2 with four actions (note that a is used both for the first and the last statement, and recall that whenever it is needed to distinguish two equally labelled events we use $a^{(1)}$ and $a^{(2)}$). Let us concentrate on sets of variables that are used in the statements and assume the precedence relationships between pairs of statements with nonempty intersection of those sets. This way we obtain that (b) and (c) precede (d), but (b) does not need to precede (c). We then obtain two total orders depicted in Fig. 3(a, b) as well as an acyclic order Fig. 3(c) with its closure (partial order) depicted in Fig. 3(d).

$(a)\ x = x + 1$
$(b)\ y = y + 3$
$(c)\ z = 2 * x$
$(d)\ y = y + z$
$(a)\ x = x + 1$

5.2 Relational Structures for Stratified Order Runs

We would now like to develop a model suitable for specifying sets of stratified order runs by repeating the treatment for total order runs presented above. In this case, we also implicitly assume that events are instantaneous.

The first issue we note is that relational structures with a single relation are not sufficiently expressive to capture three essential relationships between events at the level of closed specifications, viz. simultaneity in addition to precedence and independence. We will therefore seek a solution in the domain of relational structures $\langle \Delta, \prec, \sqsubset \rangle$ based on two relations. The intuitive meaning of $x \prec y$ is the same as in the case of acyclic relations (i.e., x occurred 'earlier than' y), whereas $x \sqsubset y$ means that x occurred 'not later' than y (i.e., 'earlier than' or 'simultaneously' with y; in other words, one can think about $\sqsubset$ as 'weak precedence'). Thus, in particular, we interpret $x \sqsubset y \sqsubset x$ as indicating that x and y occurred 'simultaneously'.

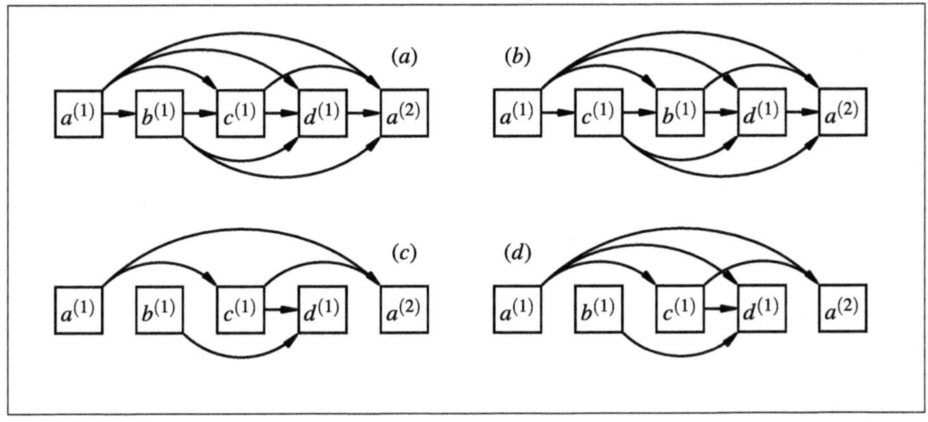

Fig. 3. (a,b) Total orders with different precedence relationship for statements b and c. (c,d) Acyclic relation which is not closed and its closure which is not maximal.

Remark 3. We do not require at this point that $\prec$ be transitive nor $\sqsubset$ enjoy a similar property. However, such properties will hold for their closures and will follow from the axioms SO:1, SO:2, and SO:3 introduced later on. Note that this is similar to the treatment of acyclic relations which only 'become' transitive after applying the closure mapping (transitive closure). $\diamond$

Relational structures with two relations cannot be directly compared with partial orders which are based on just one relation. However, any partial order $po = \langle \Delta, \prec \rangle$ can be uniquely lifted to the following relational structure:

$$\eth(po) = \langle \Delta, \prec, \{\langle x,y \rangle \in \Delta \times \Delta \mid y \not\prec x \neq y\} \rangle .$$

Note that we then have $\prec = \prec_{\eth(po)} \subseteq \sqsubset_{\eth(po)}$ and $\frown_{po} = \sqsubset_{\eth(po)} \cap \sqsubset^{-1}_{\eth(po)}$ (which means that unordered events are simultaneous). Hence, the key modelling question can be rephrased as:

What relational structures $\mathscr{R}$ provide a suitable specification model for $\eth(\mathsf{SO})$?

And, similarly as before, all one needs to require is that $\mathscr{R}^{max} = \eth(\mathsf{SO})$. In such a case, $rs \in \mathscr{R}$ implies $\varnothing \neq \text{maxext}_{\mathscr{R}}(rs) \subseteq \eth(\mathsf{SO})$, and so rs specifies a non-empty set of stratified order runs.

Structures. We start the presentation of a suitable domain of relational structures by introducing a generalisation of the concept of acyclicity defined for directed graphs. In what follows, for every relational structure $rs = \langle \Delta, \prec, \sqsubset \rangle$, we denote:

$$\lll_{rs} = (\prec \cup \sqsubset)^* \circ \prec \circ (\prec \cup \sqsubset)^* \quad \text{and} \quad \Subset_{rs} = (\prec \cup \sqsubset)^+ \setminus id_\Delta .$$

The above two relations generalise the notion of transitive closure to relational structures involving two relationships, $\prec$ and $\sqsubset$. The first relation will yield the precedence, and the second weak precedence in the definition of the closure mapping for the relational structures dealt with in this section. Referring to the graph of rs, $x \ll_{rs} y$ is equivalent to stating that there is a path in G_{rs}, beginning at x and ending at y, such that at least one arc traversed belongs to $\prec$. Similarly, $x \Subset_{rs} y$ is equivalent to stating that there is a path in G_{rs} beginning at x and ending at $y \neq x$.

A relational structure $rs = \langle \Delta, \prec, \sqsubset \rangle$ is *weakly cyclic* if no cycle in G_{rs} traverses an arc belonging to $\prec$. Weak cyclicity has a clear interpretation in operational terms:

In a given run, there are no events $x_1, x_2, \ldots, x_n$ $(n \geq 2)$ such that 'each x_i happened before or simultaneously with x_{i+1}' (i.e., $x_i \prec x_{i+1}$ or $x_i \sqsubset x_{i+1}$), while 'x_n happened (strictly) before x_1 (i.e., $x_n \prec x_1$).

We are now in a position to characterise relational structures which can play the role of specifications for sets of stratified order runs, in a similar way as acyclic relations play the role of specifications for sets of total order runs.

A *combined order structure (or* CO*-structure)* is a weakly cyclic relational structure rs such that $x \ll_{rs} y$, for all $x, y \in \Delta_{rs}$ satisfying $\ell_x = \ell_y$ and $\iota_x < \iota_y$. The set of all combined order structures is denoted by COS.

Note that the second part of the above definition will ensure that all the occurrences of the same action are ordered according to the increasing order of their indices, as described in Remark 1.

Maximal Structures. Maximal CO-structures can be characterised by a set of axioms.

A *layered concurrent structure (or* LC*-structure)* is a label-linear relational structure $lcs = \langle \Delta, \prec, \sqsubset \rangle$ such that, for all $x, y, z \in \Delta$:

$$
\begin{array}{lcl}
x \prec y \Longrightarrow x \sqsubset y \not\sqsubset x & : & \text{LC:1} \\
x \prec y \Longrightarrow x \prec z \lor z \prec y & : & \text{LC:2} \\
x \neq y \Longrightarrow x \sqsubset y \sqsubset x \lor x \prec y \lor y \prec x & : & \text{LC:3}
\end{array}
$$

The set of all LC-structures is denoted by LCS and, as stated below, LC-structures are the maximal CO-structures.

Theorem 6. $\mathsf{COS}^{max} = \mathsf{LCS} = \partial(\mathsf{SO})$.

The mapping $\mathrm{cos2LCS} : \mathsf{COS} \to 2^{\mathsf{LCS}}$, given by $cos \mapsto \mathrm{maxext}_{\mathsf{COS}}(cos)$, yields LC-structures extending CO-structures.

The close link between LC-structures and stratified orders can be captured using a pair of mappings:

- $\mathrm{lcs2so} : \mathsf{LCS} \to \mathsf{SO}$ such that $lcs \mapsto \langle \Delta_{lcs}, \prec_{lcs} \rangle$.
- $\mathrm{so2lcs} : \mathsf{SO} \to \mathsf{LCS}$ such that $so \mapsto \partial(so)$.

There is also a close link between LC-structures and step sequences, resembling that between total orders and action sequences. We can capture it using another pair of mappings:

- $\mathrm{lcs2ssq} : \mathsf{LCS} \to \mathsf{SSQ}$ such that $lcs \mapsto \mathrm{so2ssq} \circ \mathrm{lcs2so}(lcs)$.
- $\mathrm{ssq2lcs} : \mathsf{SSQ} \to \mathsf{LCS}$ such that $ssq \mapsto \mathrm{so2lcs} \circ \mathrm{ssq2so}(ssq)$.

Theorem 7. lcs2so *and* lcs2ssq *are two bijections with the inverses* so2lcs *and* ssq2lcs, *respectively.*

Closed Structures. Recall that, by Eq. (1), a closed CO-structure is any $cos \in \mathsf{COS}$ such that, for every $cos' \in \mathsf{COS}$:

$$cos \lhd cos' \implies \mathrm{cos2LCS}(cos') \subset \mathrm{cos2LCS}(cos)\ .$$

We first introduce an axiomatisation of the closed CO-structures.

A *stratified order structure (or* SO-*structure)* is a label-linear relational structure $\langle \Delta, \prec, \sqsubset \rangle$ such that, for all $x, y, z \in \Delta$:

$$\begin{aligned} x \prec y &\implies x \sqsubset y \quad : \quad \text{SO:1} \\ x \sqsubset y \sqsubset z \neq x &\implies x \sqsubset z \quad : \quad \text{SO:2} \\ x \sqsubset y \prec z \vee x \prec y \sqsubset z &\implies x \prec z \quad : \quad \text{SO:3} \end{aligned}$$

The set of all SO-structures is denoted by SOS.

It turns out that SO-structures are the closed CO-structures. Moreover, the closure of CO-structures can be expressed directly by adding all the implied precedences and weak precedences, as shown in the next result.

Theorem 8. $\mathsf{COS}^{clo} = \mathsf{SOS}$ *and the mapping* $\mathrm{cos2sos} : \mathsf{COS} \to \mathsf{SOS}$*, given by the formula* $cos \mapsto \langle \Delta, \ll_{cos}, \Subset_{cos} \rangle$*, is the closure mapping for* CO*-structures.*

A generalisation of Szpilrajn's theorem for CO-structures also holds.

Theorem 9. $\mathrm{cos2LCS}(sos) \neq \varnothing$ *and* $sos = \bigcap \mathrm{cos2LCS}(sos)$*, for every* $sos \in \mathsf{SOS}$.

Note that for $sos = \langle \Delta, \prec, \sqsubset \rangle \in \mathsf{SOS}$ understood as a specification of a set of stratified orders $\mathrm{lcs2so} \circ \mathrm{cos2LCS}(sos)$, we have the following:

- $x \prec y$ indicates the *precedence* of x over y in all the stratified orders belonging to $\mathrm{lcs2so} \circ \mathrm{cos2LCS}(sos)$,
- $x \sqsubset y \sqsubset x$ indicates the *simultaneity* of x and y in all the stratified orders belonging to $\mathrm{lcs2so} \circ \mathrm{cos2LCS}(sos)$,
- $x \sqsubset y \not\sqsubset x \not\prec y$ indicates the *(true) weak precedence* of x over y (this means that there is at least one stratified order $so \in \mathrm{lcs2so} \circ \mathrm{cos2LCS}(sos)$ such that $x \prec_{so} y$, and at least one stratified order $so' \in \mathrm{lcs2so} \circ \mathrm{cos2LCS}(sos)$ such that $y \frown_{so'} x$), and
- $x \not\sqsubset y \not\sqsubset x \neq y$ indicates that x and y are *independent*.

Consider again the program fragment in Table 2. Note that the roles of a variable on the left and right side of the assignment operator are different. We will try to make this explicit by using weak precedence in cases where the common variable of the first instruction occurs on its left side. This way statement (c) is in weak precedence relationship with statement (a). We will denote the weak precedence by dashed arcs. Recalling the intuitive meaning of weak precedence (not later than), we allow for simultaneous execution of some statements and this is manifested as cycles (cliques) of dashed arcs. Two LC-structures with weak precedence arcs are shown in Fig. 4(a, b). Note that we would get stratified orders if we omitted dashed cycles. Figure 4 depicts a CO-structure which can be used as a specification of the LC-structures in Fig. 4(a, b), and its SO-structure closure shown in Fig. 4(d).

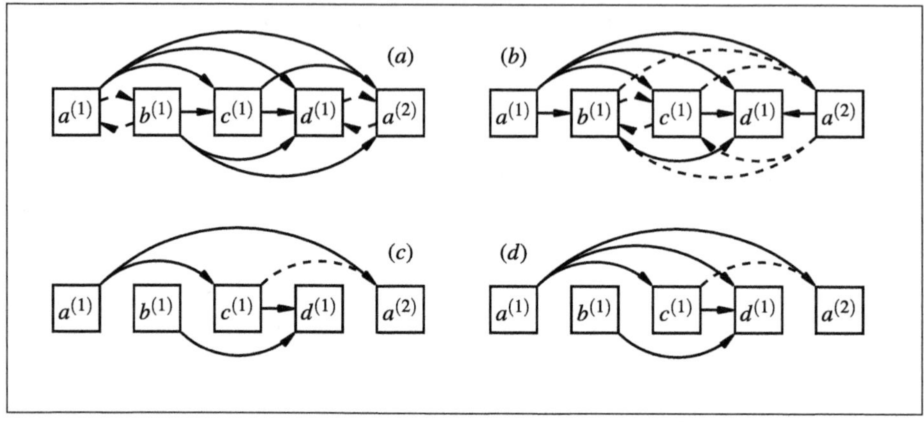

Fig. 4. (a,b) LC-structures with different simultaneous steps. (c,d) CO-structure specifying these LC-structures and its SO-structure closure. In this and subsequent diagrams, solid arrows represent $\prec$ and dashed arrows represent $\sqsubset$.

5.3 Relational Structures for Interval Order Runs

A model for specifying sets of interval order runs employs relational structures of the same form as those used in the treatment for stratified order runs presented above. That is, we use relational structures $\langle\Delta,\prec,\sqsubset\rangle$ based on two relations with the same intuitive meaning of $x \prec y$ (i.e., x occurred 'earlier than' y) and $x \sqsubset y$ (i.e., x occurred 'not later' than y). However, the interpretation of more complex relationships is not the same. In particular, whereas before $x \sqsubset y \sqsubset x$ was interpreted as indicating that x and y occurred 'simultaneously', in the current interpretation this will indicate that the corresponding time intervals 'overlap'. As a result, the transitivity of simultaneity in the model developed for stratified order runs will no longer hold. For example, it is possible to have x overlapping with both y and z (i.e., $x \sqsubset y \sqsubset x$ and $x \sqsubset z \sqsubset x$) as well as y preceding z (i.e., $y \prec z$ which implies $z \not\sqsubset y$).

Moreover, the key modelling question now takes the form:

What relational structures $\mathscr{R}$ provide a suitable specification model for $\partial(\mathsf{IPO})$?

Similarly as before, all one needs to require is that $\mathscr{R}^{max} = \partial(\mathsf{IPO})$ as, in such a case, $rs \in \mathscr{R}$ implies $\varnothing \neq \mathrm{maxext}_{\mathscr{R}}(rs) \subseteq \partial(\mathsf{IPO})$, and so rs specifies a non-empty set of interval order runs.

Structures. We again start the presentation of a suitable relational structures by introducing a generalisation of the original concept of acyclicity defined for directed graphs. In what follows, for every relational structure $rs = \langle\Delta,\prec,\sqsubset\rangle$, we denote:

$$\lll_{rs} = \prec \circ (\prec \cup (\sqsubset \circ \prec))^* \text{ and } \measuredangle_{rs} = (\prec \cup (\sqsubset \circ \prec))^+ \cup (\prec \cup (\sqsubset \circ \prec))^* \circ \sqsubset .$$

Again, the above two relations generalise the notion of transitive closure with the first relation yielding the precedence, and the second weak precedence in the definition of the closure mapping for the relational structures dealt with in this section. Referring to the graph of rs, $x \lll_{rs} y$ is equivalent to stating that there is a path in G_{rs}, beginning at x and ending at y, such that: no two consecutive arcs belong to $\sqsubset$, and the first and last arcs traversed belong to $\prec$. Similarly, $x \measuredangle_{rs} y$ is equivalent to stating that there is a path in G_{rs} beginning at x and ending at y such that: no two consecutive arcs belong to $\sqsubset$, and the first or the last arc (or both) traversed belong to $\prec$.

In the case of interval orders, the notion of behavioural acyclicity is more involved than in the previous two cases. Although it should be expected that $\prec$ is acyclic, and $\sqsubset$ allows cycles (as the time intervals corresponding to two or more events can overlap at some point), it is also necessary to state what kinds of mixed cycles, involving both $\prec$ and $\sqsubset$ relationships, might be allowed. What now follows is the concept of behavioural acyclicity which is suitable for interval order runs.

A relational structure $rs = \langle \Delta, \prec, \sqsubset \rangle$ is *combined interval structure acyclic* (or *cis-acyclic*) if every cycle in the graph G_{rs} contains at least one pair of consecutive arcs belonging to $\sqsubset \setminus \prec$.

Example 2. Figure 5(a) shows a cycle forbidden by the total order semantics but allowed in the stratified and interval order semantics, Fig. 5(b,c) show cycles forbidden by the total and stratified order semantics but allowed in the interval order semantics, and Fig. 5(d) shows a cycle forbidden in all the considered semantics. ◇

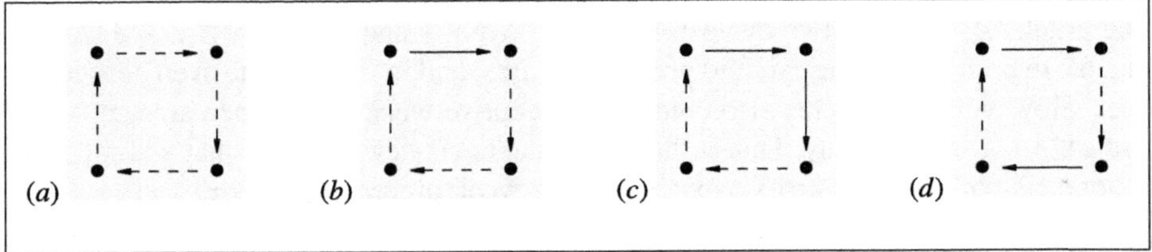

Fig. 5. The hierarchy of forbidden cycles.

The graph G_{rs} is also suitable for generalising the concept of transitive closure. First, a directed path in G_{rs} is a *cis-path* if it does not contain any pair of consecutive arcs representing the relation $\sqsubset$. Then, a cis-path from x to y which begins and ends with arcs in $\prec$ induces a precedence relationship between x and y (cf. the definition of $\lll_{rs}$). Similarly, a cis-path from x to y induces a weak precedence relationship between x and y unless it begins and ends with arcs in $\sqsubset$ (cf. the definition of $\measuredangle_{rs}$).

Remark 4. Paths in G_{rs} like $x \sqsubset y \sqsubset z$ are not taken into account in the definition of cis-paths, as weak precedence is not transitive in the interval setting (unlike in the stratified order setting). Indeed, it is possible to assign intervals to x, y, and z so that $x \sqsubset y \sqsubset z$ and $x \not\sqsubset z$ as follows: $I(x) = [3,5]$, $I(z) = [0,2]$, and $I(y) = [1,4]$. ◇

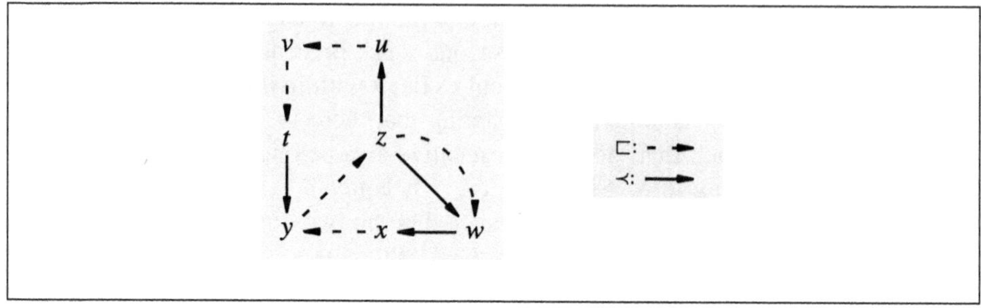

Fig. 6. The graph of the relational structure in Example 3.

Individual runs are 'acyclic' as re-visiting the past is not possible. Bearing this in mind, the essence of cis-acyclicity can be explained using the following simple example involving three events: $x \sqsubset y \prec z \sqsubset x$. Within the concurrency models discussed in [19] (and in Sect. 5.2), such a cyclic behaviour would mean that x occurred before itself. However, this view is based on the implicit assumption that events are instantaneous. But, if events have duration, the cycle $x \sqsubset y \prec z \sqsubset x$ is not inconsistent. Indeed, similarly as in Remark 4, it is possible to assign intervals to x, y, and z so that $x \sqsubset y \prec z \sqsubset x$, e.g., $I(x) = [1,4]$, $I(y) = [0,2]$, and $I(z) = [3,5]$.

Example 3. Consider the following relational structure with seven events:

$$rs = \langle \{x,y,z,w,u,v,t\}, \{\langle z,w\rangle, \langle z,u\rangle, \langle w,x\rangle, \langle t,y\rangle\}, \{\langle x,y\rangle, \langle y,z\rangle, \langle z,w\rangle, \langle u,v\rangle, \langle v,t\rangle\}\rangle \,.$$

The graph G_{rs} contains two cycles: $y \sqsubset z \prec w \prec x \sqsubset y$ and $v \sqsubset t \prec y \sqsubset z \prec u \sqsubset v$ (see Fig. 6). In both cycles one can find precedence arcs, and in the first one even consecutive ones. However, both cycles also contain consecutive weak precedence arcs, $x \sqsubset y \sqsubset z$ and $u \sqsubset v \sqsubset t$, respectively. This suffices to make rs cis-acyclic. Note that $w \prec x \sqsubset y \sqsubset z$ is not a cis-path as it traverses two consecutive weak precedence arcs $x \sqsubset y \sqsubset z$. ◇

We now characterise relational structures which can be used to specify sets of interval order runs.

A *combined interval structure* (or CI-*structure*) is a cis-acyclic relational structure rs such that $x \lll_{rs} y$, for all $x,y \in \Delta_{rs}$ satisfying $\ell_x = \ell_y$ and $\iota_x \lll_{rs} \iota_y$. The set of all CI-structures is denoted by CIS.

Note that the second part of the above definition ensures that all the occurrences of the same action are ordered according to the increasing order of their indices, as described in Remark 1.

Maximal Structures. Maximal CI-structures can be characterised by a set of axioms given below.

An *interval partial order structure* (or IP-*structure*) is a label-linear relational structure $ips = \langle \Delta, \prec, \sqsubset \rangle$ such that, for all $x,y,z,w \in \Delta$:

$$x \prec y \implies x \sqsubset y \not\sqsubset x \quad : \quad \text{IP:1}$$
$$x \prec y \wedge z \prec w \implies x \prec w \vee z \prec y \quad : \quad \text{IP:2}$$
$$x \neq y \implies x \sqsubset y \sqsubset x \vee x \prec y \vee y \prec x \quad : \quad \text{IP:3}$$

The set of all IP-*structures* is denoted by IPS.

As stated below, IP-structures are the maximal CI-structures.

Theorem 10. $\mathsf{CIS}^{max} = \mathsf{IPS} = \partial(\mathsf{IPO})$.

The mapping cis2IPS : $\mathsf{CIS} \to 2^{\mathsf{IPS}}$, given by $cis \mapsto \text{maxext}_{\mathsf{CIS}}(cis)$, yields IP-structures extending CI-structures.

Closed Structures. Recall that, by Eq. (1), a closed CI-structure is $cis \in \mathsf{CIS}$ such that, for every $cis' \in \mathsf{CIS}$:

$$cis \lhd cis' \implies \text{cis2IPS}(cis') \subset \text{cis2IPS}(cis)\ .$$

We first provide an axiomatisation of the closed CI-structures.

An *interval combined structure* (or IC-*structure*) is a label-linear relational structure $ics = \langle \Delta, \prec, \sqsubset \rangle$ such that, for all $x, y, z, w \in \Delta$:

$$\begin{array}{rll} x \prec y & \Longrightarrow x \sqsubset y \not\sqsubset x & : \ \text{IC:1} \\ x \prec y \prec z & \Longrightarrow x \prec z & : \ \text{IC:2} \\ x \prec y \sqsubset z \prec w & \Longrightarrow x \prec w & : \ \text{IC:3} \\ x \sqsubset y \prec z \sqsubset w \neq x & \Longrightarrow x \sqsubset w & : \ \text{IC:4} \\ x \sqsubset y \prec z \ \vee \ x \prec y \sqsubset z & \Longrightarrow x \sqsubset z & : \ \text{IC:5} \end{array}$$

The set of all IC-structures is denoted by ICS.

It turns out that IC-structures are the closed CI-structures. Moreover, the closure of CI-structures can be expressed directly by adding all the implied precedences and weak precedences, as shown in the next result.

Theorem 11. $\mathsf{CIS}^{clo} = \mathsf{ICS}$ *and the mapping* cis2ics : $\mathsf{CIS} \to \mathsf{ICS}$, *given by the formula* $cis \mapsto \langle \Delta, \lll_{cis}, \measuredangle_{cis} \setminus id_{\Delta_{cis}} \rangle$, *is the closure mapping for* CI-*structures.*

A generalisation of Szpilrajn's theorem for CI-structures also holds.

Theorem 12. $\text{cis2IPS}(ics) \neq \varnothing$ *and* $ics = \bigcap \text{cis2IPS}(ics)$, *for every* $ics \in \mathsf{ICS}$.

$(a)\ x = x + 1$
$(b)\ y = y + 3$
$(c)\ z = 2 * x$
$(d)\ y = y + z$
$(a)\ x = x + 1$

Let us continue the discussion of the program fragment in Table 2. By splitting every instruction into two phases (reads together with the calculation of the expression value followed by writing to the variable on the left side of the assignment operator) we would obtain the same set of weak precedences as in the previous section. Also the closed structure is the same. However, note that the closure operation differs; for example, if $rs = \langle \{x, y, z\}, \{\langle y, z\rangle\}, \{\langle x, y\rangle\}\rangle$, then

$$\begin{aligned} \text{cos2sos}(rs) &= \langle \{x,y,z\}, \{\langle y,z\rangle, \langle x,z\rangle\}, \{\langle x,y\rangle, \langle x,z\rangle, \langle y,z\rangle\rangle\} \\ \text{cis2ics}(rs) &= \langle \{x,y,z\}, \{\langle y,z\rangle\}, \{\langle x,y\rangle, \langle x,z\rangle, \langle y,z\rangle\rangle\}\ . \end{aligned}$$

Another important difference concerns the cycles of weak precedence arcs. In contrast to stratified order semantics, each such cycle means that the lifetimes of connected instructions have a nonempty intersection, i.e., in every maximal extension we observe first both reads and then both writes.

Sample maximal structures of a purely interval nature (not belonging to the stratified order semantics) are given in Fig. 7. In the IP-structure on the left one can observe two statements (c) and (d) in the precedence relation, while both of them overlap with the second occurrence of (a). Note also that we get interval orders if we omit the dashed cycles. As we already mentioned, both CI-structure specification and IC-structure closure are the same as CO-structure specification and SO-structure closure depicted in Fig. 4.

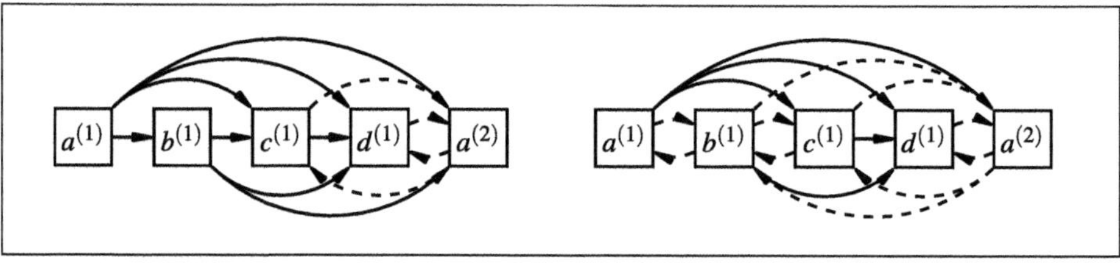

Fig. 7. Two IP-structures.

6 Traces

The original goal of (Mazurkiewicz) traces [46] was to use formal language theory to analyse behaviours of concurrent systems. Individual runs of concurrent systems are often defined in terms of sequences (i.e., total orders) or step-sequences (i.e., stratified orders) or duration intervals (i.e., interval orders) of events.

When a partial order is interpreted as a specification of individual runs, all its total extensions may be treated as equivalent sequential observations, and each individual element of an equivalence class represents fully all the relevant properties of the entire class. Such an approach is especially useful when there is an effective way of deriving the entire equivalence class from a single representative, and traces provide such a method.

The aim of this section is to show that it is possible to develop fully consistent semantics of concurrent behaviours, one based on relational structures, and the other based on language-theoretic concepts.

The three subsections that now follow again focus separately on the total, stratified, and interval order runs, and each subsection is organised under the following headings:

- **Alphabet:** Here we define relations between actions, such as independence, which are then used to define the corresponding language-theoretic representations of individual runs.
- **Sequences:** Here we define language-theoretic representations of individual runs corresponding to a given class of partial orders $\mathscr{P}$.

- **Structures:** Here we restrict the relational structures $\mathscr{R}$ which can serve as specifications for a given class of partial orders representing individual runs $\mathscr{P}$ so that they obey the rules imposed by the alphabet.
- **Maximal structures:** Here we restrict the maximal relational structures of $\mathscr{R}$ to those which obey the rules imposed by the alphabet.
- **Traces and histories:** Here we introduce equivalence classes of semantically equivalent sequences and the corresponding equivalence classes of semantically equivalent partial order runs.
- **Dependence graphs:** Here we characterise the core relational structures of $\mathscr{R}$ obeying the rules imposed by the alphabet.
- **Closed structures:** Here we restrict the closed structures of $\mathscr{R}$ to those which obey the rules imposed by the alphabet. We also discuss consistency between the language-theoretic and structure-based approaches, and discuss algebraic trace-based frameworks.

6.1 Traces for Sequential Semantics

Alphabet. A *concurrency alphabet* is a pair $\Gamma = \langle \mathbb{A}, \mathsf{ind} \rangle$, where $\mathsf{ind} \subseteq \mathbb{A} \times \mathbb{A}$ is an irreflexive and symmetric *independence* relation on actions. Independent actions have no direct influence on each other, and so ind is symmetric. Moreover, different occurrences of the same action are not independent, and so ind is irreflexive. Throughout this section, Γ is *fixed.*

Sequences. The language-theoretic representations of individual runs are all the finite sequences of actions $\mathsf{SQ} = \mathbb{A}^*$.

Structures. Traces of purely sequential runs can be treated in a framework based on acyclic relations. However, not all acyclic relations are relevant as in a given specification of total order runs only dependent events should be ordered. Therefore, we only deal with acyclic relations reflecting the intended meaning of the relationships between events captured by Γ.

A *concurrency order over* Γ is an acyclic relation $\langle \Delta, \prec \rangle$ such that, for all $x \neq y \in \Delta$, $\langle \ell_x, \ell_y \rangle \notin \mathsf{ind}$ implies $x \prec^+ y$ or $y \prec^+ x$. The set of all concurrency orders over Γ is denoted by CO_Γ.

That is, in concurrency orders over Γ dependent events are always ordered (directly or indirectly). On the other hand, independent events can be unordered or ordered. Note also that independent actions can only be ordered in the closed specifications defined later if transitivity and the ordering of dependent actions implies this.

Maximal Structures. It is immediate to observe that the maximal concurrency orders over Γ are all the total orders.

Theorem 13. $\mathsf{CO}_\Gamma^{max} = \mathsf{AR}^{max} \cap \mathsf{CO}_\Gamma = \mathsf{TO}$.

Moreover, $\mathrm{maxext}_{\mathsf{CO}_\Gamma}(co) = \mathrm{maxext}_{\mathsf{AR}}(co)$, for every $co \in \mathsf{CO}_\Gamma$. Hence, the total orders extending concurrency orders over Γ are given by $\mathrm{ar2TO}|_{\mathsf{CO}_\Gamma \to 2^{\mathsf{TO}}}$.

Traces and Histories. Action sequences represent individual runs. To identify some of them as equivalent, we will employ the independence relation ind such that two action sequences are deemed equivalent if it is possible to transform one into the other by successively swapping pairs of adjacent independent actions.

Two action sequences, $sq, sq' \in \mathsf{SQ}$, are in the *local swapping* relation if there is a pair of independent actions $\langle a,b\rangle \in \mathsf{ind}$ and action sequences $\tau, \tau' \in \mathbb{A}^*$ such that $sq = \tau ab\tau'$ and $sq' = \tau ba\tau'$. We denote this by $sq \approx_\Gamma sq'$.

The *trace equivalence over* Γ, denoted by $\equiv_\Gamma$, is the reflexive and transitive closure of $\approx_\Gamma$. Trace equivalence is an event-preserving equivalence relation. Moreover, it is characterised by consistency in the ordering of dependent events, i.e., if $sq, sq' \in \mathsf{SQ}$ then $sq \equiv_\Gamma sq'$ if and only if $\mathbb{E}_{sq} = \mathbb{E}_{sq'}$ and, for all $x, y \in \mathbb{E}_{sq}$:

$$\langle \ell_x, \ell_y\rangle \notin \mathsf{ind} \implies (\mathrm{pos}_{sq}(x) < \mathrm{pos}_{sq}(y) \iff \mathrm{pos}_{sq'}(x) < \mathrm{pos}_{sq'}(y)) .$$

Intuitively, trace equivalent orders arrange dependent events in exactly the same way. It is then natural to look at the resulting equivalence classes of action sequences.

Concurrency traces over Γ, denoted by CT_Γ, are the equivalence classes of the trace equivalence relation $\equiv_\Gamma$. Hence, a concurrency trace can be identified by a single action sequence belonging to it. The mapping sq2ct : $\mathsf{SQ} \to \mathsf{CT}_\Gamma$, given by $sq \mapsto [\![sq]\!]_{\equiv_\Gamma}$, associates concurrency traces to action sequences.

Trace equivalence is a central notion for representations based on action sequences. To extend it to order based representations of runs (in this case, total orders), we introduce two relations for TO which can be seen as direct counterparts of the local swapping and trace equivalence relations defined for SQ.

Two total orders, $to, to' \in \mathsf{TO}$, are in the *local swapping* relation if they have the same domain Δ, and there exist domain elements $x, y \in \Delta$ and sequences of domain elements $\tau, \tau' \in \Delta^*$ such that $\langle \ell_x, \ell_y\rangle \in \mathsf{ind}$, line$(to) = \tau xy\tau'$ and line$(to') = \tau yx\tau'$. We denote this by $to \ddot{\approx}_\Gamma to'$.

The above local swapping relation leads to an equivalence relation for total orders, called the *history equivalence over* Γ, denoted by $\ddot{\equiv}_\Gamma$, and defined as the reflexive and transitive closure of $\ddot{\approx}_\Gamma$. We also define the *concurrency histories over* Γ, denoted by CH_Γ, as the equivalence classes of the history equivalence $\ddot{\equiv}_\Gamma$.

Similarly as trace equivalence, history equivalence can be characterised by the consistency of the orderings of dependent events, i.e., if $to, to' \in \mathsf{TO}$ then $to \ddot{\equiv}_\Gamma to'$ if and only if $\Delta_{to} = \Delta_{to'}$ and, for all $x, y \in \Delta_{to}$:

$$\langle \ell_x, \ell_y\rangle \notin \mathsf{ind} \implies (x \prec_{to} y \iff x \prec_{to'} y) .$$

History equivalence reflects trace equivalence through the mappings linking action sequences and total orders.

Theorem 14. *For all $sq, sq' \in \mathsf{SQ}$ and $to, to' \in \mathsf{TO}$:*

$$\begin{aligned} sq \equiv_\Gamma sq' &\iff \mathrm{sq2to}(sq) \ddot{\equiv}_\Gamma \mathrm{sq2to}(sq') \\ to \ddot{\equiv}_\Gamma to' &\iff \mathrm{to2sq}(to) \equiv_\Gamma \mathrm{to2sq}(to') . \end{aligned}$$

The mapping to2ch : $\mathsf{TO} \to \mathsf{CH}_\Gamma$, given by $to \mapsto [\![to]\!]_{\doteqdot_\Gamma}$, associates concurrency histories with total orders. We then obtain a direct correspondence between concurrency traces and concurrency histories.

Theorem 15. to2sq : $\mathsf{CH}_\Gamma \to \mathsf{CT}_\Gamma$ *is a bijection with the inverse* sq2to : $\mathsf{CT}_\Gamma \to \mathsf{CH}_\Gamma$.

The next result validates the soundness of the trace approach for the sequential semantics.

Theorem 16. $\mathsf{SQ} = \biguplus \mathsf{CT}_\Gamma$ *and* $\mathsf{TO} = \biguplus \mathsf{CH}_\Gamma$.

Let us continue the discussion on the program fragment from Table 2. Now we are able to formalise the source of the precedence relationships after defining an independence relation. Recall that we treat all pairs of statements involving disjoint sets of variables as independent. Therefore, we obtain:

$$\Gamma = \langle \{a,b,c,d\}, \{\langle a,b\rangle, \langle a,d\rangle, \langle b,a\rangle, \langle b,c\rangle, \langle c,b\rangle, \langle d,a\rangle\}\rangle.$$

Moreover, one can compute all sequences equivalent with the original sequencing of statements $abcda$. Note that

$$acbda \approx_\Gamma \underline{abcda} \approx_\Gamma bacda \approx_\Gamma bacad \approx_\Gamma abcad \approx_\Gamma acbad \approx_\Gamma acabd$$

Hence, $[\![abcda]\!]_{\equiv_\Gamma} = \{abcad, abcda, acabd, acbad, acbda, bacad, bacda\}$.

Dependence Graphs. Concurrency traces and concurrency histories capture a fundamental notion of equivalence among sequential runs based on action independence. To analyse intrinsic invariant relationships between events involved in a concurrency trace/history, we need to lift independence to the level of (executed) events. To this end, we now introduce structures with (partially) ordered events in which dependent events (i.e., executions of dependent actions) are always ordered, and any ordering between independent events should be derived from those holding between dependent ones.

The *dependence graphs over* Γ, denoted by DG_Γ, are the minimal concurrency orders, i.e., $\mathsf{DG}_\Gamma = \mathsf{CO}_\Gamma^{min}$. An alternative characterisation of dependence graphs is based on the relationships between pairs of events, i.e., a concurrency order $co = \langle \Delta, \prec \rangle$ is a dependence graph if $x \prec y \vee y \prec x \iff \langle \ell_x, \ell_y \rangle \notin \mathsf{ind}$, for all $x \neq y \in \Delta$.

For each concurrency order co there is a unique dependence graph dg such that $dg \trianglelefteq co$, obtained from co by removing arcs between independent events. We will denote the latter by co2dg$_\Gamma(co)$, implicitly defining a mapping co2dg$_\Gamma$: $\mathsf{CO}_\Gamma \to \mathsf{DG}_\Gamma$.

Dependence graphs have the distinguishing power of history equivalence.

Theorem 17. $to \doteqdot_\Gamma to'$ *if and only if* co2dg$_\Gamma(to) =$ co2dg$_\Gamma(to')$, *for all* $to, to' \in \mathsf{TO}$.

Therefore, it is possible to associate dependence graphs with histories through the mapping ch2dg : $\mathsf{CH}_\Gamma \to \mathsf{DG}_\Gamma$, given by $[\![to]\!]_{\doteqdot_\Gamma} \mapsto$ co2dg$_\Gamma(to)$. We then obtain a direct correspondence between concurrency histories and dependence graphs.

Theorem 18. ch2dg : $\mathsf{CH}_\Gamma \to \mathsf{DG}_\Gamma$ *is a bijection with the inverse* ar2TO : $\mathsf{DG}_\Gamma \to \mathsf{CH}_\Gamma$.

Closed Structures. Recall that, by Eq. (1), a closed acyclic relation over Γ is $co \in \mathsf{CO}_\Gamma$ such that, for every $co' \in \mathsf{CO}_\Gamma$, $co \lhd co' \implies \text{ar2TO}(co') \subset \text{ar2TO}(co)$.

Suppose now that we were given (or observed) a concurrency order co and, on this basis, we would find out as many as possible relationships which can still be derived. We are ultimately interested in the properties of the runs which are consistent with co, i.e., the set $\text{maxext}_{\mathsf{CO}_\Gamma}(co)$. We may, for example, add the derived relationship $x \prec z$ whenever $x \prec y \prec z$. The reason why adding such a relationship is legitimate is that the extended structure co' is an order structure satisfying $\text{maxext}_{\mathsf{CO}_\Gamma}(co') = \text{maxext}_{\mathsf{CO}_\Gamma}(co)$, and so all the runs in $\text{maxext}_{\mathsf{CO}_\Gamma}(co)$ satisfy $x \prec z$. (Note that such an argument is fully consistent with the intuitive meaning of the precedence relation $\prec$.) Following this line of thinking, we arrive at the crucial observation that co provides 'complete' information about the runs consistent with it, if there is no way of extending it without shrinking the set of consistent runs. In such a case, co can be thought of as capturing all the invariant relationships attributable to the runs consistent with co. Moreover, the process of adding relationships like $x \prec z$, resembles (not surprisingly) the way in which the transitive closure of an acyclic relation is applied. And, indeed, each co can be transitively closed to yield a causal partial order in which all the invariant relationships implicit in co are made explicit.

We also need to take into account the fact that in the present context all dependence and independence relationships between events are ultimately underpinned by the static concurrency alphabet Γ. This leads to the following definition of invariant orders respecting the concurrency alphabet.

(The above discussion has wider ramifications as it can be applied after suitable adaptations to other semantical frameworks.)

An *invariant order over* Γ is $ios \in \mathsf{IO}_\Gamma = (\mathsf{CO}_\Gamma \cap \mathsf{PO})^{min}$. Moreover, $\text{ar2po}|_{\mathsf{CO}_\Gamma \to \mathsf{PO}_\Gamma}$ is the closure mapping for CO_Γ.

An alternative characterisation of invariant orders over Γ is based on the relationships between events, in the following way: A concurrency order $\langle \Delta, \prec \rangle$ is an invariant order if and only if it is a partial order such that $x \prec^{dir} y$ implies $\langle \ell_x, \ell_y \rangle \notin \mathsf{ind}$, for all $x \neq y \in \Delta$.

We then obtain a direct correspondence between invariant orders and dependence graphs.

Theorem 19. $\text{co2dg}_\Gamma|_{\mathsf{IO}_\Gamma \to \mathsf{DG}_\Gamma}$ *is a bijection with the inverse* $\text{ar2po}|_{\mathsf{DG}_\Gamma \to \mathsf{IO}_\Gamma}$.

What we would like to stress is that, in general, reversing the transitive closure is not possible. However, this is possible for the specific case of dependence graphs and invariant orders, as the above result demonstrates.

Invariant orders and concurrency histories are in a one-to-one relationship which is 'universal' in the sense that it is established by mappings which do not depend on the concurrency alphabet Γ. More precisely, the invariant partial order corresponding to a concurrency history can be obtained through *intersection*, and the concurrency history corresponding to an invariant order can be derived through *total order extension.*

Theorem 20. $\text{ar2TO} : \mathsf{IO}_\Gamma \to \mathsf{CH}_\Gamma$ *is a bijection with the inverse* $\text{AR2ar} : \mathsf{CH}_\Gamma \to \mathsf{IO}_\Gamma$, *where* $\text{AR2ar}(AO) = \bigcap AO$.

We also have in an instance of Szpilrajn's theorem.

Theorem 21. $\mathrm{ar2TO}(po) \neq \varnothing$ *and* $po = \bigcap \mathrm{ar2TO}(po)$, *for every* $po \in \mathsf{PO}_\Gamma$.

We can now summarise relationships between all the domains and mappings introduced so far in this section.

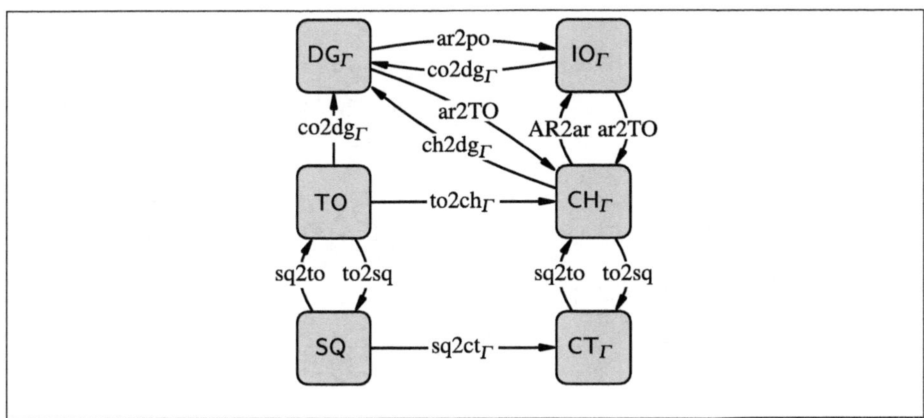

Fig. 8. Commutative diagram for the sequential semantical framework.

Theorem 22. *Figure 8 depicts a commutative diagram.*

As a direct consequence of Theorem 22, the domains TO and SQ can be considered as equivalent, and the same holds for IO_Γ, DG_Γ, CH_Γ and CT_Γ. Also, by diagram chasing, one can work out explicit mappings between different domains not shown in Fig. 8.

Figure 9 'instantiates' the commutative diagram in Fig. 8 using concrete objects based on Table 2. One can see the original sequence of instructions (left bottom) together with accompanying total order (left middle). We have also the entire concurrency trace comprising seven equivalent sequences (right bottom) together with accompanying concurrency histories (right middle). Finally, we provide the dependence graph (left top) and invariant order (right top) of the considered sequence and concurrency alphabet. For clarity, we omit the mappings on arcs (see Fig. 8).

Note that 'by chasing the arcs' one can distinguish between the single execution perspective (SQ and TO) and the process perspective which depends on concurrency alphabet (CT_Γ, CH_Γ, DG_Γ and IO_Γ).

Finally, the *concurrency trace monoid (or trace monoid)* is the equational monoid $\mathbb{CT}_\Gamma = \langle \mathsf{CT}_\Gamma, \widehat{\odot}, \{\lambda\}\rangle$ with the monoid operation given by

$$[\![sq]\!]_{\equiv_\Gamma} \widehat{\odot} [\![sq']\!]_{\equiv_\Gamma} = [\![sq \odot sq']\!]_{\equiv_\Gamma} .$$

Moreover, the domains IO_Γ, DG_Γ and CH_Γ—which are equivalent to CT_Γ—generate isomorphic monoids (with the respective monoid operations being derived from $\odot$ by

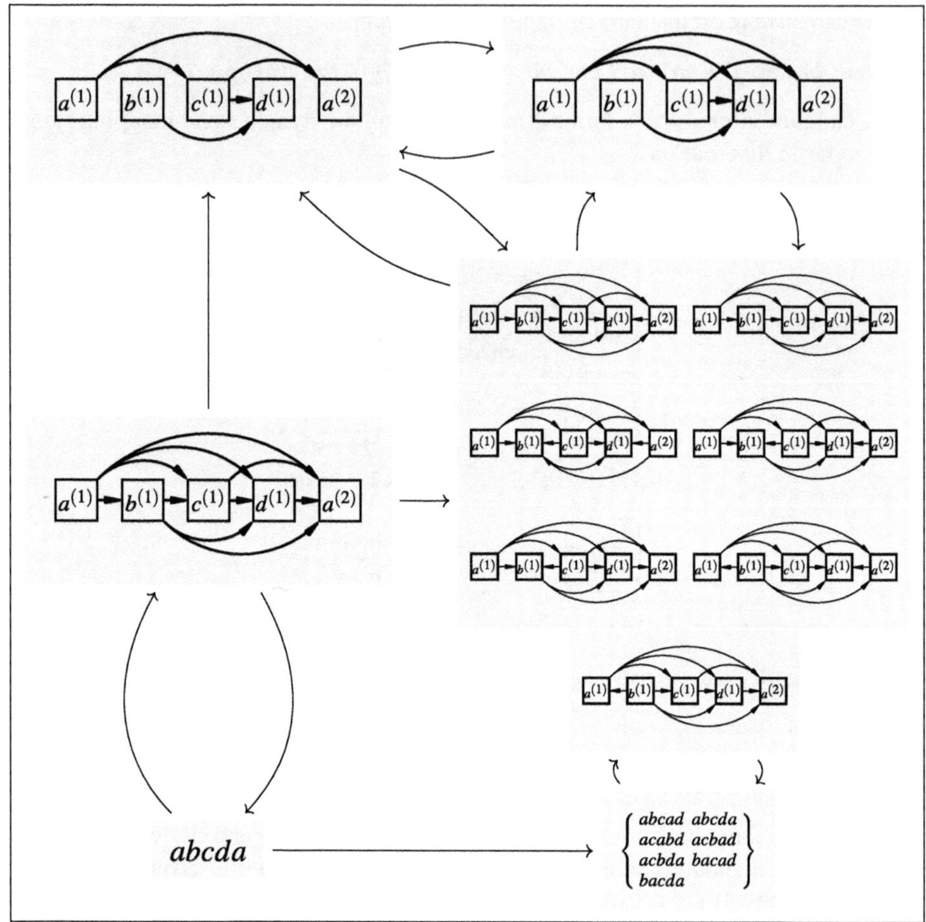

Fig. 9. An instantiation of the commutative diagram for the sequential semantical framework of Fig. 8 using concrete objects.

'diagram chasing' in Fig. 8). For example, the monoid operation for IO_Γ can be obtained by taking two invariant orders, *io* and *io'*, and defining:

$$io \otimes io' = \mathrm{AR2ar} \circ \mathrm{sq2to} \circ \mathrm{sq2ct}_\Gamma(sq \odot sq') ,$$

where $sq \in \mathrm{to2sq} \circ \mathrm{ar2TO}(io)$ and $sq' \in \mathrm{to2sq} \circ \mathrm{ar2TO}(io')$ are arbitrarily chosen. It is a matter of convenience or efficiency which of the five monoids is used in a specific context.

6.2 Traces for Step Semantics

Alphabet. A *combined concurrency alphabet* is a triple $\Theta = \langle \mathbb{A}, \mathsf{sim}, \mathsf{ser} \rangle$, where $\mathsf{sim} \subseteq \mathbb{A} \times \mathbb{A}$ is an irreflexive and symmetric *simultaneity* relation, and $\mathsf{ser} \subseteq \mathsf{sim}$ is a *serialisability* relation. Throughout this section, Θ is *fixed*.

Sequences. A *step over* Θ is a non-empty $A \subseteq \mathbb{A}$ such that $\langle a,b\rangle \in \mathsf{sim}$, for all $a \neq b \in A$. Then, a *step sequence over* Θ is a finite sequence of steps over $\mathbb{A}$. The set of all step sequences over Θ is denoted by SSQ_Θ.

Structures. A CO-*structure over* Θ is a weakly cyclic relational structure $cos = \langle \Delta, \prec, \sqsubset\rangle$ such that, for all $x \neq y \in \Delta$ (below $\lll = \lll_{cos}$ and $\Subset = \Subset_{cos}$):

$$\begin{array}{ll}\langle \ell_x,\ell_y\rangle \notin \mathsf{sim} & \Longrightarrow x \lll y \ \vee\ y \lll x\\ \langle \ell_x,\ell_y\rangle \in \mathsf{sim} \setminus (\mathsf{ser} \cup \mathsf{ser}^{-1}) & \Longrightarrow x \lll y \ \vee\ y \lll x \ \vee\ x \Subset y \Subset x\\ \langle \ell_x,\ell_y\rangle \in \mathsf{ser} \setminus \mathsf{ser}^{-1} & \Longrightarrow y \lll x \ \vee\ x \Subset y\\ \langle \ell_x,\ell_y\rangle \in \mathsf{ser}^{-1} \setminus \mathsf{ser} & \Longrightarrow x \lll y \ \vee\ y \Subset x\,.\end{array}$$

The set of all combined order structures over Θ is denoted by COS_Θ. Note that there are no restrictions for $\langle \ell_x,\ell_y\rangle \in (\mathsf{ser} \cap \mathsf{ser}^{-1})$. Those pairs of events are independent - as in the sequential semantics. Other cases are different facets of possible causal dependence.

Maximal Structures. The maximal CO-structures over Θ are derived from the general concept of LC-structure.

LC-*structures over* Θ are defined as $\mathsf{LCS}_\Theta = \mathsf{LCS} \cap \mathsf{COS}_\Theta$ and, as stated below, they are the maximal CO-structures over Θ.

Theorem 23. $\mathsf{COS}_\Theta^{max} = \mathsf{LCS}_\Theta = \partial(\mathsf{SO}_\Theta)$.

Moreover, $\mathrm{maxext}_{\mathsf{COS}_\Theta}(cos) = \mathrm{maxext}_{\mathsf{COS}}(cos)$, for every $cos \in \mathsf{COS}_\Theta$. Hence, the LC-structures extending CO-structures over Θ are given by $\mathrm{cos2LCS}\,|_{\mathsf{COS}_\Theta \to 2^{\mathsf{LCS}_\Theta}}$.

A close link between the LC-structures over Θ and the stratified orders over Θ, as well as between the LC-structures over Θ and step sequences over Θ, is captured by the next result.

Theorem 24. $\mathrm{lcs2so}\,|_{\mathsf{LCS}_\Theta \to \mathsf{SO}_\Theta}$ *and* $\mathrm{lcs2ssq}\,|_{\mathsf{LCS}_\Theta \to \mathsf{SSQ}_\Theta}$ *are bijections with the inverses* $\mathrm{so2lcs}\,|_{\mathsf{SO}_\Theta \to \mathsf{LCS}_\Theta}$ *and* $\mathrm{ssq2lcs}\,|_{\mathsf{SSQ}_\Theta \to \mathsf{LCS}_\Theta}$, *respectively.*

Traces and Histories. Two sequences $ssq, ssq' \in (2^{\mathbb{A}})^*$ are in the *local swapping* relation if there are steps A,B,C and sequences $\upsilon, \upsilon' \in (2^{\mathbb{A}})^*$ such that $A \times B \subseteq \mathsf{ser}$, $C = A \cup B$, $ssq = \upsilon AB\upsilon'$ and $ssq' = \upsilon C \upsilon'$. We denote this by $ssq \approx_\Theta ssq'$. Then the *comtrace equivalence* $\equiv_\Theta$ is the symmetric, reflexive and transitive closure of $\approx_\Theta$. Note that $ssq \equiv_\Theta ssq'$ implies that $ssq \in \mathsf{SSQ}_\Theta \iff ssq' \in \mathsf{SSQ}_\Theta$.

Comtrace equivalence is an event-preserving equivalence relation, and if $ssq \equiv_\Theta ssq'$ then $ssq \in \mathsf{SSQ}_\Theta \iff ssq' \in \mathsf{SSQ}_\Theta$. Moreover, it is characterised by consistency in the ordering of dependent events, i.e., if $ssq, ssq' \in \mathsf{SSQ}_\Theta$ then $ssq \equiv_\Theta ssq'$ if and only if $\mathbb{E}_{ssq} = \mathbb{E}_{ssq'}$ and, for all $x,y \in \mathbb{E}_{ssq}$:

$$\begin{array}{ll}\langle \ell_x,\ell_y\rangle \notin \mathsf{sim} & \Longrightarrow (k<m \iff k'<m') \wedge (k>m \iff k'>m')\\ \langle \ell_x,\ell_y\rangle \in \mathsf{sim} \setminus (\mathsf{ser} \cup \mathsf{ser}^{-1}) & \Longrightarrow (k<m \iff k'<m') \wedge (k>m \iff k'>m')\\ & \qquad \wedge\ (k=m \iff k'=m')\\ \langle \ell_x,\ell_y\rangle \in \mathsf{ser} \setminus \mathsf{ser}^{-1} & \Longrightarrow (k>m \iff k'>m') \wedge (k \le m \iff k' \le m')\\ \langle \ell_x,\ell_y\rangle \in \mathsf{ser}^{-1} \setminus \mathsf{ser} & \Longrightarrow (k<m \iff k'<m') \wedge (k \ge m \iff k' \ge m')\,,\end{array}$$

where $k = \mathrm{pos}_{ssq}(x)$, $k' = \mathrm{pos}_{ssq'}(x)$, $m = \mathrm{pos}_{ssq}(y)$, $m' = \mathrm{pos}_{ssq'}(y)$.

Intuitively, comtrace equivalent step sequences are those which order dependent events in the same way. Having introduced equivalence for step sequences over Θ, it is natural to define and investigate the resulting equivalence classes.

Combined concurrency traces (or comtraces) over Θ, CCT_Θ, are equivalence classes of the comtrace equivalence relation $\equiv_\Theta$ which comprise step sequences over Θ. To identify a comtrace it suffices to provide a single step sequence over Θ belonging to it. The mapping ssq2cct : $\mathsf{SSQ}_\Theta \to \mathsf{CCT}_\Theta$, given by $ssq \mapsto [\![ssq]\!]_{\equiv_\Theta}$, associates comtraces with step sequences over Θ.

We next introduce two relations on LCS_Θ which are counterparts of the local swapping relation and comtrace equivalence defined for SSQ_Θ.

Two LC-structures $lcs, lcs' \in \mathsf{LCS}$ are in the *local swapping* relation if they have the same domain Δ, $\mathrm{strata} \circ \mathrm{lcs2so}(lcs) = \tau XY\tau$ and $\mathrm{strata} \circ \mathrm{lcs2so}(lcs') = \tau Z\tau'$, $X \cup Y = Z$, $X \cap Y = \varnothing$, and $\ell_X \times \ell_Y \subseteq \mathsf{ser}$. We denote this by $lcs \mathrel{\dot{\approx}}_\Theta lcs'$. Then the *comtrace history equivalence* $\mathrel{\dot{\equiv}}_\Theta$ is the reflexive and transitive closure of $\mathrel{\dot{\approx}}_\Theta$. Note that $lcs \mathrel{\dot{\approx}}_\Theta lcs'$ implies $lcs \in \mathsf{LCS}_\Theta \iff lcs' \in \mathsf{LCS}_\Theta$.

In this way, the local swapping relation defined above for LC-structures can be used to introduce an equivalence relation for LC-structures. Crucially, comtrace history equivalence reflects comtrace equivalence through the mappings linking step sequences and total LC-structures.

Theorem 25. *For all* $ssq, ssq' \in \mathsf{SSQ}_\Theta$ *and* $lcs, lcs' \in \mathsf{LCS}_\Theta$*:*

$$\begin{aligned} ssq \equiv_\Theta ssq' &\iff \mathrm{ssq2lcs}(ssq) \mathrel{\dot{\equiv}}_\Theta \mathrm{ssq2lcs}(ssq') \\ lcs \mathrel{\dot{\equiv}}_\Theta lcs' &\iff \mathrm{lcs2ssq}(lcs) \equiv_\Theta \mathrm{lcs2ssq}(lcs')\,. \end{aligned}$$

Similarly as comtrace equivalence, comtrace history equivalence can be characterised by consistency of the orderings of dependent events, i.e., if $lcs, lcs' \in \mathsf{LCS}_\Theta$ then $los \mathrel{\dot{\equiv}}_\Theta los'$ if and only if $\Delta_{lcs} = \Delta_{lcs'}$ and, for all $x, y \in \Delta_{lcs}$:

$$\begin{array}{ll} \langle \ell_x, \ell_y \rangle \notin \mathsf{sim} & \Longrightarrow (x \prec_{lcs} y \iff x \prec_{lcs'} y) \wedge (y \prec_{lcs} x \iff y \prec_{lcs'} x) \\ \langle \ell_x, \ell_y \rangle \in \mathsf{sim} \setminus (\mathsf{ser} \cup \mathsf{ser}^{-1}) & \Longrightarrow (x \prec_{lcs} y \iff x \prec_{lcs'} y) \wedge (y \prec_{lcs} x \iff y \prec_{lcs'} x) \\ & \qquad \wedge\ (y \sqsubset_{lcs} x \sqsubset_{lcs} y \iff y \sqsubset_{lcs'} x \sqsubset_{lcs'} y) \\ \langle \ell_x, \ell_y \rangle \in \mathsf{ser} \setminus \mathsf{ser}^{-1} & \Longrightarrow (y \prec_{lcs} x \iff y \prec_{lcs'} x) \wedge (x \sqsubset_{lcs} y \iff x \sqsubset_{lcs'} y) \\ \langle \ell_x, \ell_y \rangle \in \mathsf{ser}^{-1} \setminus \mathsf{ser} & \Longrightarrow (x \prec_{lcs} y \iff x \prec_{lcs'} y) \wedge (y \sqsubset_{lcs} x \iff y \sqsubset_{lcs'} x)\,. \end{array}$$

We now introduce relational domains based on history equivalence.

Combined concurrency histories (comtrace histories) CCH_Θ are the equivalence classes of the comtrace history equivalence. The mapping lcs2cch : $\mathsf{SO}_\Theta \to \mathsf{CCH}_\Theta$, given by $lcs \mapsto [\![lcs]\!]_{\dot{\equiv}_\Theta}$, associates comtrace histories with stratified orders.

We also obtain a one-to-one correspondence between concurrency traces and concurrency histories.

Theorem 26. $\mathrm{lcs2ssq}|_{\mathsf{CCH}_\Theta \to \mathsf{CCT}_\Theta}$ *is a bijection with the inverse* $\mathrm{ssq2lcs}|_{\mathsf{CCT}_\Theta \to \mathsf{CCH}_\Theta}$.

The next result validates the soundness of the comtrace approach for the stratified order run model.

Theorem 27. $\mathsf{SSQ}_\Theta = \biguplus \mathsf{CCT}_\Theta$ *and* $\mathsf{LCS}_\Theta = \biguplus \mathsf{CCH}_\Theta$.

Consider again Sect. 6.1 and change from the order semantics to stratified order semantics. Taking inspiration from Sect. 5.2, we can reveal some subtle relationships between program statements.

We still have three symmetric pairs of independent (hence simultaneous and, at the same time, serialisable) statements and two new, asymmetric, relationships between (c) and (a) as well as between (d) and (c). Therefore, we define the following combined concurrency alphabet:

$$\Theta = \langle \{a,b,c,d\}, \{\langle a,b\rangle, \langle a,c\rangle, \langle a,d\rangle, \langle b,a\rangle, \langle b,c\rangle, \langle c,a\rangle, \langle c,b\rangle, \langle c,d\rangle, \langle d,a\rangle, \langle d,c\rangle\}, \{\langle a,b\rangle, \langle a,d\rangle, \langle b,a\rangle, \langle b,c\rangle, \langle c,a\rangle, \langle c,b\rangle, \langle d,a\rangle, \langle d,c\rangle\}\rangle .$$

According to Θ, we have the following valid steps:

$$\{a, b, c, d, (ab), (ac), (ad), (bc), (cd), (abc), (acd)\} .$$

Note that we have four singletons, five steps of size two, and two steps of size three. Moreover, to increase readability, for step consisting of (a) and (b) we use the notation (ab) (or equivalently (ba)) instead of the usual set notation $\{a,b\}$ and omit the parenthesis in the case of singletons (we write a instead of (a)).

The set of all step sequences equivalent with the original *abcda* consist of the seven sequences known from Example 6.1, nine step sequences grouping independent statements into steps and five more step sequences making use of the relationship $\langle c,a\rangle \in \mathsf{ser}_\Theta$. Note that the statement (d) occurs after (c), hence the relationship $\langle d,c\rangle \in \mathsf{ser}_\Theta$ is not manifested in this trace (and we have no step including both c and d). Finally, we obtain:

$$[\![abcda]\!]_{\equiv_\Theta} = \{abcad, abcda, acabd, acbad, acbda, bacad, bacda, abc(ad), (ab)cad, a(bc)(ad), (ab)cda, (ab)c(ad), a(bc)da, ac(ab)d, acb(ad), bac(ad), a(abc)d, a(ac)bd, ab(ac)d, (ab)(ac)d, ba(ac)d\}$$

which is the comtrace over Θ containing *abcda*.

Dependence Graphs. As in the case of concurrency traces, we now wish to single out CO-structures over Θ which provide a concise capture of intrinsic relationships between events in comtraces.

Combined dependence graphs (or CD*-graphs) over* Θ, CDG_Θ, are the minimal CO-structures over Θ, i.e., $\mathsf{CDG}_\Theta = \mathsf{COS}_\Theta^{min}$.

For each CO-structure over Θ, *cos*, there is a unique CD-graph *cdg* such that $cdg \trianglelefteq cos$. We will denote the latter by $\mathrm{cos2cdg}_\Theta(cos)$, implicitly defining a mapping $\mathrm{cos2cdg}_\Theta : \mathsf{COS}_\Theta \to \mathsf{CDG}_\Theta$. Crucially, deriving CD-graphs is preserved through history equivalence.

Theorem 28. $lcs \doteqdot_\Theta lcs'$ *if and only if* $\mathrm{cos2cdg}_\Theta(lcs) = \mathrm{cos2cdg}_\Theta(lcs')$, *for all* $lcs, lcs' \in \mathsf{LCS}_\Theta$.

Therefore, it is possible to associate CD-graphs with combined histories through the mapping cch2cdg : $\mathsf{CCH}_\Theta \to \mathsf{CDG}_\Theta$, given by $[\![lcs]\!]_{\doteqdot_\Theta} \mapsto \mathrm{cos2cdg}_\Theta(lcs)$. We then obtain a one-to-one correspondence between combined concurrency histories and CD-graphs.

Theorem 29. $\mathrm{cch2cdg}_\Theta$ *is a bijection with the inverse* $\mathrm{cos2LCS}\,|_{\mathsf{CDG}_\Theta \to \mathsf{CCH}_\Theta}$.

Closed Structures. A *stratified order structure (or* SO*-structure) over* Θ is $sos \in \mathsf{SOS}_\Theta = (\mathsf{COS}_\Theta \cap \mathsf{SOS})^{min}$. Moreover, $\mathrm{cos2sos}\,|_{\mathsf{COS}_\Theta \to \mathsf{SOS}_\Theta}$ is the structure closure for COS_Θ.

We also have a generalisation of Szpilrajn's theorem for SO-structures over Θ.

Theorem 30. $\mathrm{cos2LCS}(sos) \neq \varnothing$ *and* $sos = \bigcap \mathrm{cos2LCS}(sos)$*, for every* $sos \in \mathsf{SOS}_\Theta$.

We can now summarise the relationships between all the domains and mappings introduced so far in this section.

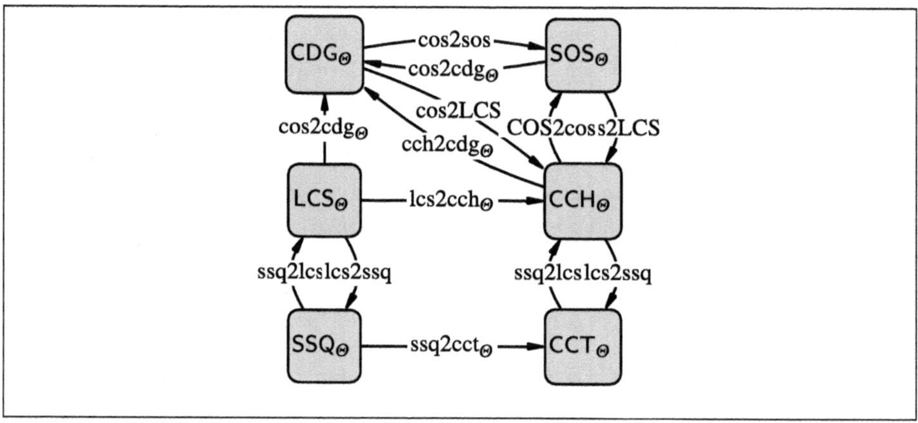

Fig. 10. Commutative diagram for the step semantics framework.

Theorem 31. *Figure 10 depicts a commutative diagram.*

As a direct consequence of Theorem 31, the domains LCS_Θ and SSQ_Θ can be considered as equivalent, and the same holds for SOS_Θ, CDG_Θ, CCH_Θ and CCT_Θ.

Finally, the *comtrace monoid* is the equational monoid $\mathbb{CCT}_\Theta = \langle \mathsf{CCT}_\Theta, \widehat{\odot}, \{\lambda\}\rangle$ with the monoid operation given by

$$[\![ssq]\!]_{\equiv_\Theta} \widehat{\odot} [\![ssq']\!]_{\equiv_\Theta} = [\![ssq \odot ssq']\!]_{\equiv_\Theta} .$$

Moreover, the domains SOS_Θ, CDG_Θ and CCH_Θ—which are equivalent to CCT_Θ—generate isomorphic monoids (with the respective monoid operations being derived from $\odot$ by 'diagram chasing' in Fig. 10). It is a matter of convenience or efficiency which of these monoids is used in a specific context.

The paper [49] introduced efficient data structures and algorithms for manipulating comtraces.

6.3 Traces for Interval Semantics

To develop a language-theoretic representation of interval order runs, we will extend the sets of actions and events by adding annotations indicating their beginnings and endings. That is, for each $x \in \mathbb{A} \cup \mathbb{E}$, we will use $x_\lceil$ and $x_\lfloor$ to denote the *beginning* and the *ending* of x, respectively. Moreover, for every set $X \subseteq \mathbb{A}$ or $X \subseteq \mathbb{E}$, we denote $X_{\lceil\lfloor} = \{x_\lceil, x_\lfloor \mid x \in X\}$.

Alphabet. We will use two kinds of alphabets, one for dealing with representations based on CI-structures, and the other (derived) for dealing with (annotated) action sequences from which CI-structures can be generated.

An *interval trace alphabet* is a pair $\Phi = \langle \mathbb{A}, \mathsf{wind} \rangle$, where $\mathsf{wind} \subseteq \mathbb{A} \times \mathbb{A}$ is an irreflexive relation called *weak independence*. Intuitively, if $\langle a,b \rangle \in \mathsf{wind}$ then a and b (treated as execution intervals) may overlap, or a may occur before b, with both runs being equivalent. In general, wind is not symmetric and so Φ is not a concurrency alphabet as defined in Sect. 6.1.

A *derived interval trace alphabet* is a pair $\phi = \langle \mathbb{A}_{\lceil\lfloor}, \mathsf{dind} \rangle$, where $\mathsf{dind} \subseteq \mathbb{A}_{\lceil\lfloor} \times \mathbb{A}_{\lceil\lfloor}$ is a symmetric and irreflexive relation, called *derived independence*, given by:

$$\mathsf{dind} = \{\langle a_\lceil, b_\lceil \rangle, \langle a_\lfloor, b_\lfloor \rangle \mid a \neq b \in \mathbb{A}\} \cup \{\langle a_\lfloor, b_\lceil \rangle, \langle b_\lceil, a_\lfloor \rangle \mid \langle a,b \rangle \in \mathsf{wind}\} .$$

The derived alphabet ϕ is always a concurrency alphabet as defined in Sect. 6.1. Throughout this section, $\Phi = \langle \mathbb{A}, \mathsf{wind} \rangle$ and $\phi = \langle \mathbb{A}_{\lceil\lfloor}, \mathsf{dind} \rangle$ are fixed.

Sequences. Interval orders can be represented by sequences of action beginnings and action endings.

A sequence isq over $\mathbb{A}_{\lceil\lfloor}$ is *interval* if $\pi_{\{a_\lceil, a_\lfloor\}}(isq) \in (a_\lceil a_\lfloor)^*$, for every $a \in \mathbb{A}$, where $\pi_{\{a_\lceil, a_\lfloor\}}(isq)$ is obtained from isq by deleting all the actions different from $a_\lceil$ and $a_\lfloor$. We also denote $\mathbb{E}^o_{isq} = \{x \in \mathbb{E} \mid x_\lceil \in \mathbb{E}_{isq}\}$, and so $(\mathbb{E}^o_{isq})_{\lceil\lfloor} = \mathbb{E}_{isq}$. The set of all interval sequences is denoted by ISQ.

Example 4. $w = a_\lceil b_\lceil a_\lfloor a_\lceil c_\lceil b_\lfloor c_\lfloor d_\lceil a_\lfloor d_\lfloor$ is an interval sequence, but neither $a_\lfloor b_\lceil b_\lfloor a_\lceil$ nor $b_\lceil b_\lfloor a_\lceil c_\lfloor$ nor $a_\lceil a_\lceil a_\lfloor a_\lfloor$ is. Moreover, $\mathbb{E}^o_w = \{a^{(1)}, a^{(2)}, b, c, d\}$. ◇

Although interval sequences could be used to generate total orders in the same way as action sequences did, we will use them to generate interval order runs. To achieve the desired result, we use a mapping $\mathrm{isq2ipo} : \mathsf{ISQ} \to \mathsf{IPO}$ such that

$$isq \mapsto \langle \mathbb{E}^o_{isq}, \{\langle x,y \rangle \in \mathbb{E}^o_{isq} \times \mathbb{E}^o_{isq} \mid \mathrm{pos}_{isq}(x_\lfloor) < \mathrm{pos}_{isq}(y_\lceil)\} \rangle ,$$

returning *interval orders generated* by interval sequences.

Example 5. Figure 11 shows a total order ipo_1 which is generated by a unique interval sequence $a_\lceil a_\lfloor b_\lceil b_\lfloor c_\lceil c_\lfloor d_\lceil d_\lfloor a_\lceil a_\lfloor$. It also shows a stratified order ipo_2 generated by interval sequence $a_\lceil a_\lfloor a_\lceil b_\lceil c_\lceil a_\lfloor b_\lfloor c_\lfloor d_\lceil d_\lfloor$ and thirty five other interval sequences.

Figure 11 shows also interval orders ipo_3 and ipo_4, which are not stratified (see Fig. 7), generated by interval sequences $a_\lceil a_\lfloor b_\lceil b_\lfloor c_\lceil a_\lceil c_\lfloor d_\lceil a_\lfloor d_\lfloor$ and $a_\lceil b_\lceil a_\lfloor a_\lceil c_\lceil b_\lfloor c_\lfloor d_\lceil a_\lfloor d_\lfloor$, respectively. ◇

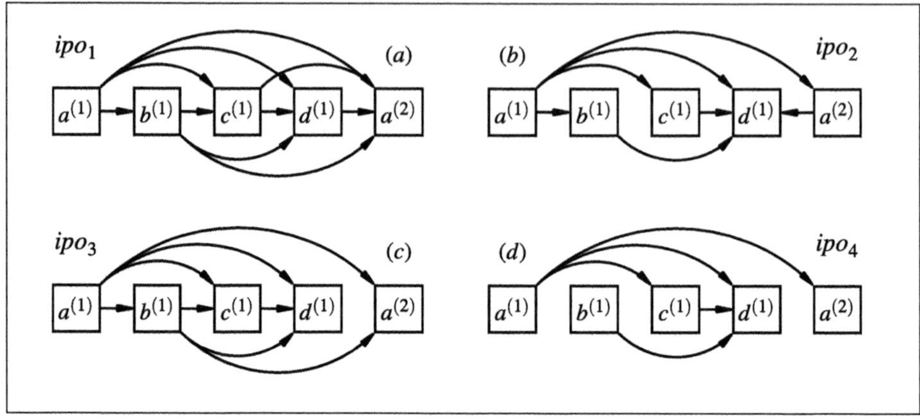

Fig. 11. (*a*) A total order. (*b*) A stratified order. (*c*, *d*) Two interval orders which are not stratified.

The mapping isq2ipo is surjective but not injective. In fact, interval sequences generating the same interval orders form a trace over another derived concurrency alphabet $\phi' = \langle \mathbb{A}_{\lceil\lfloor}, \mathsf{dind}' \rangle$, where $\mathsf{dind}' = \{\langle a_\lceil, b_\lceil \rangle, \langle a_\lfloor, b_\lfloor \rangle \mid a \neq b \in \mathbb{A}\} \subseteq \mathsf{dind}$. Then, for all $isq, isq' \in \mathsf{ISQ}$:

$$[\![isq]\!]_{\equiv_{\mathsf{dind}'}} \subseteq \mathsf{ISQ} \text{ and } \mathrm{isq2ipo}(isq) = \mathrm{isq2ipo}(isq') \iff isq \equiv_{\mathsf{dind}'} isq' .$$

Example 6. The interval sequences $a_\lceil b_\lceil a_\lfloor b_\lfloor$, $b_\lceil a_\lceil a_\lfloor b_\lfloor$, $a_\lceil b_\lceil b_\lfloor a_\lfloor$, and $b_\lceil a_\lceil b_\lfloor a_\lfloor$ form a concurrency trace over dind', and all four generate the same interval order representing run with two overlapping events. ◇

Structures. A CI-*structure over* Φ is $cis = \langle \Delta, \prec, \sqsubset \rangle \in \mathsf{CIS}$ such that, for all $x \neq y \in \Delta$ (below $\lll = \lll_{cis}$ and $\measuredangle = \measuredangle_{cis}$):

$$\begin{array}{ll} \ell_x = \ell_y & \Longrightarrow x \lll y \vee y \lll x \\ \text{and for } \ell_x \neq \ell_y & \\ \langle \ell_x, \ell_y \rangle \notin \mathsf{wind} \cup \mathsf{wind}^{-1} & \Longrightarrow x \lll y \vee y \lll x \vee x \measuredangle y \measuredangle x \\ \langle \ell_x, \ell_y \rangle \in \mathsf{wind} \setminus \mathsf{wind}^{-1} & \Longrightarrow y \lll x \vee x \measuredangle y \\ \langle \ell_x, \ell_y \rangle \in \mathsf{wind}^{-1} \setminus \mathsf{wind} & \Longrightarrow x \lll y \vee y \measuredangle x . \end{array}$$

The set of all CI-structures over Φ is denoted by CIS_Φ.

We also define the *interval orders over* Φ as $\mathsf{IPO}_\Phi = \{ipo \in \mathsf{IPO} \mid \partial(ipo) \in \mathsf{CIS}_\Phi\}$.

Maximal Structures. The maximal CI-structures over Φ are derived from the general notion of IP-structures, i.e., the IP-*structures over* Φ are defined as $\mathsf{IPS}_\Phi = \mathsf{IPS} \cap \mathsf{CIS}_\Phi$.

Theorem 32. $\mathsf{CIS}_\Phi^{max} = \mathsf{IPS}_\Phi = \partial(\mathsf{IPO}_\Phi)$.

We also have $\text{maxext}_{\mathsf{CIS}_\Phi}(cis) = \text{maxext}_{\mathsf{CIS}}(cis)$, for every $cis \in \mathsf{CIS}_\Phi$. Hence, the IP-structures extending CI-structures over Φ are given by $\text{cis2IPS}|_{\mathsf{CIS}_\Phi \to 2^{\mathsf{IPS}_\Phi}}$.

We also introduce a mapping returning IP-structures over Φ generated by interval sequences as $\text{isq2ips} : \mathsf{ISQ} \to \mathsf{IPS}_\Phi$, given by $isq \mapsto \partial(\text{isq2ipo}(isq))$.

Traces and Histories. For the concurrency alphabet ϕ defining interval sequences, we can import all the notions and results concerning concurrency traces from the treatment presented in Sect. 6.1 for the concurrency alphabet Γ, assuming that the action alphabet is now $\mathbb{A}_{\uparrow\downarrow}$. This leads to the notion of the *interval sequence equivalence over* ϕ, denoted $\equiv_{\mathsf{dind}}$, and the *interval traces over* ϕ given as $\mathsf{IT}_\phi = \{[\![isq]\!]_{\equiv_{\mathsf{dind}}} \mid isq \in \mathsf{ISQ}\}$.

The interval equivalence over ϕ is event-preserving. Moreover, for all interval sequences $sq, sq' \in \mathsf{ISQ}$, $sq \equiv_{\mathsf{dind}} sq'$ if and only if $\mathbb{E}_{sq} = \mathbb{E}_{sq'}$ and, for all $x, y \in \mathbb{E}_{sq}$ satisfying $\langle \ell_x, \ell_y \rangle \notin \mathsf{wind}$:

$$\text{pos}_{sq}(x_\downarrow) < \text{pos}_{sq}(y_\uparrow) \iff \text{pos}_{sq'}(x_\downarrow) < \text{pos}_{sq'}(y_\uparrow) \,.$$

To define notions corresponding to $\equiv_{\mathsf{dind}}$ and IT_ϕ in the domain of CI-structures, we turn to the interval alphabet Φ. A key notion here is the definition of a local swapping relation.

Let $ips, ips' \in \mathsf{IPS}_\Phi$ and $ipo, ipo' \in \mathsf{IPO}_\Phi$ be such that:

$$ips = \partial(ipo) = \langle \Delta, \prec, \sqsubset \rangle \;\text{ and }\; ips' = \partial(ipo') = \langle \Delta, \prec', \sqsubset' \rangle \,.$$

Then $ips \stackrel{\approx}{\approx}_\Phi ips'$ if there are $x, y \in \Delta$ such that the following hold:

- $\prec' = \prec \setminus \{\langle x, y \rangle\}$.
- $\langle \ell_x, \ell_y \rangle \in \mathsf{wind}$.
- $x \prec^{dir} y$.
- $x \prec^{dir} z \wedge w \prec^{dir} y \implies w \prec z$, for all $z \neq w \in \Delta \setminus \{x, y\}$.

Then the *interval equivalence*, denoted by $\stackrel{\equiv}{\equiv}_\Phi$, is the symmetric and transitive closure of $\stackrel{\approx}{\approx}_\Phi$. Moreover, the *interval histories over* Φ are $\mathsf{IH}_\Phi = \{[\![ips]\!]_{\stackrel{\equiv}{\equiv}_\Phi} \mid ips \in \mathsf{IPS}_\Phi\}$. The interval traces over ϕ are in one-to-one relationship with the interval histories over Φ, and the following result validates the soundness of the trace approach for the interval order run model.

Theorem 33. $\mathsf{ISQ} = \biguplus \mathsf{IT}_\phi$ *and* $\mathsf{IPS}_\Phi = \biguplus \mathsf{IH}_\Phi$.

Dependence Graphs. As in the two previous cases, we now single out CI-structures over Φ which provide a concise capture of intrinsic relationships between events.

Interval dependence graphs (or ID*-graphs) over* Φ, IDG_Θ, are the minimal CI-structures over Φ, i.e., $\mathsf{IDG}_\Phi = \mathsf{CIS}_\Phi^{min}$.

For each CI-structure over Φ, cis, there is a unique ID-graph idg such that $idg \trianglelefteq cis$. We will denote the latter by $\text{cis2idg}_\Phi(cis)$, implicitly defining a mapping $\text{cis2idg}_\Phi : \mathsf{CIS}_\Phi \to \mathsf{IDG}_\Phi$. Crucially, deriving ID-graphs is preserved through interval history equivalence.

Theorem 34. *$ips \,\ddot{\equiv}_\Phi\, ips'$ if and only if* $\text{cis2idg}_\Phi(ips) = \text{cis2idg}_\Phi(ips')$*, for all* $ips, ips' \in \mathsf{IPS}_\Phi$.

Therefore, it is possible to associate ID-graphs with interval histories through the mapping $\text{ih2idg}_\Theta : \mathsf{IH}_\Phi \to \mathsf{IDG}_\Phi$, given by $[\![ips]\!]_{\ddot{\equiv}_\Phi} \mapsto \text{cis2idg}_\Phi(ips)$, which yields a one-to-one correspondence between interval histories and ID-graphs.

Closed Structures. A *closed* CI*-structure over* Φ is $cis \in \mathsf{ICS}_\Phi = (\mathsf{ICS} \cap \mathsf{CIS}_\Phi)^{min}$. Moreover, $\text{cis2ics}|_{\mathsf{CIS}_\Phi \to \mathsf{ICS}_\Phi}$ is the structure closure for CIS_Φ.

We also have a generalisation of Szpilrajn's theorem for CI-structures.

Theorem 35. $\text{cis2IPS}(ics) \neq \varnothing$ *and* $ics = \bigcap \text{cis2IPS}(ics)$*, for every* $ics \in \mathsf{ICS}_\Phi$.

As interval sequences are closed under concatenation, i.e., $isq \odot isq' \in \mathsf{ISQ}$, for all $isq, isq' \in \mathsf{ISQ}$, one can introduce *interval trace monoid* is the equational monoid $\mathbb{IT}_\Phi = \langle \mathsf{IT}_\phi, \widehat{\odot}, \{\lambda\} \rangle$ with the monoid operation given by:

$$[\![isq]\!]_{\equiv_\phi} \widehat{\odot} [\![isq']\!]_{\equiv_\phi} = [\![isq \odot isq']\!]_{\equiv_\phi} .$$

Moreover, the domains IH_Φ, IDG_Φ and ICS_Φ—which are equivalent to IT_ϕ—generate isomorphic monoids.

7 Petri Net Semantics

In this section, we will show how the sequential semantical framework can provide a behavioural model for a *fundamental* class of Petri nets.

A *(Petri) net* is a triple $pn = \langle P, T, F \rangle$, where P and T are disjoint finite sets of *nodes*, called *places* and *transitions*, respectively, and $F \subseteq (T \times P) \cup (P \times T)$ is the *flow relation*. We require, for every $t \in T$:

$$^\bullet t \neq \varnothing \neq t^\bullet \;\text{ and }\; ^\bullet t \cap t^\bullet = \varnothing ,$$

where the *inputs* and *outputs* of a node x are the sets $^\bullet x$ and $x^\bullet$ of all y such that $\langle y, x \rangle \in F$ and $\langle x, y \rangle \in F$, respectively. The dot-notations extend to sets of nodes X in the usual way, e.g., $^\bullet X = \bigcup \{ ^\bullet x \mid x \in X \}$.

A *marking* $M \subseteq P$ is a set of places. In diagrams, places (local states) are represented by circles, transitions (actions) by rectangles, the flow relation by directed arcs, and a marking (global state) by tokens (small black dots) drawn inside each place belonging to the marking.

7.1 Nets with Sequential Semantics

An *elementary net system (or* EN*-system)* is a tuple $en = \langle P, T, F, M^{init} \rangle$ such that: $pn = \langle P, T, F \rangle$ is a net from which en inherits the defining properties, as well as the graphical representations; and $M^{init} \subseteq P$ is a non-empty *initial* marking. The set of all EN-systems is denoted by EN.

The dynamic behaviour of an EN-system *en* is introduced through the transition firing rule.

A transition $t \in T$ is *enabled* at marking $M \subseteq P$ if ${}^\bullet t \subseteq M$ and $t^\bullet \cap M = \varnothing$. If t is enabled at marking M, then it can be *fired* leading to the marking $M' = (M \setminus {}^\bullet t) \cup t^\bullet$. This is denoted by $M[t\rangle_{en}$ and $M[t\rangle_{en} M'$.

A sequence of transitions $fs = t_1 \dots t_n \in T^*$ is a *firing sequence from marking $M \subseteq P$ to marking M'* if there are markings

$$(M =)M_0, M_1, \dots, M_n(= M')$$

such that $M_{i-1}[t_i\rangle_{en} M_i$, for every $1 \leq i \leq n$. This is denoted by $M[fs\rangle_{en} M'$ and $M[fs\rangle_{en}$ (the latter to indicate that fs can be fired from M).

The *firing sequences* FS_{en} of *en* are the firing sequences from the initial marking M^{init}, and the *reachable markings* RM_{en} of *en* are the markings to which such firing sequences lead. We will treat transitions of EN-system as actions.

Marking reachability does not depend on the order in which transitions are fired, i.e., if $M[fs\rangle_{en} M'$ and $M[fs'\rangle_{en} M''$, then $\mathbb{E}_{fs} = \mathbb{E}_{fs'} \implies M' = M''$.

An EN-system is *contact-free* if, for every reachable marking M and every transition t, ${}^\bullet t \subseteq M$ implies $t^\bullet \cap M = \varnothing$. In such a case, it suffices to check whether ${}^\bullet t \subseteq M$ to assert whether transition t is enabled at a reachable marking M. As contact-freeness simplifies the technical treatment of causality (and is easy to enforce statically), we will assume EN-systems are contact-free.

In the rest of this section, $en = \langle P, T, F, M^{init} \rangle$ is a *fixed* contact-free EN-system.

Example 7. Consider again the program from Sect. 1.1 and the EN-system related to its total order semantics depicted in Fig. 1(a) (in Fig. 12 we omitted program statements annotating transitions and provided names of places).

In the initial marking $M^{init} = \{p_1, p_2, p_4\}$ we have two enabled transitions, a and b (all input places are marked, and all output places are empty). Transition c is not enabled at the initial marking, because the input place p_3 is not marked. Firing a at M^{init} leads to marking $M_1 = \{p_2, p_3, p_4\}$, i.e., $M^{init}[a\rangle_{en} M_1$. At marking M_1 transition c is enabled and we have $M_1[c\rangle_{en} M_2$, where $M_2 = \{p_1, p_2, p_6\}$. Transition a is again enabled at M_2.

One of the firing sequences enabled at the initial marking is *abcda* and we have $M^{init}[abcda\rangle_{en} M_3$, where $M_3 = \{p_3, p_7\}$. At marking M_3 no transition is enabled.

The *en*-system from Fig. 12 is contact-free, and its set of firing sequences FS_{en} is equal to $\mathsf{FS}_{\max} = \{abcad, abcda, acabd, acbad, acbda, bacad, bacda\}$ together with all the prefixes of the firing sequences in $\mathsf{FS}_{\max}$. $\diamond$

Trace Semantics of EN-Systems. To specialise concurrency traces to EN-systems, we start by defining the *concurrency alphabet* of *en* as $\Gamma_{en} = \langle T, \mathsf{ind}_{en} \rangle$, where:

$$\mathsf{ind}_{en} = \{\langle t, u \rangle \in T \times T \mid ({}^\bullet t \cup t^\bullet) \cap ({}^\bullet u \cup u^\bullet) = \varnothing\}.$$

That is, ind_{en} comprises pairs of transitions with disjoint neighbourhoods and so embodies the essence of being a pair of 'independent transitions', which is captured by the following result:

$$\langle t, u \rangle \in \mathsf{ind}_{en} \wedge M \in \mathsf{RM}_{en} \implies (M[tu\rangle_{en} M' \iff M[ut\rangle_{en} M').$$

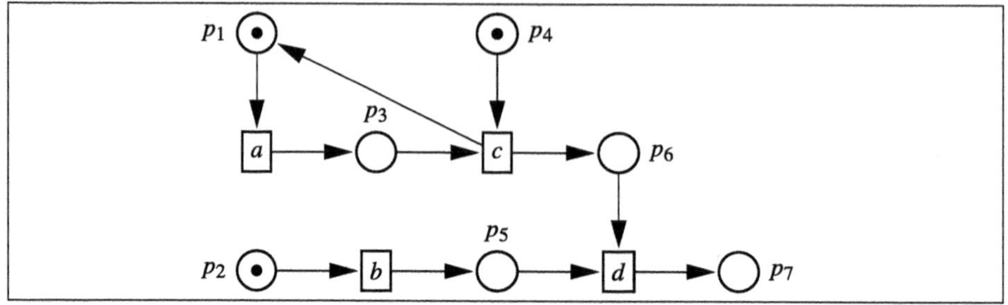

Fig. 12. EN-system *en* modelling the program from Table 2.

$\Gamma = \Gamma_{en}$ induces relations $\approx_\Gamma$ and $\equiv_\Gamma$ on the sequences in SQ, as well as relations $\ddot{\approx}_\Gamma$ and $\ddot{\equiv}_\Gamma$ on the total orders in TO, in the way described in Sect. 6.1. Other domains involved in the framework described there are: $\mathsf{CT}_\Gamma = \mathsf{SQ}/_{\equiv_\Gamma}$, $\mathsf{CH}_\Gamma = \mathsf{TO}/_{\ddot{\equiv}_\Gamma}$, and IO_Γ.

The domains SQ, TO, CT_Γ, and CH_Γ need to be restricted to only those behaviours which can be generated by *en*.

To start with, we restrict SQ to the set FS_{en} of firing sequences of *en*. After that, the modifications of other notions are straightforward. A key result is that the general notion of trace equivalence fits the restricted domain of action sequences.

Theorem 36. $\llbracket fs \rrbracket_{\equiv} \subseteq \mathsf{FS}_{en}$, *for every* $fs \in \mathsf{FS}_{en}$.

The required restriction of TO is to consider precisely those total orders which generate FS_{en}, i.e., $\mathsf{FO}_{en} = \mathrm{sq2to}(\mathsf{FS}_{en})$ are the *firing orders of en*. Similarly, the general notion of history equivalence fits the restricted domain of total orders.

Theorem 37. $\llbracket fo \rrbracket_{\ddot{\equiv}} \subseteq \mathsf{FO}_{en}$, *for every* $fo \in \mathsf{FO}_{en}$.

The above two results mean that one can switch to the restricted framework without losing results developed for the general one presented in Sect. 6.1:

- $\mathsf{CT}_{en} = \{\llbracket fs \rrbracket_{\equiv} \mid fs \in \mathsf{FS}_{en}\}$ are the *concurrency traces* of *en*.
- $\mathsf{CH}_{en} = \{\llbracket fo \rrbracket_{\ddot{\equiv}} \mid fo \in \mathsf{FO}_{en}\}$ are the *concurrency histories* of *en*.
- $\mathsf{IO}_{en} = \mathrm{AR2ar}(\mathsf{CH}_{en})$ are the *invariant orders* of *en*.

We then obtain a fundamental link between the traces and firing sequences of EN-systems.

Theorem 38. $\mathsf{FS}_{en} = \biguplus \mathsf{CT}_{en}$ *and* $\mathsf{FO}_{en} = \biguplus \mathsf{CH}_{en}$.

Hence, the firing sequences of the EN-system *en* can be structured after identifying (in a static way) some transitions as being independent.

For the restricted traces we can re-establish a number of properties which hold in the general model presented in Sect. 6.1.

Theorem 39. $\mathrm{sq2to}|_{\mathsf{CT}_{en} \to \mathsf{CH}_{en}}$ *and* $\mathrm{ar2TO}|_{\mathsf{IO}_{en} \to \mathsf{CH}_{en}}$ *are two bijections with the inverses* $\mathrm{to2sq}|_{\mathsf{CH}_{en} \to \mathsf{CT}_{en}}$ *and* $\mathrm{AR2ar}|_{\mathsf{CH}_{en} \to \mathsf{IO}_{en}}$, *respectively.*

Occurrence Nets. An alternative causality semantics of EN-systems uses a class of acyclic Petri nets, called occurrence nets, which can be regarded as acyclic relations. In what follows, we add the indexes to places from P and to the actions from T and so $\mathbb{E}_P$ can be regarded as a set of place occurrences while $\mathbb{E}_T$ as a set of transition occurrences. We also allow $\mathbb{E}_P$ to serve as places of occurrence nets, and $\mathbb{E}_T$ to serve as transitions of occurrence nets.

An *occurrence net* is a net $on = \langle B, E, G \rangle$ such that $B \subseteq \mathbb{E}_P$, $E \subseteq \mathbb{E}_T$, $\langle B \cup E, G \rangle$ is an acyclic relation, and, for every $b \in B$:

$$|{}^\bullet b| \leq 1 \text{ and } |b^\bullet| \leq 1 .$$

The set of all occurrence nets is denoted by ON. Given a place $b \in B$, we will use ${}^\bullet b$ (or $b^\bullet$) to denote the unique transition $e \in E$ with an arc leading to (resp. originating from) b if such a transition does exist.

We also define a mapping $\ell_{aon} : B \cup E \to P \cup T$, given by $x \mapsto \ell_x$.

Occurrence nets record possible ways of executing system models, such as EN-systems. Their transitions represent events, and their places represent the occurrences of tokens which are consumed and produced during system executions. Using occurrence nets to represent executions of EN-systems allows one to capture causality and concurrency between executed transitions using structural properties.

The transitions of an occurrence net form an *(acyclic) relation on transitions*, represented by the mapping $\mathrm{on2ao} : \mathsf{ON} \to \mathsf{AR}$, given by $\langle B, E, G \rangle \mapsto \langle E, (G \circ G)|_{E \times E} \rangle$.

Each $\mathrm{on2ao}(on)$ captures direct causality between transitions of on, and an arc $\langle t, u \rangle$ in $\mathrm{on2ao}(on)$ means that the event t has produced a token consumed by the event u, and so t is a direct causal predecessors of u. Such an interpretation of causality is consistent with that present in on, i.e., $G^+|_{E \times E} = ((G \circ G)|_{E \times E})^+$.

Having captured direct causalities between transitions of occurrence nets, we introduce three mappings:

- $\mathrm{on2po}(= \mathrm{ar2po} \circ \mathrm{on2ao}) : \mathsf{ON} \to \mathsf{PO}$ (returning *causal partial order*)
- $\mathrm{on2TO}(= \mathrm{ar2TO} \circ \mathrm{on2ao}) : \mathsf{ON} \to 2^{\mathsf{TO}}$ (returning *total order observations*)
- $\mathrm{on2SQ}(= \mathrm{to2sq} \circ \mathrm{on2TO}) : \mathsf{ON} \to 2^{\mathsf{SQ}}$ (returning *action sequence observations*)

Example 8. Figure 13 shows an occurrence net which consists of 8 place instances and 5 transition instances. Note that the graph of the net is acyclic. $\diamond$

Executing Occurrence Nets. Although the total order observations $\mathrm{on2TO}(on)$ of occurrence net on were captured in a *structural* way, they are consistent with the standard Petri net semantics. To see this, we introduce the default *initial* and *final* markings of on as $M_{on}^{init} = \{b \in B_{on} \mid {}^\bullet b = \varnothing\}$ and $M_{on}^{fin} = \{b \in B_{on} \mid b^\bullet = \varnothing\}$, respectively.

Adding the default initial marking to an occurrence net and dropping the labelling turns it into a contact-free EN-system, i.e., we have a mapping $\mathrm{on2en} : \mathsf{ON} \to \mathsf{EN}$, given by $\langle B, E, G \rangle \mapsto \langle B, E, G, M_{on}^{init} \rangle$.

Since an occurrence net on models concurrent execution rather than concurrent system, its *firing sequences* are those leading from the default initial to the default final marking:

$$\mathsf{FS}_{on} = \{fs \in \mathsf{FS}_{\mathrm{on2en}(on)} \mid M_{on}^{init} [fs\rangle_{\mathrm{on2en}(on)} M_{on}^{fin}\} .$$

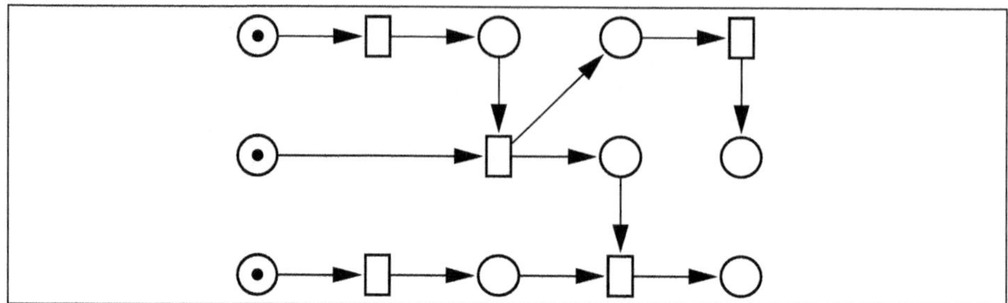

Fig. 13. An occurrence net with the default initial marking.

Moreover, the *reachable markings* of *on* are:

$$\mathsf{RM}_{on} = \{M \mid \exists fs \in \mathrm{pref}(\mathsf{FS}_{on}) : M_{on}^{init}[fs\rangle_{\mathrm{on2en}(on)} M\} .$$

Processes of EN-Systems. We will now show how to associate occurrence nets (processes) with EN-systems, providing their causality semantics in which both places and transitions are taken into account.

All valid behaviours of EN-systems can be expressed through a class of occurrence nets defined next.

A *process* of *en* is an occurrence net $on = \langle B, E, G \rangle$ such that the following are satisfied:

- $\ell_{on}|_{M_{on}^{init} \to M_{en}^{init}}$ is a bijection.
- $\ell_{on}|_{{}^{\bullet}e \to {}^{\bullet}\ell_e}$ and $\ell_{on}|_{e^{\bullet} \to \ell_e^{\bullet}}$ are bijections, for every $e \in E$.

The set of all processes of *en* is denoted by CP_{en}.

Note that the default initial marking of a process reflects the initial marking of the EN-system, and each transition in a process has the same local environment (in terms of tokens consumed and produced) as the transition of the EN-system it represents.

It is also possible to derive processes from single firing sequences of EN-systems. The construction below builds an occurrence net, for each firing sequence $fs = t_1 \ldots t_n$ of *en*. In the construction, $\mathrm{fs2on}_{en}(fs) = \langle B, E, G \rangle$ is the last occurrence net in the sequence of occurrence nets $on_0, \ldots, on_n$ (with $on_i = \langle B_i, E_i, G_i \rangle$ for every $0 \leq i \leq n$), derived as follows:

- $B_0 = \{p^{(1)} \mid p \in M^{init}\}$ and $E_0 = G_0 = \varnothing$.
- For every $0 < i \leq n$:

$$\begin{aligned} B_i &= B_{i-1} \cup \{p^{new} \mid p \in t_i^{\bullet}\} \\ E_i &= E_{i-1} \cup \{t_i^{new}\} \\ G_i &= G_{i-1} \cup \{\langle p^{last}, t_i^{new} \rangle \mid p \in {}^{\bullet}t_i\} \cup \{\langle t_i^{new}, p^{new} \rangle \mid p \in t_i^{\bullet}\} , \end{aligned}$$

where, for every $x \in P \cup T$ with $k = |\{y \in B_{i-1} \cup E_{i-1} \mid \ell_y = x\}|$, we denote:

$$x^{last} = x^{(k)} \text{ and } x^{new} = x^{(k+1)} .$$

The resulting occurrence nets $\mathsf{CP}_{en} = \mathrm{fs2on}_{en}(\mathsf{FS}_{en})$ are called *(concurrency) processes* of *en*. We also derive *orders on transitions* of *en* by $\mathsf{OT}_{en} = \mathrm{on2ao}(\mathsf{CP}_{en})$.

A process generated from a firing sequence has this sequence as one of its observation sequences. Also, generating processes from two observation sequences derived from a single process always yields the same result.

Theorem 40. *Let* $fs \in \mathsf{FS}_{en}$ *and* $on \in \mathsf{CP}_{en}$.

1. $fs \in \mathrm{on2SQ} \circ \mathrm{fs2on}_{en}(fs)$.
2. $fs', fs'' \in \mathrm{on2SQ}(on)$ *implies* $\mathrm{fs2on}_{en}(fs') = \mathrm{fs2on}_{en}(fs'')$.

Example 9. Consider again the EN-system *en* from Example 7. One can see that the occurrence net from Example 8 corresponds to the process of *en* related with the firing sequence *abcda*. The occurrence net with the appropriate names assigned to place and transition instances as well as default initial marking is depicted in Fig. 14. Note that all maximal firing sequences provided in Example 7 also lead to the same occurrence net. ◇

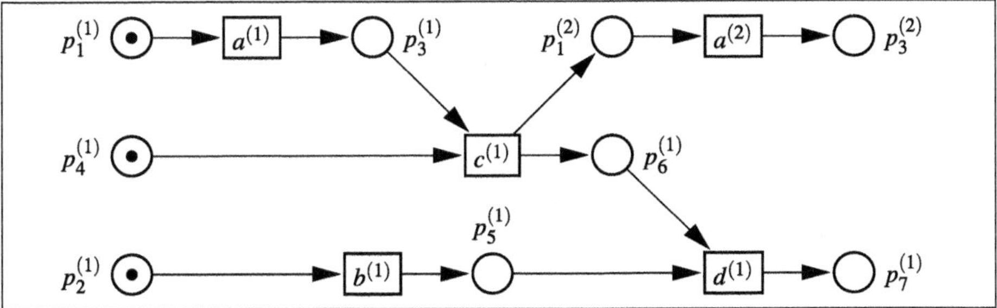

Fig. 14. The occurrence net $on = \mathrm{fs2on}_{en}(abcda)$.

Processes and Traces of EN-System. We are now in a position to link together semantical notions coming from two different perspectives of defining causality semantics.

Theorem 41. $\mathrm{on2TO}(\mathsf{CP}_{en}) = \mathsf{CH}_{en}$, $\mathrm{on2SQ}(\mathsf{CP}_{en}) = \mathsf{CT}_{en}$ *and* $\mathrm{on2po}(\mathsf{CP}_{en}) = \mathsf{IO}_{en}$.

It is also possible to associate a unique process with every trace of *en*, through the mapping $\mathrm{FS2on}_{en} : \mathsf{CT}_{en} \to \mathsf{CP}_{en}$, given by $[\![fs]\!]_{\equiv} \mapsto \mathrm{fs2on}_{en}(fs)$.

Theorem 42. $\mathrm{FS2on}_{en}$ *is a bijection with the inverse* $\mathrm{on2SQ}|_{\mathsf{CP}_{en} \to \mathsf{CT}_{en}}$.

One can also show that

Theorem 43. $\mathrm{ao2on}_{en} : \mathsf{OT}_{en} \to \mathsf{CP}_{en}$, $\mathrm{po2on}_{en} : \mathsf{IO}_{en} \to \mathsf{CP}_{en}$, *and* $\mathrm{po2ao}_{en} : \mathsf{IO}_{en} \to \mathsf{OT}_{en}$ *are three bijections with the inverses* $\mathrm{on2ao} : \mathsf{CP}_{en} \to \mathsf{OT}_{en}$, $\mathrm{on2po} : \mathsf{CP}_{en} \to \mathsf{IO}_{en}$, *and* $\mathrm{ar2po} : \mathsf{OT}_{en} \to \mathsf{IO}_{en}$, *respectively.*

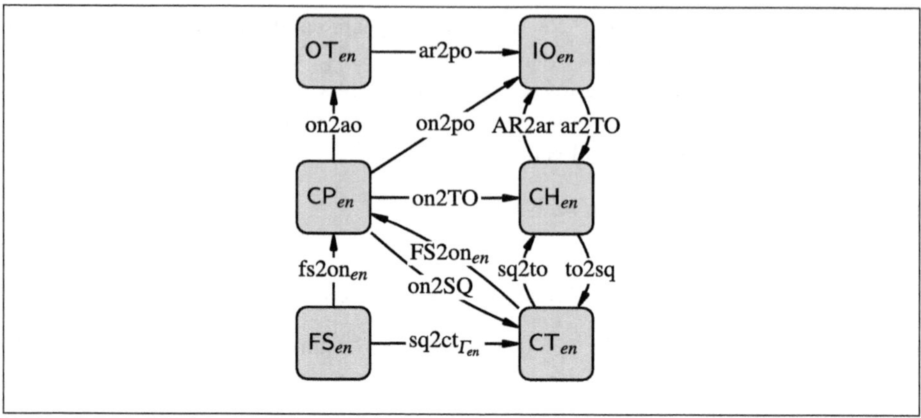

Fig. 15. Commutative diagram relating different domains associated with the EN-system *en*.

We can now summarise relationships between the various semantical domains introduced for the EN-system *en*.

Theorem 44. *Figure 15 depicts a commutative diagram.*

The orders on transitions of processes are different from the dependence graphs of traces of an EN-system. The reason is that processes record dependencies which actually occurred during an execution, and may therefore not record some potential dependencies. At the same time orders on transitions of processes are different from transitive reductions of dependence graphs as they still might contain some redundant relationships. This indicates that partial orders are *the* right representations of causal dependencies in the behaviours of concurrent systems modelled by EN-systems. The trace semantics and the process semantics of EN-systems lead to the same partial order semantics. This provides a strong argument in favour of the view that both approaches capture the essence of causality in the semantics of EN-systems.

Many formal notions related to EN-systems were discussed since the publication of the original 1962 paper introducing Petri nets [53]. Their current formalisation follows mainly from [52,57] and [58]. Occurrence nets were first discussed in [55], and then developed in [2,14]. The way in which the process semantics of EN-systems discussed is presented follows [32].

Adding conflicts between transitions in occurrence nets leads to branching processes [9] and is the basis for an efficient verification technique [10,30,47]. Moreover, only considering relationships between events leads to the abstract model of event structures [16,51,63].

7.2 Nets with Other Semantics

The treatment presented in the previous section for the standard EN-systems and total order runs can be extended to EN-systems with activator arcs and stratified order runs (note that a more general model that covers also mutual exclusion and true interleaving can be found in [19]), and EN-systems and EN-systems with interval order runs covered in another part of this volume entitled “From Behaviour to Nets via Regions”. We will now briefly discuss the leading example and the second choice of label assignment shown in Fig. 1(*c*).

Intuitively, EN-systems with activator arcs are not only EN-systems with another type of arcs $A \subseteq P \times T$ (depicted as edges with black dots instead of arrowheads). Another important difference is the firing rule. First of all, apart from the enabledness of individual transitions, we allow non-empty sets of transitions (called *steps*) to be enabled and fired simultaneously. More precisely, a step $U \subseteq T$ is *enabled at marking* M if, for all $t, t' \in U$ and $p \in P$:

- $^\bullet t \subseteq M$ and $t^\bullet \cap M = \varnothing$ (enabledness as before)
- $t \neq t' \implies {^\bullet t} \cap {^\bullet t'} = \varnothing$ (no conflicts between transitions)
- $\langle p, t \rangle \in A \implies p \in M$. (activator places are marked)

Moreover, the *firing* of such U results in the marking $M' = (M \setminus {^\bullet U}) \cup U^\bullet$.

Then, according to the step enabling and step firing rules, one can easily define step firing sequences as sequences of steps enabled and fired starting from the initial marking M^{init}.

Example 10. Figure 16 shows the EN-system with activator arcs *ena* of Fig. 1(*c*) after omitting the program statements annotating transitions and adding names for the places. At the initial marking $M^{init} = \{p_1, p_2\}$ three steps are enabled, namely *a*, *b* and (ab). Moreover, we have two firing sequences *ab* and *ba* enabled at this marking. Executing step (ab) at M^{init} leads to $M_1 = \{p_3, p_4, p_5\}$. At marking M_1 again three steps are enabled: *c*, *e* and (ce). This time, however, *ec* is not a firing sequence enabled at M_1 since, after firing *e*, transition *c* is no longer enabled as p_3 connected with *c* by activator arc is empty. ◇

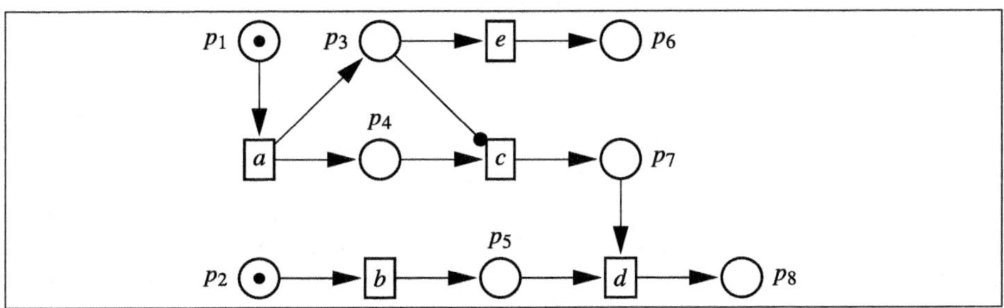

Fig. 16. EN-system with activator arcs whose behaviour refers to the sample program from Example 1.1 when considering the stratified order semantics.

Similarly, one can generalise occurrence nets by adding activator arcs and allowing one to execute sequences of steps of transitions.

Example 11. The EN-system with activators *ena* from Fig. 16 is acyclic and all its transitions are used in the step sequence $a(bce)d$ which is enabled at the initial marking. It is therefore not surprising that a suitable activator occurrence net shown in Fig. 17 (where we indicated the shape of steps of the generating step sequence) is almost the same as *ena*. ◇

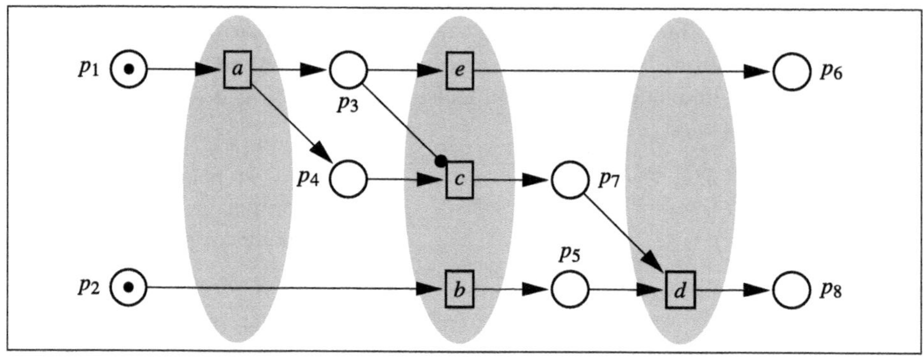

Fig. 17. The activator occurrence net generated by step firing sequence $a(bce)d$.

8 Final Remarks

This paper is focused on the modelling of concurrent behaviours emphasising assumptions about individual runs—represented by the total, stratified, and interval partial orders—emphasising relationships between events, and the potential to model phenomena like 'weak precedence'. For each of these three classes of partial orders a model of relational structures was presented, which is suitable for representing groups of closely related individual runs. In fact, each case took advantage of the more generic approach expounded in [18,19].

The second part of this paper presented a language-theoretic framework for abstract captures of concurrent histories, for each of the three models of concurrent behaviours. These captures—called traces—have been introduced by Cartier and Foata in 1969 [4], and independently reinvented by Mazurkiewicz in 1977 [44] with a different motivation to provide a tool to model causality in Petri nets. Dependence graphs have been introduced in [45] and analysed in [15]. An extensive account of trace theory is provided by [7]. Applications of traces in combinatorics can be found in [4,5,8]. The COSY [27] model of concurrency assumes that concurrent systems are compositions of sequential components, and to capture this semantically [59] introduced the concept of vector firing sequences. It turned out that traces and vector firing sequences can be considered as different representations of the same kind of partially commutative monoids [27]. There are also several strands of related research on traces which have not even been mentioned, e.g., infinite traces [12,13,39]. Algebraic properties of traces can be found in, e.g., [6,7].

The development of (finite and infinite) process semantics based on stratified order structures for different classes of Petri nets with context arcs was presented in, e.g., [31,33,34]. The treatment was also extended to other models of concurrent systems in, e.g., [25,36–38].

For the model of step traces, [48] introduced and applied the notion of indivisible steps, the lexicographical form of step traces, as well as the representation of a step trace utilising its linear projections to binary action sub-alphabets. Also, it solved in an efficient way, the problem of step sequence equivalence in the context of step traces. Moreover, [43] provides and analyses a detailed representation of step traces by the stratified order structures and combined dependency graphs of [35].

The paper [28] deals with the algebraic properties, such as projections, hiding, and normal forms of step traces and interval traces (where the structures underlying observation are interval orders). In [26] a representation of interval orders by sequences of antichains is discussed, and a semantics based on sequences of maximal antichains investigated for a class of safe Petri nets with contextual arcs.

The third part of this paper presents *en*-systems working according to the sequential semantics, together with their concurrent processes in the form of occurrence nets. Their connection with concepts covered in the first two parts of the paper are discussed in detail.

We finish with a short discussion of Petri net models working according to the step and interval semantics. Activator arcs, introduced in [23] and used in this paper, are closely related to inhibitor arcs checking for the absence rather than the presence of tokens. Both types of arcs are instances of contextual arcs [50]. A trace and process semantics of EN-systems with inhibitor arcs with step sequence semantics were developed in [23], and the proposed process semantics was later extended to a larger class of inhibitor nets in [32]. An alternative process semantics for place/transition nets with inhibitor and read arcs can be found in [3].

Acknowledgement. Partial support by the Discovery NSERC of Canada grant No. 6466-15, and the Leverhulme Trust grant RPG-2022-025 is acknowledged. The authors are grateful to the anonymous referees, whose comments significantly contributed to the revised version of this paper.

Disclosure of Interests. The authors have no competing interests to declare that are relevant to the content of this article.

References

1. Best, E., Fernández, C.: Nonsequential Processes: A Petri Net View. EATCS Monographs on Theoretical Computer Science. Springer (1988)
2. Best, E., Devillers, R.R.: Sequential and concurrent behaviour in Petri net theory. Theoret. Comput. Sci. **55**(1), 87–136 (1987)
3. Busi, N., Pinna, G.M.: Process semantics for place/transition nets with inhibitor and read arcs. Fundam. Informaticae **40**(2–3), 165–197 (1999)
4. Cartier, P., Foata, D.: Problèmes combinatoires de commutation et réarrangements. LNM, vol. 85. Springer-Verlag, Berlin (1969)

5. Choffrut, C.: Combinatorics in trace monoids I. In: Diekert, V., Rozenberg, G. (eds.) The Book of Traces, pp. 71–82. World Scientific (1995)
6. Diekert, V., Métivier, Y.: Partial commutation and traces. In: Rozenberg, G., Salomaa, A. (eds.) Handbook of Formal Languages, pp. 457–533. Springer, Heidelberg (1997). https://doi.org/10.1007/978-3-642-59126-6_8
7. Diekert, V., Rozenberg, G. (eds.): The Book of Traces. World Scientific (1995)
8. Duchamp, G., Krob, D.: Combinatorics in trace monoids II. In: Diekert, V., Rozenberg, G. (eds.) The Book of Traces, pp. 83–129. World Scientific (1995)
9. Engelfriet, J.: Branching processes of Petri nets. Acta Infortmatica **28**(6), 575–591 (1991)
10. Esparza, J., Römer, S., Vogler, W.: An improvement of McMillan's unfolding algorithm. In: Margaria, T., Steffen, B. (eds.) TACAS 1996. LNCS, vol. 1055, pp. 87–106. Springer, Heidelberg (1996). https://doi.org/10.1007/3-540-61042-1_40
11. Gaifman, H., Pratt, V.R.: Partial order models of concurrency and the computation of functions. In: Proceedings of the Symposium on Logic in Computer Science (LICS '87), Ithaca, New York, USA, 22–25 June 1987, pp. 72–85. IEEE Computer Society (1987)
12. Gastin, P.: Infinite traces. In: Guessarian, I. (ed.) LITP 1990. LNCS, vol. 469, pp. 277–308. Springer, Heidelberg (1990). https://doi.org/10.1007/3-540-53479-2_12
13. Gastin, P., Petit, A.: Poset properties of complex traces. In: Havel, I.M., Koubek, V. (eds.) MFCS 1992. LNCS, vol. 629, pp. 255–263. Springer, Heidelberg (1992). https://doi.org/10.1007/3-540-55808-X_24
14. Goltz, U., Reisig, W.: The non-sequential behavior of Petri nets. Inf. Control **57**(2/3), 125–147 (1983)
15. Hoogeboom, H.J., Rozenberg, G.: Dependence graphs. In: Diekert, V., Rozenberg, G. (eds.) The Book of Traces, pp. 43–67. World Scientific (1995)
16. Hoogers, P.W., Kleijn, H.C.M., Thiagarajan, P.S.: An event structure semantics for general Petri nets. Theoret. Comput. Sci. **153**(1&2), 129–170 (1996)
17. Janicki, R., Kleijn, J., Koutny, M., Mikulski, Ł.: Characterising concurrent histories. Fund. Inform. **139**(1), 21–42 (2015)
18. Janicki, R., Kleijn, J., Koutny, M., Mikulski, Ł.: Relational structures for concurrent behaviours. Theor. Computut. Sci. **862**, 174–192 (2021)
19. Janicki, R., Kleijn, J., Koutny, M., Mikulski, Ł.: Paradigms of Concurrency - Observations, Behaviours, and Systems - a Petri Net View. Studies in Computational Intelligence, vol. 1020. Springer, Heidelberg (2022)
20. Janicki, R., Kleijn, J., Koutny, M., Mikulski, Ł.: Relational structures for interval order semantics of concurrent systems. In: Kristensen, L.M., van der Werf, J.M.E.M. (eds.) Application and Theory of Petri Nets and Concurrency - 45th International Conference, PETRI NETS 2024, Geneva, Switzerland, 26–28 June 2024, Proceedings. LNCS, vol. 14628, pp. 153–174. Springer, Cham (2024). https://doi.org/10.1007/978-3-031-61433-0_8
21. Janicki, R., Koutny, M.: Invariants and paradigms of concurrency theory. In: Aarts, E.H.L., van Leeuwen, J., Rem, M. (eds.) PARLE 1991. LNCS, vol. 506, pp. 59–74. Springer, Heidelberg (1991). https://doi.org/10.1007/3-540-54152-7_58
22. Janicki, R., Koutny, M.: Structure of concurrency. Theor. Computut. Sci. **112**(1), 5–52 (1993)
23. Janicki, R., Koutny, M.: Semantics of inhibitor nets. Inf. Comput. **123**(1), 1–16 (1995)
24. Janicki, R., Koutny, M.: Fundamentals of modelling concurrency using discrete relational structures. Acta Informatica **34**(5), 367–388 (1997)
25. Janicki, R., Koutny, M.: On causality semantics of nets with priorities. Fund. Inform. **38**(3), 223–255 (1999)
26. Janicki, R., Koutny, M.: Operational semantics, interval orders and sequences of antichains. Fund. Inform. **169**(1–2), 31–55 (2019)
27. Janicki, R., Lauer, P.E.: Specification and Analysis of Concurrent Systems - The COSY Approach, 2nd edn. EATCS Monographs on Theoretical Computer Science. Springer (2012)

28. Janicki, R., Mikulski, Ł.: Algebraic structure of step traces and interval traces. Fund. Inform. **175**(1–4), 253–280 (2020)
29. Janicki, R., Yin, X.: Modeling concurrency with interval traces. Inf. Comput. **253**, 78–108 (2017)
30. Khomenko, V., Koutny, M., Vogler, W.: Canonical prefixes of Petri net unfoldings. Acta Infortmatica **40**(2), 95–118 (2003)
31. Kleijn, H.C.M., Koutny, M.: Causality semantics of petri nets with weighted inhibitor arcs. In: Brim, L., Křetínský, M., Kučera, A., Jančar, P. (eds.) CONCUR 2002. LNCS, vol. 2421, pp. 531–546. Springer, Heidelberg (2002). https://doi.org/10.1007/3-540-45694-5_35
32. Kleijn, H.C.M., Koutny, M.: Process semantics of general inhibitor nets. Inf. Comput. **190**(1), 18–69 (2004)
33. Kleijn, H.C.M., Koutny, M.: Infinite process semantics of inhibitor nets. In: Donatelli, S., Thiagarajan, P.S. (eds.) ICATPN 2006. LNCS, vol. 4024, pp. 282–301. Springer, Heidelberg (2006). https://doi.org/10.1007/11767589_16
34. Kleijn, J., Koutny, M.: Processes of Petri nets with range testing. Fund. Inform. **80**(1–3), 199–219 (2007)
35. Kleijn, J., Koutny, M.: Formal languages and concurrent behaviours. In: Enguix, G.B., Jiménez-López, M.D., Martín-Vide, C. (eds.) New Developments in Formal Languages and Applications, Studies in Computational Intelligence, vol. 113, pp. 125–182. Springer (2008). https://doi.org/10.1007/978-3-540-78291-9_5
36. Kleijn, J., Koutny, M.: Processes of membrane systems with promoters and inhibitors. Theor. Computut. Sci. **404**(1–2), 112–126 (2008)
37. Kleijn, J., Koutny, M.: Causality in structured occurrence nets. In: Jones, C.B., Lloyd, J.L. (eds.) Dependable and Historic Computing. LNCS, vol. 6875, pp. 283–297. Springer, Heidelberg (2011). https://doi.org/10.1007/978-3-642-24541-1_22
38. Kleijn, J., Koutny, M.: Mutex causality in processes and traces of general elementary nets. Fund. Inform. **122**(1–2), 119–146 (2013)
39. Kwiatkowska, M.Z.: Fairness for non-interleaving concurrency. Ph.D. thesis, University of Leicester (UK) (1989)
40. Lämmel, R.: Google's MapReduce programming model - revisited. Sci. Comput. Program. **70**(1), 1–30 (2008)
41. Lamport, L.: Time, clocks, and the ordering of events in a distributed system. Commun. ACM **21**(7), 558–565 (1978)
42. Lamport, L.: The mutual exclusion problem: part I - a theory of interprocess communication. J. ACM **33**(2), 313–326 (1986)
43. Lê, D.T.M.: On three alternative characterizations of combined traces. Fund. Inform. **113**(3–4), 265–293 (2011)
44. Mazurkiewicz, A.: Concurrent program schemes and their interpretations. DAIMI Rep. PB 78, Aarhus University (1977)
45. Mazurkiewicz, A.W.: Trace theory. In: Brauer, W., Reisig, W., Rozenberg, G. (eds.) Petri Nets: Central Models and Their Properties, Advances in Petri Nets 1986, Part II, Proceedings of an Advanced Course, Bad Honnef, Germany, 8–19 September 1986. LNCS, vol. 255, pp. 279–324. Springer, Boston (1986)
46. Mazurkiewicz, A.W.: Introduction to trace theory. In: Diekert, V., Rozenberg, G. (eds.) The Book of Traces, pp. 3–41. World Scientific (1995)
47. McMillan, K.L.: Using unfoldings to avoid the state explosion problem in the verification of asynchronous circuits. In: von Bochmann, G., Probst, D.K. (eds.) CAV 1992. LNCS, vol. 663, pp. 164–177. Springer, Heidelberg (1993). https://doi.org/10.1007/3-540-56496-9_14
48. Mikulski, Ł.: Algebraic structure of combined traces. Logical Methods Comput. Sci. **9**(3) (2013)

49. Mikulski, Ł., Koutny, M.: Folded Hasse diagrams of combined traces. Inf. Process. Lett. **114**(4), 208–216 (2014)
50. Montanari, U., Rossi, F.: Contextual nets. Acta Infortmatica **32**(6), 545–596 (1995)
51. Nielsen, M., Plotkin, G.D., Winskel, G.: Petri nets, event structures and domains, part I. Theoret. Comput. Sci. **13**, 85–108 (1981)
52. Nielsen, M., Rozenberg, G., Thiagarajan, P.S.: Behavioural notions for elementary net systems. Distrib. Comput. **4**, 45–57 (1990)
53. Petri, C.A.: Fundamentals of a theory of asynchronous information flow. In: Information Processing, Proceedings of the 2nd IFIP Congress 1962, Munich, Germany, 27 August–1 September 1962, pp. 386–390. North-Holland (1962)
54. Petri, C.A.: Concepts of net theory. In: Mathematical Foundations of Computer Science: Proceedings of Symposium and Summer School, Strbské Pleso, High Tatras, Czechoslovakia, 3–8 September 1973, pp. 137–146. Mathematical Institute of the Slovak Academy of Sciences (1973)
55. Petri, C.A.: Non-sequential processes. GMD-ISF Report 77.05, Gesellschaft fuer Mathematik und Datenverarbeitung mbH, Bonn (1977)
56. Pratt, V.R.: Modeling concurrency with partial orders. Int. J. Parallel Prog. **15**(1), 33–71 (1986)
57. Reisig, W.: Petri Nets (An Introduction). EATCS Monographs on Theoretical Computer Science. Springer-Verlag, Heidelberg (1985)
58. Rozenberg, G., Engelfriet, J.: Elementary net systems. In: Reisig, W., Rozenberg, G. (eds.) Lectures on Petri Nets I: Basic Models, Advances in Petri Nets, the volumes are based on the Advanced Course on Petri Nets, held in Dagstuhl, September 1996. LNCS, vol. 1491, pp. 12–121. Springer (1996)
59. Shields, M.W.: Adequate path expressions. In: Kahn, G. (ed.) Semantics of Concurrent Computation, Proceedings of the International Symposium, Evian, France, 2–4 July 1979. LNCS, vol. 70, pp. 249–265. Springer (1979)
60. Szpilrajn, E.: Sur l'extension de l'ordre partiel. Fundam. Math. **16**, 386–389 (1930)
61. Vogler, W.: Partial order semantics and read arcs. Theoret. Comput. Sci. **286**(1), 33–63 (2002)
62. Wiener, N.: A contribution to the theory of relative position. Proc. Cambridge Philosophical Soc. **33**(2), 313–326 (1914)
63. Winskel, G.: An introduction to event structures. In: de Bakker, J.W., de Roever, W.-P., Rozenberg, G. (eds.) REX 1988. LNCS, vol. 354, pp. 364–397. Springer, Heidelberg (1989). https://doi.org/10.1007/BFb0013026

From Behaviour to Nets via Regions

Maciej Koutny[1(✉)], Łukasz Mikulski[2], and Marta Pietkiewicz-Koutny[1]

[1] School of Computing, Newcastle University, 1 Science Square, Newcastle upon Tyne NE4 5TG, UK
{maciej.koutny,marta.koutny}@ncl.ac.uk

[2] Faculty of Mathematics and Computer Science, Nicolaus Copernicus University in Toruń, Chopina 12/18, Toruń, Poland
lukasz.mikulski@mat.umk.pl

Abstract. The behaviour of concurrent systems is often given in the form of graphs/transition systems that show the execution of systems' actions (or transitions). The extraction of the systems' topology from the transition systems' specification—with every transition and its environment (places) clearly identified—is possible by synthesising Petri net models from given transition systems. A particularly successful technique is based on the notion of a region of a transition system, where each region is used to define a place in the synthesised Petri net.

The class of Elementary Net systems is a fundamental Petri net model with markings that can be represented by sets of the marked places. Their standard semantics is based on sequences of executed transitions, which can be understood as (labelled) total orders. In this paper, and in its workshop precursor [32], we consider a newly proposed semantics based on (labelled) interval (partial) orders which allows one to describe behaviours where transitions have non-atomic duration. For such a semantical model, we consider the net synthesis problem, and show that the standard notion of a region of a transition system can still be applied.

Keywords: theory of concurrency · Petri net · structure and behaviour of nets · elementary net system · transition system · step transition system · interval transition system · theory of regions · synthesis problem · step firing policy

1 Introduction

Petri nets are a general model of concurrent systems which emerged in the 1960's as a counterpart to state machines that were successfully used to model sequential systems. An advantage of Petri nets is that the model allows one to both specify concurrent system designs as well as their different behavioural semantics. It is generally acknowledged that concepts related to fundamental notions of concurrency theory, such as causality and independence, can be particularly well

F. Kordon et al. (Eds.): *Transactions on Petri Nets and Other Models of Concurrency XVIII*, LNCTPN 16260, pp. 93–122, 2026.
https://doi.org/10.1007/978-3-662-73305-9_4

explained using the framework provided by Petri nets [18,29,42,46]. A fundamental class of Petri nets in that respect is the class of Elementary Net systems (EN-systems) [47].

An attractive way of constructing complex computing systems (in a Petri net form) is automated synthesis from behavioural specifications given in terms of suitable transition systems. The synthesis problem is usually stated as follows:

> *Given a labelled transition system lts, provide necessary and sufficient conditions for lts to be* realised *by some Petri net N (i.e., $lts \cong RG(N)$, where $\cong$ is transition system isomorphism preserving the initial states and transition labels, and $RG(N)$ is the reachability graph/transition system generated by N.*

The synthesis procedure is often based on the regions of a labelled transition system *lts*, a notion introduced in [21], and later used to solve the synthesis problem for a number of different classes of Petri nets, e.g., in [4,7,11,12,39,40,43]. A comprehensive and systematic survey of the synthesis problem and region theory is presented in [5]. Though in a majority of the existing works dealing with synthesis problem(s) it was assumed that the actions/transitions have atomic duration and are executed sequentially, there were also papers dealing with non-atomic durations and partial order executions, e.g., [8,10,32]. In particular, the recent paper [32] considered behaviours where transitions have non-atomic duration and the proposed solution was still based on an idea of a region that was suitably adapted to this new setting. The aim of this paper is to further explain the approach and techniques used in [32].

To show the results of [32] in historical context, in Sect. 1.1 we briefly sketch the idea of a region as it was originally defined for the transition system specifications with 'atomic' transitions. Then, in Sect. 1.2, we present the challenges posed by the assumption of having transitions of non-atomic duration as it was done in [32], which we will use as a case study in the later parts of the paper.

1.1 Synthesis of Systems with Transitions of Atomic Duration

To illustrate the evolution of an idea of a region that is a key 'tool' in the process of synthesising Petri nets from transition systems (or, indeed, other behavioural specifications), we consider the fundamental class of nets, viz. EN-systems. According to the standard definition, an EN-system is a tuple $en = \langle P, T, F, M^{init} \rangle$, where P and T are sets of places and transitions (i.e., nodes in the Petri net graph), $F \subseteq (T \times P) \cup (P \times T)$ is the flow relation defining the arcs in Petri net graph, and $M^{init} \subseteq P$ is the initial marking (or configuration) showing the initial satisfaction of conditions given by the places (in diagrams, places belonging to markings have tokens—black dots—inside them). The standard sequential execution semantics of *en* is given by the Elementary Transition System (sequential transition system) $ts_{en} = RG(en) = \langle Q, T, A, q_0 \rangle$, where Q is the set of states, T is the set of transitions labelling its arcs $A \subseteq Q \times T \times Q$ and $q_0 \in Q$ is an initial state. ts_{en} will be called the *interleaving reachability graph* of *en* in order to distinguish it from other reachability graphs produced by applying different execution semantics to *en*. The interleaving reachability graph for a net (EN-system) in Fig. 1(a) is shown in Fig. 1(b).

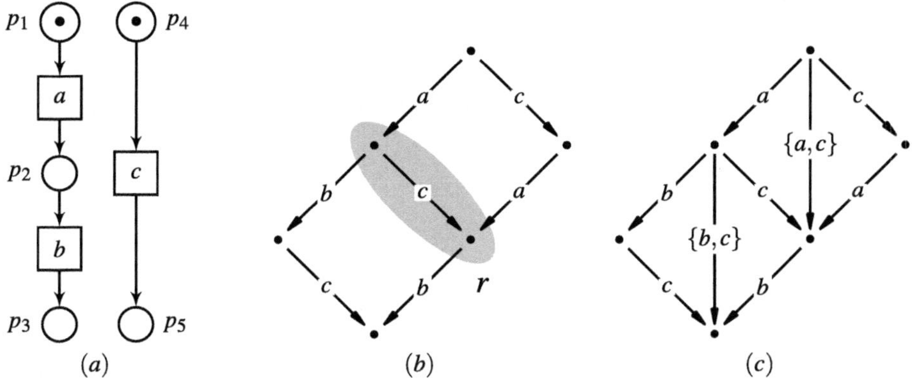

Fig. 1. (a) EN-system; (b) its interleaving reachability graph (the topmost node is the initial state), where one of its regions, r, has been highlighted; and (c) its step reachability graph.

The synthesis procedure describes the transformation in the reverse direction, viz. from a given transition system to a net. In this procedure the idea of a region is used, and its standard definition for EN-systems (see [40]) is as follows: a region is a set of states in a transition system with which all arcs labelled with the same transition have the same 'crossing' relationship (either they all enter the region, or all exit it, or all do not cross its 'border'). For example, in Fig. 1(b), the two highlighted states form a region r as all the arcs labelled by a enter it, all the arcs labelled by b exit it, and none of the arcs labelled by c crosses its border.

The standard definition of a region introduced for interleaving executions can be generalised to the *step semantics* of EN-systems, where several transitions, enabled at a given marking, might be allowed to execute simultaneously. Such transitions form *steps* that can be represented as sets (or, in the case of more general net classes, multi-sets) of transitions. In the case of step semantics, the behaviour of a net can be represented by its 'step transition system' (see Fig. 1(c)), where a region is a set of states such that the 'crossing' relationship of a step with respect to this region depends on the step containing a special 'leading' transition. For a fixed step and a fixed region such a transition is unique (see, for example, [43]).

In [6], a uniform approach to the synthesis problem was proposed. It is based on regions defined as morphisms from a given transition system into a classifying transition system—called a *type of nets*—which describes the behaviour of the class of nets under consideration. To synthesise a net from a sequential transition system $ts = \langle Q, T, A, q_0 \rangle$ one needs to find regions in the form of morphisms

$\langle \sigma, \eta \rangle : \langle Q, T, A \rangle \to \tau$, where τ is an uninitialised classifying transition system[1]. For Elementary Transition Systems, a region $r \subseteq Q$ can be represented as a morphism $\langle \sigma, \eta \rangle$, where σ is a characteristic function $\sigma = \chi_r : Q \to \{0, 1\}$ and $\eta : T \to \{-1, 0, 1\}$ is such that $\eta(t) = \sigma(q') - \sigma(q)$, for every arc $\langle q, t, q' \rangle$ in A. The classifying transition system is then

$$\tau_{en} = \langle \{0, 1\}, \{-1, 0, 1\}, \{\langle 0, 0, 0 \rangle, \langle 0, 1, 1 \rangle, \langle 1, -1, 0 \rangle, \langle 1, 0, 1 \rangle\} \rangle .$$

Figure 2, taken from [6], illustrates the concept of regions as morphisms for Elementary Transition Systems.

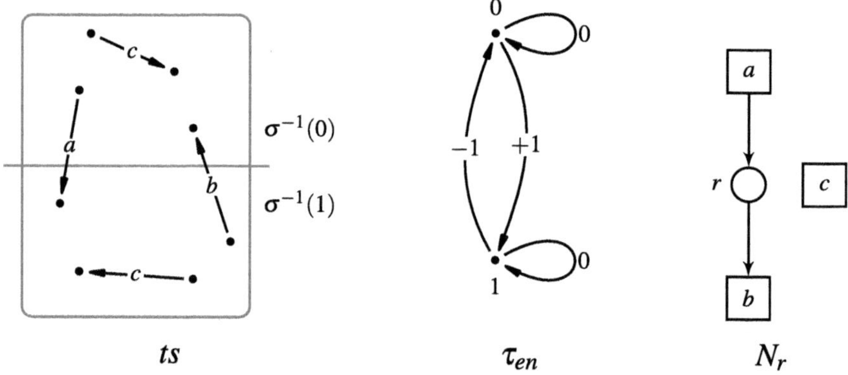

Fig. 2. Elementary Transition System ts, classifying transition system τ_{en}, and atomic net corresponding to a region r, N_r.

By identifying every place in the net with a region in the form $r = \langle \sigma, \eta \rangle$, one can build atomic nets $N_r = \langle \{r\}, T, F, M^{init} \rangle$, where the flow relation F is given by η ($\eta(a) = +1$ means that a deposits a token in r; $\eta(b) = -1$ means that b consumes a token from r; and $\eta(c) = 0$ means that c does not make any changes to r) and the initial marking, M^{init}, by σ (r is initially marked if $q_0 \in \sigma^{-1}(1)$). Solving the synthesis problem amounts then to gluing such atomic net systems (on common transitions), provided that the set of regions is *admissible* [19], i.e., it contains witnesses for the satisfaction of every instance of two 'separation axioms'. The first one, called the state separation property, ensures that there are enough regions to distinguish every two different states in the transition system. The second axiom, usually referred to as the event/state separation property (or forward closure), states that for every transition t and every state q at which this transition is <u>not</u> enabled, there is a region which disallows t at q. For all considered classes of nets—whatever the definition of a region—a solution to the synthesis problem requires some variants of these two

[1] A morphism for uninitialised transition systems $\langle \sigma, \eta \rangle : \langle Q, T, A \rangle \to \langle Q', T', A' \rangle$ is a pair of maps $\sigma : Q \to Q'$ and $\eta : T \to T'$ such that $\langle q, t, q' \rangle \in A$ implies $\langle \sigma(q), \eta(t), \sigma(q') \rangle \in A'$.

regional axioms to be fulfilled. When representing regions as morphisms, the two axioms can be uniformly expressed in terms of functions σ and η, for all types of nets τ. A classifying transition system, τ, which is needed to define regions as morphisms, characterises the behaviour of synthesised nets. Most precisely, it describes all possible 'quantitative' changes which may happen in a place of a net of that type.

Observe that the intention of Fig. 2 was to show the general idea for discovering regions. In the transition system *ts* of Fig. 2, if we want to link it to Fig. 1(b), we see that some arcs and states are missing in the picture and some states should be glued. Also notice that region r highlighted in Fig. 1(b) models place p_2 in Fig. 1(a).

As the standard set definition of a region in a sequential transition system can be generalised to cope with step semantics of nets, similarly the definition of a region that uses functions σ and η and the classifying transition system τ can also be generalised to deal with step semantics of nets. For this adaptation, treated thoroughly for Boolean nets in [30], a useful tool for forming steps is a *connection monoid*, $\mathbb{S} = \langle S, \oplus, \mathbf{0}\rangle$, with a set S of *connections* together with a commutative and associative binary composition operation $\oplus$, and a neutral element (identity) $\mathbf{0}$. For a given Petri net class, the elements of S describe all possible connections between places and transitions of nets from this class. The effect of simultaneous execution of a set or a multi-set of transitions (a step) on a given place is calculated using $\oplus$, which returns the composite connection between that place and the step. For example, the connection monoid for EN-systems can be defined as

$$\mathbb{S}_{en} = \langle\{\top, \mathtt{out}, \mathtt{in}, \bot\}, \oplus_{en}, \top\rangle\ ,$$

where names are given to arc annotations/connections of τ_{EN} of Fig. 2 as follows: $\top = 0$, $\mathtt{out} = +1$ and $\mathtt{in} = -1$. In addition to the three standard types of connections, τ_{EN} of [30] has a special 'blocking' connection $\bot$, which does not label any arc (and is never enabled). The connection $\bot$ is used to capture 'structural conflict' between transitions. As such, it is a convenient device to capture precisely these steps which are not allowed, because of internal conflicting relationships between transitions w.r.t. a place. The monoid operation, $\oplus_{en}$, is defined as follows (we omit compositions with $\top$ as $\top$ acts as an identity element):

$$\mathtt{out} \oplus_{en} \mathtt{out} = \mathtt{out} \oplus_{en} \mathtt{in} = \mathtt{in} \oplus_{en} \mathtt{out} = \mathtt{in} \oplus_{en} \mathtt{in} = \bot\ .$$

The above corresponds to the requirement that the neighbourhoods of transitions of an executable step in EN-systems must be disjoint. Furthermore,

$$\mathtt{out} \oplus_{en} \bot = \mathtt{in} \oplus_{en} \bot = \bot \oplus_{en} \bot = \bot\ .$$

A type of nets classifying transition system (*net-type*, for short) can be then generalised to support step semantics by using a connection monoid $\mathbb{S}$, $\tau = \langle\mathbb{Q}, \mathbb{S}, \Delta\rangle$, and may be conveniently used as a parameter in the definition of a class of nets, called τ*-nets*. The parameter τ specifies the values (markings) that can be stored within net places ($\mathbb{Q}$), the operations and tests (inscriptions on the arcs) that a net transition may perform on these values ($\mathbb{S}$), and the enabling condition and the newly generated values for steps of transitions (Δ). Petri nets can be then defined in the form of τ-nets by using net-types τ as follows:

> A τ*-net* is a bi-partite graph $\langle P, T, F\rangle$, where P and T are disjoint sets of places and transitions, respectively, and $F : (P \times T) \to \mathbb{S}$ is a (generalised) flow mapping, which can be extended for steps as follows: $F(p, \{t_1, \ldots, t_n\}) = F(p, t_1) \oplus \cdots \oplus F(p, t_n)$. A *marking* of the τ-net is a map $M : P \to \mathbb{Q}$. A τ*-net system* N is a τ-net with an initial marking M^{init}.

Let us recall the EN-system from Fig. 1(a). If we treated it as τ-net, we would have, for example, $F(p_2, a) = \texttt{out}$, $F(p_2, b) = \texttt{in}$ and $F(p_2, c) = \top$. Hence

$$F(p_2, \{a, c\}) = \texttt{out} \oplus_{en} \top = \texttt{out} \quad \text{and} \quad F(p_2, \{b, c\}) = \texttt{in} \oplus_{en} \top = \texttt{in}\ ,$$

while

$$F(p_2, \{a, b\}) = \texttt{out} \oplus_{en} \texttt{in} = \bot\ .$$

As a consequence, step $\{a, b\}$ is forbidden for this system.

The notion of a region was also generalised to synthesise τ-nets in [30]. First of all, it was assumed that the specification for their synthesis is coming in the form of finite step transition systems. Then the starting point for the synthesis procedure is a step transition system $ts = \langle Q, 2^T, \delta, q_0\rangle$ over T, where Q is a finite set of states, q_0 is the initial state, and $\delta : Q \times 2^T \to Q$ is a partial (transition) function. The paper [30] assumed that steps are sets of transitions rather than multi-sets. For a given $q \in Q$ and $U \in 2^T$ (a step), for whom δ is defined, the related arc in the transition system was defined by the triple $\langle q, U, \delta(q, U)\rangle$.

Assuming that ts is defined as above and recalling that $\tau = \langle \mathbb{Q}, \mathbb{S}, \Delta\rangle$ and $\mathbb{S} = \langle S, \oplus, \mathbf{0}\rangle$, a region for synthesising general τ-nets, a τ-region, was defined in [30] as follows:

> A τ*-region* of ts is a pair of mappings $\langle \sigma : Q \to \mathbb{Q}\ ,\ \eta : 2^T \to \mathbb{S}\rangle$ where
>
> $$\eta(\{t_1, \ldots, t_n\}) = \eta(\{t_1\}) \oplus \ldots \oplus \eta(\{t_n\})$$
>
> and for every $q \in Q$ and every step U enabled at q in ts:
>
> $$\eta(U) \text{ is enabled at } \sigma(q) \text{ in } \tau \text{ and } \Delta(\sigma(q), \eta(U)) = \sigma(\delta(q, U))\ .$$

We can see that again (like in the sequential case) the mappings σ and η, if they are going to represent a region, they need to satisfy the properties which ensure that every arc in the specifying ts has its 'equivalent' arc in the classifying transition system τ. Therefore, the σ and η mappings of a region define a morphism, as they allow to retrace the 'moves' of ts in τ.

Describing step semantics in terms of connection monoids makes it possible to apply results from the general theory of Petri net synthesis as outlined in [5,7,17]. In these references nets are represented as τ-nets, the connections between places and steps of transitions in the nets are represented using connection monoids (so steps can be formed in a formal way), the regions are generalised to τ-regions, and the state separation and forward closure axioms are expressed in terms of the σ and η mappings.

Although the τ-nets framework and its definition of regions proved to be very robust (see, for example, [31]) allowing the specification of many synthesis problems in a uniform fashion, new research attempts usually start solving the synthesis problems from 'scratch', proposing new definitions of regions that are tailored for the new classes of nets and their particular semantics. The task of checking whether the new class of nets with its new execution semantics would fit into the existing τ-nets framework is left for future considerations. This is indeed the case in this paper, where we take the challenge of synthesising EN-systems with the semantics assuming that transitions take time to execute.

1.2 Synthesis of Systems with Transitions of Non-atomic Duration

In general, as discussed in the previous section, the execution semantics of Petri nets (i.e., the representation of individual runs or observations) is captured by total orders of executed transitions (or, equivalently, by firing sequences), or stratified orders of executed transitions (or, equivalently, by step sequences), where simultaneity is transitive. Having said that, it has also been argued that any execution should be based on interval orders, where simultaneity is often non-transitive.

In this paper, using EN-systems as a system model, we first show how one can generate interval order observations of their executions in a direct way, without the need to modify the original system specification (e.g., by splitting transitions into explicit beginnings and endings) as it was done, for example, in [14,28,52]. We also define interval reachability graphs (IR-graphs) which can be seen as finite generators of potentially infinite sets of interval orders defined by EN-systems. IR-graphs are a subclass of interval transition systems (ITR-systems) which differ from the standard transition systems since instead of having their arcs labelled by executed transitions, they have states labelled by sets of transitions (interpreted as transitions currently being executed). The latter feature is related to having the so-called lifecycle information in event logs (see, e.g., [38]). Then, assuming the interval order semantics of EN-systems, we consider the problem of synthesising EN-systems from given ITR-systems.

We approach the new synthesis problem using the standard synthesis approach based on the theory of regions [5,22,23]. If one considers sequential behaviours of nets, a transition system is realised by a net *iff* it is isomorphic to the sequential reachability graph (or case graph) of this net. Ehrenfeucht and Rozenberg investigated the realisation of transition systems by Elementary Net systems and produced an axiomatic characterisation of the realisable transition systems in terms of regions [22,23]. As in the existing literature about Petri net synthesis, the net realisable ITR-systems are characterised by suitably adapted State Separation and Forward Closure axioms.

2 Partial Orders

Labelled partial orders with domain elements representing executed actions (events) are commonly used in concurrency theory to formalise different notions of dynamic semantics.

A (*strict labelled*) *partial order* is a triple $po = \langle X, \prec, \ell \rangle$ such that $X (= X_{po})$ is a set, $\prec (=\prec_{po})$ is a binary relation over X which is irreflexive and transitive, and $\ell (= \ell_{po})$ is a labelling for the elements of X. The *maximal* elements of po are defined as $\max_{po} = \{x \in X \mid \neg \exists y \in X : x \prec y\}$. For all $x \neq y \in X$, $x \frown y$ if $x \not\prec y \not\prec x$. In this paper, all partial orders are assumed to have a *finite* domain X.

The partial order is *total* whenever, for all $x \neq y \in X$, $x \prec y$ or $y \prec x$. Moreover, it is *interval* whenever, for all $x, y, z, w \in X$, if $x \prec z$ and $y \prec w$ then $x \prec w$ or $y \prec z$. The adjective 'interval' derives from the following result (c.f. [24]):

> *A partial order $\langle X, \prec, \ell \rangle$ is interval iff there are two integer-valued mappings on X, β and ε, such that, for all $x,y \in X$, $\beta(x) < \varepsilon(x)$ and $x \prec y \iff \varepsilon(x) < \beta(y)$.*

The mappings β and ε above are usually interpreted as 'beginnings of' and 'endings of' events represented by the elements of X.

The relevance of interval orders follows from an observation, credited to Wiener [51], that any execution of a physical system that can be observed by a single observer must be an interval order. It implies that the most precise observational semantics should be defined in terms of interval orders (cf. [26]). In the area of concurrency theory, the use of interval orders can be traced back to [26,35,36,45], and processes of concurrent systems with interval order semantics were studied in [27,28]. Interval orders were used to investigate communication protocols in [1], using the approach of [34]. Interval semantics (ST-semantics) was investigated for Petri nets with read arcs [49] and used in discussions on distributability of concurrent systems [25].

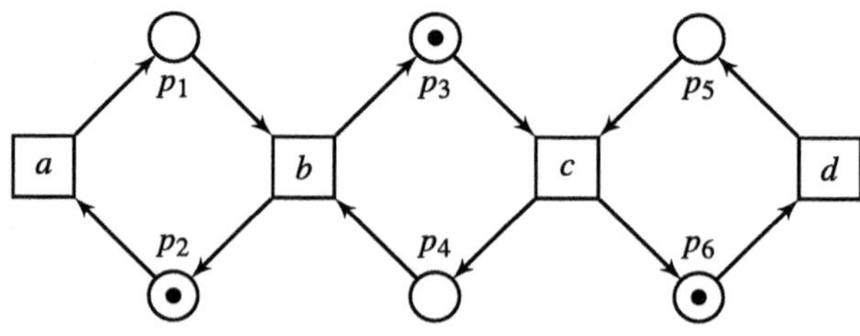

Fig. 3. EN-system where $\overline{p_1} = p_2$, $\overline{p_3} = p_4$, and $\overline{p_5} = p_6$.

As an example, consider four (database) transactions in the distributed environment: a, b, c, and d. Moreover, suppose that a precedes b and c precedes d. Suppose further that a does not precede d and c does not precede b. Then, it is possible for two messages α (from d to a) and β (from b to c) to be communicated by the respective transactions. Hence $\alpha_{snd} \prec \alpha_{rcv} \prec \beta_{snd} \prec \beta_{rcv} \prec \alpha_{snd}$, which is impossible. Hence a precedes d or c precedes b, and so the precedence relationship between the four transactions is an interval order.

3 Elementary Net Systems and Their Standard Semantics

Definition 1 (EN -system). *An* elementary net system *(or* EN*-system) is a tuple* $en = \langle P, T, F, M^{init} \rangle$*, where* P *and* T *are disjoint finite sets of* nodes, *called respectively* places *and* transitions, $F \subseteq (T \times P) \cup (P \times T)$ *is the* flow relation, *and* $M^{init} \subseteq P$ *is the* initial marking *(in general, any subset of places is a* marking*). We denote:*

- $^\bullet x = \{y \mid \langle y, x \rangle \in F\}$ *and* $x^\bullet = \{y \mid \langle x, y \rangle \in F\}$*, for every* $x \in P \cup T$.
- $^\bullet X = \bigcup \{^\bullet x \mid x \in X\}$ *and* $X^\bullet = \bigcup \{x^\bullet \mid x \in X\}$*, for every* $X \subseteq P \cup T$.

We then require that the following hold, for all transitions t *and places* p*:*

1. $^\bullet t \neq \varnothing \neq t^\bullet$ *and* $^\bullet t \cap t^\bullet = \varnothing$.
2. *There is a unique (complement) place* $\overline{p}$ *such that:* $^\bullet p = \overline{p}^\bullet$, $p^\bullet = {}^\bullet \overline{p}$*, and* $p \in M^{init} \iff \overline{p} \notin M^{init}$.

Note that the last part of Definition 1 is added to the standard one in order to simplify Definition 2.

In diagrams, places are represented by circles, transitions by rectangles, the flow relation by directed arcs, and a marking by small black dots drawn inside places belonging to the marking.

Example 1. Figure 3 shows an EN-system. Intuitively, its three components represented by cyclic sub-nets progress independently, but any action shared by two components can be executed only if both of them do so.

Until Sect. 4.4, we assume that $en = \langle P, T, F, M^{init} \rangle$ is a fixed EN-system.

The dynamic behaviour of EN-systems is introduced by defining valid sequences of executed transitions, called *firing sequences.*

Definition 2 (firing sequence). *The* firing sequences *of* en*, denoted by* SEQ_{en}*, are generated as follows.*

- *The empty sequence* λ *is a firing sequence of* en*, leading to marking* $\mathrm{mar}_\lambda = M^{init}$.

– *Let* σ *be a firing sequence of en leading to marking* mar_σ*, and* t *be a transition such that* ${}^\bullet t \subseteq \mathrm{mar}_\sigma$ *(*t *is enabled at* mar_σ*). Then* σt *is a firing sequence of en leading to marking* $\mathrm{mar}_{\sigma t} = \mathrm{mar}_\sigma \setminus {}^\bullet t \cup t^\bullet$.

Proposition 1. *Let* $\sigma \in \mathsf{SEQ}_{en}$*,* $t \in T$*, and* $p, q \in P$*.*

1. *If* ${}^\bullet p = q^\bullet$ *and* $p^\bullet = {}^\bullet q$ *and* $p \in M^{init} \iff q \notin M^{init}$*, then* $p \in \mathrm{mar}_\sigma \iff q \notin \mathrm{mar}_\sigma$.
2. *If* ${}^\bullet t \subseteq \mathrm{mar}_\sigma$*, then* $t^\bullet \cap \mathrm{mar}_\sigma = \varnothing$.

Proof. (1) It follows directly from Definitions 1 and 2.

(2) Suppose that there is $p \in P$ such that $p \in t^\bullet \cap \mathrm{mar}_\sigma$. The complement place $\overline{p}$ of p which belongs to P (Definition 1) is such that $\overline{p} \in {}^\bullet t \subseteq \mathrm{mar}_\sigma$. But $p \in \mathrm{mar}_\sigma$ as well, which is not possible as p and $\overline{p}$ are complementary places (see Proposition 1(1)). Hence we obtained a contradiction. □

One can also associate labelled total orders of transition occurrences with the executed interleaving sequences of transitions. In what follows, the n-th occurrence of transition t will be denoted by $t^{(n)}$ and called *event*.

Definition 3 (total orders of EN-system). *The* total orders *of en, denoted by* TO_{en}*, are generated as follows.*

– $to_\varnothing = \langle \varnothing, \varnothing, \varnothing \rangle$ *is a total order of en, and it leads to marking* $\mathrm{mar}_{to_\varnothing} = M^{init}$.
– *Let* $to = \langle X, \prec, \ell \rangle$ *be a total order of en leading to marking* mar_{to}*, and* t *be a transition such that* ${}^\bullet t \subseteq \mathrm{mar}_{to}$*. Then,*

$$to' = \langle X \cup \{x\}, \prec \cup (X \times \{x\}), \ell \cup \{\langle x, t \rangle\} \rangle$$

is a total order of en leading to marking $\mathrm{mar}_{to'} = (\mathrm{mar}_{to} \setminus {}^\bullet t) \cup t^\bullet$*, where* $x = t^{(1+|\ell^{-1}(t)|)}$.

Proposition 2. TO_{en} *is a set of labelled total orders.*

Proof. It follows directly from Definition 3. □

There is a canonical way of associating a labelled total order with a finite sequence of transitions $\sigma = t_1 \ldots t_k$ ($k \geq 0$), namely $\xi(\sigma) = \langle \{x_1, \ldots, x_k\}, \prec, \ell \rangle$, where $x_1 \prec \cdots \prec x_k$ and, moreover, each $x_i = t_i^{(k_i)}$ is such that $\ell(x_i) = t_i$, and k_i is the number of occurrences of t_i in $t_1 \ldots t_i$.

Proposition 3. ξ *induces a bijection between* SEQ_{en} *and* TO_{en}.

Proof. It follows directly from Definitions 2 and 3. □

In what follows, we will assume that each transition of an EN-system occurs in at least one firing sequence, i.e., there are no dead transitions.

4 Interval Order Semantics of EN-systems

The standard execution semantics of EN-systems implicitly assumes that events are executed instantaneously, or that their duration is negligible. Let us now assume that transitions are fired over intervals of arbitrary duration. Moreover, the firing of a transition t is *transaction-like*. By this we mean that the places in $t^\bullet$ are locked when t starts its execution, and when the execution is finished, then the tokens present in these places become available for firing other transitions.

Our aim is to define a simple abstract interval order semantics for *en*. We start with the standard approach in which the execution is carried out by taking a firing sequence $t_1 \dots t_k$. The firings are instantaneous (or at least non-overlapping), and so they are implicitly ordered $t_1{}^{(m_1)} \prec \cdots \prec t_k{}^{(m_k)}$, where $t_i{}^{(m_i)}$ represents the m_i-th firing of t_i, for every $1 \leq i \leq k$ (in particular, $m_1 = 1$). Then there exists an easy way of relating the executed transitions which only takes into account the direct causal dependencies resulting from creating and consuming resources (tokens), viz. $t_i{}^{(m_i)} \prec_{causal} t_j{}^{(m_j)}$ whenever $(t_i^\bullet \cap {}^\bullet t_j) \setminus {}^\bullet\{t_{i+1}, \dots, t_{j-1}\} \neq \varnothing$, for all $1 \leq i < j \leq k$.

When working towards a sound interval order semantics for *en* in the case of interval overlapping, we could proceed by noting down the beginnings and ends of all the executed transitions and convert the 'interval sequence' obtained in this way into the corresponding interval order. It is crucial now to observe that, in general, the result is in no way based on the fundamental *causality* relationship (i.e., $\prec_{causal}$) which is inherent in EN-systems.

Similarly as in Definitions 2 and 3, we will use an inductive approach to define interval order semantics of EN-systems. This leads to the following question: Having observed a hypothetical interval order execution *ipo*, resulting from extending the initial empty interval order by observed events $t_1{}^{(m_1)}, \dots, t_k{}^{(m_k)}$, what could we say about the interval order obtained after firing of the beginning of another transition? In other words, what could we say about *ipo*$'$ derived from *ipo* after adding a single event $x = t^{(n)}$? Our answer is based on the following key observations:

(i) If v is a non-maximal event in *ipo* then, for sure, we should have $v \prec_{ipo'} x$.
(ii) If $v \in \max_{ipo}$ is a maximal event in *ipo* such that $\ell(v)^\bullet \cap {}^\bullet t \neq \varnothing$, then v must have terminated before x started, and we should have $v \prec_{ipo'} x$.
(iii) If $v \in \max_{ipo}$ is a maximal event in *ipo* such that $\ell(v)^\bullet \cap {}^\bullet t = \varnothing$, then all we can be sure of is that v has not started after x finished, and so we should have either $v \prec_{ipo'} x$ or $v \frown_{ipo'} x$.

Intuitively, the maximal events in *ipo* can be considered 'unfinished' before starting x, and can either be ended 'just before' x started or continued to be finished after the execution of x has started. Note that the first two cases above, (i) and (ii), are deterministic (there is only one possibility of the relationship between v and x). However, case (iii) is a source of non-determinism which is not present in the standard interleaving semantics of *en*.

4.1 Interval Orders Generated by EN-systems

Definition 4 (interval orders of EN-system). *The* interval orders *of en, denoted by* IPO_{en}*, are generated as follows.*

- $ipo_\varnothing = \langle \varnothing, \varnothing, \varnothing \rangle$ *is an interval order of en, and it leads to marking* $\mathrm{mar}_{ipo_\varnothing} = M^{init}$.
- *Let* $ipo = \langle X, \prec, \ell \rangle$ *be an interval order of en leading to marking* mar_{ipo}*, and t be a transition such that* ${}^\bullet t \subseteq \mathrm{mar}_{ipo}$*. Then*

$$ipo' = \langle X \cup \{x\}, \prec \cup ((X \setminus Exec) \times \{x\}), \ell \cup \{\langle x, t \rangle\} \rangle$$

is an interval order of en, and it leads to marking $\mathrm{mar}_{ipo'} = (\mathrm{mar}_{ipo} \setminus {}^\bullet t) \cup t^\bullet$*, where* $Fin = \{z \in \max_{ipo} \mid \ell(z)^\bullet \cap {}^\bullet t \neq \varnothing\}$*,* $Exec \subseteq \max_{ipo} \setminus Fin$*, and* $x = t^{(1+|\ell^{-1}(t)|)}$*. also denote* $ipo \rightarrow_{en} ipo'$ *and* $ipo \xrightarrow{t:\ell(Exec)}_{en} ipo'$*.*

Intuitively, *Exec* are all those maximal events of *ipo* which we keep 'executing' simultaneously with x (and so $Fin \cap Exec = \varnothing$). Hence, the nondeterministic execution of t results from having 2^k, where $k = |\max_{ipo} \setminus Fin|$, possibilities for choosing *Exec*.

Proposition 4. *Assume the notation as in Definition 4. Then:*

1. $t \notin \ell(\max_{ipo})$.
2. $t^\bullet \cap \mathrm{mar}_{ipo} = \varnothing$.
3. $\max_{ipo'} \setminus \max_{ipo} = \{x\}$.
4. $\ell_{ipo'}(\max_{ipo'} \setminus \max_{ipo}) = \{t\}$.
5. $\ell_{ipo'}(\max_{ipo'} \setminus \{x\}) = \ell(Exec) \subseteq \ell(\max_{ipo} \setminus Fin)$.
6. *If* $x \neq y \in X$ *are such that* $\ell(x) = \ell(y)$*, then* $x \prec y$ *or* $y \prec x$*.*
7. *If* $ipo \xrightarrow{t:V}_{en} ipo'$ *and* $ipo \xrightarrow{t:V}_{en} ipo''$*, then* $ipo' = ipo''$*.*

Proof. It follows directly from Definition 4. □

Proposition 5. IPO_{en} *is a set of labelled interval orders such that* $\mathsf{TO}_{en} \subseteq \mathsf{IPO}_{en}$*.*

Proof. Clearly, as we can always set $Exec = \varnothing$, we have $\mathsf{TO}_{en} \subseteq \mathsf{IPO}_{en}$.

To show that IPO_{en} is a set of interval orders, we show that, for every $ipo \in \mathsf{IPO}_{en}$, there exist suitable integer-valued functions β_{ipo} and ϵ_{ipo} such that there is $k_{ipo} \geq 0$ satisfying $\epsilon_{ipo}(y) \leq k_{ipo}$ (for all $y \notin \max_{ipo}$) and $\epsilon_{ipo}(z) = k_{ipo} + 1$ (for all $z \in \max_{ipo}$). We proceed by induction on the derivation of *ipo*.

In the base case there is nothing to show, and if *ipo* has one element x we set $\beta_{ipo}(x) = 0$, $\epsilon_{ipo}(x) = 1$ and $k_{ipo} = 0$.

In the inductive case, we assume that *ipo*, x, and *ipo'* are as in Definition 4. We then set $\beta_{ipo'}(x) = k_{ipo} + 2$, $\epsilon_{ipo'}(x) = k_{ipo} + 3$, and keep β and ϵ unchanged except for re-setting $\epsilon_{ipo'}(z) = k_{ipo} + 3$, for all $z \in \max_{ipo'} \setminus \{x\}$. Moreover, $k_{ipo'} = k_{ipo} + 2$. □

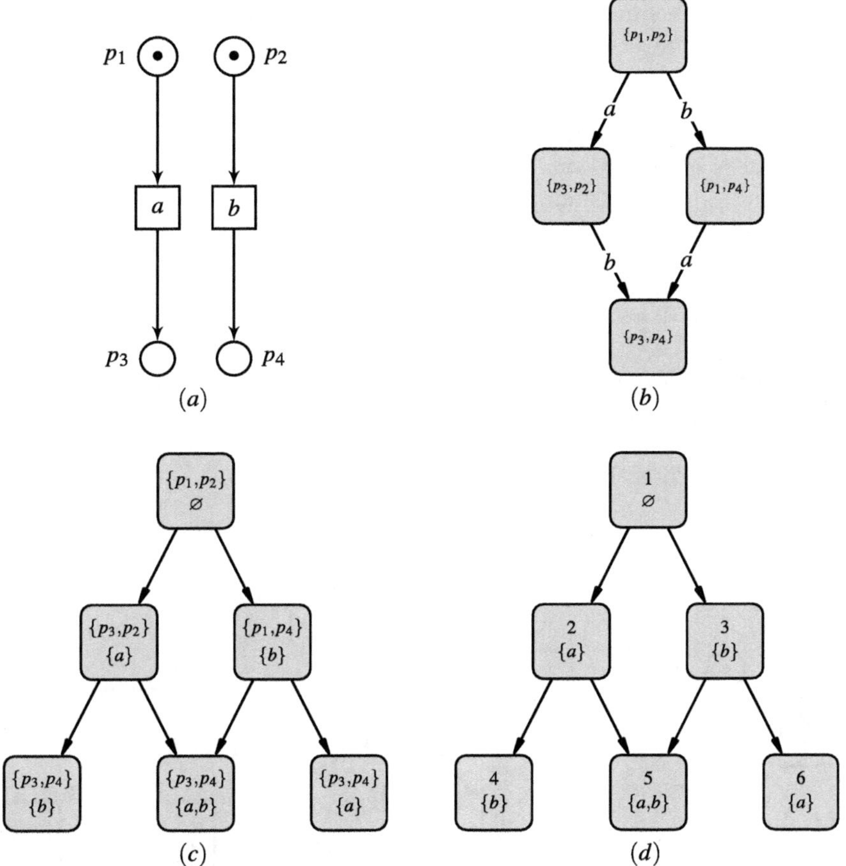

Fig. 4. (*a*) EN-system; (*b*) its interleaving reachability graph; (*c*) its IR-graph; and (*d*) an isomorphic ITR-system.

Remark 1. The construction of interval orders in Definition 4 is not only a natural generalisation of that for the total orders of *en*, but it also can capture other semantics which might be used to define execution semantics of EN-systems. There are two obvious possibilities, using the extreme choices of *Exec*. (Note that the same option is taken at all the stages of execution.)

- $Exec = \varnothing$. Then the construction generates all the total orders of *en*, as in Definition 3. Intuitively, this defines an 'interleaving' semantics of *en*.
- $Exec = \max_{ipo} \setminus Fin$. To our knowledge this option does not correspond to any semantical framework considered in the literature. Intuitively, it can be regarded as a 'maximally prolonged' semantics, where events are not terminated unless other actions need their execution to finish.

Leading to the same marking is not enough to ensure that two generated interval orders have the same extensions. The next definition adds another requirement.

Definition 5. (extension equivalent interval orders of EN-system). *Two interval orders of en, ipo and ipo′, are* extension equivalent *if* $\text{mar}_{ipo} = \text{mar}_{ipo'}$ *and* $\ell_{ipo}(\text{max}_{ipo}) = \ell_{ipo'}(\text{max}_{ipo'})$.
We denote this by $ipo \sim_{en} ipo'$.

The above relation is an equivalence relation. Moreover, the following result will be needed to define states of EN-systems.

Proposition 6. *If* $ipo \sim_{en} ipo'$ *and* $ipo \xrightarrow{t:V}_{en} ipo_o$, *then there is* ipo'_o *such that* $ipo' \xrightarrow{t:V}_{en} ipo'_o$ *and* $ipo_o \sim_{en} ipo'_o$.

Proof. It follows directly from Definition 4. □

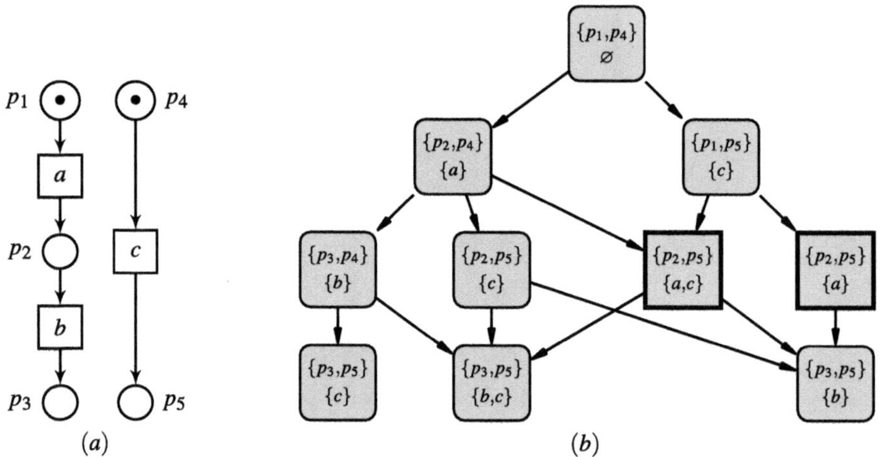

Fig. 5. (a) EN-system (some of complement places are omitted); and (b) its IR-graph.

4.2 Reachable States and Interval Reachability Graphs

In the standard semantics of EN-systems, one usually associates the notion of 'a reachable system state' with that of the marking reached after executing a firing sequence. This, in turn, leads to the notion of the reachability graph of an EN-system (see Fig. 4(a, b) for a simple EN-system and its reachability graph). Such graphs can be seen, in particular, as generators of all the firing sequences that can be executed.

It is not difficult to see that markings alone are insufficient to identify states of EN-systems under the interval order semantics. Consider, for example, the EN-system *en* depicted in Fig. 5(a). It generates two interval orders, ipo_1 and ipo_2, both with the domain $\{a^{(1)}, c^{(1)}\}$ and such that $c^{(1)} \prec_{ipo_1} a^{(1)}$ and $a^{(1)} \frown_{ipo_2} c^{(1)}$ (the states/squares of the graph in Fig. 5(b) that are reached when generating ipo_1 and ipo_2 have thicker borders). Both orders lead to the same marking $\{p_2, p_5\}$ which enables transition b. However, following Definition 4, ipo_1 can only be extended in one way (with $a^{(1)} \prec b^{(1)}$ as in Fig. 7(c)), whereas ipo_2 can be extended in two ways (one with $a^{(1)} \prec b^{(1)}$ and $c^{(1)} \frown b^{(1)}$ as in Fig. 7(f), and the other with $a^{(1)} \prec b^{(1)}$ and $c^{(1)} \prec b^{(1)}$ as in Fig. 7(e)).

Clearly, each $ipo \in \mathsf{IPO}_{en}$ leads to a 'state'. However, associating a state with each individual interval order could generate a huge (infinite) state space. This is not the way to go. It turns out that we can associate a state of *en* with all those interval orders which lead to the same marking, and have the same set of labels of maximal events. The reason is that all the 'continuations' for such interval orders are the same. So, each state of *en* can represent an equivalence class of the relation $\sim_{en}$ (see Definition 5).

We can then define the reachability graph of an EN-system.

Definition 6 (interval reachability graph of EN-system). *The* interval reachability graph (or IR-graph) *of en is* $irg_{en} = \langle Q, \rightarrow, q_0, \iota\rangle$, *where:*

1. $Q = \{state_{en}(ipo) \mid ipo \in \mathsf{IPO}_{en}\}$, *where* $state_{en}(ipo) = \langle \mathrm{mar}_{ipo}, \ell_{ipo}(\mathrm{max}_{ipo})\rangle$ *is the state corresponding to* $ipo \in \mathsf{IPO}_{en}$.
2. $\rightarrow = \{\langle state_{en}(ipo), state_{en}(ipo')\rangle \mid ipo \rightarrow_{en} ipo'\}$ *are the arcs.*
3. $q_0 = state_{en}(ipo_{\varnothing})$ *is the initial state.*
4. $\iota : Q \rightarrow 2^T$ *is the labelling such that* $\iota(state_{en}(ipo)) = \ell_{ipo}(\mathrm{max}_{ipo})$, *for every* $ipo \in \mathsf{IPO}_{en}$.

In the next section, we will show that irg_{en} is a generator of all interval orders of *en*.

Remark 2. Remark 1 mentioned two different kinds of semantics which can be applied to EN-systems. Figure 6 shows reachability graphs generated by these two semantics applied to the EN-system in Fig. 5(a)/Figure 1(a) using the equivalence relation on interval orders introduced in Definition 5. Observe that in the case of the interleaving semantics, we can 'move' the singleton sets from the states to annotate the arcs that directly lead to them, and 'glue' the so obtained states which have the same markings, to obtain the reachability graph of Fig. 1(b) as expected.

4.3 Transition Systems Generating Interval Orders

In general, we are interested in transition systems which are capable of generating interval orders.

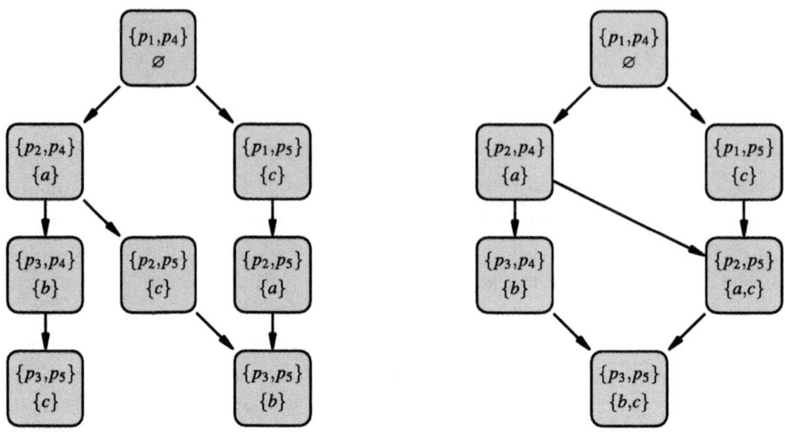

Fig. 6. Reachability graphs for other semantical models described in Remark 1 of the EN-system in Fig. 5(a): interleaving semantics (left); and maximally prolonged semantics (right).

Definition 7 (interval transition system). *An* interval transition system over T (or ITR-system) *is $itrs = \langle S, \rightarrow, s_0, \iota\rangle$, where S is a finite set of states, $\rightarrow \subseteq S \times S$ is the set of arcs, $s_0 \in S$ is the initial state, and $\iota : S \rightarrow 2^T$ is the labelling of states. The following hold, for every $s \in S$:*

1. *All states are reachable from s_0.*
2. *$\iota(s) = \varnothing$ iff $s = s_0$.*
3. *If $s \rightarrow r$, then there are $t \in T \setminus \iota(s)$ and $V \subseteq \iota(s)$ such that $\iota(r) = V \cup \{t\}$. We also denote $s \xrightarrow{t:V} r$, and $s \xrightarrow{t:V}$ if there is $r \in S$ such that $s \xrightarrow{t:V} r$.*
4. *For every $t \in T$, there are $r \in S$ and $V \subseteq T$ such that $r \xrightarrow{t:V}$.*
5. *If $s \xrightarrow{t:V} r$ and $s \xrightarrow{t:V} q$, then $r = q$.*

Proposition 7. *irg_{en} is an* ITR*-system. Moreover, for every $ipo \in \mathsf{IPO}_{en}$:*

$$\begin{aligned} ipo \xrightarrow{t:V}_{en} ipo' &\implies state_{en}(ipo) \xrightarrow{t:V} state_{en}(ipo') \\ state_{en}(ipo) \xrightarrow{t:V} q &\implies \exists ipo' \in \mathsf{IPO}_{en} : ipo \xrightarrow{t:V}_{en} ipo' \wedge q = state_{en}(ipo') . \end{aligned} \tag{1}$$

Proof. The first part follows directly from Definitions 6 and 7. To show the second part, we first observe that, by Definition 6, $state_{en}(ipo) \xrightarrow{t:V} q$ implies that there are $ipo'', ipo''' \in \mathsf{IPO}_{en}$ such that $ipo'' \xrightarrow{t:V}_{en} ipo'''$ as well as $state_{en}(ipo'') = state_{en}(ipo)$ and $state_{en}(ipo''') = q$. Then, by $state_{en}(ipo'') = state_{en}(ipo)$, we have $\mathrm{mar}_{ipo} = \mathrm{mar}_{ipo''}$ and $\ell_{ipo}(\mathrm{max}_{ipo}) = \ell_{ipo''}(\mathrm{max}_{ipo''})$. It then follows from $ipo'' \xrightarrow{t:V}_{en} ipo'''$, Definition 4, and Proposition 4, that there is $ipo' \in \mathsf{IPO}_{en}$ such that $ipo \xrightarrow{t:V}_{en} ipo'$ as well as $\mathrm{mar}_{ipo'} = \mathrm{mar}_{ipo'''}$ and $\ell_{ipo'}(\mathrm{max}_{ipo'}) = \ell_{ipo'''}(\mathrm{max}_{ipo'''})$. Hence $state_{en}(ipo') = state_{en}(ipo''') = q$.

To show that irg_{en} is an ITR-system, we proceed as follows.

Definition 7(2,3) follow directly from Definitions 4 and 6.

Definition 7(1,4) follow from the first part of Eq.(1), $q_0 = state_{en}(ipo_\varnothing)$, the assumption made after Proposition 3(see also Remark 1), and the fact that, for every $ipo \in \mathsf{IPO}_{en}$, there are $ipo_1, \ldots, ipo_k \in \mathsf{IPO}_{en}$ such that $(ipo_\varnothing =) ipo_1 \rightarrow_{en} \cdots \rightarrow_{en} ipo_k (= ipo)$.

Finally, suppose that $q \xrightarrow{t:V} q'$ and $q \xrightarrow{t:V} q''$. By Definition 6 and $q \xrightarrow{t:V} q'$, there are $ipo, ipo' \in \mathsf{IPO}_{en}$ such that $ipo \xrightarrow{t:V} ipo'$ as well as $state_{en}(ipo) = q$ and $state_{en}(ipo') = q'$. Moreover, by $q \xrightarrow{t:V} q'$ and the second part of Eq.(1), there is $ipo'' \in \mathsf{IPO}_{en}$ such that $ipo \xrightarrow{t:V}_{en} ipo''$ and $q'' = state_{en}(ipo'')$. Hence, by Proposition 4(7), $ipo'' = ipo'$. As a result, $q' = q''$ and so Definition 7(5) holds. □

Note that Definition 7(5) reflects the deterministic nature of EN-systems. See Fig. 4(c) for a sample IR-graph and Fig. 4(d) for another ITR-system that differs from it only in state names.

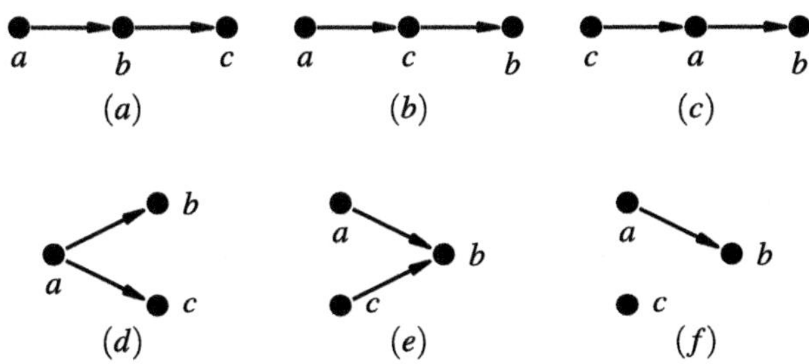

Fig. 7. Interval orders generated by different paths in the transition system of Fig. 5(b).

Each ITR-system generates a set of interval orders.

Definition 8 (interval orders of ITR-system). *Let $itrs = \langle S, \rightarrow, s_0, \iota \rangle$ be an* ITR-*system. Its* interval orders, *denoted by IPO_{itrs}, are the interval orders ipo_π derived from paths (sequences of states) π originating at the initial state. They are generated as follows:*

- *$ipo_\pi = ipo_\varnothing$ is the interval order generated by $\pi = s_0$.*
- *Let $\pi = s_0 \ldots s_k$ be a path such that $ipo = ipo_{s_0 \ldots s_{k-1}} = \langle X, \prec, \ell \rangle$ and $s_{k-1} \xrightarrow{t:V} s_k$. Then the interval order generated by π is*

$$ipo_\pi = \langle X \cup \{x\}, \prec \cup ((X \setminus Exec) \times \{x\}), \ell \cup \{\langle x, t\rangle\}\rangle \ ,$$

where $Exec = \max_{ipo} \cap\, \ell^{-1}(V)$ and $x = t^{(1+|\ell^{-1}(t)|)}$.

Proposition 8. $\mathsf{IPO}_{en} = \mathsf{IPO}_{irg_{en}}$.

Proof. First note that, by Proposition 7, the IR-graph of *en* is an ITR-system. Hence, Definition 8 can be applied.

In both Definition 4 and Definition 8 interval orders are generated inductively, hence we will provide a proof by structural induction. Both constructions start from $ipo_\varnothing = ipo_\pi = \langle \varnothing, \varnothing, \varnothing \rangle$, for the path $\pi = s_0$. The inductive steps are dealt with as follows.

($\subseteq$) Let $ipo' = \langle X \cup \{x\}, \prec \cup ((X \setminus Exec) \times \{x\}), \ell \cup \{\langle x, t\rangle\}\rangle$ for $x = t^{(1+|\ell^{-1}(t))|}$ and $Exec \subseteq \max_{ipo} \setminus Fin$, where $ipo = \langle X, \prec, \ell\rangle$, *Fin* as in Definition 4 and t such that ${}^\bullet t \subseteq \mathrm{mar}_{ipo}$. Let $V = \ell(Exec)$, hence $Exec = \max_{ipo} \cap \ell^{-1}(V)$. By the induction hypothesis, there exists a path $\pi = s_0 \dots s_{k-1}$ such that $ipo_\pi = ipo$. Then, by Definition 6, π leads from s_0 to $state_{en}(ipo) = s_k$ and, by Proposition 7, there exists s_{k+1} such that $s_k \xrightarrow{t:V} s_{k+1}$. Hence, by Definition 8, $ipo_{\pi s_{k+1}} = ipo'$.

($\supseteq$) Let $ipo_\pi = \langle X \cup \{x\}, \prec \cup ((X \setminus Exec) \times \{x\}), \ell \cup \{\langle x, t\rangle\}\rangle$, where $ipo = \langle X, \prec, \ell\rangle$, $s_{k-1} \xrightarrow{t:V} s_k$, $Exec = \max_{ipo} \cap \ell^{-1}(V)$ and $x = t^{(1+|\ell^{-1}(t))|}$. Then, by Definition 6 and Proposition 7, $ipo \rightarrow ipo'$ and $s_k = state_{en}(ipo')$. Hence ${}^\bullet t \subseteq \mathrm{mar}_{ipo}$ and we can apply Definition 4 obtaining $ipo' = ipo_\pi$. □

4.4 Isomorphic ITR-systems

The standard definition of transition system isomorphism can be adapted for ITR-systems as shown below, where $itrs = \langle S, \rightarrow, s_0, \iota\rangle$ and $itrs' = \langle S', \Rightarrow, s'_0, \iota'\rangle$ are fixed ITR-systems over T.

Definition 9 (isomorphism of ITR-systems). *itrs and itrs′ are* isomorphic *if there is a bijection* $\psi : S \rightarrow S'$ *such that* $\psi(s_0) = s'_0$, $\iota = \iota' \circ \psi$, *and* $s \rightarrow r \iff \psi(s) \Rightarrow \psi(r)$, *for all* $s, r \in S$.
We denote this by $itrs \approx_\psi itrs'$ *and* $itrs \approx itrs'$.

Proposition 9. $\approx$ *is an equivalence relation.*

ITR-system isomorphism is validated by the following immediate result.

Proposition 10. $itrs \approx itrs'$ *implies* $\mathsf{IPO}_{itrs} = \mathsf{IPO}_{itrs'}$.

The next three results are straightforward consequences of the fact that if in an ITR-system we replace each arc $s \rightarrow r$ by a labelled arc $s \xrightarrow{t:V} r$, where $\{t\} = \iota(r) \setminus \iota(s)$ and $V = \iota(r) \cap \iota(s)$, and remove the mapping ι, then the result is a deterministic finite state automaton such that each state is reachable from the initial state.

Proposition 11. *If* $itrs \approx itrs'$ *then there is exactly one* ψ *such that* $itrs \approx_\psi itrs'$.

Proposition 12. *If* $itrs \approx_\psi itrs'$ *and* $s \in S$, *then:*

1. $s \xrightarrow{t:V} r$ *implies that there is exactly one* $r' \in S'$ *such that* $\psi(s) \overset{t:V}{\Longrightarrow} r'$; *moreover,* $\psi(r) = r'$.
2. $\psi(s) \overset{t:V}{\Longrightarrow} r'$ *implies that there is exactly one* $r \in S$ *such that* $s \xrightarrow{t:V} r$; *moreover,* $\psi(r) = r'$.

ITR-system isomorphism can be established in a rather simple way.

Proposition 13. *Let* $\psi : S \to S'$ *be an injective mapping such that* $\psi(s_0) = s_0'$, *and the following hold, for all* $s \in S$, $t \in T$, *and* $V \subseteq T$:

- $s \xrightarrow{t:V}$ *implies that* $\psi(s) \overset{t:V}{\Longrightarrow}$.
- $\psi(s) \overset{t:V}{\Longrightarrow} r'$ *implies that* $s \xrightarrow{t:V} r$, *for some* $r \in S$ *such that* $r' = \psi(r)$.

Then $itrs \approx_\psi itrs'$.

5 Synthesis

The synthesis procedure to be introduced in this section follows the standard approach applied in [3,5,13,15,22,23,39,43], where a transition system with its global states is used as an initial specification from which local states (places of Petri nets) are inferred in the form of regions. In our case, transitions systems are ITR-systems. The verification that a given ITR-system is realisable by an EN-system with interval order semantics is essentially done by checking whether the derived regions satisfy suitable state separation and forward closure properties.

Until Definition 11, we assume that $itrs = \langle S, \to, s_0, \iota \rangle$ is a fixed ITR-system over T.

Definition 10 (int-region of ITR-system). *An* int-region *of itrs is* $\mathfrak{r} = \langle In_\mathfrak{r}, Out_\mathfrak{r}, S_\mathfrak{r} \rangle$, *where* $In_\mathfrak{r}$, $Out_\mathfrak{r} \subseteq T$, *and* $S_\mathfrak{r} \subseteq S$ *are such that the following hold, for all* $s \xrightarrow{t:V} r$ *and* $v \in T$:

1. $t \in In_\mathfrak{r}$ *iff* $s \notin S_\mathfrak{r}$ *and* $r \in S_\mathfrak{r}$.
2. $t \in Out_\mathfrak{r}$ *iff* $s \in S_\mathfrak{r}$ *and* $r \notin S_\mathfrak{r}$.
3. *If* $t \in Out_\mathfrak{r}$ *and* $v \in In_\mathfrak{r} \cap \iota(s)$, *then* $v \notin \iota(r)$.
4. *If* $t \in In_\mathfrak{r}$ *and* $v \in Out_\mathfrak{r} \cap \iota(s)$, *then* $v \notin \iota(r)$.

Figure 8 illustrates the last two conditions in Definition 10.

There are two trivial int-regions, $\langle \varnothing, \varnothing, S \rangle$ and $\langle \varnothing, \varnothing, \varnothing \rangle$. The set of all non-trivial int-regions of *itrs* is denoted by $\mathfrak{R}_{itrs}$, and $\mathfrak{R}_s = \{\mathfrak{r} \in \mathfrak{R}_{itrs} \mid s \in S_\mathfrak{r}\}$ are the non-trivial int-regions comprising a state $s \in S$. We also denote, for all $t \in T$ and $U \subseteq T$:

$$\begin{array}{ll} {}^\blacklozenge t = \{\mathfrak{r} \in \mathfrak{R}_{itrs} \mid t \in Out_\mathfrak{r}\} & {}^\blacklozenge U = \bigcup\{{}^\blacklozenge t \mid t \in U\} \\ t^\blacklozenge = \{\mathfrak{r} \in \mathfrak{R}_{itrs} \mid t \in In_\mathfrak{r}\} & U^\blacklozenge = \bigcup\{t^\blacklozenge \mid t \in U\}\,. \end{array} \tag{2}$$

Proposition 14. *If* $\mathfrak{r} \in \mathfrak{R}_{itrs}$ *then* $\overline{\mathfrak{r}} = \langle Out_\mathfrak{r}, In_\mathfrak{r}, S \setminus S_\mathfrak{r} \rangle \in \mathfrak{R}_{itrs}$.

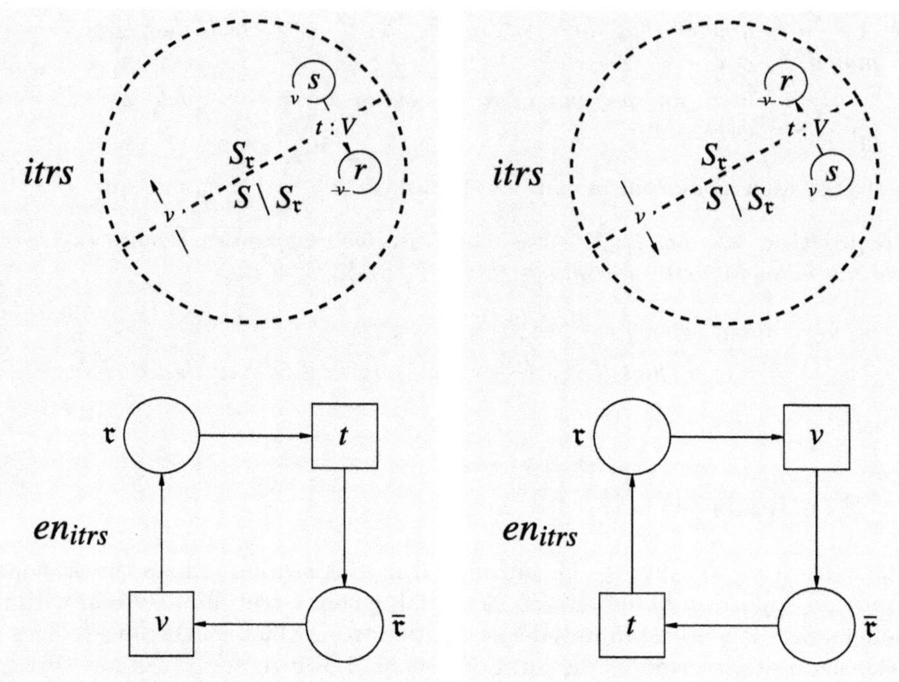

Fig. 8. Visualisation of Definition 10(3) on the left, and Definition 10(4) on the right. The upper pictures illustrate the definition from the point of view of *itrs*, and the lower ones from the point of view of the synthesised net understanding that regions will become places there.

Proof. It follows from Definition 10. □

Note that $\bar{\mathfrak{r}}$ defined above will be referred to as the *complement* int-region of $\mathfrak{r} \in \mathfrak{R}_{itrs}$.

To provide some intuition for Definition 10, we need to look ahead and imagine that regions will become places of the synthesised net. Then, $S_{\mathfrak{r}}$ is the set of states where region/place $\mathfrak{r}$ is marked or will be marked by currently executed transition. The transitions from $In_{\mathfrak{r}}$ will deposit tokens in $\mathfrak{r}$ (Definition 10(1)), and transitions from $Out_{\mathfrak{r}}$ will be consuming tokens from $\mathfrak{r}$ (Definition 10(2)). As the transition t will be executing in the context of some currently active transitions, Definition 10(3, 4) must make sure that some previously active transitions, like v, which share parts of their environment with t, should finish their executions before t starts, respecting the properties of places in EN-systems (see Fig. 8).

The next result relates int-regions involved in a transition between two states of *itrs*.

Proposition 15. *Let* $s \xrightarrow{t:V} r$. *Then:*

1. ${}^{\blacklozenge}t \cap t^{\blacklozenge} = \varnothing$.
2. ${}^{\blacklozenge}t \subseteq \mathfrak{R}_s$ *and* ${}^{\blacklozenge}t \cap \mathfrak{R}_r = \varnothing$.
3. $\mathfrak{R}_s \setminus \mathfrak{R}_r = {}^{\blacklozenge}t$ *and* $\mathfrak{R}_r \setminus \mathfrak{R}_s = t^{\blacklozenge}$.

Proof. (1) Suppose that $\mathfrak{r} \in {}^{\blacklozenge}t \cap t^{\blacklozenge}$. Then $t \in Out_{\mathfrak{r}} \cap In_{\mathfrak{r}}$. Hence, by Definition 10(1,2), we have $s \in S_{\mathfrak{r}}$ and $s \notin S_{\mathfrak{r}}$, yielding a contradiction.

(2) It follows from Definition 10(1,2).

(3) We only show $\mathfrak{R}_s \setminus \mathfrak{R}_r = {}^{\blacklozenge}t$ as the second part can be shown in a similar way.

By part (2), ${}^{\blacklozenge}t \subseteq \mathfrak{R}_s \setminus \mathfrak{R}_r$. Suppose that $\mathfrak{r} \in \mathfrak{R}_s \setminus \mathfrak{R}_r$, i.e., $s \in S_{\mathfrak{r}}$ and $r \notin S_{\mathfrak{r}}$. Then, by Definition 10(2), we have $t \in Out_{\mathfrak{r}}$, and so $\mathfrak{r} \in {}^{\blacklozenge}t$. Thus, $\mathfrak{R}_s \setminus \mathfrak{R}_r \subseteq {}^{\blacklozenge}t$. □

Proposition 16. *Let* $s \xrightarrow{t:V}$. *Then* ${}^{\blacklozenge}t \subseteq \mathfrak{R}_s$ *and* $V \subseteq \iota(s) \setminus fin$, *where* $fin = \{v \in \iota(s) \mid v^{\blacklozenge} \cap {}^{\blacklozenge}t \neq \varnothing\}$.

Proof. Let $\mathfrak{r} \in {}^{\blacklozenge}t$, and so $t \in Out_{\mathfrak{r}}$. By Proposition 15, we have ${}^{\blacklozenge}t \subseteq \mathfrak{R}_s$. Moreover, by Definitions 7 and 10(3), $V \subseteq \iota(s) \setminus fin$. □

We can now provide a precise definition of all those ITR-systems which could be translated into semantically equivalent EN-systems.

Definition 11 (EN-ITR-system). *An interval transition system itrs is an* EN-ITR-*system if the following hold, for all* $t \in T$, $V \subseteq T$, *and* $s \neq r \in S$:

1. $t^{\blacklozenge} \neq \varnothing \neq {}^{\blacklozenge}t$.
2. *If* $\iota(s) = \iota(r)$, *then there is* $\mathfrak{r} \in \mathfrak{R}_{itrs}$ *such that* $|S_{\mathfrak{r}} \cap \{s, r\}| = 1$. *(state separation)*
3. *If* $s \overset{t:V}{\not\longrightarrow}$, *then at least one of the following holds:* *(forward closure)*
   - $t \in \iota(s)$
   - $V \not\subseteq \iota(s)$
   - ${}^{\blacklozenge}t \not\subseteq \mathfrak{R}_s$
   - $V \not\subseteq \iota(s) \setminus fin$, *where* $fin = \{v \in \iota(s) \mid v^{\blacklozenge} \cap {}^{\blacklozenge}t \neq \varnothing\}$.

The above three 'axioms' characterise the EN-system realisable ITR-systems. 'State separation' requires that if two distinct states are not distinguished by at least one int-region, then they are distinguished by the labels of the maximal elements of their associated interval orders. 'Forward closure' is a variation of similar axioms that can be found in the literature for solving synthesis problems, e.g., [3,5,13,15,39,43]. Note, however, that both the state separation and the forward closure axioms for EN-ITR-systems differ from their standard formalisation as they do not rely only on int-regions, but also on sets of transitions labelling the states.

Definition 12. *The tuple associated with an* EN-ITR-*system itrs is given by*

$$en_{itrs} = \langle \mathfrak{R}_{itrs}, T, F_{itrs}, \mathfrak{R}_{s_0} \rangle ,$$

where $F_{itrs} = \{\langle \mathfrak{r}, t \rangle \in \mathfrak{R}_{itrs} \times T \mid t \in Out_{\mathfrak{r}}\} \cup \{\langle t, \mathfrak{r} \rangle \in T \times \mathfrak{R}_{itrs} \mid t \in In_{\mathfrak{r}}\}$.

Until the end of this section, we assume that $en = en_{itrs} = \langle \mathfrak{R}_{itrs}, T, F_{itrs}, \mathfrak{R}_{s_0} \rangle$ is the tuple associated with an EN-ITR-system $itrs = \langle S, \rightarrow, s_0, \iota \rangle$, and $irg_{en} = \langle Q, \rightarrow_o, q_0, \iota_o \rangle$ is the IR-graph of en_{itrs}.
Moreover, we use the dot-notation for $t \in T$ in the context of en_{itrs}, and the diamond-notation for $t \in T$ in the context of *itrs*.

Referring to irg_{en} as the 'IR-graph of en_{itrs}' is justified as en_{itrs} is a valid EN-system.

Proposition 17.

1. en_{itrs} *is an* EN*-system.*
2. ${}^\bullet t = {}^\blacklozenge t$ *and* $t^\bullet = t^\blacklozenge$*, for every* $t \in T$.
3. ${}^\bullet \mathfrak{r} = In_{\mathfrak{r}}$ *and* $\mathfrak{r}^\bullet = Out_{\mathfrak{r}}$*, for every* $\mathfrak{r} \in \mathfrak{R}_{itrs}$.

Proof. Parts (2) and (3) follow from Definition 12 and Eq.(2). With this in mind, we show part (1) in the following way: Definition 1(1) follows from Definition 11(1) and Proposition 15(1), while Definition 1(2) follows from Propositions 14. □

We then obtain a result validating the proposed approach to the synthesis of EN-systems with interval order semantics, where the EN-system en_{itrs} is a solution for the synthesis problem with the initial specification given by the ITR-system *itrs*.

Theorem 1. *itrs* $\approx_{\mathfrak{s}} irg_{en}$, *where* $\mathfrak{s} : S \rightarrow Q$ *is such that* $\mathfrak{s}(s) = \langle \mathfrak{R}_s, \iota(s) \rangle$*, for every* $s \in S$.

Proof. (The aim is to show that Proposition 13 can be applied.)

By Definition 11(2), $\mathfrak{s}$ is an injective mapping.

By Proposition 17, *en* is an EN-system and, by Definition 7(1), all the states of *itrs* are reachable from s_0. Also all the states of irg_{en} are reachable from q_0, which follows from the construction of irg_{en} and the inductive approach of Definition 4. Furthermore, from Definition 6(3) we have $q_0 = \langle \mathfrak{R}_{s_0}, \varnothing \rangle$, and from Definition 7(2) we have $\iota(s_0) = \varnothing$. Hence, $\mathfrak{s}(s_0) = q_0$.

Suppose now that $s \in S$ and $q \in Q$ are such that $q = \mathfrak{s}(s)$. Then there is an interval order $ipo = \langle X, \prec, \ell \rangle \in \mathsf{IPO}_{en}$ such that

$$q = state_{en}(ipo) = \langle \mathrm{mar}_{ipo}, \ell_{ipo}(\mathrm{max}_{ipo}) \rangle = \langle \mathfrak{R}_s, \iota(s) \rangle = \mathfrak{s}(s) \ .$$

Hence $\mathrm{mar}_{ipo} = \mathfrak{R}_s$ and $\ell_{ipo}(\mathrm{max}_{ipo}) = \iota(s)$. We then prove two lemmas.

Lemma 1. *If* $q \xrightarrow{t:V}_o q'$*, then there is* $s' \in S$ *such that* $s \xrightarrow{t:V} s'$ *and* $q' = \mathfrak{s}(s')$.

Proof. By $q \xrightarrow{t:V}_o q'$, there is $ipo' \in \mathsf{IPO}_{en}$ such that $ipo \xrightarrow{t:V}_{en} ipo'$ and

$$q' = state_{en}(ipo') = \langle \mathrm{mar}_{ipo'}, \ell_{ipo'}(\mathrm{max}_{ipo'}) \rangle$$

and the following hold:

- ${}^{\bullet}t \subseteq \mathrm{mar}_{ipo}$
- $ipo' = \langle X \cup \{x\}, \prec \cup ((X \setminus \mathit{Exec}) \times \{x\}), \ell \cup \{\langle x, t\rangle\}\rangle$
- $\mathrm{mar}_{ipo'} = (\mathrm{mar}_{ipo} \setminus {}^{\bullet}t) \cup t^{\bullet}$
- $V = \ell(\mathit{Exec})$
- $\mathit{Exec} \subseteq \max_{ipo} \setminus \mathit{Fin}$, where $\mathit{Fin} = \{z \in \max_{ipo} \mid \ell(z)^{\bullet} \cap {}^{\bullet}t \neq \varnothing\}$ and $x = t^{(1+|\ell^{-1}(t)|)}$.

Hence, by Proposition 17, $\mathrm{mar}_{ipo} = \mathfrak{R}_s$, and $\ell_{ipo}(\max_{ipo}) = \iota(s)$, we have:

- ${}^{\blacklozenge}t \subseteq \mathfrak{R}_s$
- $\ell_{ipo'}(\max_{ipo'}) = V \cup \{t\}$
- $\mathrm{mar}_{ipo'} = (\mathfrak{R}_s \setminus {}^{\blacklozenge}t) \cup t^{\blacklozenge}$
- $V \subseteq \iota(s) \setminus \mathit{fin}$, where $\mathit{fin} = \{v \in \iota(s) \mid v^{\blacklozenge} \cap {}^{\blacklozenge}t \neq \varnothing\}$.

Hence, by Definition 11, there is $s' \in S$, such that $s \xrightarrow{t:V} s'$. Then, by Propositions 15 and 17,

$$\mathrm{mar}_{ipo'} = (\mathrm{mar}_{ipo} \setminus {}^{\bullet}t) \cup t^{\bullet} = (\mathfrak{R}_s \setminus {}^{\blacklozenge}t) \cup t^{\blacklozenge} = \mathfrak{R}_{s'} \ .$$

Moreover, $\ell_{ipo'}(\max_{ipo'}) = V \cup \{t\} = \iota(s')$. Hence, $\mathit{state}_{en}(ipo') = \langle \mathfrak{R}_{s'}, \iota(s')\rangle = \mathfrak{s}(s')$. This concludes the proof of Lemma 1.

Lemma 2. *If* $s \xrightarrow{t:V}$ *then* $q(= \mathfrak{s}(s)) \xrightarrow{t:V}_{o}$.

Proof. As $s \xrightarrow{t:V}$, by Proposition 16 and Definition 7, we have:

- $t \notin \iota(s)$
- $V \subseteq \iota(s)$
- ${}^{\blacklozenge}t \subseteq \mathfrak{R}_s$
- $V \subseteq \iota(s) \setminus \mathit{fin}$, where $\mathit{fin} = \{v \in \iota(s) \mid v^{\blacklozenge} \cap {}^{\blacklozenge}t \neq \varnothing\}$.

Hence, by Proposition 17, $\mathrm{mar}_{ipo} = \mathfrak{R}_s$, and $\ell_{ipo}(\max_{ipo}) = \iota(s)$, we have:

- $t \notin \ell_{ipo}(\max_{ipo})$ and $V \subseteq \ell_{ipo}(\max_{ipo})$
- ${}^{\bullet}t \subseteq \mathrm{mar}_{ipo}$
- $V \subseteq \ell_{ipo}(\max_{ipo}) \setminus \mathit{fin}$, where $\mathit{fin} = \{v \in \ell_{ipo}(\max_{ipo}) \mid v^{\bullet} \cap {}^{\bullet}t \neq \varnothing\}$.

Let $\mathit{Exec} = \ell_{ipo}^{-1}(V) \cap \max_{ipo}$ and $x = t^{(1+|\ell^{-1}(t)|)}$. We then have $ipo \xrightarrow{t:V}_{en} ipo'$, where:

$$ipo' = \langle X \cup \{x\}, \prec \cup ((X \setminus \mathit{Exec}) \times \{x\}), \ell \cup \{\langle x, t\rangle\}\rangle \ .$$

Hence $ipo \xrightarrow{t:V}_{en}$, and so $q \xrightarrow{t:V}_{o}$ (see Proposition 7). This concludes the proof of Lemma 2.

Returning to the proof of Theorem 1 we observe that, from $\mathfrak{s}(s_0) = q_0$ and Lemma 1 and the fact that all states in Q are reachable from q_0, it follows that $Q \subseteq \mathfrak{s}(S)$. Hence $\mathfrak{s}$ is well-defined mapping. The theorem then follows from Proposition 13, Lemmas 1 and 2, $\mathfrak{s}(s_0) = q_0$, and the fact that $\mathfrak{s}$ is a well-defined injective mapping. □

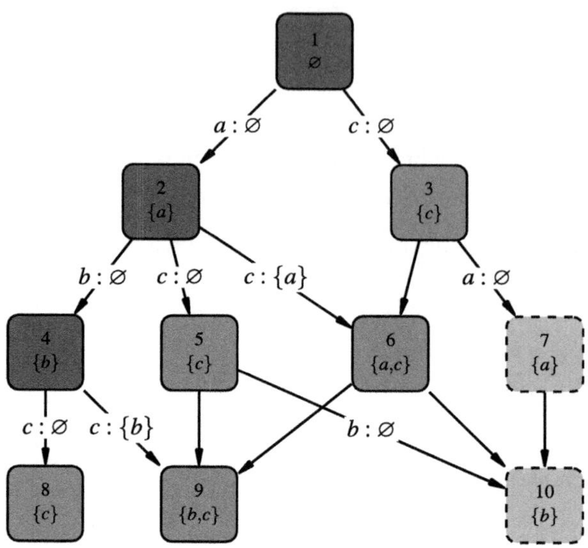

Fig. 9. ITR-system *itrs* for the discussion of the derivation of int-region $\mathfrak{r}$ such that $c \in In_{\mathfrak{r}}$. States that are surely in $S_{\mathfrak{r}}$ are shown in green (medium shade), states that are surely outside $S_{\mathfrak{r}}$ are shown in red (dark shade), and states whose status is uncertain are shown in yellow (light shade). Moreover, all the implicit arc labels used in the discussion are provided. (Color figure online)

Synthesis Example. We will now apply the proposed synthesis procedure to the ITR-system *itrs* shown in Fig. 5(*b*). First, we rename all the states (similarly to the way in which Fig. 4(*d*) was derived from Fig. 4(*c*)) and extract all the non-trivial int-regions in $\mathfrak{R}_{itrs}$.

We start by finding all the int-regions entered by c (i.e., $\mathfrak{r} \in c^{\blacklozenge}$ or $c \in In_{\mathfrak{r}}$). Looking at Fig. 9, we can see that $1, 2, 4 \notin S_{\mathfrak{r}}$ and $3, 5, 6, 8, 9 \in S_{\mathfrak{r}}$ since there are arcs labelled with transition c that go from the first group of states to the states of the second one. There are two uncertain states to consider, viz. 7 and 10. Suppose that $7 \notin S_{\mathfrak{r}}$. This means that $a \in Out_{\mathfrak{r}}$, but a labels the transition from 1 to 2, and so $a \notin Out_{\mathfrak{r}}$. Similarly, 10 must belong to $S_{\mathfrak{r}}$ because of transition b. Consequently, 7 and 10 must belong to $S_{\mathfrak{r}}$. In this way, we have found the only int-region $\mathfrak{r} = \langle \{c\}, \varnothing, \{3, 5, 6, 7, 8, 9, 10\} \rangle$ for which $c \in In_{\mathfrak{r}}$. Note that this int-region corresponds to the place p_5 in Fig. 5(*a*).

In the second step we attempt to find all the int-regions $\mathfrak{r} \in b^{\blacklozenge}$. Repeating the same reasoning as before (see Fig. 10), we can see that $2, 5, 6, 7 \notin S_{\mathfrak{r}}$ and $4, 9, 10 \in S_{\mathfrak{r}}$. Suppose that $8 \notin S_{\mathfrak{r}}$. Then $c \in Out_{\mathfrak{r}}$, but there is an arc labelled by c between $2 \notin S_{\mathfrak{r}}$ and $5 \notin S_{\mathfrak{r}}$, and so $c \notin Out_{\mathfrak{r}}$ implying $8 \in S_{\mathfrak{r}}$. The only states that remain to be considered are 1 and 3. There is an arc labelled with c between 1 and 3, hence they need to be together either in $S_{\mathfrak{r}}$ or outside $S_{\mathfrak{r}}$. And indeed both situations are possible. Moreover, if $1, 3 \in S_{\mathfrak{r}}$ then $a \in Out_{\mathfrak{r}}$.

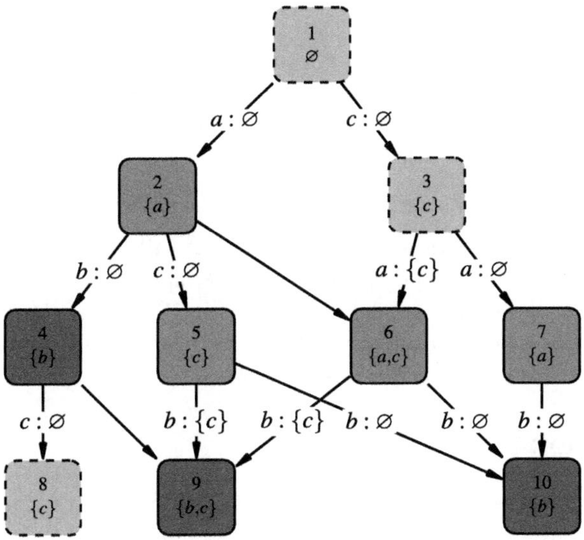

Fig. 10. ITR-system *itrs* for the discussion of finding int-region $\mathfrak{r}$ such that $b \in In_{\mathfrak{r}}$.

We therefore obtain

$$b^{\blacklozenge} = \{\langle \{b\}, \varnothing, \{4, 8, 9, 10\}\rangle, \langle \{b\}, \{a\}, \{1, 3, 4, 8, 9, 10\}\rangle\} \; .$$

Next we search for all the int-regions $\mathfrak{r} \in a^{\blacklozenge}$. Note that we already 'discovered' one int-region in $a^{\blacklozenge}$, namely the complement of the int-region $\langle \{b\}, \{a\}, \{1, 3, 4, 8, 9, 10\}\rangle$, i.e., $\langle \{a\}, \{b\}, \{2, 5, 6, 7\}\rangle$. Then, using reasoning similar as in the two previous cases, we can see that $2, 6, 7 \in S_{\mathfrak{r}}$. Because of the arc labelled by c between 2 and 6, $c \notin In_{\mathfrak{r}}$ as well as $c \notin Out_{\mathfrak{r}}$. Hence $5 \in S_{\mathfrak{r}}$, while either $4, 8 \in S_{\mathfrak{r}}$ or $4, 8 \notin S_{\mathfrak{r}}$. If $4 \in S_{\mathfrak{r}}$, then $b \notin Out_{\mathfrak{r}}$, and so $9, 10 \in S_{\mathfrak{r}}$. If $4 \notin S_{\mathfrak{r}}$, then $b \in Out_{\mathfrak{r}}$, and we end up with the already known $\langle \{a\}, \{b\}, \{2, 5, 6, 7\}\rangle$. We therefore obtain

$$a^{\blacklozenge} = \{\langle \{a\}, \{b\}, \{2, 5, 6, 7\}\rangle, \langle \{a\}, \varnothing, \{2, 4, 5, 6, 7, 8, 9, 10\}\rangle\} \; .$$

To complete the search for non-trivial int-regions, we derive all the missing complements of the already found int-regions, ending with eight non-trivial int-regions. They precisely correspond to the five places shown in Fig. 5(a) and the omitted complements of p_1, p_2, and p_3.

Let us now check all the conditions from Definition 11. The first one is clearly satisfied, as we have nonempty sets of pre-regions and post-regions for each of three considered transitions. The state separation condition needs to be checked between each pair of distinct states within the following three sets as the states of these sets have the same labels: $\{2, 7\}$, $\{3, 5, 8\}$ and $\{4, 10\}$. We start by observing that the states within the first set and within the third set are separated by the int-region $\mathfrak{r}$ with $S_{\mathfrak{r}} = \{1, 2, 4\}$. To separate 5 from both 3 and 8, we can use the int-region $\mathfrak{r}$ with $S_\mathfrak{r} = \{2, 5, 6, 7\}$. Finally, 3 is separated from 8 by the int-region $\mathfrak{r}$ with $S_\mathfrak{r} = \{1, 3\}$. The most time-consuming part of Definition 11 is to check the forward closure condition. Most of the cases can be checked using the clauses ${}^\blacklozenge t \not\subseteq \mathfrak{R}_s$ and $V \not\subseteq \iota(s)$. Thanks to them we can, for instance, validate the absence of arcs $\xrightarrow{t:V}$, for $V \neq \varnothing$ or $t = b$, outgoing from state 1. The only cases that remain to be validated are the missing arcs $\xrightarrow{b:\{a\}}$ outgoing from states 2, 6 and 7, and the missing arc $\xrightarrow{b:\{a,c\}}$ outgoing from state 6. In all these cases, the validation comes from the last clause and the int-region $\langle\{a\}, \{b\}, \{2, 5, 6, 7\}\rangle \in a^\blacklozenge \cap {}^\blacklozenge b$.

After finding all the non-trivial int-regions in $\mathfrak{R}_{itrs}$ and checking that all the conditions in Definition 11 are satisfied, we can use Definition 12 to construct a solution to the example synthesis problem we were dealing with in this section.

6 Conclusion

In this paper, we presented a new class of transition systems (interval transition systems, or ITR-systems) whose paths are associated with interval orders and whose states are labelled with the maximal elements of these interval orders. Also, we explained how EN-systems can generate interval orders and produce their interval reachability graphs (IR-graphs, a subclass of ITR-systems). Note that transitions in EN-systems are started sequentially, but there is an assumption that every transition execution takes time and may (partially) overlap with transitions that started earlier. We provided an axiomatisation of ITR-systems that can be synthesised to EN-systems with interval order semantics (Definition 11 of EN-ITR-system). We then showed how to adapt the synthesis approach based on the concept of regions of the standard sequential transition systems to the case of the EN-ITR-systems.

We expect that the theoretical concepts and results presented in this paper can provide a foundation to develop practical methods and tools for synthesising nets operating according to the interval order semantics. In particular, since many algorithms developed in the area of process mining (process discovery) were inspired by the results obtained for synthesising Petri nets from regions of the standard transition systems, we feel that a similar development is possible in the case of event logs that record events with duration. Such event logs could be derived, e.g., from records of transaction-like executions in distributed environments, where the start and finish of a transaction indicate its duration, and the overlapping of transactions is possible. Such event logs could be represented by interval orders (intuitively corresponding to paths in ITR-systems). We believe that the approach outlined in this paper can provide a line of work in the area of process discovery which is an alternative to the existing approaches pursued in, e.g., [9,16,20,37,50]. However, this would still require new results allowing one to deal with large logs, noise, and similar challenges. Also, we envisage more theoretical work on the synthesis problems with interval order semantics, for example, by considering more expressive net models (see, e.g., [33]).

As already mentioned, in this paper we presented a solution to the problem of synthesising EN-systems from ITR-systems, whose states are labelled by sets of currently active transitions (there might be more than one), and whose arcs are implicitly labelled by single transitions representing new actions/activities that are fired in the context of some of the previously active transitions and are responsible for the changes of states. As with any type of initialised transition systems, they capture the behaviour of a system starting from its initial state and show its progress from state to state when transitions are executed.

The ITR-systems (including IR-graphs) *do not* directly show all the relationships between transitions/actions, but these relationships can be inferred from them during the synthesis procedure and become evident in the synthesised EN-systems. However, these relationships are not as precise as in other approaches found in the literature, where systems are discovered/synthesised from behavioural information about the activities that are treated as non-instantaneous (i.e., taking some time to complete). For example, Context-Aware Temporal Network Representation (TNR) graphs of [48] that are extracted from event logs capture the global relationships between different non-instantaneous activities/actions and use 13 relationships to relate the intervals of any two activities as described by Allen's Interval Algebra [2]. In our approach, we use an abstraction that recognises only two relationships between the intervals related to two transitions, viz. one can precede the other or they can overlap. Moreover, assuming that it is not possible to observe the beginnings (or endings) of two intervals simultaneously, the relationships expressible in Allen's Interval Algebra can be embedded in the present framework using additional intervals. For example, we can express the fact that x and y overlap and x started before y started, provided that there is z such that $z \prec y$ and $z \frown x \frown y$ (recall that the relation $\frown$ does not need to be transitive). As a result, at every state of an ITR-system, a new active transition can follow the previously active transitions or join some of them to form a new set of active transitions.

In essence, the approaches of [2,48] are semantically close to real-time semantics whereas the approach pursued in this paper is more abstract. For similar reasons, the interval order semantics used in this paper and the 'interval semantics' or 'interval time semantics' of, e.g., [41,44], are incomparable.

Acknowledgement. Partial support by the Leverhulme Trust grant RPG-2022-025 is acknowledged. The authors are grateful to the anonymous referees, whose comments contributed to the final version of this paper.

Disclosure of Interests. The authors have no competing interests to declare that are relevant to the content of this article.

References

1. Abraham, U., Ben-David, S., Magidor, M.: On global-time and inter-process communication. In: Kwiatkowska, M., Shields, M.W., Thomas, R.M. (eds.) Semantics for Concurrency, Proceedings, pp. 311–323. Springer, Workshops in Computing (1990). https://doi.org/10.1007/978-1-4471-3860-0_19
2. Allen, J.F.: Maintaining knowledge about temporal intervals. Commun. ACM **26**(11), 832–843 (1983)
3. Badouel, E., Bernardinello, L., Darondeau, P.: Polynomial algorithms for the synthesis of bounded nets. In: Mosses, P.D., Nielsen, M., Schwartzbach, M.I. (eds.) CAAP 1995. LNCS, vol. 915, pp. 364–378. Springer, Heidelberg (1995). https://doi.org/10.1007/3-540-59293-8_207
4. Badouel, E., Bernardinello, L., Darondeau, P.: The synthesis problem for elementary net systems is np-complete. Theoret. Comput. Sci. **186**(1–2), 107–134 (1997)
5. Badouel, E., Bernardinello, L., Darondeau, P.: Petri Net Synthesis. Texts in Theoretical Computer Science. An EATCS Series, Springer (2015)
6. Badouel, E., Darondeau, P.: Dualities between nets and automata induced by schizophrenic objects. In: Pitt, D., Rydeheard, D.E., Johnstone, P. (eds.) CTCS 1995. LNCS, vol. 953, pp. 24–43. Springer, Heidelberg (1995). https://doi.org/10.1007/3-540-60164-3_18
7. Badouel, E., Darondeau, P.: Theory of regions. In: Reisig, W., Rozenberg, G. (eds.) ACPN 1996. LNCS, vol. 1491, pp. 529–586. Springer, Heidelberg (1998). https://doi.org/10.1007/3-540-65306-6_22
8. Bergenthum, R.: Synthesizing petri nets from hasse diagrams. In: Carmona, J., Engels, G., Kumar, A. (eds.) BPM 2017. LNCS, vol. 10445, pp. 22–39. Springer, Cham (2017). https://doi.org/10.1007/978-3-319-65000-5_2
9. Bergenthum, R.: Prime miner - process discovery using prime event structures. In: International Conference on Process Mining, ICPM 2019, Aachen, Germany, 24-26 June 2019, pp. 41–48. IEEE (2019)
10. Bergenthum, R., Desel, J., Lorenz, R., Mauser, S.: Synthesis of Petri nets from finite partial languages. Fund. Inform. **88**(4), 437–468 (2008)
11. Bernardinello, L.: Synthesis of net systems. In: Ajmone Marsan, M. (ed.) ICATPN 1993. LNCS, vol. 691, pp. 89–105. Springer, Heidelberg (1993). https://doi.org/10.1007/3-540-56863-8_42
12. Bernardinello, L., Michelis, G.D., Petruni, K., Vigna, S.: On the synchronic structure of transition systems. In: Desel, J. (ed.) STRICT 1995, pp. 69–84, Workshops in Computing. Springer (1995). https://doi.org/10.1007/978-1-4471-3078-9_5
13. Bernardinello, L., De Michelis, G., Petruni, K., Vigna, S.: On the synchronic structure of transition systems. In: Desel, J. (eds.) Structures in Concurrency Theory. Workshops in Computing. Springer, London (1995). https://doi.org/10.1007/978-1-4471-3078-9_5
14. Best, E., Koutny, M.: Petri net semantics of priority systems. Theoret. Comput. Sci. **96**(1), 175–174 (1992)
15. Busi, N., Pinna, G.M.: Synthesis of nets with inhibitor arcs. In: Mazurkiewicz, A., Winkowski, J. (eds.) CONCUR 1997. LNCS, vol. 1243, pp. 151–165. Springer, Heidelberg (1997). https://doi.org/10.1007/3-540-63141-0_11
16. Carmona, J., Cortadella, J., Kishinevsky, M.: A region-based algorithm for discovering petri nets from event logs. In: Dumas, M., Reichert, M., Shan, M.-C. (eds.) BPM 2008. LNCS, vol. 5240, pp. 358–373. Springer, Heidelberg (2008). https://doi.org/10.1007/978-3-540-85758-7_26

17. Darondeau, P., Koutny, M., Pietkiewicz-Koutny, M., Yakovlev, A.: Synthesis of nets with step firing policies. Fund. Inform. **94**(3–4), 275–303 (2009)
18. Desel, J., Reisig, W.: Place/transition petri nets. In: Reisig, W., Rozenberg, G. (eds.) ACPN 1996. LNCS, vol. 1491, pp. 122–173. Springer, Heidelberg (1998). https://doi.org/10.1007/3-540-65306-6_15
19. Desel, J., Reisig, W.: The synthesis problem of Petri nets. Acta Inform. **33**(4), 297–315 (1996)
20. Dumas, M., García-Bañuelos, L.: Process mining reloaded: event structures as a unified representation of process models and event logs. In: Devillers, R., Valmari, A. (eds.) PETRI NETS 2015. LNCS, vol. 9115, pp. 33–48. Springer, Cham (2015). https://doi.org/10.1007/978-3-319-19488-2_2
21. Ehrenfeucht, A., Rozenberg, G.: Partial (set) 2-structures. part II: state spaces of concurrent systems. Acta Informatica **27**(4), 343–368 (1990)
22. Ehrenfeucht, A., Rozenberg, G.: Theory of 2-structures, part I: clans, basic subclasses, and morphisms. Theoret. Comput. Sci. **70**(3), 277–303 (1990)
23. Ehrenfeucht, A., Rozenberg, G.: Theory of 2-structures, part II: representation through labeled tree families. Theoret. Comput. Sci. **70**(3), 305–342 (1990)
24. Fishburn, P.C.: Intransitive indifference with unequal indifference intervals. J. Math. Psychol. **7**, 144–149 (1970)
25. Glabbeek, R.J.v., Goltz, U., Schicke-Uffmann, J.W.: On characterising distributability. Logical Methods Comput. Sci. **9**(3), 1–58 (2013)
26. Janicki, R., Koutny, M.: Structure of concurrency. Theoret. Comput. Sci. **112**(1), 5–52 (1993)
27. Janicki, R., Koutny, M.: Fundamentals of modelling concurrency using discrete relational structures. Acta Informatica **34**(5), 367–388 (1997)
28. Janicki, R., Yin, X.: Modeling concurrency with interval traces. Inf. Comput. **253**, 78–108 (2017)
29. Jensen, K.: Coloured Petri Nets. Basic Concepts, Analysis Methods and Practical Use. Volume 1, Basic Concepts. Monographs in Theoretical Computer Science, Springer-Verlag (1997)
30. Kleijn, J., Koutny, M., Pietkiewicz-Koutny, M., Rozenberg, G.: Step semantics of boolean nets. Acta Informatica **50**(1), 15–39 (2013)
31. Kleijn, J., Koutny, M., Pietkiewicz-Koutny, M., Rozenberg, G.: Applying regions. Theor. Comput. Sci. **658**, 205–215 (2017)
32. Koutny, M., Pietkiewicz-Koutny, M.: Synthesising elementary net systems with interval order semantics. In: Joint Proceedings of the Workshop on Algorithms & Theories for the Analysis of Event Data and the International Workshop on Petri Nets for Twin Transition. CEUR Workshop Proceedings, vol. 3424. CEUR-WS.org (2023)
33. Koutny, M., Pietkiewicz-Koutny, M.: Synthesising ENI-systems with interval order semantics. In: Köhler-Bussmeier, M., Moldt, D., Rölke, H. (eds.) Proceedings of the International Workshop on Petri Nets and Software Engineering 2024 co-located with the 45th International Conference on Application and Theory of Petri Nets and Concurrency (PETRI NETS 2024),24 - 25 June 2024, Geneva, Switzerland. CEUR Workshop Proceedings, vol. 3730, pp. 33–52. CEUR-WS.org (2024)
34. Lamport, L.: Time, clocks, and the ordering of events in a distributed system. Commun. ACM **21**(7), 558–565 (1978)
35. Lamport, L.: The mutual exclusion problem: part I - a theory of interprocess communication. J. ACM **33**(2), 313–326 (1986)
36. Lamport, L.: On interprocess communication: part i: basic formalism. Distrib. Comput. **1**, 77–85 (1986)

37. Leemans, S.J.J., Fahland, D., van der Aalst, W.M.P.: Using Life cycle information in process discovery. In: Reichert, M., Reijers, H.A. (eds.) BPM 2015. LNBIP, vol. 256, pp. 204–217. Springer, Cham (2016). https://doi.org/10.1007/978-3-319-42887-1_17
38. Leemans, S.J.J., van Zelst, S.J., Lu, X.: Partial-order-based process mining: a survey and outlook. Knowl. Inf. Syst. **65**(1), 1–29 (2023)
39. Mukund, M.: Petri nets and step transition systems. Int. J. Found. Comput. Sci. **3**(4), 443–478 (1992)
40. Nielsen, M., Rozenberg, G., Thiagarajan, P.S.: Elementary transition systems. Theoret. Comput. Sci. **96**(1), 3–33 (1992)
41. Pelz, E.: Full axiomatisation of timed processes of interval-timed Petri nets. Fund. Inform. **157**(4), 427–442 (2018)
42. Petri, C.A.: Concepts of net theory. In: Mathematical Foundations of Computer Science: Proceedings of Symposium and Summer School, Strbské Pleso, High Tatras, Czechoslovakia, 3-8 September 1973, pp. 137–146. Mathematical Institute of the Slovak Academy of Sciences (1973)
43. Pietkiewicz-Koutny, M.: The synthesis problem for elementary net systems with inhibitor arcs. Fund. Inform. **40**(2–3), 251–283 (1999)
44. Popova-Zeugmann, L., Pelz, E.: Algebraical characterisation of interval-timed Petri nets with discrete delays. Fund. Inform. **120**(3–4), 341–357 (2012)
45. Pratt, V.R.: Modeling concurrency with partial orders. Int. J. Parallel Prog. **15**(1), 33–71 (1986)
46. Reisig, W.: Understanding Petri Nets - Modeling Techniques, Analysis Methods. Springer, Case Studies (2013)
47. Rozenberg, G., Engelfriet, J.: Elementary net systems. In: Petri Nets. pp. 12–121 (1996)
48. Senderovich, A., Weidlich, M., Gal, A.: Context-aware temporal network representation of event logs: model and methods for process performance analysis. Inf. Syst. **84**, 240–254 (2019)
49. Vogler, W.: Partial order semantics and read arcs. Theoret. Comput. Sci. **286**(1), 33–63 (2002)
50. van der Werf, J.M.E.M., van Dongen, B.F., Hurkens, C.A.J., Serebrenik, A.: Process discovery using integer linear programming. In: van Hee, K.M., Valk, R. (eds.) PETRI NETS 2008. LNCS, vol. 5062, pp. 368–387. Springer, Heidelberg (2008). https://doi.org/10.1007/978-3-540-68746-7_24
51. Wiener, N.: A contribution to the theory of relative position. Proc. Cambridge Philos. Soc. **17**, 441–449 (1914)
52. Zuberek, W.M.: Timed Petri nets and preliminary performance evaluation. In: Lenfant, J., Borgerson, B.R., Atkins, D.E., Irani, K.B., Kinniment, D., Aiso, H. (eds.) Proceedings of the 7th Annual Symposium on Computer Architecture, La Baule, France, 6-8 May 1980, pp. 88–96. ACM (1980)

The Reachability Problem in Petri Nets: Decidability and Hardness

Sławomir Lasota(✉)

University of Warsaw, Warsaw, Poland
sl@mimuw.edu.pl

Abstract. Petri nets, equivalently presentable as vector addition systems with states, are an established model of concurrency with widespread applications. The reachability problem, where we ask whether from a given initial configuration there exists a sequence of valid execution steps reaching a given final configuration, is the central algorithmic problem for this model. Its complexity has remained, over four decades, one of the hardest open questions in verification of concurrent systems. Only very recently, a number of breakthrough results led to establishing exact complexity of the problem.

This note is an attempt of an easy introduction to the problem and to some of ideas underlying the complexity bounds. It is intended to be neither rigorously formal nor complete, but rather to be an intuitive but precise enough description of main concepts.

1 Introduction

Petri nets [43] are an established model of concurrency with extensive and diverse applications in various fields, including modelling and analysis of hardware [6,30], software [5,19,23] and database [4] systems, as well as chemical [2], biological [3] and business [1,37] processes (the references on applications are illustrative). The model admits various alternative but essentially equivalent presentations, most notably *vector addition systems* (VAS) [25], and *vector addition systems with states* (VASS) [20,22]. The central algorithmic question for this model is the *reachability problem* that asks whether from a given initial configuration there exists a sequence of valid execution steps reaching a given final configuration. Each of the alternative presentations admits its own formulation of the reachability problem, all of them being equivalent due to straightforward polynomial-time translations that preserve reachability, see e.g. Schmitz's survey [46, Section 2.1]. For instance, in terms of VAS, the problem is stated as follows: given a finite set T of integer vectors in d-dimensional space and two d-dimensional vectors $\mathbf{v}$ and $\mathbf{w}$ of nonnegative integers, does there exist a walk from $\mathbf{v}$ to $\mathbf{w}$ such that it stays within the nonnegative orthant, and every step modifies the current position by adding some vector from T? The model of VASS is a natural extension of VAS with finite control, where $\mathbf{v}$ is additionally equipped with an initial control

F. Kordon et al. (Eds.): *Transactions on Petri Nets and Other Models of Concurrency XVIII*, LNCTPN 16260, pp. 123–149, 2026.
https://doi.org/10.1007/978-3-662-73305-9_5

state, $\mathbf{w}$ with a final one, and each vector in T is additionally equipped with a source-target pair of control states.

Following [10–12,46], we recall the widespread importance of the Petri nets reachability problem, as many diverse problems from formal languages [8], logic [7,14,15,24], concurrent systems [16,18], process calculi [42], linear algebra [21] and other areas (the references are again illustrative) are known to admit reductions to or from the VASS reachability problem; for more such problems and a wider discussion, we refer to [46].

Brief History of the Problem. The complexity of the Petri nets reachability problem has remained unsettled since 70ties. Concerning the decidability status, after an incomplete proof by Sacerdote and Tenney in 1970s [44], decidability of the problem was established by Mayr [40,41] in 1981, whose proof was then simplified by Kosaraju [26]. On the other hand, the exponential space lower bound for the problem has been established even before decidability by Lipton [38]. The landmark Lipton's construction applies to a wide range of decision problems, for instance to the coverability problem, and has remained the state of the art for over 40 years.

Next, during almost four decades, no significant progress has been reported towards establishing exact complexity of the problem. Worth mentioning are two works: further refinement of the decision procedure by Lambert in the 1990s [27]; and a different approach to decidability, based on Presburger inductive invariants, that has emerged from a series of papers by Leroux, more than a decade ago [31–33].

As the first breakthrough, a substantial improvement of our understanding of the complexity of the problem has been achieved by Leroux and Schmitz, who provided the first explicit upper complexity bound in 2015 [35], consequently improved to the Ackermannian upper bound in 2019 [36]. The complexity gap has been therefore narrowed down slightly: the reachability is ExpSpace-hard and belongs to Ackermann, the class of decision problems solvable in time or space bounded by Ackermann function of the input size.

The second, and complementary, breakthrough happened soon afterwards: a non-elementary lower bound has been achieved by Czerwiński, Lasota, Lazic, Leroux and Mazowiecki [10] (see also [11]). Therefore the problem turned out hard for the class Tower of decision problems solvable in time or space bounded by a tower of exponentials whose height is an elementary function of input size. A further refinement of Tower-hardness, in terms of fine-grained complexity classes closed under polynomial-time reductions, has been subsequently reported by Czerwiński, Lasota and Orlikowski [12]. Finally, as the last step, Ackermannian lower bound has been announced soon afterwards, independently by Czerwiński and Orlikowski [13], and by Leroux [34] (the two constructions underlying the proofs seem to be significantly different). These results finally close the long standing complexity gap, and yield Ackermann-completeness of the Petri nets reachability problem.

Under more fine-grained view the story is not finished yet, namely exact complexity of the reachability problem is still open, once measured in terms of levels in Grzegorczyk hierarchy of fast-growing functions [39,45]. The Grzegorczyk hierarchy allows to define a hierarchy of complexity classes $\mathcal{F}_\alpha$, indexed by ordinals $\alpha = 0, 1, 2, \ldots, \omega$, that includes as special cases $\mathcal{F}_3 =$ TOWER and $\mathcal{F}_\omega =$ ACKERMANN. One mostly considers the parametric complexity with respect to the dimension of vector addition systems with states (or, equivalently, the number of places of Petri nets[1]). Results of [13,34] can be stated in parametric terms as follows: the former shows $\mathcal{F}_d$-hardness of the reachability problem for VASS in dimension $6d$, while the latter one shows $\mathcal{F}_d$-hardness for VASS in dimension $4d + 5$. In this note we present a conceptually simpler and more direct construction [29] which also yields a better lower bound: $\mathcal{F}_d$-hardness already in dimension $3d + 2$. This bound has been further improved by [9], which shows $\mathcal{F}_d$-hardness already in dimension $2d + 4$. On the other hand, the upper bound of [36] amounts to $\mathcal{F}_d$-membership in dimension $d - 4$, which has been very recently improved to $\mathcal{F}_d$-membership in dimension d by [17]. The sequence of results still leaves a parametric complexity gap for the reachability problem in VASS in dimension d, which is between $\mathcal{F}_{\frac{d-4}{2}}$ and $\mathcal{F}_d$.

Outline. This paper is split into two parts: one devoted to the classical decidability proof, and the other one to the crucial recent advances, namely to the hardness construction that matches the upper complexity bound. In the first part (Sects. 2–4) we sketch the decision procedure [26,40,41,44] (the presentation follows [28]), while in the second part (Sects. 5–9) we present one of the lower bound constructions, namely the one of [29]. In each part we prefer to work with a slighly different model, in each case equivalent to Petri nets [46, Section 2.1]: in the decidability part we work with the model of VASS which is the most convenient for algorithmic considerations, while in the lower bound part we conveniently work with counter machines without zero tests, which are the most amenable for construction of gadgets used in the hardness argument.

We focus on intuitive presentation of main ideas underlying the complexity bounds. Therefore, the presentation is not always rigorously formal and complete, attempting to be intuitive, while precise enough, description of main concepts.

2 The Reachability Problem in VASS

A *vector addition system with states* (VASS) consists of a finite set of control states Q and a finite set $E \subseteq Q \times \mathbb{Z}^d \times Q$ of transitions. The number $d \geqslant 1$ is the *dimension* of the VASS. A pseudo-configuration is a pair $(q, v) \in Q \times \mathbb{Z}^d$; it is a *configuration* if $v \in \mathbb{N}^d$. A transition $e = (q, z, q')$ induces a step

$$(q, v) \xrightarrow{e} (q', v + z)$$

[1] We remark that a Petri net corresponding to a VASS of dimension d has $d + 3$ places, due to 3 extra places for encoding the control states of VASS [22]. Likewise, a VAS corresponding to a VASS of dimension d has dimension $d + 3$.

between pseudo-configurations. We write $(q, v) \dashrightarrow (q', v')$ if there is a sequence of steps from (q, v) to (q', v'); every such sequence we call *pseudo-run*. We reserve this term for a sequence of steps, as well as for an (inducing) sequence of transitions. If all vectors appearing in a pseudo-run belong to $\mathbb{N}^d$ we call it a *run*, and write $(q, v) \longrightarrow (q', v')$; this implies in particular that (q, v) and (q', v') themselves are configurations. We describe an algorithm for the following decision problem:

VASS REACHABILITY PROBLEM:

Input: a VASS (d, Q, E) and two configurations $(q, v), (q', v')$.

Question: does $(q, v) \longrightarrow (q', v')$ hold?

Vector addition systems with states can be viewed as a syntactic subclass of Petri nets: replace states by places that store jointly exactly one token. Conversely, the standard translation of Petri nets into VASS [22] yields also a reduction of the reachability problem in Petri nets to the reachability problem in VASS. Therefore we focus on proving decidability of the latter problem:

Theorem 1 ([26,40,41,44]). VASS REACHABILITY PROBLEM *is decidable.*

We now embark on proving decidability. Very roughly, the overall idea is to have a decidable condition $\Theta \equiv \Theta_1 \wedge \Theta_2$ on a VASS such that Θ implies reachability and $\neg\Theta$ implies that the well-founded *rank* of VASS can be reduced. With these two properties, the algorithm iteratively reduces the rank of input until either Θ eventually holds, or the problem becomes trivial. We proceed in three steps: we first formulate the condition Θ for plain VASS, then adapt it to more general VASS *with unconstrained coordinates*, and finally to *generalized* VASS of [26], for which we also describe a reduction step of the algorithm.

Sufficient Condition. As a warm-up, we prove a sufficient condition for reachability. For a VASS and two configurations (q, v), (q', v'), define the following two conditions:

Θ_1: For every $m \geqslant 1$, $(q, v) \dashrightarrow (q', v')$ by a pseudo-run that uses every transition at least m times.

Θ_2: There are vectors $\Delta, \Delta' \geqslant \mathbf{1}$ such that

$$(q, v) \longrightarrow (q, v + \Delta)$$

$$(q', v') \longleftarrow (q', v' + \Delta')$$

Proposition 1. $\Theta_1 \wedge \Theta_2$ *implies* $(q, v) \longrightarrow (q', v')$.

Proof. We will use the following claim, to be proved later:

Lemma 1. $(q', \Delta) \dashrightarrow (q', \Delta')$.

Here and in the sequel we silently use *monotonicity* of VASS: $(p, w) \longrightarrow (p', w')$ implies $(p, w + \delta) \longrightarrow (p', w' + \delta)$ for every $\delta \in \mathbb{N}^d$. The required run from (q, v) to (q', v') is of the following shape (for readability we omit brackets):

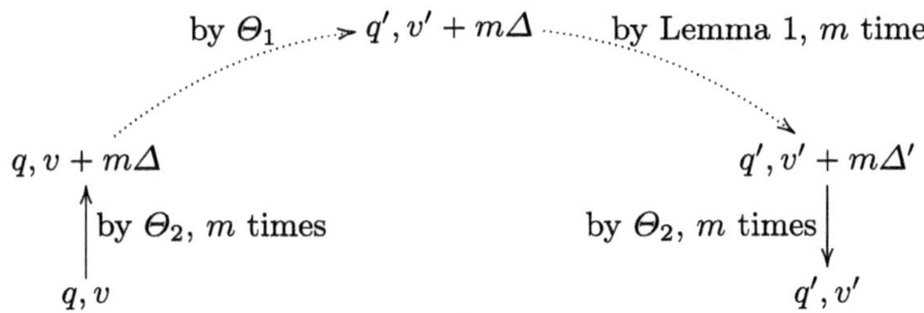

Observe that when m increases, the three intermediate points also increase on all coordinates. Therefore, for a sufficiently large m, the two pseudo-runs become runs: $(q, v + m\Delta) \longrightarrow (q', v' + m\Delta)$ and $(q', v' + m\Delta) \longrightarrow (q', v' + m\Delta')$. For both claim we use monotonicity. Furthermore, in the latter one we use the observation that the whole pseudo-run $(q', v' + m\Delta) \dashrightarrow (q', v' + m\Delta')$, consisting of m segments, becomes a run as soon as its first and last segment becomes so.

Proof of Lemma 1. Consider the underlying graph of the VASS, whose vertices are control states and edges are transitions (note that there may be parallel edges). Every pseudo-run induces a path in the graph. For a pseudo-run from (p, w) to (p', w'), we shortly speak of a pseudo-run from p to p' when vectors w, w' are irrelevant (contrarily to runs, in case of pseudo-runs the initial vector w may be arbitrary). Let E denote the set of transitions. By the *folding* of a pseudorun π we mean the vector $\text{fold}(\pi) \in \mathbb{N}^E$ that says how many times every transition is used by π. The following lemma, roughly speaking, allows us to subtract one pseudo-run from another (it is proved using Kirchhoff equalities, similarly as in the greedy construction of an Eulerian cycle in a directed graph):

Lemma 2. *Let τ, ρ be two pseudo-runs from p to p' such that*[2]

$$\mathit{fold}(\tau) - \mathit{fold}(\rho) \geqslant \mathbf{1}_E.$$

For every non-isolated control state p'' there is a pseudo-run σ from p'' to p'' with $\mathit{fold}(\sigma) = \mathit{fold}(\tau) - \mathit{fold}(\rho)$.

By $\text{shift}(\pi) \in \mathbb{Z}^d$ we mean the effect of a pseudo-run π, namely the difference between its final vector and its initial one. Note that the shift of a pseudo-run is

[2] We write $\boldsymbol{m}_C$ for a constant vector in $\mathbb{Z}^C$ having m on all coordinates. In the sequel we prefer to omit the subscript C and write simply $\boldsymbol{m}$ whenever this does not lead to confusion.

completely determined by its folding. To prove Lemma 1, we need to show that there is a pseudo-run from q' to q' with shift $\Delta' - \Delta$.

Basing on condition Θ_1, we know that we can pick two pseudo-runs τ, ρ from (q, v) to (q', v') with arbitrarily large difference $\text{fold}(\tau) - \text{fold}(\rho)$. Fix (due to Θ_2) a run π from (q, v) to $(q, v + \Delta)$, and a run π' from $(q', v' + \Delta')$ to (q', v'). Then fix two pseudoruns τ, ρ from (q, v) to (q', v') such that

$$\text{fold}(\tau) - \text{fold}(\rho) - \text{fold}(\pi) - \text{fold}(\pi') \geqslant \mathbf{1}.$$

Finally, apply Lemma 2 three times in a sequence, to deduce that there is a pseudo-run ν from q' to q' satisfying

$$\text{fold}(\nu) = \text{fold}(\tau) - \text{fold}(\rho) - \text{fold}(\pi) - \text{fold}(\pi').$$

Indeed, $\text{shift}(\nu) = \text{shift}(\tau) - \text{shift}(\rho) - \text{shift}(\pi) - \text{shift}(\pi') = \Delta' - \Delta$ as required. This completes the proof of Lemma 1. □

3 Partially Constrained Reachability Problem

We now slightly generalize the reachability problem and the sufficient condition. In the next section we will provide a yet further generalization that will be finally suitable for designing a decision procedure for reachability.

We will need a bit of concise notation. From now on we identify $\mathbb{Z}^d$ and $\mathbb{Z}^{\{1...d\}}$; for instance, the set of configurations is $Q \times \mathbb{N}^{\{1...d\}}$. For two disjoint subsets $C, B \subseteq \{1 \dots d\}$ and two vectors $v \in \mathbb{Z}^C$ and $w \in \mathbb{Z}^B$, we write $v \oplus w$ for the unique vector in $\mathbb{Z}^{C \cup B}$ obtained by glueing together v and w. Formally:

$$(v \oplus w)(i) = \begin{cases} v(i) & \text{if } i \in C \\ w(i) & \text{if } i \in B. \end{cases}$$

From now on, by convention $\overline{C}$ will always denote the complement $\{1 \dots d\} - C$.

The generalization of the reachability problem amounts to considering only some subset $C \subseteq \{1 \dots d\}$ of coordinates as *constrained*, while the remaining coordinates (i.e., those in $\overline{C}$) are considered as *unconstrained.* The input and output configuration is specified only on constrained coordinates, and left unspecified on the remaining ones. Nevertheless, a run we ask for should remain nonnegative on all coordinates. Here is a precise formulation:

PARTIALLY CONSTRAINED VASS REACHABILITY PROBLEM:

Input: a VASS (d, Q, E), two subsets $C, C' \subseteq \{1 \dots d\}$, $(q, v) \in Q \times \mathbb{N}^C$ and $(q', v') \in Q \times \mathbb{N}^{C'}$.

Question: does $(q, v \oplus \overline{v}) \longrightarrow (q', v' \oplus \overline{v}')$ hold for some vectors $\overline{v} \in \mathbb{N}^{\overline{C}}$, $\overline{v}' \in \mathbb{N}^{\overline{C}'}$?

We remark that we do not assume $C = C'$. The setting of the previous section is the special case $C = C' = \{1 \ldots d\}$.

Sufficient Condition. Here is a generalization of Θ_1 and Θ_2 to the more general setting. We write $(q, v) \overset{C}{\dashrightarrow} (q', v')$, for $C \subseteq \{1 \ldots d\}$, to say that there is a pseudo-run from (q, v) to (q', v') whose all vectors are non-negative on coordinates from C (such pseudo-runs we call *C-runs*). We write shortly $\mathbb{N}{+}m$ for $\mathbb{N} - \{0 \ldots m-1\}$.

Θ_1: For every $m \geqslant 1$, there are some vectors $\overline{v} \in (\mathbb{N}{+}m)^{\overline{C}}$, $\overline{v}' \in (\mathbb{N}{+}m)^{\overline{C}'}$ such that $(q, v \oplus \overline{v}) \dashrightarrow (q', v' \oplus \overline{v}')$ by a pseudo-run that traverses every transition at least m times.

Θ_2: There are vectors $\Delta \in (\mathbb{N}{+}1)^C$, $\Delta' \in (\mathbb{N}{+}1)^{C'}$, $\bar{\Delta} \in \mathbb{Z}^{\overline{C}}$ and $\bar{\Delta}' \in \mathbb{Z}^{\overline{C}'}$ such that

$$\pi : \quad (q, v \oplus \mathbf{0}) \overset{C}{\dashrightarrow} (q, (v + \Delta) \oplus \bar{\Delta})$$

$$\pi' : \quad (q', v' \oplus \mathbf{0}) \overset{C'}{\dashleftarrow} (q', (v' + \Delta') \oplus \bar{\Delta}')$$

Proposition 2. *$\Theta_1 \wedge \Theta_2$ implies $(q, v \oplus \overline{v}) \longrightarrow (q', v' \oplus \overline{v}')$ for some vectors $\overline{v} \in \mathbb{N}^{\overline{C}}$, $\overline{v}' \in \mathbb{N}^{\overline{C}'}$.*

Proof. The general idea of the proof is similar to the previous section, namely pumping up by a multiplicity of Δ (and de-pumping down by the same multiplicity of Δ') in order to make some pseudorun $(q, v \oplus \overline{v}) \dashrightarrow (q', v' \oplus \overline{v}')$ into a run. The new difficulty is that pumping involves $\Delta \oplus \bar{\Delta}$, with $\bar{\Delta}$ possibly negative on some coordinates (and likewise for de-pumping). This issue is solved by starting from $v \oplus \overline{v}$, for a sufficiently large $\overline{v} \geqslant \boldsymbol{m}$.

We will need a couple of facts. The first one easily follows from Θ_1:

Lemma 3. *There are vectors $\overline{v} \in \mathbb{N}^{\overline{C}}$, $\overline{v}' \in \mathbb{N}^{\overline{C}'}$ and a pseudo-run*

$$\pi_0 : \quad (q, v \oplus \overline{v}) \dashrightarrow (q', v' \oplus \overline{v}')$$

such that for every $m > 0$ there is a pseudo-run

$$\pi_1 : \quad (q, v \oplus (\overline{v} + \overline{\delta})) \dashrightarrow (q', v' \oplus (\overline{v}' + \overline{\delta}'))$$

with $fold(\pi_1) - fold(\pi_0) \geqslant \boldsymbol{m}_E$ and $\overline{\delta} \geqslant \boldsymbol{m}_{\overline{C}}$ and $\overline{\delta}' \geqslant \boldsymbol{m}_{\overline{C}'}$.

In other words, π_0 and π_1 can be chosen to make the three vectors $\text{fold}(\pi_1) - \text{fold}(\pi_0)$, $\overline{\delta}$ and $\overline{\delta}'$ arbitrarily large on all coordinates. Therefore we conclude:

Lemma 4. *The pseudo-runs π_0 and π_1 can be chosen so that:*

(a) $\overline{\delta} + \bar{\Delta} \geqslant \mathbf{1}_{\overline{C}}$, $\overline{\delta}' + \bar{\Delta}' \geqslant \mathbf{1}_{\overline{C}'}$;

(b) pseudo-runs in Θ_2*, lifted by* $\mathbf{0} \oplus (\overline{v} + \overline{\delta})$ *and* $\mathbf{0} \oplus (\overline{v}' + \overline{\delta}')$*, respectively, become runs:*

$$\pi : \qquad (q, v \oplus (\overline{v} + \overline{\delta})) \longrightarrow (q, (v + \Delta) \oplus (\overline{v} + \overline{\delta} + \bar{\Delta}))$$

$$\pi' : \quad (q', v' \oplus (\overline{v}' + \overline{\delta}')) \longleftarrow (q', (v' + \Delta') \oplus (\overline{v}' + \overline{\delta}' + \bar{\Delta}')) \ ;$$

(c) $\mathit{fold}(\pi_1) - \mathit{fold}(\pi_0) - \mathit{fold}(\pi) - \mathit{fold}(\pi') \geqslant \mathbf{1}_E$.

Using Lemma 4(a)–(b) together with the monotonicity of VASS, we deduce that for an arbitrary $m > 0$, the runs π and π' can be repeated m times when lifted further by $\mathbf{0} \oplus m\overline{\delta}$ and $\mathbf{0} \oplus m\overline{\delta}'$, respectively:

Lemma 5. *For every* $m \geqslant 1$ *it holds*

$$(q, v \oplus (\overline{v} + m\overline{\delta})) \longrightarrow (q, (v + m\Delta) \oplus (\overline{v} + m(\overline{\delta} + \bar{\Delta})))$$

$$(q', v' \oplus (\overline{v}' + m\overline{\delta}')) \longleftarrow (q', (v' + m\Delta') \oplus (\overline{v}' + m(\overline{\delta}' + \bar{\Delta}'))) \ .$$

The last claim generalizes Lemma 1 from the previous section.

Lemma 6. $(q', \Delta \oplus (\overline{\delta} + \bar{\Delta})) \dashrightarrow (q', \Delta' \oplus (\overline{\delta}' + \bar{\Delta}'))$.

Proof. We have $\text{shift}(\pi_1) - \text{shift}(\pi_0) = (\mathbf{0} \oplus \overline{\delta}') - (\mathbf{0} \oplus \overline{\delta})$ and $\text{shift}(\pi) = \Delta \oplus \bar{\Delta}$ and $\text{shift}(\pi') = (-\Delta') \oplus (-\bar{\Delta}')$. By Lemma 4(c) we can apply Lemma 2 three times, to deduce that there is a pseudo-run ν from q' to q' satisfying

$$\text{fold}(\nu) = \text{fold}(\pi_1) - \text{fold}(\pi_0) - \text{fold}(\pi) - \text{fold}(\pi').$$

We check: $\text{shift}(\nu) = (\text{shift}(\pi_1) - \text{shift}(\pi_0)) - \text{shift}(\pi) - \text{shift}(\pi') = \Delta' \oplus (\overline{\delta}' + \bar{\Delta}') - \Delta \oplus (\overline{\delta} + \bar{\Delta})$, as required. □

We are now prepared to draw a shape of a required run (for readability, the primed items are depicted in blue):

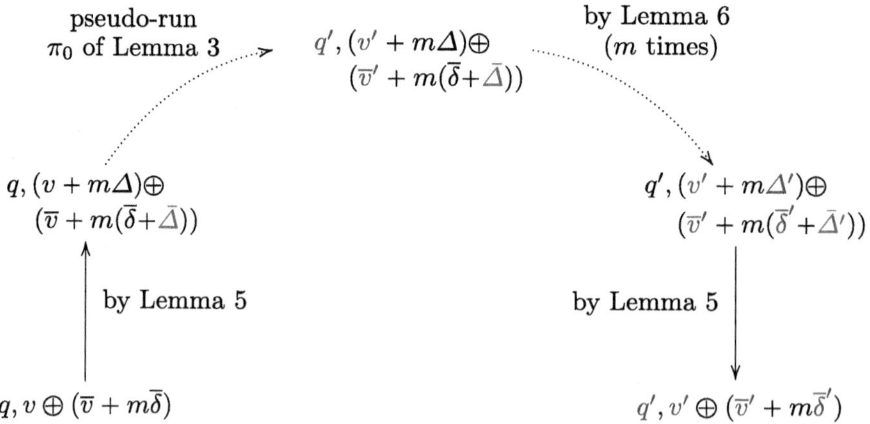

When m increases, each of the three intermediate points increases on all coordinates. In consequence, for sufficiently large m, all the pseudo-runs become runs.

Remark 1. Before advancing to the next section it is important to note that we have actually shown $(q, v \oplus (\overline{v} + m\overline{\delta})) \longrightarrow (q', v' \oplus (\overline{v}' + m\overline{\delta}'))$ for all sufficiently large m.

4 Generalized Reachability Problem

We do now the last generalization in order to complete the decidability proof. By a *component* we mean a VASS (d, Q, E) together with the following data:

- initial and final state $q, q' \in Q$;
- subset of rigid coordinates $R \subseteq \{1 \ldots d\}$; we assume that all transitions in E are 0 on all coordinates in R and hence, intuitively speaking, $d - |R|$ may be considered as the actual dimension of the component;
- rigid vector $r \in \mathbb{N}^R$; it provides the (fixed) values on rigid coordinates;
- two partitions $\{1 \ldots d\} - R = C \cup U = C' \cup U'$ of non-rigid coordinates into initial constrained coordinates C and initial unconstrained coordinates U, and into final constrained coordinates C' and final unconstrained coordinates U';
- initial and final vector $v \in \mathbb{N}^C$, $v' \in \mathbb{N}^{C'}$.

Note that a component does not essentially differ from input of the partially unconstrained reachability problem from the previous section. The *generalized* VASS (GVASS) $\mathcal{G}$ consists of $l \geqslant 1$ components

$$\mathcal{V}_i = (d, Q_i, E_i, q_i, q_i', R_i, r_i, C_i, U_i, C_i', U_i', v_i, v_i')$$

of the same dimension d, with pairwise disjoint state sets Q_i, plus $l-1$ transitions of the form $e_i = (q_i', z_i, q_{i+1})$, where $z_i \in \mathbb{Z}^d$, for $i \in \{1 \ldots i-1\}$. We will be interested in pseudo-runs π from q_1 to q_l' of the following form:

$$\begin{aligned} (q_1, r_1 \oplus v_1 \oplus u_1) &\dashrightarrow (q_1', r_1 \oplus v_1' \oplus u_1') \overset{e_1}{\rightsquigarrow} \\ (q_2, r_2 \oplus v_2 \oplus u_2) &\dashrightarrow (q_2', r_2 \oplus v_2' \oplus u_2') \overset{e_2}{\rightsquigarrow} \ldots \\ \ldots \overset{e_{l-1}}{\rightsquigarrow} (q_l, r_l \oplus v_l \oplus u_l) &\dashrightarrow (q_l', r_l \oplus v_l' \oplus u_l') \end{aligned} \tag{1}$$

for some $u_1 \in \mathbb{N}^{U_1}, u_1' \in \mathbb{N}^{U_1'}, \ldots, u_l \in \mathbb{N}^{U_l}, u_l' \in \mathbb{N}^{U_l'}$. Each such pseudo-run π passes through every transition e_i exactly once, and thus splits into l pseudo-runs $\pi = \pi_1 e_1 \pi_2 e_2 \ldots e_{l-1} \pi_l$, each π_i being a pseudo-run in $\mathcal{V}_i$. When each of π_i is a run, π is a run;

GENERALIZED VASS REACHABILITY PROBLEM:

Input: a GVASS $\mathcal{G}$.

Question: does $\mathcal{G}$ have a run?

The setting of the previous section is the special case of one component without rigid coordinates: $l = 1$, $R_1 = \emptyset$.

Sufficient Condition. The condition Θ_2 below is essentially the conjunction of conditions Θ_2 of the previous section for each of the VASS $\mathcal{V}_i$ separately; the only difference is taking rigid coordinates into account. On the other hand, the condition Θ_1 below speaks jointly about all the VASS $\mathcal{V}_i$.

Θ_1: For every $m \geqslant 1$, there is a pseudo-run from q_1 to q'_l of the form (1) that traverses every transition in every E_i at least m times, for some $u_1 \in (\mathbb{N}+m)^{U_1}, u'_1 \in (\mathbb{N}+m)^{U'_1}, \ldots, u_l \in (\mathbb{N}+m)^{U_l}, u'_l \in (\mathbb{N}+m)^{U'_l}$.

Θ_2: For every $i \in \{1 \ldots l\}$ there are vectors $\Delta \in (\mathbb{N}+1)^{C_i}$, $\Delta' \in (\mathbb{N}+1)^{C'_i}$, $\bar{\Delta} \in \mathbb{Z}^{U_i}$ and $\bar{\Delta}' \in \mathbb{Z}^{U'_i}$ such that

$$(q_i, r_i \oplus v_i \oplus \mathbf{0}) \overset{C_i}{\dashrightarrow} (q_i, r_i \oplus (v_i + \Delta) \oplus \bar{\Delta}) \tag{2}$$

$$(q'_i, r_i \oplus v'_i \oplus \mathbf{0}) \overset{C'_i}{\dashleftarrow} (q'_i, r_i \oplus (v'_i + \Delta') \oplus \bar{\Delta}') \tag{3}$$

Observe that Θ_1 implies $C'_i = C_{i+1}$ for $i \in \{1 \ldots l-1\}$. The sufficient condition for reachability is proved similarly as in the previous section:

Proposition 3. *If $\mathcal{G}$ satisfies $\Theta_1 \wedge \Theta_2$ then $\mathcal{G}$ has a run.*

Indeed, in Lemma 3 one should consider all components simultaneously and recall the remark at the end of Sect. 3; for the other claims and the construction of a run, one can consider the components separately.

Furthermore, the sufficient condition can be effectively tested:

Proposition 4. *Both Θ_1 and Θ_2 are decidable.*

Proof. Pseudo-runs (1) can be encoded as the set of nonegative integer solutions of a system of linear equations. Then condition Θ_1 can be decided by inspecting the (hybrid-linear) set of solutions (cf. Lemma 7 below). Checking condition $\Theta_2(2)$ reduces to the coverability problem, namely to checking, for every i, whether $(q_i, v_i) \longrightarrow (q_i, v_i + \Delta)$ in the projection of the component to coordinates C_i. Likewise for $\Theta_2(3)$. □

Refinement. Let $|\mathcal{V}_i| = (d - |R_i|, |E_i|, |U_i| + |U'_i|) \in \mathbb{N}^3$. Thus the size of $\mathcal{V}_i$ is a triple consisting of: the number of non-rigid coordinates, the number of transitions, the number of unconstrained coordinates. For a GVASS $\mathcal{G}$, we define its *rank* $|\mathcal{G}|$ as the multiset of sizes of all components $\mathcal{V}_i$.

Order triples in $\mathbb{N}^3$ lexicographically. For two finite ranks, i.e., finite multisets of triples m and m', we say that m' *refines* m if m' is obtained by removing one triple from m, and replacing it by a finite number of lexicographically strictly smaller triples.

Claim. The refinement relation is well-founded.

We shortly say that $\mathcal{G}'$ refines $\mathcal{G}$ when the rank $|\mathcal{G}'|$ refines $|\mathcal{G}|$. We can assume wlog. that every component of $\mathcal{G}$ is strongly connected:

Claim. If the underlying graph[3] of some component of $\mathcal{G}$ is not strongly-connected then one can compute $\mathcal{G}_1 \dots \mathcal{G}_n$ refining $\mathcal{G}$ such that $\mathcal{G}$ has a run if, and only if some of $\mathcal{G}_1 \dots \mathcal{G}_n$ has.

Indeed, it suffices to decompose the component into strongly connected components.

For *trivial* $\mathcal{G}$, whose rank contains only zero triples $(0,0,0)$, the reachability problems trivializes. Otherwise, either $\mathcal{G}$ satisfies $\Theta_1 \wedge \Theta_2$ and thus has a run, or $\mathcal{G}$ can be refined, as shown in Propositions 5 and 6 below.

Proposition 5. *If a non-trivial $\mathcal{G}$ violates Θ_1 then one can compute $\mathcal{G}_1 \dots \mathcal{G}_n$ refining $\mathcal{G}$ such that $\mathcal{G}$ has a run if, and only if some of $\mathcal{G}_1 \dots \mathcal{G}_n$ has.*

Proof. Wlog. assume that the underlying graphs of all components $\mathcal{V}_i$ are strongly connected. Let $k = \sum_{i=1}^{l} |U_i| + E_i + |U_i'|$. Consider the set $L \subseteq \mathbb{N}^k$ of all vectors

$$(u_1, f_1, u_1', \dots, u_l, f_l, u_l') \in \mathbb{N}^k \tag{4}$$

such that there is a pseudo-run $\pi = \pi_1 e_1 \pi_2 e_2 \dots e_{l-1} \pi_l$ of the form (1) with $\text{fold}(\pi_1) = f_1 \geqslant \mathbf{1}, \dots, \text{fold}(\pi_l) = f_l \geqslant \mathbf{1}$. The set L is the set of nonnegative integer solutions of a system of linear equations, and thus we have:

Lemma 7. *One can compute finite sets $B, P \subseteq \mathbb{N}^k$ such that $L = B + P^*$.*

Suppose $\mathcal{G}$ does not satisfy Θ_1. Hence for some coordinate in $\{1 \dots k\}$, all vectors in P are zero on that coordinate. This *zero coordinate* corresponds either to some transition, or to some unconstrained (input or output) coordinate.

Suppose the first case holds, and let $e \in E_i$ be the transition corresponding to the zero coordinate. By Lemma 7 one can compute a number c such that every pseudo-run (1) passes through e at most c times. We refine $\mathcal{G}$ by $c+1$ GVASS $\mathcal{G}_0 \dots \mathcal{G}_c$, each $\mathcal{G}_m$ obtained by replacing $\mathcal{V}_i$ by a sequence of $m+1$ copies of $\mathcal{V}_i - \{e\}$, i.e. of $\mathcal{V}_i$ without the transition e. The rigid coordinates and rigid vector of all copies are as in $\mathcal{V}_i$. The initial constrained coordinates of the first copy are C_i, the final constrained coordinates of the last copy are C_i', and the remaining initial or final constrained coordinates of all copies are empty sets. The initial vector of the first copy is v_1 and the final vector of the last copy is v_l'; all other initial and final vectors are empty ones.

Now suppose the second case holds, i.e., the zero coordinate corresponds to some, say, initial unconstrained coordinate $j \in U_i$ (final unconstrained coordinate is treated symmetrically). By Lemma 7 one can compute a number c such that the value on coordinate j in u_i (cf. (4)) is at most c, for every pseudo-run π. We refine $\mathcal{G}$ by constraining the coordinate j to some value in $\{0 \dots c\}$. We define $c+1$ refining GVASS $\mathcal{G}_0 \dots \mathcal{G}_c$, where $\mathcal{G}_m$ differs from $\mathcal{G}$ only by making the coordinate j in $\mathcal{V}_i$ an initial constrained coordinate, with value m. □

[3] We ignore here one inessential detail: this is a *multigraph*, i.e., parallel edges are allowed.

Proposition 6. *If a non-trivial $\mathcal{G}$ violates Θ_2 then one can compute $\mathcal{G}_1 \ldots \mathcal{G}_n$ refining $\mathcal{G}$ such that $\mathcal{G}$ has a run if, and only if some of $\mathcal{G}_1 \ldots \mathcal{G}_n$ has.*

Proof. Wlog. assume that the underlying graphs of all components $\mathcal{V}_i$ are strongly connected. Suppose that $\mathcal{G}$ does not satisfy Θ_2, i.e. condition (2) fails for some i (condition (3) is treated symmetrically). Thus all initial constrained coordinates cannot be simultaneously increased arbitrarily, which means that for some number c, in every pseudo-configuration reachable in $\mathcal{V}_i$ from $v_i \oplus \mathbf{0}$ via the relation $\overset{C_i}{\dashrightarrow}$, some of initial constrained coordinates $j \in C_i$ is bounded by c. From the coverability tree for $\mathcal{V}_i$ one can extract c with a stronger property:

Claim. For every C_i-run π in $\mathcal{V}_i$ from $v_i \oplus \mathbf{0}$ there is an initial constrained coordinate $j \in C_i$ which is bounded by c in π.

Relying on the claim, we refine $\mathcal{G}$ by a finite family of GVASS. For every $j \in C_i \cap C'_i$ the family contains one GVASS $\mathcal{G}_j$, and for every $j \in C_i \cap U'_i$ the family contains $c+1$ GVASS $\mathcal{G}_{j,0} \ldots \mathcal{G}_{j,c}$, as outlined below:

$j \in C_i \cap U'_i$: Thus j is a final unconstrained coordinate. We define GVASS $\mathcal{G}_{j,0} \ldots \mathcal{G}_{j,c}$, where $\mathcal{G}_{j,m}$ differs from $\mathcal{G}$ only by making the coordinate j a final constrained coordinate in $\mathcal{V}_i$, and fixing its value to m.

$j \in C_i \cap C'_i$: Thus j is a final constrained coordinate. Let a and a' be the values of initial and final vectors v_i, v'_i on coordinate j. We define $\mathcal{G}_j$ by replacing $\mathcal{V}_i$ with two components $\mathcal{V}'$ and $\mathcal{V}''$. $\mathcal{V}'$ behaves exactly as $\mathcal{V}_i$ with the only exception that the value of the jth coordinate is kept between 0 and c. This can be achieved using a cross-product of $\mathcal{V}_i$ with a finite state automaton, with states $\{0, \ldots, c\}$, the initial state a, the final state a', and transitions induced by the jth coordinate of transitions in E_i. This allows to set the jth coordinate of all transitions in $\mathcal{V}'$ to 0; in consequence, the coordinate j can be moved to rigid coordinates of $\mathcal{V}'$. Thus $\mathcal{V}'$ has $(c+1)$ times more states and transitions than $\mathcal{V}_i$ but one less non-rigid coordinate. The rigid vector of $\mathcal{V}'$ is set to a on coordinate j. The difference $a' - a$ is easily compensated by adding one transition-less component $\mathcal{V}''$ to $\mathcal{G}_j$, connected to $\mathcal{V}'$ by an transition that adds $a' - a$ on coordinate j and preserves all other coordinates. □

We have shown decidability of the VASS reachability problem by providing a decidable condition $\Theta \equiv \Theta_1 \wedge \Theta_2$ that implies reachability, together with a reduction step that, assuming $\neg\Theta$, decreases the rank while preserving reachability. The complexity of the decision procedure is very high: the blowups introduced in the reduction steps result in the upper complexity bound as bad as Ackermannian [17] (see [36] for the detailed analysis of the blowups). The bad upper complexity bound is related to the similarly bad upper bound on the lengths of decreasing sequences of ranks [36].

In the remaining part of the paper we concentrate on the maching lower complexity bound.

5 The Reachability Problem in Counter Programs

Following [10–13, 34], in this section we work with a convenient presentation of VASS as counter programs without zero tests, where the dimension of a VASS corresponds to the number of counters of a program.

Counter Programs. A *counter program* (or simply a *program*) is a sequence of (line-numbered) commands, each of which is of one of the following types:

$\mathsf{x} \mathrel{+}= 1$	(increment counter x)
$\mathsf{x} \mathrel{-}= 1$	(decrement counter x)
goto L **or** L'	(nondeterministically jump to either line L or line L')
zero? x	(zero test: continue if counter x equals 0)

Counters are only allowed to have nonnegative values. We are particularly interested in counter programs *without zero tests*, i.e., ones that use no zero test command. Whenever we use zero tests in the sequel, it is always in view of faithfully simulating them by programs without zero tests.

Convention: In the sequel, unless specified explicitly, counter programs are implicitly assumed to be without zero tests.

Example 1. We write $\mathsf{x} \mathrel{+}= m$ (resp. $\mathsf{x} \mathrel{-}= m$) as a shorthand for for m consecutive increments (resp. decrements) of x. As an illustration, consider the program with three counters $\mathsf{C} = \{\mathsf{x}, \mathsf{y}, \mathsf{z}\}$ (on the left), and its more readable presentation using a syntactic sugar **loop** (on the right):

```
1: goto 2 or 6              1: loop
2: x -= 1                   2:     x -= 1
3: y += 1                   3:     y += 1
4: z += 2                   4:     z += 2
5: goto 1 or 1              5: z += 1
6: z += 1
```

The program repeats the block of commands in lines 2–4 some number of times chosen nondeterministically (possibly zero, although not infinite because x is decreasing, and hence its initial value bounds the number of iterations) and then increments z. In the sequel we conveniently use **loop** construct instead of explicit **goto** commands. (A dummy command is implicitly added after a **loop** in case it appears at the very end of a program.)

We emphasise that counters are only permitted to have nonnegative values. In the program above, that is why the decrement in line 2 works also as a non-zero test.

A counter programs is easily conversed into a VASS whose dimension is the number of counters, and whose control states correspond to control locations of the program.

Consider a program with counters C. By $\mathbb{N}^{\mathsf{C}}$ we denote the set of all valuations of counters. Given an initial valuation of counters, a *run* (or *execution*) of a counter program is a finite sequence of executions of commands, as expected. W.l.o.g. we may assume that the last-line command is not a **goto**. A run which has successfully finished (i.e., executed its last-line command) we call *complete*; otherwise, the run is *partial*. Observe that, due to a decrement that would cause a counter to become negative, a partial run may fail to continue because it is blocked from further execution. Moreover, due to nondeterminism of **goto**, a program may have various runs from the same initial valuation.

Two programs $\mathcal{P}, \mathcal{Q}$ may be *composed* by concatenating them, written $\mathcal{P}\ \mathcal{Q}$. We silently assume the appropriate re-numbering of lines referred to by **goto** command in $\mathcal{Q}$.

Fast-Growing Hierarchy. For a positive integer k, let $\mathbb{N}_k = k \cdot (\mathbb{N}+1) = \{k, 2k, 3k, \ldots\} \subseteq \mathbb{N}$ denote positive multiplicities of k. We define the complexity classes $\mathcal{F}_i$ corresponding to the ith level in the Grzegorczyk Hierarchy [45, Sect. 2.3, 4.1]. The standard family of approximations $\mathbf{A}_i : \mathbb{N}_1 \to \mathbb{N}_1$ of Ackermann function, for $i \in \mathbb{N}_1$, can be defined as follows:

$$\mathbf{A}_1(n) = 2n, \qquad \mathbf{A}_{i+1}(n) = \underbrace{\mathbf{A}_i \circ \mathbf{A}_i \circ \ldots \circ \mathbf{A}_i}_{n}(1) = \mathbf{A}_i^n(1).$$

In particular, $\mathbf{A}_2(n) = 2^n$ and $\mathbf{A}_i(1) = 2$ for all $i \in \mathbb{N}_1$. Using functions $\mathbf{A}_i$, we define the complexity classes $\mathcal{F}_i$, indexed by $i \in \mathbb{N}_1$, of problems solvable in deterministic time $\mathbf{A}_i(p(n))$, where $p : \mathbb{N}_1 \to \mathbb{N}_1$ ranges over functions computable in deterministic time $\mathbf{A}_{i-1}^m(n)$, for some $m \in \mathbb{N}_1$:

$$\mathcal{F}_i = \bigcup_{p \in \mathcal{FF}_{<i}} \text{DTIME}(\mathbf{A}_i(p(n))), \qquad \text{where } \mathcal{FF}_{<i} = \bigcup_{m \in \mathbb{N}_1 j<i} \text{FDTIME}(\mathbf{A}_j^m(n)).$$

Intuitively speaking, the class $\mathcal{F}_i$ contains all problems solvable in time $\mathbf{A}_i(n)$, and is closed under reductions computable in time of lower order $\mathbf{A}_{i-1}^m(n)$, for some fixed $m \in \mathbb{N}_1$. In particular, $\mathcal{F}_3 = \text{TOWER}$ (problems solvable in a tower of exponentials of time or space, whose height is an elementary function of input size). The classes $\mathcal{F}_k$ are robust with respect to the choice of fast-growing function hierarchy (see [45, Sect. 4.1]). For $k \geqslant 3$, instead of deterministic time, one could equivalently take nondeterministic time, or space.

Ackermann function $\mathbf{A}_\omega : \mathbb{N}_1 \to \mathbb{N}_1$ is defined by diagonalisation: $\mathbf{A}_\omega(n) = \mathbf{A}_n(n)$. Having $\mathbf{A}_\omega$, we define the Ackermannian complexity class $\text{ACKERMANN} = \mathcal{F}_\omega$ exactly as above.

The Reachability Problem Redefined. Given a subset $R \subseteq \mathbb{N}^{\mathsf{C}}$ of valuations, by a run *from* R we mean any run whose initial valuation belongs to R. A complete run is called X-*zeroing*, for a subset $\mathsf{X} \subseteq \mathsf{C}$ of counters, if it ends with $\mathsf{x} = 0$ for all $\mathsf{x} \in \mathsf{X}$. When $\mathsf{X} = \{\mathsf{x}\}$ and/or $R = \{r\}$ are a singleton we write simply "x-zeroing" and/or "from r". For instance, the program from Example 1 has exactly one x-zeroing run from the valuation $\mathsf{x} = 10$, $\mathsf{y} = \mathsf{z} = 0$, where the final values of counters are $\mathsf{x} = 0$, $\mathsf{y} = 10$, $\mathsf{z} = 21$.

By $\mathbf{0}$ we denote the valuation where all counters are 0. We investigate the complexity of the following variant of the reachability problem (with a partially constrained final valuation of counters) that asks if the given program has a run starting with all counters equal to 0, and ending with the given subset of counters equal to 0 (while the final value of the remaining counters may be arbitrary):

REACHABILITY PROBLEM:

Input: A program $\mathcal{P}$ without zero tests, and a subset X of its counters.

Question: Does $\mathcal{P}$ have an X-zeroing run from the zero valuation $\mathbf{0}$?

Since counter programs are easily translated to VASS, the above decision problem translates to a variant of the reachability problem for the latter model, where all coordinates of the initial vector are 0, and a subset of coordinates of the final vector must be 0 (namely coordinates corresponding to counters X), while the remaining coordinates are unrestricted. According to the encoding of VASS as Petri nets, the latter problem translates to the *submarking reachability* problem for Petri nets, where all places (except for the place encoding the initial control state) are initially empty, and only the places corresponding to counters X, and places corresponding to control states of a VASS, have specified final values. Finally, the submarking reachability problem is polynomially reducible to the classical reachability problem, where the final content of all places is fully specified.

In the rest of this paper we prove $\mathcal{F}_k$-hardness for programs with the fixed number $3k + 2$ of counters, and ACKERMANN-hardness when the number of counters is not fixed:

Theorem 2. *For every $k \geqslant 3$, the reachabilty problem for programs with $3k + 2$ counters is $\mathcal{F}_k$-hard. Without fixing the number of counters, the reachability problem for counter programs is* ACKERMANN*-hard.*

Here are the main ideas underlying the hardness proof (presented in Sect. 9). Speaking slightly informally, suppose some three counters $\mathsf{b}, \mathsf{c}, \mathsf{d}$ satisfy initially

$$\mathsf{b} = B, \qquad \mathsf{c} > 0, \qquad \mathsf{d} = \mathsf{b} \cdot \mathsf{c}, \tag{5}$$

for some fixed positive integer $B \in \mathbb{N}$. Furthermore, suppose that the initial values of c and d may be arbitrary, in a nondeterministic way, as long as they satisfy the latter equality in (5); they are hence unbounded (this is assured by *mulipliers*, to be constructed in Sects. 6 and 8). Under these assumptions, the *ratio* technique allows one to correctly simulate exactly $B/2$ zero tests (for B even) on unbounded counters (in fact, on counters bounded by the initial value of c which may be arbitrarily large). The ratio technique was introduced originally in [10]; we rely on its variant, as described in Sect. 7. Simulation of a large number of zero tests (namely simulation of roughly $\mathbf{A}_k(n)/2$ zero tests by a program with $3k + 2$ counters of size n) is a key feature in our reduction given in Sect. 9.

6 Multipliers

Consider a program $\mathcal{P}$ with counters C, a set of counters $\mathsf{X} \subseteq \mathsf{C}$ and $R \subseteq \mathbb{N}^{\mathsf{C}}$. We define the set X-*computed by* $\mathcal{P}$ *from* R as the set of all valuations of counters at the end of all X-zeroing (and hence forcedly complete) runs of $\mathcal{P}$ from R. Formally, denoting by $\text{RUNS}_{\mathcal{P}}(R, \mathsf{X})$ the set of all X-zeroing runs of $\mathcal{P}$ from R, and by $\text{FIN}(\pi)$ the final counter valuation of a complete run π of $\mathcal{P}$, the set X-computed by $\mathcal{P}$ from R is

$$\text{COMP}_{\mathcal{P}}(R, \mathsf{X}) \quad = \quad \{\text{FIN}(\pi) \mid \pi \in \text{RUNS}_{\mathcal{P}}(R, \mathsf{X})\}.$$

As before, when $\mathsf{X} = \{\mathsf{x}\}$ and/or $R = \{r\}$ are a singleton we write simply'x-computed' and/or'from r'.

Example 2. The program in Example 1 above, x-computes from the set of all valuations satisfying $\mathsf{y} = \mathsf{z} = 0$ (no constraint for x), the set of all valuations satisfying $\mathsf{x} = 0$ (trivially) and $\mathsf{z} = 2\mathsf{y} + 1$.

Likewise, for a fixed integer $m \in \mathbb{N}$ and a program $\mathcal{P}$ with zero tests, we define the set X-computed by $\mathcal{P}$ from R *using* m *zero tests*, by restricting the above definition to runs $\pi \in \text{RUNS}_{\mathcal{P}}(R, \mathsf{X})$ that do exactly m zero tests. This finer variant of the definition will be used in the next section.

Multipliers. Let $\mathsf{b}, \mathsf{c}, \mathsf{d} \in \mathsf{C}$ be some three distinguished counters, and $B \in \mathbb{N}_4$. We define the subset $\text{RATIO}(B, \mathsf{b}, \mathsf{c}, \mathsf{d}, \mathsf{C}) \subseteq \mathbb{N}^{\mathsf{C}}$, called informally the *ratio of* B, consisting of all valuations that satisfy the three conditions (5) and assign 0 to all other counters $\mathsf{x} \in \mathsf{C} \setminus \{\mathsf{b}, \mathsf{c}, \mathsf{d}\}$.

Definition 1. *A program* $\mathcal{M}$ *(with no zero tests) with counters* C *that* z*-computes from the zero valuation* $\mathbf{0}$ *the set* $\text{RATIO}(B, \mathsf{b}, \mathsf{c}, \mathsf{d}, \mathsf{C})$*, for some four of its counters* $\mathsf{z}, \mathsf{b}, \mathsf{c}, \mathsf{d} \in \mathsf{C}$*, we call* B-**multiplier**. *In formula:*

$$\text{COMP}_{\mathcal{M}}(\mathbf{0}, \mathsf{z}) = \text{RATIO}(B, \mathsf{b}, \mathsf{c}, \mathsf{d}, \mathsf{C}).$$

Example 3. As a simple example, for every fixed $B \in \mathbb{N}_4$, the following program is a B-multiplier of size $\mathcal{O}(B)$ (several commands are written in one line to save space). Counter z is not used at all.

Program $\mathcal{M}_B(\mathsf{b}, \mathsf{c}, \mathsf{d})$:

$\mathsf{b} \mathrel{+}= B \quad \mathsf{d} \mathrel{+}= B \quad \mathsf{c} \mathrel{+}= 1$

loop

$\quad \mathsf{d} \mathrel{+}= B \quad \mathsf{c} \mathrel{+}= 1$

Directly from the definition we derive the following fundamental property of multipliers, to be used in the proofs in Sects. 8 and 9:

Lemma 8. *Let* $\mathcal{M}$ *be a* B*-multiplier with counters* C *as in Definition 1, let* $\mathcal{P}$ *be a counter program with counters* $\mathsf{C} \setminus \{\mathsf{z}\}$*, and let* $\mathsf{Y} \subseteq \mathsf{C}$*. Then the set* Y*-computed by* $\mathcal{P}$ *from* $\text{RATIO}(B, \mathsf{b}, \mathsf{c}, \mathsf{d}, \mathsf{C})$ *is equal to the set* $(\{\mathsf{z}\} \cup \mathsf{Y})$*-computed by the composed program* $\mathcal{M}\ \mathcal{P}$ *from* $\mathbf{0}$*:*

$$\text{COMP}_{\mathcal{P}}(\text{RATIO}(B, \mathsf{b}, \mathsf{c}, \mathsf{d}, \mathsf{C}), \mathsf{Y}) \quad = \quad \text{COMP}_{\mathcal{M}\,\mathcal{P}}(\mathbf{0}, \{\mathsf{z}\} \cup \mathsf{Y}).$$

Proof. The claim is a special case of the following general composition rule: for two programs $\mathcal{P}$ and $\mathcal{Q}$, if $\textsc{Comp}_{\mathcal{P}}(A, \mathsf{X}) = B$ and $\mathcal{Q}$ does not use counters X, then $\textsc{Comp}_{\mathcal{P}\,\mathcal{Q}}(A, \mathsf{X} \cup \mathsf{Y}) = \textsc{Comp}_{\mathcal{Q}}(B, \mathsf{Y})$. Indeed, under the above assumptions $(\mathsf{X} \cup \mathsf{Y})$-zeroing runs of $\mathcal{P}\ \mathcal{Q}$ from A are in mutual correspondence with Y-zeroing runs of $\mathcal{Q}$ from B. □

Computing Multipliers. For technical convenience we prefer to rely on the following family of functions $\mathbf{F}_i : \mathbb{N}_4 \to \mathbb{N}_4$, indexed by $i \in \mathbb{N}_1$, closely related to functions $\mathbf{A}_i$ (cf. Lemma 9 below):

$$\mathbf{F}_1(n) = 2n, \qquad \mathbf{F}_{i+1} = \widetilde{\mathbf{F}_i} \quad \text{where} \quad \widetilde{F}(n) = \underbrace{F \circ F \circ \ldots \circ F}_{n/4}(4). \tag{6}$$

By induction on i one easily shows that $\mathbf{F}_i$ is a linear re-scaling of $\mathbf{A}_i$:

Lemma 9. *$\mathbf{F}_i(4 \cdot n) = 4 \cdot \mathbf{A}_i(n)$, for $i, n \in \mathbb{N}_1$.*

Proof. As $\mathbf{F}_1(n) = 2n$ and $\mathbf{A}_1(n) = 2n$, the claim holds for $i = 1$. Assuming the claim for $i \in \mathbb{N}_1$, by n-fold application thereof we derive the required equality for $i + 1$:

$$\mathbf{F}_{i+1}(4 \cdot n) \;=\; \underbrace{\mathbf{F}_i \circ \ldots \circ \mathbf{F}_i}_{n}(4) \;=\; 4 \cdot \underbrace{\mathbf{A}_i \circ \ldots \circ \mathbf{A}_i}_{n}(1) \;=\; 4 \cdot \mathbf{A}_{i+1}(n).$$

□

As a technical core of the proof of Theorem 2, we provide an effective construction of B-multipliers with $3k + 2$ counters, where $B = \mathbf{F}_k(n)$, of size polynomial in k and n.

Theorem 3. *Given $k \in \mathbb{N}_1$ and $n \in \mathbb{N}_4$ one can compute, in time polynomial in k and n, an $\mathbf{F}_k(n)$-multiplier with $3k + 2$ counters.*

The proof is in Sect. 8.

7 Bounded Number of Zero Tests

In this section we provide a construction that enables simulating a bounded number m of zero tests (cf. Lemma 12) at the cost of introducing 3 additional counters initialised to the ratio of $B = 2(m + 1)$. This construction is a core ingredient of the proofs of Theorems 2 and 3.

Whenever analysing a single run of a program, we denote by $\overline{\mathsf{x}}$ the initial value of a counter x, and by $\underline{\mathsf{x}}$ the final value thereof.

Maximal Iteration. In the sequel we intensively use loops of the following form that, intuitively, flush the value from some counter f to some other counter e, decreasing simultaneously yet another third counter d (and possibly execute some further commands):

$$\begin{array}{l}\textbf{loop}\\ \quad \mathsf{f} \mathrel{-}= 1 \quad \mathsf{e} \mathrel{+}= 1 \quad \mathsf{d} \mathrel{-}= 1 \\ \quad \ldots\end{array} \tag{7}$$

Assuming $\overline{\mathsf{d}} \geqslant \overline{\mathsf{f}}$, we observe that the amount $\overline{\mathsf{d}} - \underline{\mathsf{d}}$ by which d is decreased as an effect of execution (we use the word *execution* as a synonym to *complete run*) of the above loop may be any value between 0 and $\overline{\mathsf{f}}$. Furthermore, assuming $\overline{\mathsf{d}} \geqslant \overline{\mathsf{e}} + \overline{\mathsf{f}}$, the equality $\overline{\mathsf{d}} - \underline{\mathsf{d}} = \overline{\mathsf{e}} + \overline{\mathsf{f}}$ holds if and only if

$$\overline{\mathsf{e}} = 0 = \underline{\mathsf{f}}. \tag{8}$$

This simple observation will play a crucial role in the sequel, and deserves a definition:

Definition 2. *Whenever an execution of a loop of the form* (7) *satisfies the two equalities* (8) *we call this execution* **maximally iterated**.

The Construction. Let $\mathcal{P}$ be a counter program with counters C, and assume that $\mathcal{P}$ uses zero tests only on two its counters $\mathsf{x}, \mathsf{y} \in \mathsf{C}$ (the construction easily extends to programs with an arbitrary number of zero-tested counters). We add to $\mathcal{P}$ three fresh counters $\mathsf{b}, \mathsf{c}, \mathsf{d}$ (let $\mathsf{C}^* = \mathsf{C} \cup \{\mathsf{b}, \mathsf{c}, \mathsf{d}\}$), and transform $\mathcal{P}$ into a program $\mathcal{P}^*$ *without zero tests* that, assuming its initial valuation of counters belongs to $\textsc{Ratio}(2(m+1), \mathsf{b}, \mathsf{c}, \mathsf{d}, \mathsf{C}^*)$ for some $m \in \mathbb{N}$, simulates correctly m zero tests (jointly) on counters x, y, as long as their sum is bounded by the initial value of c (cf. Lemma 12).

The transformation proceeds in three steps. First, we accompany every increment (decrement) on x with a decrement (increment) of c, and likewise we do for y:

command	replaced by
$\mathsf{x} \mathrel{+}= 1$	$\mathsf{x} \mathrel{+}= 1 \quad \mathsf{c} \mathrel{-}= 1$
$\mathsf{x} \mathrel{-}= 1$	$\mathsf{x} \mathrel{-}= 1 \quad \mathsf{c} \mathrel{+}= 1$

command	replaced by
$\mathsf{y} \mathrel{+}= 1$	$\mathsf{y} \mathrel{+}= 1 \quad \mathsf{c} \mathrel{-}= 1$
$\mathsf{y} \mathrel{-}= 1$	$\mathsf{y} \mathrel{-}= 1 \quad \mathsf{c} \mathrel{+}= 1$

In the resulting program $\overline{\mathcal{P}}$ counters x, y are, intuitively speaking, put on a shared 'budget' c. Assuming x and y initially 0, this clearly enforces $\mathsf{x} + \mathsf{y}$ to not exceed the initial value of c, and the sum $s = \mathsf{c} + \mathsf{x} + \mathsf{y}$ to remain invariant.

As the second step, we replace in $\overline{\mathcal{P}}$ every **zero?** x command by the following macro $\textsc{Zero?}\,\mathsf{x}$. Likewise we replace every **zero?** y command by an analogous macro $\textsc{Zero?}\,\mathsf{y}$ obtained from $\textsc{Zero?}\,\mathsf{x}$ by swapping x and y.

<u>ZERO? x:</u>

```
1: loop
2:     y -= 1   x += 1   d -= 1
3: loop
4:     c -= 1   y += 1   d -= 1
5: loop
6:     y -= 1   c += 1   d -= 1
7: loop
8:     x -= 1   y += 1   d -= 1
9: b -= 2
```

This yields the program $\widehat{\mathcal{P}}$ without zero tests. We note that each of the two ZERO? macros preserves the sum $s = \mathsf{c} + \mathsf{x} + \mathsf{y}$, and decrements the counter b by 2. Furthermore, each of the two ZERO? macros decrements d by at most $2s$ (cf. Lemma 10 below), and hence the macros preserve the inequality $d \geqslant \mathsf{b} \cdot s$ (recall that $\mathsf{d} = \mathsf{b} \cdot s$ holds initially).

As the final step we adjoint at the end of $\widehat{\mathcal{P}}$ the following program, thus obtaining the transformed program $\mathcal{P}^*$:

<u>SET-C-TO-ZERO:</u>

```
loop
    c -= 1   d -= 2
ZERO? c
```

The macro ZERO? c is obtained from ZERO? x by swapping x and c. We note that an execution of SET-C-TO-ZERO may decrease the sum $\mathsf{c} + \mathsf{x} + \mathsf{y}$ (but ZERO? c preserves it).

Correctness. Recall that $\widehat{\mathcal{P}}$ preserves the sum $\mathsf{c} + \mathsf{x} + \mathsf{y}$; we denote by s the value of this sum. An execution of ZERO? x is called *maximally iterated* if all four loops are so. Observe that every such execution is forcedly *correct*, i.e. satisfies:

$$\overline{\mathsf{x}} = \underline{\mathsf{x}} = 0, \qquad \overline{\mathsf{y}} = \underline{\mathsf{y}}, \qquad \overline{\mathsf{c}} = \underline{\mathsf{c}}. \tag{9}$$

(Likewise in case of ZERO? y and ZERO? c.) The idea behind ZERO? x is to flush from y to a zero-tested counter x and back, but also flush from c to y and back, in an appropriately nested way that guarantees that the amount $\overline{\mathsf{d}} - \underline{\mathsf{d}}$ by which d is decreased equals $2s$ exactly in maximally iterated executions:

Lemma 10. *Consider an execution of* ZERO? x *(resp.* ZERO? y*) macro, assuming* $\overline{\mathsf{d}} \geqslant 2s$*. Then* $0 \leq \overline{\mathsf{d}} - \underline{\mathsf{d}} \leq 2s$*. Furthermore, the equality* $\overline{\mathsf{d}} - \underline{\mathsf{d}} = 2s$ *holds if and only if the execution is maximally iterated.*

Proof. Consider an execution of ZERO? x, assuming $\overline{\mathsf{d}} \geqslant 2s$, and let $\dot{\mathsf{y}}$ denote the value of y at the exit from the first loop. The amount by which d is decreased in the two loops in lines 1–2 and 7–8 is at most

$$\Delta_1 = 2(\overline{\mathsf{y}} - \dot{\mathsf{y}}) + \overline{\mathsf{x}}.$$

Furthermore, the amount by which d is decreased in the two loops in lines 3–6 is at most

$$\Delta_2 = 2\overline{\mathsf{c}} + \dot{\mathsf{y}}.$$

The sum $\Delta_1 + \Delta_2$ clearly satisfies $\Delta_1 + \Delta_2 \leq 2s = 2(\overline{\mathsf{c}} + \overline{\mathsf{x}} + \overline{\mathsf{y}})$. It equals $2s$ if and only if $\Delta_1 = 2\overline{\mathsf{y}}$ and $\Delta_2 = 2\overline{\mathsf{c}}$, i.e., exactly when all four loops are maximally iterated. □

In consequence, as b is decreased by 2, if the invariant $\mathsf{d} = \mathsf{b} \cdot s$ is preserved by an execution of ZERO? x (resp. ZERO? y) then the zero test is forcedly correct. Furthermore notice that once the invariant is violated, i.e., $\mathsf{d} > \mathsf{b} \cdot s$, due to the first part of Lemma 10 the invariant cannot be recovered later. These observations lead to the correctness claim stated in Lemma 12.

In the proof of Lemma 12 we will also need the following corollary of Lemma 10, where s denotes, as before, the sum $\mathsf{c} + \mathsf{x} + \mathsf{y}$ at the start of SET-c-TO-ZERO(c):

Lemma 11. *Consider an execution of* SET-c-TO-ZERO(c)*, assuming* $\overline{\mathsf{d}} \geqslant 2s$*. Then* $0 \leq \overline{\mathsf{d}} - \underline{\mathsf{d}} \leq 2s$*. Furthermore, the equality* $\overline{\mathsf{d}} - \underline{\mathsf{d}} = 2s$ *holds if and only if the* ZERO? c *macro is maximally iterated.*

Proof. Consider an execution of SET-c-TO-ZERO(c) and denote by $\dot{s}$ the value of $\mathsf{c} + \mathsf{x} + \mathsf{y}$ just before entering ZERO? c. Thus d decrease by $2(s - \dot{s})$ before entering ZERO? c. Moreover, due to Lemma 10, the macro ZERO? c decreases d by at most $2\dot{s}$, and furthermore the macro decreases d by exactly $2\dot{s}$ if and only if it is maximally iterated. These observations imply the claim. □

Recall that $\mathsf{C}^* = \mathsf{C} \cup \{\mathsf{b}, \mathsf{c}, \mathsf{d}\}$. We define the C^*-*extension* of a counter valuation $v \in \mathbb{N}^{\mathsf{C}}$ as the counter valuation that extends v by assigning 0 to b, c and d. The C^*-extension of a set $R \subseteq \mathbb{N}^{\mathsf{C}}$ is defined as the set of C^*-extensions of all valuations in R.

Lemma 12. *The following sets are equal (as subsets of* $\mathbb{N}^{\mathsf{C}^*}$*):*

- *the* C^**-extension of the set computed by* $\mathcal{P}$ *from* $\mathbf{0}$ *using* m *zero tests.*
- *the set* d*-computed by* $\mathcal{P}^*$ *from* RATIO$(2(m+1), \mathsf{b}, \mathsf{c}, \mathsf{d}, \mathsf{C}^*)$.

Proof. For the inclusion of the former set in the latter, we show that for each complete run π of $\mathcal{P}$ from $\mathbf{0}$ that does m zero tests on x, y, there is a corresponding d-zeroing run of $\mathcal{P}^*$ from RATIO$(2(m+1), \mathsf{b}, \mathsf{c}, \mathsf{d}, \mathsf{C}^*)$, for any initial value $\overline{\mathsf{c}}$ at least as large as the maximal value of the sum $\mathsf{x}+\mathsf{y}$ along π. The run iterates maximally ZERO? x and ZERO? y macros, decrements c to 0 in line 2 in SET-c-TO-ZERO(c), and then iterates maximally ZERO? c. Thus the final counter valuation of the run is the C^*-extension of the final counter valuation of π.

For the converse direction, consider a d-zeroing run π of $\mathcal{P}^*$ from RATIO$(2(m+1), \mathsf{b}, \mathsf{c}, \mathsf{d}, \mathsf{C}^*)$. The initial counter valuation satisfies the equalities $\mathsf{b} = 2(m+1)$ and $\mathsf{d} = 2(m+1) \cdot s$. Each execution of ZERO? x or ZERO? y or SET-c-TO-ZERO(c) decreases b by 2, and d by at most $2s$ (by the first part of Lemmas 10 and Lemma 11). Therefore, since b and d are not affected elsewhere and $\underline{\mathsf{d}} = 0$ finally, we deduce:

Claim. Each execution of ZERO? x, ZERO? y or ZERO? c in π decreases d by *exactly* $2s$.

Claim. There are exactly m executions of ZERO? x or ZERO? y in π.

Claim. Finally, $\underline{\mathsf{b}} = 0$.

By the first claim combined with the second part of Lemmas 10 and 11, respectively, we derive:

Claim. Each execution of ZERO? x in π is correct, i.e. satisfies the equalities (9). Likewise for ZERO? y.

Claim. Finally, $\underline{\mathsf{c}} = 0$.

Due to the second and fourth claim above, once we remove counters $\mathsf{b}, \mathsf{c}, \mathsf{d}$ from π we obtain a complete run of $\mathcal{P}$ from $\mathbf{0}$ that does exactly m zero tests, as required. Finally, due to the third and fifth claim above, the C^*-extension of the final counter valuation of the obtained run is exactly the final counter valuation of π. □

8 Computing Large Multipliers (Proof of Theorem 3)

The proof proceeds by combining the concept of amplifier lifting of [13] with the program transformation of Sect. 7.

Amplifiers. Let $F : \mathbb{N}_4 \to \mathbb{N}_4$ be a monotone function satisfying $F(n) \geqslant n$ for $n \in \mathbb{N}_4$. Informally speaking, an F-*amplifier* is a program without zero tests that computes the ratio of $F(B)$ from the ratio of B, for every $B \in \mathbb{N}_4$.

Definition 3. *Consider a program* $\mathcal{P}$ *with counters* C *without zero tests and distinguished three* input counters $\mathsf{b}, \mathsf{c}, \mathsf{d} \in \mathsf{C}$ *and three* output counters $\mathsf{b}', \mathsf{c}', \mathsf{d}' \in \mathsf{C}$. *The program is called* F**-amplifier** *if for every* $B \in \mathbb{N}_4$, *it* d*-computes from* $\textsc{Ratio}(B, \mathsf{b}, \mathsf{c}, \mathsf{d}, \mathsf{C})$ *the set* $\textsc{Ratio}(F(B), \mathsf{b}', \mathsf{c}', \mathsf{d}', \mathsf{C})$.

We note that no condition is imposed on d-zeroing runs from counter valuations not belonging to any set $\textsc{Ratio}(B, \mathsf{b}, \mathsf{c}, \mathsf{d}, \mathsf{C})$. As an example, consider the following program $\mathcal{L}_\ell$, for $\ell \in \mathbb{N}_1$, with input counters $\mathsf{b}, \mathsf{c}, \mathsf{d}$ and output counters $\mathsf{b}', \mathsf{c}', \mathsf{d}'$:

Program $\mathcal{L}_\ell(\mathsf{b}, \mathsf{c}, \mathsf{d}, \mathsf{b}', \mathsf{c}', \mathsf{d}')$:

```
loop
    loop
        c -= 1    c' += 1    d -= 1    d' += ℓ
    loop
        c' -= 1   c += 1     d -= 1    d' += ℓ
    b -= 2    b' += 2ℓ
loop
    c -= 1    c' += 1    d -= 2    d' += 2ℓ
b -= 2    b' += 2ℓ
```

Claim. The above program is an L_ℓ-amplifier, where $L_\ell : \mathbb{N}_4 \to \mathbb{N}_4 = (x \mapsto \ell \cdot x)$.

Proof. Writing counter valuations as vectors $(\mathsf{b}, \mathsf{c}, \mathsf{d}, \mathsf{b}', \mathsf{c}', \mathsf{d}')$, one shows that the program d-computes, from the set containing just one counter valuation $(B, c, d, 0, 0, 0)$, the set containing one counter valuation $(0, 0, 0, \ell \cdot B, c, \ell \cdot d)$. Indeed, as $\mathsf{d} = 0$ finally, each of the two inner loops in lines 2–5, as well as the last loop in lines 7–8, is forcedly maximally iterated. □

Putting $\ell = 1$ we get an identity-amplifier $\mathcal{L}_1(\mathsf{b}, \mathsf{c}, \mathsf{d}, \mathsf{b}', \mathsf{c}', \mathsf{d}')$.

Amplifier Lifting. Recall the definition (6) of functions $\mathbf{F}_i$; in particular $\mathbf{F}_1 = L_2$. Let $\mathcal{P}$ be a program with counters C, without zero tests, with distinguished input counters $\mathsf{b}_1, \mathsf{c}_1, \mathsf{d}_1 \in \mathsf{C}$ and output counters $\mathsf{b}_2, \mathsf{c}_2, \mathsf{d}_2 \in \mathsf{C}$. We describe a transformation of the program $\mathcal{P}$ to a program $\widetilde{\mathcal{P}}$, also without zero tests, such that assuming that $\mathcal{P}$ is an F-amplifier for some function $F : \mathbb{N}_4 \to \mathbb{N}_4$, the program $\widetilde{\mathcal{P}}$ is an $\widetilde{F}$-amplifier. The program $\widetilde{\mathcal{P}}$ uses, except for the counters of $\mathcal{P}$, three fresh counters $\mathsf{b}, \mathsf{c}, \mathsf{d}$. Thus counters of $\widetilde{\mathcal{P}}$ are $\mathsf{C}^* = \mathsf{C} \cup \{\mathsf{b}, \mathsf{c}, \mathsf{d}\}$. We let input counters of $\widetilde{\mathcal{P}}$ be $\mathsf{b}, \mathsf{c}, \mathsf{d}$, and its output counters be $\mathsf{b}_2, \mathsf{c}_2, \mathsf{d}_2$.

In the transformation we use the identity-amplifier $\mathcal{L} = \mathcal{L}_1(\mathsf{b}_2, \mathsf{c}_2, \mathsf{d}_2, \mathsf{b}_1, \mathsf{c}_1, \mathsf{d}_1)$ with input counters $\mathsf{b}_2, \mathsf{c}_2, \mathsf{d}_2$ and output counters $\mathsf{b}_1, \mathsf{c}_1, \mathsf{d}_1$, and the 4-multiplier $\mathcal{M} = \mathcal{M}_4(\mathsf{b}_1, \mathsf{c}_1, \mathsf{d}_1)$ of Example 3, both without zero tests. For defining the program $\widetilde{\mathcal{P}}$ we apply the transformation of Sect. 7 (with counters d_1 and d_2 in place of x and y) to the following program $\mathcal{Q}$ built using $\mathcal{P}$, $\mathcal{L}$ and $\mathcal{M}$:

Program $\mathcal{Q}$:

$\mathcal{M}$
loop
  $\mathcal{P}$
  zero? d_1
  $\mathcal{L}$
  zero? d_2
$\mathcal{P}$
zero? d_1

Program $\widetilde{\mathcal{P}}$:

$\overline{\mathcal{M}}$
loop
  $\overline{\mathcal{P}}$
  ZERO? d_1
  $\overline{\mathcal{L}}$
  ZERO? d_2
$\overline{\mathcal{P}}$
ZERO? d_1
SET-c-TO-ZERO

Formally, $\widetilde{\mathcal{P}} = \mathcal{Q}^*$. Intuitively speaking, the program $\mathcal{Q}$ directly implements the computation of $\widetilde{F}$ according to the definition: with $2\ell + 1$ zero tests it computes, from $\mathbf{0}$, the ratio of $F^{\ell+1}(4)$. Note that counters of $\mathcal{Q}$ are C while counters of $\widetilde{\mathcal{P}}$ are C^*. Lemma 13 states the crucial amplifier-lifting property of the program transformation $\mathcal{P} \mapsto \widetilde{\mathcal{P}}$.

Lemma 13. *If $\mathcal{P}$ is an F-amplifier, then $\widetilde{\mathcal{P}}$ is an $\widetilde{F}$-amplifier.*

Proof. Let $\mathcal{P}$ be an F-amplifier. Thus for every $B \in \mathbb{N}_4$, we have

$$\text{COMP}_{\mathcal{P}}(\text{RATIO}(B, \mathsf{b}_1, \mathsf{c}_1, \mathsf{d}_1, \mathsf{C}), \mathsf{d}_1) = \text{RATIO}(F(B), \mathsf{b}_2, \mathsf{c}_2, \mathsf{d}_2, \mathsf{C}).$$

$\mathcal{L}$, being an identity-amplifier, d_2-computes from $\text{RATIO}(B, \mathsf{b}_2, \mathsf{c}_2, \mathsf{d}_2, \mathsf{C})$ the set $\text{RATIO}(B, \mathsf{b}_1, \mathsf{c}_1, \mathsf{d}_1, \mathsf{C})$. Let $B = 4(\ell + 1) \in \mathbb{N}_4$ for an arbitrary $\ell \in \mathbb{N}$. As $\mathcal{P}$ is an F-amplifier and $\mathcal{L}$ is an identity-amplifier, we deduce:

Claim. $\mathcal{Q}$ computes from $\mathbf{0}$ the set $\text{RATIO}(F^{\ell+1}(4), \mathsf{b}_2, \mathsf{c}_2, \mathsf{d}_2, \mathsf{C})$, using $2\ell + 1$ zero tests.

As $\widetilde{\mathcal{P}} = \mathcal{Q}^*$, by Lemma 12 we deduce:

Claim. $\text{COMP}_{\widetilde{\mathcal{P}}}(\text{RATIO}(4(\ell+1), \mathsf{b}, \mathsf{c}, \mathsf{d}, \mathsf{C}^*), \mathsf{d}) = \text{RATIO}(F^{\ell+1}(4), \mathsf{b}_2, \mathsf{c}_2, \mathsf{d}_2, \mathsf{C})$.

As $B \in \mathbb{N}_4$ was chosen arbitrarily and $\widetilde{F}(B) = F^{\ell+1}(4)$, the last claim says that $\widetilde{\mathcal{P}}$ is an $\widetilde{F}$-amplifier. □

Remark 2. The program $\mathcal{P}$ appears twice in the body of $\widetilde{\mathcal{P}}$. This doubling can be easily avoided by re-structuring the loop using explicit **goto** commands. In this way, the size of $\widetilde{\mathcal{P}}$ becomes larger than the size of $\mathcal{P}$ only by a constant.

Proof of Theorem 3 We rely on Lemma 13. Given $k \in \mathbb{N}_1$ and $n \in \mathbb{N}_4$ we compute, in time linear in k, the $\mathbf{F}_k$-amplifier $\mathcal{A}_k$ with $3k+3$ counters C, by $(k-1)$-fold application of the amplifier lifting transformation $\mathcal{P} \mapsto \widetilde{\mathcal{P}}$ described above, starting from the $\mathbf{F}_1$-amplifier $\mathcal{L}_2$. The construction is linear in k due to Remark 2. Let $\mathsf{b}, \mathsf{c}, \mathsf{d} \in \mathsf{C}$ be input counters of $\mathcal{A}_k$. Relying on Lemma 8 in Sect. 6, the $\mathbf{F}_k(n)$-multiplier is obtained by pre-composing $\mathcal{A}_k$ with an n-multiplier (e.g. $\mathcal{M}_n(\mathsf{b}, \mathsf{c}, \mathsf{d})$ from Sect. 5) that outputs the set $\text{RATIO}(n, \mathsf{b}, \mathsf{c}, \mathsf{d}, \mathsf{C})$. The whole construction is thus linear in n.

Finally we observe that the counter b is bounded by n and hence can be eliminated: we encode its values in control locations, by cloning the program into $n+1$ copies, where ith (for $i = 0, \ldots, n$) copy corresponds to the value $\mathsf{b} = i$. The resulting program has $3k+2$ counters. □

9 Hardness Proof

Relying on Lemma 12 and Theorem 3, we prove in this section Theorem 2. Fix $k \geqslant 3$. The proof proceeds by a polynomial-time reduction from the following $\mathcal{F}_k$-hard problem:

$\mathbf{F}_k$-BOUNDED HALTING PROBLEM:

Input: A program $\mathcal{P}$ of size n (w.l.o.g. assume $n \in \mathbb{N}_4$) with 2 zero-tested counters.

Question: Does $\mathcal{P}$ have a complete run from $\mathbf{0}$ that does at most $(\mathbf{F}_k(n) - 1)/2$ zero tests?

Claim. The above problem is $\mathcal{F}_k$-hard.

Proof. Indeed, the standard $\mathcal{F}_k$-hard halting problem (does a program $\mathcal{P}$ with *arbitrarily many* zero-tested counters $\mathsf{x}_1, \ldots, \mathsf{x}_\ell$ have a complete run that does at most $(\mathbf{F}_k(n) - 1)/2$ *steps*?) reduces polynomially to the above one using the standard simulation of arbitrarily many zero-tested counters by 2 such counters $\mathsf{y}_1, \mathsf{y}_2$. The simulation stores the values of all counters $\mathsf{x}_1, \ldots, \mathsf{x}_\ell$ on one of $\mathsf{y}_1, \mathsf{y}_2$ (e.g., using Gödel encoding), and the simulation of each command involves flushing the value of that counter to the other, followed by the zero test. Thus a bound on time of computation is translated to the same bound on the number of zero tests. □

Given $\mathcal{P}$ as above with two counters x, y, we transform it to a counter program $\mathcal{P}'$ with $3k + 2$ counters C but without zero tests, such that $\mathcal{P}$ has a complete run from $\mathbf{0}$ that does at most $m = (\mathbf{F}_k(n) - 1)/2$ zero tests if and only if $\mathcal{P}'$ has a $\{\mathsf{d}, \mathsf{z}\}$-zeroing run from $\mathbf{0}$ (for some $\mathsf{d}, \mathsf{z} \in \mathsf{C}$).

First, we post-compose $\mathcal{P}$ with a simple program $\mathcal{L}$ that first decrements x nondeterministically many times, and then zero tests it nondeterministically many times:

```
loop
    x −= 1
loop
    zero? x
```

Thus $\mathcal{P}$ has a complete run that does *at most* m zero tests if and only if the composed program $\mathcal{P}\ \mathcal{L}$ has a complete run that does *exactly* m zero tests. We will apply the transformation of Sect. 7 to the composed program $\mathcal{P}\ \mathcal{L}$. Let $\mathsf{b}, \mathsf{c}, \mathsf{d}$ be the three counters added in the course of the transformation.

Second, using Theorem 3 we compute a $2(m+1)$-multiplier $\mathcal{M}$ (recall that $2(m+1) = \mathbf{F}_k(n)$) with $3k + 2$ counters C that z-computes from $\mathbf{0}$ the set $\text{RATIO}(2(m+1), \mathsf{b}, \mathsf{c}, \mathsf{d}, \mathsf{C})$, for some counter z different than x, y. Thus $\mathsf{z}, \mathsf{b}, \mathsf{c}, \mathsf{d} \in \mathsf{C}$.

Finally, we define $\mathcal{P}'$ as a composition of $\mathcal{M}$ with the transformed program $(\mathcal{P}\ \mathcal{L})^*$, and get the required equivalence:

Claim (Correctness). The following conditions are equivalent:

- $\mathcal{P}$ has a complete run from $\mathbf{0}$ that does at most m zero tests;
- $\mathcal{P}\ \mathcal{L}$ has a complete run from $\mathbf{0}$ that does exactly m zero tests;
- $(\mathcal{P}\ \mathcal{L})^*$ has a d-zeroing run from $\text{RATIO}(2(m+1), \mathsf{b}, \mathsf{c}, \mathsf{d}, \mathsf{C})$;
- $\mathcal{P}' = \mathcal{M}\ (\mathcal{P}\ \mathcal{L})^*$ has a $\{\mathsf{z}, \mathsf{d}\}$-zeroing run from $\mathbf{0}$.

The second and the third point are equivalent due to Lemma 12, while the equivalence of the third and the last point follows by Lemma 8 in Sect. 6.

The program $\mathcal{P}'$ has $3k + 4$ counters ($3k + 2$ counters of $\mathcal{M}$ plus x, y) but, since $k \geqslant 3$, this number can be decreased back to $3k + 2$, by re-using some of $3k - 2$ counters from $\mathsf{C}' = \mathsf{C} - \{\mathsf{b}, \mathsf{c}, \mathsf{d}, \mathsf{z}\}$ in place of x, y. The latter equivalence in the correctness claim remains true, as z-zeroing runs of $\mathcal{M}$ from $\mathbf{0}$ are necessarily C'-zeroing too, by the definition of multipliers.

This completes the proof of the first part of Theorem 2. The second part, namely ACKERMANN-hardness, is shown in exactly the same way, but using $k = n$ instead of a fixed k.

Acknowledgments. This work has been partially supported by the ERC grant INFSYS, agreement no. 950398, and by NCN grant 2021/41/B/ST6/00535.

References

1. van der Aalst, W.M.P.: Business process management as the "killer app" for Petri nets. Softw. Syst. Model. **14**(2), 685–691 (2015). https://doi.org/10.1007/s10270-014-0424-2
2. Angeli, D., Leenheer, P.D., Sontag, E.D.: Persistence results for chemical reaction networks with time-dependent kinetics and no global conservation laws. J. SIAM Appl. Math. **71**(1), 128–146 (2011)
3. Baldan, P., Cocco, N., Marin, A., Simeoni, M.: Petri nets for modelling metabolic pathways: a survey. Nat. Comput. **9**(4), 955–989 (2010). https://doi.org/10.1007/s11047-010-9180-6
4. Bojańczyk, M., David, C., Muscholl, A., Schwentick, T., Segoufin, L.: Two-variable logic on data words. ACM Trans. Comput. Log. **12**(4), 27:1–27:26 (2011). http://doi.acm.org/10.1145/1970398.1970403
5. Bouajjani, A., Emmi, M.: Analysis of recursively parallel programs. ACM Trans. Program. Lang. Syst. **35**(3), 10:1–10:49 (2013). http://doi.acm.org/10.1145/2518188
6. Burns, F.P., Koelmans, A., Yakovlev, A.: WCET analysis of superscalar processors using simulation with coloured Petri nets. Real-Time Syst. **18**(2/3), 275–288 (2000). https://doi.org/10.1023/A:1008101416758
7. Colcombet, T., Manuel, A.: Generalized data automata and fixpoint logic. In: FSTTCS. LIPIcs, vol. 29, pp. 267–278. Schloss Dagstuhl (2014). https://doi.org/10.4230/LIPIcs.FSTTCS.2014.267
8. Crespi-Reghizzi, S., Mandrioli, D.: Petri nets and Szilard languages. Inf. Control **33**(2), 177–192 (1977). https://doi.org/10.1016/S0019-9958(77)90558-7
9. Czerwiński, W., Jecker, I., Lasota, S., Leroux, J., Orlikowski, Ł.: New lower bounds for reachability in vector addition systems. In: Proceedings of FSTTCS 2023. LIPIcs, vol. 284, pp. 35:1–35:22. Schloss Dagstuhl - Leibniz-Zentrum für Informatik (2023). https://doi.org/10.4230/LIPICS.FSTTCS.2023.35
10. Czerwiński, W., Lasota, S., Lazic, R., Leroux, J., Mazowiecki, F.: The reachability problem for Petri nets is not elementary. In: Charikar, M., Cohen, E. (eds.) Proceedings of STOC 2019, pp. 24–33. ACM (2019)
11. Czerwiński, W., Lasota, S., Lazic, R., Leroux, J., Mazowiecki, F.: The reachability problem for Petri nets is not elementary. J. ACM **68**(1), 7:1–7:28 (2021). https://doi.org/10.1145/3422822
12. Czerwiński, W., Lasota, S., Orlikowski, Ł.: Improved lower bounds for reachability in vector addition systems. In: Proceedings of ICALP. LIPIcs, vol. 198, pp. 128:1–128:15 (2021)
13. Czerwiński, W., Orlikowski, Ł.: Reachability in vector addition systems is Ackermann-complete. In: Proceedings of FOCS 2021. pp. 1229–1240. IEEE (2021)
14. Decker, N., Habermehl, P., Leucker, M., Thoma, D.: Ordered Navigation on Multi-attributed Data Words. In: Baldan, P., Gorla, D. (eds.) CONCUR 2014. LNCS, vol. 8704, pp. 497–511. Springer, Heidelberg (2014). https://doi.org/10.1007/978-3-662-44584-6_34

15. Demri, S., Figueira, D., Praveen, M.: Reasoning about data repetitions with counter systems. Logical Methods Comput. Sci. **12**(3) (2016). https://doi.org/10.2168/LMCS-12(3:1)2016
16. Esparza, J., Ganty, P., Leroux, J., Majumdar, R.: Verification of population protocols. Acta Inf. **54**(2), 191–215 (2017). https://doi.org/10.1007/s00236-016-0272-3
17. Fu, Y., Yang, Q., Zheng, Y.: Improved algorithm for reachability in d-VASS. In: Proceedings of ICALP 2024. LIPIcs, vol. 297, pp. 136:1–136:18 (2024). https://doi.org/10.4230/LIPICS.ICALP.2024.136
18. Ganty, P., Majumdar, R.: Algorithmic verification of asynchronous programs. ACM Trans. Program. Lang. Syst. **34**(1), 6:1–6:48 (2012). http://doi.acm.org/10.1145/2160910.2160915
19. German, S.M., Sistla, A.P.: Reasoning about systems with many processes. J. ACM **39**(3), 675–735 (1992). http://doi.acm.org/10.1145/146637.146681
20. Greibach, S.A.: Remarks on blind and partially blind one-way multicounter machines. Theor. Comput. Sci. **7**, 311–324 (1978). https://doi.org/10.1016/0304-3975(78)90020-8
21. Hofman, P., Lasota, S.: Linear equations with ordered data. In: Proceedings of CONCUR. LIPIcs, vol. 118, pp. 24:1–24:17. Schloss Dagstuhl (2018). https://doi.org/10.4230/LIPIcs.CONCUR.2018.24
22. Hopcroft, J.E., Pansiot, J.: On the reachability problem for 5-dimensional vector addition systems. Theor. Comput. Sci. **8**, 135–159 (1979). https://doi.org/10.1016/0304-3975(79)90041-0
23. Kaiser, A., Kroening, D., Wahl, T.: A widening approach to multithreaded program verification. ACM Trans. Program. Lang. Syst. **36**(4), 14:1–14:29 (2014). http://doi.acm.org/10.1145/2629608
24. Kanovich, M.I.: Petri nets, Horn programs, linear logic and vector games. Ann. Pure Appl. Logic **75**(1–2), 107–135 (1995). https://doi.org/10.1016/0168-0072(94)00060-G
25. Karp, R.M., Miller, R.E.: Parallel program schemata. J. Comput. Syst. Sci. **3**(2), 147–195 (1969). https://doi.org/10.1016/S0022-0000(69)80011-5
26. Kosaraju, S.R.: Decidability of reachability in vector addition systems (preliminary version). In: Proceedings of STOC. pp. 267–281. ACM (1982). http://doi.acm.org/10.1145/800070.802201
27. Lambert, J.: A structure to decide reachability in Petri nets. Theor. Comput. Sci. **99**(1), 79–104 (1992). https://doi.org/10.1016/0304-3975(92)90173-D
28. Lasota, S.: VASS reachability in three steps. CoRR **abs/1812.11966** (2018). http://arxiv.org/abs/1812.11966
29. Lasota, S.: Improved Ackermannian lower bound for the Petri nets reachability problem. In: Proceedings of STACS 2022. LIPIcs, vol. 219, pp. 46:1–46:15. Schloss Dagstuhl - Leibniz-Zentrum für Informatik (2022). https://doi.org/10.4230/LIPICS.STACS.2022.46
30. Leroux, H., Andreu, D., Godary-Dejean, K.: Handling exceptions in Petri net-based digital architecture: from formalism to implementation on FPGAs. IEEE Trans. Ind. Inf. **11**(4), 897–906 (2015)
31. Leroux, J.: The general vector addition system reachability problem by Presburger inductive invariants. Logical Methods Comput. Sci. **6**(3) (2010). https://doi.org/10.2168/LMCS-6(3:22)2010
32. Leroux, J.: Vector addition system reachability problem: a short self-contained proof. In: POPL, pp. 307–316. ACM (2011). http://doi.acm.org/10.1145/1926385.1926421

33. Leroux, J.: Vector addition systems reachability problem (A simpler solution). In: Turing-100. EPiC Series in Computing, vol. 10, pp. 214–228. EasyChair (2012). http://www.easychair.org/publications/paper/106497
34. Leroux, J.: The reachability problem for Petri nets is not primitive recursive. In: Proceedings of FOCS 2021. IEEE (2021)
35. Leroux, J., Schmitz, S.: Demystifying reachability in vector addition systems. In: Proceedings of LICS, pp. 56–67 (2015)
36. Leroux, J., Schmitz, S.: Reachability in vector addition systems is primitive-recursive in fixed dimension. In: Proceedings of LICS, pp. 1–13. IEEE (2019)
37. Li, Y., Deutsch, A., Vianu, V.: VERIFAS: A practical verifier for artifact systems. PVLDB **11**(3), 283–296 (2017). http://www.vldb.org/pvldb/vol11/p283-li.pdf
38. Lipton, R.J.: The reachability problem requires exponential space. Tech. rep. 62, Yale University (1976). http://cpsc.yale.edu/sites/default/files/files/tr63.pdf
39. Löb, M.H., Wainer, S.S.: Hierarchies of number-theoretic functions. I. Archiv für mathematische Logik und Grundlagenforschung **13**(1–2), 39–51 (1970). https://doi.org/10.1007/BF01967649
40. Mayr, E.W.: An algorithm for the general Petri net reachability problem. In: STOC, pp. 238–246. ACM (1981). http://doi.acm.org/10.1145/800076.802477
41. Mayr, E.W.: An algorithm for the general Petri net reachability problem. SIAM J. Comput. **13**(3), 441–460 (1984). https://doi.org/10.1137/0213029
42. Meyer, R.: A theory of structural stationarity in the *pi*-calculus. Acta Inf. **46**(2), 87–137 (2009). https://doi.org/10.1007/s00236-009-0091-x
43. Petri, C.A.: Kommunikation mit Automaten. Ph.D. thesis, Universität Hamburg (1962). http://edoc.sub.uni-hamburg.de/informatik/volltexte/2011/160/
44. Sacerdote, G.S., Tenney, R.L.: The decidability of the reachability problem for vector addition systems (preliminary version). In: STOC, pp. 61–76. ACM (1977). http://doi.acm.org/10.1145/800105.803396
45. Schmitz, S.: Complexity hierarchies beyond elementary. TOCT **8**(1), 3:1–3:36 (2016)
46. Schmitz, S.: The complexity of reachability in vector addition systems. SIGLOG News **3**(1), 4–21 (2016)

Model Checking Timed and Strategic Properties

Étienne André[1,2], Wojciech Penczek[3], and Laure Petrucci[1(✉)]

[1] Université Sorbonne Paris Nord, LIPN, CNRS UMR 7030, 93430 Villetaneuse, France
laure.petrucci@lipn.univ-paris13.fr
[2] Institut Universitaire de France (IUF), Paris, France
[3] Institute of Computer Science, PAS, Warsaw, Poland

1 Introduction

The verification of real-time systems is a crucial area of research, driven by the growing need to ensure the safety of time-sensitive distributed systems. Failure in these systems can lead to severe consequences, both for human lives and hardware. For instance, hardware components with specific response times must adhere to strict deadlines. Temporal logic methods have proven valuable for verifying these systems, particularly in the context of finite abstract models that can be analyzed using model checking techniques. Essentially, this method involves determining whether a temporal formula holds true for a model that represents all possible system computations.

In this article, we review the most widely studied models of real-time systems in the literature. These models are either synchronous, such as Tight Durational Concurrent Game Structures [78], or asynchronous, including Timed Automata [4], Time Petri Nets [87], and Timed Petri Nets [102]. Temporal logics are employed to formally express system properties, such as behavior and reachability, where specific events or states must occur at designated times.

Unfortunately, the practical applicability of model checking methods is significantly constrained by the state explosion problem. This issue arises when models grow exponentially with the number of concurrent processes in a system. In real-time systems, the problem is particularly severe due to the infinite nature of the dense time domain. To address this issue, we discuss various methods used to mitigate the state explosion problem, including abstractions, equivalence-based reductions, symbolic model checking (involving different types of BDDs, SAT- and SMT-based verification, and bounded model checking), partial order reductions, upper and lower approximations, as well as different smart exploration strategies such as on-the-fly exploration and selecting the exploration order.

Despite sharing a similar underlying timed structure, model checking methods for Time(d) Petri Nets and Timed Automata have largely been developed independently. However, several efforts have been made to bridge the two approaches. These include attempts to structurally translate one model into the other [45,48,58,61,82,100,104], as well as efforts to adapt existing verification techniques [55,93,107].

F. Kordon et al. (Eds.): *Transactions on Petri Nets and Other Models of Concurrency XVIII*, LNCTPN 16260, pp. 150–194, 2026.
https://doi.org/10.1007/978-3-662-73305-9_6

Systems are frequently designed in a modular or compositional manner, where multiple parties—or autonomous agents, as seen in multi-agent systems—are modeled individually. Each agent has its own behavior, yet they can interact through shared actions and employ strategic abilities to collaborate toward a common goal. Networks of autonomous agents are commonly used to model and verify socio-technical systems, where agents make autonomous decisions based on either a local or global perspective of the environment. In this context, we consider two types of models that incorporate strategic abilities: synchronous models like Tight Durational Concurrent Game Structures [78], and asynchronous models such as Asynchronous Multi-Agent Systems [65].

There are two key modal logics that facilitate reasoning about strategic interactions in agent systems by extending temporal logic with the game-theoretic concept of strategic ability. These are alternating-time temporal logic (ATL^*) and its fragment ATL [6]. Recently, a further extension of CTL with strategic operators, known as SCTL, was introduced [23]. These logics enable the expression of statements regarding what groups of agents can achieve collaboratively.

Such properties are crucial for specifying, verifying, and reasoning about interactions in agent systems [60,72,73], as well as for ensuring security and usability in e-voting protocols [28]. They have gained prominence due to the rapid development of verification algorithms and tools [64,65,85], where "correctness" is determined by the agents' strategic abilities.

In this article, we also explore timed extensions of strategic logics. We start with TATL [15,78] (the discrete-time extension of ATL) and proceed to discuss Strategic Timed CTL (STCTL) [23], the real-time extension of SCTL.

Each of these (timed) strategic logics is interpreted over two types of structures: synchronous (Timed) Multi-Agent Systems (MAS) and asynchronous (Timed) Multi-Agent Systems (AMAS). We consider several semantic variants. Furthermore, Timed MAS and Timed AMAS can be either discrete (D) or continuous (C).

Additionally, we examine the complexity of the model checking problem for different combinations of these semantics. For instance, the complexity of model checking for $\mathsf{SCTL[ir]}$ is equivalent to that of $\mathsf{ATL[ir]}$, whereas the complexity for $\mathsf{STCTL[ir]}$ aligns with that of TCTL. We give hints on approaches to combat the state space explosion or undecidability of model checking in order to enable model checking in practice.

We also show how the previous models can be extended with parametric time, so as to handle systems where the actual timing constraints are unknown.

Finally, we give a short overview of the major tools dealing with time and strategies, with automata or Petri nets based models.

2 Timed Models

In this section, we present two main formalisms that allow for modelling timed systems: Timed Automata and Time Petri Nets. Each of them is defined and illustrated with examples. Their behaviour is explained, first as concrete behaviour with actual timing values. Then the need for a symbolic behaviour arises, which is introduced.

2.1 Timed Automata

A *Timed Automaton* (TA) is a finite state automaton, with sets of locations and actions, augmented with a set of clocks [4]. Figure 1 depicts such an automaton.

Clocks are real-valued variables evolving at the same rate. They can be compared to integer constants in invariants and guards associated with locations and actions, respectively. Location *invariants* express properties to be verified in order to stay at a location. Transition *guards* must be verified to enable a transition. When taking a transition, some clocks can be *reset*, i.e. set to 0.

Example 1. The Timed Automaton in Fig. 1 models a simple coffee machine. It has 3 locations ℓ_0, ℓ_1 and ℓ_2. Location ℓ_0 is the initial one, i.e. the initial state of the system, denoted by a short incoming arrow. The dotted boxes next to locations ℓ_1 and ℓ_2 contain their respective invariants. Location ℓ_0 has no invariant pictured, as it is always `true`. When in ℓ_0, a user can ask the machine to prepare a coffee. This is modelled by transition start which resets both clocks x and y. Then, the state of the system becomes ℓ_1. The invariant of ℓ_1 indicates that the machine can remain in this location as long as $y \leq 5$, i.e. at most 5 time units. While in ℓ_1, sugar can be added, using transition sugar. The guard $x \geq 1$ indicates that 1 time unit must have passed, measured by clock x before this action can happen. When adding sugar, clock x is reset. Thus, at least 1 time unit elapses between 2 sugars. When clock y reaches 5, transition prepare can be taken, leading to location ℓ_2, where the coffee is poured. When y is 8, the coffee is served, and the machine is ready to start again in ℓ_0.

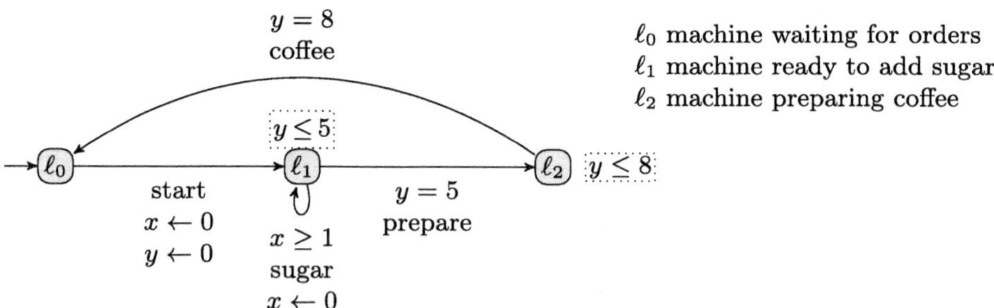

Fig. 1. Timed Automaton for the coffee machine

Formal Definition of Timed Automata

To capture the clock constraints, we first define clock guards:

Definition 1. *Let $X = \{x_1, \ldots, x_n\}$ be a set of variables. A* zone *is a convex polyhedron in $\mathbb{R}^n$ which can be described by a finite set of inequalities of the form $x_i \sim c$ or $x_i - x_j \sim c$, where $\sim \in \{<, \leq, =, \geq, >\}$ and $c \in \mathbb{Q}$. A* clock guard *is a zone made from inequalities only of the form $x_i \sim c$. Let $\mathcal{CG}(n)$ be the set of all clock guards over $\{x_1, \ldots, x_n\}$.*

Given a clock guard g, we write $v \models g$ if the expression obtained by replacing each x with $v(x)$ in g evaluates to true.

Remark 1. Timed Automata were originally defined with integer constants in [4], while our definition allows *rational*-valued constants. By assuming a rescaling of the constants (i.e. by multiplying all constants in a TA by the least common multiple of their denominators), we obtain an equivalent (integer-valued) TA.

Example 2. Let us consider $X = \{x_1, x_2\}$. Figure 2 graphically represents the zone corresponding to $x_1 \leq 3 \wedge x_1 \geq 1 \wedge x_2 - x_1 \geq 0$.

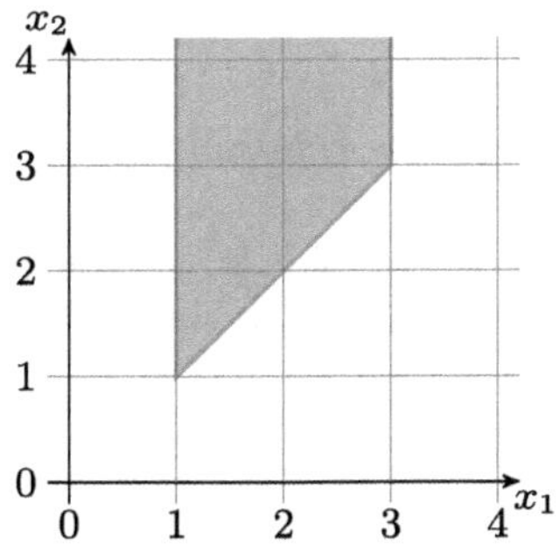

Fig. 2. $x_1 \leq 3 \wedge x_1 \geq 1 \wedge x_2 - x_1 \geq 0$

We can now formally define Timed Automata:

Definition 2. *A* Timed Automaton *is a tuple $\mathcal{A} = \langle L, \ell_0, \Sigma, X, E, I \rangle$ where:*

- *L is a finite set of locations*
- *$\ell_0 \in L$ is an initial location*
- *Σ is a finite set of actions*
- *$X = \{x_1, \ldots, x_n\}$ is a finite set of clocks*
- *$E \subseteq L \times \mathcal{CG}(n) \times \Sigma \times \mathcal{P}(X) \times L$ is a transition relation whose elements are a source location, a clock guard (called "transition guard"), an action, clocks to be reset, and a target location*
- *$I : L \to \mathcal{CG}(n)$ is a clock guard called location invariant.*

Remark 2. Allowing *zones* instead of *clock guards* in guards is sometimes considered, and referred to as *diagonal constraints.* Such diagonal constraints have an impact in some decidability situations, and may require specific algorithms. See, e.g. [39,40,56].

Remark 3. Allowing *real*-valued constants instead of *rational* ones in clock constraints renders the reachability problem undecidable [89], which is why we do not allow them in our definition.

Concrete Semantics of Timed Automata

The concrete semantics of a Timed Automaton allows for expressing its behaviour with actual time values. At any time in the life of a system, its state is described by its location and the values of its clocks.

Definition 3. *The* concrete state *of a Timed Automaton is a pair* (ℓ, v)*, where*

- ℓ *is a location*
- v *is a valuation of all clocks*

The system can evolve from one concrete state to the next by either taking an enabled transition that satisfies the clocks constraints, or by letting time pass.

Definition 4. *Let* $s = (\ell, v)$ *be a state. The concrete behavior of the timed automaton from state s is defined by:*

- *(time elapse* $\delta \in \mathbb{R}_+$*)* $s \xrightarrow{\delta} s'$ *with* $s' = (\ell, v')$ *iff* $\forall x \in X : v'(x) = v(x) + \delta$ *and* $v' \models I(\ell)$
- *(action* $a \in \Sigma$*)* $s \xrightarrow{a} s'$ *with* $s' = (\ell', v')$ *iff* $\exists (\ell, g, a, R, \ell') \in E$ *such that* $v \models g$, $\forall x \in R : v'(x) = 0 \wedge \forall x \notin R : v'(x) = v(x)$*, and* $v' \models I(\ell')$

Definition 5. *A* concrete run *is an alternating sequence of concrete states and actions or time elapse.*

Example 3. Here are some possible concrete runs for the coffee machine of Fig. 1 (also remember that due to the guards on the arcs exiting ℓ_1 and ℓ_2, it is necessary to wait there):

- Coffee with no sugar:

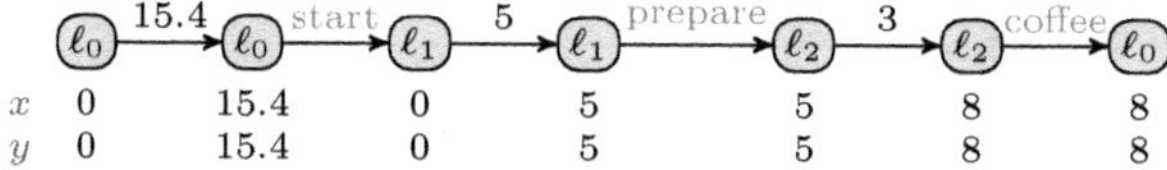

In this run, we first wait for 15.4 time units, thus both clocks x and y, initially with value 0, increase to 15.4. This value is arbitrary, since it is the time for a user to start ordering a coffee. Then, the user presses the start button, leading to location ℓ_1 and resetting both clocks. Afterwards, we wait for 5 time units, and the machine delivers a prepare. Both clocks then have value 5. After waiting for another 3 time units, they reach value 8 which allows for serving the coffee and return to ℓ_0.

- Coffee with 2 doses of sugar:

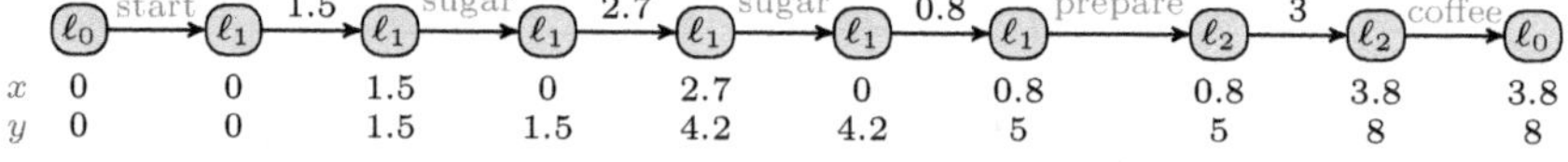

Now, the user immediately presses the start button. The machine goes to location ℓ_1 with both clocks having value 0. If the user wants some sugar, they must wait for x to be at least 1 in order the satisfy the guard of transition sugar. Here the wait is 1.5 time units. This action resets x but not y. They thus have different values. This way, in location ℓ_1, x measures the time for having a sugar while y measures the time since the start button was pressed.

2.2 Time Petri Nets

Time Petri Nets are Petri Nets [98] (containing places and transitions) augmented with firing time intervals of transitions [87]. Transitions can be fired when a time in this interval has passed since the transition was enabled.

Time Petri Nets should not be confused with Time**d** Petri Nets which are another formalism with a global clock and where time is associated to the availability of tokens [102].

Example 4. Let us consider the Time Petri Net of Fig. 3. The initial marking has only places p1 and p2 marked with one token each. This marking enables transitions t1 and t2. The intervals specified denote that transition t2 can be fired between times 0 and 3 (from the time it is enabled) while t1 can be fired between 1 and 2. As in Timed Automata, an action can be taken provided the time constraints are satisfied, or time can elapse.

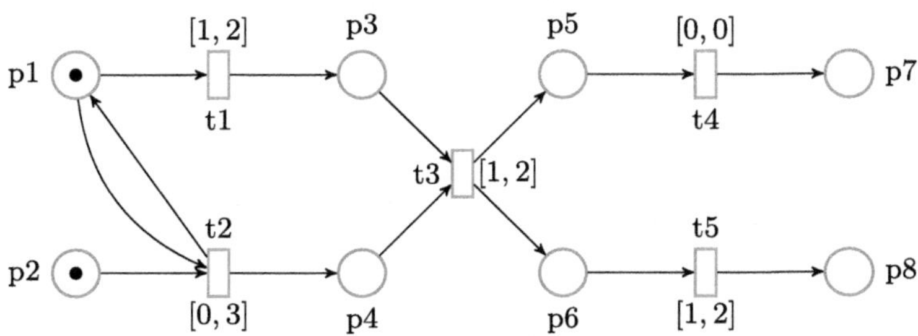

Fig. 3. A Time Petri Net

Formal Definition of Time Petri Nets

Time Petri Nets are formally defined as follows.

Definition 6. *A* Time Petri net *is a tuple* $\mathcal{N} = \langle P, T, Pre, Post, Eft, Lft, M_0 \rangle$ *where:*

- P *is a finite set of places*
- T *is a finite set of transitions*
- $Pre, Post : P \times T \to \mathbb{N}$ *and are the* pre- *and* post- *conditions*
- $Eft : T \to \mathbb{N}$ *and* $Lft : T \to \mathbb{N} \cup \{\infty\}$ *are the earliest and latest firing times of transitions:* $\forall t \in T : Eft(t) \leq Lft(t)$
- $M_0 : P \to \mathbb{N}$ *is the initial marking*

Enabledness of transitions only depends on the current marking:

Definition 7. *Enabled transitions*

- *A transition* $t \in T$ *is* enabled *at a marking* m*, denoted* $m[t\rangle$*, iff* $\forall p \in P$: $Pre(p, t) \leq m(p)$
- $en(m) = \{t \in T | m[t\rangle\}$ *denotes the set of enabled transitions at marking* m.

Concrete Semantics of Time Petri Nets

As with Timed Automata, we define first the concrete states of a Time Petri Net and then its concrete behaviour.

Definition 8. *A* concrete state *of a Timed Petri Net is a pair* (m, f)*, where:*

- m *is a marking*
- f *is a firing interval function assigning to each* $t \in en(m)$ *the time interval in which* t *can fire*
- $s_0 = (m_0, f_0)$ *with* $\forall t \in en(m_0) : f_0(t) = [Eft(t), Lft(t)]$

The time elapse is not allowed to disable an enabled transition[1]. Note that this definition of the semantics uses the interval as a kind of sliding window in which the time of firing will occur, i.e. the remaining time to fire the transition.

Definition 9. *The concrete behaviour of a Time Petri Net from a state* (m, f) *is defined by:*

- *(time elapse* $\delta \in \mathbb{R}_+$*)* $(m, f) \xrightarrow{\delta} (m, f')$ *with* $\forall t \in en(m), f(t) = [a, b], \delta \leq b$ *:* $f'(t) = [\max(0, a - \delta), b - \delta]$
- *(transition* $t \in E$*)* $(m, f) \xrightarrow{t} (m', f')$ *with* $t \in en(m), f(t) = [0, b]$ $\forall p \in P, m'(p) = m(p) - Pre(p, t) + Post(p, t)$
$\forall t' \in en(m')$ *: if* $t' \notin en(m - Pre(., t))$
then $f'(t') = [Eft(t'), Lft(t')]$
else $f'(t') = f(t')$

Definition 10. *A* concrete run *is an alternating sequence of concrete states and actions or time elapse.*

Example 5. Let us consider again the Time Petri Net in Fig. 3. Here is a possible concrete run:

$p1 + p2$, $f(t1) = [1, 2]$, $f(t2) = [0, 3]$ $\xrightarrow{0.5}$ $p1 + p2$, $f(t1) = [0.5, 1.5]$, $f(t2) = [0, 2.5]$ $\xrightarrow{t2}$ $p1 + p4$, $f(t1) = [1, 2]$ $\xrightarrow{1}$ $p1 + p4$, $f(t1) = [0, 1]$ $\xrightarrow{t1}$

$p3 + p4$, $f(t3) = [1, 2]$ $\xrightarrow{1.5}$ $p3 + p4$, $f(t3) = [0, 0.5]$ $\xrightarrow{t3}$ $p5 + p6$, $f(t4) = [0, 0]$, $f(t5) = [1, 2]$ $\xrightarrow{t4}$ $p6 + p7$, $f(t5) = [1, 2]$ $\xrightarrow{2}$

$p6 + p7$, $f(t5) = [0, 0]$ $\xrightarrow{t5}$ $p7 + p8$

Initially, only places $p1$ and $p2$ hold a token. Transitions $t1$ and $t2$ have just been enabled, so their corresponding firing intervals in the initial state has

[1] Note that other semantics exist, where time can go beyond the intervals boundaries, but we do not consider them here.

their earliest and latest firing times as bounds. Then, this run waits for 0.5 time units. The new state holds the same marking, while the intervals are shifted by 0.5 (without becoming negative). Hence $f(t2) = [0, 2.5]$. In this state only t2 can be fired, and t1 still has to wait for at least another 0.5 time units (and no more than 1.5). In the run, transition t2 is fired. Since it removes one token from p1 it disables momentarily t1. When firing, it puts back a token in p1, enabling t1 again. Thus, the interval $f(t1)$ is set to its initial value. In the 7th state, there is no possible choice. Indeed, $f(t4) = [0, 0]$, so we cannot wait and t4 must be fired as t5 is enabled but not yet ready to be fired.

2.3 Concrete Models

A concrete model is composed of states, transitions, and propositional variables assigned to states. This assignment is used later for interpreting temporal logics over concrete models.

Definition 11. *A* concrete model *is a tuple* $\mathcal{M}_c = \langle (S, s_0, \rightarrow), V_c \rangle$ *where:*

- *S is the set of concrete states*
- *s_0 is the initial state*
- *$\rightarrow$ is the transition relation, comprising both action and delay transitions*
- *$V_c : S \rightarrow \mathcal{P}(\mathcal{PV})$ is a valuation function with $\mathcal{PV}$ a set of propositional variables*

Example 6. For Time Petri Nets, a valuation function is such that $\forall s = (m, f)$: $V_c(s) = \{p \mid m(p) \neq 0\}$ where $\mathcal{PV} = P$, indicating the marked places.

2.4 Symbolic Semantics

Using the concrete semantics of a timed model has drawbacks: it is impossible to enumerate all timings, and the generated state spaces may be infinite. In order to alleviate these problems, it is desirable to use symbolic semantics instead. This is achieved by grouping similar states within a symbolic representation, and using an abstract model instead of a concrete one.

Abstract Models

We first define an abstract model of a concrete model, and we will then explicit how it applies to Time Petri Nets and Timed Automata.

Definition 12. $\mathcal{M}_a = \langle (W, w_0, \rightarrow), V_a \rangle$ *is an* abstract model *for a concrete model* $\mathcal{M}_c = \langle (S, s_0, \rightarrow), V_c \rangle$ *if:*

- *each node $w \in W$ is a set of states of S*
- $s_0 \in w_0$
- $w_1 \xrightarrow{b} w_2$ *if* $\exists s_1 \in w_1, \exists s_2 \in w_2 : s_1 \xrightarrow{b} s_2$
- $V_a(w) = V_c(s)$ *for each* $s \in w$

Example 7. Let us consider the concretemodel in blue. The red model is an abstract model for this concrete model. Indeed, each abstract node contains two concrete nodes, and each abstract transition has a corresponding concrete transition.

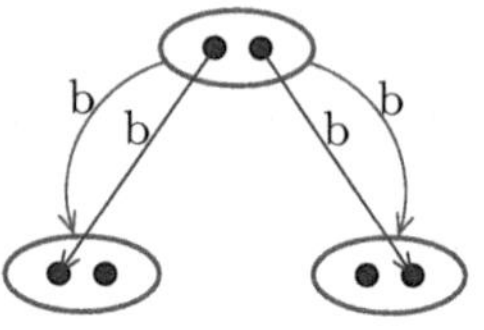

Abstract models may satisfy some desirable properties such as surjectivity or bisimulation.

Definition 13. *An abstract model is* surjective *when:*
$w_1 \xrightarrow{b} w_2$ *iff* $\forall s_2 \in w_2 : \exists s_1 \in w_1, s_1 \xrightarrow{b} s_2$

Example 8. Let us consider the concrete model in blue. The red model is a surjective abstract model for this concrete model. First, it is obvious that it is an abstract model. Then, let us consider $w_0 \xrightarrow{b_1} w_1$. Each concrete state in w_1 has a predecessor by $\xrightarrow{b_1}$ in w_0. Similarly for $w_0 \xrightarrow{b_2} w_2$. Note that a concrete node in w_0 has no successor, which is compatible with surjectivity.

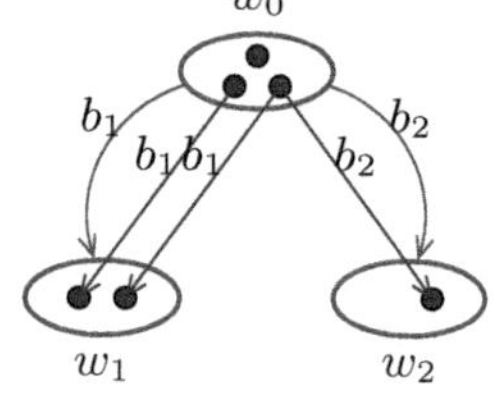

Definition 14. *An abstract model is* bisimulating *(or is a* b-model*) when:*
$w_1 \xrightarrow{b} w_2$ *iff* $\forall s_1 \in w_1 : \exists s_2 \in w_2, s_1 \xrightarrow{b} s_2$

Example 9. Let us consider the concrete modelin blue. The red model is a b-model for this concrete model. First, it is obvious that it is an abstract model. Then, let us consider $w_0 \xrightarrow{b_1} w_1$. Each concrete state in w_0 has a successor by $\xrightarrow{b_1}$ in w_1. Similarly for $w_0 \xrightarrow{b_2} w_2$. Note that a concrete node in w_2 has no predecessor, which is compatible with bisimulation.

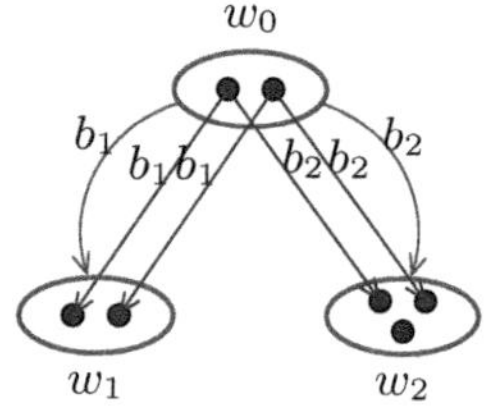

Time Petri Nets: State Classes

Definition 15. *A* state class *of a TPN is a pair* $C = (m, I)$ *where* m *is a marking and* I *is a set of inequalities built over variables corresponding to transitions.*

Example 10. In the figure in the right,we have several states with the same marking m but different time intervals. They are grouped according to the interval for transition t_1, leading to 3 groups where $f(t_1) = [0, 1)$, $f(t_1) = [1, 1]$ and $f(t_1) = (0.5, 1)$. These can be represented by a single state class with marking m and $I = \{0 \leq t_1 \leq 1\}$.

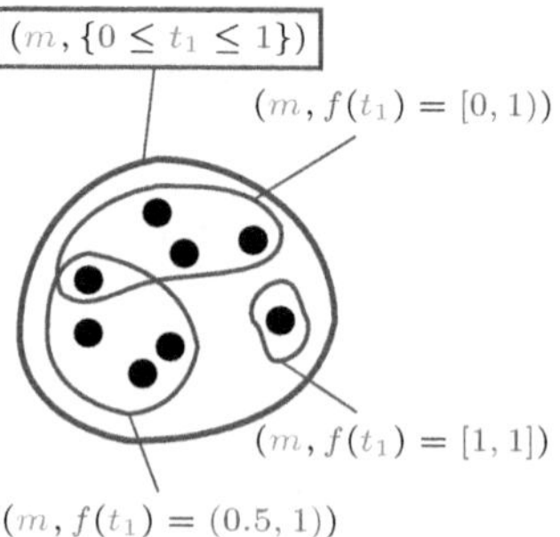

Timed Automata: Zones

Definition 16. *A* zone *of a TA is a pair* $\mathcal{Z} = (\ell, Z)$ *where* ℓ *is a location and* Z *is a zone.*

Example 11. Let us consider again the coffee machine of Fig. 1. Below is a symbolic run of the automaton. Initially, both clocks have the same positive value. This is still valid when letting time elapse. Then after action start, another symbolic state is reached where both clocks are still equal and y is less than 5. Intuitively, this is due to both clocks being reset by the action, so as long as the system remains in ℓ_1 (just letting time elapse) their values are the same. Due to the invariant $I(\ell_1)$ the value of y cannot go beyond 5. When taking prepare, y is exactly 5, both clocks are equal, and time can elapse in ℓ_2 until 8, as indicated by the invariant $I(\ell_2)$, hence the associated zone $5 \leq y \leq 8$. When taking coffee, y has value 8, and time can elapse when in ℓ_0 without an upper bound since the invariant is `true`.

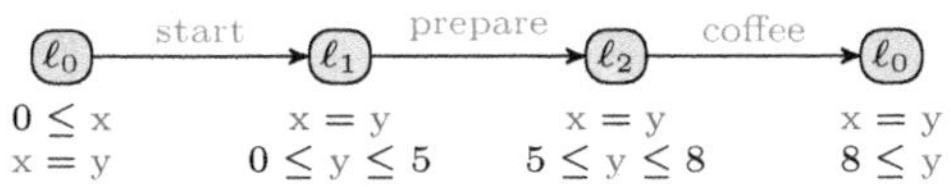

ℓ_0 —start→ ℓ_1 —prepare→ ℓ_2 —coffee→ ℓ_0

ℓ_0	ℓ_1	ℓ_2	ℓ_0
$0 \leq x$ $x = y$	$x = y$ $0 \leq y \leq 5$	$x = y$ $5 \leq y \leq 8$	$x = y$ $8 \leq y$

2.5 From Time Petri Nets to Timed Automata

Building a Timed Automaton equivalent to a given Time Petri Net is easy. Locations in the automaton are labelled with the marking in the Petri net. There is one clock for each transition. The invariants on locations are built from the enabled transitions clocks and their interval upper bound. The value of clocks should not exceed it. The guards of transitions correspond to their intervals. Moreover, a clock is reset whenever its transition in the Petri net is newly enabled (either because it becomes enabled or because it is disabled and then enabled again by the transition firing).

Equivalence between Timed Automata and Time Petri Nets and translations between these two formalisms were considered notably in [44,45,49].

Example 12. Let us apply such a procedure to the Time Petri Net in Fig. 3. Both the Time Petri Net and the obtained Timed Automaton are displayed in Fig. 4.

The initial location corresponds to the initial marking {p1,p2}. Transitions t1 and t2 are enabled. Their corresponding clocks in the automaton should not exceed their latest firing time in the Petri net. Hence the invariant $x_1 \leq 2 \wedge x_2 \leq 3$.

Transition t1 can be fired only if the earliest firing time has been reached and the latest firing time not exceeded. This is modelled by the guard $1 \leq x_1 \leq 2$ in the automaton. The marking obtained by firing t1 is {p2,p3}, labelling the target location.

Transition t2 has, similarly, the guard $0 \leq x_2 \leq 3$. It consumes the token required for t1 to fire and immediately puts it back. Thus t1 is newly enabled and its clock is reset by action t2 ($x_1 \leftarrow 0$). The marking obtained by firing t2 in the Petri net only enables t1, hence no other clock is reset. The target location, labelled by {p1,p4}, has invariant $x_1 \leq 2$, guaranteeing that the latest firing time of t1 is not exceeded. The other locations and transitions of the automaton are constructed in a similar manner.

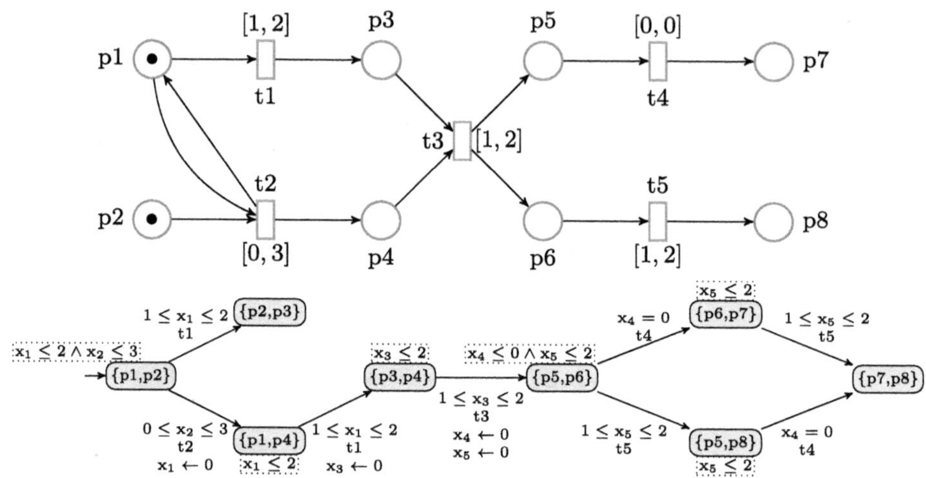

Fig. 4. The Time Petri Net from Fig. 3 and an equivalent Timed Automaton

3 Temporal Logics for Timed Systems

Temporal logics allow for expressing properties of the *dynamic behaviour* of the system. It provides a *formal syntax and semantics* to avoid any ambiguity. Temporal logics formulae capture statements and reasoning that involve the notion of *order in time*.

Here, we first recall the basics of temporal logics, and then extend them to timed systems and systems with additional strategic abilities. More details on the basic logics can be found in paper [111] in this volume.

3.1 Temporal Logic CTL*

The general framework for temporal logics is captured by CTL* which uses the following propositions and operators:

- Propositional variables: $\mathcal{PV} = \{\pi_1, \pi_2, \ldots\}$
- Boolean combinators: `true`, `false`, $\neg$ (negation), $\wedge$ (and), $\vee$ (or), $\implies$ (logical implication), $\iff$ (if and only if)
- Temporal combinators: X (neXt), F (Future), G (Globally), U (Until), W (Weak until), R (Release)
- Quantifiers: A (Always), E (Exists)

Syntax

The *syntax of* CTL*is expressed by state formulas φ_s defined using path formulas φ_p, according to the following grammar:

$$\varphi_s ::= \pi \mid \neg\varphi_s \mid \varphi_s \wedge \varphi_s \mid \varphi_s \vee \varphi_s \mid \varphi_s \implies \varphi_s \mid \varphi_s \iff \varphi_s \mid \mathsf{A}\varphi_p \mid \mathsf{E}\varphi_p$$

$$\varphi_p ::= \varphi_s \mid \varphi_p \wedge \varphi_p \mid \varphi_p \vee \varphi_p \mid \mathsf{X}\varphi_p \mid \mathsf{F}\varphi_p \mid \mathsf{G}\varphi_p \mid \varphi_p\mathsf{U}\varphi_p \mid \varphi_p\mathsf{W}\varphi_p \mid \varphi_p\mathsf{R}\varphi_p$$

Semantics

Let σ be a run and $\pi \in \mathcal{PV}$ a propositional variable.

$\sigma, i \models \varphi$ denotes that at step i of its execution, σ satisfies formula φ.

Table 1 formalises the semantics of operators. In line 1, a run satisfies an propositional variable π at step i iff the state at this step is labelled with π.

Lines 2–6 are for the boolean combinators. The negation of a formula φ is satisfied iff φ is not. The conjunction of two formulae φ and ψ is satisfied iff both φ and ψ hold. Their disjunction holds whenever one of them holds. The implication $\varphi \implies \psi$ is satisfied when either φ does not hold, or when it does and ψ holds as well. The equivalence $\varphi \iff \psi$ is satisfied when either both φ and ψ hold, or both do not.

Lines 7–9 are for unary temporal operators. The next operator ($\mathsf{X}\varphi$) indicates that the formula φ should hold in the next state, i.e. at step $i+1$. The future operator ($\mathsf{F}\varphi$) says it is in the future (or at the current step), and not necessarily on the immediate next one, i.e. at some step $j, i \leq j \leq |\sigma|$. The globally operator ($\mathsf{G}\varphi$) indicates that formula φ holds at all steps, starting from step i.

In lines 10–14 are the binary temporal operators. They express an order in time for the satisfaction of two formulae. For Until ($\varphi\mathsf{U}\psi$), formula φ must hold until at least some step j where ψ becomes true. Note that it is possible that it is the current step, i.e. $i = j$. The weak until ($\varphi\mathsf{W}\psi$) is similar, but also allows for ψ never becoming true, in which case φ must always hold (line 10). Finally, the release operator ($\varphi\mathsf{R}\psi$) is such that ψ should hold until some step j where φ holds as well.

Last, the quantifiers are defined in lines 15 and 16. The existential quantifier $\mathsf{E}\varphi$ is such that there exists a run σ' identical to σ until step i such that σ' satisfies φ at step i. The always quantifier $\mathsf{A}\varphi$ is similar, but applies to all possible runs σ'.

Example 13. Let us consider the coffee machine example. The CTL* formula $\ell_1 \Rightarrow \mathsf{F}(\ell_2\mathsf{U}\ell_0)$ expresses that whenever the machine is in ℓ_1, it will eventually reach a state where the machine is preparing the coffee in ℓ_2 and remains there before delivering the coffee and going back to the initial state ℓ_0.

3.2 Temporal Logic CTL

There are two main temporal logics: CTL and LTL, which are subsets of CTL*. The Linear Time temporal Logic expresses properties on individual runs, and

Table 1. Semantics of CTL*

$\sigma, i \models \pi$	iff $\pi \in V_c(\sigma(i))$
$\sigma, i \models \neg\varphi$	iff $\sigma, i \not\models \varphi$
$\sigma, i \models \varphi \wedge \psi$	iff $\sigma, i \models \varphi$ and $\sigma, i \models \psi$
$\sigma, i \models \varphi \vee \psi$	iff $\sigma, i \models \varphi$ or $\sigma, i \models \psi$
$\sigma, i \models \varphi \implies \psi$	iff $\sigma, i \not\models \varphi$ or ($\sigma, i \models \varphi$ and $\sigma, i \models \psi$)
$\sigma, i \models \varphi \iff \psi$	iff ($\sigma, i \models \varphi$ and $\sigma, i \models \psi$) or ($\sigma, i \not\models \varphi$ and $\sigma, i \not\models \psi$)
$\sigma, i \models \mathsf{X}\varphi$	iff $i < \lvert\sigma\rvert$ and $\sigma, i+1 \models \varphi$
$\sigma, i \models \mathsf{F}\varphi$	iff $\exists j, i \leq j \leq \lvert\sigma\rvert : \sigma, j \models \varphi$
$\sigma, i \models \mathsf{G}\varphi$	iff $\forall j, i \leq j \leq \lvert\sigma\rvert : \sigma, j \models \varphi$
$\sigma, i \models \varphi\mathsf{U}\psi$	iff $\exists j, i \leq j \leq \lvert\sigma\rvert : \sigma, j \models \psi$ and $\forall k, i \leq k < j : \sigma, k \models \varphi$
$\sigma, i \models \varphi\mathsf{W}\psi$	iff $\exists j, i \leq j \leq \lvert\sigma\rvert : \sigma, j \models \psi$ and $\forall k, i \leq k < j : \sigma, k \models \varphi$ or$\forall k, i \leq k \leq \lvert\sigma\rvert : \sigma, k \models \varphi$
$\sigma, i \models \varphi\mathsf{R}\psi$	iff $\exists j, i \leq j \leq \lvert\sigma\rvert : \sigma, j \models \varphi$ and $\forall k, i \leq k \leq j : \sigma, k \models \psi$ or$\forall k, i \leq k \leq \lvert\sigma\rvert : \sigma, k \models \psi$
$\sigma, i \models \mathsf{E}\varphi$	iff $\exists\sigma' : \sigma(0)\ldots\sigma(i) = \sigma'(0)\ldots\sigma'(i)$ and $\sigma', i \models \varphi$
$\sigma, i \models \mathsf{A}\varphi$	iff $\forall\sigma' : \sigma(0)\ldots\sigma(i) = \sigma'(0)\ldots\sigma'(i)$ we have $\sigma', i \models \varphi$

thus does not include quantifiers.[2] The Computation Tree Logic CTL allows for expressing properties on the entire tree of possible executions.

In CTL, each use of a temporal operator (X, F, G, U, W, R) is in the immediate scope of a quantifier (E, A).

Figure 5 illustrates the different combinations of quantifier and temporal operator[3] on a tree of executions starting from a step i. For $\mathsf{EX}\varphi$, there must exist an immediate successor satisfying φ (Fig. 5a), while for $\mathsf{AX}\varphi$, all immediate successors must satisfy φ (Fig. 5f). Similarly, for $\mathsf{EF}\varphi$ to be satisfied, there must exist an execution where φ holds for some state (Fig. 5b), whereas for $\mathsf{AF}\varphi$, it must be true for all possible executions, i.e. all branches of the tree (Fig. 5g). For $\mathsf{EG}\varphi$ (Fig. 5c) and $\mathsf{AG}\varphi$ (Fig. 5h) φ should hold at every step of the execution. For $\mathsf{E}\varphi\mathsf{U}\psi$ (Fig. 5d) and $\mathsf{A}\varphi\mathsf{U}\psi$ (Fig. 5i), ψ holds in some state and φ holds from the root to the predecessor of that state. Note that the case where ψ holds in the root of the tree is not pictured. Finally, for $\mathsf{E}\varphi\mathsf{R}\psi$ (Fig. 5e) and $\mathsf{A}\varphi\mathsf{R}\psi$ (Fig. 5j), φ holds in some state where ψ is also true, and ψ is satisfied by all states from the root of the tree to that state. Note that the case where φ never holds is not pictured.

Example 14. Let us consider the coffee machine example. A desirable property of the coffee machine is that when a user has asked for a coffee, they will eventually get it and the coffee machine then eventually goes back to the initial state. This

[2] We will not detail LTL here but the reader can refer to [43].

[3] The weak until W is not pictured since it is very similar to U and can be expressed with it, as we shall see later.

is expressed by the CTL formula: $\mathsf{AG}(\ell_1 \Rightarrow \mathsf{AF}(\mathsf{A}\ell_2\mathsf{U}\ell_0))$. It is similar to Example 13, where the use of A enforces the formula to hold on all possible runs.

Reducing the Necessary Set of Operators

One can note that some operators are convenient for writing temporal logic properties, but can be expressed by a combination of the other operators. Reducing the set of operators to the essential ones allows for simpler model checking algorithms considering only these.

Proposition 1. *Let φ and ψ be two* CTL *formulae.*

1. $(\sigma, i \models \varphi \wedge \psi) \equiv (\sigma, i \models \neg(\neg\varphi \vee \neg\psi))$
2. $(\sigma, i \models \varphi \implies \psi) \equiv (\sigma, i \models \neg\varphi \vee (\varphi \wedge \psi))$
3. $(\sigma, i \models \varphi \iff \psi) \equiv (\sigma, i \models (\varphi \wedge \psi) \vee (\neg\varphi \wedge \neg\psi))$
4. $(\sigma, i \models \mathsf{F}\varphi) \equiv (\sigma, i \models \mathit{true}\mathsf{U}\varphi)$
5. $(\sigma, i \models \mathsf{G}\varphi) \equiv (\sigma, i \models \neg\mathsf{F}\neg\varphi)$
6. $(\sigma, i \models \varphi\mathsf{W}\psi) \equiv (\sigma, i \models (\varphi\mathsf{U}\psi) \vee \mathsf{G}\varphi)$
7. $(\sigma, i \models \varphi\mathsf{R}\psi) \equiv (\sigma, i \models \psi\mathsf{W}(\varphi \wedge \psi))$

Item 1 is the usual relation between disjunction and conjunction with the negation operator. Items 2 and 3 are the usual relations for implication and equivalence. In Item 4, `true` holds in any state. Therefore, whenever φ becomes satisfied there is an execution in which $\mathsf{F}\varphi$ holds. For Item 5, the execution must satisfy φ at all states. Hence, no state in the execution can satisfy $\neg\varphi$. Item 6 follows directly from the definition of W in Table 1, lines 9 and 10. Finally, Item 7 follows from the definitions of R and W in Table 1, lines 11, 12 and lines 9, 10. Note that Items 2, 3, 6 and 7 can be further rewritten using Items 1, 5 and 6. Hence, the only operators $\neg$, $\vee$, X and U and quantifiers E and A are necessary for CTL formulae.

3.3 Adding Time to CTL: TCTL

Temporal logics allow for expressing properties, with the order in time. However, this is limited for analysing timed models, where the actual time value is important. Therefore, they were extended to TCTL (Timed CTL) where temporal operators also carry time constraints [3].

Syntax of TCTL

TCTL formulae φ are defined by the following grammar, where $\pi \in \mathcal{PV}$ and I is an interval with bounds in $\mathbb{N}$:[4]

$$\varphi ::= \pi \mid \neg\varphi \mid \varphi \vee \varphi \mid \mathsf{A}(\varphi\mathsf{U}_I\varphi) \mid \mathsf{A}(\varphi\mathsf{R}_I\varphi) \mid \mathsf{E}(\varphi\mathsf{U}_I\varphi) \mid \mathsf{E}(\varphi\mathsf{R}_I\varphi)$$

[4] Bounds could also be equivalently defined in $\mathbb{Q}$, using an appropriate rescaling of the constants in the model and in the property.

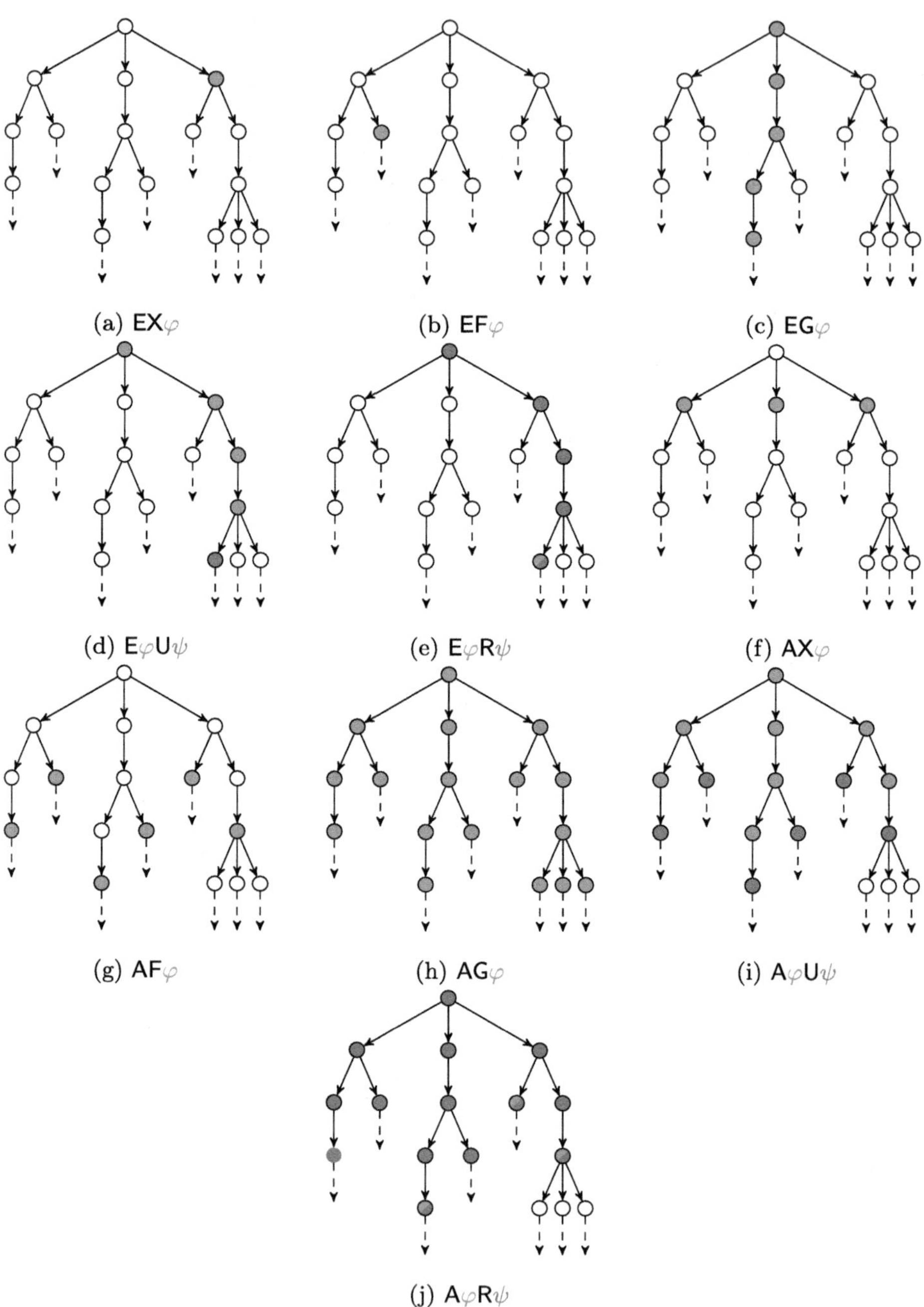

Fig. 5. Illustration of the CTL semantics

Note that operators $\wedge$, F, G and R can be expressed from the other operators, similar to the untimed case. For example, $\mathsf{F}_I\varphi$ can be defined using $\mathtt{true}\mathsf{U}_I\varphi$. Or $\varphi\mathsf{R}_I\psi$ can be defined using $\neg((\neg\varphi)\mathsf{U}_I(\neg\psi))$. Finally, operator X is irrelevant as the next state is not defined in a continuous time context.

Semantics of TCTL

The time interval I indicates the time period when the change from one sub-formula to the other should happen. Since some formulae should hold over a period of time, it is not possible to discretise the execution, but rather consider the time associated with the specific states that intervene in the formula verification.

Let $\sigma' = s_0, \delta_0, s_0', a_0, s_1, \delta_1, s_1', a_1 \ldots$ be a concrete run, where $s_i = (l_i, v_i)$ for $i \geq 0$. We define the dense path $\pi_{\sigma'}$ corresponding to σ' as a mapping from $\mathbb{R}_+$ to a set of concrete states given by $\pi_{\sigma'}(r) = (l_i, v_i + \delta)$, for $r = \Sigma_{j=0}^{i-1}\delta_j + \delta$, where $i \geq 0$ and $0 \leq \delta < \delta_i$.

Table 2 gives a formal definition of $\mathsf{E}\varphi\mathsf{U}_I\psi$ with $I = [a, b]$.[5] Notice that in case of the semantics of TCTL the notions of $\sigma, i \models \phi$ and $\sigma(i) \models \phi$ are equivalent, i.e., the TCTL formulas are evaluated in concrete states. The case $\mathsf{A}\varphi\mathsf{U}_I\psi$ is obtained in a similar manner by replacing appropriately $\exists$ with $\forall$.

Table 2. Semantics of TCTL(assuming $I = [a, b]$)

$\sigma, i \models \mathsf{E}\varphi\mathsf{U}_I\psi$	iff $\exists\sigma' = s_0, \delta_0, s_0', a_0, s_1, \delta_1, s_1', a_1 \ldots$ with $\sigma(i) = \sigma'(0)$ and	1
	$\exists r \in [a, b]$ such that $\pi_{\sigma'}(r) \models \psi$ and	2
	$\pi_{\rho'}(r') \models \varphi$ for all $0 \leq r' < r$	3

The semantics is illustrated in Fig. 6 where the axis represents the time, starting from step i, where $\theta(i)$ is the time at state i. The structure of the executions for the TCTL formulae are not described, as it was previously presented. We instead focus on the timing aspects. As shown in Fig. 6a, for $\mathsf{E}(\varphi\mathsf{U}_{[a,b]}\psi)$ to hold, ψ should be satisfied by some state reached from step i within the time interval $[a, b]$ (corresponding to Table 2, line 2) and φ must always hold until then (Table 2, line 3).

As an illustration, let us now consider $\mathsf{E}(\varphi\mathsf{R}_{[a,b]}\psi)$. There are two possible cases. In the first one, pictured in Fig. 6b, φ is satisfied by some state within the interval $[a, b]$ from step i and ψ holds from the beginning of the interval, i.e. a, until that state included. In the second case, pictured in Fig. 6c, there is no state within the interval $[a, b]$ where φ holds. Then formula ψ must be satisfied during the whole time interval.

Example 15. Let us consider again the coffee machine example, and a TCTL variant of the CTL property in Example 14: $\mathsf{AG}(\ell_1 \Rightarrow \mathsf{AF}(\mathsf{A}\ell_2\mathsf{U}_{[3,3]}\ell_0))$. It additionally indicates that the machine remains 3 time units in ℓ_2.

[5] I could also be an open interval on one or both sides, by changing $\leq$ to $<$ where appropriate.

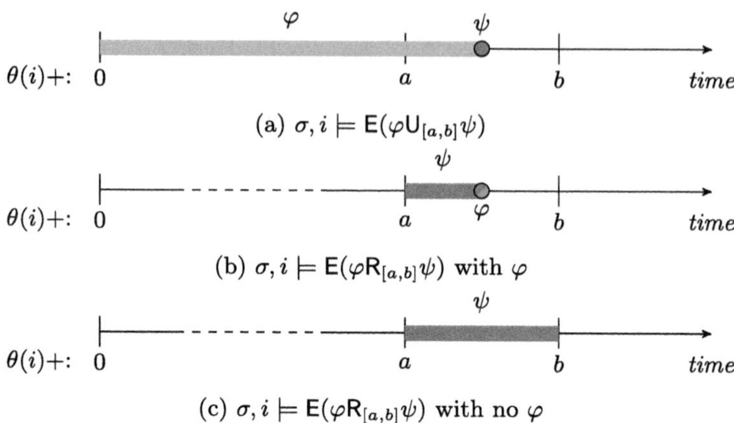

Fig. 6. Illustration of the TCTL semantics

4 Systems of Agents with Strategic Abilities

Systems are often designed in a modular or compositional way, rather than monolithically. This way, several parties (or *agents* as in multi-agents systems) are modelled individually, each having its own individual behaviour. In such systems, different agents can compete or collaborate to reach their own individual or collective goal.

In order to achieve their goal, agents can use *strategic abilities*: they have a strategy to choose an action according to the situation in the system.

Example 16. As an example, users capabilities match some desired properties such as *functionality* (ability of authorized users to complete some tasks) or *security* (inability of unauthorized users to complete certain tasks).

Therefore, there is a need for both formalisms and logics to express their properties to capture these users' abilities.

An application domain of such multi-agent models is voting systems. Desired properties are ballot confidentiality, coercion resistance, end-to-end voter verifiability, the existence (or not) of a suitable strategy for a voter or a coercer.

There is a large diversity of approaches, and thus formalisms to describe the systems and logics to express their properties.

The first paradigm concerns agents performing their actions in a synchronous or asynchronous manner.

In *synchronous models*, agents perform actions *simultaneously*. Thus, actions are global, in the sense that all agents participate, and have a fixed duration, i.e. an action takes a fixed amount of time.

In *asynchronous models*, the agents behave somewhat independently of one another. They can perform their own *individual actions*, regardless of other agents' behaviour. But an agent can also participate in *synchronised actions* together with some other agents. There, as actions are asynchronous, they all have their *own timing* constraints or durations.

A second major difference between agent models resides in time. It can either be *discrete* with only possible individual values of timings being specified, or *continuous* where any value within an interval can be considered.

A third aspect concerns the strategic abilities: *semantic variants* encapsulate different assumptions about agents strategic abilities [1,35,63]. The main variants, detailed in Sect. 4.2, concern:

- **Memory** of agents: *perfect recall* (R) vs. *imperfect recall* (r) strategies.
  With perfect recall, agents' strategies base on the history of what happened before reaching the current state, whereas imperfect recall strategies decide of the next action based solely on the current state. Counting strategies (#) are in this category an intermediate semantics, where the next action depends on the number of times the state has been visited.
- Available **Information**: *perfect information* (I) vs. *imperfect information* (i) strategies.
  With imperfect information, the agent has a partial view of the system state, whereas with perfect information it is aware of the whole picture.

Both memory and information capabilities are combined in a semantic variant.

4.1 Synchronous Models and Logics

Here we first start with untimed models, and then extend them with timing features.

Synchronous Untimed Models: Concurrent Game Structures

Concurrent Game Structures (CGS) are an automata-based formalism where transitions are labelled with a tuple of actions, one per agent in the system. A protocol indicates for each agent and each location which actions the agents can take in that location.

Definition 17. *A* Concurrent Game Structure *is a tuple* $\mathcal{A} = (Agents, \Sigma, \mathcal{Q}, \mathcal{PV}, \mathcal{V}, prot, trans)$*, where:*

- *Agents is a finite set of all the* agents
- Σ *is a finite set of* actions
- $\mathcal{Q}$ *is a finite set of* global locations
- $\mathcal{PV}$ *is a set of* propositional variables
- $\mathcal{V} : \mathcal{Q} \times \mathcal{PV} \to \{\bot, \top\}$ *is a* valuation function
- $prot : Agents \times \mathcal{Q} \to \mathcal{P}(\Sigma) \setminus \{\emptyset\}$ *is a* protocol function
- $trans : \mathcal{Q} \times \Sigma^{|Agents|} \to \mathcal{Q}$ *is a* transition function *consistent*[6] *with* $prot$ *for each agent of Agents*

[6] This means that $trans(s, (a_1, \ldots, a_n))$ is defined if $a_i \in prot(i, s)$.

Example 17. Let us consider the ConcurrentGame Structure on the right. The system can be in 3 different locations: ℓ_0, ℓ_1 and ℓ_2. A propositional variable π is `true` in ℓ_1, `false` in ℓ_2 and undefined in ℓ_0. There are 2 agents. The first one can perform actions a, b or c, while the second agent can perform actions x or y. Each transition in the CGS is thus labelled with a pair of actions, one for each agent. For example, the arc from ℓ_0 to ℓ_1 represents two transitions: one where the first agent does b and the second x, and another where the first agent also does b but the second does y. This arc thus represents the first agent choosing b to go to ℓ_1, regardless of the second agent's action.

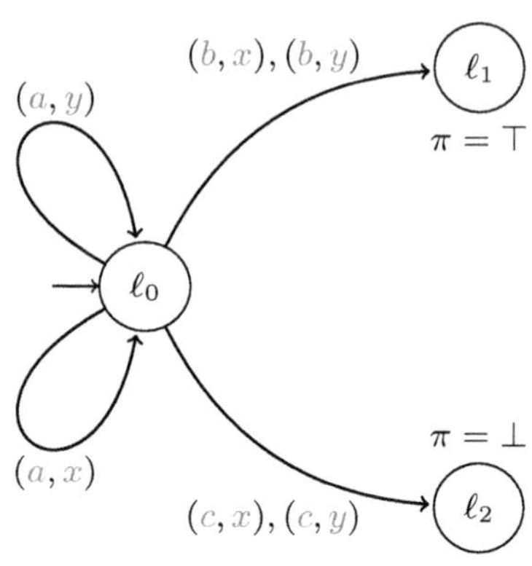

Logic for CGS properties: ATL

The *Alternating-time Temporal Logic* [5] (ATL) allows for expressing properties on the strategic abilities of one agent or a group of agents. Informally, the strategy of an agent describes the action the agent should take in a given state of the system.

The syntax of ATL is defined by formulas φ where $\pi \in \mathcal{PV}$ and $A \subseteq \mathit{Agents}$, according to the following grammar:

$$\varphi ::= \pi \mid \neg\varphi \mid \varphi \vee \varphi \mid \langle\langle A\rangle\rangle \mathsf{X}\varphi \mid \langle\langle A\rangle\rangle \varphi \mathsf{U} \varphi \mid \langle\langle A\rangle\rangle \varphi \mathsf{R} \varphi$$

$\langle\langle A\rangle\rangle\phi$ means that agent(s) in coalition A have a collective strategy to enforce ϕ, where ϕ equals to $\mathsf{X}\varphi$, $\varphi\mathsf{U}\varphi$, or $\varphi\mathsf{R}\varphi$ (and also $\mathsf{F}\varphi$ or $\mathsf{G}\varphi$).

Example 18. Let us consider the following formula for the CGS in Example 17: $\langle\langle ag_1\rangle\rangle \mathsf{F}(\pi = \top)$. This formula means that the first agent, ag_1, has a strategy to reach in the future a state where $\pi = \top$. It suffices for ag_1 to choose action b. Indeed, when choosing b, whatever the second agent chooses, the transition will lead to ℓ_1 where the property holds.

Formula $\langle\langle ag_2\rangle\rangle \mathsf{F}(\pi = \top)$ does however not hold: the second agent has no strategy to reach in the future a state where $\pi = \top$. Indeed, whatever the second agent chooses, the action of the first agent determines the next location.

This example also exhibits two different problems to address: 1. proving the ATL property, i.e. the existence of a strategy; 2. *synthesizing* strategies, i.e. finding the strategies that make the property hold.

Adding Time: Tight-Durational Concurrent Game Structures As Concurrent Game Structures are a synchronous model, *time* is added by assigning a duration to each transition. Thus, all synchronous actions that happen together start and finish simultaneously.

Definition 18. *A* Tight-Durational Concurrent Game Structure *is a tuple* $\mathcal{A} = (Agents, \Sigma, \mathcal{Q}, \mathcal{PV}, \mathcal{V}, prot, trans)$, *where:*

- *Agents is a finite set of all the* agents
- Σ *is a finite set of* actions
- $\mathcal{Q}$ *is a finite set of* global locations
- $\mathcal{PV}$ *is a set of* propositional variables
- $\mathcal{V} : \mathcal{Q} \times \mathcal{PV} \rightarrow \{\bot, \top\}$ *is a* valuation function
- $prot : Agents \times \mathcal{Q} \rightarrow \mathcal{P}(\Sigma) \setminus \{\emptyset\}$ *is a* protocol function
- $trans : \mathcal{Q} \times \Sigma^{|Agents|} \rightarrow \mathcal{Q} \times \mathbb{N}^{+}$ *is a* transition function *consistent with* $prot$ *for each agent of Agents*

The state of a TDCGS comprises both the location and the time at which it is reached:

Definition 19. *A* global state *of a TDCGS is a pair* (q, v) *where:*

- $q \in \mathcal{Q}$ *is a global location*
- $v \in \mathbb{N}^{+}$ *is a time value*

Example 19. The Tight-Durational ConcurrentGame Structure on the right extends the CGS of Example 17 with time. Transitions are labelled with triples representing the actions of the two agents and its duration. Note that the duration is not related to the action of an agent, but to the transition itself: e.g. the self-loops on location ℓ_0 have timings 1 and 2 even though ag_1 performs action a in both.

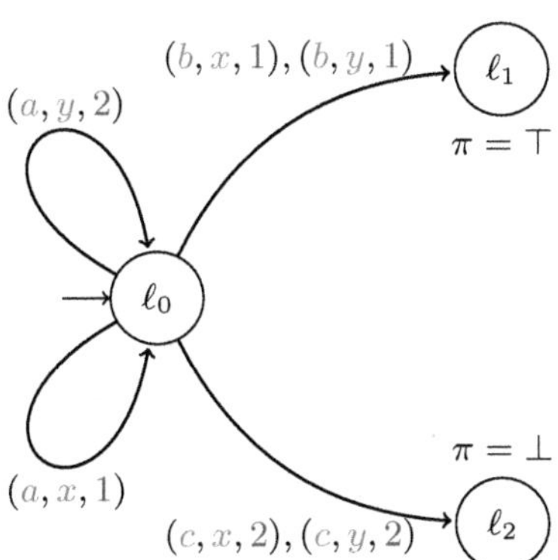

Logic for TDCGS Properties: TATL

Similarly to TCTL extending CTL with time, the Timed Alternating-time Temporal Logic (TATL) is built from ATL by associating time constraints to the temporal operators.

The syntax of TATL is defined by formulas φ where $\pi \in \mathcal{PV}$, $A \subseteq Agents$, $\sim \in \{\leq, =, \geq\}$[7] and $\eta \in \mathbb{N}$, according to the following grammar:

$$\varphi ::= \pi \mid \neg\varphi \mid \varphi \vee \varphi \mid \langle\langle A\rangle\rangle \mathsf{X}\varphi \mid \langle\langle A\rangle\rangle \varphi \mathsf{U}_{\sim\eta}\varphi \mid \langle\langle A\rangle\rangle \varphi \mathsf{R}_{\sim\eta}\varphi$$

[7] Note that TCTL was defined with time intervals whereas TATL uses inequalities.

Example 20. Let us consider the following formula for the TDCGS in Example 19: $\langle\langle ag_1\rangle\rangle \texttt{true}\, \mathsf{U}_{\geq 2}\pi = \top$. This formula means that the first agent, ag_1, has a strategy to reach in at least 2 time units a state where $\pi = \top$. A possible strategy is for ag_1 to choose action a first and then action b.

The strategy exhibited in Example 20 is a possible solution only with some semantic variants of the strategic abilities of agents, that we explain next.

4.2 Strategic Abilities

Let $ag \in Agents$ and α_F: be *the final global location* of sequence α.

Perfect Information Strategies (I)

Perfect information strategies are such that each agent knows its individual states of the system.

Definition 20. *A* perfect recall *(R) and* perfect information *(I)* strategy *($\Sigma_{R,I}$) is a function $\sigma_{ag} : \mathcal{Q}^+ \rightarrow \Sigma$ such that $\forall \alpha \in \mathcal{Q}^+ : \sigma_{ag}(\alpha) \in prot(ag, \alpha_F)$.*

When also considering a perfect recall, agents have knowledge of the history of the execution as the sequence of locations traversed. Thus, there is no specific constraint on the strategy of agent ag, apart from agreeing to its protocol.

Definition 21. *An* imperfect recall *(r),* perfect information *(I)* strategy *($\Sigma_{r,I}$) is a function σ_{ag} such that $\forall \alpha, \alpha' \in \mathcal{Q}^+ : \alpha_F = \alpha'_F \implies \sigma_{ag}(\alpha) = \sigma_{ag}(\alpha')$.*

With imperfect recall and perfect information, agent ag selects an action based on the *last location* in α, i.e. the current location only.

Example 21. Let us revisit Example 20 and the possible strategies to verify the TATL formula: $\langle\langle ag_1\rangle\rangle \texttt{true}\, \mathsf{U}_{\geq 2}\pi = \top$. Assume perfect information.

In case of perfect recall, ag_1 can use a taking a self-loop on ℓ_0 that takes 1 or 2 units of time, depending on the action selected by ag_2. Then it does b, which leads to ℓ_1 in 1 unit of time. So, the total time spent is either 2 or 3 and the TATL property holds.

Now assume we have an imperfect recall. If ag_1 chooses a, a self-loop is always taken in ℓ_0 and thus $\pi = \top$ never holds. c is obviously also a bad choice. The choice of b when in ℓ_0 leads to ℓ_1 where $\pi = \top$ holds, but in 1 unit of time only, thus violating the time constraint of the TATL property. Hence $\langle\langle ag_1\rangle\rangle \texttt{true}\, \mathsf{U}_{\geq 2}\pi = \top$ is not satisfied in an Ir semantics.

Imperfect Information Strategies (i)

In an imperfect information setting, the agents have a partial view of the state of the system. Therefore, there are some states that they cannot distinguish: $\forall ag \in Agents : \sim_{ag} \subseteq \mathcal{Q} \times \mathcal{Q}$ is an *indistinguishability relation.*

Definition 22. *A* perfect recall *(R),* imperfect information *(i)* strategy *($\Sigma_{R,i}$) is a strategy σ_{ag} such that $\forall \alpha, \alpha' \in \mathcal{Q}^+ : \alpha(0) \sim_{ag} \alpha'(0), \ldots, \alpha_F \sim_{ag} \alpha'_F \implies \sigma_{ag}(\alpha) = \sigma_{ag}(\alpha')$.*

With perfect recall and imperfect information, agent *ag* selects an action based on its view of the history.

Definition 23. *An* imperfect recall *(r),* imperfect information *(i)* strategy *($\Sigma_{r,i}$) is a strategy σ_{ag} such that $\forall \alpha, \alpha' \in \mathcal{Q}^+ : \alpha_F \sim_{ag} \alpha'_F \implies \sigma_{ag}(\alpha) = \sigma_{ag}(\alpha')$.*

With imperfect information and imperfect recall, agent *ag* selects an action based on its view of the last location in α, i.e. its view of the current location.

Example 22. Let us consider a variant of the Blind bartender with boxing gloves problem [52].

This problem is a two-player game where a blind bartender has to put four glasses either all upright or all upside down. The glasses are on a rotating square tray, one glass in each corner of the tray. The bartender has boxing gloves (so they cannot feel whether a glass is upright or not), and is authorised to move as many glasses as they want. If the goal is reached, the bartender wins the game, otherwise a customer spins the tray randomly. The process is repeated until the game is won.

Figure 7 shows a model for this problem. Note that there is a single agent for which we want to know whether there exists a winning strategy. There are four locations that show the configuration on the tray: in ℓ_1, three glasses are in a position and the other glass in the opposite position (e.g. 3 upright and 1 upside down); in ℓ_2, two glasses are in each position but those in the same position are on a diagonal; in ℓ_3, two glasses are in each position but those in the same position are next to one another; in ℓ_4, all glasses are in the same position. Obviously ℓ_4 is the winning location.

There are three possible actions: turn 1 glass (t1); turn 2 glasses in diagonal (t2d); turn 2 adjacent glasses (t2a). Turning 3 glasses gives a configuration similar to that obtained by turning only one glass, and such an action is thus useless. Let us look at the actions from location ℓ_1. With t1, either the glass represented by the black dot is turned and the game moves to ℓ_4. Or one of the 3 glasses pictured as circles is turned. If it is adjacent to the black one, the resulting location is ℓ_3, or it is the glass is diagonal with the black one and the resulting location is ℓ_2. Remember that the bartender is blind and has boxing gloves, so they have no means to distinguish anything on the tray. When turning 2 glasses in location ℓ_1, the configuration of the tray remains the same, i.e. 3 glasses in a position and the other in the opposite position. Actions from ℓ_2 and ℓ_3 are modelled in a similar manner.

The main question of interest is: Is there a strategy for the bartender to win? This can be formalised by: $\langle\langle bar \rangle\rangle F \ell_4$. Let us consider the different semantics. With perfect information, we assume the bartender knows the initial location, whereas with imperfect information they do not, but is told if winning (hence

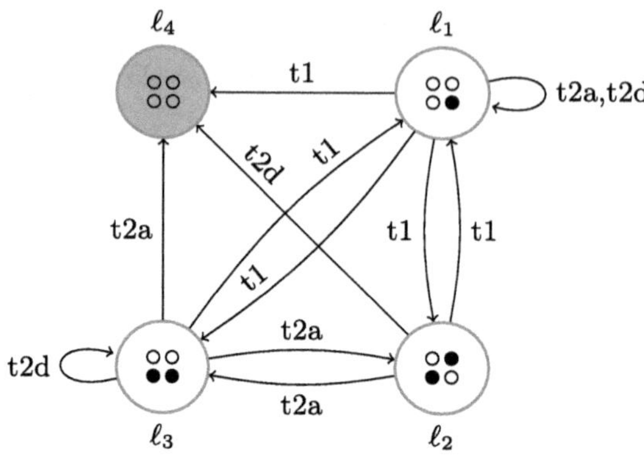

Fig. 7. The blind bartender with boxing gloves problem

ℓ_1, ℓ_2 and ℓ_3 are undistinguishable). Examples of winning strategies for the four semantics are:

- *Perfect information, perfect recall:* depending on the initial location: ℓ_1: t1, then if not in ℓ_4 apply the strategy as if starting in that new location; ℓ_2: t2d; ℓ_3: t2a, t2d.
- *Perfect information, imperfect recall:* ℓ_1: t1; ℓ_2: t2d; ℓ_3: t2a.
- *Imperfect information, perfect recall:* t2d, t2a, t2d, t1, t2d, t2a, t2d.
- *Imperfect information, imperfect recall:* no strategy.

Let us now extend the problem with time, assuming that turning one glass takes one unit of time, i.e. t1 takes 1 time unit, and both t2a and t2d take 2 time units.

The question of interest now becomes: Is there a strategy for the bartender to win in less than 5 units of time? This can be formalised by: $\langle\langle bar\rangle\rangle F_{\leq 5}\ell_4$. We again consider the different semantics.

- *Perfect information, perfect recall:* depending on the initial location: ℓ_1: t1 which takes 1 time unit, or it leads to another location where the strategy is as if starting from this location, thus all possible durations for this strategy from ℓ_1 can be 1, 3 or 5 (from what follows); ℓ_2: t2d, which takes 2 time units; ℓ_3: t2a, t2d, which takes 2 or 4 time units.
- *Perfect information, imperfect recall:* ℓ_1: t1; ℓ_2: t2d; ℓ_3: t2a. So all possible durations for this strategy are 1, 2, 3, 4 or 5 time units.
- *Imperfect information, perfect recall:* no strategy. Indeed the solution for the untimed case takes up to 11 time units. The winning location can be reached within this time limit (of 5 according to the formula), for example with durations 2 or 4 time units, but without guarantee.
- *Imperfect information, imperfect recall:* no strategy.

Joint Strategies

A set of agents can collaborate to achieve a common goal. To do so, they apply a joint strategy.

Definition 24. *A* joint strategy σ_A *for agents* $A \subseteq Agents$ *is a tuple of strategies, one per agent* $ag \in A$.

The outcome *of* σ_A *in location* $q \in \mathcal{Q}$ *is the set* $out(q, \sigma_A) \subseteq \mathcal{Q}^\omega$ *such that* $\alpha \in out(q, \sigma_A)$ *iff* $\alpha(0) = q$ *and for each* $i \in \mathbb{N} : \alpha(i) \xrightarrow{a} \alpha(i+1)$ *for some* $a \in \Sigma$ *s.t.* $a|_A = \sigma_A(\alpha_i)$ *and* $a|_{\overline{A}} \in prot_{\overline{A}}(\alpha(i))$.

When coalition A follows σ_A, then in every location, A selects actions according to the joint strategy while the remaining agents in $\overline{A}$ can choose any action.

Counting Strategies

Counting strategies [15] are a middle term between perfect and imperfect recall. They do consider a simple abstraction of the history.

Definition 25. Counting strategies *with* perfect information *($\Sigma_{\#,I}$) are functions* σ_{ag} *such that* $\forall \alpha, \alpha' \in \mathcal{Q}^+ : (\alpha_F = \alpha'_F \wedge \#_F(\alpha) = \#_F(\alpha')) \implies \sigma_{ag}(\alpha) = \sigma_{ag}(\alpha')$ *where* $\#_F(\alpha)$ *is the number of occurrences of the location of* α_F *in sequence* α.

Definition 26. Counting strategies *with* imperfect information *($\Sigma_{\#,i}$) are functions* σ_{ag} *such that* $\forall \alpha, \alpha' \in \mathcal{Q}^+ : (\alpha_F \sim_{ag} \alpha'_F \wedge \#_F(\alpha) = \#_F(\alpha')) \implies \sigma_{ag}(\alpha) = \sigma_{ag}(\alpha')$ *where* $\#_F(\alpha)$ *is the number of occurrences of the location of* α_F *in sequence* α.

With counting strategies, the action selection depends on the *number of visits* to the current location α_F.

Example 23. Let us consider Example 20 and couting strategies to verify the TATL formula: $\langle\langle ag_1 \rangle\rangle \texttt{true}\, \mathsf{U}_{\geq 2} \pi = \top$.

If ag_1 chooses a when visiting ℓ_0 the first time, and then b the second time, it reaches ℓ_1 where $\pi = \top$ holds, in 2 or 3 units of time, thus the TATL property holds. In this case, it is the same behaviour as for perfect recall, but the counting strategy only requires recording the number of times a location has been visited instead of the entire path stored for perfect recall.

4.3 Adding Strategic Abilities to TCTL: STCTL

STCTL [23] extends TCTL with the strategic modality.

Asynchronous Models

In this general framework, models are *based on timed automata* (one per agent) that communicate, either in a *synchronous* or an *asynchronous* manner, and can use *discrete* or *continuous* time. Here, we focus on the (more complex) case of asynchronous agents with continuous time[8].

Definition 27. *A* Continuous-time Asynchronous Multi Agent System *(*CAMAS*) is:*

- *a* family of agents $\mathcal{A}_i = \langle L_i, \ell_{0i}, \Sigma_i, X_i, E_i, I_i, prot_i \rangle$
  - *similar to Timed Automata equipped with a* protocol *function* $prot_i : L_i \to \mathcal{P}(\Sigma_i)$ *(set of authorised actions in each location)*
  - *a* local transition *must agree with the protocol:* $\forall t = (\ell, -, a, -, -) \in E_i : a \in prot_i(\ell)$
- *a* global transition *in* $E \subseteq \bigtimes_i L_i \times Z(n) \times \Sigma \times \mathcal{P}(\bigcup_i X_i) \times \bigtimes_i L_i$ *is* $t = ((\ell_1, \dots, \ell_{|Agents|}), \bigwedge_i Z_i, a, \bigcup_i x_i, (\ell_1', \dots, \ell_{|Agents|}') \in E$ *iff*

$$\begin{cases} (\ell_i, Z_i, a, x_i, \ell_i') \in E_i & \text{if } i \in Agent(a) \\ \ell_i = \ell_i' & \text{otherwise} \end{cases}$$

Syntax of STCTL

STCTL formulas φ are defined by the following grammar, where $\pi \in \mathcal{PV}$ and I is an interval, and $\langle\langle A \rangle\rangle\gamma$ means that agent(s) in A have a strategy to enforce γ.

$$\varphi ::= \pi \mid \neg\varphi \mid \varphi \wedge \varphi \mid \langle\langle A \rangle\rangle\gamma$$

$$\gamma ::= \varphi \mid \neg\gamma \mid \gamma \wedge \gamma \mid \forall(\gamma \mathsf{U}_I \gamma) \mid \forall(\gamma \mathsf{R}_I \gamma) \mid \exists(\gamma \mathsf{U}_I \gamma) \mid \exists(\gamma \mathsf{R}_I \gamma)$$

Semantics of STCTL

The existential and universal path quantifiers $\exists$ and $\forall$ are interpreted within the context of the strategic modality $\langle\langle\rangle\rangle$.

Definition 28. $q \models \langle\langle A \rangle\rangle\gamma$ *iff there exists a joint strategy* σ_A *such that we have* $out(q, \sigma_A) \models \gamma$*, where:*

- $out(q, \sigma_A) \models \forall\varphi$ *iff for each* $\alpha \in out(q, \sigma_A)$ *we have* $\pi, \sigma_A \models \varphi$
- $out(q, \sigma_A) \models \exists\varphi$ *iff for some* $\alpha \in out(q, \sigma_A)$ *we have* $\pi, \sigma_A \models \varphi$

with π *is an execution and* TCTL *operators are defined as usual.*

Example 24. Let us revisit the coffee machine of Fig. 1. Figure 8 presents a CAMAS version with two agents: the user and the machine. They synchronise on the start action where the user has pressed the button and the machine starts operating, and on coffee where the user gets it. Between these two actions, the user can ask for sugar. Clock x, used for the sugar, is handled on the user side

[8] The full set of models and associated logics is detailed in [23].

while clock y, used for monitoring the coffee delivery process, is handled by the machine[9].

We want to know whether there is a strategy for the user to get a sugar after 5 time units. Note that it is impossible in the original problem without agents since sugar can be obtained exactly every time unit for 5 occurrences of the self-loop and then immediately the preparation starts without any possibility of getting an additional sugar.

In STCTL, the property is expressed by the formula $\langle\langle user \rangle\rangle \exists \mathsf{F}_{>5}(\mathrm{sugar})$[10] This formula holds[11] e.g. with strategy: start, sugar ^{6}. A corresponding global concrete run is:

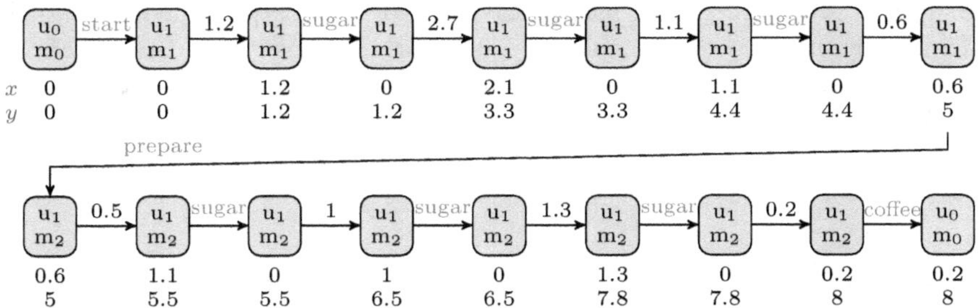

Note that in this model, the user can ask for sugar while the coffee is being poured, i.e. the machine in location m_2. Also notice that in the run action prepare is in the middle of the 6 actions sugar, which still agrees with the strategy since prepare is an action of the machine and not the user agent.

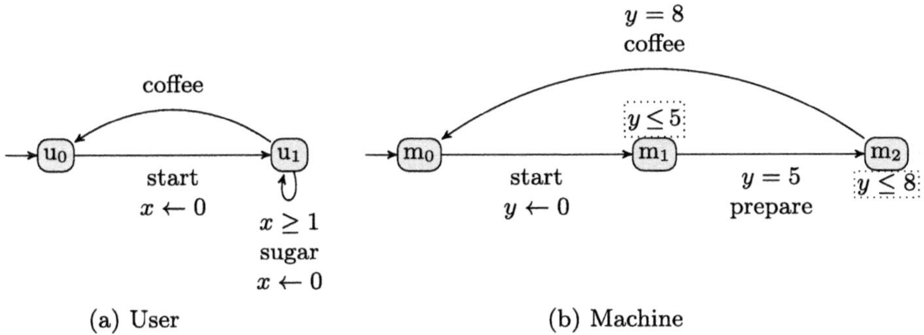

Fig. 8. CAMAS for the coffee machine

---

[9] On such a small and simple example this decomposition is somewhat artificial.

[10] This assumes that there is a way to know the action taking a sugar has been triggered, which is easily feasible with a slight modification of the model or by the use of discrete variables. We do not present this modified version for consistency of the presentation.

[11] Of course, the strategy depends on the chosen semantics for strategic abilities.

5 Model Checking Algorithms

In this section, we examine the complexity of the model checking problem for both timed and strategic logics, followed by a discussion of model checking algorithms

5.1 Complexity of Model Checking [23]

Table 3 displays the complexity of the model checking problem w.r.t. the model size for STCTL and its subsets, also compared with $\mathsf{ATL}^{*\mathsf{U}}$ and $\mathsf{TATL}^{*\mathsf{C}}$. Surprisingly, the complexity of model checking for SCTL[ir] is equivalent to that of ATL[ir], whereas the complexity for STCTL[ir] aligns with that of TCTL. Notice that undecidability of $\mathsf{ATL}^{\mathsf{U}}_{\mathsf{iR}}$ and of MTL[12] propagates to more expressive logics.

Δ_2^P denotes the complexity class of decision problems that can be solved in deterministic polynomial time with access to an NP oracle (such as SAT) a polynomial number of times.

Table 3. Complexity of Model Checking timed and strategic logics, where the superscripts C, D, and U mean continuous time, discrete time, and untimed, respectively

<table>
<tr><th></th><th>Ir</th><th>IR</th><th>ir</th><th>iR</th></tr>
<tr><td>$\mathsf{ATL}^{\mathsf{U}}$</td><td colspan="2">PTIME
(Ir, IR semantics coincide)</td><td>Δ_2^{P}</td><td rowspan="6">Undecidable (⊃ ATL[iR])</td></tr>
<tr><td>$\mathsf{SCTL}^{\mathsf{U}}$</td><td>$\Delta_2^{\mathsf{P}}$</td><td>EXPTIME</td><td>Δ_2^{P}</td></tr>
<tr><td>$\mathsf{ATL}^{*\mathsf{U}}$</td><td>PSPACE</td><td>2EXPTIME</td><td>PSPACE</td></tr>
<tr><td>$\mathsf{TATL}^{\mathsf{D}}$</td><td colspan="2">PTIME
(Ir, IR semantics coincide)</td><td>Δ_2^{P}—PSPACE</td></tr>
<tr><td>$\mathsf{STCTL}^{\mathsf{C}}$</td><td>PSPACE</td><td>Undecidable</td><td>PSPACE</td></tr>
<tr><td>$\mathsf{TATL}^{*\mathsf{C}}$</td><td colspan="3">Undecidable (⊃ MTL)</td></tr>
</table>

Table 3 shows that the complexity of model checking for (timed) strategic logics under the ir-semantics is high and, in case of the continuous semantics is at least PSPACE-complete. Therefore we need methods that aim at making the verification feasible, mainly by alleviating the state explosion problem. These methods can be divided into the following groups:

- Abstractions: generating abstract models,

[12] MTL - Metric Temporal Logic is a continuous time extension of Linear Time Temporal Logic, see [38].

- Equivalence-based reductions,
- Symbolic model checking: different types of BDDs, SAT- and SMT-based verification,
- Bounded model checking,
- Partial order reductions,
- Upper and lower approximations,
- Smart exploration strategies.

Generating abstract models for Timed Automata or Time(d) Petri Nets in order to model check temporal formulas over them is one of the fundamental approaches to verification. Abstract models are (usually) finite and possibly minimal w.r.t. the properties they preserve. Clearly, some information from concrete models is lost, but this information is not taken into account by the properties to be checked. Abstract models for Timed Automata include: detailed region graphs [3, 59] and region graphs typically represented by Difference Bound Matrices (DBMs) [51].

Abstract models for Time(d) Petri Nets include these based on state classes or region graphs: linear state class graphs [31,32,34], geometric region graphs, atomic state class graphs [114], and pseudo-atomic state class graphs [95]. Besides the state class methods, other approaches to building abstract models for Time Petri Nets also exist. In many cases they correspond to the solutions known for Timed Automata. This includes, e.g. the detailed region graph for Time Petri Nets [93,107], or a method for computing the state spaces of Time Petri Nets based on a construction of the forward-reachability graph for Timed Automata [55].

One of the main methods for generating abstract models are minimization algorithms [36,81,94], which produce *bisimulating models*. A method for building *pseudo-bisimulating models*, preserving reachability properties, was introduced in [99]. However, the verification based on reachability analysis is usually performed on an abstract model known as *simulation graph* or *forward-reachability graph*. The nodes of this graph can be defined as (not necessarily convex) sets of detailed regions [37] or as regions [50,79,113], which follows from a convenient representation of zones by Difference Bound Matrices (DBMs) [51].

The existing verification techniques often employ symbolic representations of state spaces. These include operations on Difference Bound Matrices (DBMs) [51] and similar structures [31] to represent the states of abstract models. Additionally, various forms of decision diagrams are used, such as Clock Decision Diagrams (CDDs) [27,109], Numeric Decision Diagrams (NDDs) [24], Difference Decision Diagrams (DDDs) [90,91], and Clock Restriction Diagrams (CRDs) [110]. SAT-related algorithms, including both bounded [8,25,97,105,112] and unbounded model checking [68–70,103] are also commonly supported by SAT- or SMT-solvers [96]. In bounded model checking, the existential fragment of a (timed) strategic logic can only be verified. The verification is on finite paths of the model, of size which is increased step by step. The algorithm stops when either the formula holds true in the model or the length of the paths reaches the size of the model.

In addition to unbounded model checking for ATL [71,72], methods based on upper and lower approximations [64] and partial order reductions [65] turned out to be quite efficient. Partial order reductions can be viewed as an abstraction method which consists in obtaining a reduced model in which for each trace equivalence class of runs at least one run (but as few as possible) is generated only. Intuitively, two runs are trace equivalent if they differ only in the ordering of independent actions, i.e. actions belonging to different agents.

5.2 CTL Model Checking with State Labelling

Model checking CTL properties is based on states labelling, as introduced in [47]. We here recall the general principles, and refer the reader to [111] in this volume for going further.

General Principle. The CTL model checking algorithm operates by *marking* states where a formula is satisfied, *memorising* the already computed results and *reusing* the computed results of sub-formulae to compute new formulae. Hence, when checking a formula it is first decomposed as much as possible in sub-formulae.The sub-formulae are checked, and the results are reused to verify other formulas embedding them. For CTL, there are 6 cases to consider:

1. $\psi = \pi$: the formula ψ is a propositional variable. It suffices to mark states labelled with π.
2. $\psi = \neg\varphi$: mark states where φ does not hold
3. $\psi = \varphi_1 \wedge \varphi_2$: mark states where both φ_1 and φ_2 hold
4. $\psi = \mathsf{EX}\varphi$: mark states for which a successor is marked with φ
5. $\psi = \mathsf{E}\varphi_1\mathsf{U}\varphi_2$ (see below)
6. $\psi = \mathsf{EG}\varphi$ (see below)

CTL Model-Checking: $\psi = \mathsf{E}\varphi_1\mathsf{U}\varphi_2$ Let us assume the marking of states for sub-formulae φ_1 and φ_2 has already been done. From the definition of the U operator, all states satisfying φ_2 also satisfy ψ. Thus, they are immediately marked as such. Then we have to explore their predecessors as long as they satisfy φ_1, as follows:

- find all predecessors of states marked with ψ
- if they are marked with φ_1, mark them with ψ
- repeat until all states marked with ψ have been visited

CTL Model-Checking: $\psi = \mathsf{EG}\varphi$ Let us assume the marking of states for sub-formula φ has already been done. Consider the sub-graph formed by the states marked with φ, and construct its strongly connected components (SCCs). Note that within a SCC, all states are marked φ and are reachable from one another, provided there is an arc in the SCC. Thus, they also satisfy ψ. Hence all states in these SCCs with at least an arc are marked with ψ. Then we need to explore the paths backwards from these, as follows:

- find all predecessors of states marked with ψ
- if they are marked with φ, mark them with ψ
- repeat until all states marked with ψ have been visited

Example 25. Let us consider the state space in Fig. 9. We want to check the CTL formula $\psi = \mathsf{E}\pi_1\mathsf{U}(\mathsf{EG}\pi_2)$. The marking of formulae π_1 and π_2 is pictured by the colour of nodes, i.e. s_0 to s_3 satisfy π_1; s_5 to s_9 satisfy π_2; and s_4 satisfies none of these two propositions.

Let us now do the marking procedure for $\psi' = \mathsf{EG}\pi_2$. The sub-graph of the state space with nodes satisfying π_2 has 3 SCCs (pictured as dashed rectangles). Since the SCC containing s_5 does not have an arc, s_5 is not marked with ψ', while states s_6 to s_9 are. Then we apply the loop for backward exploration: s_5 is a predecessor of s_6 which is marked with ψ'. Moreover, s_5 is marked with π_2. Thus s_5 can now be marked with ψ'. The other predecessors are s_2 and s_4 which do not satisfy π_2, and thus cannot be marked with ψ'. Hence, the states marked with $\psi' = \mathsf{EG}\pi_2$ are s_5 to s_9.

We can now do the marking for $\psi = \mathsf{E}\pi_1\mathsf{U}(\psi')$. First, all states marked ψ' are also marked ψ. We explore their predecessors which are marked π_1. There is only one such predecessor, s_2, which is now marked ψ. We repeat the operation with s_1, predecessor of s_2, and then s_0, predecessor of s_1 (both s_1 and s_0 are marked π_1). The algorithm is finished and all states satisfy ψ except s_3 and s_4.

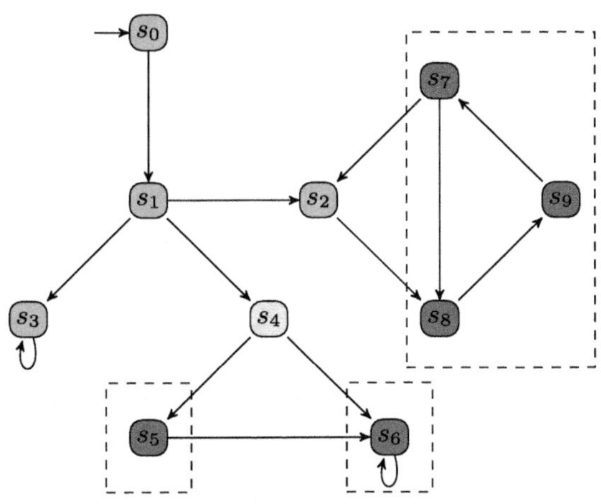

Fig. 9. Model checking $\psi = \mathsf{E}\pi_1\mathsf{U}(\mathsf{EG}\pi_2)$

5.3 Smart Exploration Strategies for Timed Models

The time and strategic dimensions of systems lead, as can already be seen in Table 3, to state spaces that may be infinite, and even worse, some cases are undecidable. Therefore, state spaces cannot be generated before applying model checking approaches such as state labelling. It is thus necessary to operate other methods for model checking. Note that for Timed Automata (TA), the state spaces are *zone graphs* so that classes of states are already grouped, according to the symbolic semantics[13].

First, *on-the-fly* model checking allows for computing the property satisfaction (or not) while constructing the state space. As soon as the positive or negative conclusion is obtained, the exploration can be stopped. Let us note that due to infinity and undecidability the exploration might never terminate. Hence, the algorithms are semi-algorithms that provide the exact answer when they terminate, or an over/under-approximation otherwise.

Second, the space to explore can be reduced so that less states are to be checked, and useless ones, w.r.t. the reduction, are discarded. Using subsumption ([77] for TA) is such an approach.

Definition 29. *A zone $\mathcal{Z} = (\ell, Z)$ is* subsumed *by another zone $\mathcal{Z}' = (\ell', Z')$, denoted $\mathcal{Z} \sqsubseteq \mathcal{Z}'$ iff $\ell = \ell'$ and $Z \subseteq Z'$.*

The subsumption abstraction *is a total mapping α over the zones such that for all reachable zones $\mathcal{Z}$, we have $\mathcal{Z} \sqsubseteq \alpha(\mathcal{Z})$.*

Example 26. Consider the TA in Fig. 10a. Its zone graph (Fig. 10b) contains 4 states: $s_0 = (\ell_0, Z_0)$, $s_1 = (\ell_1, Z_1)$, $s_2 = (\ell_2, Z_2)$ and $s_3 = (\ell_1, Z_3)$. Note that $Z_3 \subseteq Z_1$ and thus $s_3 \sqsubseteq s_1$, leading to the reduced zone graph in Fig. 10c.

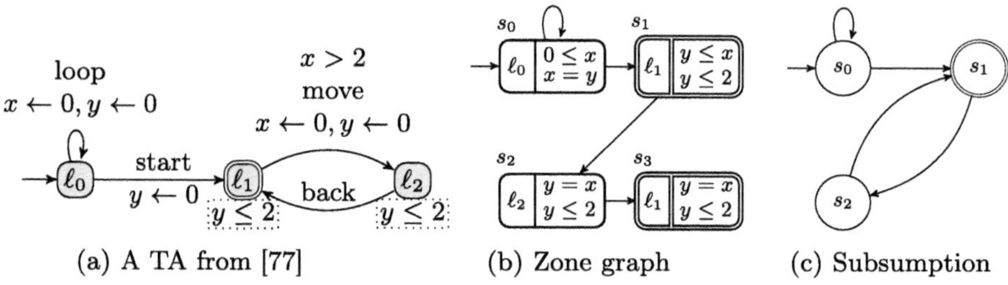

(a) A TA from [77] (b) Zone graph (c) Subsumption

Fig. 10. Reduction of the zone graph with subsumption abstraction

Third, one can adopt an *exploration strategy* adapted to the property to be checked, so that it has better chances to be successful [11,77].

Checking a *reachability* property consists in finding a path that leads to a desired state (a state satisfying the property). The state space is generally built using a *breadth-first* search (BFS), verifying on-the-fly whether the property holds. The state space can be reduced using subsumption.

---

[13] It is obvious that a concrete state space, enumerating explicitly all possible timings, is at best unpractical.

Liveness properties require the existence of a path going infinitely often through some desired state, i.e. the existence of a cycle with this state. Such a problem is tackled using *depth-first* search (DFS). Subsumption does not preserve liveness, and thus cannot be used in a straightforward way. Indeed, this can be seen in Example 26 where reachability of any state covered by s_1 is guaranteed, while a loop between s_1 and s_2, which is not feasible in the zone graph, has been introduced by the abstraction. Some simple strategies for exploration in order to find cycles are included in [11][14]. For example, a strategy consists in looking if some successor closes a cycle so as to conclude immediately without engaging in a sub-branch; or to select an accepting successor (if any) for the next exploration, so as to look for a cycle with that particular accepting state.

Moreover, going in depth for the exploration is dangerous as one might engage in an infinite branch where the state of interest is never encountered. To overcome this problem, [11] proposes *iterative deepening*, a middle ground between BFS and DFS. It consists in generating the zone graph using DFS until a given depth. Thus, when exploring a branch, when the depth is reached, the algorithm backtracks and picks a sibling, etc. When the zone graph up to the given depth has been completely explored unsuccessfully, the depth limit is increased and the exploration restarted from those states previously computed at the depth limit.

Example 27. Let us consider again the coffee machine, delivering less sugar as in Fig. 11a (in order to have small enough zone graphs), to illustrate subsumption and exploration orders.

The states in the zone graph (Fig. 11b) are numbered in the order they are encountered when building the graph using a BFS.

When using subsumption (still with BFS), states s_0–s_3 are constructed. Then, when exploring s_4, we notice that $s_4 \sqsubseteq s_0$. Thus s_4 is discarded and the coffee action leads to s_0 in the graph abstracted with subsumption (Fig. 11c). Similarly, we have $s_6 \sqsubseteq s_3$ hence the sugar self-loop on s_3. After s_7 is explored, there is no more pending state and the graph is complete.

Let us now check a reachability property: "Can I get a coffee with at least 1 sugar?" It can be expressed by $\mathsf{EF}(\ell_2 \wedge 1 \leq y - x)$. The inner property is satisfied in s_5, thus the reachability property holds. When checking it on-the-fly with BFS, states s_0–s_5 are explored. With DFS, in the best case we can choose the branch where a sugar is taken and then the prepare started, thus exploring s_0, s_1, s_3 and s_5.

For checking the liveness property "Is there a run going infinitely often through ℓ_0?", i.e. $\mathsf{EGEF}\ell_0$, when going from s_4 to s_1, a cycle is detected, on which state s_4 has location ℓ_0, thus the property holds.

6 Further Features: Adding Timing Parameters

Parametric timed automata (PTAs) are an extension of TAs where timed constraints can be expressed with timing parameters instead of integer constants,

[14] Although [11] addresses the problem for Parametric Timed Automata, the results are valid in a non-parametric context.

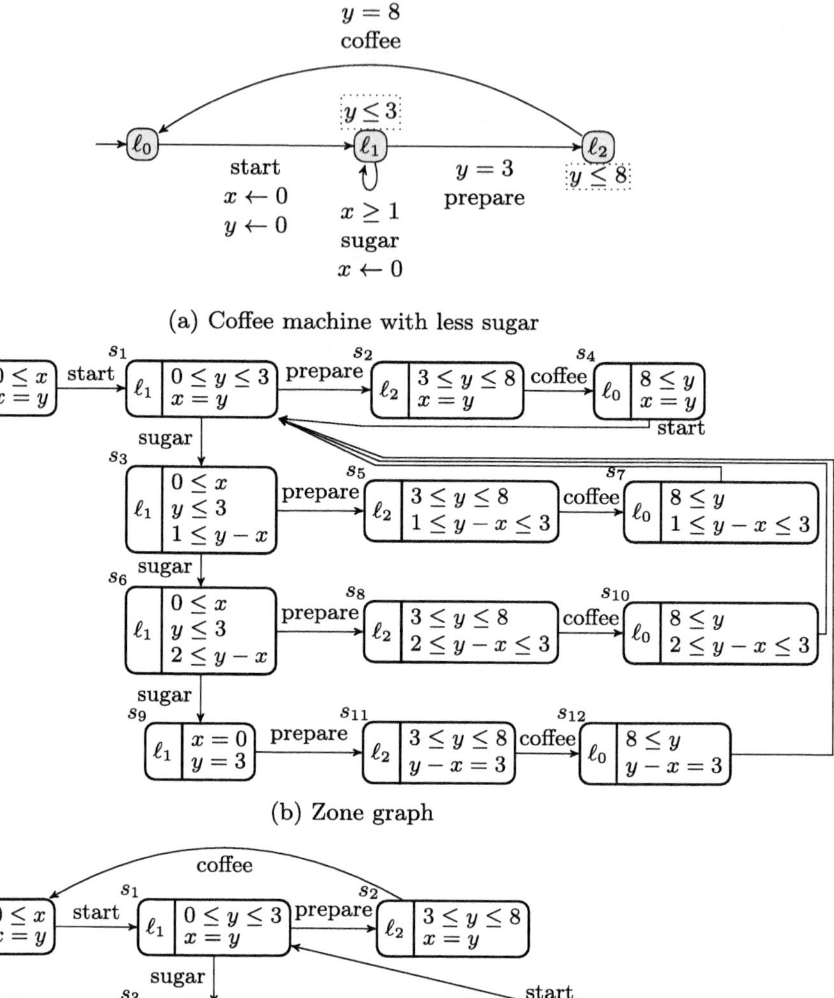

(a) Coffee machine with less sugar

(b) Zone graph

(c) Zone graph reduced with subsumption

Fig. 11. Model checking properties for the coffee machine

allowing to model uncertainty or lack of knowledge about such constants. Parametric timed automata fit into the parametric timed verification framework [16].

PTAs have several advantages such as:

- Modeling Flexibility: PTAs can model systems with unknown timing characteristics. This flexibility is essential for designing and analyzing real-time systems where exact timing details may not be known in advance or may vary between different instances of the system.

- Verification: PTAs ease the verification of temporal properties of systems under different timing constraints. By analyzing a PTA, one can ensure that a system meets safety, liveness, or performance properties across a range of possible parameter valuations.
- Optimization: PTAs can be used to optimize timing parameters to improve system performance or efficiency. By exploring different parameter valuations, designers can find optimal configurations that meet all required constraints while maximizing performance metrics.
- Robustness Analysis: PTAs allow for the analysis of system robustness with respect to timing variations (see, e.g. [41]). By examining how small changes in timing parameters affect system behavior, designers can ensure that the system is resilient to variations and uncertainties in its operating environment.

6.1 Syntax

Definition 30. *Let* $X = \{x_1, \ldots, x_n\}$ *be a set of clock variables, and* $P = \{p_1, \ldots, p_m\}$ *be a set of parameters. A* parametric clock guard *is a convex polyhedron in* $\mathbb{R}^{n+m}$ *which can be described by a finite set of inequalities of the form* $x_i \sim c$ *or* $x_i - x_j \sim c$*, where* $\sim \in \{<, \leq, =, \geq, >\}$ *and* $c \in \mathbb{Q} \cup P$*. Let* $\mathcal{PCG}(n, m)$ *be the set of all clock guards over* $\{x_1, \ldots, x_n\}$ *and* $\{p_1, \ldots, p_m\}$*.*

Definition 31. *A* parametric timed automaton *is a tuple* $\mathcal{A} = \langle L, \ell_0, \Sigma, X, P, E, I \rangle$ *where:*

- L *is a finite set of locations*
- $\ell_0 \in L$ *is an initial location*
- Σ *is a finite set of actions*
- $X = \{x_1, \ldots, x_n\}$ *is a finite set of clocks*
- $P = \{p_1, \ldots, p_m\}$ *is a finite set of parameters*
- $E \subseteq L \times \mathcal{PCG}(|X|, |P|) \times \Sigma \times \mathcal{P}(X) \times L$ *is a transition relation whose elements are a source location, a parametric clock guard (called transition guard), an action, clocks to be reset, and a target location*
- $I : L \to \mathcal{PCG}(|X|, |P|)$ *is a parametric clock guard called location invariant*

Definition 32 (Valuation of a PTA). *Given a PTA* $\mathcal{A}$ *and a parameter valuation* v*, we denote by* $v(\mathcal{A})$ *the non-parametric structure where all occurrences of a parameter* p_i *have been replaced by* $v(p_i)$*.*

Note that $v(\mathcal{A})$ is a TA as defined in Definition 2.

Example 28. The PTA in Fig. 12 is a parametric version of the coffee machine example, where the time limits are parameters. A sugar can be added every p_1 time units, the preparation starts after p_2 time units, and the coffee is served after exactly p_3 time units. The coffee machine TA in Fig. 1 is thus a valuation of this PTA, with $p_1 = 1$, $p_2 = 5$ and $p_3 = 8$.

Note that in the PTA, the invariant of location ℓ_2 compares clock y to a constant 8, while the coffee action requires it to have the same value as parameter p_3. If $p_3 \neq 8$, then this might lead to inconsistencies in the coffee machine.

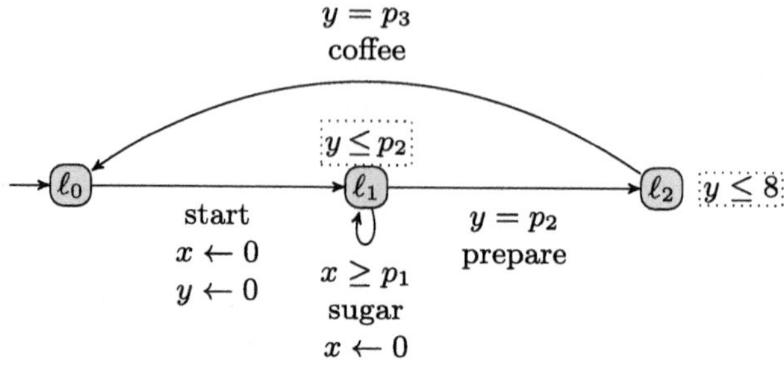

Fig. 12. Parametric coffee machine

6.2 Semantics

Concrete Semantics. The concrete semantics of PTAs can be understood as the union over all parameter valuations of the concrete semantics of the corresponding TAs (see Sect. 2.1). To this regard, a PTA is "just" the abstraction of an infinite number of concrete TAs. This is indeed one of the main advantages of PTAs.

Symbolic Semantics. While TAs can be analyzed using the zone graph (see, e.g., [30]) which, using some technical subtleties, is of finite size, PTAs cannot be analyzed using a finite structure. However, a (generally infinite) structure can be defined: the *parametric zone graph* extends the zone graph with timing parameters; zones become *parametric zones*. These zone graphs have been documented in, e.g. [12,62,67].

6.3 Decision and Computation Problems

Classical problems for PTAs come with two flavors:

1. *emptiness* problems: whether the set of parameter valuations guaranteeing a given property is empty or not, and
2. *synthesis* problems: synthesize all parameter valuations for which a given property holds.

The former are decision problems while the latter are computation problems.

Decision Problems. Due to the high expressiveness of PTAs, most non-trivial decision problems are undecidable. The mere emptiness of the parameter valuations set for which a location is reachable is undecidable [7]. Some decidable subclasses were exhibited, such as one-clock PTAs [7,29], two-clock PTAs with a single parameter over discrete time [57], L/U-PTAs [62], integer-valued PTAs [18,67], etc. See [9] for a survey on decision problems for PTAs and their subclasses.

Efficient Verification and Heuristics. Due to the aforementioned negative results, exact parameter synthesis is generally out of reach. Therefore, a number of works proposed synthesis algorithms for subclasses of PTAs, or tried to perform synthesis for the general class of PTAs using heuristics in order to obtain termination "as often as possible", but with a risk of non-termination. These works include:

- bounded model checking [74];
- synthesis for bounded parameters restricted to integer-valued valuations [67], or allowing rational valuations but without a guarantee of completeness [18];
- the use of subsumption for liveness synthesis [11,92];
- zone merging [20] and extrapolations [22];
- exploration orders [21]; and
- distributed [14] or compositional [19,26] verification.

6.4 Applications

PTAs were used to model and verify systems belonging to a number of areas, notably:

- protocols (e.g. [62,67,74]);
- verification of hardware systems (e.g. [46]);
- schedulability analysis of real-time systems under uncertainty (e.g. [2,13,54]);
- verification of software product lines [86];
- analyses of attack-trees [17];
- monitoring and parametric timed pattern matching [108]; and
- timing analyses of music scores [53].

7 Tool Support

7.1 Timed Model Checking

TINA (TIme petri Net Analyzer) [33] is a toolbox for modeling and verifying real-time systems modeled by time Petri nets, possibly extended with inhibitor arcs and priorities. The tool features notably CTL^* and LTL model checking.

Uppaal [80] is arguably the most well-known model checker for networks of timed automata extended with data types. Uppaal supports notably simulation, model checking, timed games, and statistical model checking. It relies on difference bound matrices [30], and is highly efficient in many different contexts.

7.2 Parametric Timed Model Checking

IMITATOR [10] is a parametric timed model checker taking as input models of real-time systems with timing parameters (i.e. unknown timing constants). The tool takes as inputs

1. a model in the form of a network of parametric timed automata (NPTA) [7], augmented with discrete global variables, stopwatches, multi-rate clocks, and some other useful features, and
2. a property expressed using a subset of TCTL possibly extended with timing parameters [42].

IMITATOR then synthesizes a set of parameter valuations (in the form of a possibly non-convex symbolic constraint) satisfying the property.

Roméo [83] is a parametric timed model checker taking as input parametric time Petri nets possibly extended with linear hybrid dynamics including stopwatches [106] and various data types. Roméo offers notably parameter synthesis against a subset of (parametric) TCTL [42], controller synthesis for parametric timed models, and parameter synthesis for optimal reachability with an affine cost model.

7.3 Model Checking with Strategies

MCMAS [85] is one of the leading model checkers for the verification of multi-agent systems. It takes as an input an (extended) interpreted system [69,84, 101]. MCMAS supports efficient BDD-based symbolic techniques for the model checking of multi-agent systems against specifications representing temporal, epistemic, and strategic properties.

STV (StraTegic Verifier) is an explicit-state ATL model checker, accommodating memoryless strategies and imperfect information within an asynchronous semantic framework. For verification purposes, STV deploys one of two principal algorithms: fixed-point approximations [64] or strategy synthesis utilizing a depth-first search algorithm [75]. To effectively manage the state-space explosion, STV incorporates various techniques, including partial order reductions [76] and assume-guarantee reasoning [88]. It features a user-defined text input for the specification of models and verification formulas, complemented by a web-based graphical interface for enhanced usability, available at stv.cs-htiew.com. Notably, STV has been instrumental in the verification of diverse scenarios, such as e-voting protocols [66].

Acknowledgement. This work was supported by: CNRS IRP "Le Trójkąt", NCBR Poland & FNR Luxembourg under the PolLux/FNR-CORE project SpaceVote (POLLUX-XI/14/SpaceVote/2023 and C22/IS/17232062/SpaceVote), the ANR-22-CE48-0012 project BISOUS, the PHC Polonium project MoCcA (BPN/BFR/2023/1/00045). For the purpose of open access, and in fulfilment of the obligations arising from the grant agreement, the authors have applied CC BY 4.0 license to any Author Accepted Manuscript version arising from this submission.

References

1. Ågotnes, T., Walicki, M.: A logic of reasoning, communication and cooperation with syntactic knowledge. In: Dignum, F., Dignum, V., Koenig, S., Kraus, S., Singh, M.P., Wooldridge, M.J. (eds.) AAMAS, pp. 1135–1136. ACM (2005). https://doi.org/10.1145/1082473.1082660
2. Altmeyer, S., et al.: From FMTV to WATERS: lessons learned from the first verification challenge at ECRTS (invited paper). In: Papadopoulos, A.V. (ed.) ECRTS. Leibniz International Proceedings in Informatics (LIPIcs), vol. 262, pp. 19:1–19:18. Schloss Dagstuhl – Leibniz-Zentrum für Informatik, Dagstuhl, Germany (2023). https://doi.org/10.4230/LIPIcs.ECRTS.2023.19
3. Alur, R., Courcoubetis, C., Dill, D.L.: Model-checking in dense real-time. Inf. Comput. **104**(1), 2–34 (1993). https://doi.org/10.1006/inco.1993.1024
4. Alur, R., Dill, D.L.: A theory of timed automata. Theoret. Comput. Sci. **126**(2), 183–235 (1994). https://doi.org/10.1016/0304-3975(94)90010-8
5. Alur, R., Henzinger, T.A., Kupferman, O.: Alternating-time temporal logic. In: FOCS, pp. 100–109. IEEE Computer Society (1997). https://doi.org/10.1109/SFCS.1997.646098
6. Alur, R., Henzinger, T.A., Kupferman, O.: Alternating-time temporal logic. J. ACM **49**(5), 672–713 (2002). https://doi.org/10.1145/585265.585270
7. Alur, R., Henzinger, T.A., Vardi, M.Y.: Parametric real-time reasoning. In: Kosaraju, S.R., Johnson, D.S., Aggarwal, A. (eds.) STOC, pp. 592–601. ACM, New York, NY, USA (1993). https://doi.org/10.1145/167088.167242
8. Amla, N., Kurshan, R., McMillan, K.L., Medel, R.: Experimental analysis of different techniques for bounded model checking. In: Garavel, H., Hatcliff, J. (eds.) TACAS 2003. LNCS, vol. 2619, pp. 34–48. Springer, Heidelberg (2003). https://doi.org/10.1007/3-540-36577-X_4
9. André, É.: What's decidable about parametric timed automata? Int. J. Softw. Tools Technol. Transfer **21**(2), 203–219 (2017). https://doi.org/10.1007/s10009-017-0467-0
10. André, É.: IMITATOR 3: synthesis of timing parameters beyond decidability. In: Silva, A., Leino, K.R.M. (eds.) CAV 2021. LNCS, vol. 12759, pp. 552–565. Springer, Cham (2021). https://doi.org/10.1007/978-3-030-81685-8_26
11. André, É., Arias, J., Petrucci, L., Pol, J.: Iterative bounded synthesis for efficient cycle detection in parametric timed automata. In: TACAS 2021. LNCS, vol. 12651, pp. 311–329. Springer, Cham (2021). https://doi.org/10.1007/978-3-030-72016-2_17
12. André, É., Chatain, T., Encrenaz, E., Fribourg, L.: An inverse method for parametric timed automata. Int. J. Found. Comput. Sci. **20**(5), 819–836 (2009). https://doi.org/10.1142/S0129054109006905
13. André, É., Coquard, E., Fribourg, L., Jerray, J., Lesens, D.: Parametric schedulability analysis of a launcher flight control system under reactivity constraints. Fund. Inform. **182**(1), 31–67 (2021). https://doi.org/10.3233/FI-2021-2065
14. André, É., Coti, C., Nguyen, H.G.: Enhanced distributed behavioral cartography of parametric timed automata. In: Butler, M., Conchon, S., Zaïdi, F. (eds.) ICFEM 2015. LNCS, vol. 9407, pp. 319–335. Springer, Cham (2015). https://doi.org/10.1007/978-3-319-25423-4_21
15. André, É., Jamroga, W., Knapik, M., Penczek, W., Petrucci, L.: Timed ATL: forget memory, just count. J. Artif. Intell. Res. **66**, 197–223 (2019). https://doi.org/10.1613/jair.1.11612

16. André, É., Knapik, M., Lime, D., Penczek, W., Petrucci, L.: Parametric verification: an introduction. In: Koutny, M., Pomello, L., Kristensen, L.M. (eds.) Transactions on Petri Nets and Other Models of Concurrency XIV. LNCS, vol. 11790, pp. 64–100. Springer, Heidelberg (2019). https://doi.org/10.1007/978-3-662-60651-3_3
17. André, É., Lime, D., Ramparison, M., Stoelinga, M.: Parametric analyses of attack-fault trees. Fund. Inform. **182**(1), 69–94 (2021). https://doi.org/10.3233/FI-2021-2066
18. André, É., Lime, D., Roux, O.H.: Integer-complete synthesis for bounded parametric timed automata. In: Bojańczyk, M., Lasota, S., Potapov, I. (eds.) RP 2015. LNCS, vol. 9328, pp. 7–19. Springer, Cham (2015). https://doi.org/10.1007/978-3-319-24537-9_2
19. André, É., Lin, S.-W.: Learning-based compositional parameter synthesis for event-recording automata. In: Bouajjani, A., Silva, A. (eds.) FORTE 2017. LNCS, vol. 10321, pp. 17–32. Springer, Cham (2017). https://doi.org/10.1007/978-3-319-60225-7_2
20. André, É., Marinho, D., Petrucci, L., van de Pol, J.: Efficient convex zone merging in parametric timed automata. In: Bogomolov, S., Parker, D. (eds.) FORMATS. Lecture Notes in Computer Science, vol. 13465, pp. 200–218. Springer (2022). https://doi.org/10.1007/978-3-031-15839-1_12
21. André, É., Nguyen, H.G., Petrucci, L.: Efficient parameter synthesis using optimized state exploration strategies. In: Hu, Z., Bai, G. (eds.) ICECCS, pp. 1–10. IEEE (2017). https://doi.org/10.1109/ICECCS.2017.28
22. Arcile, J., André, É.: Zone extrapolations in parametric timed automata. Innov. Syst. Softw. Eng. (2024). https://doi.org/10.1007/s11334-024-00554-5
23. Arias, J., Jamroga, W., Penczek, W., Petrucci, L., Sidoruk, T.: Strategic (timed) computation tree logic. In: Agmon, N., An, B., Ricci, A., Yeoh, W. (eds.) AAMAS, pp. 382–390. ACM (2023). https://doi.org/10.5555/3545946.3598661
24. Asarin, E., Bozga, M., Kerbrat, A., Maler, O., Pnueli, A., Rasse, A.: Data-structures for the verification of timed automata. In: Maler, O. (ed.) HART. Lecture Notes in Computer Science, vol. 1201, pp. 346–360. Springer (1997). https://doi.org/10.1007/BFB0014737
25. Audemard, G., Cimatti, A., Kornilowicz, A., Sebastiani, R.: Bounded model checking for timed systems. In: Peled, D.A., Vardi, M.Y. (eds.) FORTE 2002. LNCS, vol. 2529, pp. 243–259. Springer, Heidelberg (2002). https://doi.org/10.1007/3-540-36135-9_16
26. Aştefănoaei, L., Bensalem, S., Bozga, M., Cheng, C.-H., Ruess, H.: Compositional parameter synthesis. In: Fitzgerald, J., Heitmeyer, C., Gnesi, S., Philippou, A. (eds.) FM 2016. LNCS, vol. 9995, pp. 60–68. Springer, Cham (2016). https://doi.org/10.1007/978-3-319-48989-6_4
27. Behrmann, G., Larsen, K.G., Pearson, J., Weise, C., Yi, W.: Efficient timed reachability analysis using clock difference diagrams. In: Halbwachs, N., Peled, D. (eds.) CAV 1999. LNCS, vol. 1633, pp. 341–353. Springer, Heidelberg (1999). https://doi.org/10.1007/3-540-48683-6_30
28. Belardinelli, F., Condurache, R., Dima, C., Jamroga, W., Jones, A.V.: Bisimulations for verifying strategic abilities with an application to ThreeBallot. In: Larson, K., Winikoff, M., Das, S., Durfee, E.H. (eds.) AAMAS, pp. 1286–1295. ACM (2017). http://dl.acm.org/citation.cfm?id=3091303
29. Beneš, N., Bezděk, P., Larsen, K.G., Srba, J.: Language emptiness of continuous-time parametric timed automata. In: Halldórsson, M.M., Iwama, K., Kobayashi,

N., Speckmann, B. (eds.) ICALP 2015. LNCS, vol. 9135, pp. 69–81. Springer, Heidelberg (2015). https://doi.org/10.1007/978-3-662-47666-6_6
30. Bengtsson, J., Yi, W.: Timed automata: semantics, algorithms and tools. In: Desel, J., Reisig, W., Rozenberg, G. (eds.) ACPN 2003. LNCS, vol. 3098, pp. 87–124. Springer, Heidelberg (2004). https://doi.org/10.1007/978-3-540-27755-2_3
31. Berthomieu, B., Diaz, M.: Modeling and verification of time dependent systems using time Petri nets. IEEE Trans. Software Eng. **17**(3), 259–273 (1991). https://doi.org/10.1109/32.75415
32. Berthomieu, B., Menasche, M.: An enumerative approach for analyzing time Petri nets. In: Mason, R.E.A. (ed.) Information Processing, pp. 41–46. North-Holland/IFIP (1983)
33. Berthomieu, B., Vernadat, F.: Time petri nets analysis with TINA. In: QEST, pp. 123–124. IEEE Computer Society (2006). https://doi.org/10.1109/QEST.2006.56
34. Berthomieu, B., Vernadat, F.: State class constructions for branching analysis of time petri nets. In: Garavel, H., Hatcliff, J. (eds.) TACAS 2003. LNCS, vol. 2619, pp. 442–457. Springer, Heidelberg (2003). https://doi.org/10.1007/3-540-36577-X_33
35. Bontemps, Y., Schobbens, P.Y., Löding, C.: Synthesis of open reactive systems from scenario-based specifications, vol. 62, pp. 139–169 (2004). http://content.iospress.com/articles/fundamenta-informaticae/fi62-2-02
36. Bouajjani, A., Fernandez, J.C., Halbwachs, N., Raymond, P.: Minimal state graph generation. Sci. Comput. Program. **18**(3), 247–269 (1992). https://doi.org/10.1016/0167-6423(92)90018-7
37. Bouajjani, A., Tripakis, S., Yovine, S.: On-the-fly symbolic model checking for real-time systems. In: RTSS, pp. 25–34. IEEE Computer Society (1997). https://doi.org/10.1109/REAL.1997.641266
38. Bouyer, P., Chevalier, F., Markey, N.: On the expressiveness of TPTL and MTL. Inf. Comput. **208**(2), 97–116 (2010). https://doi.org/10.1016/J.IC.2009.10.004
39. Bouyer, P., Dufourd, C., Fleury, E., Petit, A.: Updatable timed automata. Theoret. Comput. Sci. **321**(2–3), 291–345 (2004). https://doi.org/10.1016/j.tcs.2004.04.003
40. Bouyer, P., Laroussinie, F., Reynier, P.-A.: Diagonal constraints in timed automata: forward analysis of timed systems. In: Pettersson, P., Yi, W. (eds.) FORMATS 2005. LNCS, vol. 3829, pp. 112–126. Springer, Heidelberg (2005). https://doi.org/10.1007/11603009_10
41. Bouyer, P., Markey, N., Sankur, O.: Robustness in timed automata. In: Abdulla, P.A., Potapov, I. (eds.) RP 2013. LNCS, vol. 8169, pp. 1–18. Springer, Heidelberg (2013). https://doi.org/10.1007/978-3-642-41036-9_1
42. Bruyère, V., Raskin, J.F.: Real-time model-checking: Parameters everywhere. Log. Methods Comput. Sci. **3**(1:7), 1–30 (2007). https://doi.org/10.2168/LMCS-3(1:7)2007
43. Bérard, B., et al.: Systems and Software Verification. Model-Checking Techniques and Tools. Springer (2001). https://doi.org/10.1007/978-3-662-04558-9
44. Bérard, B., Cassez, F., Haddad, S., Lime, D., Roux, O.H.: Comparison of the expressiveness of timed automata and time petri nets. In: Pettersson, P., Yi, W. (eds.) FORMATS 2005. LNCS, vol. 3829, pp. 211–225. Springer, Heidelberg (2005). https://doi.org/10.1007/11603009_17
45. Cassez, F., Roux, O.H.: Structural translation from time Petri nets to timed automata. J. Syst. Softw. **79**(10), 1456–1468 (2006). https://doi.org/10.1016/j.jss.2005.12.021

46. Chevallier, R., Encrenaz-Tiphène, E., Fribourg, L., Xu, W.: Timed verification of the generic architecture of a memory circuit using parametric timed automata. Formal Methods Syst. Des. **34**(1), 59–81 (2009). https://doi.org/10.1007/s10703-008-0061-x
47. Clarke, E.M., Emerson, E.A., Sistla, A.P.: Automatic verification of finite-state concurrent systems using temporal logic specifications. ACM Trans. Program. Lang. Syst. **8**(2), 244–263 (1986). https://doi.org/10.1145/5397.5399
48. Cortés, L.A., Eles, P., Peng, Z.: Modeling and formal verification of embedded systems based on a Petri net representation. J. Syst. Architect. **49**(12–15), 571–598 (2003). https://doi.org/10.1016/S1383-7621(03)00096-1
49. D'Aprile, D., Donatelli, S., Sangnier, A., Sproston, J.: From time petri nets to timed automata: an untimed approach. In: Grumberg, O., Huth, M. (eds.) TACAS 2007. LNCS, vol. 4424, pp. 216–230. Springer, Heidelberg (2007). https://doi.org/10.1007/978-3-540-71209-1_18
50. Daws, C., Tripakis, S.: Model checking of real-time reachability properties using abstractions. In: Steffen, B. (ed.) TACAS. Lecture Notes in Computer Science, vol. 1384, pp. 313–329. Springer (1998). https://doi.org/10.1007/BFb0054180
51. Dill, D.L.: Timing assumptions and verification of finite-state concurrent systems. In: Sifakis, J. (ed.) CAV 1989. LNCS, vol. 407, pp. 197–212. Springer, Heidelberg (1990). https://doi.org/10.1007/3-540-52148-8_17
52. Ehrenborg, R., Skinner, C.M.: The blind bartender's problem. J. Comb. Theory Ser. A **70**(2), 249–266 (1995)
53. Fanchon, L., Jacquemard, F.: Formal timing analysis of mixed music scores. In: ICMC. Michigan Publishing (2013)
54. Fribourg, L., Lesens, D., Moro, P., Soulat, R.: Robustness analysis for scheduling problems using the inverse method. In: Reynolds, M., Terenziani, P., Moszkowski, B. (eds.) TIME, pp. 73–80. IEEE Computer Society Press (2012). https://doi.org/10.1109/TIME.2012.10
55. Gardey, G., Roux, O.H., Roux, O.F.: Using zone graph method for computing the state space of a time petri net. In: Larsen, K.G., Niebert, P. (eds.) FORMATS 2003. LNCS, vol. 2791, pp. 246–259. Springer, Heidelberg (2004). https://doi.org/10.1007/978-3-540-40903-8_20
56. Gastin, P., Mukherjee, S., Srivathsan, B.: Reachability in timed automata with diagonal constraints. In: Schewe, S., Zhang, L. (eds.) CONCUR. LIPIcs, vol. 118, pp. 28:1–28:17. Schloss Dagstuhl - Leibniz-Zentrum für Informatik (2018). https://doi.org/10.4230/LIPICS.CONCUR.2018.28
57. Göller, S., Hilaire, M.: Reachability in two-parametric timed automata with one parameter is EXPSPACE-complete. In: Bläser, M., Monmege, B. (eds.) STACS. LIPIcs, vol. 187, pp. 36:1–36:18. Schloss Dagstuhl - Leibniz-Zentrum für Informatik (2021). https://doi.org/10.4230/LIPIcs.STACS.2021.36
58. Haar, S., Kaiser, L., Simonot-Lion, F., Toussaint, J.: On equivalence between timed state machines and time Petri nets. Research Report RR-4049, INRIA (2000). https://inria.hal.science/inria-00072589
59. Henzinger, T.A., Nicollin, X., Sifakis, J., Yovine, S.: Symbolic model checking for real-time systems. Inf. Comput. **111**(2), 193–244 (1994). https://doi.org/10.1006/inco.1994.1045
60. Huang, X., van der Meyden, R.: Symbolic model checking epistemic strategy logic. In: Brodley, C.E., Stone, P. (eds.) AAAI, pp. 1426–1432. AAAI Press (2014). https://doi.org/10.1609/AAAI.V28I1.8894

61. Hulgaard, H., Burns, S.M.: Efficient timing analysis of a class of petri nets. In: Wolper, P. (ed.) CAV 1995. LNCS, vol. 939, pp. 423–436. Springer, Heidelberg (1995). https://doi.org/10.1007/3-540-60045-0_67
62. Hune, T., Romijn, J., Stoelinga, M., Vaandrager, F.W.: Linear parametric model checking of timed automata. J. Logic Algebraic Program. **52–53**, 183–220 (2002). https://doi.org/10.1016/S1567-8326(02)00037-1
63. Jamroga, W., van der Hoek, W.: Agents that know how to play. Fundamenta Informaticae **63**(2-3), 185–219 (2004). http://content.iospress.com/articles/fundamenta-informaticae/fi63-2-3-05
64. Jamroga, W., Knapik, M., Kurpiewski, D., Mikulski, L.: Approximate verification of strategic abilities under imperfect information. Artif. Intell. **277** (2019). https://doi.org/10.1016/J.ARTINT.2019.103172
65. Jamroga, W., Penczek, W., Sidoruk, T., Dembinski, P., Mazurkiewicz, A.W.: Towards partial order reductions for strategic ability. J. Artif. Intell. Res. **68**, 817–850 (2020). https://doi.org/10.1613/jair.1.11936
66. Jamroga, W., et al.: Verification of multi-agent properties in electronic voting: a case study. In: Fernández-Duque, D., Palmigiano, A., Pinchinat, S. (eds.) AiML, pp. 531–556. College Publications (2022)
67. Jovanović, A., Lime, D., Roux, O.H.: Integer parameter synthesis for real-time systems. IEEE Trans. Software Eng. **41**(5), 445–461 (2015). https://doi.org/10.1109/TSE.2014.2357445
68. Kacprzak, M., Lomuscio, A., Łasica, T., Penczek, W., Szreter, M.: Verifying multi-agent systems via unbounded model checking. In: Hinchey, M.G., Rash, J.L., Truszkowski, W.F., Rouff, C.A. (eds.) FAABS 2004. LNCS (LNAI), vol. 3228, pp. 189–212. Springer, Heidelberg (2004). https://doi.org/10.1007/978-3-540-30960-4_13
69. Kacprzak, M., Lomuscio, A., Penczek, W.: Bounded versus unbounded model checking for interpreted systems. In: Dunin-Kęplicz, B., Verbrugge, R. (eds.) FAMAS, pp. 5–20. Warsaw University (2003)
70. Kacprzak, M., Lomuscio, A., Penczek, W.: Unbounded model checking for knowledge and time. In: Czaja, L. (ed.) CS&P, vol. 1, pp. 251–264. Warsaw University (2003)
71. Kacprzak, M., Penczek, W.: A SAT-based approach to unbounded model checking for alternating-time temporal epistemic logic. Synthese **142**(2), 203–227 (2004). https://doi.org/10.1007/S11229-004-2446-8
72. Kacprzak, M., Penczek, W.: Unbounded model checking for alternating-time temporal logic. In: AAMAS, pp. 646–653. IEEE Computer Society (2004). https://doi.org/10.1109/AAMAS.2004.10089
73. Kacprzak, M., Penczek, W.: Fully symbolic unbounded model checking for alternating-time temporal logic. Auton. Agent. Multi-Agent Syst. **11**(1), 69–89 (2005). https://doi.org/10.1007/S10458-005-0944-9
74. Knapik, M., Penczek, W.: Bounded model checking for parametric timed automata. In: Jensen, K., Donatelli, S., Kleijn, J. (eds.) Transactions on Petri Nets and Other Models of Concurrency V. LNCS, vol. 6900, pp. 141–159. Springer, Heidelberg (2012). https://doi.org/10.1007/978-3-642-29072-5_6
75. Kurpiewski, D., Knapik, M., Jamroga, W.: On domination and control in strategic ability. In: Elkind, E., Veloso, M., Agmon, N., Taylor, M.E. (eds.) AAMAS, pp. 197–205. International Foundation for Autonomous Agents and Multiagent Systems (2019). http://dl.acm.org/citation.cfm?id=3331693

76. Kurpiewski, D., Pazderski, W., Jamroga, W., Kim, Y.: STV+reductions: towards practical verification of strategic ability using model reductions. In: Dignum, F., Lomuscio, A., Endriss, U., Nowé, A. (eds.) AAMAS, pp. 1770–1772. ACM (2021). https://doi.org/10.5555/3463952.3464232
77. Laarman, A., Olesen, M.C., Dalsgaard, A.E., Larsen, K.G., van de Pol, J.: Multi-core emptiness checking of timed Büchi automata using inclusion abstraction. In: Sharygina, N., Veith, H. (eds.) CAV 2013. LNCS, vol. 8044, pp. 968–983. Springer, Heidelberg (2013). https://doi.org/10.1007/978-3-642-39799-8_69
78. Laroussinie, F., Markey, N., Oreiby, G.: Model-checking timed ATL for durational concurrent game structures. In: Asarin, E., Bouyer, P. (eds.) FORMATS 2006. LNCS, vol. 4202, pp. 245–259. Springer, Heidelberg (2006). https://doi.org/10.1007/11867340_18
79. Larsen, K.G., Larsson, F., Pettersson, P., Yi, W.: Efficient verification of real-time systems: compact data structure and state-space reduction. In: RTSS, pp. 14–24. IEEE Computer Society (1997). https://doi.org/10.1109/REAL.1997.641265
80. Larsen, K.G., Pettersson, P., Yi, W.: UPPAAL in a nutshell. Int. J. Softw. Tools Technol. Transfer **1**(1-2), 134–152 (1997). https://doi.org/10.1007/s100090050010
81. Lee, D., Yannakakis, M.: Online minimization of transition systems (extended abstract). In: Kosaraju, S.R., Fellows, M., Wigderson, A., Ellis, J.A. (eds.) SToC, pp. 264–274. ACM (1992). https://doi.org/10.1145/129712.129738
82. Lime, D., Roux, O.H.: State class timed automaton of a time Petri net. In: PNPM, pp. 124–133. IEEE Computer Society (2003). https://doi.org/10.1109/PNPM.2003.1231549
83. Lime, D., Roux, O.H., Seidner, C., Traonouez, L.-M.: Romeo: a parametric model-checker for petri nets with stopwatches. In: Kowalewski, S., Philippou, A. (eds.) TACAS 2009. LNCS, vol. 5505, pp. 54–57. Springer, Heidelberg (2009). https://doi.org/10.1007/978-3-642-00768-2_6
84. Lomuscio, A., Łasica, T., Penczek, W.: Bounded model checking for interpreted systems: preliminary experimental results. In: Hinchey, M.G., Rash, J.L., Truszkowski, W.F., Rouff, C., Gordon-Spears, D. (eds.) FAABS 2002. LNCS (LNAI), vol. 2699, pp. 115–125. Springer, Heidelberg (2003). https://doi.org/10.1007/978-3-540-45133-4_10
85. Lomuscio, A., Qu, H., Raimondi, F.: MCMAS: an open-source model checker for the verification of multi-agent systems. Int. J. Softw. Tools Technol. Transfer **19**(1), 9–30 (2017). https://doi.org/10.1007/S10009-015-0378-X
86. Luthmann, L., Gerecht, T., Stephan, A., Bürdek, J., Lochau, M.: Minimum/-maximum delay testing of product lines with unbounded parametric real-time constraints. J. Syst. Softw. **149**, 535–553 (2019). https://doi.org/10.1016/j.jss.2018.12.028
87. Merlin, P.M., Farber, D.J.: Recoverability of communication protocols-implications of a theoretical study. IEEE Trans. Commun. **24**(9), 1036–1043 (1976). https://doi.org/10.1109/TCOM.1976.1093424
88. Mikulski, L., Jamroga, W., Kurpiewski, D.: Assume-guarantee verification of strategic ability. In: Aydogan, R., Criado, N., Lang, J., Sánchez-Anguix, V., Serramia, M. (eds.) PRIMA. Lecture Notes in Computer Science, vol. 13753, pp. 173–191. Springer (2022). https://doi.org/10.1007/978-3-031-21203-1_11
89. Miller, J.S.: Decidability and complexity results for timed automata and semi-linear hybrid automata. In: Lynch, N., Krogh, B.H. (eds.) HSCC 2000. LNCS, vol. 1790, pp. 296–310. Springer, Heidelberg (2000). https://doi.org/10.1007/3-540-46430-1_26

90. Møller, J., Lichtenberg, J., Andersen, H.R., Hulgaard, H.: Difference decision diagrams. In: Flum, J., Rodriguez-Artalejo, M. (eds.) CSL 1999. LNCS, vol. 1683, pp. 111–125. Springer, Heidelberg (1999). https://doi.org/10.1007/3-540-48168-0_9
91. Møller, J.B., Lichtenberg, J., Andersen, H.R., Hulgaard, H.: Fully symbolic model checking of timed systems using difference decision diagrams. In: Cimatti, A., Grumberg, O. (eds.) SMC@FLoC. Electronic Notes in Theoretical Computer Science, vol. 23, pp. 88–107. Elsevier (1999). https://doi.org/10.1016/S1571-0661(04)80671-6
92. Nguyen, H.G., Petrucci, L., van de Pol, J.: Layered and collecting NDFS with subsumption for parametric timed automata. In: Lin, A.W., Sun, J. (eds.) ICECCS, pp. 1–9. IEEE Computer Society (2018). https://doi.org/10.1109/ICECCS2018.2018.00009
93. Okawa, Y., Yoneda, T.: Symbolic CTL model checking of time Petri nets. Electron. Commun. Japan Scripta Technica **80**(4), 11–20 (1997)
94. Paige, R., Tarjan, R.E.: Three partition refinement algorithms. SIAM J. Comput. **16**(6), 973–989 (1987). https://doi.org/10.1137/0216062
95. Penczek, W., Półrola, A.: Abstractions and partial order reductions for checking branching properties of time petri nets. In: Colom, J.-M., Koutny, M. (eds.) ICATPN 2001. LNCS, vol. 2075, pp. 323–342. Springer, Heidelberg (2001). https://doi.org/10.1007/3-540-45740-2_19
96. Penczek, W., Półrola, A.: Advances in Verification of Time Petri Nets and Timed Automata: A Temporal Logic Approach. Studies in Computational Intelligence, vol. 20. Springer (2006). https://doi.org/10.1007/978-3-540-32870-4
97. Penczek, W., Woźna, B., Zbrzezny, A.: Towards bounded model checking for the universal fragment of TCTL. In: Damm, W., Olderog, E.-R. (eds.) FTRTFT 2002. LNCS, vol. 2469, pp. 265–288. Springer, Heidelberg (2002). https://doi.org/10.1007/3-540-45739-9_17
98. Petri, C.A.: Kommunikation mit Automaten. Ph.D. thesis, Darmstadt University of Technology, Germany (1962)
99. Półrola, A., Penczek, W., Szreter, M.: Reachability analysis for timed automata using partitioning algorithms. Fund. Inform. **55**(2), 203–221 (2003)
100. Półrola, A., Penczek, W.: Minimization algorithms for time Petri nets. Fundamenta Informaticae **60**(1-4), 307–331 (2004). http://content.iospress.com/articles/fundamenta-informaticae/fi60-1-4-21
101. Raimondi, F., Lomuscio, A.: A tool for specification and verification of epistemic properties in interpreted systems. In: van der Hoek, W., Lomuscio, A., de Vink, E.P., Wooldridge, M.J. (eds.) LCMAS. Electronic Notes in Theoretical Computer Science, vol. 85, pp. 176–191. Elsevier (2003). https://doi.org/10.1016/S1571-0661(05)82609-X
102. Ramchandani, C.: Analysis of asynchronous concurrent systems by timed Petri nets. Ph.D. thesis, Massachusetts Institute of Technology, USA (1973). http://hdl.handle.net/1721.1/13739
103. Seshia, S.A., Bryant, R.E.: Unbounded, fully symbolic model checking of timed automata using boolean methods. In: Hunt, W.A., Somenzi, F. (eds.) CAV 2003. LNCS, vol. 2725, pp. 154–166. Springer, Heidelberg (2003). https://doi.org/10.1007/978-3-540-45069-6_16
104. Sifakis, J., Yovine, S.: Compositional specification of timed systems. In: Puech, C., Reischuk, R. (eds.) STACS 1996. LNCS, vol. 1046, pp. 345–359. Springer, Heidelberg (1996). https://doi.org/10.1007/3-540-60922-9_29

105. Sorea, M.: Bounded model checking for timed automata. In: Vogler, W., Larsen, K. (eds.) MTCS. Electronic Notes in Theoretical Computer Science, vol. 68, pp. 116–134. Elsevier (2002). https://doi.org/10.1016/S1571-0661(04)80523-1
106. Traonouez, L.M., Lime, D., Roux, O.H.: Parametric model-checking of stopwatch Petri nets. J. Univ. Comput. Sci. **15**(17), 3273–3304 (2009). https://doi.org/10.3217/jucs-015-17-3273
107. Virbitskaite, I., Pokozy, E.: A partial order method for the verification of time Petri nets. In: Ciobanu, G., Păun, G. (eds.) FCT 1999. LNCS, vol. 1684, pp. 547–558. Springer, Heidelberg (1999). https://doi.org/10.1007/3-540-48321-7_46
108. Waga, M., André, É., Hasuo, I.: Parametric timed pattern matching. ACM Trans. Softw. Eng. Methodol. **32**(1), 10:1–10:35 (2023). https://doi.org/10.1145/3517194
109. Wang, F.: Region encoding diagram for fully symbolic verification of real-time systems. In: COMPSAC, pp. 509–515. IEEE Computer Society (2000). https://doi.org/10.1109/CMPSAC.2000.884774
110. Wang, F.: Efficient verification of timed automata with BDD-like data structures. Int. J. Softw. Tools Technol. Transfer **6**(1), 77–97 (2004). https://doi.org/10.1007/S10009-003-0135-4
111. Wolf, K.: A gentle tour through a Petri net model checking tool. In: Kordon, F., et al. (eds.) Transactions on Petri Nets and Other Models of Concurrency XVIII. LNCS, vol. 16260, pp. xx-yy. Springer, Cham (2026)
112. Woźna, B., Lomuscio, A., Penczek, W.: Bounded model checking for knowledge and real time. In: Pechoucek, M., Steiner, D., Thompson, S.G. (eds.) AAMAS, pp. 165–172. ACM (2005). https://doi.org/10.1145/1082473.1082498
113. Yi, W., Pettersson, P., Daniels, M.: Automatic verification of real-time communicating systems by constraint-solving. In: Hogrefe, D., Leue, S. (eds.) FORTE. IFIP Conference Proceedings, vol. 6, pp. 243–258. Chapman & Hall (1994)
114. Yoneda, T., Ryuba, H.: CTL model checking of time Petri nets using geometric regions. IEICE Trans. Inf. Syst. **81**(3), 297–306 (1998)

Analysis and Synthesis of Some Subclasses of Petri Nets

Raymond Devillers[1] and Kamila Barylska[2](✉)

[1] Département d'Informatique, Université Libre de Bruxelles, Brussels, Belgium
raymond.devillers@ulb.be

[2] Faculty of Mathematics and Computer Science, Nicolaus Copernicus University, 87-100 Toruń, Poland
kamila.barylska@mat.umk.pl

Abstract. The present paper constitutes the material used for a lecture that took place as part of the Advanced Course on Petri Nets in September 2023. The lecture was mainly based on papers by Eike Best and Raymond Devillers [1–7], among others [8,9]. The main issues discussed here are synthesis algorithms designed for certain classes of Petri nets, enabling faster solution. These subjects (among others) are also discussed in detail in the book [10].

1 Introduction

The analysis of a dynamic system consists of deriving its behavioural properties from a static description of the system. A variant consists of deriving the behavioural properties common to all the systems belonging to some class of interest. Reversely, a synthesis problem consists of deriving a system (of some class) presenting some aimed properties. Note however that it may happen that no system presents the properties we want and, if there is one, very often many ones will also do the job, possibly with very different structures.

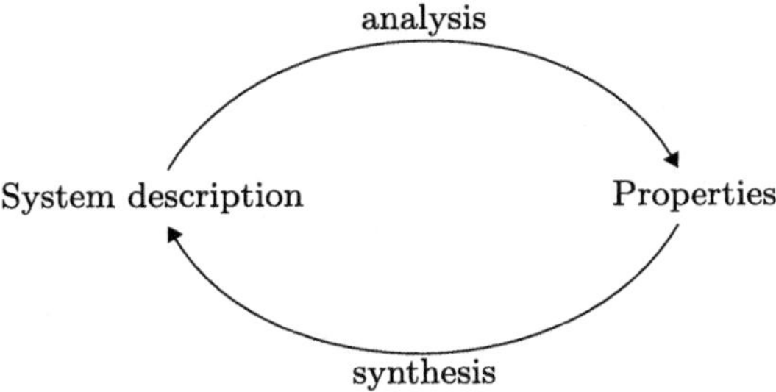

In his PhD thesis [11], Carl Adam Petri used some kinds of nets to model the interactions between the various components of a system. Since then many classes (and subclasses) of "Petri nets" have been considered in the literature, like elementary nets [12], occurrence nets [13], P/T nets [14,15], coloured nets [16], algebraic nets [17], recursive nets [18], fluid nets [19], ... They are all based on

F. Kordon et al. (Eds.): *Transactions on Petri Nets and Other Models of Concurrency XVIII*, LNCTPN 16260, pp. 195–230, 2026.
https://doi.org/10.1007/978-3-662-73305-9_7

bipartite graphs, i.e., graphs with two kinds of nodes and arcs only between nodes of different kinds. They differ in decorations, interpretations and constraints.

Here, we shall essentially be interested in (bounded, weighted) P/T nets (hereafter simply called *nets*) and some popular subclasses obtained by restricting the weights, the number of arcs into and from each node, ... The two kinds of nodes are called places and transitions. Transitions represent local activities and each place represents a local state, i.e., a type of resource. There may be many interchangeable copies of each resource and the global state is captured by a notion of marking. The arcs indicate how local activities need, absorb and produce resources. The semantics is captured by a so-called firing rule, which leads to labelled transition systems in the form of reachability graphs.

The structure of the paper is as follows. The next section recalls basic notions on graphs, transition systems and nets, as well as the general ideas about net synthesis from a labelled transition system. Section 3 will then concentrate on choice-free nets and show how separating a synthesis into a pre-synthesis and a proper synthesis; the classical case is also generalised to simultaneous syntheses. The next two sections reduce the target class to (weighted) marked graphs. Section 6 introduces the principle of a divide and conquer strategy for synthesis and details it in the case of product/sum of nets and articulations, as well as for combining these two principles. The last section, as usual, concludes.

2 Preliminaries

2.1 Basics

Let us first present some concepts and definitions used throughout this paper.

The set of non-negative integers is denoted by $\mathbb{N}$. Given a set X, the cardinality (number of elements) of X is denoted by $|X|$. A function $\mu : X \to \mathbb{N}$ may also be considered as a vector in $\mathbb{N}^{|X|}$. Having a vector $x \in \mathbb{N}^{|X|}$, the set $\{s \in X \mid |x(s) \geq 0\}$ is called the *support* of x.

To make it easier to understand the presented material, we provide several definitions from graph theory.

Definition 1. *A* directed graph *is an ordered pair $G = (V, E)$ where:*

- *V is a set of elements called* vertices *or* nodes,
- *E is a set of ordered pairs of vertices, called* (directed) edges *or* arcs.

A directed graph with an initial vertex *is a tuple $G = (V, E, v_0)$ where (V, E) is a directed graph and $v_0 \in V$ is a distinguished vertex.*

Given a directed graph $G = (V, E)$, a sequence $(e_0, e_1, \ldots, e_{n-1})$ of edges is called a *(directed) path* if it joins a sequence of vertices, i.e., there exist vertices $v_0, v_1, \ldots, v_n \in V$ such that $\forall_{k \in \{0,1,\ldots,n-1\}} : e_k = (v_k, v_{k+1}) \in E$. A *cycle* is a path $(v_0, v_1, \ldots, v_n)$ such that $v_0 = v_n$.

Let Σ be a set of *labels*, then a *graph labelling* l of G is an assignment of labels to the edges of the graph ($l : E \to \Sigma$).

Definition 2. *A* labelled directed graph with an initial vertex *is a tuple* $G = (V, E, v_0, l)$ *where* (V, E, v_0) *is a directed graph with an initial vertex and* $l : E \to \Sigma$ *is a graph labelling.*

Sometimes when analysing a labelled graph, instead of referring to the names of the edges, we use their labels directly, and instead of analysing sequences of edges, we focus only on their labels. We then adapt the concepts of path and cycle to the sequence of labels in a natural way, according to the labeling function. Namely, assuming $e_i \in E$, $l_i \in \Sigma$ for $i \in \{1, \dots, |E|\}$, and moreover $l(e_i) = l_i$, each path $(v_1, v_2, \dots, v_n)$ defines a sequence of labels $(l_1, l_2, \dots, l_n)$, which we also call a *path* (whenever this doesn't lead to misunderstandings).

Let Σ be a set of labels (also called an *alphabet*). By Σ^* we denote the set of all finite sequences of labels or *letters*.[1] A sequence $\sigma = (l_1, l_2, \dots, l_n) \in \Sigma^*$ may be denoted simply by $\sigma = l_1 l_2 \dots l_n$ (omitting the parentheses). For an alphabet $\Sigma = (a_1, a_2, \dots, a_k)$ and a sequence of labels $\sigma \in \Sigma^*$, the *Parikh vector* is defined as the function $\Psi : \Sigma^* \to \mathbb{N}^k$, given by $\Psi(\sigma) = (|\sigma|_{a_1}, |\sigma|_{a_2}, \dots, |\sigma|_{a_k})$, where $|\sigma|_{a_i}$ denotes the number of occurrences of the label a_i in the sequence σ. In other words, the Parikh vector $\Psi(\sigma)$ is a vector of natural numbers with index set Σ (i.e., a Σ-vector), where $\Psi(\sigma)(a)$ denotes the number of occurrences of a in σ.

Having two Σ-vectors $V_1, V_2 : \Sigma^* \to \mathbb{N}^k$ we say that V_1 is *smaller* than V_2 (denoted $V_1 \leq V_2$) if $\forall_{a \in \Sigma}\ V_1(a) \leq V_2(a)$. In that case we also say that V_2 *dominates* V_1.

Let us now recall basic definitions concerning finite labelled transition systems.

Definition 3. *A* finite labelled transition system *with initial state (in short: an lts) is a tuple* $TS{=}(S, \to, T, \imath)$ *with:*

- *a finite set of* states S *(*nodes*),*
- *an* alphabet T*, that is a finite set of* letters *(edge* labels*),*
- *a set of* labelled edges $\to \subseteq (S \times T \times S)$,
- *a distinguished state called the* initial state $\imath \in S$.

Finite labelled transition systems admit a natural graphical representation in the form of a labelled directed graph with an initial vertex, where the vertices are states (S), while the initial vertex is the initial state ($\imath$), and there is an edge (s, s') labelled by t in the graph if $(s, t, s') \in \to$. An example of *lts* can be found, among others, on the left hand side of the Fig. 1.

We now list definitions and notations for the enabledness and reachability in an *lts*.

· In $TS{=}(S, \to, T, \imath)$, a label $t \in T$ of is *enabled* at a state s, denoted by $s[t\rangle$, if there is some state s' such that $(s, t, s') \in \to$. In this case we also say that s' is *reachable* from s through t, and use the notation $s[t\rangle s'$.

[1] An empty sequence is denoted as ε.

- One can extend in a natural way the notions of enabledness and reachability to sequences of labels. The empty sequence ε is enabled at any state s and $s[\varepsilon\rangle s$. A sequence $\sigma = t\rho$ is enabled at s, and s'' is the resulting state (denoted $s[\sigma\rangle s''$) for $t \in T$, $\rho \in T^*$, whenever $(s,t,s') \in \rightarrow$, ρ is enabled at s' and s'' is the resulting state ($s'[\rho\rangle s''$).
- If there exist a sequence $\sigma \in T^*$ such that $s[\sigma\rangle s'$, then we say that s' is reachable from s. By $[s\rangle$ we denote the set of all the states reachable from s.

Analogously to the case of graphs, a finite sequence of labels $\rho \in T^*$, such that $s[\rho\rangle s'$ is called a *cycle (at state s)*, if $s = s'$. The *Parikh vector* $\Psi(\rho)$ is a vector of natural numbers with index set T, where $\Psi(\rho)(t)$ denotes the number of occurrences of t in ρ.

Below we recall a number of definitions and notations concerning an *lts*.

- A nonempty cycle is *small* in a transition system if no other one has a smaller Parikh vector.
- A path $\rho \in T^*$, such that $s[\rho\rangle s'$, is *short* if there is no other one with a smaller Parikh vector from s to s'.
- A cycle $\rho \in T^*$, such that $s[\rho\rangle s$, is *prime* if the greatest common divisor of the entries in its Parikh vector is 1.
- A T-vector Υ is *realisable* in an *lts* if there are two states s, s' and a directed path $\rho \in T^*$ with $s[\rho\rangle s'$ such that $\Upsilon = \Psi(\rho)$.
- The *residue* of a T-vector μ by another one ν is the T-vector $\mu \overset{\bullet}{-} \nu$ constructed in such a way that $\forall_{t \in T} : (\mu \overset{\bullet}{-} \nu)(t) = \max(\mu(t) - \nu(t), 0)$.[2]
- We sometimes use a shortened notation and say that $s[\rho\rangle s'$ is a path, instead of using the sentence "$\rho \in T^*$ is a path such that $s[\rho\rangle s'$".
- Two sequences $s[\rho\rangle s'$ and $q[\sigma\rangle q'$ are *Parikh equivalent* if $\Psi(\rho) = \Psi(\sigma)$, and *(label) disjoint* (or *Parikh disjoint*) if $\forall_{t \in T} : \Psi(\rho)(t) = 0 \vee \Psi(\sigma)(t) = 0$.

A labelled transition system is:

- *acyclic*, if all the paths from the initial state to any given reachable state have the same Parikh vector,
- *cyclic*, if all the small cycles have the same Parikh vector, with support T.

Definition 4. *Two finite labelled transition systems* $TS_1 = (S_1, \rightarrow_1, T, s_{01})$, $TS_2 = (S_2, \rightarrow_2, T, s_{02})$ *with the same label set* T *are* isomorphic *if there is a bijection* $\zeta \colon S_1 \to S_2$ *with* $\zeta(s_{01}) = s_{02}$ *and* $(s,t,s') \in \rightarrow_1 \Leftrightarrow (\zeta(s), t, \zeta(s')) \in \rightarrow_2$*, for all* $s, s' \in S_1$ *and* $t \in T$*. This will be denoted* $TS_1 \equiv TS_2$*, or* $TS_1 \equiv_T TS_2$ *to recall that the label set is the same.*

We are now ready to recall basic notions concerning nets.

A *net* is a structure $N = (P, T, W, M_0)$, where:

- P is a finite set of *places*,

[2] By $\max(m, n)$, we understand the maximum of two natural numbers m and n.

- T is a finite set of *transitions* (or actions), disjoint from P,
- W is the *weight function* $W\colon ((P \times T) \cup (T \times P)) \to \mathbb{N}$,
- M_0 is the *initial marking* (a *marking* is a mapping $M\colon P \to \mathbb{N}$ indicating the number of resources (denoted in figures by black tokens) in each place).[3]

If $x \in P \cup T$, the pre-set ${}^\bullet x$ and post-set $x^\bullet$ of x are defined as:

- ${}^\bullet x = \{y \in T \cup P \mid W(y,x) > 0\}$,
- $x^\bullet = \{y \in T \cup P \mid W(x,y) > 0\}$.

Having $x, y \in P \cup T$, if $W(x,y) > 0$, we say that x is an *input place* to y if $x \in P$, and an *input transition* to y if $x \in T$. In that case also, y is an *output transition* from x if $y \in T$, and an *output place* from x if $y \in P$.

Let us now provide basic definitions and notations regarding enabledness and reachability in nets.

- Transition $t \in T$ is *enabled* at a marking M, denoted by $M[t\rangle$, if $\forall_{p \in P}$: $M(p) \geq W(p,t)$.
- When t is enabled at M, the *firing/execution* of t leads from M to M', denoted by $M[t\rangle M'$, if $M'(p) = M(p) - W(p,t) + W(t,p)$.
- This can be extended to $M[\sigma\rangle M'$ for sequences $\sigma \in T^*$, defining the possible evolutions of the net from its initial marking. $[M\rangle$ denotes the set of markings *reachable* from M.

The net N is *bounded* if, there exists a natural number such that, for all reachable markings, the number of tokens in each place does not exceed that number, which amounts to say that $[M_0\rangle$ is finite.

Definition 5. *The* reachability graph $RG(N)$ *of a bounded net N is the finite labelled transition system with:*

- *set of nodes $[M_0\rangle$,*
- *label set T,*
- *set of edges $\{(M,t,M') \mid M, M' \in [M_0\rangle \wedge M[t\rangle M'\}$,*
- *initial state M_0.*

If a finite labelled transition system TS is *isomorphic* to the reachability graph of a net N, we say that: N *solves* TS or TS is *synthesisable* to N.

Given a net, it may be extremely difficult to analyse its behaviour and to check if it satisfies some desired properties. This is much simpler if the net is bounded, and may normally be obtained by analysing the reachability graph, but may remain uneasy. And if the observed properties are not the ones one expects, it may be uneasy to determine how the original net should be modified accordingly. Hence the idea to proceed the other way round and perform a net synthesis.

[3] We use the commonly accepted convention that markings are represented by vectors with indices corresponding to successive places.

2.2 Synthesis

The goal of a net synthesis is to derive a system modelled by a net, possibly belonging to some particular class, exhibiting certain intended properties, expressed with the use of an *lts*, that is a system with a reachability graph isomorphic to a given labelled transition system.

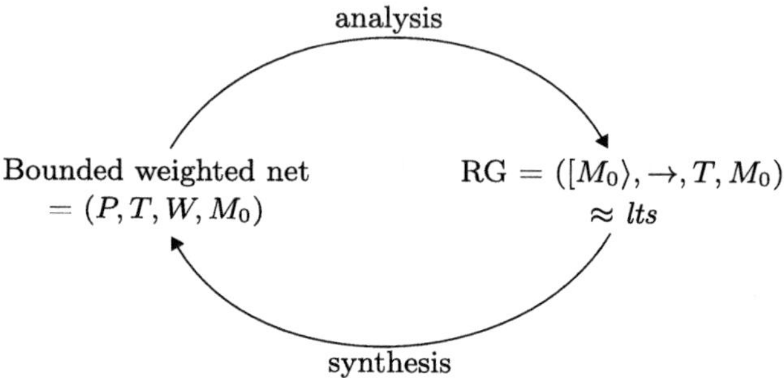

It is possible to obtain more than one net solving a particular *lts*, especially if no subclass is specified, but it is also possible that no solution exists, and it is then interesting to be able to point out the origin(s) of the problem. Figure 1 depicts the *lts* TS_1 with two rather different net solutions $PN_{1,1}$ and $PN_{1,2}$. Both are minimal, in the sense that if places are erased, a different (non-isomorphic) reachability graph is obtained.

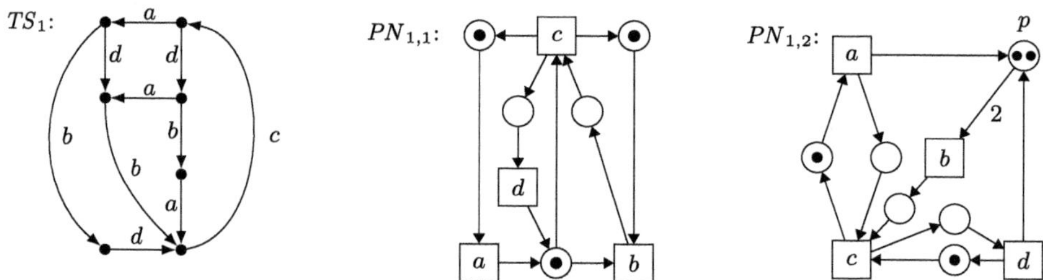

Fig. 1. An *lts* with two different net solutions.

We can also consider a more advanced variant, called "simultaneous synthesis", consisting of starting from a (finite) family of transition systems $\{TS_1, \ldots, TS_n\}$ and searching for a single net PN (of some class) together with n initial markings $\{M_{0,1}, \ldots, M_{0,n}\}$ such that the reachability graph of $(PN, M_{0,i})$ is isomorphic to TS_i for each i.

Figure 2 presents two labelled transition systems $TS_{2,1}$, $TS_{2,2}$ and their simultaneous solution PN_2. The initial marking corresponding to *lts* $TS_{2,1}$ is depicted with the use of all tokens (black and white ones), while the initial marking corresponding to *lts* $TS_{2,2}$ is pictured with black tokens only.

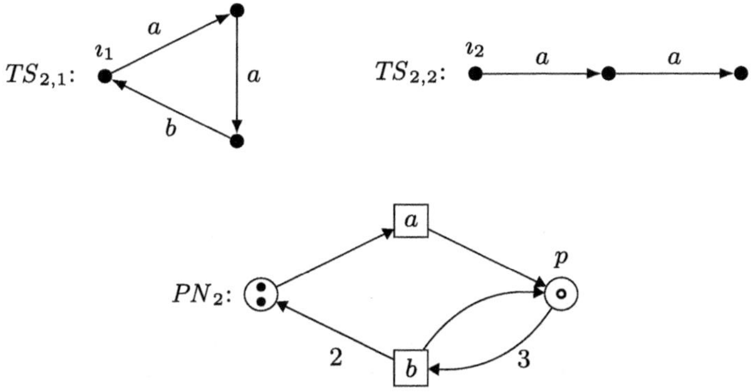

Fig. 2. $TS_{2,1}$ and $TS_{2,2}$ are simultaneously solvable by PN_2.

Classically, a synthesis problem may be solved with the use of *regions* [20,21][4]. A region $(\rho, \mathbb{B}, \mathbb{F})$ is a triple of functions ρ (from states to $\mathbb{N}$), and $\mathbb{B}, \mathbb{F}$ (both from labels to $\mathbb{N}$), satisfying the property that for any states s, s' and label a:

$$(s, a, s') \text{ is an edge of } TS \quad \Rightarrow \quad \rho(s) \geq \mathbb{B}(a) \wedge \rho(s') - \rho(s) = \mathbb{F}(a) - \mathbb{B}(a).$$

A region can be identified with a specific place p in a net, that we want to obtain (if exists), with a number of tokens corresponding to ρ during the execution of action a. The input and output transitions to p and the corresponding weight function values can be established according to $\mathbb{B}, \mathbb{F}$ to p (anywhere in TS). The only difference between a place in a weighted net and a region is that ρ yields a marking corresponding to each state in the considered *lts*, assumed to be a reachable state in the reachability graph of the searched-for net solution, while within a net we only know the initial marking of all places.

Two kinds of "separation" problems are associated to a given *lts*.

- A *state separation problem* consists of an unordered pair of states $\{s_1, s_2\}$, with $s_1 \neq s_2$, and for every such pair one needs a place that distinguishes them. In other words, to solve a SSP(s_1, s_2), we need to find an appropriate region $(\rho, \mathbb{B}, \mathbb{F})$ satisfying $\rho(s_1) \neq \rho(s_2)$.
- An *event/state separation problem* consists of a pair $(s, a) \in S \times T$ with $\neg(s[a\rangle)$. To solve an ESSP(s, a), where e is not enabled at s, we need to find a region $(\rho, \mathbb{B}, \mathbb{F})$ with $\rho(s) < \mathbb{B}(a)$.

A classical result [23] says that a given *lts* has a weighted net solution iff each SSP and each ESSP problem may be solved, and the set of separation solutions yields the places of a possible synthesis (but the solution is not necessarily unique). Let us now consider a finite labelled transition system $TS=(S, \rightarrow, T, \imath)$. To solve each separation problem, we have to find an adequate region $(\rho, \mathbb{B}, \mathbb{F})$, which means solving a system of linear constraints as explained above. The number

[4] The terminology "region" occurred first in [22] for the synthesis of elementary nets.

of unknowns is $|S| + 2 \cdot |T|$ and for each arc $(s, t, s') \in\rightarrow$ we have two linear constraints, plus one constraint for expressing the separation to be satisfied. Hence, for each separation problem, we have a system of linear constraints of the same size and the complexity CS of all the separation problems is about the same. There are $|S| \cdot (|S| - 1)/2$ SSP problems and $|S| \cdot |T| - |\rightarrow|$ (= $\sum_{s \in S}(|T| - \text{outdegree}(s))$ ESSP problems (where the outdegree of a state is the number of arcs originating from it). In large reachability graphs, the number of states is usually much larger than the number of transitions. For instance if we increase the number of initial tokens, the size of the reachability graph may increase in a dramatic manner, while the number of transitions does not change. This leads to consider complexities in terms of the number of states $|S|$, and to neglect the impact of the number of labels $|T|$. This leads to a synthesis complexity of the kind $A \cdot |S|^2 \cdot CS + B \cdot |S| \cdot CS$, where A and B are some coefficients.

Fortunately, in certain cases, the separation problems are easier to solve and the above complexity can be significantly relaxed. So this is actually an upper bound on the complexity of the synthesis problem. For instance, we shall see in Sect. 3 that, when the target class is the so-called choice-free nets, SSP problems are irrelevant: when ESSP problems are solved, SSP ones are automatically satisfied, and other simplifications apply as well.

More generally, it may be a good idea to first solve the ESSP problems and, for each SSP problem, check first if there is no region built previously which already solves it, which is very quick since there are generally few needed regions and the check is easy. This has been used for instance in the tool APT [24], and the experience shows that most of the time, no new system of linear constraints has to be solved, and otherwise only a very small number of them is needed. The same is true for ESSP problems: instead of systematically building and solving the corresponding system of linear constraints, we may first check if one of the regions built previously does not already solve the new separation problem (the efficiency of the procedure then relies on the order in which ESSP problems are considered). This may be interpreted in the following way: in the formula for the global complexity given above, in many cases $A = 0$; if this is not true, most of the time A is so small that the dominance of $A \cdot |S|^2$ over $B \cdot |S|$ only occurs for synthesis problems that are so huge that, anyway, the problem is out of practical reach, due to memory and/or execution time overflow problems. Finally, as we shall later see, for some subclasses of nets, it is possible to reduce the number of separation problems to be considered, and to reduce the size of each linear system to be solved. This is difficult to evaluate theoretically beforehand, however, and experiments may be useful for that.

In general, solving a system of linear constraints in the integer domain may be expensive (it belongs to the NP-complete problems, meaning that the known algorithms have an exponential complexity). However, here, it may be observed that, unless some numerical constraints are added (for instance, referring to Subsect. 2.3, if we search for a safe solution, in which case we must add constraints $\rho(s) \leq 1$ for each state s; and/or if we search for a plain solution, in which case we must add constraints $\mathbb{F}(a) \leq 1$ and $\mathbb{B}(a) \leq 1$ for each label a), all the systems to be solved are homogeneous, meaning that if we have a solution, any multiplication by a constant factor is also a solution. That means that we may solve the problems in the rational domain, and get an integer solution by applying an adequate multiplier. We may then use the Karmarkar algorithm [25], which has a known worse case complexity polynomial in the size of the system (here linear in $|S|$). The exact polynomial exponent is difficult to determine, but it is usually expected to be around 5, hence a degree 7 is sometimes mentioned, to solve a quadratic number of SSP problems, but we know now that we should expect a much smaller number of separation problems to be solved as a system of linear constraints of linear size. Moreover, it is known that, in practice, the Karmarkar algorithm is outperformed by the simplex algorithm [26], which however is exponential in principle [27]. The same arises with classical SMT solvers (APT uses SMTInterpol [28,29]). This seems to be due to the fact that the families of problems leading to an exponential growth are too artificial and are not met in true applications.

Finally, there is a last idea that may be used to dramatically reduce the execution times in some cases. Indeed, we mentioned the possibility to derive general behavioural properties valid for a whole subclass of nets. We may then use a pre-synthesis phase to check if these properties are satisfied by the submitted *lts*. If this is not true, we may immediately stop the synthesis, and produce an error message, more interesting than simply "that separation problem is not solvable". It is also possible to build during this pre-synthesis some algorithmic structures that may be useful during the proper synthesis phase. An example of such an approach can be found in Sect. 3.2.

2.3 Properties of *lts*'s and Nets

Let us now recall some possible basic properties of an *lts*. A labelled transition system $TS = (S, \rightarrow, T, \imath)$ is called:

- **totally reachable** if $[\imath\rangle = S$ (every state is reachable from the initial state),
- **weakly live** if $\forall_{t \in T} \exists_{s \in [\imath\rangle}\ s[t\rangle$ (every transition is reachable from the initial state),
- **live** if $\forall_{t \in T} \forall_{s \in [\imath\rangle} \exists_{\tilde{s} \in [s\rangle}\ \tilde{s}[t\rangle$ (every transition remains reachable),
- **finite** if S and T (hence also $\rightarrow$) are finite sets,
- **deterministic** if $\forall_{s \in [\imath\rangle} \forall_{t \in T}\ (s[t\rangle s' \wedge s[t\rangle s'') \implies s' = s''$ (the same label may not lead from a state to two different states),
- **generally deterministic** if $\forall_{s \in [\imath\rangle} \forall_{\sigma, \tau \in T^*}\ (s[\sigma\rangle s' \wedge s[\tau\rangle s'') \wedge \Psi(\sigma) = \Psi(\tau) \implies s' = s''$ (Parikh equivalent sequences lead to the same state)
- **reversible** $\forall_{s \in [\imath\rangle}\ \imath \in [s\rangle$ ($\imath$ always remains reachable),
- **ultimately reversible** if $\exists_{\tilde{s} \in [\imath\rangle}\ (\forall_{s \in [\imath\rangle}\ \tilde{s} \in [s\rangle)$ (there is some **home state** $\tilde{s}$, that always remains reachable),
- **persistent** if $\forall_{s \in [\imath\rangle} \forall_{t,u \in T}\ (s[t\rangle \wedge s[u\rangle \wedge t \neq u) \implies \exists_{r \in S}\ (s[tu\rangle r \wedge s[ut\rangle r)$ (the execution of an enabled action cannot disable another one),
- **backward persistent** $\forall_{s', s'' \in [\imath\rangle} :\ s'[a\rangle s \wedge s''[b\rangle s \wedge a \neq b \implies \exists_{s''' \in [\imath\rangle}\ s'''[a\rangle s'' \wedge s'''[b\rangle s'$

- **cycle coherent** if $\forall_{i\in\{1,n\}}\ s_i \in [\imath\rangle \wedge \sigma_i \in T^* \wedge s_i[\sigma_i\rangle s_i$, $\forall_{s,s'\in[\imath\rangle}\forall_{\sigma\in T^*} s[\sigma\rangle s' \wedge \Psi(\sigma) = \sum_{i\in\{1,n\}} k_i \cdot \Psi(\sigma_i) \wedge \forall_{i\in\{1,n\}} k_i \in \mathbb{N} \Rightarrow s = s'$ (a sum of cycles is a cycle).

When it comes to nets, we can distinguish two basic types of properties: structural and behavioural ones. Let us first list some basic structural properties. A net $N = (P, T, W, M_0)$ is called:

- **connected** if it is weakly connected as a graph[5],
- **plain** if arc weights do not exceed 1,
- **pure** or **side-condition free** or **self-loop free** if $\forall_{p\in P}\ p^\bullet \cap {}^\bullet p = \emptyset$,
- **ON** or **output-nonbranching** or **choice-free** if $\forall_{p\in P}\ |p^\bullet| \leq 1$,
- **marked-graph** if N is **plain** and $\forall_{p\in P}\ |p^\bullet| \leq 1 \wedge |{}^\bullet p| \leq 1$.

We can now focus on behavioural properties. A net $N = (P, T, W, M_0)$ is called:

- k**-bounded** for some k if $\forall_{M\in[M_0\rangle}\forall_{p\in P}\ M(p) \leq k$,
- **bounded** if $\exists_{k\in\mathbb{N}}\ N$ is k-bounded,
- **safe** if it is 1-bounded,
- **persistent** if $RG(N)$ is persistent,
- **backward persistent** if $RG(N)$ is backward persistent,
- **reversible** if $RG(N)$ is reversible,
- **live** if $RG(N)$ is live, which means that no transitions can be made unfireable – $\forall_{t\in T}\forall_{M\in[M_0\rangle}\exists_{M'\in[M\rangle}\ M[t\rangle$.

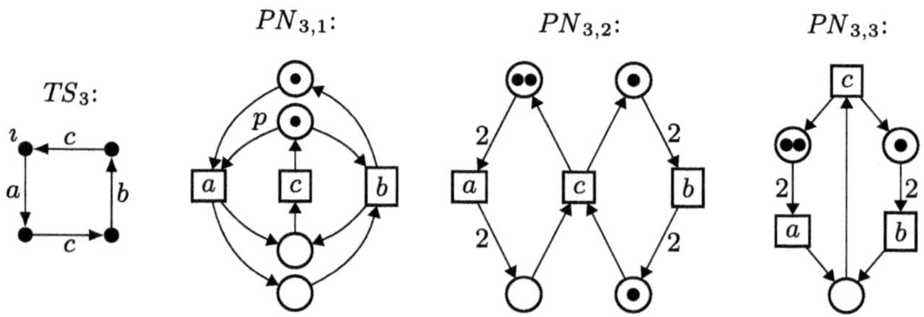

Fig. 3. Three nets solution for a same labelled transition system (on the left).

Figure 3 depicts the persistent *lts* TS_3 with three different solutions: $PN_{3,1}$, $PN_{3,2}$ and $PN_{3,3}$. The first one ($PN_{3,1}$) is:

· plain (all non-null arc weights equal 1),
· pure (no self-loops),
· safe (the content of any place at any reachable marking does not exceed 1),

[5] A directed graph is weakly connected if its underlying undirected graph is connected.

- persistent (no conflicts),
- reversible (the initial marking is reachable from every reachable marking),
- non-choice-free (place p has two outgoing transitions).

The other two solutions ($PN_{3,2}$ and $PN_{3,3}$) are both:

- non-plain (arcs with weights 2 occur),
- non-safe (at the initial marking one of the places contains 2 tokens),
- 2-bounded (at any reachable marking the content of any place does not exceed 2),
- reversible,
- choice-free (no places with more than one outgoing transition).

3 Choice-Free Nets

Those last years, several works (among others [1–6,8,9]) have been dedicated to the (simultaneous) synthesis of choice-free nets, where each place has at most one output transition. Since this means a loss of expressive power, we may wonder why this class of systems could be especially interesting from the synthesis and implementation point of view, besides the known structural properties of their behaviours (see Subsect. 3.2); the next subsection explains this point.

3.1 Implementation

As said before, a place in a net represents a type of resource; it may contain tokens representing the number of resources of that kind presently available; these (consumable) resources are considered interchangeable, and they may carry some information that will be used by the transition that will absorb them, but not to select which transition will absorb them in case of conflicts. A transition needs some number of tokens of each kind (possibly zero) in order to be able to function, and then produces some (other) tokens. As such, those nets allow to model complex intertwined mixtures of sequences, exclusive choices and concurrency, hence exhibit an interesting expressive power.

But they may also serve as static specifications of systems to build. And a (finite) finite labelled transition system may serve as a behavioural specification, from which a (bounded) synthesised net system of some class may be built and then serves itself as a structural specification. However, here we may encounter some problems. Since those models allow to represent a concurrency feature between transition firings, a natural implementation strategy would be to build a system composed of data structures to model places and tokens, and parallel agents, one for each transition, interacting only through their competition to access their needed resources, one place at a time to obtain a fully distributed realisation. Note that, in order to implement the tokens in a finite memory resource, we need to restrict our attention to bounded net systems and finite transition systems. The structure of each implemented transition could then occur as follows:

repeat
check availability of needed resources
if some are missing, retry after some time
otherwise, collect the needed tokens
process the action of the transition
produce the output tokens

There are variants of this schema however; for instance, the production of the output tokens may be performed one by one during the action process, and not all together at the end of the processing.

We can encounter two types of serious problems with this scheme, between the checking phase and the collection phase:

- the situation may have changed, due to the parallel action of other transitions: the tokens which were available during the checking phase are no longer there;
- we might need to "give back" the tokens that were absorbed during the beginning of the phase, if some needed tokens are no longer available.

This is illustrated in Fig. 4. Transition u has all of its necessary tokens available, but any of the transitions t_1, t_2 may have used them before u starts to carry out its execution. If u takes a token from one of its entries, realising that the other one is no longer available, then u must return the taken token.

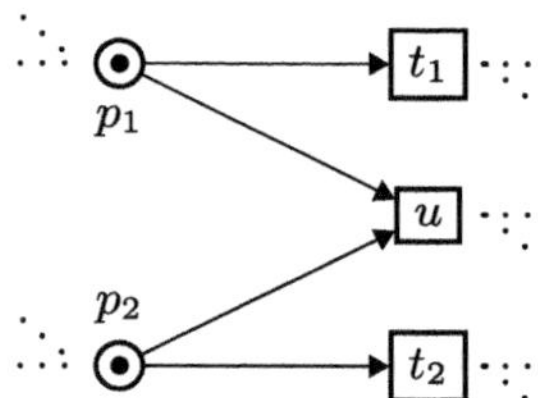

Fig. 4. A net, with a possible conflict.

There are various (partial) solutions to this problem [7], but none of them is fully satisfactory. They all reduce the parallelism expected for the transitions. However, it is possible to consider subclasses of nets for which the problem is alleviated.

For instance, the problem we described disappears, whatever the initial marking, if the places are not shared, that is if each place has (at most) a single output transition (for instance, in Fig. 4, if transition u is dropped, or t_1 and t_2), which is the definition of **choice-free nets**.

Any place of a choice-free net is schematically presented in Fig. 5. It is connected with the only outgoing transition x, which might also be its input. It may also be connected with other ingoing transitions $a_1 \dots a_m$. If we want the net to be pure, then the only output transition cannot be as well an input to any place; so in that case $h = 0$.

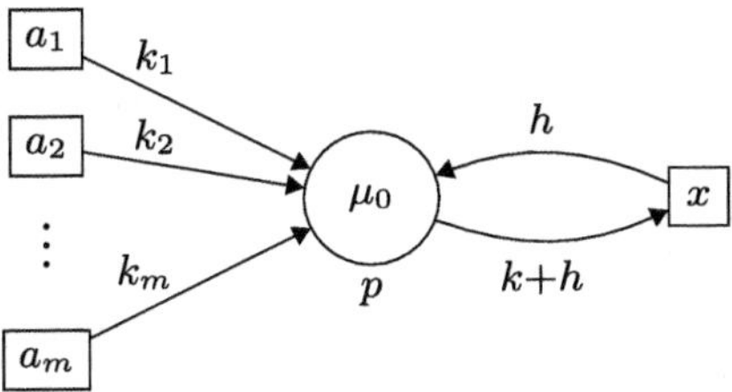

Fig. 5. A general pure ($h = 0$) or non-pure ($h > 0$) choice-free place p with initial marking μ_0 and unique output x.

In that case, it is never necessary to give back some absorbed token(s), and it is even possible to fuse the check and collect phases, leading for each transition to a (parallel) procedure of the kind:

repeat
  for each input place **do**
    while the needed tokens are not present **do** wait for some time
  grab the needed tokens,
  process the action of the transition and produce the output tokens

Of course, it is still necessary to protect the data structures representing places, by semaphore-like devices [30] or monitor-like devices [31], in order to ensure that if many producers or the user and some producer(s) access the place, the result may be serialised (for instance, if two producers add one token in some common place, the result will be to add two tokens, and not a single one, the last addition wiping out the first one as it can happen in a badly implemented parallel system).

3.2 Pre-synthesis

Interestingly, choice-free nets not only allow fully distributed implementations: they also have specific behavioural properties that may be exploited in a pre-synthesis phase. We shall here present them in the context of simultaneous choice-free pre-synthesis, but this may be applied also to the classical synthesis framework, by taking $n = 1$.

If a family of transition systems $\{TS_1, \dots, TS_n\}$ is "simultaneously choice-free synthesisable", then the following conditions hold [6] for every $TS_i, i \in \{1 \dots n\}$:

(1) **General:**
Each (finite) TS_i must be deterministic, totally reachable and persistent. (It should also be generally deterministic and cycle coherent, but this may be more difficult to check.)

(2) **The small cycles property:**
Let $\mathcal{G}$ be the set of Parikh vectors of small cycles in all the TS_i's; all the members of $\mathcal{G}$ must be prime (no non-trivial common divisor) and members must be pairwise disjoint.

(3) **The short distance property:**
For each state s_i of each TS_i, all the short directed paths from $\imath_i$ to s_i have the same Parikh vector, called the distance Δ_{s_i} to s_i and none of those distances may dominate a member of $\mathcal{G}$ ($\forall_{\Upsilon \in \mathcal{G}} : \neg(\Delta_{s_i} \geq \Upsilon)$).
(4) **The reduced distance property:**
For each $i \in \{1, \ldots, n\}$, state s_j in TS_i and member $\Phi \in \mathcal{G}$, there must be a state r_j in TS_i such that $\Delta_{r_j} = \Delta_{s_j} \stackrel{\bullet}{-} \Phi$.
(5) **The earliest Parikh cycles property:**
For any member $\Upsilon \in \mathcal{G}$ and state s in some TS_i with a small cycle at s with Parikh vector Υ and member $\Phi \in \mathcal{G}$ disjoint from Υ, there is a cycle with Parikh vector Υ around the unique state in TS_i at distance $\Delta_s \stackrel{\bullet}{-} \Phi$ (which exists by the previous property).[6]
(6) **Co-enabling:** For any $\Upsilon \in \mathcal{G}$ and x in its support, for any TS_i and $s, s' \in S_i$, if $s[x\rangle$ and $\forall_{a \in T_0 \cup T_x} : (\Delta_{s'} - \Delta_s)(a) \geq (\Delta_{s'} - \Delta_s)(x) \cdot \Upsilon(a)/\Upsilon(x)$, then $s'[x\rangle$.

Let us discuss the above properties using individual examples. Figure 6 shows a deterministic, totally reachable and persistent *lts* $TS_{4,2}$, hence Property (1) holds. However, Property (2) is not valid for this *lts*, since the small cycle at $\imath$ has Parikh vector (2,2,2), which is not prime. On the other hand, *lts* $TS_{4,1}$ presents several small cycles, two of them containing the labels a and c, the other two containing the labels b and d. Obviously these cycles are mutually either Parikh-equivalent, or label-disjoint, what causes Property (2) to hold; however Property (3) does not hold, as there are two short paths from $\imath$ to s with different Parikh vectors, namely: $\imath[bac\rangle s$ and $\imath[dae\rangle s$, dominating the vectors of small cycles $\Psi(bc)$ and $\Psi(de)$, respectively. Note that the distance from $\imath$ to s is not defined here, too. In *lts* $TS_{4,3}$, there exist: a path $\imath[abb\rangle s$ and a small cycle $s[abc\rangle s$. The reduction abb by abc gives us b but a path with such a label is not enabled from $\imath$, and for that reason Property (4) is not valid there.

Let us now look at the system $TS_{4,4}$ depicted in Fig. 6. It satisfies Properties (1)–(4), but one can find cycles $s_3[ba\rangle s_3$ and $s_2[d\rangle s_2$. It is also easy to see that $\Delta_{s_2} = (1,0,1,0)$, so that there should be a cycle d at s_1 corresponding to the distance $\Delta_{s_2} = (1,0,1,0) \stackrel{\bullet}{-} \Psi(ba)$, which, however, is not present there. As Property (5) is not valid for $TS_{4,4}$, it cannot have a choice-free solution. However, if we make minor changes to get the system $TS_{4,5}$, then we obtain a choice-free solution PN_4.

We may now make the following observations.

- These properties are rather easy and quick to check, in the order in which they were defined [6].
- If one of the properties fails, we may stop the synthesis, with an interesting **error message.**

[6] It is known [32] that in a finite deterministic and persistent transition system, loops are forward Parikh-equivalently transported in the sense that, if there is a loop $s[\tau\rangle s$ and a directed path $s[\sigma\rangle s'$, then there is a loop $s'[\phi\rangle s'$ with $\Psi(\phi) = \Psi(\tau)$. The earliest Parikh cycles property means they may also be backward transported, up to some extent.

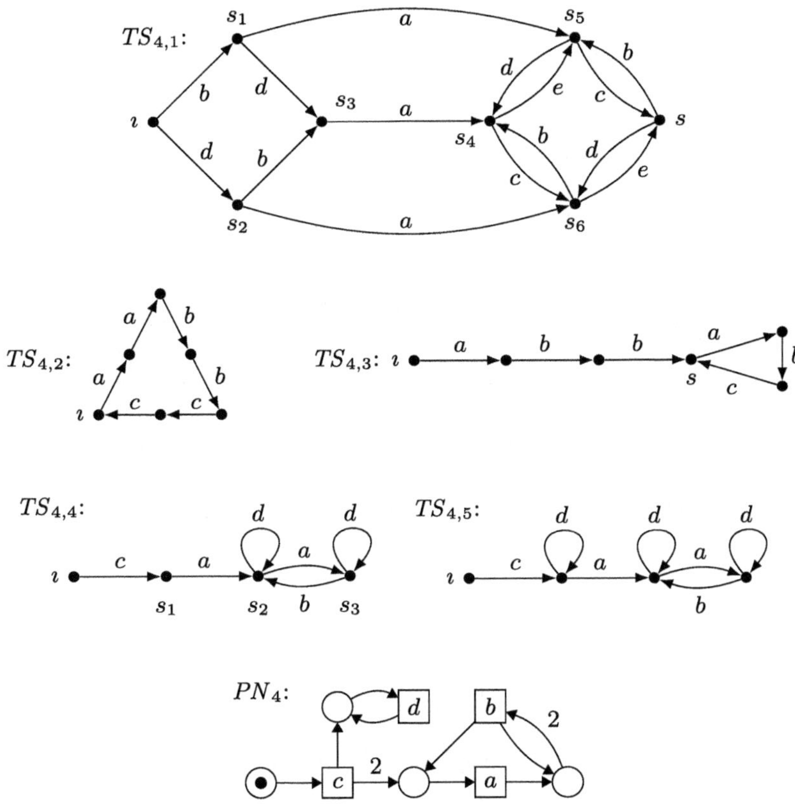

Fig. 6. Examples of transition systems satisfying (or not) some conditions needed to obtain a choice-free solution.

3.3 Proper Synthesis

Various simplifications allow to reduce the complexity to solve the needed separation properties when the target is a choice-free net (and the various pre-synthesis checks succeeded). In order to simplify the presentation, we shall first consider a single, classical synthesis problem ($n = 1$); we shall face a true simultaneous synthesis a bit later.

- SSP problems are irrelevant: it has been shown [5] that if all the ESSP problems can be solved by choice-free regions (or places), the same regions solve all the needed SSP problems if the pre-synthesis checks are satisfied. Also, we do not have to consider the case where a place has no output at all: those places are not needed to solve the ESSP problems.
- If a transition system is reversible (it is always possible to come back to the initial state) and is choice-free synthesisable, side-conditions, that is arrows leading in both directions between a place and a transition, are never necessary: in the general form of places and regions illustrated in Fig. 5, we may always assume $h = 0$ (we may reduce our attention to pure nets).

Let us thus consider an ESSP problem for s and x (there is no arc labelled x from state s). In order to assess such a non-enablingness, we only have to consider a place of the kind illustrated in Fig. 5 (with $k+h>0$). The variables we have to fix are μ_0, k, h and k_i for each $a_i \in T \setminus \{x\}$.

Let $\mathcal{G}$ be the set of Parikh vectors of small cycles occurring in the given *lts*. Since the global effect of the transitions occurring in any cycle is null, we have $\forall_{\Upsilon \in \mathcal{G}} : \sum_i k_i \cdot \Upsilon(a_i) = k \cdot \Upsilon(x)$ – then it is true for any cycle. If x does not occur in the support of some $\Upsilon \in \mathcal{G}$ (i.e. $\Upsilon(x) = 0$) while a_i does (i.e. $\Upsilon(a_i) \neq 0$), then we must have $k_i = 0$. This considerably reduces the number of variables to consider, unless $\mathcal{G}$ is a singleton and all the labels in T occur in it.

Moreover, for any state $s' \in S$, if the distance $\Delta_{s'}$ has been obtained from the examination of any short path from $\imath$ to s', we have for the place p to be constructed that $M_{s'}(p) = \mu_0 + \sum_i k_i \cdot \Delta_{s'}(a_i) - k \cdot \Delta_{s'}(x) \geq 0$. That means that μ_0, the initial marking $M_\imath(p)$ of p, has to be chosen high enough, but not too high because we also need that $M_s(p) < k+h$.

The constraints that need to be satisfied to solve the considered ESSP problem are then:

$$\sum_i k_i \cdot \Upsilon(a_i) = k \cdot \Upsilon(x) \text{ if } x \text{ belongs to } \Upsilon$$

(from Property (2), there is at most one constraint of that kind)

$$M_s(p) < k+h$$

$$\forall_{s' \in S} : s'[x\rangle \Rightarrow M_{s'}(p) \geq k+h \text{ otherwise } M_{s'}(p) \geq 0$$

But it is also possible to reduce the number of constraints of the last kind to be considered, and the number of ESSP problems to be solved. Indeed, if $s'[t\rangle s''$ and t belongs to the support of some member of $\mathcal{G}$ to which x does not belong, $M_{s'}(p) = M_{s''}(p)$ and it is not necessary to consider both s' and s'' in the constraints and the ESSP problems for x. If $s'[t\rangle s''$ and $t \neq x$, then $M_{s'}(p) \leq M_{s''}(p)$ and it is not necessary to consider s' in the constraints if s'' was already considered, and to consider ESSP(s', x) if ESSP(s'', x) was already solved.

3.4 Simultaneous Proper Synthesis

Now, let us consider a truly simultaneous choice-free synthesis problem, hence with $n > 1$; this was also detailed in [6]. We shall first solve individually each given transition system TS_i, but using the set $\mathcal{G}$ of all the Parikh vectors of small cycles occurring in all the given *lts*, and not only the ones occurring in TS_i. If one of those individual syntheses fails, the simultaneous synthesis fails too. Otherwise, we only have to synchronise all those individual solutions on the transitions and choose for the initial marking corresponding to TS_i the initial marking of the individual solution for TS_i for the places of this solution, and initial markings for the places arising from the other solutions high enough to avoid blocking a transition that should be allowed at some reachable marking. It is possible to show that this is always possible if each individual solution is compatible with all the members of $\mathcal{G}$.

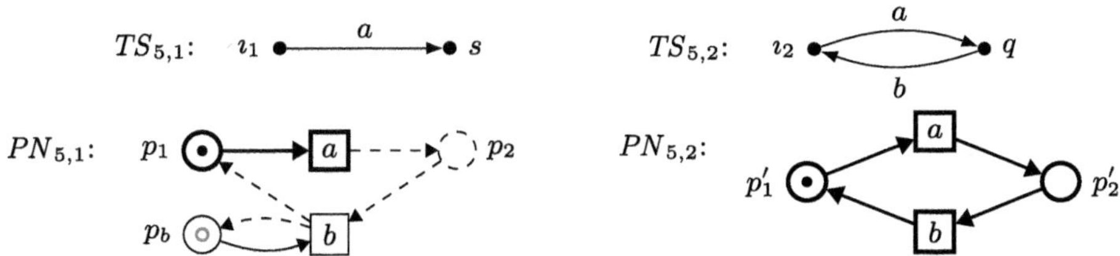

Fig. 7. Two transition systems $TS_{5,1}$ and $TS_{5,2}$, their individual solutions (thick parts of $PN_{5,1}$ and $PN_{5,2}$, respectively), as well as the simultaneous solution $PN_{5,1}$.

Let us look at the examples depicted in Fig. 7. Two individual solutions for transition systems $TS_{5,1}$ and $TS_{5,2}$ are given by the thick parts of $PN_{5,1}$ and $PN_{5,2}$, respectively. In $TS_{5,1}$, p_b and b are added by the uniformization of transition sets, and the dashed arrows by an invocation of one of the existing synthesis procedures which creates a semiflow (in $TS_{5,1}$) that corresponds to the cycle ab (in $TS_{5,2}$).

The solution for simultaneous synthesis for the family of transition systems $\{TS_6,\ TS_7\}$ is depicted as PN_a (all arcs). The initial markings of PN_a for TS_6 and TS_7 are fixed, respectively, as follows: $(p_1, p_2, p_b) \mapsto (1, 0, 0)$ and $(p_1, p_2, p_b) \mapsto (1, 0, 1)$.

4 Weighted Marked Graphs

Weighted Marked Graphs (WMG for short) are a subclass of the choice-free nets, where each place has at most one input transition in addition to having at most one output transition [33]. Examples of weighted Marked Graph PN_6 and its reachability graph TS_6 are depicted in Fig. 8.

An important general property of this subclass is that its reachability graphs are not only persistent but also backward persistent (see Sect. 2.3).

If we add that we only want to consider connected nets[7], it also arises that the reachability graph is:

- either **acyclic** (all the paths from the initial marking to any given reachable marking have the same Parikh vector),
- or **cyclic** (all the small cycles have the same Parikh vector, with support T).

[7] A net is *connected* when the underlying graph formed by its places and transitions is connected.

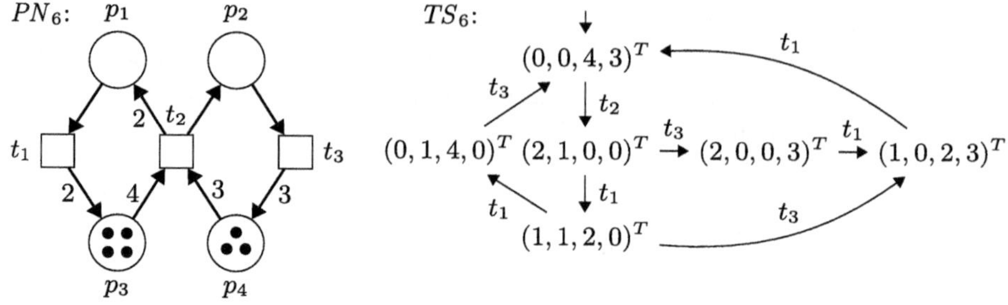

Fig. 8. A WMG system PN_6 and its reachability graph TS_6.

This may of course be incorporated in the pre-synthesis phase of any connected WMG synthesis, where all the places (corresponding to specific regions) have a very specific shape, pictured in Fig. 9. If the system is cyclic and connected, $\mathcal{F} = \Upsilon(b)$ and $\mathcal{B} = \Upsilon(a)$.

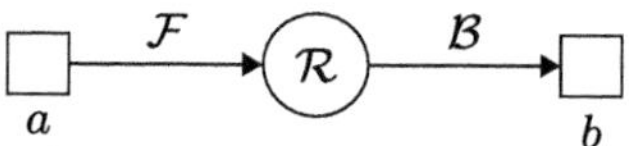

Fig. 9. Graphical interpretation of a WMG-place.

5 Marked Graphs

Marked Graphs are WMGs, where each place has exactly one input and one output, with weight 1. Moreover, they are always reversible and, when they are connected, and no transition is useless, all the small cycles in their reachability graphs have the unit Parikh vector $\mathbf{1}$[8]. In this case, the proper synthesis (where separation problems are explicitly solved) is not necessary: all the needed regions (places) are deduced from the pre-synthesis, which checks the forward and backward persistence, the reversibility and the unique small cycle Parikh vector $\mathbf{1}$. The idea is to build for each label x the (sequentialising) set

$$Seq(x) \quad = \quad \{s \in S \mid \neg s[x\rangle \wedge \forall_{a \in T}\colon s[a\rangle \Rightarrow s[ax\rangle\}.$$

The a occurring in this definition is in fact unique for each $s \in Seq(x)$, and there is a unique $s_a \in Seq(x)$ which only enables a. There is also a unique state r_x with $[x\rangle r_x$ as its unique input arc. Then a marked graph solution may be obtained by the following procedure:

[8] A transition is *useless* if it is never enabled in any reachable marking.

for every label $x \in T$ **do** **for** every state $s \in Seq(x)$ **do**
  determine $a \in T$ for which $s = s_a$;
  define a place $p{=}p^{s,x}$ with ${}^{\bullet}p{=}\{a\}, F(a,p){=}1$ and $p^{\bullet}{=}\{x\}, F(p,x){=}1$;
  compute the number n_a of occurrences of a's on any short path from r_x to $\imath$
  and put initially $M_0(p^{s,x}) = n_a$ tokens on $p^{s,x}$.
endfor **endfor**

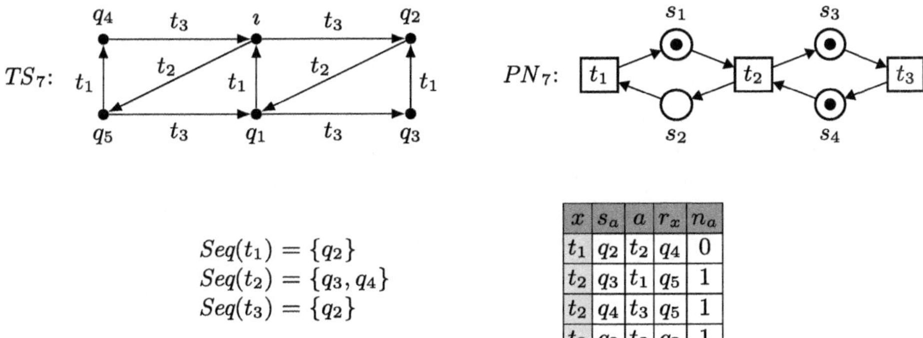

$Seq(t_1) = \{q_2\}$
$Seq(t_2) = \{q_3, q_4\}$
$Seq(t_3) = \{q_2\}$

x	s_a	a	r_x	n_a
t_1	q_2	t_2	q_4	0
t_2	q_3	t_1	q_5	1
t_2	q_4	t_3	q_5	1
t_3	q_2	t_2	q_3	1

Fig. 10. Finite labelled transition system, its solution, and sequentialising sets for its transitions.

Example 1. Figure 10 shows an example of an *lts* (TS_7) with the sequentialising sets for its individual transitions. Let us first obtain the set $Seq(t_1)$. We are looking for all states $s \in S$ such that t_1 is not enabled at s, but after the firing of one label, t_1 become enabled. Obviously q_1, q_3, q_5 cannot belong to $Seq(t_1)$, since t_1 is enabled at each of these states. Moreover, $\imath \notin Seq(t_1)$, because t_1 is not enabled at the state q_3 obtained after executing the label t_3 from $\imath$, and $q_4 \notin Seq(t_1)$, because t_1 is not enabled at the state $\imath$ obtained after executing t_2 from q_4. Hence, $Seq(t_1) = \{q_2\}$. It is easy to see, that the label, whose execution at q_2 makes t_1 enabled, denoted above by a, is t_2. Of course, the unique state $s_a \in Seq(t_1)$ which only enables t_2 is q_2 (the only state in the set). The unique state r_x with $[t_1\rangle r_x$ as its unique input arc is q_4. The number n_a of occurrences of t_1's on any short path from q_4 to $\imath$ is 1. A similar reasoning can be carried out for the remaining labels and the results are presented in the table below right in Fig. 10. However, note that the set $Seq(t_2)$ contains two elements, namely q_3 and q_4. For that reason we must look for two labels which, when executed at q_3 and q_4, respectively, make t_2 enabled - in this case such labels are t_1 and t_3, respectively. The unique state $s_a \in Seq(t_2)$ which only enables t_1 is q_3, while the unique state $s_a \in Seq(t_2)$ which only enables t_3 is q_4. All that remains for us to do is to notice that the unique state r_x with $[t_2\rangle r_x$ as its unique input arc is q_5, and the number n_a of occurrences of t_2 on any short path from q_4 to $\imath$ is 1. Having found all the necessary values for all labels, we are able to construct a solution. It is presented in the upper right corner of the figure.

6 Divide and Conquer

The synthesis problem is usually polynomial in terms of the size of the *lts*, with a degree between 2 and 7 depending on the subclass of nets one searches for [5], but can also be NP-complete if we add some constraints like plainness and/or safeness [34]. Hence the interest to apply a "divide and conquer" synthesis strategy when possible. The general idea ([10], Chap 13) is to:

1. Decompose the given *lts* into components.
2. Synthesise each component separately.
3. Recombine the results to obtain a solution for the global problem.

We thus have to find a pair of operators, one acting on transition systems and a corresponding one acting on nets, such that a composed *lts* has a net solution if and only if each component has a solution, and a possible solution for the composed net is given by the application of the net operator applied to solutions of the components. It is also necessary to be able to rapidly decompose a given *lts*, or to state it is not possible. This is summarised in Fig. 11.

$$TS = TS_1 \ \mathbf{op_{TS}} \ TS_2$$

$$TS \text{ solvable} \iff TS_1 \text{ and } TS_2 \text{ solvable}$$

$$sol(TS) = sol(TS_1) \ \mathbf{op_{PN}} \ sol(TS_2)$$

$$TS \Rightarrow \text{discovering of } TS_1 \text{ and } TS_2$$

Fig. 11. Divide and conquer strategy for synthesis.

We shall here present two such strategies, which may be combined efficiently.

1. Given by the disjoint products of *lts* – corresponding to disjoint sums of nets.
2. Given by articulations on a state of a transition system – corresponding to non-dominated reachable markings of a net.

An example of their mixed usage is illustrated in Fig. 12, where articulations are instantiated in their sequence form. On the left hand side we can see an easy transition system called $TS(x)$ with a single transition, while on the right hand side is depicted the transition system obtained by the concatenation of the following ones: $TS(start)$, the product $TS(a) \otimes TS(b)$ (described in the following subsection), and $TS(end)$. This may not only allow to simplify the net synthesis, if needed, but also to exhibit an interesting internal structure for complex systems which could otherwise be considered as "spaghetti-like"

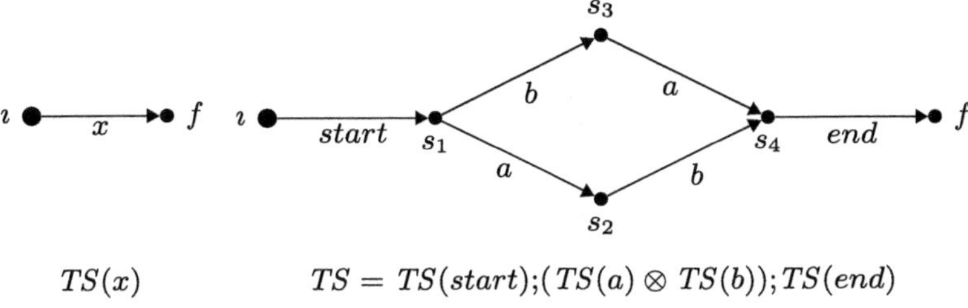

Fig. 12. Combination of sequence operators with a product.

6.1 Products and Sums [35–37]

A *product* of two disjoint *lts* is again an *lts*. Its states are pairs of states of the two *lts* and an edge exists if one of the underlying states can do the transition. An example is shown in Fig. 13 – a finite labelled transition system TS_10 is the product of TS_8 and TS_9.

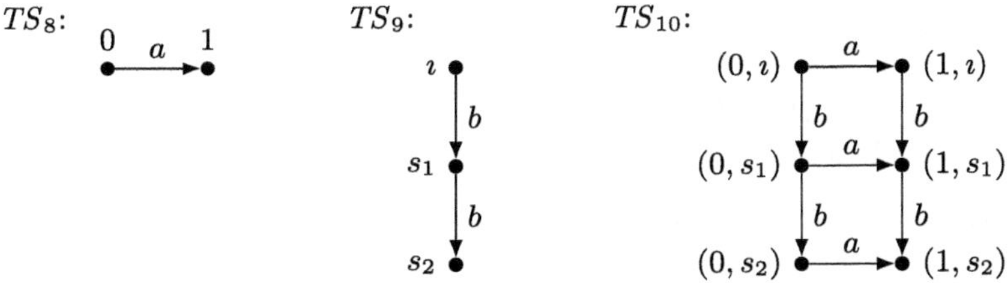

Fig. 13. Example of a disjoint product. We have $TS_9 \otimes TS_{10} = TS_8$.

Formally, let $TS_1 = (S_1, \rightarrow_1, T_1, \imath_1)$ and $TS_2 = (S_2, \rightarrow_2, T_2, \imath_2)$ be two *lts* with disjoint label sets ($T_1 \cap T_2 = \emptyset$). The (disjoint) product $TS_1 \otimes TS_2$ is the *lts* $\big(S_1 \times S_2, \rightarrow, T_1 \cup T_2, (\imath_1, \imath_2)\big)$, where $\rightarrow = \{\big((s_1, s_2), t_1, (s_1', s_2)\big) \mid (s_1, t_1, s_1') \in \rightarrow_1\} \cup \{\big((s_1, s_2), t_2, (s_1, s_2')\big) \mid (s_2, t_2, s_2') \in \rightarrow_2\}$.
It may be observed that, if $TS = (S, \rightarrow, T_1 \cup T_2, \imath) \equiv_T TS_1 \otimes TS_2$, TS is totally reachable (resp. deterministic) iff so are the factors TS_1 and TS_2.

Clearly, up to isomorphism, the disjoint product of *lts* is commutative, associative and has a neutral (the *lts* with a single state and no label). Each *lts* has itself and the neutral system as (trivial) factors; it is prime if it has exactly two factors. If $TS = (S, \rightarrow, T, \imath)$ is connected and finite, there is a finite set I of indices and a unique set of connected prime *lts*' $\{TS_i | i \in I\}$ such that $TS \equiv_T \bigotimes_{i \in I} TS_i$.

Figure 14 depicts three *lts*' (lhs) and their product (rhs).

When a product is given and the individual label sets T_1 and T_2 are known, the factors can be computed by only following edges with labels in T_1, resp. T_2, from the initial state: $(s_1, s_2)[\sigma\rangle(s_1', s_2')$ in TS iff $s_1[\sigma_1\rangle s_2$ in TS_1 and $s_2[\sigma_2\rangle s_2'$ in

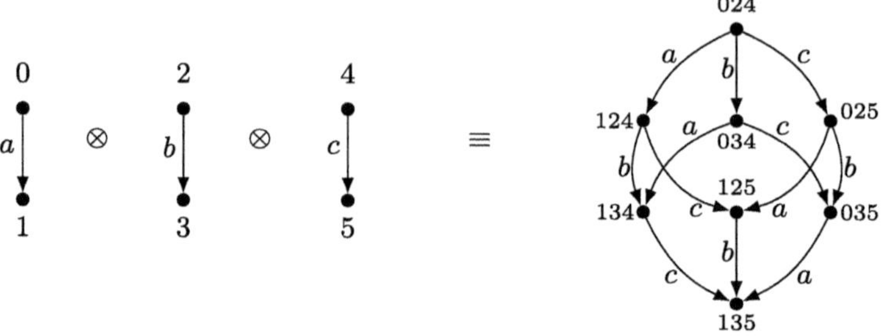

Fig. 14. *lts* obtained as a product of three *lts*'.

TS_2, where σ_1 is the projection of σ on T_1^* and similarly for σ_2. Then, $TS_1 \equiv_T (S^1, \rightarrow^1, T_1, \imath)$ with $S^1 = \{s \in S \mid \exists_{\alpha_1 \in T_1^*} : \imath[\alpha\rangle s\}$ and $\rightarrow^1 = \{(s_1, t_1, s_2) \in \rightarrow$ such that $s_1, s_2 \in S^1, t_1 \in T_1\}$, and similarly for TS_2.

There is an obvious but interesting relation between *lts* products and nets:

- If two nets are disjoint, putting them side by side yields a new net whose reachability graph is (up to isomorphism) the disjoint product of the reachability graphs of the two original nets. Note that the disjoint sum of net systems, again, up to isomorphism, is commutative, associative and has a neutral – the empty net).
- A disjoint product of *lts* has a net solution iff each composing *lts* has a net solution, and (if it exists) the solution is the disjoint sum of the latter.

An additional remark that may be valuable for applications is that many subclasses of nets found in the literature (free-choice, choice-free, join-free, fork-attribution, homogeneous, ..., not defined here) are compatible with the presented (de)composition, in the sense that a disjoint sum of nets belongs to such a subclass if and only if each component belongs to the same subclass.

Let us now examine when and how an *lts* may be decomposed into (non-trivial) disjoint factors. It is enough to discover an adequate decomposition of the label set $T = T_1 \cup T_2$. A general characterisation of such adequate decompositions is based on the following property: an *lts* $TS = (S, \rightarrow, T, \imath)$ has the *general diamond property* for two distinct labels $a, b \in T$ if $\forall_{s,s_1,s_2 \in S}$, $\forall_{u \in \{a,-a\}}, \forall_{v \in \{b,-b\}} : s[u\rangle s_1 \wedge s[v\rangle s_2 \Rightarrow (\exists_{s' \in S} : s_1[v\rangle s' \wedge s_2[u\rangle s')$, where for $t \in T$ label $-t$ means a backward arrow of t.

If $T_1, T_2 \subseteq T$ with $T_1 \cap T_2 = \emptyset$, *TS* will be said $\{T_1, T_2\}$-*gdiam* if it has the general diamond property for each pair of labels $a \in T_1$, $b \in T_2$.
In other words, *TS* has the general diamond property for $a \neq b \in T$ if whenever there are two adjacent edges in a diamond like in Fig. 15, the other two are also present. Note that any *lts* $TS = (S, \rightarrow, T, \imath)$ is $\{\emptyset, T\}$-gdiam.

General diamonds are not enough to derive a non-trivial factorisation in all generality, but it becomes so in the context of net synthesis [36]. Indeed, if a totally reachable *lts* $TS = (S, \rightarrow, T_1 \cup T_2, \imath)$ is deterministic and satisfies the general diamond property for each pair of labels $a \in T_1$ and $b \in T_2$, then it

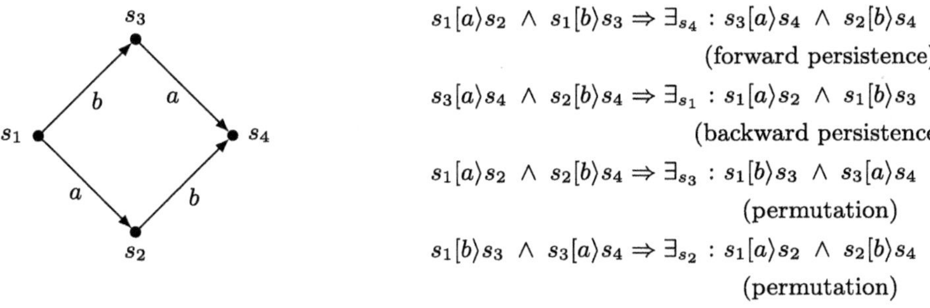

Fig. 15. General diamond property.

is net synthesisable iff so are the restrictions $[\imath\rangle^{T_1}$ and $[\imath\rangle^{T_2}$ of TS to the states reachable from $\imath$ while only using labels from T_1 or T_2, respectively; moreover, we then have $TS \equiv_T [\imath\rangle^{T_1} \otimes [\imath\rangle^{T_2}$ and therefore a possible solution for the synthesis problem for TS is the disjoint sum of a solution for $[\imath\rangle^{T_1}$ and a solution for $[\imath\rangle^{T_2}$.

It remains to find adequate subsets of labels T_1 and T_2, partitioning T and satisfying the general diamond property. To do that, one may rely on the following, which is again a local property.

Let $TS = (S, \rightarrow, T, \imath)$ be an *lts* and $a, b \in T$ be two distinct labels. We shall denote:

- by $a \leftrightarrow b$ the fact that they do not form general diamonds, i.e., there are states which do not satisfy one of the constraints in Fig. 15,
- by $\rightleftharpoons = \leftrightarrow^*$ the reflexive and transitive closure of $\leftrightarrow$, meaning in some sense that the labels are 'non-diamondisable'.

These relations mean that in any decomposition, if $a \leftrightarrow b$ they must belong to the same component, i.e., $a \in T_1 \Rightarrow [a] \subseteq T_1$, where $[a] = \{b \in T \mid a \rightleftharpoons b\}$. And we know that this is enough: for each equivalence class:

- either the synthesis works and we have a global solution by taking the disjoint sum of all the solutions,
- or one (or more) of the subproblems fails, and we know there is no global solution for the whole system.

Our proposed factorisation algorithm now works as follows:

- Iterate over all states of the given *lts*, and for each state check if the adjacent edges form general diamonds.
- If not, their labels must be in the same equivalence class.
- For each equivalence class $[a]$ try net synthesis on $[\imath\rangle^{[a]}$.
- If it works, the result is the disjoint sum of the computed nets.

This constructs the equivalence relation by repeatedly joining classes, but it also allows to stop the iteration early when only one equivalence class remains.

Note that factorising a transition system may sometimes allow to apply different specialised synthesis procedures to each connected component. This will be the case for instance if a component allows a choice-free synthesis, and another one allows a marked graph synthesis, as explained above.

6.2 Articulations [38]

Let us consider two disjoint transition systems TS_1 and TS_2 and a state in the first of them ($s \in T_1$); the general idea of their articulation[9] around s is to 'plug' the second one on the chosen state, as schematised in Fig. 16.

Let $TS_1 = (S_1, \rightarrow_1, T_1, \imath_1)$ and $TS_2 = (S_2, \rightarrow_2, T_2, \imath_2)$ be two (totally reachable and deterministic) *lts*' with $T_1 \cap T_2 = \emptyset$ and $s \in S_1$. Thanks to isomorphisms[10], we may assume that $S_1 \cap S_2 = \{s\}$ and $\imath_2 = s$. We shall then denote by $TS_1 \lhd s \rhd TS_2 = (S_1 \cup S_2, T_1 \cup T_2, \rightarrow_1 \cup \rightarrow_2, \imath_1)$ the *articulation* of TS_1 and TS_2 around s (and by $\lhd s \rhd$ the corresponding articulation operator).

Conversely, let $TS = (S, \rightarrow, T, \imath)$ be a (totally reachable and deterministic) *lts*. Let $\emptyset \subseteq T_1 \subseteq T$; we shall then denote by $adj(T_1) = \{s \in S | \exists_{t \in T_1} : s[t\rangle \text{ or } [t\rangle s\}$ if there are enabled transitions in T_1, $\{\imath\}$ otherwise. This is the *adjacency set* of T_1, i.e., the set of states connected to T_1 (with the convention that, if T_1 is empty or only contains useless labels, the result is the singleton initial state). Let $T_2 = T \setminus T_1$ and $s \in S$. We shall say that TS is *articulated* by T_1 and T_2 around s if $adj(T_1) \cap adj(T_2) = \{s\}$, $\forall_{s_1 \in adj(T_1)} \exists_{\alpha_1 \in T_1^*} : \imath[\alpha_1\rangle s_1$ and $\forall_{s_2 \in adj(T_2)} \exists_{\alpha_2 \in T_2^*} : s[\alpha_2\rangle s_2$.

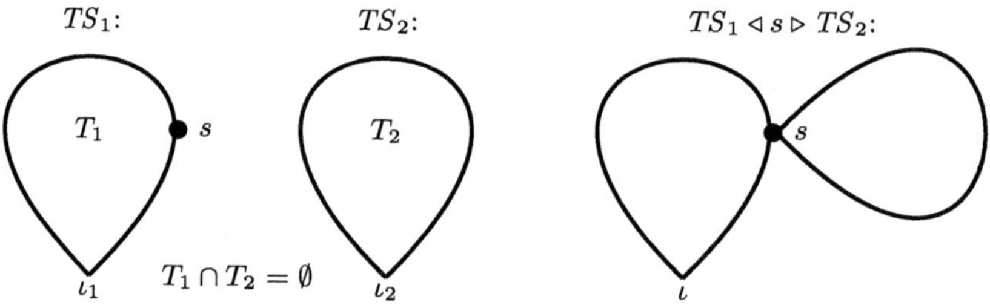

Fig. 16. General idea of articulations.

Figure 17 illustrates this operator. It also shows that the articulation highly relates on the state around which the articulation takes part. It may also be observed that, if $TS_0 = (\{\imath\}, \emptyset, \emptyset, \imath)$ is the trivial empty *lts*, we have that, for any state s of TS, $TS \lhd s \rhd TS_0 \equiv TS$, i.e., we have a kind of right neutral trivial articulation. Similarly, $TS_0 \lhd \imath \rhd TS \equiv TS$, i.e., we have a kind of left neutral

[9] In the sense of a unique contact point between two parts of a larger entity. The analogy is not perfect however since, in anatomy or mechanics, the connected parts are (partly) mobile around their articulation, while here the articulation simply allows to move from a component to the other one (and possibly back). It will be possible, however, to visit many times the articulation point s without moving out of the current component.

[10] This operator is only defined up to isomorphism since we may need to rename the state sets (usually the right one, but we may also rename the left one, or both).

trivial articulation. However, these neutrals will play no role in the following of this paper, so that we shall exclude them from our considerations (and assume the edge label sets to be non-empty, and only composed of useful labels).

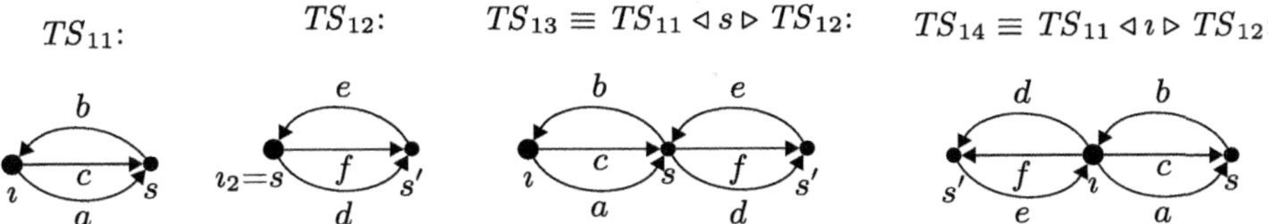

Fig. 17. Some articulations.

Several easy but interesting properties may be derived for this articulation operator.

For instance, both forms of articulation are equivalent: if $TS = (S, \rightarrow, T, \imath)$ is articulated by T_1 and T_2 around s, then the structures $TS_1 = (adj(T_1), \rightarrow_1, T_1, \imath)$ and $TS_2 = (adj(T_2), \rightarrow_2, T_2, s)$, where $\rightarrow_1$ is the restriction of $\rightarrow$ to T_1 (i.e., $\rightarrow_1 = \rightarrow \cap adj(T_1) \times T_1 \times adj(T_1)$), and similarly for $\rightarrow_2$, are (totally reachable) *lts*', $TS \equiv_{T_1 \cup T_2} TS_1 \lhd s \rhd TS_2$. Conversely, $TS_1 \lhd s \rhd TS_2$ is articulated by the label sets of TS_1 and TS_2 around s.

Concerning the evolutions of an articulation, we have that, if $TS \equiv TS_1 \lhd s \rhd TS_2$, $\imath[\alpha\rangle s'$ is an evolution of TS iff it is an alternation of evolutions of TS_1 and TS_2 separated by occurrences of s, i.e., either $\alpha \in T_1^*$ or $\alpha = \alpha_1\alpha_2 \ldots \alpha_n$ such that $\alpha_i \in T_1^*$ if i is odd, $\alpha_i \in T_2^*$ if i is even, $\imath[\alpha_1\rangle s$ and $\forall_{i \in \{1,2,\ldots,n-1\}}$: $[\alpha_i\rangle s[\alpha_{i+1}\rangle$.

For instance, for TS_{13} in Fig. 17, a possible evolution is $\imath[abc\rangle s[fede\rangle s[b\rangle \imath$, but also equivalently $\imath[a\rangle s[\varepsilon\rangle s[bc\rangle s[fe\rangle s[\varepsilon\rangle[de\rangle s[b\rangle \imath$ (where ε is the empty sequence).

Articulation operators are not always associative or commutative, but we have several interesting subcases. For instance, let us assume that TS_1, TS_2 and TS_3 are three *lts*' with label sets T_1, T_2 and T_3 respectively, pairwise disjoint. Let s_1 be a state of TS_1 and s_2 be a state of TS_2. Moreover, $S_1 \cap S_2 = s_1$ and $s_1 = i_2$, as well as $(S_1 \cup S_2) \cap S_3 = s_2$ and $s_2 = i_3$. Then, $TS_1 \lhd s_1 \rhd (TS_2 \lhd s_2 \rhd TS_3) \equiv_{T_1 \cup T_2 \cup T_3} (TS_1 \lhd s_1 \rhd TS_2) \lhd s_2' \rhd TS_3$, where s_2' corresponds in $TS_1 \lhd s_1 \rhd TS_2$ to s_2 in TS_2 (let us recall that the articulation operator may rename the states of the second operand).

This is illustrated by Fig. 18.

If $TS_1 = (S_1, \rightarrow_1, T, \imath_1)$ and $TS_2 = (S_2, \rightarrow_2, T, \imath_2)$ with disjoint label sets (i.e., $T_1 \cap T_2 = \emptyset$), then $TS_1 \lhd \imath_1 \rhd TS_2 \equiv_{T_1 \cup T_2} TS_2 \lhd \imath_2 \rhd TS_1$. For instance, in Fig. 17, $TS_{14} \equiv TS_{11} \lhd \imath \rhd TS_{12} \equiv TS_{12} \lhd \imath \rhd TS_{11}$.

Then, $(TS_1 \lhd s_2 \rhd TS_2) \lhd s_3 \rhd TS_3 \equiv_{T_1 \cup T_2 \cup T_3} (TS_1 \lhd s_3 \rhd TS_3) \lhd s_2 \rhd TS_2$ (see Fig. 19).

TS_{15}: $\quad (TS_{11} \lhd s \rhd TS_{12}) \lhd s' \rhd TS_{15} \equiv TS_{11} \lhd s \rhd (TS_{12} \lhd s \rhd TS_{15})$:

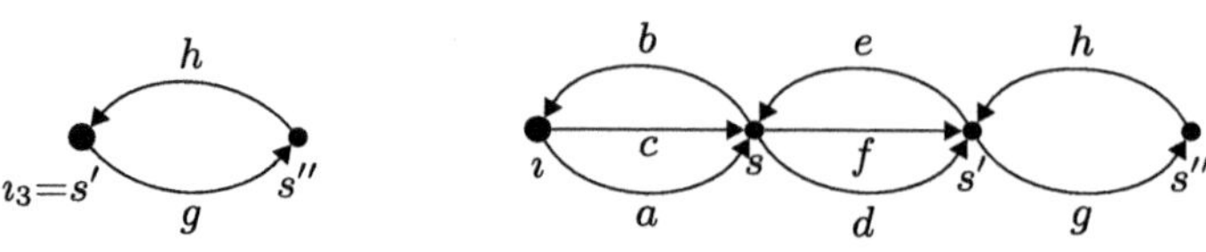

Fig. 18. Associativity of articulations.

$(TS_{11} \lhd s \rhd TS_{12}) \lhd \imath \rhd TS_{15} \equiv (TS_{11} \lhd \imath \rhd TS_{15}) \lhd s \rhd TS_{12}$:

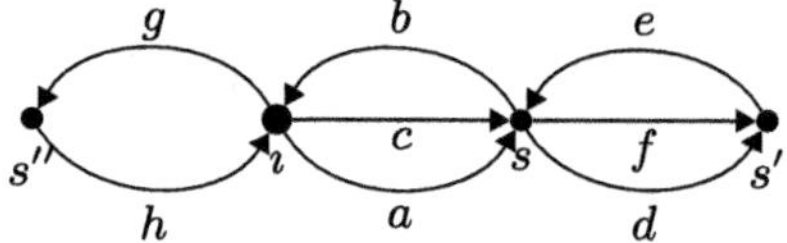

Fig. 19. Commutative associativity of articulations.

Let us now examine the connection between articulations and net synthesis. We have that, if $TS = (S, \rightarrow, T_1 \cup T_2, \imath)$ is articulated by T_1 and T_2 around s, so that $TS \equiv TS_1 \lhd s \rhd TS_2$ with $TS_1 = (adj(T_1), \rightarrow_1, T_1, \imath)$ and $TS_2 = (adj(T_2), \rightarrow_2, s)$, and is solvable, components TS_1 and TS_2 are also solvable. Moreover, in the corresponding solution for TS_1, if the decomposition is not trivial, the marking corresponding to s is not dominated by any other reachable marking.

Another phenomenon is illustrated in Fig. 20: TS_{17} has a solution in which the marking M corresponding to s is dominated (which is not true for PN_9). The *lts* TS_{16} is articulated around s_2, with $T_1 = \{a\}$ and $T_2 = \{b\}$, hence leading to TS_{17} and TS_{18}. It is solved by PN_8, and the corresponding solutions for TS_{17} and TS_{18} are PN_9 and PN_{10}, respectively. TS_{17} also has the solution PN_{11} but the marking corresponding to s_2 is then empty, hence it is dominated by the initial marking, as well as by the intermediate one. This is not the case for the other solution PN_{12} (obtained from PN_9 by erasing the useless isolated place: we never claimed that PN_9 is a minimal solution). TS_{18} also has the solution PN_{13}.

The other way round, let us now assume that $TS = TS_1 \lhd s \rhd TS_2$ is an articulated *lts* and that it is possible to solve TS_1 and TS_2. Is it possible from that to build a solution for TS?

To do that, we shall add the constraint already observed above that, in the solution for TS_1, the marking corresponding to s is not dominated by another one. If this is satisfied we shall say that the solution is *adequate* with respect to s.

Hence, in the treatment of the system in Fig. 20, we want to avoid considering the solution PN_{11} of TS_{17}; on the contrary, PN_9 or PN_{12} will be acceptable.

If TS_1 is reversible and solvable, any solution is adequate. Indeed, for any pair of distinct states $s, s' \in S_1$ we then have a path $s[\alpha\rangle s'$ with $\alpha \in T_1^*$. In the solution PN_1 of TS_1, if M is the marking corresponding to s and M' is the one

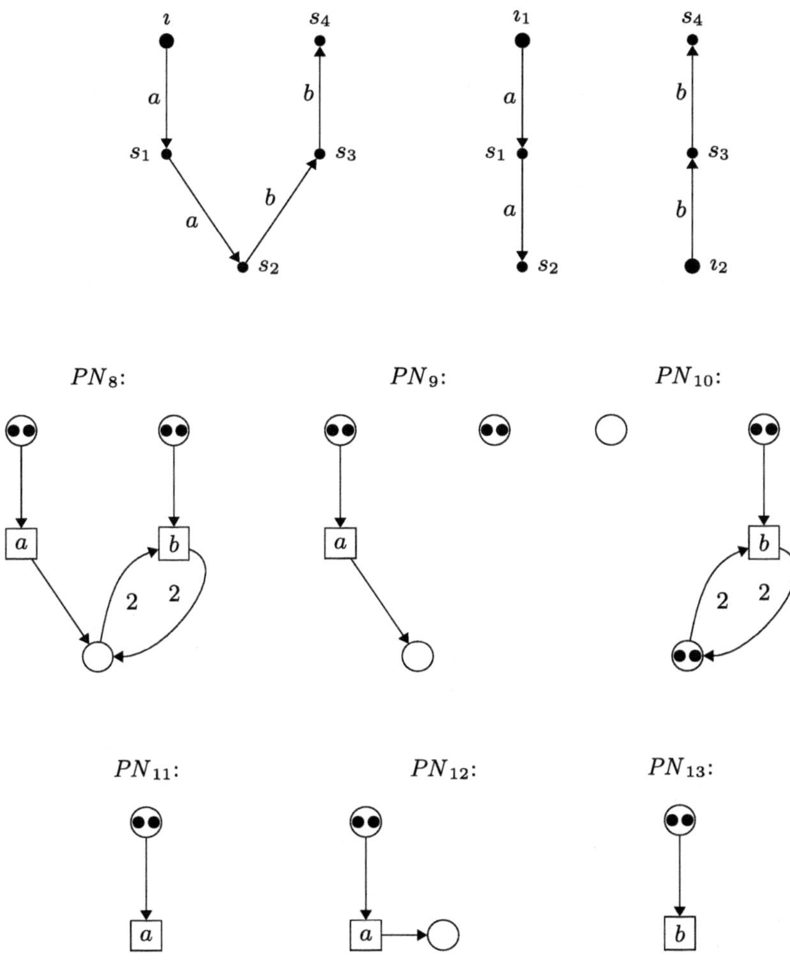

Fig. 20. Labelled transitions systems and their solutions. TS_{16} is solved by PN_8; TS_{17} is solved by PN_9, PN_{11}, PN_{12}; TS_{18} is solved by PN_{10}, PN_{13}.

corresponding to s', we have $M \neq M'$ and $M[\alpha\rangle M'$ and if $M \lneqq M'$ we also have an infinite path $M'[\alpha^\infty\rangle$. Since PN_1 is a solution for TS_1, we also have $s[\alpha^n\rangle s_i$ for an infinite series of different states s_i for $n \in \mathbb{N}$, and TS_2 as well as TS may not be finite as we assumed in this paper. Note that, from a similar argument, since TS_2 is finite, no marking reachable in PN_2 dominates the initial one, corresponding to $\imath_2 = s$.

However, if TS_1 is solvable, it is always possible to get a solution adequate at s, as for any state in fact. Indeed, if TS_1 is a (finite) solvable *lts* and s any of its states, then there is a solution for TS_1 adequate at s.

The latter may be obtained by introducing afterwards ‘complementary’ places (see [39] a. o.), but it is also possible directly to get an adequate solution (since we know there is one), in the following way. Let us add to TS_1 an arc (s, u, s), where u is a new fresh label. Let TS_1' be the *lts* so obtained. If TS_1' is not solvable, there is no (adequate) solution. Otherwise, solve TS_1' and erase u from the solution. Let N_1 be the net obtained with the procedure just described: it is a solution for TS_1 with the adequate property that the marking corresponding to s is not dominated by another one.

For instance, when applied to TS_{17} in Fig. 20, this will lead to PN_{12}, and not PN_{11} (PN_8 could also be produced, but it is likely that a ‘normal’ synthesis procedure will not construct the additional isolated place).

Now, to understand how one may generate a solution for TS_{19} from the ones obtained for TS_{20} and TS_{21}, we may first carefully examine the example illustrated in Fig. 21. The *lts* TS_{19} is articulated around s, with $T_1 = \{a, b\}$ and $T_2 = \{c, d\}$, hence leading to TS_{20} and TS_{21}. It is solved by PN_{16}, and the corresponding solutions for TS_{20} and TS_{21} are PN_{14} and PN_{15}, respectively. In PN_{16}, we may recognise PN_{14} and PN_{15}, connected by two kinds of side-conditions: the first one connects the label b out of s in TS_{20} to the initial marking of PN_{15}, the other one connects the label c out of $\imath_2$ in TS_{21} to the marking of PN_{14} corresponding to s. In the discussed example some side-conditions (i.e., pairs of place-transition with arcs going both ways, with identical weights) occur in the global solution. This leads to the following construction.

Let $PN_1 = (P_1, T_1, F_1, M_0^1)$ and $PN_2 = (P_2, T_2, F_2, M_0^2)$ be two disjoint bounded net systems and M a reachable marking of PN_1 not dominated by another one. The articulated net $PN_1 \lhd M \rhd PN_2$ is the one built first by putting side by side PN_1 and PN_2.
Then, for each transition t_1 enabled at M in PN_1, and each place $p_2 \in P_2$ such that $M_0^2(p_2) > 0$, create a side-condition $F(t_1, p_2) = F(p_2, t_1) = M(p_2)$. For each transition t_2 initially enabled in PN_2, and each place $p_1 \in P_1$ such that $M(p_1) > 0$, create a side-condition $F(t_2, p_1) = F(p_1, t_2) = M(p_1)$. No other modification is necessary.

We then have the following property about the synthesis of articulations. Let $TS = TS_1 \lhd s \rhd TS_2$. If TS_1 or TS_2 are not solvable, so is TS.
Otherwise, let PN_1 be a solution for TS_1 adequate at s, i.e., such that the marking M_s corresponding to s is not dominated by another reachable marking, and let PN_2 be a disjoint solution for TS_2. Then the net $PN_1 \lhd M \rhd PN_2$ is a solution for TS.

Note that we do not claim this is the only solution, but the goal is to find a solution when there is one.

It remains to show when and how an *lts* may be decomposed by a non-trivial articulation (or several ones). Let us thus consider some *lts* $TS = (S, \rightarrow, T, \imath)$. We may assume it is finite, totally reachable, deterministic and weakly live (there is no useless label).

First, we may observe that, for any two distinct labels $t, t' \in T$, if $|adj(\{t\}) \cap adj(\{t'\})| > 1$, t and t' must belong to a same subset for defining an articulation. Let us extend the function adj to non-empty subsets of labels by stating

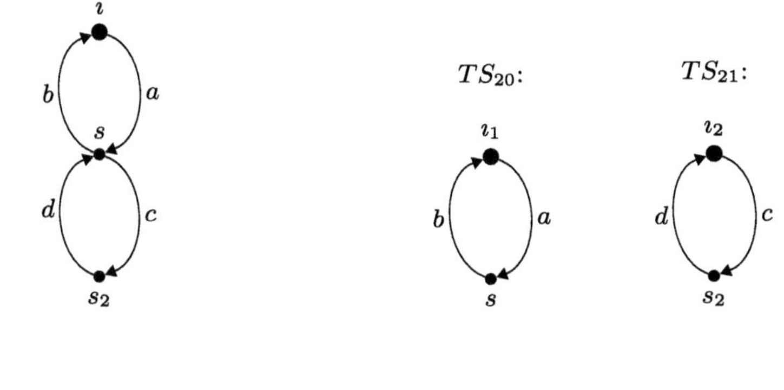

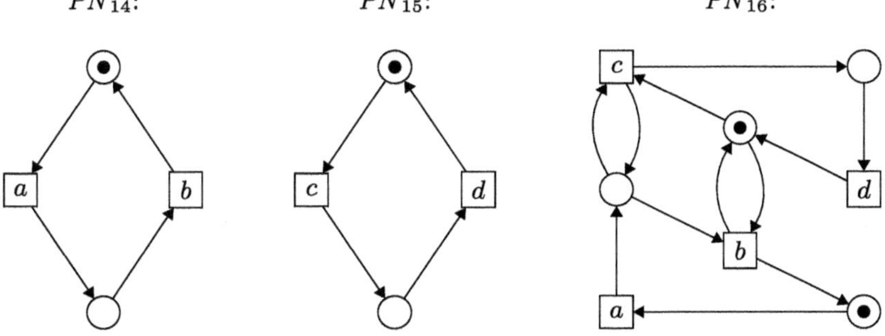

Fig. 21. Finite labelled transition systems and their solutions. TS_{19} is solved by PN_{16}, TS_{20} – by PN_{14}, TS_{21} – by PN_{15}.

$adj(T') = \cup_{t \in T'} adj(t)$ when $\emptyset \subseteq T' \subseteq T$. We then have that, if $\emptyset \subseteq T_1, T_2 \subseteq T$ and we know that all the labels in T_1 must belong to a same subset for defining an articulation, and similarly for T_2, $|adj(T_1) \cap adj(T_2)| > 1$ implies that $T_1 \cup T_2$ must belong to a same subset of labels defining an articulation. If we get the full set T, that means that there is no possible articulation (but the trivial one).

Hence, starting from any partition $\mathcal{T}$ of T (initially, if $T = \{t_1, t_2, \ldots, t_n\}$, we shall start from the finest partition $\mathcal{T} = \{\{t_1\}, \{t_2\}, \ldots, \{t_n\}\}$), we shall construct the finest partition compatible with the previous rule:

while there is $T_1, T_2 \in \mathcal{T}$ such that $T_1 \neq T_2$ and $|adj(T_1) \cap adj(T_2)| > 1$, replace T_1 and T_2 in $\mathcal{T}$ by $T_1 \cup T_2$.

At the end, if $\mathcal{T} = \{T\}$, we may stop with the result: *there is no non-trivial articulation.*

Otherwise, we may define a finite bipartite undirected graph whose nodes are the members of the partition $\mathcal{T}$ and some states of S, such that if $T_i, T_j \in \mathcal{T}, T_i \neq T_j$ and $adj(T_i) \cap adj(T_j) = \{s\}$, there is a node s in the graph, connected to T_i and T_j, and this is the only reason to have a state as a node of the graph. Since TS is weakly live and totally reachable, this graph is connected, and each state occurring in it has at least two neighbours (in contrast, a subset of labels may be connected to a single state). Indeed, since TS is weakly live, $\cup_{T'\in\mathcal{T}} adj(T') = S$. Each state s occurring as a node in the graph is connected to at least two members of the $\mathcal{T}$, by the definition of the introduction of s in the graph. Let T_1 be the member of $\mathcal{T}$ such that $\imath \in adj(T_1)$, let T_i be any other member of $\mathcal{T}$, and let us consider a path $\imath[\alpha\rangle$ (not necessarily short) ending with some $t \in T_i$. Then: each time there is a sequence $t't''$ in α such that t' and t'' belong to two different members T' and T'' of $\mathcal{T}$, we have $[t'\rangle s[t''\rangle$, where s is the only state-node connected to T' and T'', hence in the graph we have $T' \to s \to T''$. This will yield a path in the constructed graph going from T_1 to T_i, hence the connectivity.

If there is a cycle in this graph, that means that there is no way to group the members of $\mathcal{T}$ in this cycle in two subsets such that the corresponding adjacency sets only have a single common state. Hence we need to fuse all these members, for each such cycle, leading to a new partition, and we also need to go back to the refinement of the partition in order to be compatible with the intersection rule, and to the construction of the graph.

Finally, we shall get an acyclic graph G, with at least three nodes (otherwise we stopped the articulation algorithm with the information that there is no non-trivial decomposition).

We shall now define a procedure $articul(SG)$ that builds an *lts* expression based on articulations from a subgraph SG of G with a chosen state-node root. We shall then apply it recursively to G, leading finally to an articulation-based (possibly complex) expression equivalent to the original *lts* TS.

The basic case will be that, if SG is a graph composed of a state s connected to a subset node T_i, $articul(SG)$ will be the *lts* $TS_i = (adj(T_i), T_i, \to_i, s)$ (as usual $\to_i$ is the projection of $\to$ on T_i; by construction, it will always be the case that $s \in adj(T_i)$).

First, if $\imath$ is a state-node of the graph, G then has the form of a star with root $\imath$ and a set of satellite subgraphs G_1, G_2, ..., G_n (n is at least 2). Let us denote by SG_i the subgraph with root $\imath$ connected to G_i: the result will then be the (commutative) articulation around $\imath$ of all the *lts*' $articul(SG_i)$.

Otherwise, let T_1 be the (unique) label subset in the graph such that $\imath \in adj(T_1)$. G may then be considered as a star with T_1 at the center, surrounded by subgraphs SG_1, SG_2, ..., SG_n (here n may be 1), each one with a root s_i connected to T_1 (we have here that $s_i \in adj(T_1)$, and we allow $s_i = s_j$): the result is then $((\ldots((adj(T_1), T_1, \to_1, \imath) \lhd s_1 \rhd articul(SG_1)) \lhd s_2 \rhd articul(SG_2)) \ldots) \lhd s_n \rhd articul(SG_n))$. Note that, if $n > 1$, the order in which we consider the subgraphs is irrelevant.

Finally, if a subgraph starts from a state s', followed by a subset T', itself followed by subgraphs SG_1, SG_2, ..., SG_n ($n \geq 1$; if it is 0 we have the base case), each one with a root s_i connected to T' (we have here that $s' \in adj(T')$, and we allow $s_i = s_j$): the result is then $((\ldots((adj(T'), T', \rightarrow', s') \lhd s_1 \rhd articul(SG_1)) \lhd s_2 \rhd articul(SG_2))\ldots) \lhd s_n \rhd articul(SG_n))$. Again, if $n > 1$, the order in which we consider the subgraphs is irrelevant.

This procedure is illustrated in Fig. 22. The *lts* TS_{22} leads to the graph G, with easily synthesised corresponding components TS_{23} to TS_{28}. Note that, from the total reachability of TS_{22}, they are all totally reachable themselves. This leads to the following articulated expression: $TS_{22} \equiv TS_{23} \lhd s_1 \rhd (((TS_{24} \lhd s_3 \rhd TS_{25}) \lhd s_2 \rhd TS_{26}) \lhd s_2 \rhd (TS_{27} \lhd s_7 \rhd TS_{28}))$.

6.3 Mixed Decomposition

In the previous sections we have introduced two pairs of (families of) operators acting on transition systems and net systems: $TS_1 \otimes TS_2$ - $PN_1 \oplus PN_2$ and $TS_1 \lhd s \rhd TS_2$ - $PN_1 \lhd M \rhd PN_2$.

There are special cases, however, where they are equivalent. This occurs when there is a single (initial) state in each component. Indeed, each label then only occurs in a loop around the initial state since we assumed they are not useless, and the same is true for the product as for the articulation (around the initial state). This is illustrated in Fig. 23. The other way round, if $TS = (\{\imath\}, \{(t, \imath, t | t \in T\}, T, \imath)$ has a single state, we have both $TS \equiv_T \bigotimes_{t \in T}(\{\imath\}, \{(t, \imath, t)\}, \{t\}, \imath) \equiv_T \lhd s \rhd_{t \in T}(\{\imath\}, \{(t, \imath, t)\}, \{t\}, \imath)$. In this case, there is always a PN-solution, composed of isolated transitions.

If $TS = (S, \rightarrow, T, \imath)$ and $|S| > 1$, in general either there is no non-trivial decomposition, or it is a non-trivial product or it is a non-trivial articulation, but there are still exceptions where we have both a product and an articulation. This is illustrated by Fig. 24, where TS may be both decomposed as an articulation and as a product. This only occurs however when some components are singleton systems, that is, when the decompositions are not very interesting in terms of synthesis efficiency. Indeed, if TS_1 has more than one state, there is an arc $s[t\rangle s'$ in it, and for any arc $s''[u\rangle$ in TS_2 we have in $TS = TS_1 \otimes TS_2$ three arcs $(s, s'')[t\rangle(s', s'')$, $(s, s'')[u\rangle$ and $(s', s'')[u\rangle$, so that $\{(s, s''), (s', s'')\} \subseteq adj(t) \cap adj(u)$ and we must have that t, u belong to the same component in any articulation of TS. Since there is no constraint on u, we thus have that T_2 belongs to the same articulated component than t. If TS_2 has more than one state and $s_2[v\rangle s_2' \in \rightarrow_2$, by symmetry, T_1 is in the same component as v in any articulation of TS. Hence, $T_1 \cup T_2$ belongs to the same component in any articulation of TS and TS is only trivially articulated.

As a consequence, from components with at least two states, hence not only composed of loops, we may form complex expressions alternating products and articulations, and there is no ambiguity in the decomposition. For instance, in the example of Fig. 12, $TS = TS(start); (TS(a) \otimes TS(b)); TS(end)$ may be rewritten $TS = TS(start) \lhd s_1 \rhd ((TS(a) \otimes TS(b)) \lhd s_4 \rhd TS(end))$.

Using alternatively the procedures detailed at the end of Sects. 6.1 and 6.2, until a component obtained by one of them only has a trivial decomposition, we shall obtain an adequate and optimal, possibly mixed, decomposition. Initially, we may start equivalently with the decomposition in factors or in articulations.

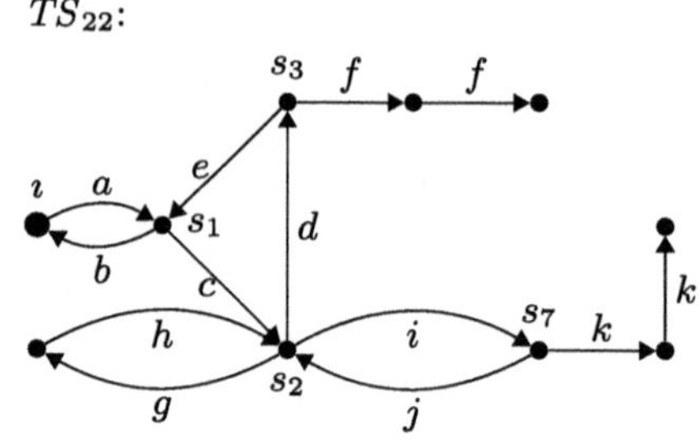

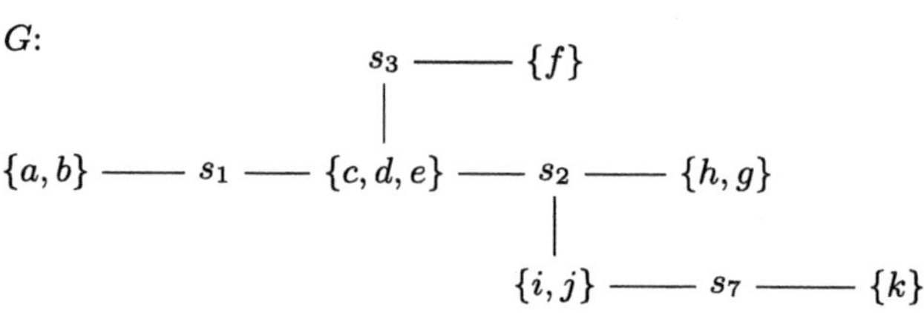

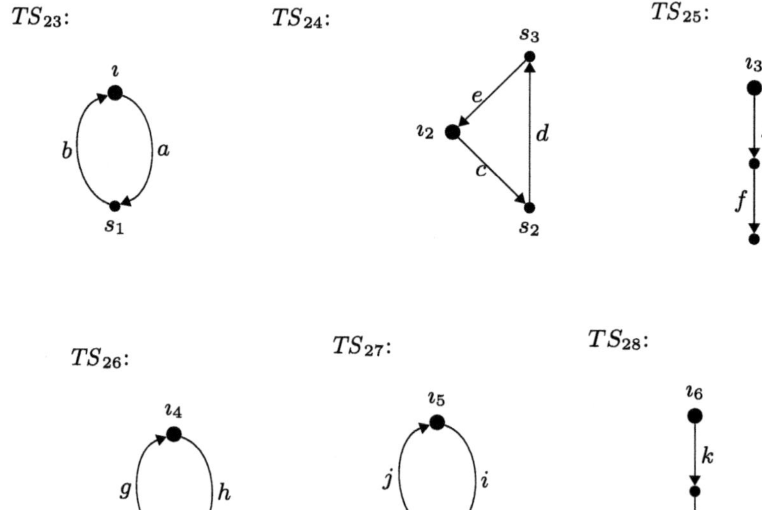

Fig. 22. $TS_{22} \equiv TS_{23} \lhd s_1 \rhd (((TS_{24} \lhd s_3 \rhd TS_{25}) \lhd s_2 \rhd TS_{26}) \lhd s_2 \rhd (TS_{27} \lhd s_7 \rhd TS_{28}))$

The result will be unique, unless we get singleton components as in the examples in Figs. 23 and 24. The recomposition of partial solutions into a global one, may be performed during a post-processing phase.

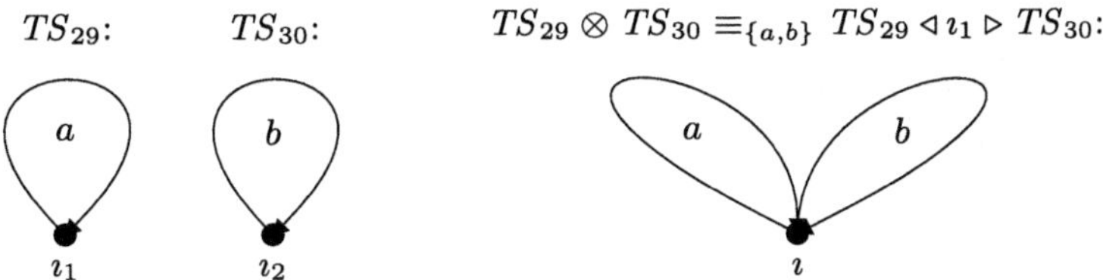

Fig. 23. Singleton case.

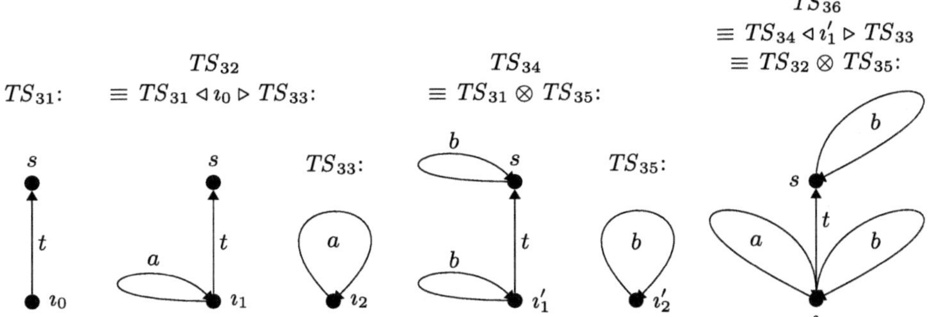

Fig. 24. Ambiguous case.

7 Conclusion

From the difficulty of analysing a given net, and to modify the latter if the found properties are not satisfactory, we have introduced the synthesis of a net (of some subclass) with a reachability graph isomorphic to a given labelled transition system. We have seen how, when the target class only constrains the transitions of its members, a solution is built by adding progressively places to solve the various needed separation properties. This works for the general class of weighted P/T nets, but also for plain and/or safe and/or pure nets. We also considered two pairs of operators allowing to apply a divide-and-conquer strategy.

We have also seen how to specialise the general net synthesis procedure rather efficiently for some target subclasses, essentially the choice-free nets, separating the synthesis process into a pre-synthesis based on general properties of this class and a proper synthesis. Moreover, we have observed, that in the case of the smaller class of Marked Graphs, a more detailed analysis allows to even avoid the need to solve systems of linear constraints.

Note that, if we have specialised techniques for a series of embedded target classes, like here, we may start by trying the narrowest class first, then extend it progressively up to the point where a solution is found. If it does not work, it is also possible to search for an approximate solution, for instance like in [9, 40], where an optimal morphism is obtained for subclasses of nets resisting to reversing the arcs.

Region-based synthesis has been extensively studied in the literature, notably in classical works [21,41–43]. Our presentation follows a specialised line of results developed for bounded and weighted nets, highlighting the cases where the structure of the behaviour allows for efficient synthesis. The comparison with other synthesis approaches confirms that choice-free nets and marked graphs form classes where the structural constraints lead to particularly transparent and tractable synthesis procedures.

Other target classes may also be considered, but some are more difficult to handle. For instance, for free-choice nets, it is necessary to check whenever we add a place, if the specific constraints on places and transitions remain fulfilled, and to backtrack if this is not the case [40]. We could of course try to find other interesting subclasses of nets, enrich the pre-synthesis by incorporating additional general structural properties, find other pairs of operators for divide-and-conquer strategies, etc.

References

1. Best, E., Devillers, R.: Synthesis of persistent systems. In: 35th International Conference on Application and Theory of Petri Nets and Concurrency (ICATPN 2014), pp. 111–129 (2014)
2. Best, E., Devillers, R.: Synthesis and reengineering of persistent systems. Acta Inf. **52**(1), 35–60 (2015)
3. Best, E., Devillers, R.: Synthesis of live and bounded persistent systems. Fund. Inform. **140**, 39–59 (2015)
4. Best, E., Devillers, R.: Synthesis of bounded choice-free Petri nets. In: Aceto, L., Frutos Escrig, D. (eds.) Proceedings of 26th International Conference on Concurrency Theory (CONCUR 2015), pp. 128–141 (2015)
5. Best, E., Devillers, R., Schlachter, U.: Bounded choice-free Petri net synthesis: algorithmic issues. Acta Inf. **55**(7), 575–611 (2018)
6. Best, E., Devillers, R., Schlachter, U., Wimmel, H.: Simultaneous Petri net synthesis. Sci. Ann. Comput. Sci. **28**(2), 199–236 (2018)
7. Best, E., Devillers, R.R., Erofeev, E.: A new property of choice-free Petri net systems. In: Application and Theory of Petri Nets and Concurrency - 41st International Conference, PETRI NETS 2020, Paris, France, 24–25 June 2020, Proceedings, pp. 89–108 (2020)
8. Teruel, E., Colom, J.M., Silva, M.: Choice-free Petri nets: a model for deterministic concurrent systems with bulk services and arrivals. IEEE Trans. Syst. Man Cybern. Part A **27**(1), 73–83 (1997)
9. Schlachter, U.: Over-approximative Petri nets synthesis for restricted subclasses of nets. In: Klein, S.T., Martín-Vide, C., Shapira, D. (eds.) LATA 2018. LNCS, vol. 10792, pp. 296–307. Springer, Cham (2018). https://doi.org/10.1007/978-3-319-77313-1_23
10. Best, E., Devillers, R.: Petri Net Primer - A Compendium on the Core Model, Analysis, and Synthesis. Computer Science Foundations and Applied Logic, Birkhäuser Cham (2024)
11. Petri, C.: Kommunikation mit Automaten. Rheinisch-Westfälisches Institut für Instrumentelle Mathematik Bonn: [Schriften des Rheinisch-Westfälischen Instituts für Instrumentelle Mathematik, Rheinisch-Westfälisches Institut f. instrumentelle Mathematik an d. Univ. (1962)

12. Rozenberg, G., Engelfriet, J.: Elementary net systems. In: Lectures on Petri Nets I: Basic Models, Advances in Petri Nets, the Volumes are Based on the Advanced Course on Petri Nets, held in Dagstuhl, September 1996, pp. 12–121 (1996)
13. Khomenko, V., Koutny, M., Vogler, W.: Canonical prefixes of Petri nets unfoldings. Acta Informatica **40**(2), 95–118 (2003)
14. Commoner, F.G., Holt, A.W., Even, S., Pnueli, A.: Marked directed graphs. J. Comput. Syst. Sci. **5**(5), 511–523 (1971)
15. Genrich, H.J., Lautenbach, K.: Synchronisationsgraphen. Acta Informatica **2**, 143–161 (1973)
16. Jensen, K.: Coloured Petri nets and the invariant-method. Theor. Comput. Sci. **14**, 317–336 (1981)
17. Vautherin, J.: Parallel systems specitications with coloured Petri Nets and algebraic specifications. In: Rozenberg, G. (ed.) APN 1986. LNCS, vol. 266, pp. 293–308. Springer, Cham (1986). https://doi.org/10.1007/3-540-18086-9_31
18. Haddad, S., Poitrenaud, D.: Recursive Petri nets. Acta Informatica **44**(7–8), 463–508 (2007)
19. Vázquez, C.R., Mahulea, C., Júlvez, J., Silva, M.: Introduction to fluid Petri nets. In: Control of Discrete-Event Systems, pp. 365–386 (2013)
20. Desel, J., Reisig, W.: The synthesis problem of Petri nets. Acta Informatica **33**, 297–315 (1993)
21. Badouel, E., Darondeau, P.: Theory of Regions, pp. 529–586. Springer, Heidelberg (1998)
22. Ehrenfeucht, A., Rozenberg, G.: Partial (set) 2-structures. Part II: state spaces of concurrent systems. Acta Informatica **27**(4), 343–368 (1990)
23. Desel, J., Reisig, W.: The synthesis problem of Petri nets. Acta Inf. **33**(4), 297–315 (1996)
24. Best, E., Schlachter, U.: Analysis of Petri nets and transition systems. In: Proceedings 8th Interaction and Concurrency Experience, ICE 2015, Grenoble, France, 4–5 June 2015, pp. 53–67 (2015)
25. Karmarkar, N.: A new polynomial-time algorithm for linear programming. Combinatorica **4**(4), 373–396 (1984)
26. Dantzig, G.: Maximization of a linear function of variables subject to linear inequalities. In: Koopmans, T. (ed.) Activity Analysis of Production and Allocation, Proceedings, pp. 339–347. Wiley, New York (1951)
27. Klee, V., Minty, G.: How good is the simplex algorithm?. In: Shisha, O. (ed.) Inequalities III, Proceedings, pp. 159–175. Academic Press, New York (1951)
28. Smtinterpol, an interpolating SMT solver. https://ultimate.informatik.uni-freiburg.de/smtinterpol/
29. Kroening, D., Leroux, J., Rümmer, P.: Interpolating quantifier-free Presburger arithmetic. In: Logic for Programming, Artificial Intelligence, and Reasoning - 17th International Conference, LPAR-17, Yogyakarta, Indonesia, 10–15 October 2010. Proceedings, pp. 489–503 (2010)
30. Dijkstra, E.W.: The structure of "the"-multiprogramming system. Commun. ACM **11**(5), 341–346 (1968)
31. Hoare, C.A.R.: Monitors: an operating system structuring concept. Commun. ACM **17**(10), 549–557 (1974)
32. Best, E., Darondeau, P.: A decomposition theorem for finite persistent transition systems. Acta Inf. **46**(3), 237–254 (2009)

33. Devillers, R., Hujsa, T.: Analysis and synthesis of weighted marked graph Petri nets. In: Application and Theory of Petri Nets and Concurrency - 39th International Conference, PETRI NETS 2018, Bratislava, Slovakia, 24–29 June 2018, Proceedings, pp. 19–39 (2018)
34. Tredup, R.: Hardness results for the synthesis of b-bounded petri nets. In: Application and Theory of Petri Nets and Concurrency - 40th International Conference, PETRI NETS 2019, Aachen, Germany, 23–28 June 2019, Proceedings, pp. 127–147 (2019)
35. Devillers, R.: Products of transition systems and additions of Petri nets. In: Desel, J., Yakovlev, A. (eds) Proceedings of 16th International Conference on Application of Concurrency to System Design (ACSD 2016), pp. 65–73 (2016)
36. Devillers, R.: Factorisation of transition systems. Acta Informatica **55**(4), 339–362 (2018)
37. Devillers, R., Schlachter, U.: Factorisation of Petri net solvable transition systems. In: Application and Theory of Petri Nets and Concurrency - 39th International Conference, PETRI NETS 2018, Bratislava, Slovakia, pp. 82–98 (2018)
38. Devillers, R.: Articulation of transition systems and its application to Petri net synthesis. In: Application and Theory of Petri Nets and Concurrency - 40th International Conference, PETRI NETS 2019, Aachen, Germany, 23–28 June 2019, Proceedings, pp. 113–126 (2019)
39. Murata, T.: Petri nets: properties, analysis and applications. Proc. IEEE **77**, 541–580 (1989)
40. Schlachter, U.: Petri net synthesis and modal specifications. Ph.D. thesis, University of Oldenburg, Germany (2018)
41. Badouel, E., Bernardinello, L., Darondeau, P.: Polynomial algorithms for the synthesis of bounded nets. In: TAPSOFT'95: Theory and Practice of Software Development, 6th International Joint Conference CAAP/FASE, Aarhus, Denmark, pp. 364–378 (1995)
42. Badouel, E., Bernardinello, L., Darondeau, P.: The synthesis problem for elementary net systems is NP-complete. Theor. Comput. Sci. **186**(1–2), 107–134 (1997)
43. Badouel, E., Bernardinello, L., Darondeau, P.: Petri Net Synthesis. Texts in Theoretical Computer Science. An EATCS Series, Springer, Cham (2015)

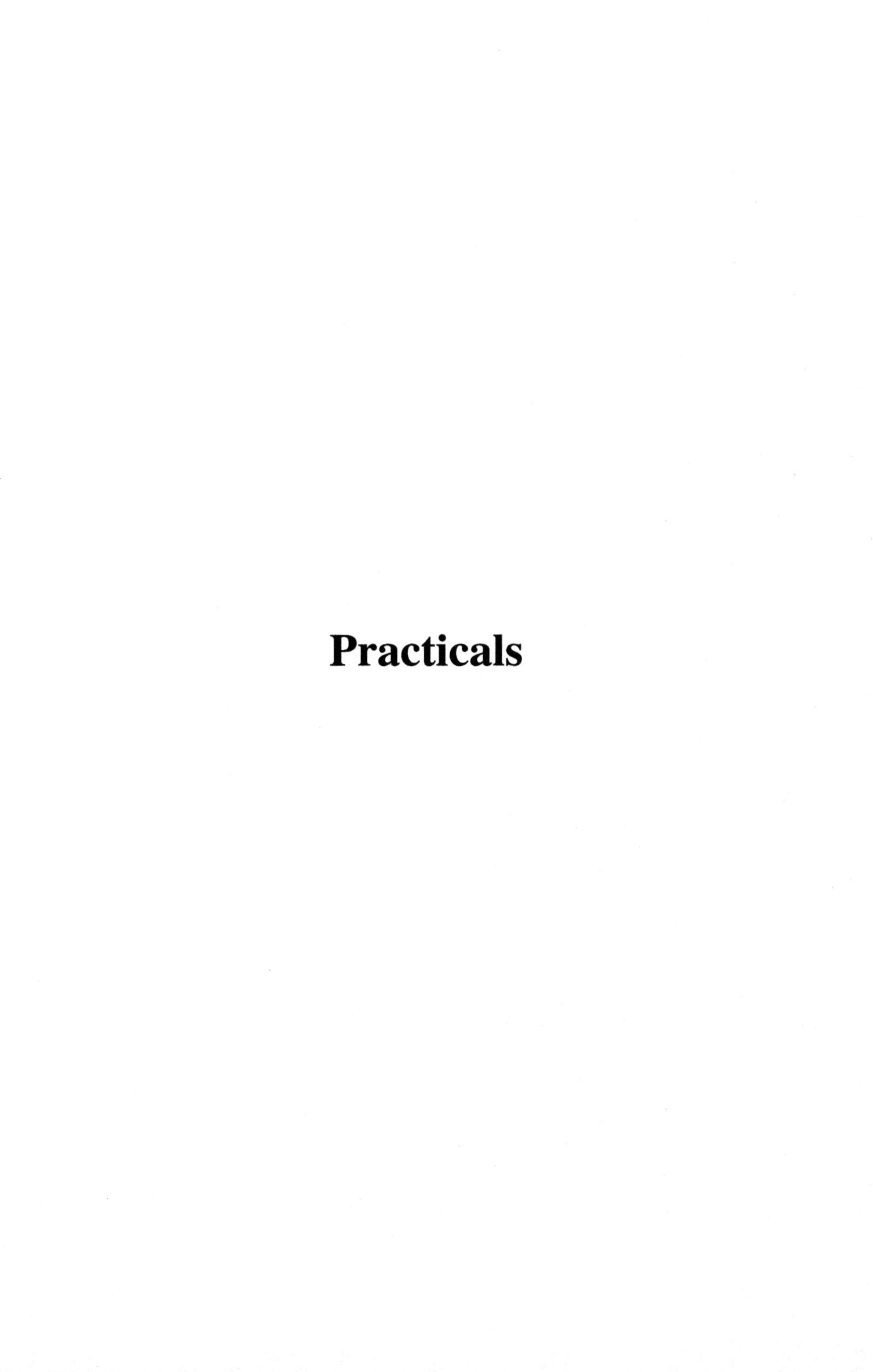

Practicals

Design Decisions in Process Discovery and the Inductive Miner Framework

D. Fahland(✉)

Eindhoven University of Technology, Eindhoven, Netherlands
d.fahland@tue.nl

Abstract. Process discovery is the task of constructing a model that "best" describes the behaviour of a process recorded in an event log. The task can rarely be solved perfectly as the partial information in the log is usually insufficient to construct a model that is all: sound, fitting and precise wrt. the log, generalizes to future behavior of the process, and simple in its structure. Consequently, any process discovery technique has to decide how to trade between these quality aspects when constructing a process model. In this text, we study several fundamental design decisions and heuristics used in process discovery for resolving the trade-off between fitness and the other quality criteria. We specifically study discovery algorithms built on the "directly-follows abstraction" of an event log. In exploring these questions, we also show how to create variations of existing process discovery techniques or design new ones that may be more suitable for a particular analysis task.

1 Tradeoffs and Decisions in Process Discovery

Process mining techniques aim at extracting information from event logs. The *task of process discovery* [14] is to construct for a given log L a model $M = d(L)$ so that the following properties hold:

- M is sound [24] meaning the set $\mathcal{L}(M)$ of all traces described by M[1] is well-defined. Specifically, every partial execution of M can be extended to complete execution of M.
- M *fits* (or recalls) L perfectly ($L \subseteq \mathcal{L}(M)$) or as much as possible (maximize $L \cap \mathcal{L}(M)$).
- M is "*simple enough*" to be understood by a human analyst, i.e. the model "fits the human mind").
- M is *specific* enough to be useful for answering an *analysis task*, i.e. "fitness for purpose".

[1] For example, for a transition system TS, $\mathcal{L}(TS)$ is the set of runs from the initial state of TS to an accepting state of TS; for a Petri net N, $\mathcal{L}(N)$ is the set of firing sequences from the initial marking of N to a final marking of N.

F. Kordon et al. (Eds.): *Transactions on Petri Nets and Other Models of Concurrency XVIII*,
LNCTPN 16260, pp. 233–259, 2026.
https://doi.org/10.1007/978-3-662-73305-9_8

These properties can rarely be satisfied on a given log, forcing a process discovery techniques into striking a *tradeoff* between the different desired properties. Consequently, various *design decisions* in a discovery algorithm $d(.)$ influence how $d(.)$ strikes this tradeoff between desired properties as we discuss next.

Tradeoffs. Process discovery has to support many analysis tasks. The generic task is to describe the entire process recorded in L. Thereby, the ideal process discovery technique d is able to construct a "perfect" model of the original data generating process P. P exists and is being executed in reality with the potential behavior $\mathcal{L}(P)$ (all executions allowed by the process design and its participants). The log $L \subseteq \mathcal{L}(P)$ is a sample of this potential behavior. We ideally would like to discover a model $M = d(L)$ that has exactly the same behavior $\mathcal{L}(M) = \mathcal{L}(P)$ as the original process P, i.e., d *rediscovers* P from the sample L.

More specific tasks are to summarize the main behavior of the process, revealing particular deviations and performance bottlenecks, or "drilling-down" to particular behavior of interest. Thereby, the latter tasks are typically solved by pre-processing L to a more specific log L' and then discovering a model $M' = d(L')$.

However, true rediscovery of P is typically not achievable, and we will discuss later why this is the case. Further, as the log $L \subseteq \mathcal{L}(P)$ contains only positive samples of P (traces that happened) but no negative samples (traces that cannot happen in P), we cannot measure *specificity* of M wrt. L, i.e., the rate by which M correctly identifies negatives. This also means, we cannot use "behavior that cannot happen" as information to guide the construction of M.

Instead, we typically use *precision* (the amount of additional traces in $\mathcal{L}(M) \setminus L$ not observed in the log) and *generalization* (the likelihood that another trace of the "original" from which L was recorded will still fit M) to estimate how specific M is regarding the underlying process P. Both measures together indicate whether M really does *not* describe traces that cannot happen in the process – where generalization estimates whether traces $\mathcal{L}(M) \setminus L$ not recorded in the log L are likely to happen in the future.

State-of-the-art techniques therefore approach the process discovery task as an *unsupervised* learning problem trying to achieve pareto-optimality of M regarding *fitness* and *precision* wrt. L, *generalization* wrt. future traces not seen in L yet, and structural *simplicity* of M [12].

Design Decisions. Process discovery is primarily solved algorithmically by synthesizing a graph from behavioral abstractions of L [7,10,17], as optimization problem over linear [26] or logical constraints [23], or genetic algorithms searching for optima in the space of models [12].

Reviews and benchmarks observe that, despite impressive progress, no *unsupervised process discovery technique* consistently returns fitting, precise, simple, *and* sound models on all problem instances in feasible time [8,25]. Specifically, each technique is based on *different algorithmic design decisions* and uses *different heuristics* for efficiently finding models in the available search space, resulting in an inherent bias favoring some quality criteria over others that cannot be overcome [8].

In the following, we study *some* fundamental design decisions and heuristics and their use for *resolving the trade-off between fitness and the other quality criteria.* We do this by exploring solutions to the following challenges.

- *Maximizing fitness.* How to design a process discovery technique $d(.)$ that returns for any given event log L a process model $M = d(L)$ that is (1) is sound, (2) perfectly fits L ($L \subseteq \mathcal{L}(M)$), (3) is simple, and (4) as specific as possible wrt. L (i.e., ideally d rediscovers the process that generated L).
- *Trading fitness.* If simplicity or high specificity cannot be achieved, how to trade fitness wrt. L to improve simplicity or specificity? In other words, how to obtain a model M' that may not perfectly fit L but is better in answering the analysis question than $d(L)$? Can we obtain M' only by filtering $L' \subseteq L$ or can we introduce parameters to d to return M' instead of M?

In exploring these questions, we also show how to create variations of existing process discovery techniques or design new ones that may be more suitable for a particular analysis task.

In the remainder, we first study the above two questions for discovering directly-follows graphs in Sect. 2 and discuss their fundamental limitations. We then discuss in Sect. 3 the relevance of choosing stronger modeling constructs and how to limit the search space of process discovery algorithms to ensure soundness. We then show how to systematically link patterns in event logs to modeling constructs in Sect. 4. We then show in Sect. 5 how the *Inductive Miner* (IM) was designed to solve the first challenge of maximizing fitness; Sect. 7 discusses when IM even ensure rediscoverability. We discuss the second challenge of trading fitness both for directly-follows graphs in Sect. 2 in for the Inductive Miner in Sect. 8.

2 Discovery with Directly-Follows Graphs

The most basic form of process discovery is based on directly-follows graphs (DFGs), who are still the de-facto "model" in industry. We write "model" in quotation marks, because: a DFG M does not always have well-defined set $\mathcal{L}(M)$ of traces described by M, and a DFG M may provide little helpful abstraction to be specific and simple. In the following, we discuss these shortcomings in detail and how they can be overcome.

Simple Event Logs. Let Σ be the set of all process activity names we consider; Σ is also called *alphabet.* A *trace* is a (possibly empty) sequence $t \in \Sigma^*$; an occurrence of an activity $a \in t$ is also called an *event*[2]. A simple event *log* L is a finite multiset of traces: $L \in \mathbb{N}^{\Sigma^*}$; we write $L(t)$ for the *frequency* of trace t in L. For example, the log $L = [\langle a, b, c\rangle^3, \langle a, c, b\rangle]$ has two trace variants:

[2] Note that we may now refer to a as an activity, e.g., $a \in \Sigma$, but also as an event, e.g., $a \in t$. This dual interpretation of a originates from the projection of events to their activity names. It is crucial to remember that generally an activity is different from an event.

a, b, c (occurring with *frequency* 3) and a, c, b (occurring with frequency 1); a, b, c denotes that first a occurred, then b, and finally c. If we are not interested in the frequency of a trace, we denote $L \subseteq \Sigma^*$ as a set of traces, e.g., $L = \{\langle a, b, c\rangle, \langle a, c, b\rangle\}$. We write $\Sigma(L)$ for the alphabet of all activities occurring in L.

A *language* $L \subseteq \Sigma^*$ is any finite or infinite set of traces, i.e., every log is a language, but not every language is a log.

Directly-Follows Graph. The *directly-follows graph* (DFG) expresses when two activities in a log L follow each other as a graph $G(L) = (\Sigma(L) \cup \{\top, \bot\}, \twoheadrightarrow)$ with

- nodes $\Sigma(L) \cup \{\top, \bot\}$ (one node per activity; and artificial start/end),
- an edge $(a, b) \in \twoheadrightarrow$ iff some trace $\langle \cdots, a, b, \cdots\rangle \in L$,
- an edge $(\top, a) \in \twoheadrightarrow$ iff some trace $\langle a, \cdots\rangle \in L$, and
- an edge $(a, \bot) \in \twoheadrightarrow$ iff some trace $\langle \cdots, a\rangle \in L$

We also write $Start(G(L)) = \{a \mid (\top, a) \in \twoheadrightarrow\}$ and $End(G(L)) = \{a \mid (a, \bot) \in \twoheadrightarrow\}$ for the *start* and *end* nods of G. A *weighted* DFG $G(L) = (\Sigma(L) \cup \{\top, \bot\}, \twoheadrightarrow, w)$ additionally assigns to each $a \in \Sigma(L)$ the weight $w(a)$ of how often a occurs in L, and to each $(a, b) \in \twoheadrightarrow$ how often $\langle \cdots, a, b, \cdots\rangle$, $\langle a, \cdots\rangle$, or $\langle \cdots, a\rangle$ occurs in L.

A sequence $\langle a_1, a_2, \ldots, a_n\rangle$ is in the *language* $\mathcal{L}(G)$ of DFG G iff $\langle \top, a_1, a_2, \ldots, a_n, \bot$ is a path in G. By definition, $L \subseteq \mathcal{L}(G(L))$, i.e., the log L always fits the DFG $G(L)$.

For example, the weighted DFG $G(L)$ of the log $L = [\langle A, E, G\rangle^{60}, \langle A, B, F, E, G\rangle^{15}, \langle A, B, F, G\rangle^{5}, \langle A, C, F, G\rangle^{10}, \langle A, D, F\rangle^{10}]$ is shown in Fig. 1. The trace $\langle A, D, F, G\rangle$ is in $\mathcal{L}(G(L))$ but not in L, i.e., it is part of the language of G not observed in the log.

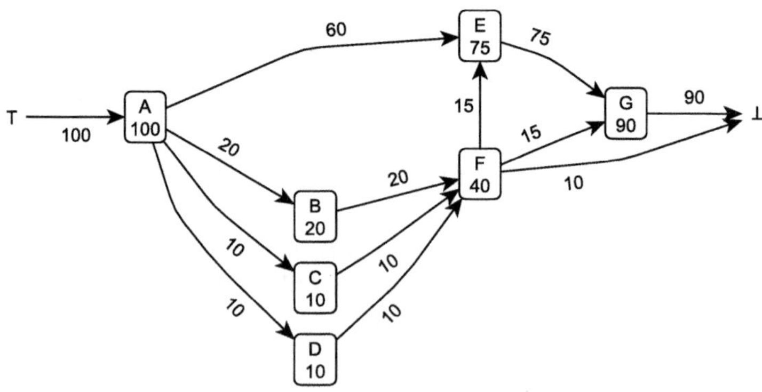

Fig. 1. Weighted DFG of $L = [\langle A, E, G\rangle^{60}, \langle A, B, F, E, G\rangle^{15}, \langle A, B, F, G\rangle^{5}, \langle A, C, F, G\rangle^{10}, \langle A, D, F\rangle^{10}]$.

Figure 2 shows the DFG of the public real-life event log of a Road Traffic Fines Management process [20]. This DFG illustrates, at a small scale, the disadvantages of DFGs:

1. A DFG only models the *sum of all temporal observations* "a occurred directly before b", but no higher-order behavioral logic.
2. Thus, it is not possible to distinguish *choices* between two alternative activities from *parallel* or *concurrent* executions of two activities that can be executed in an arbitrary order and *repetitions* of activities.

This makes DFGs of real-life event logs typically both complex and not specific, i.e., DFGs allow for many more traces than in the log or in the underlying process.

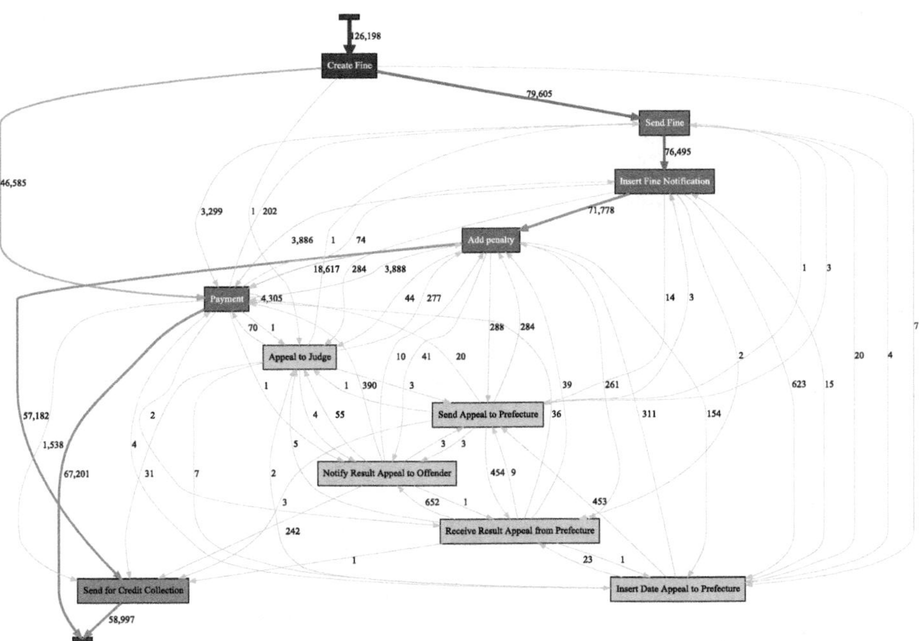

Fig. 2. Weighted DFG of the Road Traffic Fines Management Process [20].

Obtaining Simplicity Through Filtering. A standard technique to obtain simpler DFGs and possibly "reveal structure" in the graph is filtering. Most process mining tools offer functionality to filter a weighted DFG $G(L) = (\Sigma(L) \cup \{\top, \bot\}, \twoheadrightarrow, w)$ by removing infrequent nodes or infrequent edges wrt. some threshold $f_{activity}$ and f_{edge}:

- A naive DFG filter for nodes is to remove each node a with $w(a) \leq f_{activity} \cdot \max_{b \in \Sigma(L)} w(b)$ and all adjacent edges.

– A naive DFG filter for edges is to remove each edge $(a, b) \in \twoheadrightarrow$ with $w(a, b) \leq f_{edge} \cdot \max_{(c,d) \in \twoheadrightarrow} w(c, d)$; and then removing all isolated nodes.

If we apply the naive DFG filter for nodes on the DFG of Fig. 1 with $f_{activity} = 0.25$, we remove ndoes B, C, D. Now node F no longer has any incoming edges and F no longer appears in any trace of the resulting graph, i.e., F is no longer part of any path from $\top$ to $\bot$.

If we apply the naive DFG filter for edges on the DFG of Fig. 1 with $f_{edge} = 0.15$, we remove $(A, C), (A, D), (C, F), (D, F), (F, E), (F, G)(F, \bot)$ and nodes C, D. Now F no longer has any outgoing edges and any trace reaching F cannot be completed, i.e., F is no longer part of any path from $\top$ to $\bot$.

Although these naive filtering options are widely used in industrial implementations, both can make the graph $G(L)$ *unsound* [18] as there can be partial executions starting in $\top$ that cannot be completed to reach $\bot$, or there are activities that can never be executed. A DFG $G(L)$ is *sound* iff every node $a \in \Sigma(L)$ is on a path from $\top$ to $\bot$.

Figure 3 illustrates the problem of naively filtering the DFG of Fig. 2.

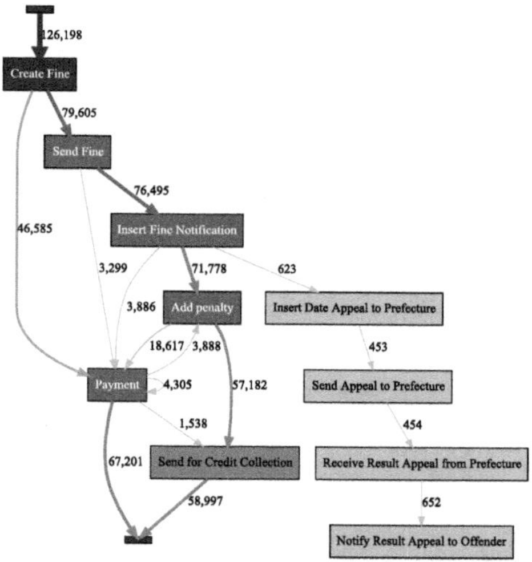

Fig. 3. Weighted DFG of the Road Traffic Fines Management Process [20] after filtering edges occurring < 400 times.

A proper frequency-based activity and edge filter of a DFG has to filter the underlying event log L to obtain the filtered log L', and then compute $G(L')$. For example:

– Let $\Sigma' = \{a \in \Sigma \mid w(a) > f_{activity} \cdot \max_{b \in \Sigma(L)} w(b)\}$ be the *frequent activities* wrt. threshold $0 \leq f_{activity} \leq 1$. We write $t|_{\Sigma'}$ for the projection of simple trace t onto the subset $\Sigma' \subseteq \Sigma$ of frequent activities. The projected log is $L' = L|_{\Sigma'} = \{t|_{\Sigma'} \mid t \in L\}$. The DFG of L over the frequent activities wrt. $f_{activity}$ is $G(L')$.

- A trace $t \in L$ with frequency $L(t)$ is *frequent* wrt. $0 \leq f_{trace} \leq 1$ iff $L(t) > f_{trace} \cdot \max_{s \in L} L(s)$. The log selecting only frequent traces is $L' = [t \in L \mid L(t) > f_{trace} \cdot \max_{s \in L} L(s)]$. The DFG of L over the frequent traces of L is $G(L')$.

Note that both filters can be combined. Filtering the log $L = [\langle A, E, G\rangle^{60}, \langle A, B, F, E, G\rangle^{15}, \langle A, B, F, G\rangle^{5}, \langle A, C, F, G\rangle^{10}, \langle A, D, F\rangle^{10}]$ for the frequent activities with $f_{activity} = 0.25$ yields $L' = [\langle A, E, G\rangle^{60}, \langle A, F, E, G\rangle^{15}, \langle A, F, G\rangle^{15}, \langle A, F\rangle^{10}]$. Filtering for the frequent traces with $f_{trace} = 0.10$ yields $L'' = [\langle A, E, G\rangle^{60}, \langle A, F, E, G\rangle^{15}, \langle A, F, G\rangle^{15}]$. Figure 4 shows $G(L'')$.

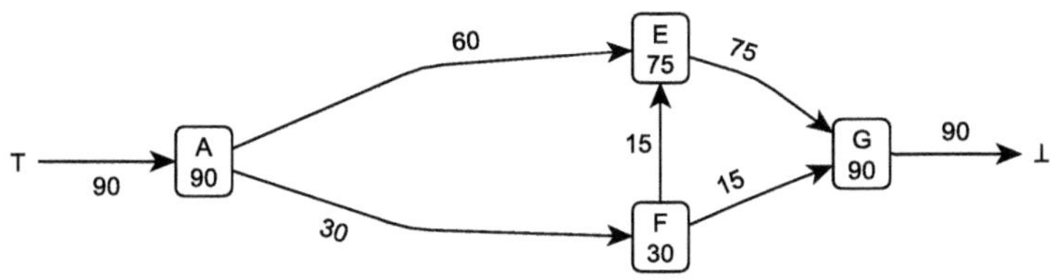

Fig. 4. Weighted DFG after frequency-based filtering of the event-log.

Filtering a DFG reduces fitness (by design not all traces of L fit the model) but usually increase specificity. Removing nodes and edges from $G(L)$ reduces the language that can be generated and thereby specifically removes traces of $G(L)$ that are neither in L nor in the process P from which L was recorded.

Applying corresponding filters on the DFG of the Road Traffic Fine Management log yields the DFG in Fig. 5(left).

Other definitions for filtering in directly-follows based mining are possible as explored in [18] and [2]. **ProM** supports directly-follows based mining with filtering in the Inductive Visual Miner and in the Interactive Data-Aware Heuristics Miner (choose directly-follows miner in the configuration in each).

Heuristics Filtering. While the DFG of Fig. 5(left) is sound, it still cannot model choices, parallelism, and loops appropriately. Parallelism introduces spurious edges in the directly-follows graph: We observe two activities $(a, b) \in \twoheadrightarrow$ following each other *temporally* but not *causally*. There is no reason that b occurred after a; b could also have occurred *before* a, i.e., $(b, a) \in \twoheadrightarrow$. The α-algorithm uses $(a, b), (b, a) \in \twoheadrightarrow$ to infer that a and b are concurrent. But if $w(a, b) = 100$ and $w(b, a) = 1$, then this inference is not necessarily reliable.

A *heuristic filter* to remove edges due to parallelism is to keep only those edges (a, b) where $w(a, b) >> w(b, a)$, i.e., (a, b) occurs much more often than (b, a) does. Thus, to remove every edge $(a, b) \in \twoheadrightarrow$ where the *relative strength* $(w(a, b) - w(b, a))/(w(a, b) + w(b, a) + 1) > f$ for some threshold $0 \leq f \leq 1$. This heuristic filtering is used by the *Heuristic Miner*. Figure 5(right) shows the result of applying this heuristic filter on the Road Traffic Fine Management log for $f = 0.1$ (edge annotation indicate the relative strength).

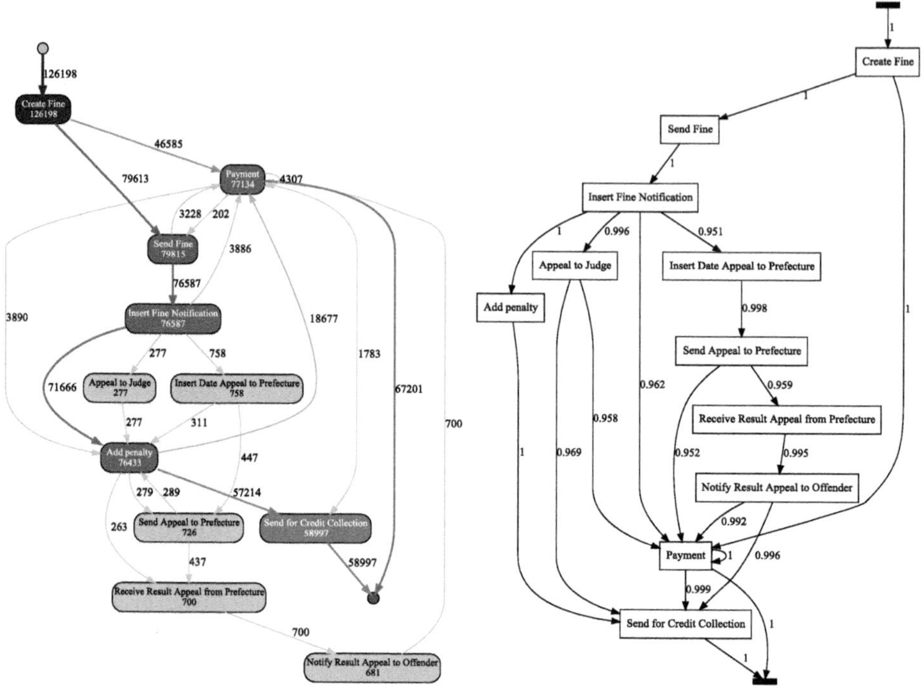

Fig. 5. Weighted DFG of the Road Traffic Fines Management Process [20] after filtering infrequent traces (left) and after heuristic edge filtering (right).

The shown edges no longer describe spurious temporal ordering, and thus loops and parallelism are easier to distinguish. This heuristic filtering of edges also makes the discovery result "robust" against infrequent behavioral features: a few new traces that deviate from the features already shown in the model will not lead to changes in the model. This makes this heuristic particularly useful for identify the main behavior in a process (but less useful for showing deviations).

However, we still cannot distinguish whether two outgoing edges of an activity describe a choice between two alternative or parallelism (both get executed). The *Heuristics Miner* [1,21] discovers whether two edges (a, b) and (a, c) in a filtered DFG describe a choice or parallelism by checking whether a is followed by b and c in a trace ($\langle \ldots a \ldots b \ldots c \ldots \rangle$) or whether only one of them occurs ($\langle \ldots a \ldots b \ldots \rangle$ or $\langle \ldots a \ldots c \ldots \rangle$). The *Split Miner* [7] distinguishes choices from parallelism by remembering whether b and c had edges $(b, c), (c, b) \in \twoheadrightarrow$ prior to filtering. While this results in results in models of high fitness and precision [7,10]; the models may be unsound and have high complexity [8]; the heuristics may not generalize to new data [19] or larger samples [27].

ProM supports heuristics-based mining in the Interactive Data-Aware Heuristics Miner. The discovered heuristics models can be exported to Petri nets for follow-up analysis.

3 Stronger Modeling Constructs

If we want to distinguishing choices from parallelism in a process model, but also properly model loops, we need stronger modeling constructs. These constructs are provided by formal process models.

Petri Nets, Workflow Nets and Block-structured Workflow Nets. A *Petri net* is a bipartite graph containing places and transitions, interconnected by directed arcs. A transition models a process activity, places and arcs model the ordering of process activities. We assume the standard semantics of Petri nets here, see [22]. A *workflow net* is a Petri net having a single start place and a single end place, modeling the start and end state of a process. Moreover, all nodes are on a path from start to end [6]. A *block-structured workflow net* is a hierarchical workflow net that can be divided recursively into parts having single entry and exit points. Figure 7 shows a block-structured workflow net.

Process Trees. A *process tree* is a compact abstract representation of a block-structured workflow net: a rooted tree in which leaves are labeled with activities (or with τ for an invisible step) and all other nodes are labeled with operators. A process tree describes a language, an operator describes how the languages of its subtrees are to be combined.

We formally define process trees recursively. We assume a finite alphabet Σ of activities and a set $\bigoplus$ of operators to be given. Symbol $\tau \notin \Sigma$ denotes the silent activity.

- a with $a \in \Sigma \cup \{\tau\}$ is a process tree;
- Let $M_1, \ldots, M_n$ with $n > 0$ be process trees and let $\oplus$ be a process tree operator, then $\oplus(M_1, \ldots, M_n)$ is a process tree. We also write this as $\overset{\oplus}{\overbrace{M_1 \;\ldots\; M_n}}$.

There are a few standard operators that we consider in the following: operator $\times$ means the exclusive choice between one of the subtrees, $\rightarrow$ means the sequential execution of all subtrees, $\circlearrowleft$ means the structured loop of loop body M_1 and alternative loop back paths $M_2, \ldots, M_n$, and $\wedge$ means a parallel (interleaved) execution as defined below. Please note that for $\circlearrowleft$, n must be ≥ 2.

Each process tree describes a language: an activity describes the execution of that activity, a silent activity describes the empty trace, while an operator node describes a combination of the languages of its children. Each operator combines the languages of its children in a specific way.

Figure 6 illustrates how each process tree translates to a sound, block-structured workflow Petri net template [5,11]. These Petri net templates can be composed hierarchically. For instance, the Petri net shown in Fig. 7 corresponds to the process tree $\rightarrow(a, \circlearrowleft(\rightarrow(\wedge(\times(b,c),d),e),f),\times(g,h))$. If one would come up with another process tree operator, soundness of the translation follows if the translation of the new process tree operator is sound in isolation. The four operators presented here translate to well-structured, free-choice Petri nets [3]; other operators might not.

The behavior of a process tree $\mathcal{L}(M)$ is the set of firing sequences $\mathcal{L}(M) = \mathcal{L}(N_M)$ described by the Petri net N_M that we obtain by translating M to a Petri net using the patterns in Fig. 6. Thus also allows us to define the directly-follows graph of a process tree M as $G(\mathcal{L}(M))$ (without weights).

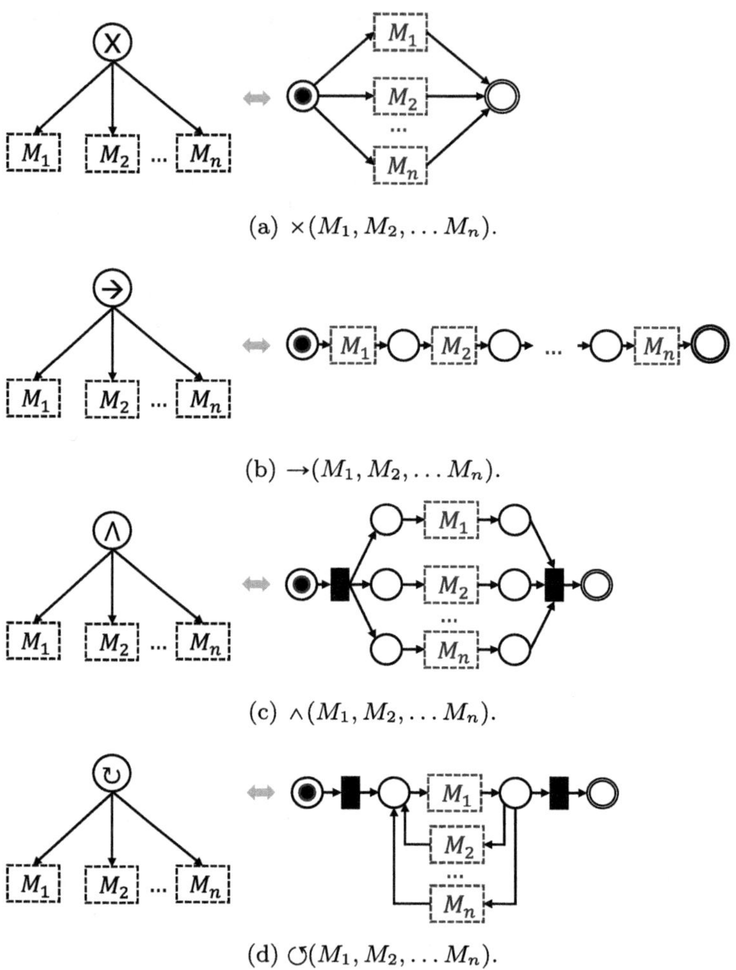

(a) $\times(M_1, M_2, \ldots M_n)$.

(b) $\rightarrow(M_1, M_2, \ldots M_n)$.

(c) $\wedge(M_1, M_2, \ldots M_n)$.

(d) $\circlearrowleft(M_1, M_2, \ldots M_n)$.

Fig. 6. Recursive Petri-net translations of process trees.

If M is a process tree and L is a log, then L *fits* M if and only if every trace in L is in the language of M: $L \subseteq \mathcal{L}(M)$. A *flower model* is a process tree that can produce any sequence of Σ. An example of a flower model is the model $\circlearrowleft(\tau, a_1, \ldots, a_m)$ where $a_1, \ldots, a_m = \Sigma$.

As additional notation, we write $\Sigma(L)$ and $\Sigma(M)$ for the activities occurring in log L or model M respectively, not including τ. Furthermore, $Start(L)$,

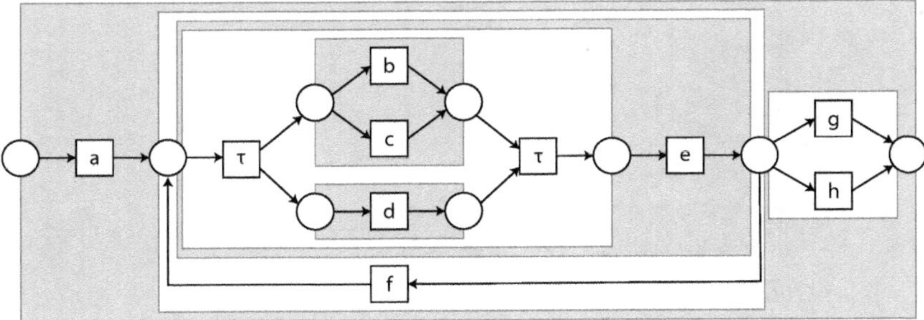

Fig. 7. A Petri net, modified from [4, page 196]. The rectangle regions denote the process tree nodes in $\rightarrow(a, \circlearrowleft(\rightarrow(\wedge(\times(b, c), d), e), f), \times(g, h))$.

Start(M) and *End*(L), *End*(M) denote the sets of activities with which log L and model M start or end.

4 Finding Structures in Directly-Follows Graphs

We now make a very important observation: although we cannot easily distinguish choices, loops, and parallelism in a DFG, the DFG actually contains patterns from which we can safely recover the "most dominant" operator in the process. The section provides a semi-formal introduction to the concept; Sect. 6 provides the full formal definitions.

If we assume the original process P from which the log $L \subseteq \mathcal{L}(P)$ was recorded is a block-structured process (or process tree), then the DFG $G(L)$ holds information about the top-level operator of P that we can recover.

The idea is to find in $G(L)$ structures that indicate the 'dominant' operator that orders the behaviour. For instance, the DFG of the log $L = \{\langle a, b, c\rangle, \langle a, c, b\rangle, \langle a, d, e\rangle, \langle a, d, e, f, d, e\rangle\}$ is shown in Fig. 8a. $G(L)$ of Fig. 8a can be partitioned into two sets of activities as indicated by the dashed line such that edges cross the line only from left to right. This pattern corresponds to a *sequence* where the activities left of the line precede the activities right of the line.

Cuts of Basic Process Operators. Each of the four operators $\times$, $\rightarrow$, $\circlearrowleft$, $\wedge$ has a characteristic pattern in $G(L)$ that can be identified by finding a partitioning of the nodes of $G(L)$ into n sets of nodes with characteristic edges in between.

Let $G(L) = (\Sigma(L) \cup \{\top, \bot\}, \twoheadrightarrow)$ be the directly-follows graph of a log L; recall that *Start*($G(L)$) and *End*($G(L)$) denote the start and end nodes of G. An *n-ary cut* c of $G(L)$ is a partition of the nodes of the graph into disjoint sets $\Sigma_1 \cup \ldots \cup \Sigma_n = \Sigma$.

We characterise a different cut for each operator $\times$, $\rightarrow$, $\circlearrowleft$, $\wedge$ based on edges between the nodes.

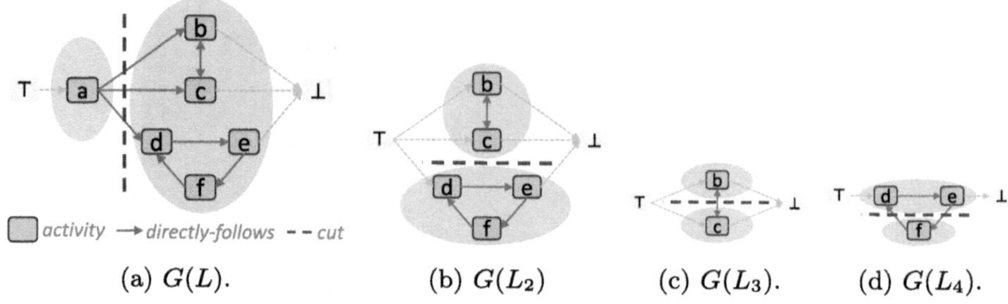

(a) $G(L)$. (b) $G(L_2)$ (c) $G(L_3)$. (d) $G(L_4)$.

Fig. 8. Directly-follows graphs of the running example with cuts; dashed red lines denote cuts (modified from [16, page 320] (Color figure online)).

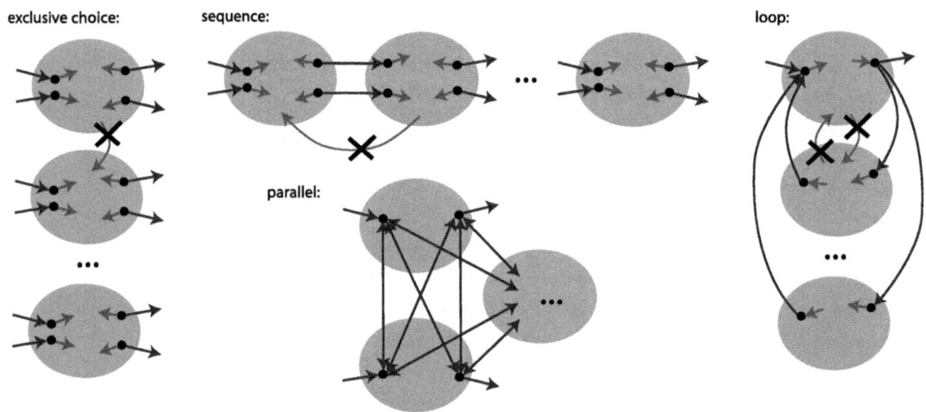

Fig. 9. General characterization of cuts in directly-follows graph for operators $\times$, $\rightarrow$, $\wedge$ and $\circlearrowleft$, from [16, page 321].

- In an *exclusive choice cut* $(\times, \Sigma_1, \ldots, \Sigma_n)$, each Σ_i has a start node and an end node, and there is no edge between two different $\Sigma_i \neq \Sigma_j$, as illustrated by Fig. 9(left) and Fig. 8b.
- In a *sequence cut* $(\rightarrow, \Sigma_1, \ldots, \Sigma_n)$, the sets $\Sigma_1 \ldots \Sigma_n$ are ordered such that for any two nodes $a \in \Sigma_i, b \in \Sigma_j, i < j$, there is a path from a to b along the edges of $G(L)$, but not vice versa; see Fig. 9(top) and Fig. 8a.
- In a *parallel cut* $(\wedge, \Sigma_1, \ldots, \Sigma_n)$, each Σ_i has a start node and an end node, and any two nodes $a \in \Sigma_i, b \in \Sigma_j, i \neq j$ are connected by edges (a, b) and (b, a); see Fig. 9(bottom) and Fig. 8c.
- In a *loop cut* $(\circlearrowleft, \Sigma_1, \ldots, \Sigma_n)$, Σ_1 has all start and all end nodes of $G(L)$, there is no edge between nodes of different $\Sigma_i \neq \Sigma_j, i, j > 1$, and any edge between Σ_1 and $\Sigma_i, i > 1$ either leaves an end node of Σ_1 or reaches a start node of Σ_1; see Fig. 9(right).

A cut c is *nontrivial* if $n > 1$. An n-ary cut is *maximal* if there exists no cut of G of which n is bigger. We are only interested in maximal cuts. Appendix 6.1 provides the formal definitions for each of the cuts.

5 Recursively Findings Structures with Inductive Miner

We now use the idea of the cuts from Sect. 4 in a process discovery algorithm. We explain how the discovery algorithm works in several steps while the example in Sect. 5.6 brings it all together. Alongside, we make a number of important design decisions by which we ensure that the resulting model has perfect fitness; we revisit this property in Sect. 7).

The cuts introduced in Sect. 4 allow to recognize the top-level operator of the process recorded in the log. Most processes have more complex behavior that is described by further operators underneath the top-level operator. Their footprints are "hidden" in the partitions of the top-level cut. To identify them, we use recursion on each of the partitions.

For example, the DFG of the log $L = \{\langle a, b, c\rangle, \langle a, c, b\rangle, \langle a, d, e\rangle, \langle a, d, e, f, d, e\rangle\}$ in Fig. 8a revealed a sequence cut $(\rightarrow, \{a\}, \{b, c, d, e, f\})$. To recurse on each partition, we split L according to the partition into a log L_a and a log $L_{b,c,d,e,f}$, and continue the analysis on each of these logs.

5.1 IM Framework

We introduce a generic process discovery framework function called *IMframework*. This framework uses four functions that have to be instantiated (or defined) to obtain a concrete process discovery algorithm.

- BaseCase(L) tells when the event log L only contains trivial, basic information that can be identified by just "looking" at log L, for example, all traces only have the same single activity $\langle a\rangle$ or all traces are empty.
- FindCut(L) abstracts the event log into a finite structure (e.g., the directly-follows graph of L and finds a way to partition the activities in L into k different subsets $\Sigma_1, \ldots, \Sigma_k$ that are related to each other in a uniform way by a specific process tree operator $\oplus$, e.g., they are mutually exclusive.
- SplitLog($L, (\oplus, \Sigma_1, \ldots, \Sigma_k)$) splits the event log L into k sublogs according to the operator $\oplus$, e.g., put each trace into one sublog if $\oplus = \times$.
- FallThrough(L) applies if no meaningful structure could be found in L and allows for example to find a generic fitting model, e.g., the flower model, to ensure fitness.

The framework works independently of the chosen process tree operators. The only requirement is that each operator $\oplus$ is explicitly checked for in FindCut(L) and explicitly handled in SplitLog($L, (\oplus, \Sigma_1, \ldots, \Sigma_k)$).

Given a set $\bigoplus$ of process tree operators for which the above functions are defined, *IMframework* discovers a process model using a divide and conquer approach. Given a log L, *IMframework* searches for possible splits of L into smaller logs $L_1, \ldots, L_n \leftarrow$ SPLITLOG$(L, (\oplus, \Sigma_1, \ldots, \Sigma_k))$ (according to the partitioning $(\oplus, \Sigma_1, \ldots, \Sigma_k)$). Then *IMframework* is applied on each smaller log L_i and the returned model M_i becomes a child under the operator $\oplus$.

```
function IMFRAMEWORK(L)
    bc ← BASECASE(L)
    if bc ≠⊥ then
        return base
    end if
    (⊕, Σ1, ..., Σk) ← FINDCUT(L)
    if (⊕, Σ1, ..., Σk) ≠⊥ then
        L1, ..., Ln ← SPLITLOG(L, (⊕, Σ1, ..., Σk))
        return (⊕, IMFRAMEWORK(L1), ..., IMFRAMEWORK(Lk))
    else
        return FALLTHROUGH(L)
    end if
end function
```

The above framework has to be instantiated with concrete functions for BASECASE, FINDCUT, SPLITLOG, and FALLTHROUGH(L).

5.2 Ensuring Fitness

In the following, we introduce the algorithm *IM* (Inductive Miner) which instantiates *IMframework*. In analogy to the basic DFG-based process discovery, we want to obtain a baseline discovery algorithm that ensures that the discovered model M perfectly fits the log.

To ensure fitness, we have to pay attention that FINDCUT(L) $=$ $(\oplus, \Sigma_1, \ldots, \Sigma_k)$ and SPLITLOG$(L, (\oplus, \Sigma_1, \ldots, \Sigma_k)) = L_1, \ldots, L_n$ only produce logs, such that these logs combined with the operator $\oplus$ can produce L again.

For example, splitting the traces $\langle a, b, c, d\rangle$ and $\langle a, e, f\rangle$ for $(\rightarrow, \{a, b\}, \{c, d, e, f\})$ yields the traces

- $\langle a, b\rangle$ and $\langle c, d\rangle$;
- $\langle a\rangle$ and $\langle e, f\rangle$.

The semantics of the sequence operator $\rightarrow$ then allows to recombine these traces again into $\langle a, b, c, d\rangle$ and $\langle a, e, f\rangle$ but also $\langle a, c, d\rangle$ and $\langle a, b, e, f\rangle$.

Thus, splitting a log L into $L_1 = [\langle a, b\rangle, \langle a\rangle]$ and $L_2 = [\langle c, d\rangle, \langle e, f\rangle]$ allows to construct a partial process tree with operator $\rightarrow$. The children of this tree are models M_1 and M_2 to be discovered from L_1 and L_2.

If $L_1 \subseteq \mathcal{L}(M_1)$ and $L_2 \subseteq \mathcal{L}(M_2)$, i.e., the models fit the logs, then the $\rightarrow$ ensures that recombining the traces $L_1 \subseteq \mathcal{L}(M_1)$ and $L_2 \subseteq \mathcal{L}(M_2)$ will yield a model $M = (\rightarrow, M_1, M_2)$ where $L \subseteq \mathcal{L}(M) = \mathcal{L}((\rightarrow, M_1, M_2))$.

If we adhere to this principle, we can ensure fitness.

5.3 Detecting Trivial Cases with BaseCase

The purpose of BASECASE(L) is to directly "see" from L which model M describes L best, so that $L \subseteq \mathcal{L}(M)$.

The basic function BASECASE$_{IM}$ (formally defined in Appendix 6.2) returns

- an activity a if the log only contains traces $\langle a \rangle$,
- τ if the log is empty (contains no trace), and
- $\perp$ otherwise, i.e., the log has complex information that requires further analysis.

5.4 Finding Cuts

The cut detection FINDCUT (formally defined in Sect. 6.3) works by constructing the directly follows graph $G(L)$ of the input log L. After that, the function tries to find one of the four cuts in $G(L)$ characterised above in this specific order:

- choice cut,
- sequence cut,
- parallel cut, and finally
- loop cut.

If FINDCUT cannot find a cut, it returns $\perp$ and *IM* will reach the FALLTHROUGH(L) which we discuss in the next section.

5.5 Splitting the Event Log According to a Cut

If FINDCUT finds a cut, *IM* has to split the log according to the cut, which we explain next. We define the log split functions together with a running example; the formal definitions are given in Appendix 6.4.

Consider the log $L = \{\langle a, b, c \rangle, \langle a, c, b \rangle, \langle a, d, e \rangle, \langle a, d, e, f, d, e \rangle\}$.

SequenceSplit. $G(L)$ (in Fig. 8a) has the sequence cut $\{a\}, \{b, c, d, e, f\}$. The log is then split by projecting each trace of L onto the different activity sets of the cut.

For a sequence cut $(\rightarrow, \Sigma_1, \ldots, \Sigma_n)$, the *sequence split* of L splits each trace $t \in L$ into sub-traces $t = t_1 \cdot t_2 \cdots t_n$ so that $t_i \in \Sigma_i^*$ (i.e., the sub-trace t_i can be generated by the sub-alphabet Σ_i). Each sub-log L_i holds all the sub-traces t_i.

In the example, SEQUENCESPLIT($L, (\{a\}, \{b, c, d, e, f\})$) $=$ $\{\langle a \rangle\}, \{\langle b, c \rangle, \langle c, b \rangle, \langle d, e \rangle, \langle d, e, f, d, e \rangle\}$. Call the second log L_2.

XorSplit. $G(L_2)$ (in Fig. 8b) has the exclusive choice cut $\{b, c\}, \{d, e, f\}$. The log is then split by moving each trace of L into the log of the corresponding activity set.

For a choice cut $(\times, \Sigma_1, \ldots, \Sigma_n)$, the *xor split* of L puts each trace $t \in L$ into log L_i iff $t \in \Sigma^*$ (i.e., the sub-trace t_i can be generated by the sub-alphabet Σ_i).

In the example, $\textsc{XorSplit}(L_2, (\{b,c\}, \{d,e,f\})) = \{\langle b,c\rangle, \langle c,b\rangle\}, \{\langle d,e\rangle, \langle d,e,f,d,e\rangle\}$. Call the first log L_3 and the second log L_4.

ParallelSplit. $G(L_3)$ (in Fig. 8c) has the parallel cut $\{b\}, \{c\}$. The log is split by projecting each trace for each activity set in the cut.

For a parallel cut $(\wedge, \Sigma_1, \ldots, \Sigma_n)$, the *parallel split* of L projects each trace $t \in L$ onto sub-traces $t_i = t|_{\Sigma_i}, i = 1, \ldots, n$ and placing t_i in L_i. Note that $t_i \in \Sigma_i^*$ can be generated by the sub-alphabet Σ_i.

In our example, $\textsc{ParallelSplit}(L_3, (\{b\}, \{c\})) = \{\langle b\rangle\}, \{\langle c\rangle\}$.

LoopSplit. The directly-follows graph of the log $L_4 = \{\langle d,e\rangle, \langle d,e,f,d,e\rangle\}$ is shown in Fig. 8d and has the loop cut $\{d,e\}, \{f\}$. The log is split by splitting each trace into subtraces of the loop body and of the loopback condition which are then added to the respective sublogs.

For a loop cut $(\circlearrowleft, \Sigma_1, \ldots, \Sigma_n)$, the *loop split* of L splits each trace $t \in L$ into sub-traces $t = t_1 \cdot t_2 \cdots t_k$ so that

- for $j = 1, 3, \ldots, k$ holds $t_j \in \Sigma_1^*$ (execution of the loop body), and
- for $j = 2, 4, \ldots, k = 1$ holds $t_j \in \Sigma_i^*, i > 1$ (execution of the loopback condition).

Add each sub-trace $t_j, j = 1, \ldots, k$ to sub-log L_i iff $t_j \in \Sigma_i^*$ (the partition that can generate t_j). In our example, $\textsc{LoopSplit}(L_4, (\{d,e\}, \{f\})) = \{\langle d,e\rangle\}, \{\langle f\rangle\}$.

The complete log splitting function $\textsc{SplitLog}_{IM}$ is just a case distinction on the operator $\oplus$ in the cut and defined in Appendix 6.4.

5.6 Example

Instantiating $\textsc{IMframework}$ with $\textsc{BaseCase}_{IM}$, $\textsc{FindCut}_{IM}$, and $\textsc{SplitLog}_{IM}$ yields the algorithm IM.

IM allows us to discover a process tree from the log $L = \{\langle a,b,c\rangle, \langle a,c,b\rangle, \langle a,d,e\rangle, \langle a,d,e,f,d, e\rangle\}$ as follows.

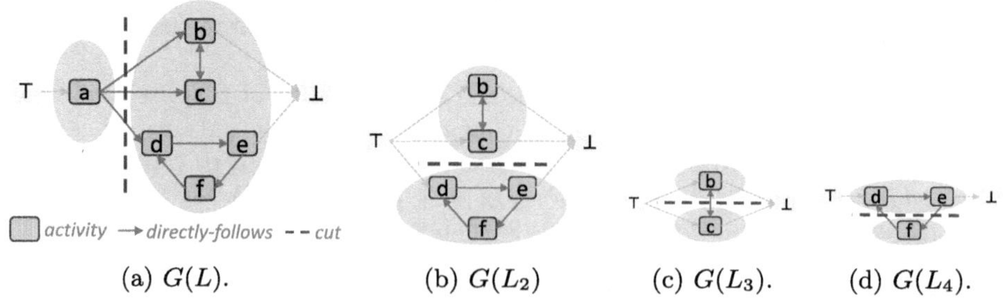

(a) $G(L)$. (b) $G(L_2)$ (c) $G(L_3)$. (d) $G(L_4)$.

Fig. 10. Several directly-follows graphs. Dashed lines denote cuts. (Repetition of Fig. 8)

.

- First, $\text{BASECASE}_{IM}(L)$ returns $\bot$ as none of the trivial cases hold in L.
- Next, $\text{FINDCUT}_{IM}(L)$ is called. Calculating $G(L)$ yields the DFG shown in Fig. 10a.
  - The only exclusive choice cut for $G(L)$ is $\{a, b, c, d, e, f\}$, which is a trivial cut, so $\text{XORCUT}(L)$ returns $(\times, \{a, b, c, d, e, f\})$, and the conditions $k > 1$ does not hold.
  - As we have shown before, a sequence cut for $G(L)$ is $\{a\}, \{b, c, d, e, f\}$ and $\text{SEQUENCECUT}(L)$ returns $(\rightarrow, \{a\}, \{b, c, d, e, f\})$. The condition $k > 1$ holds and SEQUENCESPLIT is called, which returns two sublogs:
    1. $L_1 = \{\langle a\rangle\}$
    2. $L_2 = \{\langle b, c\rangle, \langle c, b\rangle, \langle d, e\rangle, \langle d, e, f, d, e\rangle\}$
  - Then IM constructs the partial model $M = \rightarrow(\text{IM}(L_1), \text{IM}(L_2))$, i.e., a process tree with sequence $\rightarrow$ as root operator and two process trees as children that still have to be computed by $\text{IM}(L_1)$ and $\text{IM}(L_2)$ through recursion.
- IM first calls $\text{IM}(L_1)$ which calls $\text{BASECASE}_{IM}(L_1)$ which returns $base = a$. IM returns a as the process-tree consisting of the single leaf activity a, with which the partially discovered model becomes $M = \rightarrow(a, \text{IM}(L_2))$.
- For $\text{IM}(L_2)$, no base case is found. The directly-follows graph $G(L_2)$ is shown in Fig. 10b. Here, XORCUT finds the cut $(\times, \{b, c\}, \{d, e, f\})$ and XORSPLIT splits the log into
  1. $L_3 = \{\langle b, c\rangle, \langle c, b\rangle\}$
  2. $L_4 = \{\langle d, e\rangle, \langle d, e, f, d, e\rangle\}$
- The partially discovered model then becomes $M = \rightarrow(a, \times(\text{IM}(L_3), \text{IM}(L_4)))$.
- For $\text{IM}(L_3)$,
  - no base case is found by $\text{BASECASE}_{IM}(L_3)$ and
  - $\text{FINDCUT}(L_3)$ constructs $G(L_3)$ shown in Fig. 10c.
  - There is only a trivial exclusive choice cut $(\times, \{b, c\})$ and only a trivial sequence cut $(\rightarrow, \{b, c\})$, but $\text{PARALLELCUT}(L_3) = (\wedge, \{b\}, \{c\})$. So, PARALLELSPLIT splits L_3 into $L_5 = \{\langle b\rangle\}$ and $L_6 = \{\langle c\rangle\}$.
  - M becomes $\rightarrow(a, \times(\wedge(\text{IM}(L_5), \text{IM}(L_6)), \text{IM}(L_4)))$.
  - For $\text{IM}(L_5)$, $\text{BASECASE}_{IM}(L_5)$ returns leaf activity b and for $\text{IM}(L_6)$, $\text{BASECASE}_{IM}(L_6)$ returns leaf activity c. M becomes $\rightarrow(a, \times(\wedge(b, c), \text{IM}(L_4)))$.
- For $\text{IM}(L_4)$,
  - no base case is found by $\text{BASECASE}_{IM}(L_4)$ and
  - $\text{FINDCUT}(L_4)$ constructs $G(L_4)$ shown in Fig. 10d.
  - There are only trivial cuts for $\times$, $\rightarrow$, and $\wedge$, but $\text{LOOPCUT}(L_4) = (\circlearrowleft, \{d, e\}, \{f\})$.
  - LOOPSPLIT splits L_4 into $L_7 = \{\langle d, e\rangle\}$ and $L_8 = \{\langle f\rangle\}$, such that M becomes $\rightarrow(a, \times(\wedge(b, c), \circlearrowleft(\text{IM}(L_7), \text{IM}(L_8))))$
- After one more sequence cut ($\text{IM}(L_7)$) and a few base cases for d, e, and f, IM returns the model $\rightarrow(a, \times(\wedge(b, c), \circlearrowleft(\rightarrow(d, e), f)))$.

6 Fully Formal Definition of Inductive Miner

We now provide the complete formal definition of IM. It repeats all the steps of Sect. 5.

6.1 Cut Definitions

Let $a \rightsquigarrow b \in G$ denote that there exists a directed edge chain (path) from a to b in G. Definitions 1, 2, 3 and 4 show the formal cut definitions.

Definition 1. *An* exclusive choice cut *is a cut $\Sigma_1, \ldots, \Sigma_n$ of a directly-follows graph G, such that*

1. *No part is connected to any other part:*
   $\forall i \neq j \wedge a_i \in \Sigma_i \wedge a_j \in \Sigma_j : (a_i, a_j) \notin G$

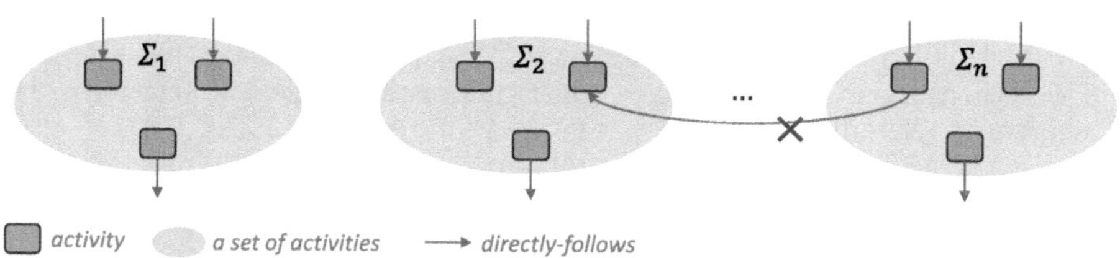

Definition 2. *A* sequence cut *is an ordered cut $\Sigma_1, \ldots, \Sigma_n$ of a directly-follows graph G such that each node in a part is indirectly and only connected to all nodes in the parts "after" it:*

1. $\forall 1 \leq i < j \leq n \wedge a_i \in \Sigma_i \wedge a_j \in \Sigma_j : a_j \rightsquigarrow a_i \notin G$
2. $\forall 1 \leq i < j \leq n \wedge a_i \in \Sigma_i \wedge a_j \in \Sigma_j : a_i \rightsquigarrow a_j \in G$

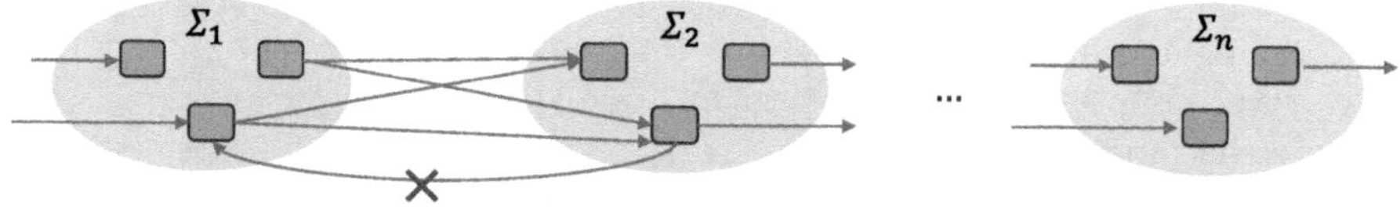

Definition 3. *A* parallel cut *is a cut $\Sigma_1, \ldots, \Sigma_n$ of a directly-follows graph G such that*

1. *Each part contains a start and an end activity:*
   $\forall i : \Sigma_i \cap Start(G) \neq \emptyset \wedge \Sigma_i \cap End(G) \neq \emptyset$
2. *All parts are fully interconnected:*
   $\forall i \neq j \wedge a_i \in \Sigma_i \wedge a_j \in \Sigma_j : (a_i, a_j) \in G \wedge (a_j, a_i) \in G$

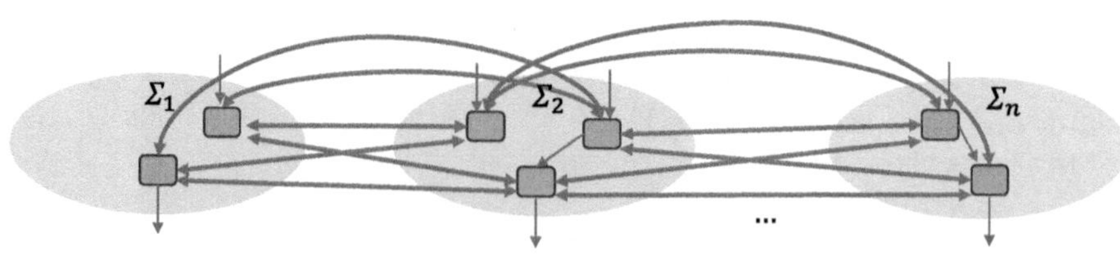

Definition 4. *A* loop cut *is a partially ordered cut $\Sigma_1, \ldots, \Sigma_n$ of a directly-follows graph G such that*

1. *All start and end activities are in the body (i.e. the first) part:* $Start(G) \cup End(G) \subseteq \Sigma_1$
2. *Only start/end activities in the body part have connections from/to other parts:*
   $\forall i \neq 1 \wedge a_i \in \Sigma_i \wedge a_1 \in \Sigma_1 : (a_1, a_i) \in G \Rightarrow a_1 \in End(G)$
   $\forall i \neq 1 \wedge a_i \in \Sigma_i \wedge a_1 \in \Sigma_1 : (a_i, a_1) \in G \Rightarrow a_1 \in Start(G)$
3. *Redo parts have no connections to other redo parts:*
   $\forall 1 \neq i \neq j \neq 1 \wedge a_i \in \Sigma_i \wedge a_j \in \Sigma_j : (a_i, a_j) \notin G$
4. *If an activity from a redo part has a connection to/from the body part, then it has connections to/from all start/end activities:*
   $\forall i \neq 1 \wedge a_i \in \Sigma_i \wedge a_1 \in Start(G) : (\exists a'_1 \in \Sigma_1 : (a_i, a'_1) \in G) \Leftrightarrow (a_i, a_1) \in G$
   $\forall i \neq 1 \wedge a_i \in \Sigma_i \wedge a_1 \in End(G) : (\exists a'_1 \in \Sigma_1 : (a'_1, a_i) \in G) \Leftrightarrow (a_1, a_i) \in G$

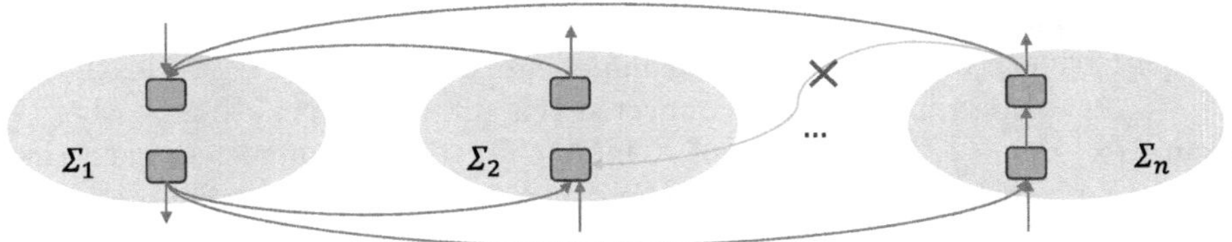

6.2 Base Case

```
function BaseCase_IM(L)
    if L = {ε} then
        base ← τ
    else if ∃a ∈ Σ : L = {⟨a⟩} then
        base ← a
    else
        base ← ⊥
    end if
    return base
end function
```

6.3 Findings Cuts

```
function FindCut_IM(L)
    G ← G(L) (the directly-follows graph of L)
    (×, Σ1, ..., Σk) ← XorCut(G)
    if k > 1 then
        return (×, Σ1, ..., Σk)
    end if
    (→, Σ1, ..., Σk) ← SequenceCut(G)
    if k > 1 then
```

```
            return (→, Σ1, ..., Σk)
        end if
        (∧, Σ1, ..., Σk) ← ParallelCut(G)
        if k > 1 then
            return (∧, Σ1, ..., Σk)
        end if
        (↺, Σ1, ..., Σk) ← LoopCut(G)
        if k > 2 then
            return (↺, Σ1, ..., Σk)
        end if
        return ⊥ (none of the cuts were found)
    end function
```

For the curious, the explanation below details how to find cuts algorithmically in a directly-follows graph.

Each of the cuts of Sect. 4 can be detected on a directly-follows graph $G = (\Sigma, \twoheadrightarrow)$ as follows.

XorCut(G): Find all connected components $G_1, \ldots, G_k$ of G, i.e., each $G_i = (\Sigma_i, \twoheadrightarrow_i)$ is a sub-graph of G not connected (via directed edges) to any other G_j. Return $(\times, \Sigma_1, \ldots, \Sigma_k)$ as result of XorCut(G). If G is connected, then there is only one connected component G_1 and $k = 1$ and then there is no choice in G.

SequenceCut(G): Create a singleton set $\Sigma_a = \{a\}$ for each $a \in \Sigma$. Keep merging any two sets Σ', Σ'' if any two nodes $a \in \Sigma', b \in \Sigma''$ are either pairwise reachable $a \twoheadrightarrow b$ and $b \twoheadrightarrow a$ or pairwise unreachable $\not{a} \twoheadrightarrow b$ and $\not{b} \twoheadrightarrow a$, until no more sets can be merged. We obtain sets $\Sigma_1, \ldots, \Sigma_k$. The nodes within each Σ_i cannot be sequentially ordered, while the nodes between the different Σ_i are only sequentially ordered. Sort the Σ_i along $\twoheadrightarrow$. Return $(\rightarrow, \Sigma_1, \ldots, \Sigma_k)$ as result of SequenceCut(G). If all nodes in Σ are pairwise reachable or unreachable, then $k = 1$ (there is no sequence ordering in G).

ParallelCut(G): Create a singleton set $\Sigma_a = \{a\}$ for each $a \in \Sigma$. Keep merging any two sets Σ', Σ'' if any two nodes $a \in \Sigma', b \in \Sigma''$ or *not* fully connected, i.e., when $a \twoheadrightarrow b$ and $b \twoheadrightarrow a$ does not hold for some $a \in \Sigma', b \in \Sigma''$. Also merge any Σ' which has no start activity or end activity, i.e., $\Sigma' \cap \mathit{Start}(G) = \emptyset$ or $\Sigma' \cap \mathit{End}(G) = \emptyset$, with some other Σ''. We obtain sets $\Sigma_1, \ldots, \Sigma_k$ where any two nodes $a \in \Sigma_i, b \in \Sigma_j$ are pairwise directly reachable $a \twoheadrightarrow b$ and $b \twoheadrightarrow a$ and each Σ_i has a start and an end activity. Return $(\wedge, \Sigma_1, \ldots, \Sigma_k)$ as result of AndCut(G). It returns just a single set $k = 1$ if no two sets with the above properties can be found (then there is no and relation between sets of activities in G).

LoopCut(G): Create a set Σ_1 that contains all start activities $\mathit{Start}(G)$ and end activities $\mathit{End}(G)$. Add to Σ_1 all activities x on a path $a \rightsquigarrow x \rightsquigarrow b$ with $a \in \mathit{Start}(G)$ and $b \in \mathit{End}(G)$. Remove from Σ_1 all activities x on a path $b \rightsquigarrow x \rightsquigarrow a$ with $a \in \mathit{Start}(G)$ and $b \in \mathit{End}(G)$. Now Σ_1 contains all activities which can only be reached between the start and end activities of G (the loop body). $\Sigma_2, \ldots, \Sigma_k$ are the connected components of G with Σ_1 (as in XorCut).

Return $(\circlearrowleft, \Sigma_1, \ldots, \Sigma_k)$ as result of ANDCUT(G). It returns just a single set $k = 1$ if there is no looping path from $End(G)$ to $Start(G)$ that involves at least one other activity.

6.4 Splitting Logs

The complete log splitting function SPLITLOG$_{IM}$ is just a case distinction on the operator $\oplus$ in the cut.

```
function SPLITLOG_IM(L, (⊕, Σ_1, ..., Σ_k))
    if ⊕ = × then
        return LOOPSPLIT(L, Σ_1, ..., Σ_k)
    end if
    if ⊕ = → then
        return SEQUENCESPLIT(L, Σ_1, ..., Σ_k)
    end if
    if ⊕ = ∧ then
        return PARALLELSPLIT(L, Σ_1, ..., Σ_k)
    end if
    if ⊕ = ↺ then
        return LOOPSPLIT(L, Σ_1, ..., Σ_k)
    end if
end function
```

```
function SEQUENCESPLIT(L, (Σ_1, ..., Σ_n))
    ∀j : L_j ← {t_j | t_1 · t_2 ··· t_n ∈ L ∧ ∀i ≤ n ∧ e ∈ t_i : e ∈ Σ_i}
    return L_1, ..., L_n
end function
```

```
function XORSPLIT(L, (Σ_1, ..., Σ_n))
    ∀i : L_i ← {t | t ∈ L ∧ ∀e ∈ t : e ∈ Σ_i}
    return L_1, ..., L_n
end function
```

```
function PARALLELSPLIT(L, (Σ_1, ..., Σ_n))
    ∀i : L_i ← {t|_{Σ_j} | t ∈ L}
    return L_1, ..., L_n
end function
```

where $t|_X$ is a function that projects trace t onto set of activities X, such that all events remaining in $t|_X$ are in X.

```
function LOOPSPLIT(L, (Σ_1, ..., Σ_n))
    ∀i : L_i ← {t_2 | t_1 · t_2 · t_3 ∈ L ∧
                    Σ({t_2}) ⊆ Σ_i ∧
                    (t_1 = ϵ ∨ (t_1 = ⟨··· , a_1⟩ ∧ a_1 ∉ Σ_i)) ∧
                    (t_3 = ϵ ∨ (t_3 = ⟨a_3, ···⟩ ∧ a_3 ∉ Σ_i))}
    return L_1, ..., L_n
end function
```

7 Properties of IM

When defining the basic IM algorithm, we made several important design decisions by which we ensure that the returned model has perfect fitness. We now highlight these design decisions again and discuss why they ensure fitness of the returned model; here the chosen fall-through is essential. Moreover, we discuss a very special property: when IM is guaranteed to rediscover a model of the original process.

7.1 Ensuring Fitness and Other Design Decisions

The aim of IM is ensure that the discovered model fits the log. We discuss in this section, how IM can achieve this and which other design decisions can be made.

In [16] the following property is proven.

It states that for every cut $(\oplus, \Sigma_1, \ldots, \Sigma_k)$ found by IM, the log L is split in such a way that re-combining the behavior of the split logs $L_1, \ldots, L_k$ according to $\oplus$ will always fit L. In other words, in each recursion step, IM only finds operators and sublogs that can replay L.

Lemma 1. *Let L be an event log, let $(\oplus, \Sigma_1, \ldots, \Sigma_k)$ be a non-trivial $\oplus$-cut. Let $L_1, \ldots, L_k$ = $\text{LogSplit}(L, (\oplus, \Sigma_1, \ldots, \Sigma_k))$. And let $M_1, \ldots, M_k$ be process trees such that $L_i \subseteq \mathcal{L}(M_i)$ (i.e., the tree can replay L_i). Then $L \subseteq \mathcal{L}(\oplus(M_1, \ldots, M_k))$.*

If IM can find a non-trivial cut in each recursion step, then by the above Lemma, the model $M = \text{IM}(L)$ will fit the log $L \subseteq \mathcal{L}(M)$.

However, it may be that no cut can be found on L. For example, for the log $L = \{\langle a, b, c\rangle, \langle c, b, a\rangle\}$, no cut can be found.

To ensure that IM always returns a model, also in the cases where no cut is found, the FallThrough function is defined. Here, different options are possible. The default option is to ensure fitness by returning a model that always fits any log L over its alphabet $\Sigma(L) = \{a_1, \ldots, a_k\}$. This is the flower model $(\circlearrowleft, \tau, a_1, \ldots, a_k)$.

function $\text{FallThrough}_{IM}(L)$
  return $(\circlearrowleft, \tau, a_1, \ldots, a_k)$ for $\Sigma(L) = \{a_1, \ldots, a_k\}$
end function

Another option would be the trace model which defines an explicit sequence for each trace in L, i.e., a process tree $\times(\rightarrow(a_1, \ldots, a_k), \ldots, \rightarrow(z_1, \ldots, z_k))$. This fall through would ensure fitness and precision at the cost of a larger model, but could be beneficial for small logs, such as $L = \{\langle a, b, c\rangle, \langle c, b, a\rangle\}$.

Another option could be to deliberately sacrifice fitness, for example by filtering L by selecting only the most frequent trace variants (by some user-defined threshold), and running IM again on the filtered log L'.

Another option could be to invoke a different discovery algorithm for L and to add the returned model as a child model.

7.2 Language-rediscoverability

An interesting property of a discovery algorithm is whether and under which assumptions a model M can be discovered that is guaranteed to show exactly the same behavior as the original process.

More precisely, suppose there is a process described by a process tree P with behavior $\mathcal{L}(P)$. Let $L \subseteq \mathcal{L}(P)$ be a log recorded from executing P. Which properties have to hold for P and L that $\mathrm{IM}(L) = M$ is a model with $\mathcal{L}(M) = \mathcal{L}(P)$. We then say that IM *language-rediscovers* P from L.

The proof strategy for language-rediscoverability in [16] is to reduce each process tree to a normal form and then prove that IM isomorphically rediscovers this normal form from a log L that is "complete enough". Two process trees $M = \oplus(M_1, \ldots, M_n)$ and $M' = \oplus'(M'_1, \ldots, M'_n)$ are *isomorphic* if and only if they are syntactically equivalent up to reordering of children in the case of $\times$, $\wedge$ and the non-first children of $\circlearrowleft$.

Log Completeness. Earlier, we introduced the directly-follows graph. This yields the notion of *directly-follows completeness* of a log L with respect to a model M, written as $L \diamond_{\mathrm{df}} M$: $L \diamond_{\mathrm{df}} M \equiv \langle \cdots, a, b, \cdots \rangle \in \mathcal{L}(M) \Leftrightarrow \langle \cdots, a, b, \cdots \rangle \in L \wedge Start(M) = Start(L) \wedge End(M) = End(L) \wedge \Sigma(M) = \Sigma(L)$. Intuitively, the directly-follows graphs of M and L must be same.

Please note that IM does not require the log to be directly-follows complete in order to guarantee soundness and fitness.

Class of Language-rediscoverable Models. Given a model M and a generated directly-follows complete log L, one can prove [16] language-rediscoverability assuming the following model restrictions, where $\oplus(M_1, \ldots, M_n)$ is a node at any position in M:

1. Duplicate activities are not allowed: $\forall i \neq j : \Sigma(M_i) \cap \Sigma(M_j) = \emptyset$.
2. If $\oplus = \circlearrowleft$, the sets of start and end activities of the first branch must be disjoint: $\oplus = \circlearrowleft \Rightarrow Start(M_1) \cap End(M_1) = \emptyset$.
3. No τ's are allowed: $\forall i \leq n : M_i \neq \tau$.

These restrictions are similar to the rediscoverability restrictions of the α algorithm [6]. We call any process tree which has these properties a *simple* process tree.

Normal Form. Although process trees are simple models, the same behavior can be represented by two syntactically (or structurally) different process trees M_1 and M_2 with $\mathcal{L}(M_1) = \mathcal{L}(M_2)$. The following rules show how process trees can be syntactically changed (or transformed) without changing the language. All rules have in common that they combine multiple nested subtrees with the same operator into one node with that operator.

Property 1.

$$\begin{aligned}
\oplus(M) &= M\\
\times(\cdots_1, \times(\cdots_2), \cdots_3) &= \times(\cdots_1, \cdots_2, \cdots_3)\\
\rightarrow(\cdots_1, \rightarrow(\cdots_2), \cdots_3) &= \rightarrow(\cdots_1, \cdots_2, \cdots_3)\\
\wedge(\cdots_1, \wedge(\cdots_2), \cdots_3) &= \wedge(\cdots_1, \cdots_2, \cdots_3)\\
\circlearrowleft(\circlearrowleft(M, \cdots_1), \cdots_2) &= \circlearrowleft(M, \cdots_1, \cdots_2)\\
\circlearrowleft(M, \cdots_1, \times(\cdots_2), \cdots_3) &= \circlearrowleft(M, \cdots_1, \cdots_2, \cdots_3)
\end{aligned}$$

It is not hard to reason that these rules preserve language. Every process tree M that has nested operators can be made simpler by applying the above rules. Doing this repeatedly and exhaustively, yields a process tree in so-called *normal form*. This tree has the following properties a) for all nodes $\oplus(M_1, \ldots, M_n)$, $n > 1$; b) $\times$, $\rightarrow$ and $\wedge$ do not have a direct child of the same operator; and c) the first child of a $\circlearrowleft$ is not a $\circlearrowleft$ and any non-first child is not an $\times$.

Language-rediscoverability. One then can prove the following property: Let P be a simple process tree. Let L be a directly-follows complete log of P. For the model $M = \text{IM}(L)$ holds: $\mathcal{L}(M) = \mathcal{L}(P)$.

The proof [16] first transforms P into its normal form P' (which has $\mathcal{L}(P') = \mathcal{L}(P)$). The proof then shows the following central property: for the tree $P' = (\oplus, P_1, \ldots, P_k)$, the directly-follows complete log L can only show an $\oplus$-cut, and the partitions $\Sigma_1, \ldots, \Sigma_k$ can only match $\Sigma(P_1), \ldots, \Sigma(P_k)$. In other words, IM can only find back the operator $\oplus$ resulting in a model $M = (\oplus, \ldots)$. Then it is shown that log splitting preserves directly-follows completeness for $P_1, \ldots, P_k$. So the logs $L_1, \ldots, L_k$ and the models satisfy $P_1, \ldots, P_k$ the same properties as P and L. By induction, IM also rediscovers the children correctly, etc.

8 Conclusion

In this chapter, we have revisited the fundamental challenges and trade-offs inherent in the process discovery problem. Discovering a "perfect" model – one that precisely rediscovers the original process from which a log was sampled – remains an ideal yet often unattainable goal due to incompleteness of data and complexities of processes that fall outside the scope of behavior the algorithm can discover. Thus, process discovery is the problem of balancing fitness, simplicity, and specificity in the construction of process models from event logs while retaining soundness.

Extending IM to Filtering Logs During Discovery. The Inductive Miner ensures perfect fitness and rediscoverability for some cases. However, if the log L does not originate from a block-structured process model or contains deviations from a block-structured process model, then $G(L)$ contains edges that "hide" the cut and $\mathrm{IM}(L)$ will reach the fallthrough and return a very imprecise, i.e., unspecific model.

It is possible to extend the functions of the IM framework to filter $G(L)$ "on the fly" to discover a process model that is possibly less fitting but more specific (i.e., precise). **ProM** supports Inductive Mining with on-the-fly filtering and various extensions through the Inductive Miner plugin and the Visual Inductive Miner. For a detailed discussion, see [15].

Different Design Decisions: Further Extensions of IM. The fact that the Inductive Miner is a framework allows to develop other instantiations making different design decisions on how to recover structure from event logs.

For example, instead of detecting cuts on the edges of the DFG, we can compute for every pair of activities the likelihood that one of the four operators $\times$, $\rightarrow$, $\circlearrowleft$, $\wedge$ holds between them [9,13]. This then allows to formulate an optimization problem to find a cut (operator and activity partition) that has the highest likelihood. Once this cut is found, this version of IM then continues with log splitting as discussed in this paper.

The Tradeoff Remains. Our exploration of design decisions highlights that no single process discovery technique consistently achieves the optimal balance across all desired quality criteria. The diversity in algorithmic approaches, from graph synthesis to optimization problems and genetic algorithms, each with their own biases and heuristics, underscores the need for careful consideration of tradeoffs. In particular, maximizing fitness while maintaining simplicity and specificity remains a central challenge, often requiring compromises that may necessitate the adjustment of discovery parameters or the refinement of event logs. The need to trade fitness for other criteria, such as simplicity or specificity, is not just a limitation but also an opportunity to better align process discovery outputs with the specific requirements of the analysis task at hand.

Acknowledgement. This chapter greatly benefitted from the excellent examples and explanations by Sander J.J. Leemans in his various publications.

References

1. van der Aalst, W.M.P.: Process Mining - Data Science in Action. 2nd Edn. Springer (2016). https://doi.org/10.1007/978-3-662-49851-4
2. van der Aalst, W.M.P.: Foundations of process discovery. In: van der Aalst, W.M.P., Carmona, J. (eds.) Process Mining Handbook, Lecture Notes in Business Information Processing, vol. 448, pp. 37–75. Springer (2022). https://doi.org/10.1007/978-3-031-08848-3_2
3. van der Aalst, W.: Workflow verification: finding control-flow errors using petri-net-based techniques. In: Business Process Management, pp. 161–183. Springer (2000)
4. van der Aalst, W.: Process Mining: Discovery. Springer, Conformance and Enhancement of Business Processes (2011)

5. van der Aalst, W., Buijs, J., van Dongen, B.: Improving the representational bias of process mining using genetic tree mining. SIMPDA 2011 Proceedings (2011)
6. van der Aalst, W., Weijters, T., Maruster, L.: Workflow mining: discovering process models from event logs. Knowl. Data Eng. IEEE Trans. **16**(9), 1128–1142 (2004)
7. Augusto, A., Conforti, R., Dumas, M., La Rosa, M., Bruno, G.: Automated discovery of structured process models from event logs: the discover-and-structure approach. Data Knowl. Eng. **117**(April), 373–392 (2018)
8. Augusto, A., et al.: Automated discovery of process models from event logs: review and benchmark. IEEE Trans. Knowl. Data Eng. **31**(4), 686–705 (2019)
9. Brons, D., Scheepens, R., Fahland, D.: Striking a new balance in accuracy and simplicity with the probabilistic inductive miner. In: 2021 3rd International Conference on Process Mining (ICPM), pp. 32–39 (2021)
10. vanden Broucke, S.K.L.M., Weerdt, J.D.: Fodina: a robust and flexible heuristic process discovery technique. Decis. Support Syst. **100**, 109–118 (2017)
11. Buijs, J., van Dongen, B., van der Aalst, W.: A genetic algorithm for discovering process trees. In: Evolutionary Computation (CEC), 2012 IEEE Congress on, pp. 1–8. IEEE (2012)
12. Buijs, J.C.A.M., van Dongen, B.F., van der Aalst, W.M.P.: Quality dimensions in process discovery: the importance of fitness, precision, generalization and simplicity. Int. J. Cooperative Inf. Syst. **23**(1) (2014)
13. van Detten, J.N., Schumacher, P., Leemans, S.J.J.: An approximate inductive miner. In: 2023 5th International Conference on Process Mining (ICPM), pp. 129–136 (2023). https://api.semanticscholar.org/CorpusID:263837928
14. Leemans, S.J.J.: Automated process discovery. In: Encyclopedia of Big Data Technologies. Springer (2019)
15. Leemans, S.J.J.: Discovery Algorithms, pp. 215–325. Springer International Publishing, Cham (2022). https://doi.org/10.1007/978-3-030-96655-3_6
16. Leemans, S.J.J., Fahland, D., van der Aalst, W.M.P.: Discovering block-structured process models from event logs - a constructive approach. In: Colom, J.M., Desel, J. (eds.) Application and Theory of Petri Nets and Concurrency - 34th International Conference, PETRI NETS 2013, vol. 7927, pp. 311–329, Milan, June 24-28, 2013. Proceedings. Lecture Notes in Computer Science. Springer (2013). https://doi.org/10.1007/978-3-642-38697-8_17
17. Leemans, S.J.J., Fahland, D., van der Aalst, W.M.P.: Discovering block-structured process models from event logs containing infrequent behaviour. In: BPM 2013 Workshops. LNBIP, vol. 171, pp. 66–78 (2013)
18. Leemans, S.J.J., Poppe, E., Wynn, M.T.: Directly follows-based process mining: exploration & a case study. In: International Conference on Process Mining, ICPM 2019, pp. 25–32, Aachen, Germany, June 24-26, 2019. IEEE (2019). https://doi.org/10.1109/ICPM.2019.00015
19. Leemans, S.J.J., Tax, N., ter Hofstede, A.H.M.: Indulpet miner: combining discovery algorithms. In: OTM 2018. LNCS, vol. 11229, pp. 97–115. Springer (2018)
20. de Leoni, M.M., Mannhardt, F.: Road Traffic Fine Management Process (2015). https://data.4tu.nl/articles/dataset/Road_Traffic_Fine_Management_Process/12683249
21. Mannhardt, F., de Leoni, M., Reijers, H.A.: Heuristic mining revamped: an interactive, data-aware, and conformance-aware miner. In: Clarisó, R., et al., (eds.) Proceedings of the BPM Demo Track and BPM Dissertation Award co-located with 15th International Conference on Business Process Modeling (BPM 2017), Barcelona, Spain, September 13, 2017. CEUR Workshop Proceedings, vol. 1920. CEUR-WS.org (2017). http://ceur-ws.org/Vol-1920/BPM_2017_paper_167.pdf

22. Reisig, W., Schnupp, P., Muchnick, S.: Primer in Petri Net Design. Springer-Verlag, New York, Inc (1992)
23. Solé, M., Carmona, J.: Encoding process discovery problems in SMT. Softw. Syst. Model. **17**(4), 1055–1078 (2018)
24. Verbeek, H.M.W., Basten, T., van der Aalst, W.M.P.: Diagnosing workflow processes using woflan. Comput. J. **44**(4), 246–279 (2001)
25. Weerdt, J.D., Backer, M.D., Vanthienen, J., Baesens, B.: A multi-dimensional quality assessment of state-of-the-art process discovery algorithms using real-life event logs. Inf. Syst. **37**(7), 654–676 (2012). https://doi.org/10.1016/j.is.2012.02.004
26. van der Werf, J.M.E.M., van Dongen, B.F., Hurkens, C.A.J., Serebrenik, A.: Process discovery using integer linear programming. Fundam. Inf. **94**(3–4), 387–412 (2009)
27. van der Werf, J.M.E.M., Polyvyanyy, A., van Wensveen, B.R., Brinkhuis, M., Reijers, H.A.: All that glitters is not gold - towards process discovery techniques with guarantees. In: CAiSE 2021. LNCS, vol. 12751, pp. 141–157. Springer (2021)

Building and Pre-processing Event Logs

Dirk Fahland[1(✉)] and Xixi Lu[2]

[1] Eindhoven University of Technology, Eindhoven, The Netherlands
d.fahland@tue.nl

[2] Utrecht University, Utrecht, The Netherlands

Abstract. Event data is the basis for all process mining analysis. Most process mining techniques assume their input to be an *event log*. However, event data is rarely recorded in an event log format, but has to be *extracted* from raw data. Event log extraction itself is an act of *modeling* as the analyst has to consciously choose which features of the raw data are used for describing which behavior of which entities. Being aware of these choices and subtle but important differences in concepts such as trace, case, activity, event, table, and log is crucial for mastering advanced process mining analyses.

This text provides fundamental concepts and formalizations and discusses design decisions in event log extraction from a raw event table and for event log pre-processing. It is intended as study material for an advanced lecture in a process mining course.

1 Event Data

Event data is the basis for all process mining analysis. Most process mining techniques assume that their input is in the form of a *simple event log* such as the following:

$$\begin{aligned} L = [&\langle A, B, C, D\rangle^{10},\\ &\langle A, C, B, D\rangle^{5},\\ &\langle A, B, A, D\rangle^{3},\\ &\langle A, E, D\rangle^{1}]. \end{aligned}$$

This simple event log is defined over an *alphabet* $\Sigma = \{A, B, C, D, E\}$ which is a *set* of activity names that have been observed. Each $a \in \Sigma$ is the name of an *activity*, i.e., a specific action that can be executed or observed. For now, we consider each activity name as "atomic" — later in this chapter we will see that activities themselves can have some "structure" themselves.

A *trace* $\sigma \in \Sigma^*$ is a finite sequence of activities[1]. It describes that this sequence of activities had been observed at some point in the past. Each occurrence of an activity in a trace σ is called an *event*. For example, the trace

[1] Recall that the star * after Σ is the *Kleene star* [10] which we use when constructing the set of all possible finite sequences over the elements of set Σ.

F. Kordon et al. (Eds.): *Transactions on Petri Nets and Other Models of Concurrency XVIII*,
LNCTPN 16260, pp. 260–279, 2026.
https://doi.org/10.1007/978-3-662-73305-9_9

$\langle A, B, A, D \rangle$ describes we first observed A, then B followed by another occurrence of A, and finally we observed D.

A *simple event log* $L \in \mathbb{B}(\Sigma^*)$ is a multiset[2] of traces describing that various traces that have been observed and *how often* each trace has been observed, e.g., $\langle A, B, A, D \rangle^3$ was observed 3 times.

Question 1. Why do we only study finite sequences of activities when analyzing event logs (recorded historic executions) of processes?

However, event data is *not* recorded in this form in practice. First of all, an event records multiple attributes, not just the name of an activity. Secondly, event data is recorded as it occurs, and thus never grouped into traces or event logs.

A central part of process mining comprises actually obtaining event data from various data sources, and transforming it into an event log. We will see that both steps are non-trivial and allow for many choices. After the event log has been created, it rarely has sufficient quality to be used for any process mining analysis. Consequently, we have to pre-process the event log.

In the following, we first introduce a generic event data model and the notion of an event table in Sect. 2. Then, we explain in Sect. 3 how to extract structured event logs from such an event table and kinds of choices that can be made. We then introduce in Sect. 4 the notion of event classifiers required to turn structured event logs into the simple event logs explained above. We introduce the three central pre-processing operations on structured event logs in Sect. 5. We discuss limitations of event logs in Sect. 7 before we conclude in Sect. 8.

2 Events and Event Table

The most common direct or "raw" logging format for events is an *event table* or *event stream* as shown in Table 1. Each row in this table is one *event record.* Each column is an *attribute* where the column header defines the *attribute name.* The contents of a table cell for event e in column a is the *attribute value* event e has for attribute a.

The event table can be considered as "raw" data as besides providing attributes per event, the data has no further structure. Specifically notice that no traces are recognizable in this event table.

The following definitions formally define events described by attributes and an event table.

- Let AN be a set of *attribute names.*
- Let Val a set of *values.*
- Let $\mathcal{E}$ be the universe of events.

[2] A multi-set is also called a *bag*, which explains the symbol $\mathbb{B}$ we use for constructing the multiset over Σ^*. Recall that a multiset can contain the same element $\sigma \in \Sigma^*$ multiple times; see details in [4].

Table 1. An event table with 32 events, ordered by their timestamps.

order	time	action	life-cycle	user	customer	item	delivery	type
23	19/12/2018 15:46	receive payment	complete	System	A7001			online
23	19/12/2018 16:30	archive	complete	Diana				online
35	20/12/2018 11:02	receive order	complete	System	A8760			phone
41	20/12/2018 11:03	receive order	complete	Ellen	A8920			phone
56	20/12/2018 11:04	receive order	complete	System	A7001			online
72	20/12/2018 11:05	receive order	complete	Charles	A9494			online
56	20/12/2018 11:12	pack order	start	Bob	A7001			online
35	20/12/2018 12:09	pack order	start	Alice	A8760			phone
35	20/12/2018 12:10	add item	complete	Bob	A8760	Walkman	432	phone
35	20/12/2018 12:10	add item	complete	Bob	A8760	Gameboy	432	phone
35	20/12/2018 12:15	ship parcel	complete	Charles	A8760		432	phone
72	20/12/2018 14:05	pack order	start	Alice	A9494			online
72	20/12/2018 14:08	add item	complete	Alice	A9494	VHS Player	775	online
72	20/12/2018 14:10	pack order	suspend	Diana	A9494			online
35	20/12/2018 16:00	pack order	complete	Alice	A8760			phone
56	21/12/2018 09:06	receive payment	complete	System	A7001			online
56	21/12/2018 09:17	add item	complete	Alice	A7001	Walkman	623	online
56	21/12/2018 09:23	pack order	abort	Charles	A7001			online
56	21/12/2018 10:15	archive	complete	Diana				online
72	22/12/2018 03:36	receive payment	complete	Diana	A9494			online
35	22/12/2018 07:23	receive payment	complete	System	A8760			phone
35	22/12/2018 07:24	archive	complete	Diana				phone
72	22/12/2018 08:05	pack order	resume	Alice	A9494			online
72	22/12/2018 08:07	add item	complete	Alice	A9494	VHS Tapes	775	online
72	22/12/2018 09:01	ship parcel	complete	Charles	A9494		775	online
41	23/12/2018 23:11	pack order	start	Bob	A8920			phone
41	23/12/2018 23:46	add item	complete	Bob	A8920	VHS Player	514	phone
41	23/12/2018 23:49	ship parcel	complete	Ellen	A8920		514	phone
41	23/12/2018 23:51	add item	complete	Bob	A7001	Gameboy	623	phone
41	23/12/2018 23:59	ship parcel	complete	Bob	A7001		623	phone
41	27/12/2018 09:01	pack order	complete	Alice	A8920			phone
41	27/12/2018 09:02	archive	complete	Alice				phone

Definition 1 (Event). *An event* $e \in \mathcal{E}$ *describes that a specific discrete observation has been made (by a sensor, a system, a human observer, etc.). The observation itself is described by attribute-value pairs through the partial*[3] *function* $\pi : \mathcal{E} \times AN \nrightarrow Val$.

For each event $e \in \mathcal{E}$ *and each attribute name* $a \in AN$, $\pi(e, a) = v$ *defines the value* v *of attribute* a. *We write* $\pi(e, a) = \perp$ *if attribute* a *is undefined for* e *(has no value). We also write* $\pi_a(e) = v$ *or* $e.a = v$ *for* $\pi(e, a) = v$.

For each event $e \in \mathcal{E}$, *we require that*

- *the attribute time is defined, i.e.,* $\pi_{time}(e) \neq \perp$.
- e *carries a value* $\pi_a(e) \neq \perp$ *for some other attribute* $a \in AN, a \neq time$.

In other process mining literature, you also find the notation $\#_a(e) = v$ instead of $\pi_a(e) = v$ or $e.a = v$ to describe that event e has attribute a with value v.

[3] A partial function does not have a value for each argument.

By the two requirements on each event $e \in \mathcal{E}$ in Definition 1, we ensure that each event has a timestamp $\pi_{time}(e)$ and records at least *one* meaningful observation $\pi_a(e)$ (but it can record more). To be able to analyze processes in a meaningful way, we need the events we analyze to share some common ground: They should refer to the same kinds of observations, i.e., share some attributes. Therefore, an event table is a sequence of events, that all have the same attribute a defined. We can think of attribute a as the activity name or measurement that was recorded.

Definition 2 (Event Table). *An* event table $ET = \langle e_1, \dots, e_n \rangle$ *is a finite sequence of events* $e_1, \dots, e_n \in \mathcal{E}$ *of events with* $\pi_a(e_i) \neq \perp$ *for some attribute* $a \in ET, a \neq time$ *and all* $1 \leq i \leq n$.

We write $e_i \in ET, 1 \leq i \leq n$ *when referring to an event in* ET.

Definitions 1 and 2 define the absolute bare minimum for analyzing events: all events e have a timestamp $\pi_{time}(e)$ and record the some observation (or value) $\pi_a(e_i)$. In this bare form, an event table could even specify a time-series. However, most events carry many additional attributes which we exploit in process mining.

Table 1 shows an event table according to Definition 1 and Definition 2.

Strictly speaking, Definition 2 does not define an event *table* in the sense of the data model of relational databases, but rather just a finite stream of events of attribute-value pairs. However, the table format representation is convenient and data in this form is often stored and exchanged using the *Comma Separated Value (CSV)* format.

Question 2. What are the differences between Definition 2 and the data model of relational databases?

We can reorder the events/rows in an event table to better understand its contents. Table 2 reorders the events of Table 1 by grouping them by attribute *order* and then sorting all events per order on attribute *time*. In Table 2, we added a column assigning each event a unique identifier to be able to refer to them individually, e.g., e_1 is the first event in this table.

In this sorted event table, we can start recognizing the traces we discussed in Sect. 1. However, the traces are no objects yet in their own right. We discuss how to obtain traces and structured event logs next.

3 Extracting Structured Event Logs from an Event Table

An event table only records for each event its timestamp and some observation such as an activity name. The essential difference between an event table and an event *log* is the presence of an additional attribute called the *case identifer*. It allows to group events into cases and traces and compare multiple sequences of events to each other.

3.1 Entities and Case

We use the term *Case* to refer to an *entity* or *object* that we are "tracking" over time in terms of the events in which this entity is involved.

For example, for the first event in Table 2 we can recognize that three *types of entities* were involved:

- *order* (for which we find the order id "23" as attribute value),
- *user* (for which we find the user name "System" as attribute value), and
- *customer* (for which we find an identifier "A7001" as attribute value).

Other events also refer to a fourth entity type *delivery*.

In contrast, the attribute *item* does not refer to an entity type because its values describe sets or classes of similar objects but do not identify a unique entity or object. Recognizing which attributes of an event refer to entity types requires domain knowledge or additional context information.

To obtain a structured event log from an event table, we have to recognize from all attribute names the entity types, and then select one these attributes c referring to an entity type as the *case identifier* attribute. The attribute values for c we find among all events are the cases we find in the data.

Definition 3 (Case identifier, cases). *Let* $ET = \langle e_1, \ldots, e_n \rangle$ *be an event table. The set of attribute names in* ET *is*

$$AN(ET) = \{a \in AN \mid \exists e_i \in ET, \pi_a(e_i) \neq \perp\}.$$

If we select an attribute $id \in AN(ET)$ *as* case identifier, *then*

$$Cases(ET, id) = \{\pi_{id}(e_i) \mid e_i \in ET\}$$

is the set of cases for this case identifier.

By choosing one entity type as case identifier, we decide to reformat the event data in a way that "tracks" what has happened to all entities of this type.

Note that Definition 3 allows to pick any attribute as case identifier, not just those that refer to entity types. For example, we could even pick attribute name $action \in AN(ET)$. The next steps in building a structured event log work with any chosen case identifier. However, the subsequent analysis entirely depends on how sensible this choice of a case identifier was for the particular analysis question. In other words, we have to understand which analysis question we try to answer, and then identify the corresponding attribute name (e.g., of an entity type of interest) that we want to use as case identifier.

This also means that at this point we implicitly require that each event e has *three* mandatory attributes that are different from each other (i.e., we do not choose $a = c$ or $a = c = time$):

1. the *timestamp* $\pi_{time}(e)$ (see Definition 1),
2. a recorded action or *activity* $\pi_a(e)$ (see Definition 2), and
3. a *case identifier* $\pi_c(e)$ (see Definition 3).

However, except for $\pi_{time}(e)$, activity and case identifier are *not* pre-determined by the event table. They are choices we make.

Question 3. Can two events happen at the same time? Do they have to be in different cases? Do they have to have different activities?

Table 2. The same event table as in Table 1, ordered by order id.

e	order	time	action	life-cycle	user	customer	item	delivery	type
1	23	19/12/2018 15:46	receive payment	complete	System	A7001			online
2	23	19/12/2018 16:30	archive	complete	Diana				online
3	35	20/12/2018 11:02	receive order	complete	System	A8760			phone
4	35	20/12/2018 12:09	pack order	start	Alice	A8760			phone
5	35	20/12/2018 12:10	add item	complete	Bob	A8760	Walkman	432	phone
6	35	20/12/2018 12:10	add item	complete	Bob	A8760	Gameboy	432	phone
7	35	20/12/2018 12:15	ship parcel	complete	Charles	A8760		432	phone
8	35	20/12/2018 16:00	pack order	complete	Alice	A8760			phone
9	35	22/12/2018 07:23	receive payment	complete	System	A8760			phone
10	35	22/12/2018 07:24	archive	complete	Diana				phone
11	41	20/12/2018 11:03	receive order	complete	Ellen	A8920			phone
12	41	23/12/2018 23:11	pack order	start	Bob	A8920			phone
13	41	23/12/2018 23:46	add item	complete	Bob	A8920	VHS Player	514	phone
14	41	23/12/2018 23:49	ship parcel	complete	Ellen	A8920		514	phone
15	41	23/12/2018 23:51	add item	complete	Bob	A7001	Gameboy	623	phone
16	41	23/12/2018 23:59	ship parcel	complete	Bob	A7001		623	phone
17	41	27/12/2018 09:01	pack order	complete	Alice	A8920			phone
18	41	27/12/2018 09:02	archive	complete	Alice				phone
19	56	20/12/2018 11:04	receive order	complete	System	A7001			online
20	56	20/12/2018 11:12	pack order	start	Bob	A7001			online
21	56	21/12/2018 09:06	receive payment	complete	System	A7001			online
22	56	21/12/2018 09:17	add item	complete	Alice	A7001	Walkman	623	online
23	56	21/12/2018 09:23	pack order	abort	Charles	A7001			online
24	56	21/12/2018 10:15	archive	complete	Diana				online
25	72	20/12/2018 11:05	receive order	complete	Charles	A9494			online
26	72	20/12/2018 14:05	pack order	start	Alice	A9494			online
27	72	20/12/2018 14:08	add item	complete	Alice	A9494	VHS Player	775	online
28	72	20/12/2018 14:10	pack order	suspend	Diana	A9494			online
29	72	22/12/2018 03:36	receive payment	complete	Diana	A9494			online
30	72	22/12/2018 08:05	pack order	resume	Alice	A9494			online
31	72	22/12/2018 08:07	add item	complete	Alice	A9494	VHS Tapes	775	online
32	72	22/12/2018 09:01	ship parcel	complete	Charles	A9494		775	online

For the example of Table 1, we can see four candidates for case identifiers based on the entity-types we found in the event table: *order*, *delivery*, *user*, and *customer*.

If we have selected an attribute id as case identifier, then we say an event e is *correlated* to a case c if its id-attribute refers to c, i.e., $\pi_{id}(e) = c$.

Definition 4 (Correlation to a case). *Let ET be an event table. Let $c \in Cases(ET, id)$ be a case for a case identifier $id \in AN(ET)$.*

Event $e \in ET$ is correlated *to c iff $\pi_{id}(e) = c$. The set of all events correlated to c is*

$$corr(ET, id, c) = \{e \in ET \mid \pi_{id}(e) = c\}.$$

For example, events e_1 and e_2 are correlated to $order = 23$ in Table 2. Note that if an event e does not have attribute id defined, i.e., $\pi_{id}(e) = \perp$, then it is not correlated to any case of this case identifier. Table 2 now shows the same event table where the events are grouped by order id.

If all events correlated to a case c carry the *same* value v for an attribute x, then we call x a *case attribute* of c.

Definition 5 (Case attribute). *Let ET be an event table. Let $c \in Cases(ET, id)$ be a case for a case identifier $id \in AN(ET)$.*

Attribute $x \in AN(ET)$ is a case attribute *of c iff for all $e, e' \in corr(ET, id, c)$ holds $\pi_x(e) = \pi_x(e') = v \neq \perp$. We then lift the function $\pi(.)$ from events to cases and write $\pi_x(c) = v$.*

Attribute x is a global *case attribute iff it is a case attribute for every case $c \in Cases(ET, id)$.*

The case identifier is *always* a global case attribute. A global case attribute has to be defined for each case, but each case can have its own value.

3.2 Trace

A *trace* is the sequence of events correlated to a case and ordered by time. For example, the trace of $order = 23$ in Table 2 is $\langle e_1, e_2 \rangle$.

Definition 6 (Trace of a case). *Let $ET = \langle e_1, \ldots, e_n \rangle$ be an event table. Let $id \in AN(ET)$ be the selected case identifier.*

A sequence $\langle e_1, \ldots, e_k \rangle$ of events is a trace *of case $c \in Cases(ET, id)$ iff*

1. *$\{e_1, \ldots, e_k\} = corr(ET, id, c)$, i.e., it consists of all events of ET correlated to c, and*
2. *for each $i = 1, \ldots, k-1$ holds $\pi_{time}(e_i) \leq \pi_{time}(e_{i+1})$, i.e., events are ordered by time.*

Note that there may be more than one way to sequentialize the events $\{e_1, \ldots, e_k\} = corr(ET, id, c)$ correlated to a case c. This happens where two or more events e_i, e_{i+1} have the same time-stamp $\pi_{time}(e_i) = \pi_{time}(e_{i+1})$.

3.3 Structured Event Log

A structured event log is a set of cases where each case is associated with exactly one trace for this case as a case attribute.

Definition 7 (Structured Event Log). *Let $ET = \langle e_1, \ldots, e_n \rangle$ be an event table. Let $id \in AN(ET)$ be the selected case identifier.*

The structured *event log L is the set $L = Cases(ET, id)$ of cases for case identifier id so that additionally each case $c \in L$ gets assigned a trace $\langle e_1, \ldots, e_k \rangle$ of c as trace attribute $\pi_{trace}(c) = \langle e_1, \ldots, e_k \rangle$.*

For example, the structured event log of Table 2 has the cases $L = \{23, 35, 41, 56, s72\}$ for *order* and the following traces:

- $\pi_{trace}(23) = \langle e_1, e_2 \rangle$ where
  - e_1 has
    - $\pi_{order}(e_1) = 23$
    - $\pi_{time}(e_1) = 19/12/2018\ 15{:}46$
    - $\pi_{action}(e_1) =$ receive payment
    - ...
  - e_2 has
    - $\pi_{order}(e_2) = 23$
    - $\pi_{time}(e_2) = 19/12/2018\ 16{:}30$
    - $\pi_{action}(e_2) =$ archive
    - ...
- $\pi_{trace}(35) = \langle e_3, e_4, e_5, \ldots, e_{10} \rangle$
- $\pi_{trace}(41) = \langle e_{11}, e_{12}, e_{13}, \ldots, e_{18} \rangle$
- $\pi_{trace}(56) = \langle e_{19}, \ldots, e_{24} \rangle$
- $\pi_{trace}(72) = \langle e_{25}, \ldots, e_{32} \rangle$

A structured event log has a simple hierarchical structure. At the top-level are the cases $L = \{c_1, \ldots, c_k\} = \mathit{Cases}(ET, id)$. Each case has case attributes as "children", one of them is the trace $\pi_{trace}(c)$. Each event e in a trace has event attributes as children, including $\pi_{time}(e)$ (time-stamp), $\pi_a(e)$ (the observed activity), and $\pi_{id}(e) = c$ (the case identifier).

1. A structured event log L consists of a set of cases $L = \{c_1, \ldots, c_n\} \subseteq \mathit{Val}$, i.e., values for some case identifier.
2. Each case $c \in L$ defines a trace $\pi_{trace}(c) = \langle e_1, \ldots, e_k \rangle \in \mathcal{E}^*$ as a sequence of events ordered by time, i.e., $\pi_{time}(e_i) \leq \pi_{time}(e_{i+1})$ for each $i = 1, \ldots, k-1$.
3. The events in $\pi_{trace}(c)$ are all correlated to the case, i.e., $\pi_{id}(e_i) = c$. However, most XES event logs do not store the case identifier as an event attribute again.
4. There is at least one attribute a (e.g., the activity name) defined by each event $\pi_a(e)$ in each trace $e \in \pi_{trace}(c), c \in L$.
5. Cases do not share events, i.e., there is no event $e \in \mathcal{E}$ with $e \in \pi_{trace}(c), \pi_{trace}(c'), c, c' \in L, c \neq c'$.

This hierarchical structure is formalized in the XES-standard [2,9,11]. See also other formalizations of event logs [1].

4 Event Classifiers and Simple Event Logs

The nested hierarchy of a structured event log contains all information about all events. However, analysis techniques operating on events, prefer a flat data structure where

- a structured event $e \in \mathcal{E}$ with its various attributes is represented by a single attribute value $\pi_a(e)$, e.g., the activity name,
- a structured case c with its various case attributes is not represented its trace $\pi_{trace}(c) = \langle e_1, \ldots, e_k \rangle$ but rather in its simplified form $\langle \pi_a(e_1), \ldots, \pi_a(e_k) \rangle$.

For example, we can transform $\langle e_1, e_2 \rangle$ of Table 2 into $\langle$receive payment, archive$\rangle$. This representation allows easily searching for patterns in the sequences of activity names.

4.1 Event Classifiers and Event Classes

However, as for Definition 3 of the case identifier, events do not have a canonical or standard attribute a by which it *must* be represented in this simplified way. Rather, we again can pick.

Literature introduces for this purpose the definition of an *event classifier.*

Definition 8 (Event Classifier). *An event classifier is a function with signature*

$$class : \mathcal{E} \to Value$$

that maps each event to a value. The value class(e) is called the event class. *Any two events e, e' with $class(e) = class(e')$ belong to the same event class, which means they describe the same kind of observation.*

Usually, the event classifier is defined over event attributes which can be a single attribute or a combination of attributes. The following three event classifiers are used frequently in process mining analyses:

1. The standard event classifier is the *activity name classifier* $class_{act}(e) = \pi_a(e)$ where $a \in AN$ is the attribute we identify as the activity name. For example,
   - for Table 2, the *activity name classifier* is $class_{act}(e) = \pi_{action}(e)$;
   - events e_4, e_8 have the same activity name class $class_{act}(e_4) = class_{act}(e_8)$ = pack order.
2. The *activity+lifecycle* classifier combines the activity name a with the event life-cycle attribute lc (if it exists in the event log), i.e., $class_{act+lifecycle}(e) = (\pi_a(e), \pi_{lc}(e))$.
   - For Table 2, the *activity+lifecycle* classifier is $class_{act+lifecycle}(e) = (\pi_{action}(e), \pi_{\text{life-cycle}}(e))$.
   - For example, events e_4 belong to different event classes for this classifier: $class_{act+lifecycle}(e_4) = (\text{pack order}, \text{start})$ and $class_{act+lifecycle}(e_8) = (\text{pack order}, \text{complete})$.
   - Event classes over multiple attributes are also represented with a '+', e.g., $class_{act+lifecycle}(e_4) = \text{pack order+start}$.
3. The *resource* classifier $class_{res}(e) = \pi_r(e)$ where $r \in AN$ is the attribute deferring to the user, machines, or resource that participated in the event.
   - For Table 2, the *resource* classifier is $class_{res}(e) = \pi_{user}(e)$. For example, events e_4 and e_8 belong to the same event resource event class: $class_{res}(e_4) = class_{res}(e_8) = \text{Alice}$.

We can in principle choose any combination of attributes for the event classifier. This essentially corresponds to *feature selection* in data mining: we choose the event attributes we think are most relevant for the analysis task at hand. If the event has no value defined for the selected event classifier, e.g., $class_{item}(e) = \pi_{item}(e)$ and $class_{item}(e_1) = \perp$, then the event will be omitted from the analysis.

It is also possible to derive new event attributes based on other events in the trace or even the entire event log, and to use these subsequently as event classifiers. This would correspond to *feature engineering*.

Definition 9 (Event Classes of an Event Log). *Given a structured event log L (according to Definition 7) and an event classifier class, the* set of event classes *in L is the set* $\Sigma_{class}(L) = \{class(e) \mid c \in L, e \in \pi_{trace}(c), class(e) \neq \perp\}$.

4.2 Simple Event Log

If we have fixed an event classifier *class*, we can represent each trace in a log L by the sequence of event classes, e.g., the sequence of activity names. However, we omit all $\perp$ values.

Definition 10 (Simple Trace). *Let L be a structured event log, let* $\langle e_1, \ldots, e_k \rangle = \pi_{trace}(c), c \in L$ *be a trace. Let class be an event classifier.*

The simple trace *of c is the sequence*

$$simple_{class}(c) = \langle class(e_1), \ldots, class(e_k) \rangle|_{\Sigma_{class}(L)}$$

where we replace each event e_i *by* $class(e_i)$ *and then project*[4] *the resulting sequence onto all valid event classes* $\Sigma_{class}(L)$*, i.e., all values that are not* $\perp$.

The simple trace for case 23 and the activity event classifier $class_{act}(e) = \pi_{action}(e)$ is

$$\langle \text{receive payment, archive} \rangle.$$

The simple trace for case 23 and the activity event classifier $class(e) = \pi_{customer}(e)$ is

$$\langle \text{A7001} \rangle.$$

We obtain the simple event log of L by collecting all simple traces of all cases L in a multiset. Recall from Sect. 1 that $\sigma \in \Sigma^*$ is a finite sequence of activity names and $\mathbb{B}(\Sigma^*)$ is a multi-set (bag) of finite sequences.

Definition 11 (Simple Event Log). *Let L be a structured event log. Let class be an event classifier. Let* $\Sigma = \Sigma_{class}(L)$

The simple event log is the multiset $simple_{class}(L) = L' \in \mathbb{B}(\Sigma^*)$ *where* $L'(\sigma) = |\{c \in L \mid simple_{class}(c) = \sigma\}|$*, i.e., there are as many copies of* σ *as there are cases which have the same simple trace* $simple_{class}(c) = \sigma$.

The simple event log of Table 2 for the *action* classifier is (we abbreviate each action name for succinctness):

$$\begin{aligned} L' = [&\langle \text{RP}, \text{AR} \rangle^1, \\ &\langle \text{RO}, \text{PO}, \text{AI}, \text{AI}, \text{SP}, \text{PO}, \text{RP}, \text{AR} \rangle^1, \\ &\langle \text{RO}, \text{PO}, \text{AI}, \text{SP}, \text{AI}, \text{SP}, \text{PO}, \text{AR} \rangle^1, \\ &\langle \text{RO}, \text{PO}, \text{RP}, \text{AI}, \text{PO}, \text{AR} \rangle^1, \\ &\langle \text{RO}, \text{PO}, \text{AI}, \text{PO}, \text{RP}, \text{PO}, \text{AI}, \text{SP} \rangle^1]. \end{aligned}$$

---

[4] We write $\sigma|_{\Sigma'}$ for the projection of a trace $\sigma \subseteq \Sigma^*$ onto a subset $\Sigma' \subseteq \Sigma$ of some alphabet.

The simple traces in a simple event log are also called *trace variants* of the event log as they show the principle ways the object that is tracked by the case identifier "moves" through the data.

Note that each simple trace is a finite sequence $\sigma \in \Sigma^*$ over some alphabet of event classes $\Sigma = \Sigma_{class}(L)$ and that the simple event log is a multiset of simple traces. We now have a complete procedure for obtaining a simple event log, as outlined in Sect. 1 from event data as it is recorded in practice, i.e., an event table.

1. Find meaningful entity identifiers in the attributes of the event table that correspond to your analysis question.
2. Select one entity identifier as case identifier id.
3. Construct the structured event log L for this case identifier by correlating events and ordering them over time.
4. Find meaningful event attributes to summarize or classify the observation that is recorded in the event.
5. Select or define one event classifier $class$.
6. Derive the simple event log from L for this event classifier $class$.

Given an event table ET, any simple event log is fully defined by two decision: the case identifier id and the event classifier $class$. However, these two choices are powerful and allow you to derive many different views. For example, you could choose case identifier *customer* and event classifier *order*.

Almost all process mining software contains a view to visualize the event log in the form of a simple event logs; for example the "Explore Event Log" visualizer of ProM[5] shown in Fig. 1 visualizes event logs as simple event logs and allows identifying patterns through color-coding the event classes.

5 Pre-processing Event Logs

Analyzing event data, just like any data analysis, requires pre-processing to remove data points that are not relevant for the specific analysis question at hand.

There are three basic pre-processing operations on event logs that allow us to reduce or "filter" the data in three fundamentally different ways. Most other pre-processing operations are a combination of these three operations. They are defined on the data model of the structured event log (Definition 7).

1. *Selection* of traces reduces the set of cases in L to those that satisfy a specific property. All other cases are removed. The pre-processed log L' contains just a subset of the cases in L, i.e., $L' \subseteq L$ and each cases keeps all its properties, especially all events in its trace.

   Fig. 2 (top) illustrates the selection of L to all cases whose traces end with an

[5] ProM is an open-source framework widely used in the field of process mining for implementing, testing, and applying various process mining techniques, see http://www.promtools.org/.

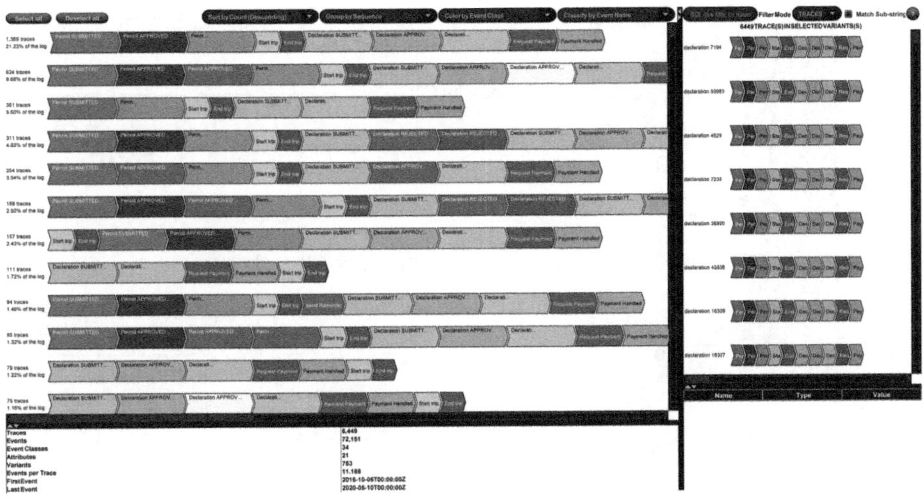

Fig. 1. The *Explore Event Log* visualizer of ProM.

event with activity name C. The resulting log L' does not contain the cases whose traces end with B or A.

2. *Projection* removes from each trace in L all events that do *not* satisfy a particular property. The resulting event log L' keeps all its cases, but their traces may contain fewer events or even be empty.
   Fig. 2 (left) illustrates the projection of L to all events with activity attribute A or C. The resulting event log does not contain any event with activity attribute B anymore.
3. *Aggregation* groups in each trace multiple subsequent events $e_1, \ldots, e_k$ with the same property into a new event e^* whose properties are derived from $e_1, \ldots, e_k$; $e_1, \ldots, e_k$ are then replaced by e^*. The pre-processed log L' keeps all its cases, but the traces may have fewer events and may contain a new aggregated event with new properties that were not explicitly visible in L.
   Fig. 2 (bottom right) illustrates the aggregation of subsequent events with the same activity name. For example, the subsequence $\langle B, B \rangle$ in the second case was replaced by a single B.

Definition 12 (Selection). *Let L be a structured event log. Let $\varphi(c)$ be a predicate over the case attributes and event attributes of L. The* selection *of L wrt. φ is the subset*

$$Select_{\varphi}(L) = \{c \in L \mid \varphi(c) = true\}.$$

Here are several example selection predicates for the event log in Table 2:

- $\varphi_1(c) \equiv \pi_{type}(c) =$ online (only cases of type "online")
- $\varphi_2(c) \equiv \pi_{trace}(c) = \langle e_1, \ldots, e_n \rangle \wedge \pi_{action}(e_1) =$ receive order (only cases starting with "receive order")

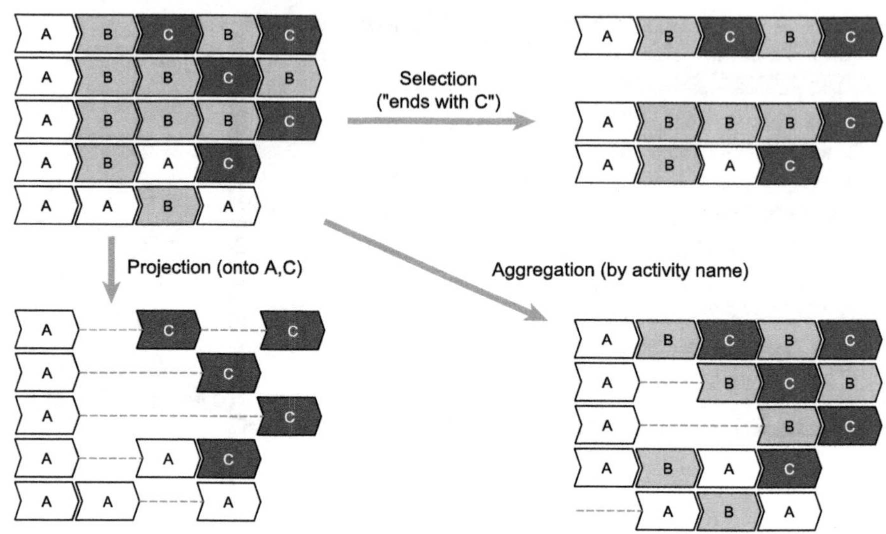

Fig. 2. Pre-processing operations on event logs.

- $\varphi_3(c) \equiv \pi_{trace}(c) = \langle e_1, \ldots, e_n \rangle \wedge \pi_{time}(e_n) - \pi_{time}(e_1) < 24h$ (only cases completing within 24 h)
- $\varphi_4(c) \equiv |\{c' \in L \mid \mathit{simple}_{class}(c) = \mathit{simple}_{class}(c')\}| \geq 10$ for some event classifier *class* (only cases whose trace variant, i.e., simple trace, occurs at least 10 times in the event log)

Note that $\varphi_4(c)$ is not purely local to the case c but rather "reaches out" into the entire event log L.

Definition 13 (Projection). *Let L be a structured event log. Let $\psi(e)$ be a predicate over the event attributes of L.*

Let $\sigma = \langle e_1, \ldots, e_n \rangle = \pi_{trace}(c), c \in L$ be a trace. The projection *of σ onto ψ is the projection of σ onto all events e_i where $\psi(e_i) = true$, i.e.,*

$$Proj_{\psi}(\sigma) = \langle e_1, \ldots, e_n \rangle|_{\psi(e_i)=true}.$$

We obtain the projection *of L into ψ, written $Proj_{\psi}(L)$, by setting $\pi_{trace}(c) := Proj_{\psi}(\pi_{trace}(c))$.*

Here are several example projection predicates for the event log in Table 2:

- $\psi_1(e) \equiv \pi_{\text{life-cycle}}(e) = \text{complete}$ (only "complete" events),
- $\psi_2(e) \equiv \pi_{\text{delivery}}(e) \neq \perp$ (only events with a reference to a delivery),
- $\psi_3(e) \equiv \pi_{\text{type}}(e) = \text{online}$,
- $\psi_4(e) \equiv \pi_{\text{user}}(e) \in \{\text{Alice}, \text{Bob}\}$ (only events where Alice or Bob are involved),
- $\psi_5(e) \equiv c = \pi_{order}(e) \wedge \pi_{trace}(c) = \langle e_1, \ldots, e_n \rangle \wedge e = e_i \wedge \forall j = i+1, \ldots, n \wedge \pi_{action}(e_i) \neq \pi_{action}(e_j)$ (only the last occurrence of each activity in a trace),

- $\psi_6(e) \equiv |\{e' \mid c' \in L, e' \in \pi_{trace}c', \pi_{act}(e) = \pi_{act}(e')| \geq 5$ (only events of activities which occur at least 5 times in the event log L).

Note that when we constructed the event log from the event table, each event e had the chosen case identifier id as event attribute, i.e., $\pi_{id}(e) = c$ refers to the case. When constructing the event log, we used the value c to construct the case itself. This means, we can "reach" the case c from an event e, and once we have the case c, we can "reach" the entire trace $\pi_{trace}(c)$ that also contains e. We use this in $\psi_5(e)$ to reason about whether e is not the last event in the trace of the same activity. Not every process mining software allows to specify such a projection predicate. It can only be defined if the event e actually has a reference to the case c and the data structure in which the event is stored allows to resolve this reference. Similarly, $\psi_6(e)$ requires that the entire event log (or statistics about the event log) are accessible.

For aggregation, we do not provide a full formal definition, but outline what has to be defined. Aggregation in a case $Agg_{g,r}(c)$ requires two functions g and r:

- A *grouping* classifier $g : \mathcal{E} \rightarrow Val$ which maps each event to a value, similar to an event classifier.
- With g, we partition the trace $\pi_{trace}(c) = \sigma$ into maximal subsequences $\sigma_i\langle e_{i_1}, \ldots, e_{i_n}\rangle$ so that $g(e_j) = g(e_{j+1})$ for all $i_1 \leq j < i_n$, e.g., all sub-sequences with the same activity name. This results in a sequence of k such sub-sequences of various lengths, i.e., $g(\sigma) = \langle \sigma_1, \ldots, \sigma_k\rangle$, for instance, $\langle\langle e_1, e_2\rangle, \langle e_3\rangle, \langle e_4, e_5\rangle\rangle$.
- A *replacement* function $r : \mathcal{E}^+ \rightarrow \mathcal{E}$ that replaces any non-empty subsequence $\langle e_i, \ldots, e_{i+m}\rangle$ by a new event $r(\langle e_i, \ldots, e_{i+m}\rangle) = e'$ and defines the event attributes for e' based on the attribute values of $\langle e_i, \ldots, e_{i+m}\rangle$; r specifically has to set the timestamp of e' to be within $\pi_{time}(e_i) \leq \pi_{time}(e') \leq \pi_{time}(e_{i+m})$. For a singleton sub-sequence $\langle e_i\rangle$, the replacement function should just return the event e_i, i.e., the event remains unchanged.
- $Agg_{g,r}(c)$ apply r to each sub-sequence $\langle e_i, \ldots, e_{i+m}\rangle$ obtained from g which results in a new sequence of events, i.e., $Agg_{g,r}(c) = \langle r(\sigma_1), \ldots, r(\sigma_k)\rangle$ where $g(\sigma) = \langle \sigma_1, \ldots, \sigma_k\rangle$ and $\sigma = \pi_{trace}(c)$. For example, $\langle r(\langle e_1, e_2\rangle), r(\langle e_3\rangle), r(\langle e_4, e_5\rangle)\rangle = \langle e_{12}, e_3, e_{45}\rangle$.
- Set $\pi_{trace}(c) := Agg_{g,r}(c)$.

For example, we can use $g(e) = \pi_{action}(e)$ to find all subsequences where the same activity occurs repeatedly. In Table 2, this would be only $\langle e_5, e_6\rangle$. We can then define a replacement function $r(\langle e_1, \ldots, e_k\rangle)$ where the new event e' gets $\pi_x(e') = \pi_x(e_k)$ for all attributes x defined for e_k, i.e., we replace the sequence by the last event. We could also define $\pi_{item}(e') = \{\pi_{item}(e_i) \mid 1 \leq i \leq k\}$ to collect the items that were involved in these events into a set.

All three event log pre-processing operations selection, projection, and aggregation always result in single event log. This allows to apply them in arbitrary combinations. For example, first project onto all events where "Bob" is involved and then aggregate on $\pi_{action}(e)$.

As in any data analysis, identifying which event log pre-processing operations to apply for the analysis question at hand is an iterative process. Process mining software supports this iterative process by letting the analyst interactively build a *stack* of filtering operations that can be modified and re-arranged alongside a visualization of the outcome of the filtering operation. Figure 3 shows the "Filter Event Log" plugin of ProM.

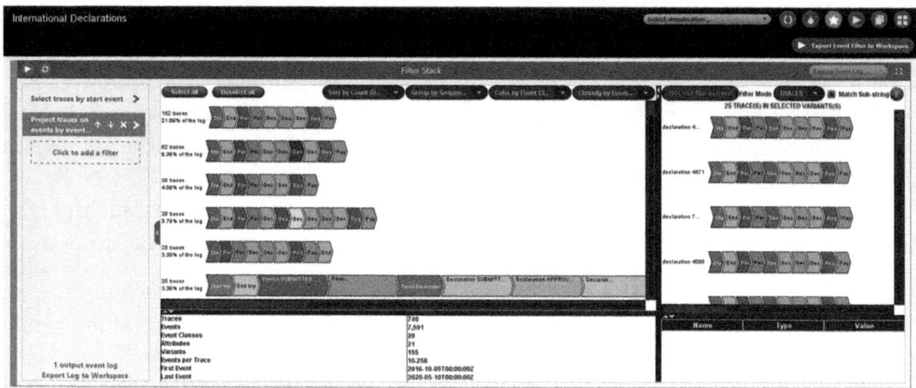

Fig. 3. Interactive event log filtering in ProM, accessible via the "Filter Event Log" plugin. The shown event data has been filtered using two filters executed one after the other.

6 Advanced Pre-processing Methods

In addition to the three basic pre-processing operations, we show three other operations on the event log that allow us to alter the event data for creating either a more precise, refined event log or a more abstract event log. Here, we define these operations on the simplified event log. Note that they can also be adapted to operate on the event data.

To introduce the operators, we use the running example shown in Fig. 4. Let L be a structured event log, as shown in Fig. 4(left), where the cases are the patients. For example, $\pi_{trace}(1) = \langle e_1, e_2, \cdots, e_8 \rangle$. Let $class_{act}(e) = \pi_{action}(e)$. For patient 1, the simple trace $simple_{class}(1) = \langle Vi, Ca, Re, Gl, Bo, Cs, Su, Cs \rangle$. We have $\Sigma_{class}(L) = \{ Vi, Ca, Re, Gl, Bo, Cs, Su \} = \Sigma$.

- A *label refinement* $\beta : \mathcal{E} \rightarrow \mathcal{E}$ replaces an event with another event by replacing the activity label of these events in L with some more precise labels. Figure 4(right) illustrates an example of a label refinement of L. In this case, $\pi_{action}(e_6) :=$ "Pre" $+ \pi_{action}(e_6)$, and $\pi_{action}(e_8) :=$ "Po" $+ \pi_{action}(e_8)$. The refined classes $\Sigma_{class}(\beta(L)) = \Sigma' = \{ Vi, Ca, Re, Gl, Bo, preCs, poCs, Su \}$. We can use two predicates ψ_7 and ψ_8 to implement this β. In essence, predicate ψ_7 checks if the event e is (1) labeled Cs and (2) directly followed by

e	patient	action	description	life-cycle	level-1	time
1	1	Vi	Visit	complete	Admin	10/10/2024
2	1	Ca	Calcium	complete	laBtest	11/10/2024
3	1	Re	Register	complete	Admin	12/10/2024
4	1	Gl	Glucose	complete	laBtest	13/10/2024
5	1	Bo	Blood test	complete	laBtest	14/10/2024
6	1	Cs	Consultation	complete	Admin	15/10/2024
7	1	Su	Surgery	complete	Medical	16/10/2024
8	1	Cs	Consultation	complete	Admin	17/10/2024
...	...	...	...	...	...	...

Label abstraction

e	patient	action	description	life-cycle	level-1	time
1	1	Vi	Visit	complete	Admin	10/10/2024
2	1	Ca	Calcium	complete	laBtest	11/10/2024
3	1	Re	Register	complete	Admin	12/10/2024
4	1	Gl	Glucose	complete	laBtest	13/10/2024
5	1	Bo	Blood test	complete	laBtest	14/10/2024
6	1	preCs	Pre-surgery Consultation	complete	Admin	15/10/2024
7	1	Su	Surgery	complete	Medical	16/10/2024
8	1	poCs	Post-surgery Consultation	complete	Admin	17/10/2024
...	...	...	...	...	...	...

Label refinement

Fig. 4. An event table that records patients' treatment trajectory; label refinement and label abstraction are illustrated.

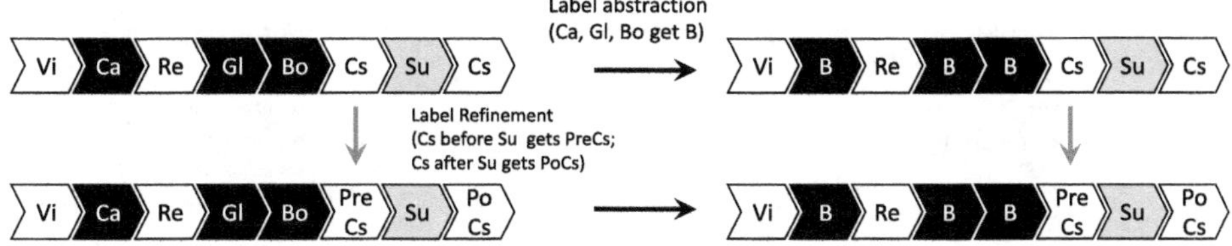

Fig. 5. The simple trace of patient 1 in Fig 4, showing label refinement and label abstraction.

an event e' labeled Su, then replace the label of e by $PreCs$. Predicate ψ_8 checks if e is labeled Cs and directly preceded by an event e' labeled Su, then replace the label of e by $PoCs$.

- A *Label abstraction* β^{-1} is the opposite of a label refinement. Figure 5(left) to Fig. 5(right) illustrates an example of a label abstraction, where the activity labels of e_2, e_4, and e_5 are abstracted and replaced by "L" (Labtest).

The label refinement and label abstraction operations retain the same number of events as in the original traces. They change the granularity of the activity labels (used as the event class) to ensure the subsequent analyses operate on the right granularity level.

Unlike label refinement and label abstraction operations, event abstraction, a form of event aggregation, may change the number of events in the traces. Here, we explain an event abstraction method that assumes the event log contains some information about hierarchical sub-processes [15]. Following the aggregation function in the previous section, we define $Agg_{g,r,\mathcal{T}}(c)$ where g is a grouping classifier, r is a replacement function, and $\mathcal{T} : \Sigma \rightarrow Val$ maps an activity to its parent (sub)process, defining a hierarchy of activities (Fig. 6).

Let's again consider the running example shown in Fig. 4(left). Assuming the event attribute *level − 1* suggests the sub-process of the corresponding action, we obtain $\mathcal{T}_A = \{Vi \rightarrow A, Re \rightarrow A, Cs \rightarrow A\}$, $\mathcal{T}_B = \{Ca \rightarrow B, Gl \rightarrow B, Bo \rightarrow B\}$, $\mathcal{T} = \mathcal{T}_A \cup \mathcal{T}_B$. Thus, sub-process A (Admin) contains activities $\mathcal{T}^{-1}(A) = \{Vi, Re, Cs\}$ and sub-process B contains $\mathcal{T}^{-1}(B) = \{Ca, Gl, Bo\}$. Figure 7 illustrates abstracting the events of sub-process A using $\mathcal{T}_A$(see Fig. 7(left to

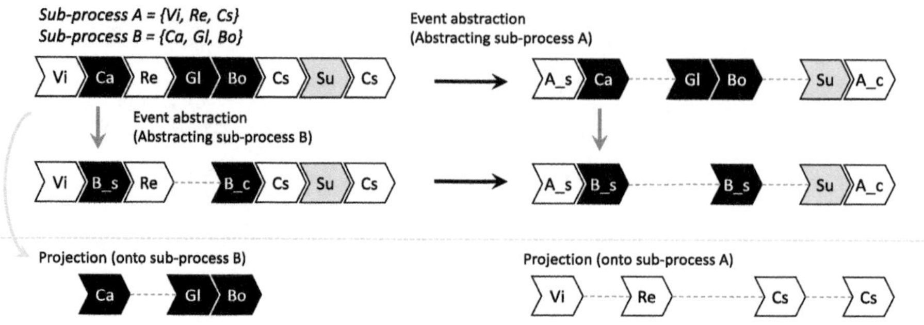

Fig. 6. The simple trace of patient 1, showing event abstraction.

e	patient	action	description	life-cycle	level-1	time
1	1	Vi	Visit	complete	Admin	10/10/2024
22	1	B_s	laBtest-start	start	-	11/10/2024
3	1	Re	Register	complete	Admin	12/10/2024
25	1	B_c	laBtest-complete	complete	-	14/10/2024
6	1	Cs	Consultation	complete	Admin	15/10/2024
7	1	Su	Surgery	complete	Medical	16/10/2024
8	1	Cs	Consultation	complete	Admin	17/10/2024
...	...	...	...	...	...	...

e	patient	action	description	life-cycle	level-1	time
31	1	A_s	Admin-start	start	-	10/10/2024
2	1	Ca	Calcium	complete	laBtest	11/10/2024
4	1	Gl	Glucose	complete	laBtest	13/10/2024
5	1	Bo	Blood test	complete	laBtest	14/10/2024
7	1	Su	Surgery	complete	Medical	16/10/2024
38	1	A_c	Admin-complete	complete	-	17/10/2024
...	...	...	...	...	...	...

Fig. 7. The event log, showing the two event abstractions; left: abstracting sub-process B; right: abstracting sub-process A.

right)) and, independently, abstracting the events of sub-process B using $\mathcal{T}_B$ (see Fig. 7(top to middle)).

– *Event abstraction* $Agg_{g,r,\mathcal{T}}(c)$ of events in an event log L is a form of *aggregation* of events. With $g_{\mathcal{T}}$, we partition the trace into maximal subsequences so that the events in the same subsequence belong to the same subprocess. For example, $g_{\mathcal{T}_A}(\pi_{trace}(1)) = \langle\langle e_1\rangle, \langle e_2\rangle, \langle e_3\rangle, \langle e_4, e_5\rangle, \langle e_6\rangle, \langle e_7\rangle, \langle e_8\rangle\rangle$. With $r_{\mathcal{T}}$, we replace the subsequences as follows: if the subsequence is the first one of a subprocess, then we replace it with an event that indicates the subprocess has started, e.g., $r_{\mathcal{T}_A}(\langle e_2\rangle) = e_{31}$; if the subsequence is the last one of a subprocess, then we replace it with an event that indicates the subprocess has completed, e.g., $r_{\mathcal{T}_A}(\langle e_8\rangle) = e_{38}$; if the subsequence does not belong to any subprocess, we keep them as-is $r_{\mathcal{T}_A}(\langle e_4, e_5\rangle)$; otherwise, remove the subsequence, e.g., $r_{\mathcal{T}_A}(\langle e_3\rangle) = r_{\mathcal{T}_A}(\langle e_6\rangle) = \langle\rangle$.

Unlike label refinement and event abstraction, clustering the cases does not necessarily change the trace of each case or its granularity. It changes the log by dividing the cases into multiple sub-logs.

– *Clustering* the cases in the event log L into multiple sub-logs $L_1, \ldots, L_k$ so that cases in a sub-log L_i have similar trace variants and cases in different sub-logs $L_i \neq L_j$ have maximally different trace variants. Technically, clustering is repeated selection. However, the selection criteria are not based on selection predicates.

Further Readings. The *label refinements* are studied for log quality issues such as duplicated tasks [14]. Many different *event abstraction* techniques have been proposed, see [5] for an overview. The event abstraction operation here is based on the technique introduced in [15]. For a survey on available clustering techniques, see [16].

7 Event Logs Have Limitations

Event logs as defined in this document face severe limitations.

The timestamp information in event data is often not reliable. For example, if events are only recorded on day-level granularity and three events e_1, e_2, e_3 occurred on the same day, then their order e_1, e_2, e_3 in the event table may not be the order in which they occurred. When creating an event log, we have to pick on ordering of these events to build a trace, but it may be the wrong one. A possible solution is to define a trace $\pi_{trace}(c)$ not as a sequence $\langle e_1, \ldots, e_n \rangle$ of events, but as a *strict partial order* $(E, <)$ where $e_i < e_j$ are ordered only iff $\pi_{time}(e_i) < \pi_{time}(e_j)$. Events with the same time-stamp remain unordered, see [13]. Additionally, if the events have read and write attributes or have attributes that explicitly record the dependencies inherited during the workflow execution, these can be used to derive such partial orders. For an overview, see [12].

Structured event logs only order event data according to a single case identifier. However, we have seen that even basic event data contains multiple entity identifiers that are in 1:n and n:m relationships to each other. For example in Table 2, customer A7001 is involved in 3 orders and deliver 623 is involved in 2 orders. The data structure of the structured event log cannot capture these relations. These limitations can be overcome through object-centric event data models [8] that allow allow tracing the behavior of multiple objects together, such as Event Knowledge Graphs [6, 7] and Object-Centric Event Logs [3].

8 Conclusion

To summarize, event data serves as the foundational input for process mining, requiring careful extraction and pre-processing to transform raw event tables into structured event logs that are suitable for analysis. This process of extraction and transformation is not merely a technical task but requiring modeling skills, necessitating conscious decisions about how to represent the observed behaviors of entities (cases) of interest. By understanding the core concepts of traces, cases, activities, events, and logs, and by carefully choosing the attributes that define these elements, analysts can create event logs that accurately reflect the process under study and most suitable for the specific analyses. This chapter has outlined these fundamental concepts, transformation steps, and considerations involved in this transformation process, equipping readers with the knowledge to make informed choices in the preparation of event logs for process mining applications.

References

1. van der Aalst, W.M.P.: Process Mining - Data Science in Action. Second Edition. Springer (2016). https://doi.org/10.1007/978-3-662-49851-4
2. Acampora, G., Vitiello, A., Di Stefano, B., Aalst, W.M.P.v.d., Günther, C.W., Verbeek, H.M.W.: IEEE 1849TM: the XES standard: the second ieee standard sponsored by ieee computational intelligence society. IEEE Comput. Intell. Mag. pp. 4–8 (2017). https://doi.org/10.1109/MCI.2017.2670420
3. Berti, A., et al.: OCEL (object-centric event log) 2.0 specification. CoRR abs/2403.01975 (2024). https://doi.org/10.48550/ARXIV.2403.01975
4. Blizard, W.D.: Multiset theory. Notre Dame J. Formal Logic **30**(1), 36–66 (1989)
5. Diba, K., Batoulis, K., Weidlich, M., Weske, M.: Extraction, correlation, and abstraction of event data for process mining. Wiley Interdiscip. Rev. Data Min. Knowl. Discov. **10**(3) (2020). https://doi.org/10.1002/widm.1346
6. Esser, S., Fahland, D.: Multi-dimensional event data in graph databases. J. Data Semant. **10**(1–2), 109–141 (2021). https://doi.org/10.1007/s13740-021-00122-1
7. Fahland, D.: Process mining over multiple behavioral dimensions with event knowledge graphs. In: van der Aalst, W.M.P., Carmona, J. (eds.) Process Mining Handbook, Lecture Notes in Business Information Processing, vol. 448, pp. 274–319. Springer, Cham (2022). https://doi.org/10.1007/978-3-031-08848-3_9
8. Fahland, D., et al.: Towards a simple and extensible standard for object-centric event data (OCED) - core model, design space, and lessons learned. CoRR abs/2410.14495 (2024). https://doi.org/10.48550/ARXIV.2410.14495
9. Günther, C.: First XES Standard Definition version 1.0. Xes standard proposal (2009). http://www.xes-standard.org/
10. Hopcroft, J.E., Motwani, R., Ullman, J.D.: Introduction to Automata Theory, Languages, and Computation. Pearson, 3rd edn. (2006)
11. IEEE 1849 (XES) WG: IEEE Standard for eXtensible Event Stream (XES) for Achieving Interoperability in Event Logs and Event Streams. IEEE Std 1849-2016 pp. 1–50 (2016). https://doi.org/10.1109/IEEESTD.2016.7740858
12. Leemans, S.J.J., van Zelst, S.J., Lu, X.: Partial-order-based process mining: a survey and outlook. Knowl. Inf. Syst. **65**(1), 1–29 (2023). https://doi.org/10.1007/S10115-022-01777-3
13. Lu, X., Fahland, D., van der Aalst, W.M.P.: Conformance checking based on partially ordered event data. In: Fournier, F., Mendling, J. (eds.) Business Process Management Workshops - BPM 2014 International Workshops, Eindhoven, The Netherlands, September 7–8, 2014, Revised Papers. Lecture Notes in Business Information Processing, vol. 202, pp. 75–88. Springer, Cham (2014). https://doi.org/10.1007/978-3-319-15895-2_7
14. Lu, X., Fahland, D., van den Biggelaar, F.J.H.M., van der Aalst, W.M.P.: Handling duplicated tasks in process discovery by refining event labels. In: Rosa, M.L., Loos, P., Pastor, O. (eds.) Business Process Management - 14th International Conference, BPM 2016, Rio de Janeiro, Brazil, September 18–22, 2016. Proceedings. Lecture Notes in Computer Science, vol. 9850, pp. 90–107. Springer, Cham (2016). https://doi.org/10.1007/978-3-319-45348-4_6

15. Lu, X., Gal, A., Reijers, H.A.: Discovering hierarchical processes using flexible activity trees for event abstraction. In: van Dongen, B.F., Montali, M., Wynn, M.T. (eds.) 2nd International Conference on Process Mining, ICPM 2020, Padua, Italy, October 4–9, 2020. pp. 145–152. IEEE (2020). https://doi.org/10.1109/ICPM49681.2020.00030
16. Zandkarimi, F., Rehse, J., Soudmand, P., Hoehle, H.: A generic framework for trace clustering in process mining. In: van Dongen, B.F., Montali, M., Wynn, M.T. (eds.) 2nd International Conference on Process Mining, ICPM 2020, Padua, Italy, October 4–9, 2020, pp. 177–184. IEEE (2020). https://doi.org/10.1109/ICPM49681.2020.00034

Application of Coloured Petri Nets for Modelling the Software Architecture of the SmartOcean Data Service Platform

Lars Michael Kristensen(✉)

Department of Computer Science, Electrical Engineering and Mathematical Sciences, Western Norway University of Applied Sciences, Bergen, Norway
lmkr@hvl.no

Abstract. We present the Coloured Petri Nets (CPNs) modelling of the SmartOcean software platform currently being developed and aimed at providing cloud-based services for data-driven systems and applications relying on marine data. The CPN model captures the systems-of-system architecture and the platform services and has evolved as a formal conceptualisation along-side the implementation of the platform and its services. The CPN model encompasses data ingestion-, data space-, messaging-, and security services with a focus on providing an abstract modelling of the services and system interaction. The work exemplifies representative CPN modelling patterns for system-of-systems modelling, service provision and consumption, and service interaction.

Keywords: Coloured Petri Nets · CPN Tools · Formal Methods · High-level Petri Nets · Software Architecture · Software Engineering

1 Introduction

Smart systems driven by the Internet-of-things (IoT), sensor- and actuator technology, and data analytics are becoming pervasive across a wide range of industry and society domains, including energy, transportation, health, buildings and homes [34]. Typical aims of smart systems are improved management, monitoring, situational awareness, decision support, and efficient- and cost-effective operation aimed at providing competitive services. An emerging domain for smart systems is the ocean space which is critical to climate and eco-systems, food- and energy production, and transportation. A recent analysis [32] shows that the ocean industries have the potential to double their economic growth in the next ten years. To realise this potential, there is a need to develop enabling technology for fact-based ocean management through ocean monitoring, sensor systems, and data services with a view towards supporting sustainable industrial operation and ocean research.

Obtaining marine- and ocean data of sufficient quality for use in smart systems represents significant challenges due to the enormous geographical areas,

F. Kordon et al. (Eds.): *Transactions on Petri Nets and Other Models of Concurrency XVIII*, LNCTPN 16260, pp. 280–308, 2026.
https://doi.org/10.1007/978-3-662-73305-9_10

the hostility of the ocean environment, accessibility for deployment and service of equipment, severe limitations in communication capabilities and availability of power. While ocean- and marine data services are now emerging, there is a huge gap in data coverage and substantial technology challenges related to interoperability, data- and meta-data standards, and APIs [24,30].

SFI SmartOcean [37] is a centre for research-based innovation funded by the Norwegian Research Council involving research and industry partners focussing on key challenges in developing smart ocean systems. The three main focus areas of the centre are: underwater sensor and measurement technology; underwater wireless sensor networks based on acoustic communication; and a platform for cloud-based data- and application services. Figure 1 sketches the type of system for which enabling technology is to be developed by the consortium partners in the course of the life-time of the centre. The system consists of an *information acquisition layer* comprised of an underwater wireless sensor network based on acoustic communication. The *information delivery layer* is comprised of sensor network communication gateways for transporting data from sub-sea to top-side and into the cloud-based *data and application service layer*. Control information may also flow from the cloud-services to the nodes in the sensor network.

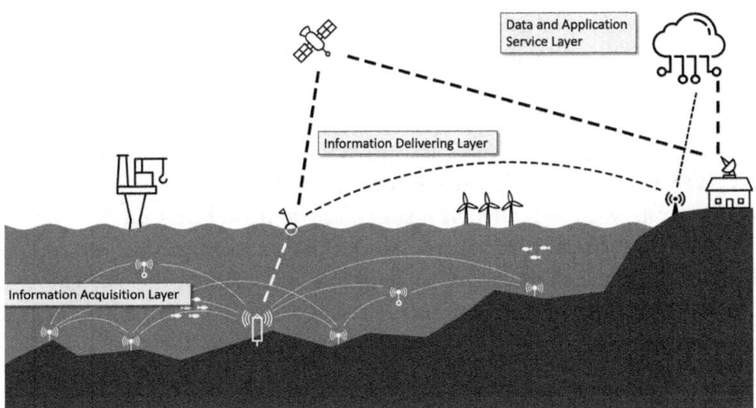

Fig. 1. Overall SmartOcean system architecture: layering and information flow

The focus of this paper is on the SmartOcean cloud platform [25] which constitute the data and application service layer. The platform is envisioned as an integration platform for the systems that constitute the SmartOcean digital ecosystem, and is being based on software components, APIs, cloud platform services and containers for developing and deploying applications and data services. Data services are services that perform computation on data ingested to the platform. Its sub-components (e.g. microservices), can have different functional requirements such as cleaning, validation, or curation of data. Such sub-components can be found in typical big data processing architectures as the one proposed by NIST [5], and are placed in between data acquisition, ingestion and the end-user application of data (data consumers systems and applications). In terms of operations, these services can perform transformations on data or retain data, preventing further propagation on the pipeline. As a first step towards development of the platform, we conducted an extensive study based on stakeholder- and focus-group interviews with the aim of identifying requirements and challenges pertinent to the development of the platform. The results from the study were published in [24], and resulted in a first sketch of the platform software architecture, its constituent systems and internal services.

The SmartOcean platform is a complex distributed system which motivated us to apply Coloured Petri Nets (CPNs) [15] modelling as a means to obtain a formal executable model that can serve as an evolving sound foundation during our research and development work on implementation of the platform. CPNs are suitable for this purpose as: 1) the hierarchical organisation into modules allows us to capture the system architecture at different levels of abstraction; and 2) the executability of the models allows us to capture the behavioral aspects related to the interactions between its constituent subsystems and services.

The actual implementation of the SmartOcean platform has been validated in operation in the context of a pilot demonstrator deployed at the Austevoll Test site of the Norwegian Institute of Marine Research. Figure 2 (left) provides a geographical overview of the test site and the top-side buoy of one of the underwater installations. Figure 2 (middle) shows one of the underwater sensor hubs deployed, and Fig. 2 (right) illustrates how the equipment are mounted on an underwater mooring line. In the pilot demonstrator, there are four underwater sensor hub nodes: two provided by Aanderaa Data Instruments (AADI) [1] (referred to as aadinorth and aadisouth) and two provided by W-Sense [49] (referred to as wsense1 and wsense2). The sensor hubs have various sensors mounted measuring marine parameters such as including oxygen, current, pressure, salinity, and temperature at different depths. In addition, there is also a virtual sensor hub node to perform basic testing of the data flow on the platform. The sensor hub nodes constitute data sources for the platform.

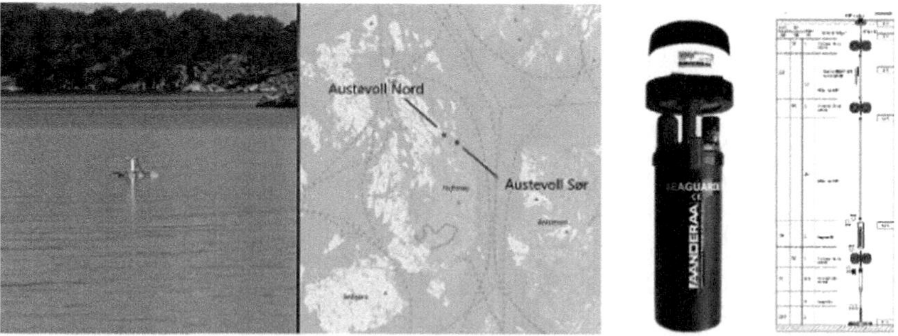

Fig. 2. Overview (left), sample sensor hub node (middle), mooring line (right) of the Austevoll pilot demonstrator

The contribution of this paper is to present the constructed CPN model focussing on the software system architecture and service interaction, and how it constitutes an abstract conceptualisation of the platform. When presenting the CPN model of the SmartOcean platform in this paper, we use base colour sets and markings corresponding to the configuration of the Austevoll pilot demonstrator. The present paper is a significantly revised and extended version of the workshop paper that appeared in [12], and is reflecting the final version of the platform architecture. The aim of this paper is not to provide a tutorial-like introduction to the CPN modelling language and CPN Tools. The reader is referred to the already existing introductory papers [16,19,20] and the comprehensive CPN textbooks [14,15].

The rest of this paper is organised as follows. Section 2 provides a brief introduction to CPNs and the CPN Tools. Section 3 presents the CPN model of the system architecture and the SmartOcean platform services. Section 4 presents the modelling of the messaging service for real-time data streams while Sect. 5 presents the modelling of the data space service for retrieving historical time series data. The modelling of the data provider and consumer clients are presented in Sect. 6. Section 7 covers the modelling of the security and identity management services. Section 8 outlines the role of the CPN model in the development of the platform and the technologies used for its implementation and cloud deployment. Finally, in Sect. 9 we sum up the conclusions and reflect upon the future development of the CPN modelling language and supporting tools. The reader is assumed to be familiar with the basic syntactical and semantical concepts of Place/Transition Nets [36], e.g., places, transitions, arcs, arc weights, tokens, markings, enabling condition and occurrence of transitions.

2 Coloured Petri Nets and CPN Tools

Coloured Petri Nets (CPNs) belong to the class of high-level Petri nets and combine Petri Nets with the Standard ML (SML) functional programming language [45]. In CPNs, Petri Nets provide the foundation of the graphical notation, and for modelling concurrency, communication, synchronisation and resource sharing. Standard ML provides the foundation for modelling data and data manipulation, and for constructing compact and parameterised models.

A main motivation behind the development of CPNs was to address the practical modelling shortcomings of Place/Transition Nets when modelling large systems containing data, data structures, and complex decisions. With CPNs, tokens can carry data values and each place has a *colour set* (data type) determining the kind of tokens that may reside on the place. Transitions in CPNs can have free *variables* that can be bound to values in *transition bindings* representing enabling and occurrence modes of the transition. Arcs in CPNs have *arc expressions* containing variables which when evaluated in transition bindings determine the *multi-sets* of tokens removed from input places and added to output places when the transition binding occurs. A boolean *guard expression* can be associated with transitions as an additional condition on enabling of the transition.

CPN models can be organised into a hierarchically organised set of modules by associating *submodules* with *substitution transitons*. The assignment of *port places* in a submodule to *socket places* connected to the corresponding substitution transition in the upper-level module determines how tokens are exchanged between a module and its submodules. The support for modules is important in order to be able to construct and maintain large models, reuse modules across a larger model, and support abstraction and management of model details. The practical application of Coloured Petri Nets is supported by CPN Tools [35] and also the more recent CPN IDE [6] web application which builds on the same underlying simulator.

CPN Tools supports editing and incremental syntax check of CPN models, and interactive and automatic simulation. CPN Tools also supports the construction of basic full state spaces for CPN models which enables state space exploration and verification of behavioral properties using model checking. The time concept of CPN models combined with monitors in CPN Tools supports simulation-based performance analysis of systems.

Figure 3 shows a screenshot of CPN Tools with some selected modules of the CPN model of the SmartOcean platform. The user interface consists of two main parts:

- an *index* (left) which contains a Tool box with *tool palettes*. Tool palettes contain tools that can be applied for editing and simulation. In addition, the index contains Options and the elements that constitute the CPN model, including Declarations, Monitors, and the hierarhically organised modules.
- a *workspace* (right) which can hold a number of *binders* containing model elements such as modules and declarations. In Fig. 3, there are two binders with the leftmost one containing the two modules System and SmartOcean-Platform, and the rightmost one containing the three modules DataProviders, DataConsumers, and Authentication.

The user of CPN Tools works directly on the graphical representation of the model using *circular menus* and the *tool palettes*. In Fig. 3, the tool palette for creating model elements such as places, transitions and arcs has been positioned in the upper right corner, while a contextual circular menu has been popped-up on an enabled transition allowing the user to, e.g., fire the transition.

The inscriptions on the places, transitions, and arcs are written in SML. SML is a statically typed functional programming language which means that computation proceeds by evaluation of expressions and that the type of expressions is inferred and checked at compile time. Furthermore, functions are first-order values and may be polymorphic, while recursion and lists are used to express iteration. CPN Tools relies on SML type constructors for defining colour sets (data types) such as enumerations, products, lists, records, and unions. The complete SML language, including functions, can be used to implement the arc expressions in the model.

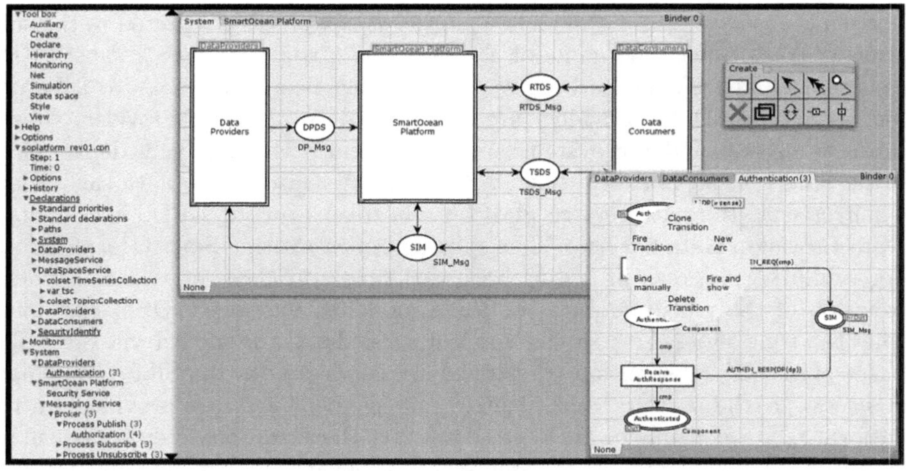

Fig. 3. CPN Tools with SmartOcean Platform CPN model

3 System Architecture and Platform Services

Figure 4 shows the top-level module of the CPN model reflecting the SmartOcean digital ecosystem at a high-level of abstraction as a system-of-systems comprised of data provider systems (left), the SmartOcean platform for development and deployment of data services and applications (middle), and data consumer systems (right).

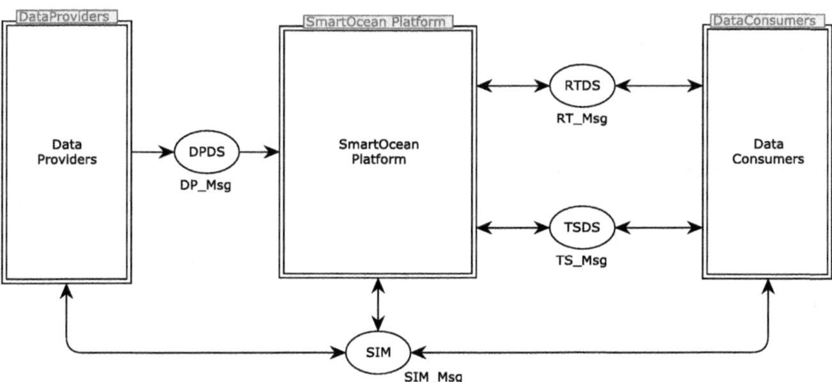

Fig. 4. Top-level module of the CPN model providing a system-of-systems perspective

The main parts of the system is represented via *substitution transitions* which by convention are drawn as rectangles with a double-lined border. Interaction between the subsystems are modelled via the *socket places* connected to the substitution transitions. The name of a submodule associated with a substitution transition is written in the blue rectangular tag positioned next to substitution transitions. Data providers are represented by the DataProviders substitution transition and are systems and applications that actively deliver data to the SmartOcean platform (e.g., AADI and W-sense cloud platforms). Data is delivered to the data service platform via tokens on the DPDS socket place (Data Provision Data Service). The substitution transition SmartOceanPlatform represents the platform providing both real-time and time series data services. Provision of the real-time data service is modelled via the RTDS socket place while the time-series data service for historical data is modelled via the TSDS socket place. All substitution transitions are connected to the SIM socket place for access to the security and identity management services provided by the platform. Data consumers are represented via the DataConsumers substitution transition, and are modelling systems and applications that actively use data services from the SmartOcean platform. Examples include NMDC [31], NORCE Enlighten [7], and client dashboard applications. The definition of the data types `DP_Msg`, `RT_Msg`, `TS_Msg`, and `SIM_Msg` used as colour sets for the socket places in Fig. 4 will be presented shortly.

Figure 5 shows the submodule of the SmartOceanPlatform substitution transition in Fig. 4. The double-bordered *port places* in Fig. 5 are associated with the accordingly named socket places in Fig. 4. The integers in the green circles positioned next to the places specify the number of tokens on the place in the current marking, and the text in the associated green box lists the data values (colours) of the individual tokens. We explain the current marking in further detail below. The three substitution transitions in Fig. 5 represents the three main services of the platform:

Messaging Service providing a real-time data service where data providers can publish marine data streams and where data consumers can subscribe to real-time data streams. The implementation of the messaging service is based on the standardised MQTT publish-subscribe protocol [28].

Data Space Service providing a data service where data consumers can access meta-data and historical time series data. The implementation of the data space service is an HTTP-based REST API [10].

Security Service providing authentication services to data providers and consumers, and authorization services for the messaging and data space service. The implementation of the security service is based on Keycloack [17].

As is evident from the arc between the RTDS place and the DataSpaceService substitution transition, then the data space service relies on the real-time messaging service to subscribe to the data streams for which it needs to provide access to the corresponding time series data. The port and socket places in Figs. 4 and 5 represent service interaction points in the platform, and tokens present on these places are representing request and response messages sent to and from the services. The (current) marking shown in Fig. 5 corresponds to a

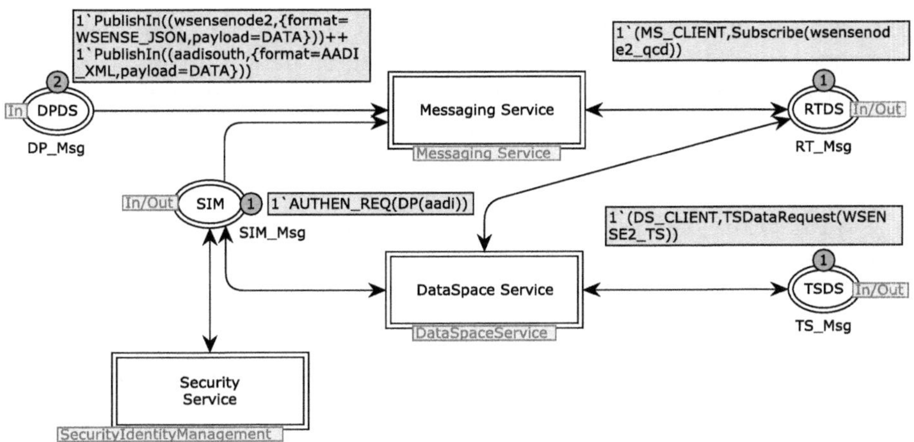

Fig. 5. The SmartOceanPatform module - platform architecture and constituent services

state in which two `PublishIn` messages with data (represented by the two tokens on place DPDS) has been sent from a `wsense` and an `aadi` sensor node to the messaging services. A data consumer client has sent a `Subscribe` request (as represented by the single token on place RTDS) to messaging system to receive data from the `wsense` sensor node 2. Furthermore, an authentication request as represented by the token on place SIM has been sent to the security service. Finally, a data request as represented by the single token on place TSDS has been sent to the data space service.

The colour sets used in the places representing points of service interaction are given in Listing 1 and will be detailed further below. A central aim of our modelling approach has been to develop a CPN model which in a compact manner can represent the subsystems (components) and their interaction which is an often used modelling pattern in CPNs. Considering Listing 1, then the `Component` union colour set has constructors for each of the main components of the system:

- `DP` used to represent *data providers* in the system. The colour set `DataProvider` is an enumeration colour set with values corresponding to each of the vendor sensor hub nodes that provides a data stream.
- `BR` for representing the *messaging brokers* which are used to implement the messaging service. The colour set `Broker` is an enumeration colour set with a value for each of the three brokers used to implement the messaging service.
- `TF` which are *transformer components* of the messaging service and responsible for transformation of data from the proprietary formats of the data providers into a common standardised JSON-based platform format for marine data.
- `PC` which are *processor components* performing processing of the data streams in the messaging service, including data quality checks, data fusion and filtering, and data forwarding.

`DATA_SPACE_SERVICE` which represents the *data space service* providing access to time series of historical data for the configured data sources.

`TSDS_CLIENT` and `RTDS_CLIENT` which represent *data consumer clients* for the time series data service and the real-time data service, respectively.

```
(* --- software system components --- *)
colset AADI_SensorHubId   = with austsouth | austnorth;
colset WSENSE_SensorHubId = int with 1..2;

colset DataProvider = with virtualnode | wsense | aadi;

colset Transformer = union AADI_XML_TR: AADI_SensorHubId
                         + WSENSE_JSON_TR:
    WSENSE_SensorHubId;

colset Processor   = union FORWARDER: INT + DQC: INT;

colset Broker = with
                INGRESS_BROKER | CORE_BROKER |
    EGRESS_BROKER;

colset Component = union DP: DataProvider  + BR: Broker
                       + TF: Transformer   + PC: Processor
                       + DATASPACE_SERVICE
                       + DS_CLIENT + MS_CLIENT;

(* --- sensor node data and payload --- *)
colset FormatSpec = with SO_JSON | AADI_XML | WSENSE_JSON;
colset Payload    = with DATA;
colset Message    = record format: FormatSpec
                         * payload: Payload;

(* --- real-time data provision and consumption  --- *)
colset DP_Msg = union PublishIn: TopicxMsg;

colset MSDC_Msg = union Subscribe: Topic
                      + Unsubscribe: Topic
                      + PublishOut: TopicxMsg;

colset RT_Msg = product Component * MSDC_Msg;

colset TSDC_Msg = union TSDataRequest:
    TimeSeriesCollection
                      + TSDataResponse:
    TimeSeriesCollection;

colset TS_Msg = product Component * TSDC_Message;

(* --- security and identitify management ---*)
```

```
colset SIM_Msg = union AUTHEN_REQ: Component
                     + AUTHEN_RESP: Component
                     + AUTHOR_REQ: Component
                     + AUTHOR_RESP: Component;
```

Listing 1. Colour set definitions for system components and service interaction

The `Message` record colour is used for representing the (sensor) data sent by the data provider clients and received by the data consumers. We have abstracted from the concrete sensor values data contained in the messages, and the `payload` of the data is represented as a `DATA` value while the `format` of the payload data is modelled via the `FormatSpec` colour set containing values corresponding to the format in which each of the data providers can provide data. The `SO_JSON` value represents the standardised JSON format used internally in the platform.

The colour sets `DP_Msg`, `RT_Msg`, `TS_Msg`, and `SIM_Msg` represents the messages that can be used for interaction with the platform services. The colour sets referred to in the definition of these colour sets are not provided in Listing 1, but will be presented when we cover the messaging-, data space-, and security services in detail in the next sections.

4 Messaging Service

The messaging service is supporting live and near real-time data streams and is based on the publish-subscribe paradigm [8]. In this paradigm, data provider clients *publish* data on *topics* while data consumer clients *subscribe* to topics in order to receive data published on the topics. When a client publishes a message on a topic, all clients subscribed to the topic will receive the message. The publish-subscribe middleware is implemented via a *broker* which manages topics and keeps track of which clients are subscribing to which topics. The broker also manages authorization related to the publishing and subscriptions.

Figure 6 shows the MessagingService module which is the submodule of the MessagingService substitution transition in Fig. 5. The messaging service employs three brokers as represented by the three substitution transitions. The IBI port place is associated with the DPDS socket place in Fig. 5 which is where the data is being provided to the messaging service by publishing clients. The port place EBO is associated with the RTDS socket place in Fig. 5 which is where data is being consumed by subscribing clients. All three broker substitution transitions are connected to the SIM place in order to perform authorization via the security and identity management services. The marking of the port places in Fig. 6 corresponds to the marking previously shown in Fig. 5, but where we have omitted the data value details of the tokens on the IBO and EBO port places and is only showing the number of tokens on each of these places.

The roles of the three brokers are as follows:

Ingress Broker receives the raw data from sensor nodes in vendor-specific formats and re-publishes them via the IBO place such that it can be picked up by *transformers* represented by the Transform substitution transition. The transformers perform data-flow control, validation, and transformation into the common JSON-based format.

Core Broker receives transformed data and re-publishes it via the CBO place where it can be picked up by *processors* represented by the Process substitution transition. The processors perform further processing of data such as data quality checks, data filtering, and data fusion.

Egress Broker receives processed data and publishes it on topics via the EBO place to make it available for data consumers which may be applications and services for visualisation, monitoring, analysis, and storage.

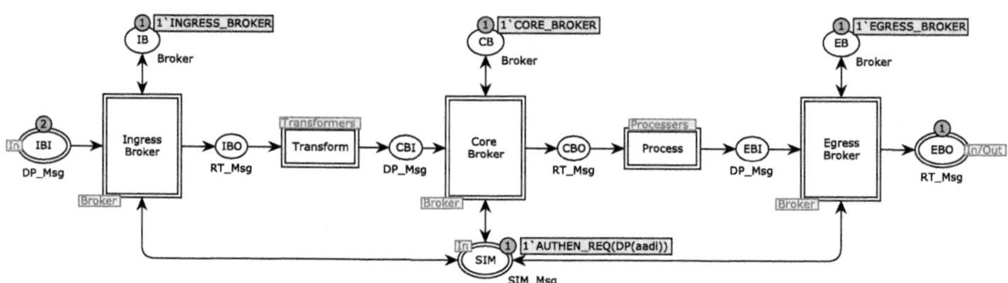

Fig. 6. The Messaging service module - modelling the publish/subscribe middleware

The marking of the IB (ingress broker), CB (core broker), and EB (egress broker) socket places corresponds to the three brokers, respectively, and are used to parameterise the module instances of the broker substitution transitions which are all based on the same underlyling Broker module. Using the initial marking of a socket place for a substitution transition to configure the underlying module instance is an often applied modelling pattern in CPN to parameterise modules. In the following subsections, we go into further details with the modelling of the brokers, transformers and processors.

4.1 Broker Modelling

The three broker substitution transition in Fig. 6 all have the Broker module shown in Fig. 7 as submodule. This means that the CPN model at simulation (run) time will have three *instances* of this module. The Broker port place is used to parameterise the module such that the initial marking of the associated socket place as explained above (see Fig. 6) can be used to specify which broker the module instance is representing. The Broker module instance shown in Fig. 7 corresponds to the core broker as is evident from the token present on the Broker place. The substitution transitions in Fig. 7 represents the main functionality of the broker which is to process publish, subscribe, and unsubscribe requests arriving from the clients via the InMsg and OutMsg port places. The place Subscriptions is used to hold a list-token representing the current set of subscriptions of clients to topics. Initially, there are no subscriptions as specified by initial marking inscription `[]` (empty list) to the upper right of the place.

The colour sets used in the modelling of the broker are provided in Listing 2. The colour set `Topic` lists the currently available topic on the platform. For each of the five data sources (virtual, wsense 1 and 2, and aadi north and south), there are three topics: one topic for the data ingested by the data source on the ingestion broker in the provider specific data format, one for the raw data transformed into the data platform JSON format by the transformers, and one for the data that has been quality checked (qcd) by the processors. The subscriptions are modelleded via the colour sets in lines 8–10. Subscription to a topic is represented by a product comprised of the `Topic` and the list of `Components` subscribing to the topic, and all current `Subscriptions` are then represented as a list of subscriptions to the individual topics and is the colour set of the place Subscriptions in Fig. 7. In the marking shown in Fig. 7 it can be seen that the single token present on place Subscriptions contains two subscriptions by processors to the `wsensenode2_raw` and `aadinorth_raw` topics.

```
1  colset Topic = with
2      virtualnode1  | virtualnode1_raw  | virtualnode1_qcd
3    | wsensenode1   | wsensenode1_raw   | wsensenode1_qcd
4    | wsensenode2   | wsensenode2_raw   | wsensenode2_qcd
5    | aadisouth     | aadisouth_raw     | aadisouth_qcd
6    | aadinorth     | aadinorth_raw     | aadinorth_qcd;
7
8  colset Components = list Component;
9  colset TopicxComponents = product Topic * Components;
10 colset Subscriptions    = list TopicxComponents;
```

Listing 2. Colour set definitions used in the modelling of brokers

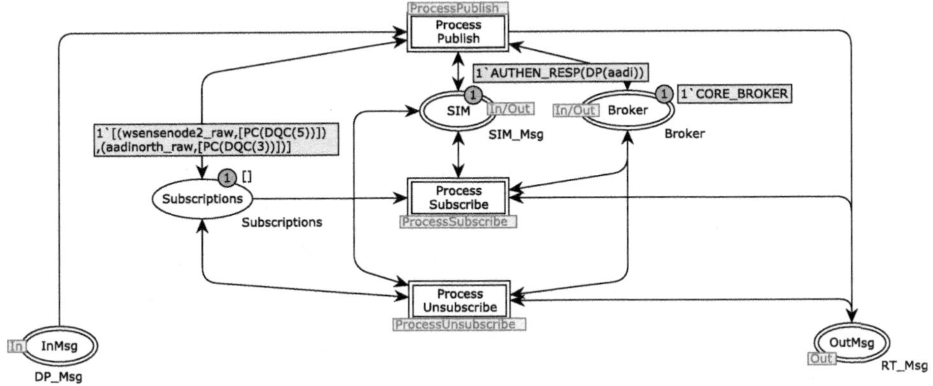

Fig. 7. The Broker module - module instances are used for modelling brokers

Figures 8, 9, 10 shows the submodules of the ProcessPublish, ProcessSubscribe, and ProcessUnsubscribe, respectively. The modules all follow the same modelling pattern with the broker in question initially being idle represented by a token on place BrokerIdle place. When idle, the broker may receive a request to publish on a topic (Fig. 8), subscribe to a topic (Fig. 9), or unsubscribe from a topic (Fig. 10). It then enters an authorization step in order to check whether the requesting client is authorized to perform the operation in question. Once the autherization step has been completed, the broker may Publish (Fig. 8) the received messages to the subscribing clients, Subscribe (Fig. 9) the client to the topic in question, or Unsubscribe (Fig. 9) the client from the topic in question. Once this has been completed, the broker will return to the idle state and is ready to process the next request.

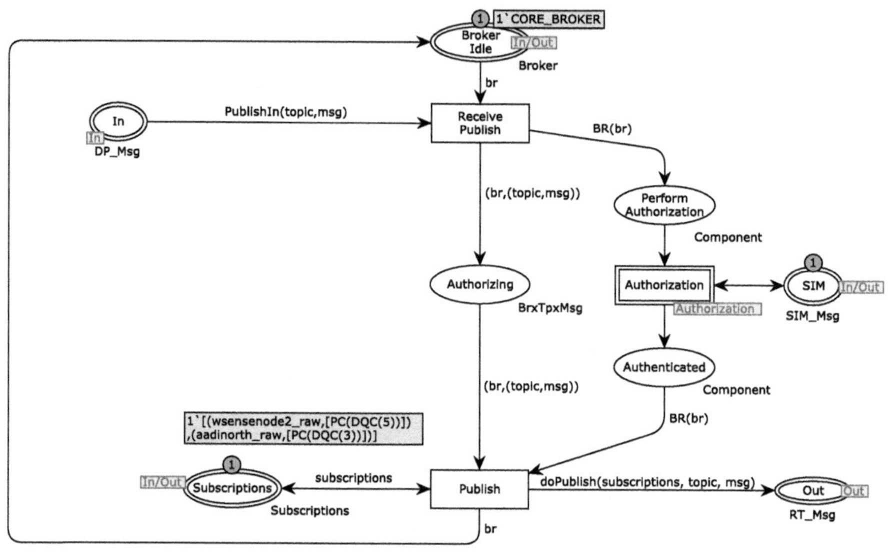

Fig. 8. The ProcessPublish module - publishing of incoming data on topics

The declaration of the colour sets and variables used in Figs. 8, 9, 10 are provided in Listing 3, and the definition of the functions are provided in Listing 4.

```
colset TopicxMsg = product Topic * Message;
colset BrxTpxMsg = product Broker * TopicxMsg;

colset BrxCxTopic = product Broker * Component * Topic;

var topic : Topic;
var msg : Message;
var br: Broker;
var subscr : Component;

var subscriptions : Subscriptions;
```

Listing 3. Colour sets and variables used in the modelling of brokers

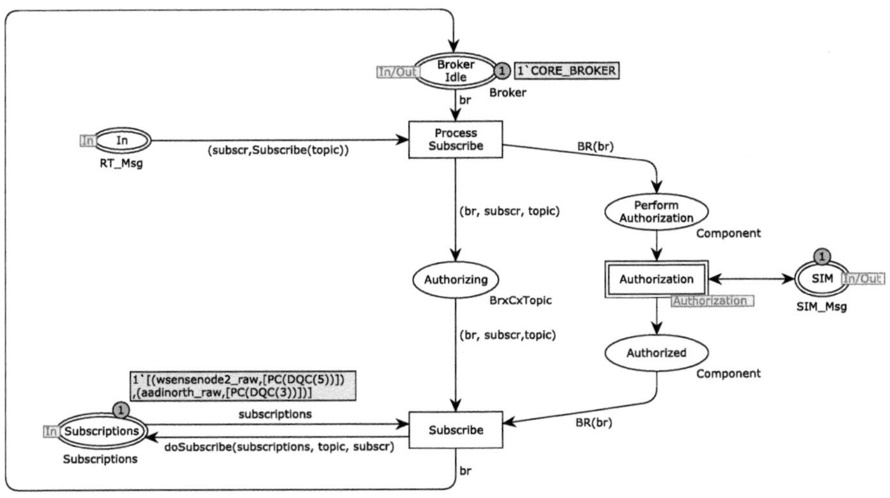

Fig. 9. The ProcessSubscribe module - subscribing clients to topics

The function `doPublish` used as part of the Publish transition in Fig. 8 is used to generate messages to the clients that are subscribing to the topic being published to. The function `doSubscribe` is used as part of the Subscribe transition in Fig. 9 to update the list of the subscription such that the requesting client is becoming subscribed to the topic in question. The function `doUnsubscribe` is

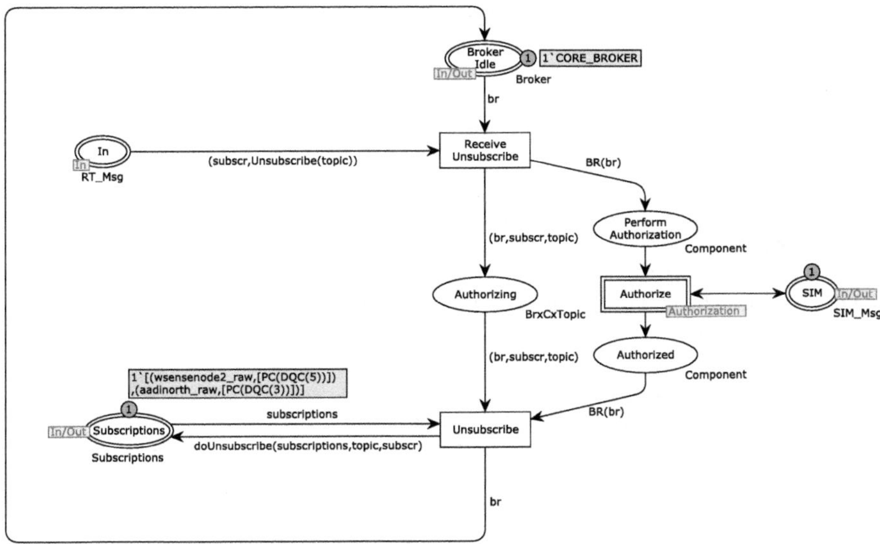

Fig. 10. The ProcessUnsubscribe module - unsubscribing clients from topics

used as part of the Unsubscribe transition in Fig. 10 to update the list of the subscription such that the requesting client is being removed from the list of components subscribing to the client in question.

```
fun doPublish (subs : Subscriptions, topic : Topic, msg) =
    let
        val consumers =
            case (List.find (fn (t,_) => t = topic)) subs of
                NONE => []
              | SOME (_,subscribers) =>
                    List.map
                        (fn dc => (dc,PublishOut(topic,msg)))
                    subscribers
    in
        consumers
    end;

fun doSubscribe (subs, topic, dc) =
    let
        val topic_exists =
                List.exists (fn (t,_) => t = topic) subs
    in
        if topic_exists
            then List.map
                (fn (t,subscriptions) =>
                    if (t = topic) andalso
                        not (List.exists
                                (fn dc' => dc = dc')
                            subscriptions)
                    then (t,dc::subscriptions)
                else (t,subscriptions))
                subs
            else
                (topic,[dc])::subs
    end

fun doUnsubscribe (subs, topic, dc) =
    List.map
        (fn (t,subscriptions) =>
            if (t = topic)
            then (t,List.filter
                    (fn dc' => dc <> dc')
                    subscriptions)
            else (t,subscriptions))
    subs
```

Listing 4. Functions used in the modelling of brokers

The functions are typical examples of functions in SML using higher-order function such as `List.map`, `List.exists`, and `List.find` used to update and manipulate lists.

4.2 Transformers and Processors

The transformers and processors constitute *connectors* in the broker pipeline and receive published data on topics corresponding to incoming data streams and republishes the transformed and processed data on topics corresponding to outgoing data streams. Figures 11 and 12 shows the modelling of the transformers and processors and are the submodules of the Transform and Process substitution transitions in Fig. 6, respectively. Both modules follow a similar modelling pattern, where interaction with the incoming broker is modelled via the InB place and where the interaction with the outgoing broker is modelled via the OutB place. The transformers and processors may Subscribe and Unsubscribe to topics on incoming brokers to receive. The configured transformers, processors and the data streams topics that they are connecting are modelled via the Transformers and Processors places. When data is being published on the topic of an incoming data stream, it will be transformed and processed, respectively, and then re-published on the corresponding outgoing data streams topic.

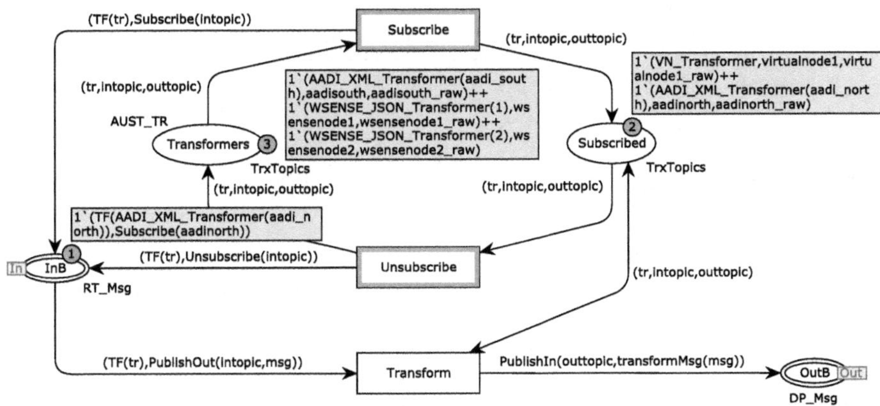

Fig. 11. The Transformers module - connecting the ingestion and core brokers

The colour set definitions and variable declaration used in Figs. 11 and 12 are shown in Listing 5. It is important to note that the messaging service provides a highly flexible scheme and can be used to implement many different data processing pipelines. As an example, subscribers may process and transform the data and republish it again (possibly on other topics) or a subscriber may store the data in the data space service by acting both as a data consumer and data provider.

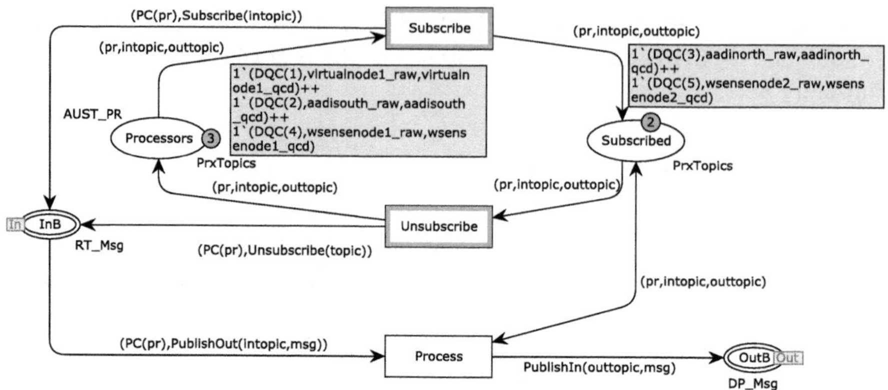

Fig. 12. The Processors module - connecting the core and egress brokers

```
var pr : Processor;
var tr : Transformer;

var intopic,outtopic : Topic;
var msg : Message;

colset TrxTopics = product Transformer * Topic * Topic;
colset PrxTopics = product Processor * Topic * Topic;
```

Listing 5. Colour sets and variables used in the modelling of connectors

5 Data Space Service

The data space service serves as storage service for time series data based upon the data streams from the real-time messaging service. Figure 13 shows the modelling of the data space service. The data space service is comprised of two main parts represented by the two substitution transitions:

Realtime Data Collection which is client component that subscribes to data streams (topics) from the real-time messaging service and stores the corresponding data in the TimeSeriesDatabase.

TimeSeriesAPI which is a server component providing a REST API that can be used by data consumer clients to access the time series data collections stored in the TimeSeriesDatabase.

Data messages are being published on the RTDS port place while the time series API can be accessed via the TSDS port place. The time series REST API service access the platform security and identity management services via the SIM port place in order to authorize the data space service requests. In the marking shown in Fig. 13 there is an incoming data request from a data consumer to access data from the `WSENSE2_TS` time series.

Listing 6 shows the SML declarations used in the modelling of the data space service. It should be noted that the CPN model abstracts from the concrete data being stored and hence only contains the names of the time series data collections as tokens on the TimeSeriesDatabase place as can be seen in Fig. 13.

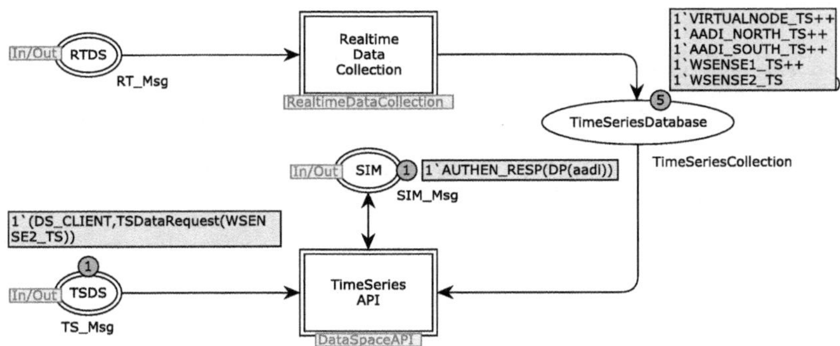

Fig. 13. The Data Space Service module - storing real-time data streams in time series collection and providing client access to historial data via an API

```
colset TimeSeriesCollection =
       with VIRTUALNODE_TS | AADI_NORTH_TS | AADI_SOUTH_TS
          | WSENSE1_TS     | WSENSE2_TS;

var tsc : TimeSeriesCollection;

colset TopicxCollection =
       product Topic * TimeSeriesCollection;
```

Listing 6. Declarations used in the data space service modelling

Figure 14 shows the submodule of the RealtimeDataCollection substitution transition in Fig. 13. The module represents a collector client that can subscribe (and unsubscribe) to the topics in the real-time messaging service according to the initial marking of the Collector place. When Subscribed to a given topic, the client will receive data being published on the topic and Persist the data into the associated time series data collection.

Figure 15 shows the submodule of the DataSpaceAPI substitution transition in Fig. 13. The API is initially in an Idle state where it may ReceiveRequest for processing via the TSDC port place. Before serving a request, the API performs an authorization step in order to check that the requesting client is authorized to perform the operation. Upon successful authorization, the API accesses the TimeSeriesDataBase in order to process the request and send back a response.

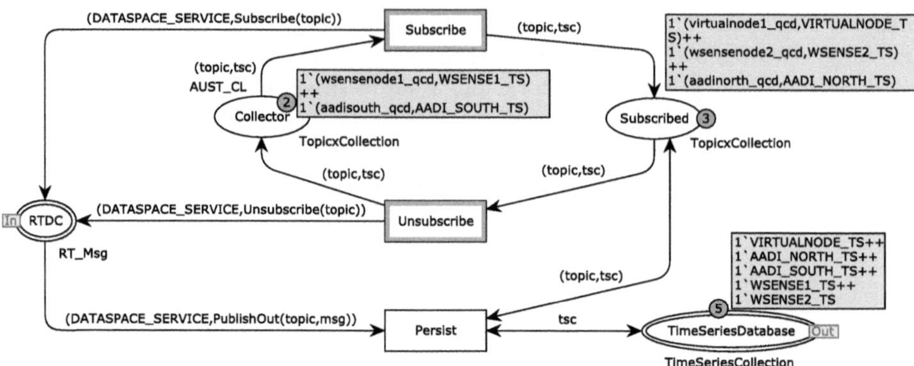

Fig. 14. The RealtimeDataColletion module - subscribing to real-time data streams for storage in time series collections

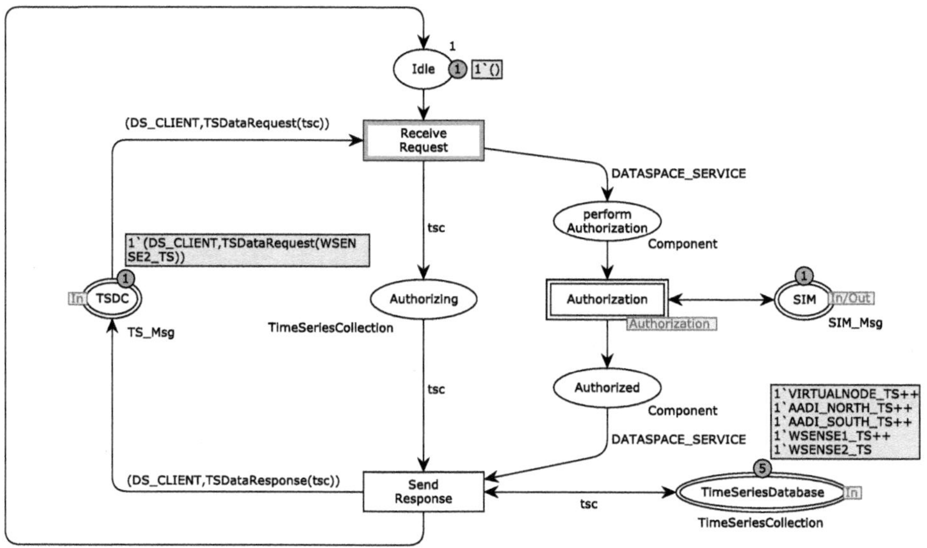

Fig. 15. The DataSpaceAPI module - providing access to historial data stored in time series collections

6 Data Providers and Consumers

The clients of the platform can be categorized into data providers and data consumers as is also evident from the system-level perspective represented in Fig. 4. Clients are providing data into the system by publishing it to the real-ingestion messaging service previously presented in Fig. 6. The primary purpose of the data providers is to support the delivery of data from the underwater wireless sensor networks (UWSNs) into the data services of the platform. Hence, it facilitates the transfer of data from the information acquisition layer into the data and application service layer (see Fig. 1). The integration point is needed since the UWSNs operate with highly specialised communication protocols intended for acoustic communication and the data will have to be provided to the cloud via a gateway service, e.g., 5G, WiFi, cabling or satellite communication.

The data providers are modelled by the DataProvider module shown in Fig. 16, which is the submodule of the DataProvider substitution transition in Fig. 4. The initial marking of place Idle (`DataProvider.all()`) specifies all possible data providers, and has been set up according to the current deployment of the platform.

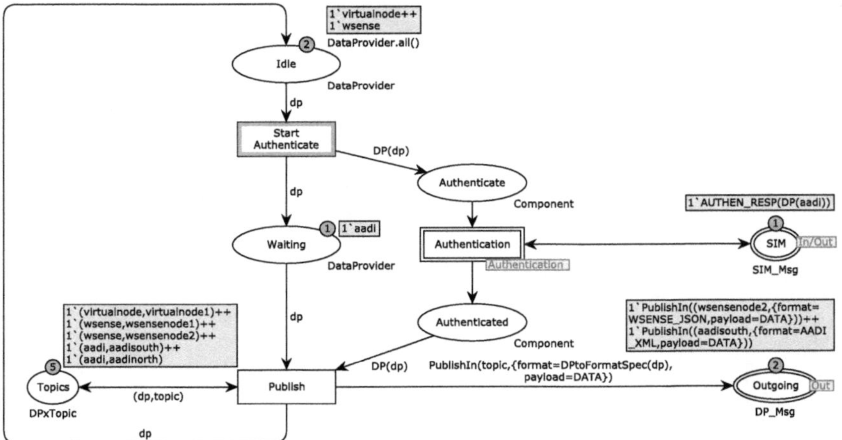

Fig. 16. The DataProvider module - modelling how clients provide data to the platform via the messaging service

Considering Fig. 16, the first step to provide data is for the data providing client to authenticate with the platform security service which is done via the StartAuthenticate transition which causes the data-providing client to enter a Waiting state until the authentication has been completed. In addition, a token representing the authenticating client is put on place Authenticate in order to trigger the actual authentication. The client-side of the authentication is modelled via the Authentication substitution transition which interacts with the platform server side of the authentication via the SIM port place. Once the client has been Authenticated, the client can publish data to the platform. The topics on which a given client may publish is configured by the initial marking of the Topics place. For each of the configured data providers, it specifies which topics the data provider will publish to.

Figure 17 shows the modelling of the data consumers, which is the submodule of the DataConsumer substitution transition in Fig. 4. There are two types of clients depending on whether they consume data from the real-time messaging service as represented by the RealtimeMessagingClient connected to the RTDS

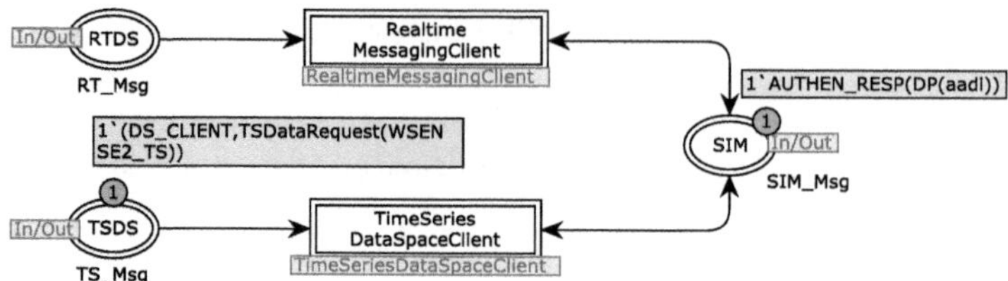

Fig. 17. The Data Consumer module - modelling how data consumers may consume real-time data via the messaging service and historical time series data via the data space service

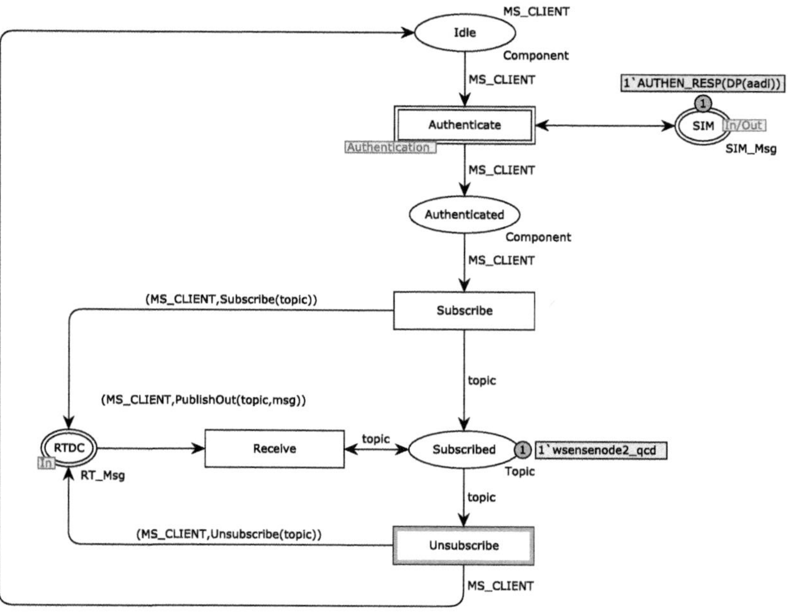

Fig. 18. The RealtimeMessagingClient module - modelling how clients may subscribe to the messaging service and receive real-time data

port place, or from the time services data space service as represented by the TimeSeriesDataSpaceClient substitution transition connected to the TSDS port place. Both types need to access the platform security and identity management services in order to perform authentication.

Figure 18 shows the module modelling the real-time messaging client. The client is initially in an Idle state and may then enter an Authenticate step, which, when completed, allows the client to subscribe to topics on the messaging service. Once subscribed, data can be received from the real-time data service. The client may also unsubscribe, after which it will return to the initial state. Figure 19 shows the module modelling the client for the data space service. The first step in retrieving historical time series data is to perform authentication. Upon com-

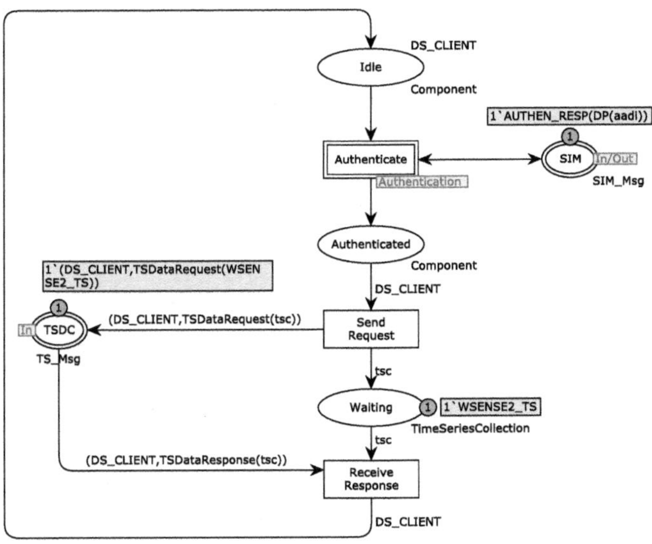

Fig. 19. The TimeSeriesDataSpaceClient module - modelling how client may send requests and receive historical time series data

pleting authentication, the client can send a request to the data space service and await a response.

7 Security and Identity Management Service

A central infrastructure service of the platform is the security and identity management service. All data provider and data consumer clients that are to use the data services of the platform will have to perform authentication for establishing their identity prior to accessing the services. The platform performs authorization of service requests in order to determine whether the client performing the request has the required privileges to use the service requested.

7.1 Server-Side Modelling

Figure 20 shows the submodule modelling the security service which is the submodule of the Security Service substitution transition in Fig. 5. The service is initially in an idle state as specified by the initial marking 1 to the upper right of the Idle place. Incoming requests for authentication and authorization are being represented as tokens on the SIM place using the `SIM_Msg` colour set previously defined in Listing 1. Occurrence of the ReceiveRequest transition will change the state of the service from Idle to Processing and place the individual requests as tokens on the Processing. Once the request has been processed, the SendResponse transition may occur, producing a response token on the SIM place signalling to the requesting client component that processing has completed. In the marking

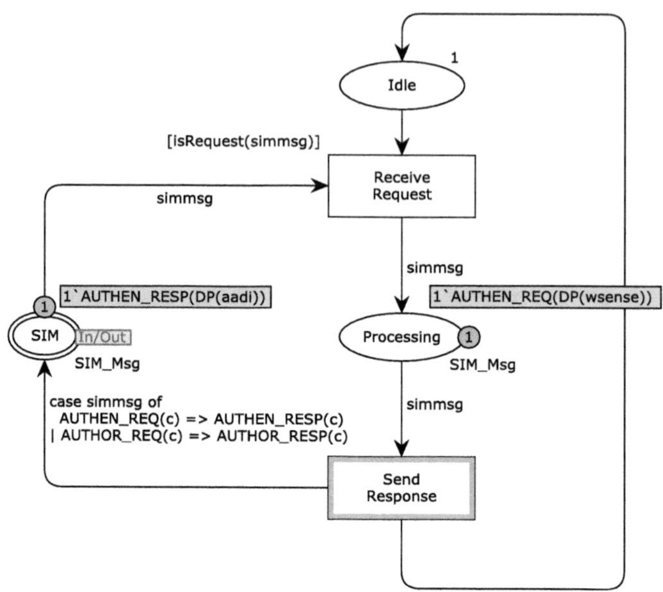

Fig. 20. The SecurityIdentityManagement module - processing authentication and authortization requests

shown in Fig. 20, there is an incoming authentication request from the wsense data provider which is being processed, and there is an outgoing authentication response to the aadi data provider client.

In line with our primary modelling focus being on service interaction, we have abstracted from the concrete outcome of the authentication and authorization process, and we have also abstracted from the concrete values of the security tokens used for authorization.

7.2 Client-Side Modelling

On the client side, the Authentication and Authorization modules shown in Fig. 21 (left) and Fig. 21(right), respectively, are being used to model the interaction with the security and identity management services. Clients that are to perform authentication will use the Authentication module, as for instance shown earlier in Fig. 16 for the data providers, where the Authentication module is the submodule of the Authentication substitution transition. Services that are to perform authorization uses the Authorization module, as for instance shown earlier in Fig. 15 for the data space service, where the Authorization module is the submodule of the Authorization substitution transition. In particular, this means that we have multiple instances of these modules when performing simulation of the CPN model.

Considering authentication (Fig. 21 (left)), then a client that is to perform authentication will place a token on the Authenticate place. A request will be

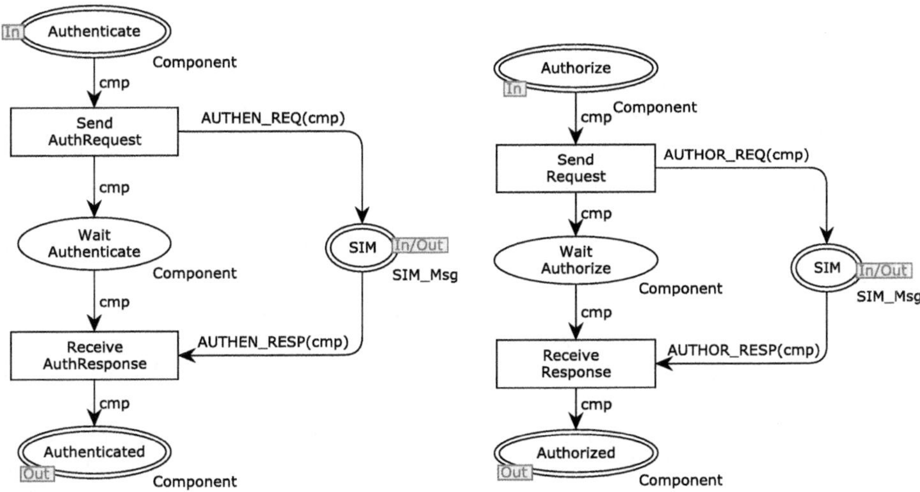

Fig. 21. The Authentication module (left) and Authorization module (right) - modelling client side authentication and authorization

sent to the service via an occurrence of the SendAuthRequest transition, which produces a `AUTHEN_REQ`-token on the SIM place. The client will then enter a Waiting state until the security service has processed the request (see Fig. 20) and send back a response as an `AUTHEN_RESP`-token in the SIM-place. The modelling of the client-side authorization as shown in (Fig. 21 (right)) is similar except that `AUTHOR_REQ`- and `AUTHOR_RESP`-tokens are being used in the interaction with the security service.

8 Platform Implementation and Deployment

The implementation of the platform and the CPN models has been developed in conjunction and in an iterative process. The CPN model has served as an important artifact to consolidate the SmartOcean platform software architecture and the service interactions. In addition, it has enabled discussions with stakeholders of the design and inception of the platform in an abstract and implementation independent manner. During the development process, the CPN model has at times been ahead of the implementation and at other times behind the actual implementation. This also reflects that at times there has been a need to undertake implementation experiments in order to determine the feasibility of particular software technologies and frameworks that have been used to implement the platform.

The resulting implementation of the SmartOcean platform is available via [41], including software development kits for consuming the data services provided by the platform. The data providers and consumers have been implemented as Python applications relying on the PahoMQTT library [33] to interact with the messaging service and the Fast API framework [9] for implementing the data space service REST API. The messaging brokers have been realised using the HiveMQ implementation of MQTT [13]. The implementation of the security and identity management services relies on Keycloak [17] in combination with JWT-tokens, to provide the authentication and authorization service. The transformers and processors connecting the brokers have been implemented as Python applications.

The platform has been deployed and validated in a configuration in accordance with the Austevoll Pilot Demonstrator of the Institute of Marine Research Facility as described in the introduction of this paper. This includes sensors and sensor hubs deployed underwater from Aanderaa Data Instruments and W-sense. The sensors measure a number of parameters at different water depths, including oxygen, pressure, salinity, and temperature. The sensors deliver data to the SmartOcean platform via underwater acoustic communication, 4G modems, and software component deployed on the sensor vendor's private and public cloud solutions. Considering Fig. 6 and Fig. 13, the SmartOcean platform itself uses the HiveMQ cloud service for cloud deployment of the messaging service brokers. The transformers and processors are deployed on virtual machines in the Microsoft Azure cloud platform, while the data space service REST API is deployed in a container on the Azure platform. The time series data collections are realised via the MongoDB Atlas cloud service [27] and time series collections using NoSQL database technology.

9 Conclusions and Future Work

We have presented a CPN model of the smart ocean data and application platform based on our recent work on identifying challenges and requirements for marine data services. The presented CPN model focused on service interaction, and as a consequence we have applied a high-level of abstraction in the modelling. A main reason for this is that our main purpose has been to make explicit the services that constitute the platform and the systems that can interact with the services. The integrated modelling approach presented in this paper has many similarities with the CPN modelling of a fire risk notification system presented in [44] which was also concerned with software architecture and services. Both used an approach where modelling was integrated with the implementation of the actual system in an iterative process. Furthermore, we have used the same modelling pattern for identifying components and for creating a parameterized CPN model. On the other hand, the modelling presented in [44] has a detailed modelling of the service endpoints in the form of REST APIs, whereas we model the service interaction at a higher level of abstraction considering messages.

The presented CPN model is based upon a series of workshops involving consortium stakeholders from both industry and research. The aim of these workshop was to define the components that constitute the platform and these have now been specified in the form of a CPN model. In particular, it has been beneficial to evolve the CPN model alongside the implementation work using an iterative methodology similar to what was that proposed in [44]. In this way, we have been able to obtain a feedback cycle between the CPN model and the platform implementation. This is important in order to integrate the CPN modelling into the development work in an agile manner. The integrated use of the CPN model in the process of designing and implementing the SmartOcean platform has demonstrated the value of formal Petri net modelling and simulation, and that the application of Petri nets in many cases can provide valuable development support even if it does not entail formal verification, e.g., in the form of model checking. We have achieved our long-term goal of using the CPN modelling as a conceptualisation and implementation independent specification of the SmartOcean platform. In particular, the CPN modelling has played a key role in supporting the work leading to an actual implementation and deployment of the platform.

From a more general perspective, the development of the CPN technology has been driven by an application-oriented research agenda based on integrated development of the underlying theory of the modelling language and the analysis method, the supporting tools and software technology, and the practical application of software tools. This has led to both research and industry picking up the CPN technology and applying it, as documenting by numerous research papers in the research literature [2,21,23,43,46,47]. A substantial number of these have also involved verification by means of model checking [3,4,11,22,48] and simulation-based performance analysis [29] exploiting that with CPNs, both verification and performance analysis are possible with the same modelling language. In addition, there are several examples where CPNs have been used as a basis for code generation of implementation artefacts [18,26,38–40,42]. Still, there has been relatively limited development of the CPN modelling language itself and the supporting software tools in recent years. As a consequence, there is a research and development gap currently present in developing more modern tool support for construction, simulation and analysis of CPN models, and also advancing the modelling language itself with features to support more efficient and elegant modelling. This would include separate compilation of CPN modules to support modelling libraries, scoped naming, local module declarations, module parameterization, and an extended set of place and transition types.

Acknowledgments. The work presented in this paper was supported by SFI Smart Ocean NFR Project 309612/F40.

References

1. Aanderaa Data Instruments AS (2024). https://www.aanderaa.com/
2. Arnold, S., Billington, J.: An initial coloured petri net model of the hypertext transfer protocol operating over the transmission control protocol. Trans. Petri Nets Other Model. Concurr. **6**, 226–250 (2012). https://doi.org/10.1007/978-3-642-35179-2_10
3. Rodríguez, A., Kristensen, L.M., Rutle, A.: Formal modelling and incremental verification of the MQTT IoT protocol. Trans. Petri Nets Other Model. Concurr. **14**, 126–145 (2019). https://doi.org/10.1007/978-3-662-60651-3_5
4. Rodríguez, A., Kristensen, L.M., Rutle, A.: Verification of the MQTT IoT protocol using property-specific CTL sweep-line algorithms. Trans. Petri Nets Other Model. Concurr. **15**, 165–183 (2021). https://doi.org/10.1007/978-3-662-63079-2_8
5. Chang, W.L., von Laszewski, G.: NIST big data interoperability framework: reference architecture interfaces (2019). https://doi.org/10.6028/NIST.SP.1500-9
6. CPN IDE (2024). https://cpnide.org/
7. Enlighten Web (2023). https://www.norceresearch.no/forskningstema/enlighten-web. Accessed 30 Mar 2023
8. Eugster, P.T., Felber, P.A., Guerraoui, R., Kermarrec, A.: The many faces of publish/subscribe. ACM Comput. Surv. **35**(2), 114–131 (2003). https://doi.org/10.1145/857076.857078
9. FastAPI framework (2024). https://fastapi.tiangolo.com/
10. Fielding, R.T.: Architectural styles and the design of network-based software architectures. Publication, University of California, Irvine (2000). https://www.ics.uci.edu/~fielding/pubs/dissertation/top.htm
11. Gkolfi, A., Johnsen, E.B., Kristensen, L.M., Yu, I.C.: Model checking starvation for resource-aware active objects with coloured petri nets. In: Proceedings of the International Workshop on Petri Nets and Software Engineering. CEUR Workshop Proceedings, vol. 2651, pp. 68–85. CEUR-WS.org (2020). https://ceur-ws.org/Vol-2651/paper5.pdf
12. Heldal, R., Kristensen, L.M., Lima, K., Oyetoyan, T.D., Nguyen, N.: Towards a formal and executable software architecture specification of the smart ocean data service platform. In: Proceedings of the 2023 International Workshop on Petri Nets and Software Engineering (PNSE 2023). CEUR Workshop Proceedings, vol. 3430, pp. 110–125. CEUR-WS.org (2023). https://ceur-ws.org/Vol-3430/paper7.pdf
13. HiveMQ MQTT Platform (2024). https://www.hivemq.com/
14. Jensen, K.: Coloured Petri Nets - Basic Concepts, Analysis Methods, and Practical Use, vol. 1-3. Springer (1996-1997)
15. Jensen, K., Kristensen, L.M.: Coloured Petri Nets - Modelling and Validation of Concurrent Systems. Springer (2009). https://doi.org/10.1007/b95112
16. Jensen, K., Kristensen, L.M.: Colored petri nets: a graphical language for formal modeling and validation of concurrent systems. Commun. ACM **58**(6), 61–70 (2015). https://doi.org/10.1145/2663340
17. Open Source Identity and Access Management (2024). https://www.keycloak.org
18. Kristensen, L.M.: An approach for the engineering of protocol software from coloured petri net models: a case study of the IETF websocket protocol. In: Proceedings of the International Workshop on Petri Nets and Software Engineering. CEUR Workshop Proceedings, vol. 1160, pp. 13–14. CEUR-WS.org (2014). https://ceur-ws.org/Vol-1160/paper1.pdf

19. Kristensen, L.M., Christensen, S., Jensen, K.: The practitioner's guide to coloured petri nets. Int. J. Softw. Tools Technol. Transf. **2**(2), 98–132 (1998). https://doi.org/10.1007/S100090050021
20. Kristensen, L.M., Jørgensen, J.B., Jensen, K.: Application of coloured petri nets in system development. In: Desel, J., Reisig, W., Rozenberg, G. (eds.) ACPN 2003. LNCS, vol. 3098, pp. 626–685. Springer, Heidelberg (2004). https://doi.org/10.1007/978-3-540-27755-2_18
21. Kristensen, L.M., Simonsen, K.I.F.: Applications of coloured petri nets for functional validation of protocol designs. Trans. Petri Nets Other Model. Concurr. **7**, 56–115 (2013). https://doi.org/10.1007/978-3-642-38143-0_3
22. Kristensen, L.M., Taentzer, G., Vaupel, S.: Towards verification of connection-aware transaction models for mobile applications. In: Proceedings of the International Workshop on Petri Nets and Software Engineering (PNSE 2017). CEUR Workshop Proceedings, vol. 1846, pp. 227–228. CEUR-WS.org (2017). https://ceur-ws.org/Vol-1846/paper15.pdf
23. Kristensen, L.M., Veiset, V.: Transforming CPN models into code for TinyOS: a case study of the RPL protocol. In: Kordon, F., Moldt, D. (eds.) PETRI NETS 2016. LNCS, vol. 9698, pp. 135–154. Springer, Cham (2016). https://doi.org/10.1007/978-3-319-39086-4_10
24. Lima, K., et al.: Marine data sharing: challenges, technology drivers and quality attributes. In: Product-Focused Software Process Improvement - 23rd International Conference, PROFES 2022. Lecture Notes in Computer Science, vol. 13709, pp. 124–140. Springer, Cham (2022). https://doi.org/10.1007/978-3-031-21388-5_9
25. Lima, K., et al.: A data-flow oriented software architecture for heterogeneous marine data streams. In: 21st IEEE International Conference on Software Architecture, ICSA 2024, Hyderabad, India, 4–8 June 2024, pp. 146–157. IEEE (2024). https://doi.org/10.1109/ICSA59870.2024.00022
26. Mailund, T., Halager, A.E., Westergaard, M.: Using colored petri nets to construct coalescent hidden Markov models: automatic translation from demographic specifications to efficient inference methods. In: Haddad, S., Pomello, L. (eds.) PETRI NETS 2012. LNCS, vol. 7347, pp. 32–50. Springer, Heidelberg (2012). https://doi.org/10.1007/978-3-642-31131-4_3
27. MongoDB Atlas Cloud Database (2024). https://www.mongodb.com/
28. Message Queue Telemetry Transport Protocol (MQTT) Specification (2019). https://mqtt.org/mqtt-specification/
29. Ndiaye, M., Pétin, J., Georges, J., Camerini, J.: Practical use of coloured petri nets for the design and performance assessment of distributed automation architectures. In: Proceedings of the International Workshop on Petri Nets and Software Engineering 2016. CEUR Workshop Proceedings, vol. 1591, pp. 113–131. CEUR-WS.org (2016). https://ceur-ws.org/Vol-1591/paper10.pdf
30. Nguyen, N.T., et al.: Engineering challenges of stationary wireless smart ocean observation systems. IEEE Internet Things J. **10**(16), 14712–14724 (2023). https://doi.org/10.1109/JIOT.2023.3283252
31. Norwegian Marine Data Centre (2023). https://www.nmdc.no/nmdc. Accessed 30 Mar 2023
32. The ocean economy in 2030. OECD Publishing (2016)
33. PahoMQTT library implementation (2024). https://eclipse.dev/paho/
34. Raggett, D.: The web of things: challenges and opportunities. Computer **48**(5), 26–32 (2015)

35. Ratzer, A.V., et al.: CPN tools for editing, simulating, and analysing coloured petri nets. In: van der Aalst, W.M.P., Best, E. (eds.) ICATPN 2003. LNCS, vol. 2679, pp. 450–462. Springer, Heidelberg (2003). https://doi.org/10.1007/3-540-44919-1_28
36. Reisig, W.: Understanding Petri Nets - Modeling Techniques, Analysis Methods, Case Studies. Springer (2013). https://doi.org/10.1007/978-3-642-33278-4
37. SFI Smart Ocean (2024). https://sfismartocean.no/. Accessed 30 Aug 2024
38. Simonsen, K.I.F.: An evaluation of automated code generation with the petricode approach. In: Proceedings of the International Workshop on Petri Nets and Software Engineering. CEUR Workshop Proceedings, vol. 1160, pp. 289–306. CEUR-WS.org (2014). https://ceur-ws.org/Vol-1160/paper17.pdf
39. Simonsen, K.I.F., Kristensen, L.M., Kindler, E.: Pragmatics annotated coloured petri nets for protocol software generation and verification. In: Proceedings of the International Workshop on Petri Nets and Software Engineering (PNSE'15). CEUR Workshop Proceedings, vol. 1372, pp. 79–98. CEUR-WS.org (2015). https://ceur-ws.org/Vol-1372/paper5.pdf
40. Simonsen, K.I.F., Kristensen, L.M., Kindler, E.: Pragmatics annotated coloured petri nets for protocol software generation and verification. Trans. Petri Nets Other Model. Concurr. **11**, 1–27 (2016). https://doi.org/10.1007/978-3-662-53401-4_1
41. SmartOcean Data Service Platform (2024). https://smartoceanplatform.github.io/
42. Somappa, A.A.K., Simonsen, K.I.F.: Model-based development for MAC protocols in industrial wireless sensor networks. In: Proceedings of the International Workshop on Petri Nets and Software Engineering 2016. CEUR Workshop Proceedings, vol. 1591, pp. 193–212. CEUR-WS.org (2016). https://ceur-ws.org/Vol-1591/paper14.pdf
43. Steinsland, V., Kristensen, L.M., Zhang, S.: Towards the application of coloured petri nets for design and validation of power electronics converter systems. In: Application and Theory of Petri Nets and Concurrency - 43rd International Conference, PETRI NETS 2022, Bergen, Norway, 19–24 June 2022, Proceedings. Lecture Notes in Computer Science, vol. 13288, pp. 3–22. Springer (2022). https://doi.org/10.1007/978-3-031-06653-5_1
44. Strand, R.D., Kristensen, L.M., Petrucci, L.: Formal specification and validation of a data-driven software system for fire risk prediction. In: Petri Nets and Software Engineering 2022. CEUR Workshop Proceedings, vol. 3170, pp. 1–20. CEUR-WS.org (2022). https://ceur-ws.org/Vol-3170/paper1.pdf
45. Ullman, J.D.: Elements of ML Programming. Pearson (1998)
46. Vanit-Anunchai, S.: Validating DCCP simultaneous feature negotiation procedure. Trans. Petri Nets Other Model. Concurr. **11**, 71–91 (2016). https://doi.org/10.1007/978-3-662-53401-4_4
47. Wang, R., Kristensen, L.M., Meling, H., Stolz, V.: Model-based testing of the gorums framework for fault-tolerant distributed systems. Trans. Petri Nets Other Model. Concurr. **13**, 158–180 (2018). https://doi.org/10.1007/978-3-662-58381-4_8
48. Westergaard, M.: Verifying parallel algorithms and programs using coloured petri nets. Trans. Petri Nets Other Model. Concurr. **6**, 146–168 (2012). https://doi.org/10.1007/978-3-642-35179-2_7
49. W-sense (2024). https://wsense.it/

A Gentle Tour Through A Petri Net Model Checking Tool

Karsten Wolf(✉)

Universität Rostock, Universitätsplatz 1, 18051 Rostock, Germany
karsten.wolf@uni-rostock.de

Abstract. Given a model of the system (in our case a Petri net) and a specification (a formula of some temporal logic), a model checking tool tries to find out whether the model satisfies the specification. A model checking tool for Petri nets may look different from a general-purpose model checker. Most differences are related to the fact that Petri nets offer a strong theory that can be used to replace or to enhance general model checking approaches.

In this paper, we survey the main ingredients of a Petri net model checking tool. For each topic, we present a selection of methods with emphasis on simplicity. In addition, we provide references to papers that study the respective topic in more depth. This paper provides a comprehensive overview on what tool developers should take care of when designing their own competitive Petri net model checking tool.

1 Introduction

The general purpose of a model checking tool is easily explained (Fig. 1). Take a system model as one input and a specification as a second input. The task is to find out whether or not the specification is valid for the model. If possible, provide additional information to support the answer (e.g. a witness or counterexample trace). The simplest way to solve that problem is to generate the state space of the system model using some search strategy such as depth-first search. As we shall see, the evaluation of the specification does also amount to depth-first search in the state space. In many cases, the search for constructing the state space and the search for evaluating the specification may be one and the same. In this case, we call our approach *on-the-fly* verification. Using on-the-fly verification, we may occasionally be able to answer the problem before all reachable states of the state space have been explored. Consequently, we may sometimes solve problems where the whole state space does not even fit into memory.

Depth-first search is an extremely efficient algorithm. It is so efficient that, according to our own profiling, about 40% of the run time is spent waiting for the run-time environment to give us fresh memory [81]. This brings us to the catch of the model checking problem. While there is virtually no room to improve upon run time, model checking is extremely memory-consuming. Realistic systems have an astronomic number of states. We refer to this observation as the *state*

F. Kordon et al. (Eds.): *Transactions on Petri Nets and Other Models of Concurrency XVIII*,
LNCTPN 16260, pp. 309–380, 2026.
https://doi.org/10.1007/978-3-662-73305-9_11

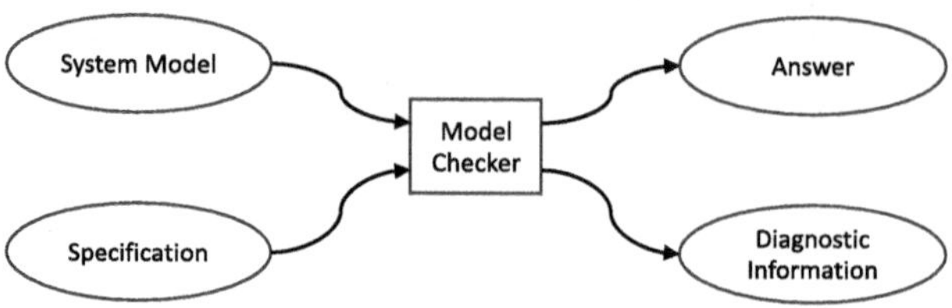

Fig. 1. The interface of a model checking tool.

explosion problem. It is the state explosion that turns a problem that seems to be simple at first glance, into a challenging area of research. For building a competitive model checking tool, we need to fight state explosion wherever we can.

Petri nets have been introduced in the early 1960s. Since then, an impressive amount of theoretical results on Petri nets has been piled up. Several results emerged in the 1970s. At this time, it was still unknown whether the reachability problem and other basic decision problem are decidable (they have been proven to be decidable in the mid 1980s [65,79]). The model checking problem has also been studied since the early 1980s [21–23,93,94]. Most fundamental approaches to model checking work for all kinds of system models. As soon as there is a notion of state space, and that state space happens to be finite, model checking algorithms can be applied. Differences between application domains and modeling formalisms such as composed transition systems, process algebra [55,83], state charts [54], programming languages, or (as in our case) Petri nets emerge when it comes to fighting state explosion. In the case of Petri nets, their unique theory turns out to be a strong ally in that endeavor. This paper actually aims to demonstrate the value of integrating Petri net theory into model checking. This way, we establish Petri net model checking as a distinguished sub-discipline of model checking.

We start our tour with inspecting our first input, the Petri net (Sect. 2). We introduce the core terminology. We then discuss three approaches to simplify the given Petri net: abstraction, reduction, and modularization. That is, we start our fight against state explosion already with our inputs. In Sect. 3, we inspect our second input, temporal logic. We continue our fight against state explosion using three methods to simplify temporal logic formulas: static analysis, tautologies, and strength reduction. The remaining sections are devoted to solving the model checking problem. We start with the basic technology for producing a state space (Sect. 4) and continue with simple explicit model checking procedures (Sect. 5). In Sect. 6, we discuss various methods to reduce the number of states that need to be explored. Finally, in Sect. 7, we briefly mention approaches to model checking that rely on data structures different from the state space.

2 Petri Nets

We introduce the basic terminology for Petri nets (Sect. 2.1). Then we discuss three approaches that we can use to simplify the net: net abstraction (Sect. 2.2), net reduction (Sect. 2.3), and modularization (Sect. 2.4). With the help of simplification, we can reduce the complexity of subsequent verification.

2.1 Basic Terminology

Most results in this paper shall be presented for place/transition Petri nets. In place/transition nets, the token game is played with indistinguishable black tokens. Let $\mathbb{N}$ denote the set of natural numbers including 0, and $\mathbb{Z}$ be the set of integer numbers.

Definition 1 (Place/transition net). *A* place/transition net *consists of a finite set P of* places, *a finite set T of transitions, disjoint to P, a set $F \subseteq (P \times T) \cup (T \times P)$ of* arcs, *a* weight function $W : (P \times T) \cup (T \times P) \to \mathbb{N}$ *such that $W(f) = 0$ if and only if $f \notin F$, and m_0 be a marking, the* initial marking. *A* marking *is a mapping $m : P \to \mathbb{N}$.*

Places and transitions are collectively called the *nodes* of the Petri net. For a node x, $\bullet x$ is its *pre-set*, i.e. $\bullet x = \{y \mid [y, x] \in F\}$. Correspondingly, the post-set $x\bullet$ of a node x is $x\bullet = \{y \mid [x, y] \in F\}$.

For a marking m, $m(p)$ represents the number of tokens on place p. Transitions model the dynamics of the system. Firing a transition, we consume tokens from the pre-places and produce tokens on the post-places. The number of tokens to be consumed or produced is given by the weight function. A transition can only fire if at least the number of tokens to be consumed are present in the pre-places. There is no obligation to fire even if that condition is satisfied.

Definition 2 (Behavior of a place/transition net). *Transition t is* enabled *in marking m if, for all places p, $p \in \bullet t$ implies $m(p) \geq W([p, t])$. If t is enabled in m, t may fire, resulting in marking m' ($m \xrightarrow{t} m'$) where, for all places p, $m'(p) = m(p) - W([p, t]) + W([t, p])$.*

A Petri net may have markings where no transition at all is enabled. Such a marking is called *deadlock*.

Using induction, we may extend the firing relation to sequences of transition. For the empty sequence ε, let $m \xrightarrow{\varepsilon} m$, for all markings m. If, for a transition sequence w and transition t, we have $m_1 \xrightarrow{w} m_2$ and $m_2 \xrightarrow{t} m_3$, then $m_1 \xrightarrow{wt} m_3$. We write $m \xrightarrow{*} m'$ if there exists a transition sequence w where $m \xrightarrow{w} m'$ and $m \to m'$ if there is a single transition t where $m \xrightarrow{t} m'$.

For a Petri net, its reachability graph represents the state space.

Definition 3 (Reachability graph). *The* reachability graph R_N *of a Petri net $N = [P, T, F, W, m_0]$ is a directed graph with labeled edges where the set*

$\{m \mid m_0 \xrightarrow{*} m\}$ of markings reachable from the initial marking forms the set of vertices while an edge $[m, t, m']$ from vertex m to vertex m' with label t is drawn whenever $m \xrightarrow{t} m'$.

A reachability graph of a place/transition net may be finite or infinite. Throughout this paper, we consider only nets with a finite reachability graph. Such nets are called *bounded* since every place has a finite bound, i.e. a maximum number of tokens on it. For bounded nets, the reachability graph is at least in principle a valid data structure for model checking algorithms. For unbounded nets, we just refer to the *coverability graph* [36,64,114], a finite abstraction for the reachability graph. A coverability graph even permits model checking in a limited way [97].

2.2 Net Abstraction

Applying abstraction, we transform a Petri net into a simpler one that represents a coarser view on the behavior of the given net. We are going to present just one particular approach to abstraction that is inspired by high-level Petri nets [46,59,120]. A high-level net can be associated with two place/transition nets: its *unfolding*[1] and its *skeleton*. The skeleton is in fact an abstraction of the unfolding. It is possible to transform a place/transition net N into an abstracted net S that, for some high-level net C, N is the unfolding and S is the skeleton of C.

In this paper, high-level nets are just a vehicle to guide abstraction, so we choose a most simple definition. The general idea of a high-level net is that every token on place p carries a value from a place-specific domain and every transition can fire in different firing modes. The inscriptions of arcs tell, for each firing mode, how many tokens with certain values are to be consumed or produced.

Definition 4 (High-Level Net). *A* high-level net *consists of a finite set P_C of places, a finite set T_C of transitions, disjoint to P_C, a set $F_C \subseteq (P_C \times T_C) \cup (T_C \times P_C)$ of arcs, a* domain mapping *χ that assigns a finite set of* colors *to every place, a weight function W_C that assigns a finite set of* variables *to every pair $[x, y] \in (P_C \times T_C) \cup (T_C \times P_C)$ such that $W_C([x, y]) = \emptyset$ if and only if $[x, y] \notin F$, a* guard mapping *γ that maps every transition to a Boolean predicate that operates on the variables $\bigcup_{p \in P}(W_C([p, t]) \cup W_C([t, p]))$ and m_{0C} is the initial marking. A marking of a high-level net is a mapping m where, for all p, $m(p) : \chi(p) \to \mathbb{N}$.*

For a place p, $\chi(p)$ is that set of values that can be carried by tokens on p. For transition t, every assignment α to the variables in $\bigcup_{p \in P_C}(W_C([p, t]) \cup W_C([t, p]))$ that satisfies the predicate $\gamma(t)$ (denoted as $\alpha \models \gamma(t)$) is a firing mode. Firing transition t in a firing mode α, every variable x attached to an arc requires to consume or produce a token with value $\alpha(x)$ from the connected place, depending on the arc direction.

---

[1] The term *unfolding* is also frequently used for the data structure that we shall call *branching prefix* in Sect. 7.3.

We can transform every high-level net into a place/transition net with equivalent behavior, i.e. isomorphic reachability graph. The idea is to have a separate place for every color and a separate transition for every firing mode. Arcs, weights, and initial marking can then be calculated such that the unfolding precisely mimics the behavior of the given high-level net. Unfolding into a place/transition net is the dominating method for model checking high-level nets.

Definition 5 (Unfolding). *Let* $N_C = [P_C, T_C, F_C, \chi, W_C, \gamma, m_{0C}]$ *be a high-level net. The* unfolding *of* N_C *is the place/transition net* $N_U = [P_U, T_U, F_U, W_U, m_{0U}]$ *where*

- $P_U = \bigcup_{p_C \in P_C}(\{p_c\} \times \chi(p))$;
- $T_U = \bigcup_{t_C \in T_C}(\{t_C\} \times \{\alpha \mid \alpha \models \gamma(t)\})$;
- $[(p,c),(t,\alpha)] \in F_U$ *if and only if* $c \in \alpha(W_C([p,t]))$;
- $[(t,\alpha),(p,c)] \in F_U$ *if and only if* $c \in \alpha(W_C([t,p]))$;
- $W_U([(p,c),(t,\alpha)]) = card\{x \mid x \in W_C([p,t]), \alpha(x) = c\}$;
- $W_U([(t,\alpha),(p,c)]) = card\{x \mid x \in W_C([t,p]), \alpha(x) = c\}$;
- $m_{0U}((p,c)) = m_{0C}(p)(c)$.

The skeleton is another place/transition net that can be associated with a high-level net. It just preserves the net structure and disregards the colors and firing modes. This way, a much coarser view on the high-level net is produced, an abstraction.

Definition 6 (Skeleton). *Let* $N_C = [P_C, T_C, F_C, \chi, W_C, \gamma, m_{0C}]$ *be a high-level net. The* skeleton *of* N_C *is the place/transition net* $N_S = [P_C, T_C, F_C, W_S, m_{0S}]$ *where, for all nodes* x *and* y *of* N_C, $W_S([x,y]) = card(W_C([x,y]))$, *and, for all places* p, $m_{0S}(P) = \sum_{c \in \chi(p)} m_0(p)(c)$.

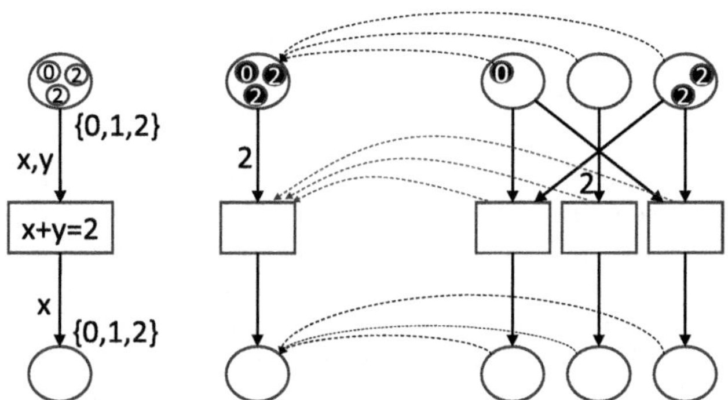

Fig. 2. A high level net (left), its skeleton (middle), its unfolding (right), and a net morphism (dashed).

The unfolding N_U and the skeleton N_S of a high-level net N_C are related by a *net morphism* [27,91]. Net morphisms preserve reachability.

Definition 7 (Net Morphism). *Let* $N_1 = [P_1, T_1, F_1, W_1, m_{0|1}]$ *and* $N_2 = [P_2, T_2, F_2, W_2, m_{0|2}]$ *be place/transition nets. A mapping* $\mu : P_1 \cup T_1 \rightarrow P_2 \cup T_2$ *is a* net morphism *if*

- $\mu(P_1) \subseteq P_2$, $\mu(T_1) \subseteq T_2$;
- *If* $[x, y] \in F_1$ *then* $[\mu(x), \mu(y)] \in F_2$ *and* $W([\mu(x), \mu(y)]) = W([x, y])$;
- *for all* $p_2 \in \mu(P_1)$, $m_{0|2}(p) = \sum_{p_1:\mu(p_1)=p_2} m_{0|1}(p_1)$.

Proposition 1 (Reachability via net morphism). *For marking* m_U *of* N_U, *let* $\mu(m_U)$ *be the marking* m_S *of* N_S *where, for all* $p \in P_S(= P_C)$, $m_S(p) = \sum_{c \in \chi(p)} m_U((p, c))$. *Then for all markings* m *and* m' *of* N_U, $m \xrightarrow{(t_1,\alpha_1)(t_2,\alpha_2)\ldots(t_n,\alpha_n)} m'$ *in* N_U *implies* $\mu(m) \xrightarrow{t_1 t_2 \ldots t_n} \mu(m')$ *in* N_S.

Figure 2 shows an example of a high level net, the two associated place/transition nets, and a net morphism.

Based on Proposition 1, some properties are preserved by the abstraction: if the property holds in the skeleton, it holds in the unfolding as well. More properties can be preserved if the mapping μ preserves deadlocks, i.e. if no transition is enabled in m in N_U then no transition is enabled in $\mu(m)$ in N_S. This is not always the case. [35] studies sufficient conditions for preservation of deadlocks via a net morphism. A net morphism that preserves deadlocks is actually a simulation relation.

Definition 8 (Simulation). *Let* N_U *and* N_S *be place/transition nets and* σ *be a relation between markings of* N_U *and markings in* N_S. σ *is a* simulation relation *if*

- $(m_{0U}, m_{0S}) \in \sigma$;
- *If no transition is enabled in* m_U *of* N_U *and* $(m_U, m_S) \in \sigma$ *then no transition is enabled in* m_S *of* N_S;
- *If* $m_U \xrightarrow{t} m'_U$ *in* N_U *and* $(m_U, m_S) \in \sigma$ *then there is a transition* t' *and a marking* m'_S *in* N_S *such that* $m_S \xrightarrow{t'} m'_S$ *in* N_S.

Simulation is a valuable tool for property preservation. We need to mention, though, that property preservation is usually an implication but not an equivalence. That is, if some property holds in the skeleton, it holds in the unfolding (i.e. in the high level net) as well, but not vice versa. For this reason, the verification of the skeleton needs to be organized in parallel to, or before the verification of the unfolding. If the verification of the skeleton yields a result that implies that result for the original net, we may be able to stop construction of the original state space early.

The paper [123] proposes a method to reverse the unfolding of a high-level net. Starting with a place/transition net N, we compute a high-level net N_C that has N as its unfolding. By deriving the skeleton N_S from N_C, we can use N_S as an abstraction of N. This way, the skeleton abstraction is applicable to both high-level nets and place/transition nets.

2.3 Net Reduction

Another approach to the simplification of a Petri net is the iterative application of net reduction rules. Reduction rules are typically local net transformations. Their application is focussed on a few connected nodes and does not depend on the shape of the remaining net (with an exception concerning the membership of the net in some net class). One goal of applying reduction rules is to reduce the number of nodes. This way, data structures (for example, to represent a marking) require less memory and loops running through all places or all transitions need fewer iterations. Some reduction rules can also have the effect of reducing the number of reachable states. If, for instance, we merge two sequentially arranged transitions into one, the intermediate marking does no longer occur. If that reduction can be applied multiple times, exponentially many combinations of intermediate markings would disappear from the state space.

Every reduction rule has four ingredients. An *anchor* defines the area of consideration. The anchor is a single node or a group of nodes from which the area of application can be defined by navigating over the neighborhood. The *guard* is a condition that states whether or not the rule is applicable in the area defined by the anchor. It may include conditions on connectivity of nodes in the application area but may also talk about arc weights or the initial marking. It may also depend on the property under verification, for example whether or not the property explicitly refers to a node in the application area. The *transformation* describes how the application of the rule changes the net in the application area. We may add or remove nodes, add, remove, or redirect arcs, change weights or initial markings. Finally *preservation* results tell us which classes of properties are preserved by rule application.

A typical reduction engine uses about 10 to 20 rules. Here, we just present a few examples and refer the reader to [6,11,86,104,109] for getting the full picture. Due to the way this paper is organized, we need to stay shallow regarding preservation.

Our first example (Fig. 3a) is a rule that removes a place p_0 if there is a parallel place p_1 such that, for every transition t, if p_0 is insufficiently marked to activate t, so is p_1. The rule can be summarized as follows:

- Name: parallel place removal [11];
- Anchor: a place p_0;
- Guard: there exists a place p_1 and a number k such that $m_0(p_0) \geq k \cdot m_0(p_1)$ and, for all transitions $t \in \bullet p_0$, $W(t, p_0) \geq k \cdot W(t, p_1)$, and, for all transitions $t \in p_0\bullet$, $W(p_0, t) \leq k \cdot W(p_1, t)$;
- Transformation: Remove p_0 and adjacent arcs;
- Preservation: Reduced reachability graph is isomorphic to original one since, for all reachable m and all t, if p_0 is insufficiently marked to fire t, so is p_1. For being preserved, property must not refer to number of tokens in p_0.

The application of this rule does not reduce the state space. It does, however, reduce memory consumption since the number of tokens on p_0 does not need to be recorded any more. It also improves the run-time since, for instance, checking activation of the post-transitions of p_0 requires less iterations. The effect sums up for all reachable markings and may therefore be substantial.

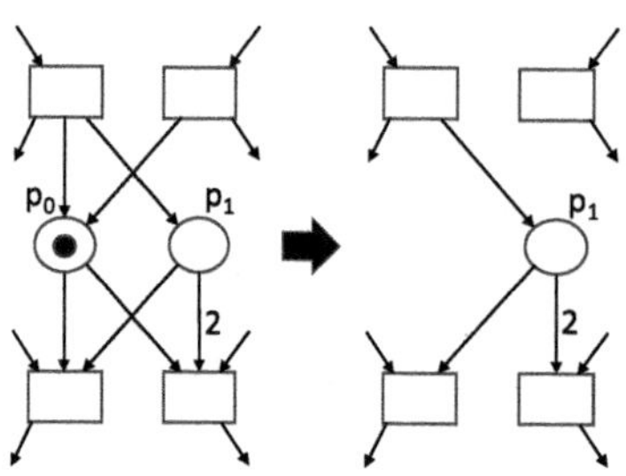

(a) Removal of a parallel place.

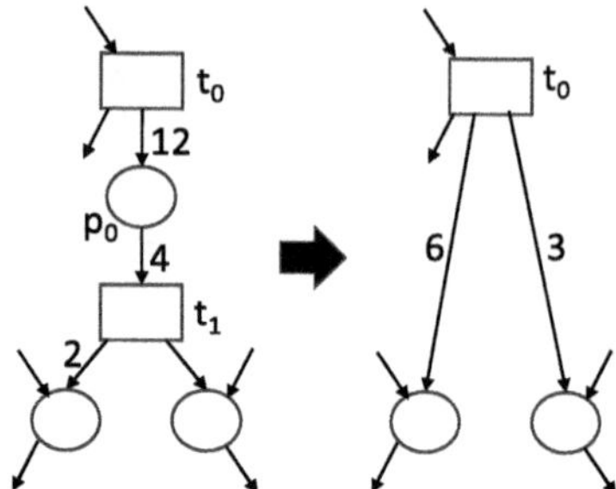

(b) Removal of a sequential place.

Fig. 3. Application of reduction rules I.

As a second example (Fig. 3b), we exhibit a rule that merges the occurrence of transitions that are causally related via a single place.

- Name: sequential place removal [11];
- Anchor: a place p_0;
- Guard: $m_0(p_0) = 0$ and there are transitions t_0 and t_1 ($t_0 \neq t_1$) as well as a number k ($k \geq 1$) such that $\bullet p_0 = \{t_0\}$, $p_0\bullet = \{t_1\}$, $\bullet t_1 = \{p_0\}$, and $W(t_0, p_0) = k \cdot W(p_0, t_1)$.
- Transformation: for every $p \in t_1\bullet$, insert a new arc $[t_0, p]$, if not yet present. For every $p \in t_1\bullet$, replace weight $W([t_0, p])$ with $W([t_0, p]) + k \cdot W([t_1, p])$. Remove p_0 and t_1.
- Preservation: If some transition sequence $w_1 t_0 u_1 t_1 u_2 t_1 \ldots u_k t_1 w_2$ can fire in the unreduced net (where t_1 does not occur in $u_1 u_2 \ldots u_k$), then sequence $w_1 t_0 t_1 \ldots t_1 u_1 u_2 \ldots u_k w_2$ with k occurrences of t_1 after t_0 can fire as well in the unreduced net since p_0 is the only pre-place of t_1 and provides sufficiently many tokens for firing t_1 k times. Firing t_0 in the reduced net has the same effect as firing $t_0 t_1 \ldots t_1$ in the unreduced net. Consequently, properties are preserved if the are not directly referring to p_0 and t_1 and if they are insensitive to the position of t_1 in a firing sequence.

This rule does not only reduce the number of places and transitions in the net. It can also substantially reduce the number of reachable markings since various distributions of tokens on the removed places are not visible in the reduced net.

Our third example (Fig. 4a) is a rule where the anchor consists of more than one node. It is a set of places that can never be marked.

- Name: empty siphon removal [109];
- Anchor: a set S of places;

- Guard: $m_0(p) = 0$ for all places $p \in S$ and, for all transitions t, if $t\bullet \cap S \neq \emptyset$ then $\bullet t \cap S \neq \emptyset$;
- Transformation: Remove all places in S and their post-transitions;
- Preservation: no place in S can ever get a token since all transitions that could produce a token in S have a pre-place in S and are therefore permanently disabled. Hence, the reachability graph of the reduced net is isomorphic to the reachability graph of the unreduced net. Every property that concerns places in S can assume that these places will invariantly contain no tokens.

One might think that places that can never be marked and transitions that can never fire would hint to a severe modeling error. This is not necessarily the case, especially if the net is the result of a transformation process from another formalism. As an example, consider a communication protocol between a set Y of participants that are connected but not necessarily directly connected. A high level net model of such a protocol would include a place for pending messages that is typed $Y \times Y$ such that every token has a value $[x, y]$ where x is the sender and y the receiver of that message. Unfolding this net to a place/transition net, we would include a separate place $p_{[x,y]}$ for every such tuple. If, however, x is not directly connected to y in the modeled network, that place will never get a token.

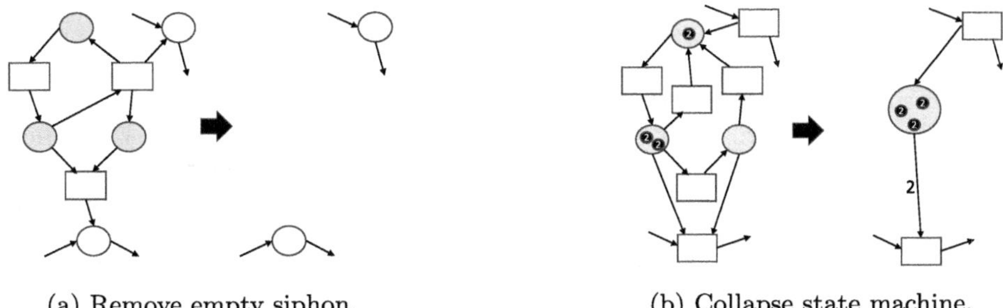

(a) Remove empty siphon.

(b) Collapse state machine.

Fig. 4. Application of reduction rules II; anchors are set in grey.

In our last example (Fig. 4b), we collapse a set of places into a single place if tokens can freely roam between the places. To this end, let t be a *state machine transition* if t has precisely one incoming and precisely one outgoing arc, and both arcs have weight 1.

- Name: Collapse state machine (inspired by [11]);
- Anchor: a set S of places;
- Guard: S is strongly connected by state machine transitions;
- Transformation: insert new place p^*. Let $[p^*, t] \in F$ iff there is a $p \in S$ where $[p, t] \in F$. Let $[t, p^*] \in F$ iff there is a $p \in F$ where $[t, p] \in F$. Let $W([p^*, t]) = \sum_{p \in S} W([p, t])$ and $W([t, p^*]) = \sum_{p \in S} W([t, p])$. Remove all places in S and all state machine transitions that have both their pre- and post-place in S;

– Preservation: Thanks to the state machine transitions, tokens may freely roam between the places in S. Consequently, the places in S do not need to be distinguished. A property is preserved if it does not explicitly mention the places in S and is not sensitive to the occurrence of the removed state machine transitions.

This rule is another example for a rule that can substantially reduce the reachability graph. All the exponentially many distributions of tokens on S are no longer distinguished in the reduced net.

Net reduction may reduce the size of the reachability graph and reduces the size of the net. This way, subsequent algorithms are accelerated. Applicability of rules may depend on the property under verification. If we want to verify multiple properties, it is recommendable to produce a separate reduced net for every property since the fight against state explosion has top priority.

2.4 Modularization

Complex Petri net models are created by glueing together simpler Petri nets. Advanced Petri net editors such as CPN Tools [96] supported this style of modeling. Another way to obtain complex Petri nets is to translate models that were created in other formalisms. Such a translation as well composes building blocks rather than single places or transitions [7,77]. That is, many Petri net models exhibit a natural modular structure. If a net does not have such a structure voluntarily, we may try to decompose it into modules [13,41,126].

We can benefit from knowing the modular structure of a Petri net. We may be able to do as much work as possible separately for every module and consider the interaction between modules on the most abstract level that is possible. We discuss this idea in Sect. 4.3. Meanwhile, we simply show how to consider a Petri net as a composition of modules. In the sequel, we shall use transition fusion as our tool for composition. Our concepts are based on [20,40].

A module is simply a place/transition net where the transitions are separated into internal transitions and interface transitions.

Definition 9 (Module). *A tuple $[P, T_{internal}, T_{interface}, F, W, m_0]$ is a module if $[P, T_{internal} \cup T_{interface}, F, W, m_0]$ is a place/transition net and $T_{internal} \cap T_{interface} = \emptyset$.*

A modular structure provides information about the modules to be composed and about the way they are composed. We compose modules by fusing interface transitions from several (not necessarily all) modules. Every fusion is described as a fusion vector. Its dimension is the number of modules. At index i, an interface transition of module N_i or the symbol $\perp$ is recorded. If it is a transition, it is part of the fusion. $\perp$ expresses that no transition of module N_i participates in the fusion. We do not permit to let more than one transition of a module participate in a single fusion. This is not a restriction for modeling since the result of the internal fusion can be added to the module as another transition.

On the other hand, with just one transition per module in the fusion vector, there is a closer relation between local and global behavior. One and the same interface transition may, however, participate in several fusions.

Definition 10 (Modular Structure). *A* modular structure *consists of a list* $N_1, \ldots, N_\ell$ *of modules (with* $N_i = [P_i, T_{i|internal}, T_{i|interface}, F_i, W_i, m_{i|0}]$*) such that the sets* $P_i \cup T_{i|internal} \cup T_{i|interface}$ *are pairwise disjoint, and a set of fusion vectors. A* fusion vector *is an* ℓ*-tuple* f *such that* $f[i] \in T_{i|interface} \cup \{\bot\}$*, for all* i*.*

A modular structure is an implicit description of a place/transition net, called the modular Petri net. The modular Petri net collects all places and internal transitions of the modules, their connections, and their initial marking. Interface transitions are not copied into the modular net. Instead, every fusion vector f defines a new transition. The effect of f is the same as the simultaneous occurrence of all the transitions contained in it.

Definition 11 (Modular Petri net). *Let* $\mathcal{M} = [\{N_1, \ldots, N_k\}, \mathcal{F}]$ *be a modular structure. The modular Petri net* $N_\mathcal{M} = [P_\mathcal{M}, T_\mathcal{M}, F_\mathcal{M}, W_\mathcal{M}, m_{0|\mathcal{M}}]$ *is defined as follows.*

- $P_\mathcal{M} = \bigcup_{i=1}^{\ell} P_i$;
- $T_\mathcal{M} = \bigcup_{i=1}^{\ell} T_{i|internal} \cup \mathcal{F}$;
- *If, for some* i, $[x, y] \in F_i$ *and* $\{x, y\} \cap T_{i|interface} = \emptyset$ *then* $[x, y] \in F_\mathcal{M}$ *and* $W([x, y]) = W_i([x, y])$;
- *If, for some* i, $p_i \in P_i$, $f \in \mathcal{F}$, $f[i] \in T_{i|interface}$, *and* $[p_i, f[i]] \in F_i$ *then* $[p_i, f] \in F_\mathcal{M}$ *and* $W_\mathcal{M}([p_i, f]) = W_i([p_i, f[i]])$;
- *If, for some* i, $p_i \in P_i$, $f \in \mathcal{F}$, $f[i] \in T_{i|interface}$, *and* $[f[i], p_i] \in F_i$ *then* $[f, p_i] \in F_\mathcal{M}$ *and* $W_\mathcal{M}([f, p_i]) = W_i([f[i], p_i])$;
- *For all other* x *and* y, $[x, y] \notin F_\mathcal{M}$ *and therefore* $W_\mathcal{M}([x, y]) = 0$;
- *for all* i *and all* $p_i \in P_i$, $m_{0|\mathcal{M}}(p_i) = m_{0|i}(p_i)$.

By this construction, all interface transitions that are not contained in any fusion set, are removed. If that effect is not desired for some transition $t_i \in T_{i|interface}$, one can simply add a fusion vector f where all but the i-th component are set to $\bot$ while $f[i] = t_i$.

Figure 5a depicts a modular structure with three modules. Transitions drawn on the boundary of a module are considered to be interface transitions. The grey ovals represent the fusion vectors $[t_3, u_3, \bot]$, $[\bot, u_2, v_1]$, and $[\bot, u_2, v_2]$, respectively. The resulting modular Petri net is drawn in Fig. 5b.

By shipping a modular structure (the modules and the rules to compose them) instead of a modular net (the result of composition) to a verification tool, the tool may take the given structure into consideration. There are cases where we want to compose several identical copies of one and the same module. Our modular structure permits such compositions as it does not rule out modules N_i and N_j that are isomorphic. The article [40] distinguishes modules and instances. From every module, we may spawn several identical instances and it is the instances that are finally composed. Knowing that some modules are in fact identical gives us the possibility to compute information only once for a module, and use for all its instances.

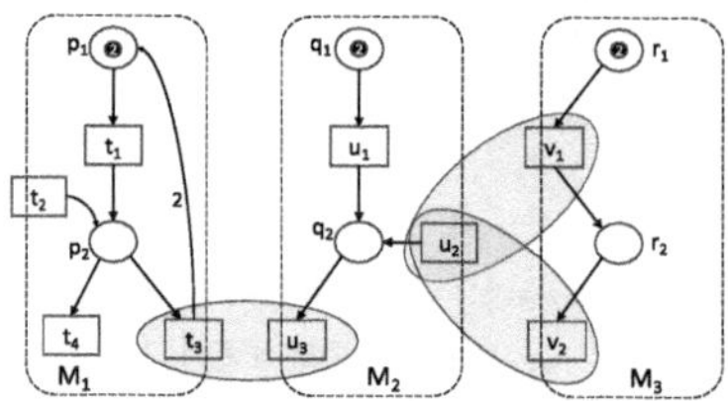

(a) A modular structure.

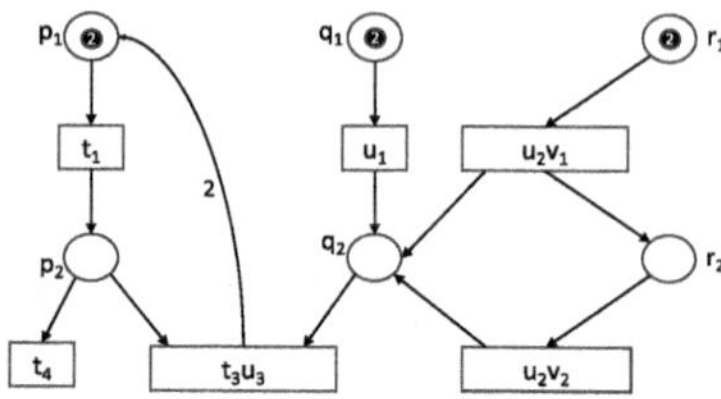

(b) Resulting modular Petri net.

Fig. 5. Modularization

2.5 Concluding Remarks

We have seen several approaches to the simplification of a Petri net, with a different way of using them. Abstraction yields a new net that may serve as an additional verification problem that, if successfully solved, allows us to skip the original problem. Net reduction can simplify the original verification task. Modularization may enable alternative strategies to explore the state space of the net.

3 Temporal Logic

In this section, we shall follow the same approach as in the previous section, but for the second input: the specification of the property to be verified. We first introduce temporal logic as our specification formalism (Sect. 3.1). Then we discuss several approaches to complexity reduction on this input. In particular, we shall study static analysis (Sect. 3.2), the application of tautologies (Sect. 3.3), and strength reduction (Sect. 3.4). In the concluding remarks of this section, we include a brief discussion on the dependencies between net reduction and formula reduction.

3.1 The Temporal Logic CTL* And Its Fragments

A temporal logic may work with properties of markings (state based logic) or properties of transitions (action based logic). We will discuss only state based logic. Temporal logic then provides temporal operators that express relations between properties of some marking and properties of successor markings. Path quantifiers specify whether the relation is meant for some successor or for all successors.

We first propose a simple language for expressing properties of markings. Then we introduce temporal operators and path quantifiers. The result is a temporal logic called CTL*. From CTL*, we shall finally derive some fragments: LTL and CTL. We shall discuss verification only for the derived fragments. CTL* model checking is possible in principle, but more involved than the other model checking procedures and therefore left out here.

An atomic proposition relates a formal sum of places to an integer number. It is evaluated in a marking m by replacing every symbol p in the proposition by $m(p)$.

Definition 12 (Atomic proposition). *Let $N = [P, T, F, W, m_0]$ be a place/transition net. An* atomic proposition *of N has the shape $\alpha = k_1 \cdot p_1 + \dots k_n \cdot p_n \leq k$ where $\{p_1, \dots, p_n\} \subseteq P$ and $\{k_1, \dots, k_n, k\} \subseteq \mathbb{Z}$. Proposition α holds in marking m (written $m \models \alpha$) if $k_1 \cdot m(p_1) + \dots + k_n \cdot m(p_n) \leq k$.*

While the proposition itself is just a string that expresses a formal sum, the evaluation in a particular marking refers to actual addition and comparison and results in a Boolean value.

We can think of other atomic propositions. However, many of them can be traced back to the defined shape. Here are a few examples.

- $k_1 \cdot p_1 + \dots k_n \cdot p_n < k$ can be expressed as $k_1 \cdot p_1 + \dots + k_n \cdot p_n \leq k - 1$;
- $k_1 \cdot p_1 + \dots k_n \cdot p_n \geq k$ can be expressed as $-k_1 \cdot p_1 - \dots - k_n \cdot p_n \leq -k$;
- $k_1 \cdot p_1 + \dots k_n \cdot p_n = k$ can be expressed as $k_1 \cdot p_1 + \dots k_n \cdot p_n \leq k \wedge k_1 \cdot p_1 + \dots k_n \cdot p_n \geq k$;
- Activation of t (written as FIREABLE(t)) can be expressed as $\bigwedge_{p \in {}^\bullet t} p \geq W([p, t])$;
- A property that is true in all deadlock markings (written as DEADLOCK) can be expressed as $\bigwedge_{t \in T} \neg FIREABLE(t)$;
- A property that is true only in the initial marking (written as INITIAL) can be expressed as $\bigwedge_{p \in P} p = m_0(p)$.

Originally, temporal logic was defined on Kripke structures. A Kripke structure consists of states and transitions (edges that lead from one state to another). A Kripke structure assumes that every state has at least one outgoing edge. Thanks to this condition, every finite path in a Kripke structure can be extended to an infinite path and the semantics of temporal logic can be defined for infinite paths only. The reachability graph of a Petri net is not a Kripke structure since we may reach deadlocks. There are two approaches to deal with this situation. The first approach adds additional edges from every deadlock to itself. This way, being stuck in a deadlock m_d is modeled as a continuous return to m_d. The resulting graph is indeed a Kripke structure. The second approach is to define the semantics both for infinite paths and for finite paths ending in a deadlock. Unfortunately, the two approaches may cause different values for some formulas. An example is discussed below. It is thus important that tool user and tool developer agree on that design decision. In the sequel, we shall follow the first approach.

Definition 13 (extended reachability graph). *The* extended reachability graph *is obtained from the actual reachability graph by adding, for every m where no transition is enabled, an edge $m \xrightarrow{\tau} m$, where τ is some symbol that is not a transition of the underlying Petri net.*

As already mentioned, the concept of a path is crucial for temporal logic.

Definition 14 (Path). *A* path starting in m_1 *in a Petri net $N = [P, T, F, W, m_0]$ is an infinite sequence $\pi = m_1 m_2 \ldots$ of markings such that, for all i, t $m_i \rightarrow m_{i+1}$ in the extended reachability graph of N.*

In the temporal logic CTL*, we distinguish state formulas and path formulas. A state formula is evaluated in a marking while a path formula is evaluated in a path. The following definition clarifies that every state formula is automatically a path formula as well. The opposite is not necessarily true. Atomic propositions are state formulas. Temporal operators refer to paths. Path quantifiers turn a path formula into a state formula.

Definition 15 (Temporal Logic). *The temporal logic CTL* is defined as follows.*

- *Every atomic proposition as well as constant expressions true and false are state formulas.*
- *Every state formula is a path formula.*
- *If ϕ and ψ are state formulas, so are $(\phi \wedge \psi)$, $(\phi \vee \psi)$, $(\phi \implies \psi)$, $(\phi \iff \psi)$, and $\neg\phi$.*
- *If ϕ and ψ are path formulas, so are $(\phi \wedge \psi)$, $(\phi \vee \psi)$, $(\phi \implies \psi)$, $(\phi \iff \psi)$, and $\neg\phi$.*
- *If ϕ and ψ are path formulas, so are $X\phi$ ("ϕ holds in the next step"), $F\phi$ ("ϕ holds eventually in the future"), $G\phi$ ("ϕ holds globally"), $\phi U \psi$ ("ϕ hold until ψ holds"), and $\phi R \psi$ ("ϕ releases ψ").*
- *If ϕ is a path formula then $A\phi$ ("ϕ holds on all paths") and $E\phi$ ("ϕ hold on some path") are state formulas.*

The semantics of CTL* states whether or not a marking m satisfies a state formula ϕ ($m \models \phi$), and whether or not a path π satisfies a path formula ϕ ($\pi \models \phi$). In addition, we specify for both state formulas and path formulas whether or not the net satisfies the formula ($N \models \phi$)

For atomic propositions, the semantics is already given by Definition 12. The meaning of Boolean constants and operators is as expected. For the remaining formulas, the following definition fixes the semantics.

Definition 16 (Semantics of CTL*). *Let m be a marking and $\pi = m_1 m_2 \ldots$ be a path starting in m_1. Let the i-*th suffix *of π (written $\pi[i \ldots]$) be the path $m_i m_{i+1} \ldots$ starting in m_i.*

- *For a state formula* ϕ, $\pi \models \phi$ *if* $m_1 \models \phi$.
- $\pi \models X\phi$ *if* $\pi[2\ldots] \models \phi$.
- $\pi \models F\phi$ *if there exists an* i *such that* $i \geq 1$ *and* $\pi[i\ldots] \models \phi$.
- $\pi \models G\phi$ *if, for all* i *with* $i \geq 1$, $\pi[i\ldots] \models \phi$.
- $\pi \models \phi U \psi$ *if, there exists an* i *such that* $i \geq 1$ *and* $\pi[i\ldots] \models \psi$ *and, for all* j $(1 \leq j < i)$, $\pi[j\ldots] \models \phi$.
- $\pi \models \phi R \psi$ *if the following holds for all* i $(i \geq 1)$: *if* $\pi[i\ldots] \not\models \psi$ *then, for some* $j (1 \leq j < i)$, $\pi[j\ldots] \models \phi$.
- $m \models A\phi$ *if, for all paths* π' *starting in* m, $\pi' \models \phi$.
- $m \models E\phi$ *if there is a path* π' *starting in* m *such that* $\pi' \models \phi$.
- *For a state formula* ϕ, $N \models \phi$ *if* $m_0 \models \phi$.
- *For a path formula* ϕ, $N \models \phi$ *if, for all paths* π' *starting in* m_0, $\pi' \models \phi$.

X, F, G, U, and R are called *temporal operators.* A and E are referred to as *path quantifiers.* The definition of $N \models \phi$ for a path formula ϕ includes an implicit universal quantifier. If there is a path starting in m_0 that satisfies ϕ and there is another path starting in m_0 that does not satisfy ϕ, we have both $N \not\models \phi$ and $N \not\models \neg\phi$. For markings and paths, however, we have the usual connection $m \models \phi$ if and only if $m \not\models \neg\phi$, and $\pi \models \phi$ if and only if $\pi \not\models \neg\phi$.

Our definition includes some syntactic sugar. Operators may be substituted by other operators using the following tautologies.

- $(\phi R \psi) \iff \neg(\neg\phi U \neg\psi)$
- $G\phi \iff \neg F \neg\phi$
- $F\phi \iff (\text{true} U \phi)$
- $A\phi \iff \neg E \neg\phi$

The net in Fig. 5b satisfies, among others, the following formulas: $p_1 > 0\ U\ p2 > 0$, $AG\ r_1{+}r_2 \leq 2$, $EF\ p_1 = 3$, $AG\ EF\ DEADLOCK$, $GF\ r_1 = 0$. The empty marking (which is reachable) satisfies EX *true*, thanks to the inserted edge in the extended reachability graph. If the semantics of temporal logic is defined separately for paths ending in a deadlock, one would usually set EX *true* to be false in a deadlock marking since there is no path in the actual reachability graph to witness that.

Only few Petri net model checkers such as GreatSPN [2] support full CTL* model checking. Most model checkers support fragments of CTL* such as LTL or CTL.

Definition 17 (Fragments of CTL*)
LTL *is the temporal logic that consists of all CTL* formulas where no path quantifier is used [78].*

CTL *is the temporal logic that consists of all CTL* formulas where every temporal operator is immediately preceded by a path quantifier [21].*

For every temporal logic F, F-X is the temporal logic that consists of all formulas in F that do not use the operator X.

In LTL, we may consider all formulas to be path formulas. In CTL, we may consider every pair consisting of a path quantifier and a temporal operator to be an operator on its own. So we could define CTL in terms of operators EX, AX, EF, AF, EG, AG, EU, AU, ER, and AR. Doing so, CTL turns out to be a logic where every formula is a state formula, so LTL and CTL are fragments where only one shape of formulas occur. As we shall see later, model checking algorithms exploit the presence of only one shape of formula.

Formula $E(F\phi \wedge G\psi)$ is in $CTL*$ but neither in LTL nor CTL. Atomic propositions are both in LTL and CTL. Since the definition of $N \models \phi$ in Definition 16 implicitly uses a universal path quantifier, we may relax the definition of LTL and allow an LTL formula to start a single universal path quantifier. Taking this point of view, $A(\phi U \psi)$ is contained both in CTL and LTL. The CTL formula $AG\ EF\ INITIAL$ cannot be expressed in LTL, and the LTL formula $(F\ p_1 = 1 \wedge F\ p_2 = 1)$ cannot be expressed in CTL.

Many properties that have been prominently studied in Petri net theory, can be expressed in at least one of the logics LTL or CTL. Some examples are listed here.

- Reachability of a marking m^* can be expressed in CTL as $EF \bigwedge_{p \in P} p = m^*(p)$. In LTL, we can only express unreachability as $G\neg \bigwedge_{p \in P} p = m^*(p)$.
- A transition t is dead if it is never enabled. This property can be expressed in CTL $(AG\neg FIREABLE(t))$ and LTL $(G\neg FIREABLE(t))$.
- A transition is live if it can be enabled from every reachable marking. In CTL, we express this as $AG\ EF\ FIREABLE(t)$. Liveness cannot be expressed in LTL.
- A net is reversible if we can reach the initial marking from every reachable marking. In CTL, this spells as $AG\ EF\ INITIAL$ and there is not LTL formula expressing reversibility.

3.2 Static Analysis

In this section, we present methods that allow us to simplify atomic propositions. We try to prove, without generating the reachability graph, that they are invariantly true or false. In this case, we can replace them with constant expressions true or false. In other cases, we may replace an atomic proposition by an equivalent one that mentions fewer places. Mentioning less places may enable additional net reduction, as discussed in Sect. 2.3. In Sect. 6, we shall see more benefits from mentioning less places in atomic propositions.

The methods for static analysis are core elements of the Petri net structure theory. Consequently, it is not straight forward to transfer these methods to other modeling formalisms. We shall employ the *Petri net state equation*, *place invariants*, and *siphons* and *traps*, in this order.

The Petri net state equation is a linear system of equations that establishes a necessary condition for reachability. We may consider a marking to be a column vector using the set of places P as indices. The effect of a transition t can also be written as a column vector $\underline{t}$ with same dimension, where $\underline{t}[p] = W(t,p) - W(p,t)$. With this setting, we can see immediately that $m \xrightarrow{t} m'$ implies $m' = m + \underline{t}$. For a transition sequence w, let the Parikh vector $\Psi(w)$ be the column vector with index set T such that $\Psi(w)[t]$ is the number of occurrences of transition t in the sequence w. Let the incidence matrix C of a place/transition net N consist of the columns $\underline{t}$, for all transitions t. That is, C has row indices in P and column indices in T. With these settings, the above observation can be generalized to transition sequences: if $m \xrightarrow{w} m'$ then $m' = m + C \cdot \Psi(w)$. From this equation, we may derive the aforementioned necessary condition for reachability. Marking m' is reachable from marking m only if the integer linear program (i.e. a system of equations and inequations, abbreviated ILP in the sequel) $m' = m + C \cdot \underline{x}$, $\underline{x} \geq \underline{0}$ is feasible in the integers. $\underline{x}$ is a vector of variables with index set T, and $\underline{0}$ is the vector of all zeros. If m' is reachable from m using sequence w then $\Psi(w)$ proves that the system is feasible. Feasibility of the considered ILP is not sufficient for reachability since the solution found may only correspond to the Parikh vector of transition sequences that are not enabled in m.

With the help of the state equation, we can derive a condition that is sufficient for an atomic proposition to be invariantly true and a condition that is sufficient for an atomic proposition to be invariantly false [10]. To this end, let $\underline{y}$ be a vector of variables with index set P.

Lemma 1 (static analysis with state equation, [10]). *Let $\alpha = k_1 \cdot p_1 + \cdots + k_n \cdot p_n \leq k$ be an atomic proposition.*

If the ILP $\underline{y} = m_0 + C \cdot \underline{x}, k_1 \cdot \underline{y}[p_1] + \cdots + k_n \cdot \underline{y}[p_n] \leq k, \underline{x} \geq 0, \underline{y} \geq \underline{0}$ is infeasible then there is no reachable marking m holding $m \models \alpha$.

If the ILP $\underline{y} = m_0 + C \cdot \underline{x}, k_1 \cdot \underline{y}[p_1] + \cdots + k_n \cdot \underline{y}[p_n] > k, \underline{x} \geq 0, \underline{y} \geq \underline{0}$ is infeasible then there is no reachable marking m holding $m \not\models \alpha$.

Proof. If there is a marking m and a transition sequence w such that $m_0 \xrightarrow{w} m$ and $m \models \alpha$ then m provides values for $\underline{y}$ and $\Psi(w)$ provides values for $\underline{x}$ that prove feasibility of the first ILP. For the second claim, we may argue accordingly. □

That is, infeasibility of the first system allows us to replace α with false while infeasibility of the second ILP allows us to replace α with true. If $m_0 \models \alpha$, proposition α cannot be invariantly false, and if $m_0 \not\models \alpha$, proposition α cannot be invariantly true. Consequently, only one of the two ILP needs to be tried for a proposition α.

A place invariant assigns a weight (an integer number) to every place such that the weighted sum of all tokens in the net does not change when transitions fire.

Definition 18 (place invariant). *Let N be a place/transition net and C its incidence matrix. A column vector $\underline{i}$ of integers with index set P is called* place invariant *of N if $C^T \cdot \underline{i} = \underline{0}$.*

Lemma 2 (invariance). *If $\underline{i}$ is a place invariant of place/transition net N then, for all markings of N, $m \xrightarrow{*} m'$ implies $\underline{i}^T \cdot m = \underline{i}^T \cdot m'$.*

Proof. Using the state equation, $m \xrightarrow{w} m'$ implies $m' = m + C \cdot \Psi(w)$. Multiplying $\underline{i}^T$ from left leads to $\underline{i}^T \cdot m' = \underline{i}^T \cdot m + \underline{i}^T \cdot C \cdot \Psi(w)$. By the definition of place invariance, $\underline{i}^T \cdot C = C^T \cdot \underline{i} = \underline{0}$, so the claimed equation $\underline{i}^T \cdot m = \underline{i}^T \cdot m'$ remains. □

From a place invariant, we may derive an atomic proposition ι that is invariantly true: $\sum_{p \in P} \underline{i}[p] \cdot p = \underline{i}^T \cdot m_0$ (the right hand side of this equation is a constant). We can use this proposition to transform other propositions [74]. If $\alpha = k_1 p_1 + \cdots + k_n p_n \leq k$ is a proposition, then we can obtain a proposition that is equivalent to α by adding ι: $\sum_{p \in P} \underline{i}[p] \cdot p + k_1 p_1 + \cdots + k_n p_n \leq k + \underline{i}^T \cdot m_0$. The resulting proposition may indeed be simpler than the original one. As an example, consider a net with four places, a place invariant $(-1, -1, 1, 0)^T$ and initial marking $(1, 0, 0, 0)^T$. The resulting equation is $-p_1 - p_2 + p_3 = -1$. Applying this to the atomic proposition $\alpha = p_1 - p_2 - p_3 + p_4 \leq 3$ results in the new atomic proposition $-2p_2 + p_4 \leq 2$ which is indeed simpler as it no longer refers to p_1 and p_3. That is, net reduction may now be applied in the vicinity of p_1 and p_3. In addition, we need less time to evaluate the new proposition. This seemingly small effect adds up to a substantial gain in run time since we may need to evaluate the propositions in millions of reachable markings. In best case, invariant and proposition match perfectly and the remaining proposition contains no place at all.

Given a proposition $\alpha = k_1 p_1 + \cdots + k_n p_n \leq k$, a good invariant to simplify α would be one where the coefficients for p_i are between 0 and k_i and otherwise have an absolute value that is as large as possible. The application of such an invariant would not introduce new places but has the opportunity to remove some. If we assume without loss of generality that there is a number r such that places $p_1, \ldots, p_r$ have coefficients in α that are greater or equal to 0 while places $p_{r+1}, \ldots, p_n$ have coefficients in α that are less or equal to 0, we can obtain a suitable invariant as a solution to the ILP

$$\text{maximize } \underline{i}[p_1] + \cdots + \underline{i}[p_r] - \underline{i}[r+1] - \cdots - \underline{i}[n] \text{ in}$$

$$C^T \cdot \underline{i} = \underline{0}, 0 \leq \underline{i}[p_j] \leq k_j (\text{ for } j \leq r), k_j \leq \underline{i}[p_j] \leq 0 (\text{ for } j > r).$$

A trap is a set Q of places such that every transition that removes at least one token from any place in Q, also produces at least one token on some place in Q. The fundamental property of traps is that, once Q contains at least one token, it will contain at least one token in every subsequent marking. As a consequence, a proposition of shape $\sum_{p \in Q} k_p \cdot p + \sum_{p \in P \setminus Q} k_p \cdot p \geq 1$ is invariantly true if the coefficients k_p in the first sum are greater than 0 and the coefficients k_p in the second sum are greater or equal to 0. This may be a small gain but it covers cases that are left open by the state equation and the place invariant approaches.

Traps can also applied for refining the state equation approach discussed above [33]. If some ILP in Lemma 1 turns out to be feasible, we cannot simplify the considered proposition. In this case, however, we get values for the variables in $\underline{y}$ that correspond to a marking m_y. If there is a trap Q such that Q has at least one token in m_0 but no token at all in m_y, marking m_y cannot be reachable from

m_0 due to the fundamental property of traps. In this case, the solution found is actually spurious. Since every reachable marking must satisfy the proposition $\sum_{p \in Q} 1 \cdot p \geq 1$, we can add this inequation to the ILP (and actually to all ILP that we consider subsequently for this and other propositions). The new ILP may turn out to be infeasible and we have proven the proposition to be invariant. It may also be feasible and have another trap that is initially marked but unmarked in the solution vector, so we may add another inequation and proceed. Only if none of these cases applies, we need to give up in our attempt to prove the proposition to be invariant.

A siphon is a set of places S such that every transition that produces at least one token on any place in S, also removes at least one token from some place in S. As its fundamental property, once a siphon becomes empty, it can never get marked again. Siphons are closely related to deadlocks. For this reason, siphons are sometimes called *structural deadlocks.*

Proposition 2 (siphon versus deadlock). *Let N be a place/transition net where all arc weights are equal to one. Then, for every marking m where no transition is enabled, the set $S = \{p \mid m(p) = 0\}$ is a siphon.*

Proof. In m, every transition is disabled, so it has an unmarked pre-place. Consequently, *every* transition removes a token from S which trivially includes those transitions that produce tokens to S.

The siphon exhibited in Proposition 2 is obviously empty. In consequence, if we consider a net N where all arc weights are equal to one, and every siphon contains a marked trap, N must be deadlock-free and we can set all atomic propositions $DEADLOCK$ to be invariantly false.

Checking the property "every siphon includes a marked trap" [28] is challenging since a net may have exponentially many siphons. In [89], it is shown that the property can be translated into a satisfiability problem of propositional logic. Existing SAT checkers [50] can solve most of the resulting satisfiability problems in reasonable time.

Checking feasibility of an ILP is NP-complete. It is still recommendable to apply the proposed simplifications since NP-completeness is much more efficient than the complexity of the model checking problem. For Petri nets, the reachability problem which is just a simple example of a model checking problem, is known to be EXPSPACE-hard. There exist tools that routinely solve very large ILP instances in a matter of seconds.

A trap that is marked in one marking and unmarked in another, can be found in polynomial time. However, a net may have exponentially many traps, so the refinement of the state equation may need prohibitively many iterations. This problem can be alleviated by introducing a limit to the number of iterations and to give up if that limit is reached.

3.3 Logical Tautologies

Logical tautologies can be used to rewrite the given temporal logic formula [10]. We can replace the left-hand side of the formula with the corresponding right-hand-side. This process can be organized using a term rewriting system such as kimwitu [116]. Using a term rewriting system has the advantage that the tautologies are explicitly represented in the specification of the term rewriting system and can be easily extended. The tool LoLA [125], for example, uses hundreds of tautologies.

The application of tautologies has several objectives:

- to expand the results of the static analysis from Sect. 3.2;
- to separate the formula into subformulas;
- to simplify the structure of the formula;
- to enable simpler model checking algorithms.

We briefly discuss every objective and give a few examples for suitable tautologies.

The result of static analysis may be a formula where some subformulas are invariantly true or false. These findings can be expanded into the temporal structure of the formula by tautologies like:

$$G\,\text{true} \iff \text{true},\ \text{true}\,U\phi \iff F\phi,\ \phi\,U\,\text{true} \iff \text{true},\ A\,\text{true} \iff \text{true}.$$

Occasionally, the rewriting process ends up in rewriting the whole formula to true or false and we can answer the model checking problem without performing any state space exploration. This is not necessarily a sign that the given problem was trivial in the first place. It is rather a sign that the structural methods used in Sect. 3.2 (state equation, place invariants, and traps) are powerful tools to gain insights about the system under verification. With the combination of static analysis and application of tautologies, the power of the mentioned structural methods extends far beyond the analysis of a fixed set of standard properties (e.g. liveness, deadlock freedom, reachability) that these methods were actually invented for in the 1960s and 1970s.

Some tautologies can be used to split a property into a Boolean combination of subformulas. Examples are:

$$EF(\phi \vee \psi) \iff (EF\phi \vee EF\psi),\ \ ((G\phi)U\psi) \iff (\psi \vee (G\phi \wedge F\psi))$$

Applying such tautologies particularly in the top region of the formula, we may end up in a Boolean combination of temporal logic subformulas. These subformulas can then be processed separately. Every subformula has a simpler structure and mentions less places than the whole formula. In some constellations, some subformulas become obsolete by the verification of others (for instance, the second part of a disjunction if the first one has been proven to be true). So the separate consideration of the subformulas gives us better opportunities to solve the whole problem. The tool LoLA provides both an LTL model checker and a CTL model checker. Its uniform specification language is CTL*. Using the separation into a Boolean combination of subformulas, we may verify an LTL subformula with the LTL model checker and a CTL subformula with a CTL model checker. This way, LoLA has a limited capability of solving problems that, as a whole, are neither in LTL nor CTL. Only if some subformula is neither in CTL nor LTL, it cannot be verified using LoLA.

We may use tautologies to simplify the structure. We may get rid of the $\Longrightarrow$ and $\Longleftrightarrow$ operators using the well-known transformations of propositional logic, and we may push negations down to the atomic propositions using tautologies like

$$\neg X\phi \iff X\neg\phi, \quad \neg F\phi \iff G\neg\phi, \quad \neg(\phi U\psi) \iff (\neg\phi R\neg\psi)$$

Other tautologies allow us to get rid of repeated applications of temporal operators.

$$FF\phi \iff F\phi, \quad AG\ EF\ AG\ EF\phi \iff AG\ EF\phi, \quad (\phi U(\phi U\psi)) \iff (\phi U\psi)$$

Again, applicability of such tautologies does not hint to an incompetent user but may be the result of previous simplifications enabled by static analysis.

Tautologies may finally be used to trim the formula such that simpler model checking algorithms become applicable. For instance, we can try to push path quantifiers down to match a temporal operator to become a CTL operator. As another example, we can rewrite the CTL* formula $A(G\phi \wedge G\psi)$ to the CTL formula $(AG\phi \wedge AG\psi)$. The article [74] lists several classes of CTL formulas that permit simpler verification than using a generic CTL model checking algorithm. We may apply tautologies such that the resulting formula falls into one of these classes as often as possible. As a last example, consider a tautology like $EF\ EX\phi \iff EX\ EF\phi$. The right hand side has a subformula $(EF\phi)$ that does not use the X operator. A model checker can use state space reduction methods to the evaluation of this subformula that are not available for the formula at the left hand side. We refer to Sect. 6 for details.

3.4 Strength Reduction

Temporal logic formulas pose different challenges to model checking. Some formulas permit the use of alternative verification approaches. For some formulas, state space reduction methods respond better than to other formulas. Not always are the simpler formulas equivalent to the given formula. We can, however, benefit from such formulas even if their validity is only sufficient, or only necessary for the given formulas. In such a case, we may verify the simpler formula before, in parallel to, or as a reaction to an unsuccessful verification attempt of the original formula.

We just give a few examples.

- $EF\psi$ is necessary for $E(\phi U\psi)$ and necessary for $AF\phi$;
- $EG\phi \wedge AF\psi$ is sufficient for $E(\phi U\psi)$;

- $AG\phi$ is sufficient and $EF\phi$ is necessary for $AG\ EF\phi$.

Whether or not it is useful to run verification with strength reduced formulas (in addition to the original formula), depends on the particular capabilities of the model checker.

3.5 Concluding Remarks

The simplification of formulas is a uniform method to let Petri net structure theory solve parts of model checking problems. The strong collaboration between structural methods and state space methods makes Petri net model checking a distinct sub-discipline in the realm of model checking. For a competitive Petri net model checker, providing advanced simplification methods is compulsory.

Simplification of the net and simplification of the formula have some dependencies. Net reduction benefits from an already simplified formula since the simplified formula may address less places and thus permits application of reduction rules in additional areas of the net. The other way round, computing the state equation and place invariants may be faster if they can be performed for an already reduced net. For this reason, processing the two inputs to the model checking problem is a process that deserves a careful design where we have a tradeoff between the quality of the result and the required computation time. We believe that, unless we have severe time restrictions as in a model checking contest (MCC) [8], time spent for careful simplification pays off. We would also recommend to reduce a net separately for subformulas that are verified independently. In the end, the fight against state explosion dominates all design decisions in model checking.

4 State Space Generation

The most popular method for computing the state space is depth-first search. Starting with the initial marking, we explore successor markings and descend recursively before exploring the next successor of a given marking. Depth-first search has very lightweight implementations. According to our own profiling, it is so efficient that about 40% of the run time is spent waiting for the operating system to assign more memory for storing the explored markings. The decisive advantage of depth-first search is, however, that we can easily instrument it for detecting the strongly connected components of the reachability graph [108]. We shall see in Sect. 5 that the evaluation of temporal logic formulas is heavily based on strongly connected components.

One disadvantage of depth-first search is that the call stack of the algorithm tends to get quite large. This is indeed a disadvantage since the content of the call stack can be used as diagnostic information in addition to the value of the formula under verification. Another disavantage is that depth-first search resists parallelization. There exist parallel algorithms for state space exploration [3,43, 57,105] and it is in principle possible to detect strongly connected components during parallel search [4,5,37], but depth-first search is still the number one method for state space exploration.

We present the algorithm for detecting strongly connected components in Sect. 4.1. Since depth-first search is used in the core of most explicit model checking algorithms, we discuss a few implementation issues in Sect. 4.2. Finally, we spend Sect. 4.3 for exhibiting a state space exploration method that is dedicated to modular Petri nets.

4.1 Depth-First Search

Algorithm 1 explores all reachable markings and numbers them consecutively using the $m.dfs$ label attached to every marking m. It also computes the strongly connected components of the reachability graph of a given place/transition net.

Definition 19 (strong connectivity). *Two markings m_1 and m_2 are* strongly connected *($m_1 \sim m_2$) if $m_1 \xrightarrow{*} m_2 \xrightarrow{*} m_1$. The equivalence classes of the set of reachable markings with respect to the equivalence relation $\sim$ are called* strongly connected components (SCC).

Algorithm 1. Depth-first search with SCC detection [108]

```
m0.dfs ← 0; m0.lowlink ← 0; nextdfs ← 1;
Visited ← ∅;
dfs(m0);

procedure DFS(m: marking)
    m.dfs ← nextdfs; m.lowlink ← nextdfs; nextdfs ← nextdfs + 1;
    Visited ← Visited ∪ {m}; push(m, sccStack);
    for all t: t enabled in m do
        m' ← m + t;
        if m' ∈ Visited then
            if m' ∈ sccStack then
                m.lowlink ← MIN(m.lowink, m'.dfs);
            end if
        else
            dfs(m');
            m.lowlink ← MIN(m.lowlink, m'.lowlink);
        end if
    end for
    if m.dfs = m.lowlink then
        repeat
            m* = pop(sccStack):
        until m = m*
    end if
end procedure
```

In the algorithm, every marking goes exactly once through the following life cycle[2]:

unexplored → open → processed → closed

Marking m is *unexplored* until **dfs**(m) is being called. As long as the procedure frame for **dfs**(m) is running, m is *open*. m is *processed* if it is no longer open but is still contained in *sccStack*. After it has been popped from *sccStack*, m is *closed* and remains closed until the search terminates. We call a marking *visited* if it is open, processed, or closed. Markings that satisfy the test in line 19, proceed immediately from *open* to *close*. All other markings proceed through stage *processed*. Markings that are popped together in lines 20 to 22, form an SCC. This is due to the semantics of the lowlink value of every marking.

Definition 20 (Lowlink [108]**).** *For a marking m, its* lowlink *is the smallest dfs value of markings m^* where a sequence $m_1 m_2 \dots m_k$ with the following two properties exists. First, $m = m_1$ and, for all i $(1 \leq i < k)$,* ***dfs***(m_{i+1}) *has been called in the frame for* ***dfs***(m_i)*, that is, $m_1 m_2 \dots m_k$ once formed a consecutive range on the call stack. Second, $m^* = m_k$ or (m_k, m^*) is an edge in the reachability graph such that m_k and m^* are strongly connected.*

In the algorithm, the update of lowlink in line 16 takes care of the first property while the update in line 12 takes care of the second condition. Tarjan indeed showed that the condition in line 11 asserts strong connectivity of m and m' in line 12. He further showed that there is only one marking in every SCC where the dfs and lowlink values are equal and this marking is the one that has been opened first and closed last. This fact is used for detecting the SCC in lines 19 to 23.

Figure 6 shows a graph and the result of two depth-first searches. The searches explore their successors in different order. The dfs numbers (left) determine the order in which the graph has been explored. The figure also shows the final values of lowlink and the SCC structure. The nodes with bold numbers are the one where the test in line 19 is true.

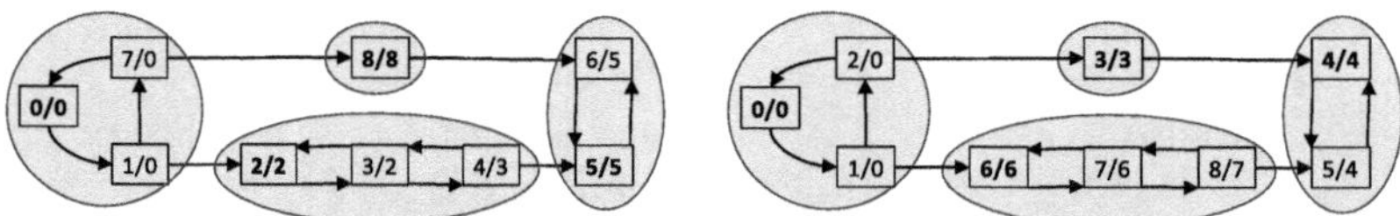

(a) Successors explored right to left (b) Successors explored left to right

Fig. 6. A graph with dfs number (left), lowlink (right) and SCC (grey). Nodes with bold numbers are the entries into their SCC.

[2] Many authors use *processed* and *closed* as synonyms for all states that are no longer open. In our terminology, *processed* and *closed* are distinct stages, and we will refer to that distinction in the sequel.

The algorithm has complexity $O(|V| + |E|)$ where V is the set of vertices, i.e. reachable markings, and E is the set of edges in the reachability graph.

4.2 Implementation Issues

In an actual implementation, the recursion in Algorithm 1 is replaced by iteration. In the iterative version, the call stack is handled explicitly, in addition to *sccStack*. However, we have just one marking *currentMarking* that represents marking m in the active frame of the recursive version. As in line 9, we proceed to a successor marking by adding the effect vetor of the fired transition t. For backtracking to a previous marking, we just subtract that effect vector. That is, the call stack does not need to carry markings. Instead, it can be restricted to information about the progress of the loop in line 8. From this information, we know for which transition the effect vector needs to be added or subtracted when navigating through the reachability graph.

The crucial data structure in depth-first search is the set $Visited$. According to our profiling, the test $m' \in Visited$ in line 9, together with the update $Visited \leftarrow Visited \cup \{m'\}$ in line 7, consumes more than 90% of the run time of the algorithm. Moreover, $Visited$ dominates the memory consumption. For this reason, $Visited$ must be implemented with great care. The currently most competitive tools (according to the model checking contest MCC [8]) use some kind of prefix tree for implementing $Visited$. A marking is considered to be a vector of bits or bytes. In a bit vector, the marking of place p can either be represented as a sequence of $\lceil \log(b+1) \rceil$ bits if b is a known bound for the number of tokens on p, or it can be represented using a Huffman style coding [39], if no good value for b is known. Such a code can, for instance, represent 0 as 10, 1 as 11, 2 as 0100, 3 as 0101, 4 as 0110, 5 as 0111, 6 as 001000, 7 as 001001, and so on.

A marking vector is represented in the prefix tree as a path from the root to a leaf. If two markings share a common prefix, that part of the path is the same for both markings. A prefix tree on the bit level is a binary tree. On byte level, [61] proposes a highly optimized implementation. Every marking corresponds to a unique leaf of the prefix tree. Consequently, the leaves carry marking specific information that includes but is not restricted to dfs and lowlink values. The search and insert operations in a prefix tree require linear run time. We insert a marking only if a prior search for the marking failed. The search for a marking terminates in precisely the branch of the tree where it needs to be inserted subsequently. This observation adds to the efficiency of the data structure. Figure 7 shows a binary prefix tree. It represents the binary vectors (from top to bottom) 10110100, 100110, 1101001, 11100, and 0110100. Every line in Fig. 7 can be organized as a bit array. This way, only the dashed edges need to be explicitly stored.

The performance of a prefix tree can be further improved with the help of place invariants (already seen in Sect. 3.2). For a place invariant $\underline{i}$, we already know that, for all markings m, $\underline{i}^T \cdot m = \underline{i}^T \cdot m_0$. For some place p^* holding

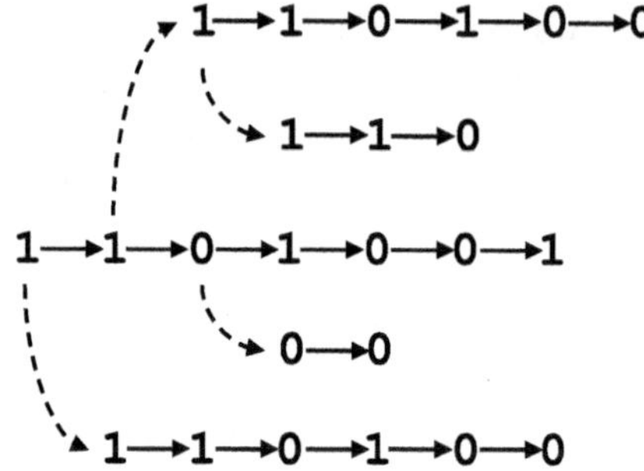

Fig. 7. A binary prefix tree. Every path represents a bit vector. Using a dashed edge from x to y, the value of x needs to be toggled.

$\underline{i}[p^*] \neq 0$, this equation can be transformed to

$$m[p^*] = \frac{\underline{i}^T \cdot m_0 - \sum_{p \neq p^*} \underline{i}[p] \cdot m[p]}{\underline{i}[p^*]}$$

That is, every marking is uniquely determined by the places in $P \setminus \{p^*\}$ which means that the prefix tree does not need to record the marking of p^* and does still have sufficient information to answer $m \in Visited$ in depth-first search [101]. If a net has k linearly independent place invariants, there are k distinct places like p^* that we do not need to store in the prefix tree. In typical Petri nets, the dimension of the space of place invariants is between 40% to 60% of the number of places. That is, the size of marking vectors shrinks by this 40% to 60%. In addition, the execution of the two main operations $m \in Visited$ and $Visited \leftarrow Visited \cup \{m\}$ is also accelerated by 40% to 60%. The reduced marking vector can be interpreted as a unique fingerprint of the marking and, as a generalization of our considerations, we observe that storing a unique fingerprint is sufficient for the implementation of the set $Visited$ to do its job.

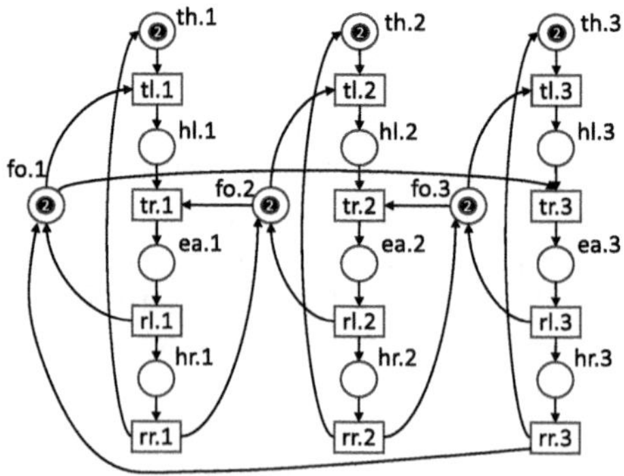

Fig. 8. The three dining philosophers.

As an example, consider the three dining philosophers example in Fig. 8. We have, for every fork i ($1 \leq i \leq 3$), a place $fo.i$ (for "fork"). For every philosopher i, there is a place $th.i$ ("thinking"). Transition $tl.i$ ("take left fork") consumes tokens from $fo.i$ and $th.i$, and produces a token on a place $hl.i$ ("has left fork"). Transition $tr.i$ ("take right fork") consumes from $fo.((i+1) \mod 3)$ and $hl.i$ and produces a token on a place $ea.i$ ("eating"). Transition $rl.i$ ("release left fork") consumes from $ea.i$ and produces tokens on a place $hr.i$ ("has right fork") and on $fo.i$. Finally, transition $rr.i$ ("release right fork") consumes from $hr.i$ and produces on $th.i$ and $fo.((i+1) \mod 3)$. For every i, there is a place invariant expressing the "preservation of philosopher i" law. It has weight 1 for $th.i$, $hl.i$, $ea.i$, and $hr.i$, and weight 0 for all other places. For every i, there is another invariant expressing the "preservation of fork i" law. It has weight 1 for $fo.i$, $hl.i$, $ea.i$, $ea.((i-1) \mod 3)$, $hr.((i-1) \mod 3)$, and weight 0 on the remaining places. Using the total of 6 place invariants, we need to permanently store only $th.i$, $hl.i$, and $ea.i$, for all i. We reduce the size of a marking vector to 40% of the original size.

4.3 Modular State Space

As an alternative to depth-first exploration of the search space, we may construct the *modular state space* [20,40] of a place/transition net if information on the modular structure of the net is available, see Sect. 2.4.

A modular state space consists of the local reachability graphs of its modules and a unique synchronization graph. The local reachability graph of a module is a subgraph of the actual reachability graph of that module. It skips those parts of the actual reachability graph that are blocked due to restrictions that are imposed on the interface transitions by the other modules. For this reason, the modular state space is always finite if the modular Petri net is bounded, even if some or all modules are unbounded when considered in isolation. It is indeed possible to compute the local reachability graph instead of the potentially unbounded actual reachability graph. We achieve this by exploring the local reachability graphs of *all* modules and the synchronization graph jointly. While we explore the internal transitions of modules concurrently, the interface transitions are only fired if all modules participating in a fusion set assert that the fused transition is activated. In this case, the synchronization graph gets a new node. The joint exploration of all local reachability graphs and the synchronization graph is an essential difference between modular state spaces and *compositional verification*. In compositional verification (in particular compositional minimization [14,25,26,51]), we assume local state spaces to be given a priori. Compositional verification tries to reduce those local state spaces one by one and only then starts computing a global data structure like the synchronization graph. While compositional verification has the advantage to be able to reduce local state spaces using the full knowledge of their size and structure, it also has major disadvantages. Without interaction with other modules, compositional verification cannot distinguish between a local reachability graph and the actual reachability graph of a module. The method is thus infeasible for unbounded modules. Even for bounded modules it has been observed that an actual reachability graph of a module may be substantially larger than the local reachability graph [42]. In addition, the requirement to have bounded modules poses much stronger restrictions for an automatic separation of a flat Petri net into modules [41]. For this reason, we believe that modular state space exploration is better suited for modular Petri nets than traditional compositional verification.

Consider first a single module $N_i = [P_i, T_{i|internal}, T_{i|interface}, F_i, W_i, m_{0|i}]$. In the local reachability graph, markings can be arranged into *segments.* A segment consists of all markings that can be reached by the same interaction at the interface of the module.

Definition 21 (segment). *A set O of markings is a* segment *if there exists a sequence $t_1 \dots t_n$ of interface transitions such that, for every $m \in O$, there are sequences $w_0 \dots w_n$ of internal transitions satisfying $m_0 \xrightarrow{w_0 t_1 w_1 t_2 \dots t_n w_n} m$.*

Segments can be disjoint, intersect, or be included in other segments. It may also happen that different sequences of interface transitions lead to the same segment.

The segment $O_{\varepsilon|i}$ corresponding to module N_i and the empty sequence ε of interface transitions is the set of markings that can be reached by internal transitions from m_0. The segment $O_{t_1 \dots t_n|i}$ corresponding to the sequence $t_1 \dots t_n$ of interface transitions can be computed from the segment $O_{t_1 \dots t_{n-1}|i}$ corresponding to $t_1 \dots t_{n-1}$ as follows. First, let E be the set of markings in $O_{t_1 \dots t_{n-1}|i}$ where t_n is enabled. Then compute the set $G = \{m' \mid m \in E, m \xrightarrow{t_n} m'\}$. Finally, $O_{t_1 \dots t_n|i}$ is the set of markings that can be reached by internal transitions from any element in G, a *generator* of $O_{t_1 \dots t_n|i}$.

Consider a modular Petri net with modules $N_1, \dots, N_\ell$. A vertex in the synchronization graph is an ℓ-vector $\langle O_1, \dots, O_\ell \rangle$ where every entry O_i is a segment of module N_i. Edges in the synchronization graph are labeled with fusion vectors. The initial vertex of the synchronization graph is $\langle O_{\varepsilon|1}, \dots, O_{\varepsilon|\ell} \rangle$. For a vertex $\langle O_1, \dots, O_\ell \rangle$, we compute a successor $\langle O'_1, \dots, O'_\ell \rangle$ for fusion vector f if, for all i where $f[i] \neq \bot$, O_i contains a marking where $f[i]$ is enabled (i.e. the fused transition is enabled in some combination of markings). In the successor segment, we have $O'_i = O_i$ if $f[i] = \bot$ and $O'_i = O_{wf[i]}$ if $O_i = O_w$ for some sequence w and $f[i] \in T_{i|interface}$.

The synchronization graph has the lead in the construction of a modular state space. For a given vertex $\langle O_1, \dots, O_\ell \rangle$ and a fusion vector f, it consults the partially created local reachability graphs N_i whether $f[i]$ is enabled in O_i. If so, it gives a signal to all modules N_i where $f[i] \neq \bot$ to compute their respective successor segment and to return a link that can be used to record the new vertex in the synchronization graph. This way, the local reachability graphs compute only those segments that correspond to markings that are reachable in the composed net. If the composed net is bounded, all local reachability graphs are finite even if modules are unbounded in isolation. If the composed net is unbounded, at least one of the local reachability graphs will be infinite while the synchronization graph may be finite or infinite, depending on whether or not the fusion transitions contribute to unboundedness.

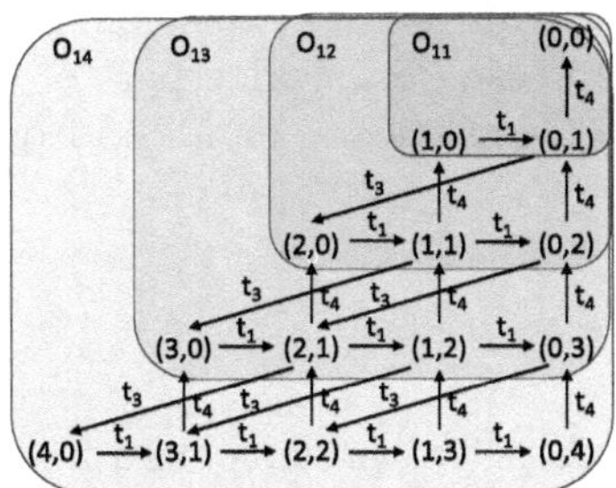

(a) Local reachability graph of M_1.

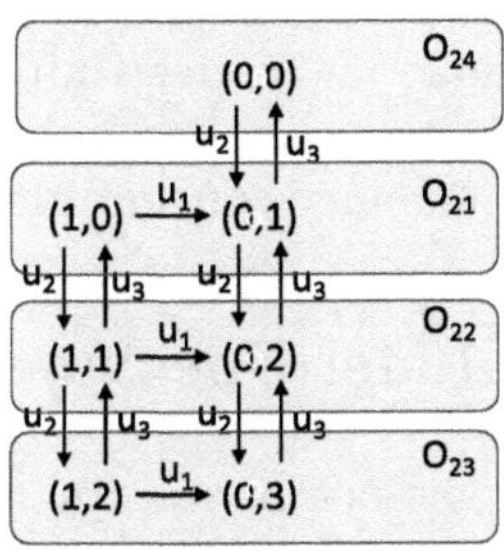

(b) Local reachability graph of M_2.

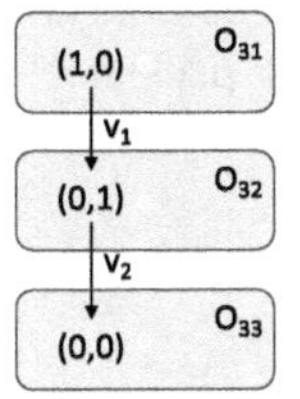

(c) Local reachability graph of M_3.

(d) Synchronization graph.

(O11,O21,O31) —u2v1→ (O11,O22,O32) —u2v2→ (O11,O23,O33)
(O12,O24,O31) —u2v1→ (O12,O21,O32) —u2v2→ (O12,O22,O33)
(O13,O24,O32) —u2v2→ (O12,O21,O33)
(O14,O24,O33)

Fig. 9. Modular state space of the net in Fig. 5.

Figure 9 depicts the modular state space of the net in Fig. 5. In this example, M_1 in isolation is indeed an unbounded net.

In the modular state space, $f_1 \dots f_n$ is a path in the synchronization graph starting in the initial vertex if and only if there exist sequences $w_{11}, w_{12}, \dots, w_{1n}$, $w_{21}, \dots, w_{\ell n}$ and marking m such that, for all j $(1 \leq j \leq \ell)$ and k $(1 \leq k \leq n)$, w_{jk} is a sequence of internal transitions of module N_j and

$$m_0 \xrightarrow{w_{11} \dots w_{\ell 1} f_1 w_{12} \dots w_{\ell 2} f_2 \dots w_{1n} \dots w_{\ell n} f_n} m$$

in the composed modular Petri net. Moreover, m is reachable in the modular net if and only if there exists a vertex $\langle O_1, \dots, O_\ell \rangle$ in the synchronization graph such that, for all i $(1 \leq i \leq \ell)$, $m \mid_{P_i} \in O_i$. Proofs of these claims can be found in [40].

There exist algorithms for model checking LTL [69, 128] and CTL [128] using the modular state space. We shall not cover these algorithms here.

4.4 Concluding Remarks

We usually construct the reachability graph using depth-first search (the modular state space being the exception from that rule). As we shall see in Sect. 5, the evaluation of a temporal logic formula also amounts to depth-first search. In fact, construction of the reachability graph and evaluation of the formula can be bundled with a single depth-first search. This approach is called *on-the-fly model checking* and has its own merits in the fight against state explosion: if the value of the formula can be determined by investigating only some part of the reachability graph, the remaining graph will not be generated at all and does not contribute to memory consumption.

5 Explicit Model Checking

Having simplified the net N and the formula ϕ as much as possible, and having an efficient implementation for the exploration of the reachability graph, we are now ready to solve the actual model checking problem: Given net N and formula ϕ, does the relation $N \models \phi$ hold? We shall present an algorithm for LTL model checking (Sect. 5.1) and an algorithm for CTL model checking (Sect. 5.2). In a separate section (Sect. 5.3), we briefly discuss model checking in presence of fairness constraints.

5.1 LTL Model Checking

In the temporal logic LTL, all formulas are path formulas and no path quantifiers occur. We can therefore focus on *sets* of infinite paths. For a marking, we mainly need the information about which atomic propositions it satisfies. We introduce some terminology to represent these ideas.

For a formula ϕ, let AP_ϕ be the set of atomic propositions that occur in ϕ. For a marking m, let $AP_\phi(m) = \{\alpha \mid \alpha \in AP_\phi, m \models \alpha\}$ be the set of atomic propositions that occur in ϕ and are satisfied in m. We can abstract a sequence of markings to a sequence of subsets of AP_ϕ. We call such a sequence a *trace*.

Definition 22 (Trace). *A* trace *corresponding to formula ϕ is an infinite sequence over the alphabet 2^{AP_ϕ}. For an infinite sequence $\pi = m_1 m_2 \ldots$ of markings, the corresponding trace $AP_\phi(\pi)$ is the infinite sequence $AP_\phi(m_1)AP_\phi(m_2)\ldots$.*

A place/transition net N induces a set of traces L_N that consists of the traces $AP_\phi(\pi)$, for all infinite paths (see Definition 14) in the extended reachability graph of N that start in m_0. Every formula ϕ also induces a set L_ϕ of those traces where ϕ is satisfied. L_ϕ does not depend on the net N under verification. From Definition 16, we get:

Proposition 3 (LTL model checking is inclusion). *For every place/transition net N and every LTL formula ϕ, $N \models \phi$ if and only if $L_N \subseteq L_\phi$.*

That is, LTL model checking amounts to an inclusion problem for sets of traces [118]. The inclusion problem can be transformed into an emptiness problem that is easier to be implemented:

Proposition 4 (inclusion versus emptiness). *$L_N \subseteq L_\phi$ if and only if $L_N \cap L_{\neg\phi} = \emptyset$.*

Both L_N and $L_{\neg\phi}$ may be infinite sets of traces. Both sets can, however, be finitely represented by some kind of automaton. From these two automata, we can construct a third automaton, called *product automaton* that represents $L_N \cap L_{\neg\phi}$. Finally, we can check whether or not the product automaton accepts the empty language. If so, we may conclude $N \models \phi$. If not, we conclude $N \not\models \phi$ and we can transform any example of a trace accepted by the product automaton back into an infinite sequence of markings of N that serves as a counterexample for the false claim $N \models \phi$.

The constructions are similar to constructions on formal languages. However, a set of traces contains *infinite* sequences rather than finite sequences that are studied in classical formal language theory. So, instead of working with finite acceptors, we need a concept of an automaton that is able to accept infinite sequences. There are several proposals for this purpose: Büchi automata [15], Street automata [106], parity automata [84], Muller automata [85], or Rabin automata [95]. Every class of automata is able to implement LTL model checking. For the presentation here, we choose Büchi automata.

Definition 23 (Büchi automaton). *A (nondeterministic)* Büchi automaton *B consists of an* alphabet *X, a set Q of* states, *a set Q_0, $Q_0 \subseteq Q$, of* initial states, *a nondeterministic* transition function *$\delta : Q \times X \to 2^Q$, and a family of* acceptance sets *$\mathcal{F} = \{F_1, \ldots, F_k\}$ such that $F_i \subseteq Q$ for all i. An infinite sequence $x_1x_2\ldots$ of elements of X is* accepted *by B if there is an infinite* run *of the automaton, i.e. an infinite sequence $q_0q_1\ldots$ such that*

- *$q_0 \in Q_0$,*
- *for all i $(i \geq 0)$, $q_{i+1} \in \delta(q_i, x_{i+1})$, and*
- *for every j there are infinitely many i where $q_i \in F_j$.*

The language *of B consists of all infinite sequences that are accepted by B.*

That is, a sequence is accepted if there exists a run for this sequence that visits every acceptance set infinitely often. In accordance with classical language theory, we call a set L of infinite sequences ω-regular if there exists a finite Büchi automaton that accepts L:

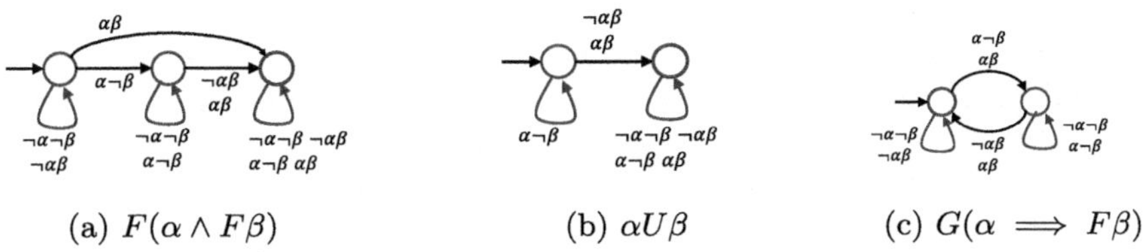

(a) $F(\alpha \wedge F\beta)$ (b) $\alpha U \beta$ (c) $G(\alpha \implies F\beta)$

Fig. 10. Büchi automata for some LTL formulas.

We can derive a Büchi automaton B_N for L_N directly from the extended reachability graph. The alphabet is 2^{AP_ϕ}, Q and F_1 both are the set of reachable markings, $\mathcal{F} = \{F_1\}$, $Q_0 = \{m_0\}$, and, for all m and m', $m' \in \delta(m, AP_\phi(m))$ if there is a transition t where $m \xrightarrow{t} m'$. That is, L_N is ω-regular for bounded nets. Every LTL formula can be translated into a finite Büchi automaton B_ϕ as well [48]. L_ϕ has $O(2^{\text{length}(\phi)})$ states which usually is acceptable since formulas tend to be small. The construction itself is beyond the scope of this paper but there exist freely available implementations [29,44]. Figure 10 shows a few examples of Büchi automata that accept exactly the paths that satisfy the given formula.

The product automaton is defined as follows.

Definition 24 (Product Büchi Automaton). *The product Büchi automaton* $B = [X, Q, Q_0, \delta, \mathcal{F}]$ *of two given automata* $B_1 = [X, Q_1, Q_{0|1}, \delta_1, \mathcal{F}_1]$ *and* $B_2 = [X, Q_2, Q_{0|2}, \delta_2, \mathcal{F}_2]$ *is defined by*

- $Q = Q_1 \times Q_2$;
- $Q_0 = Q_{0|1} \times Q_{0|2}$;
- *for all* $q_1 \in Q_1$, $q_2 \in Q_2$, *and* $x \in X$, $\delta([q_1, q_2], x) = \delta_1(q_1, x) \times \delta_2(q_2, x)$;
- $\mathcal{F} = \{F \times Q_2 \mid F \in \mathcal{F}_1\} \cup \{Q_1 \times F \mid F \in \mathcal{F}_2\}$.

The construction coincides with its well-known counterpart for finite acceptors. The only interesting part is the definition of acceptance sets that makes sure that a sequence is accepted by the product automaton if and only if it is accepted by both B_1 and B_2.

Proposition 5 (product automaton accepts intersection). *If Büchi automaton* B *is the product automaton of Büchi automata* B_1 *and* B_2 *then* $L_B = L_{B_1} \cap L_{B_2}$.

Getting back to our original model checking problem $L_N \cap L_{\neg\phi} = \emptyset$, we can provide a Büchi automaton B^* that accepts $L_N \cap L_{\neg\phi}$. It remains to find out whether B^* accepts the empty language.

Lemma 3 (Emptiness check for Büchi automata). *For a finite Büchi automaton* B, $L_B \neq \emptyset$ *if there is a nontrivial SCC* C *in* B *that is reachable from some initial state of* B *such that, for all* $F \in \mathcal{F}$, $C \cap F \neq \emptyset$.

An SCC C is nontrivial if it has an internal edge. This is the case if C has more than one element, or a single element with a self-loop.

Proof. If there is such an SCC C, we have a path in B that starts in an initial state and proceeds to some state q in C. Since the states in C are strongly connected and C is nontrivial, we can travel from q to all states in C and return to q. This circle can be repeated forever and contains acceptances states from every acceptance set. Consequently, this sequence corresponds to an accepting run.

The other way round, assume that B accepts some sequence and consider an accepting run for that sequence. let Q^∞ be the set of states that occur infinitely often in the accepting run. Since all elements of Q^∞ occur infinitely often in the considered run, all of them must be strongly connected and are therefore contained in some SCC C. C satisfies the required conditions.

If $L_N \cap L_{\neg\phi}$ is not empty, the path to and through C represents a path that can be executed in N and satisfies $\neg\phi$, i.e. violates ϕ. It is an infinite path but determined by a finite path from the initial marking to C and a finite cycle within C. That is, for every violated LTL formula we can find a finitely representable infinite sequence that serves as a counterexample. This counterexample can be animated in the model and may lead to valuable insights concerning the reasons for the violation.

Summarizing all considerations so far, we can evaluate an LTL formula ϕ for a net N using the following procedure. First, we translate ϕ into a Büchi automaton $B_{\neg\phi}$ that accepts all sequences that violate ϕ. Second, we produce the product automaton B^* that accepts $L_N \cap L_{\neg\phi}$ and check its SCC for the presence of accepting states. The reachability graph of N is explored as a part of the construction of B^*. As soon as we find an SCC C that intersects with every acceptance set, we stop the generation of B^*, report violation of ϕ in N and produce a counterexample. If the construction terminates without having an SCC C that intersects with every acceptance set, we report satisfaction of ϕ in N.

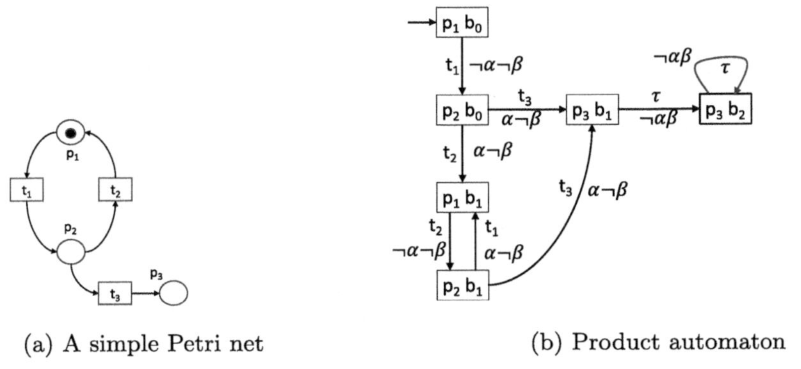

(a) A simple Petri net

(b) Product automaton

Fig. 11. Verification of an LTL formula

As an example, consider the net in Fig. 11a and suppose that we want to verify $G\ (p_2 > 0 \implies G\ p_3 = 0)$. The negation of the formula is $F\ (p_2 > 0 \wedge F\ p_3 > 0)$. A Büchi automaton for the negated formula is shown in Fig. 10a, with $\alpha = p_2 > 0$ and $\beta = p_3 > 0$. Call the states of that automaton b_0 (initial), b_1, and $b_2(final)$. Figure 11b shows the product automaton of the reachability graph of the net with the Büchi automaton of the negated formula. $p_3 b_2$ is a nontrivial SCC that contains an accepting state, so $G\ (p_2 > 0 \implies G\ p_3 = 0)$ is indeed false and the sequence $t_1 t_3 \tau^*$ is a counterexample.

According to [45], we can detect the existence of an accepting SCC C long before C is completed in Algorithm 1. To this end, consider the depth first search for constructing B^* and assume that, when processing a state q, we find one of its immediate successors q' to be open. That is, q' is on the call stack. So there is a path from q' to q, given by the call stack, and a transition from q to q'. Consequently, all states between q' and q on the search stack, including q and q', are strongly connected. If we can assert that these states intersect with all the acceptance sets, we may conclude that an accepting SCC exists long before it is completed. To find out whether the stack portion between q' and q contains accepting states, we add a separate stack for every acceptance set. On the stack for acceptance set F, we push elements of F as soon as they are entered by the search algorithm and pop them as soon as we are done processing them. Doing so, the call stack portion between q' and q contains an element of F if and only if the dfs value of the top element on the stack for F is between the dfs values of q and q'. Using this opportunity to detect non-emptiness of L_{B^*} early, we can save a tremendous amount of memory and run-time.

5.2 CTL Model Checking

In CTL, every temporal operator is immediately preceded by a path quantifier, and the two are considered to be a single operator. As a consequence, the formula and all its subformulas are state formulas. Model checking algorithms for CTL [21,30,76,121] exploit this nature of CTL formulas. We selected the algorithm form [121] for presentation in this paper.

Since all subformulas are state formulas, we can attach a vector $L(m)$ to every marking that records, for every subformula ϕ' of the formula ϕ under verification, whether $m \models \phi'$. The values of that vector range over $T, F, \perp$ representing true, false, and "not yet computed", respectively. When we evaluate a CTL operator in marking m, we pretend that all subformulas are atomic and retrieve the value from $L(m)$. If, for a subformula ϕ', it happens that $L(m)(\phi') = \perp$, we descend recursively and compute that value. The computation of the value of ϕ' at m depends on the shape of ϕ'. The general scheme of CTL model checking is given in Algorithm 2. The top level call for evaluating ϕ is $\mathbf{ctl}(\phi, m_0)$.

Atomic propositions can be evaluated on the spot. For the Boolean operators, we explore a subformula only if that is necessary for determining the value of the parent formula. Also for EX and AX, we explore only as many successors as we need to determine the value. Most of the remaining operators can be traced back to one of the CTL until operators using tautologies (see Sect. 3.3). So it remains to evaluate the until operators. Algorithm 2 delegates this effort to separate subroutines.

We consider first the evaluation of a universal until operator $A(\psi U \chi)$ in $\mathbf{searchAU}(m, \psi, \chi)$. We basically start a depth-first search in m trying to find a counterexample path starting in m. Such a counterexample may have one of two shapes. First, it may be a finite path $m_1 m_2 \dots m_k$ such that, for all i ($1 \leq i < k$), $m_i \models \psi \wedge \neg\chi$, and $m_k \models \chi$, or it may be an infinite sequence $m_1 m_2 \dots$ where, for all elements m_i, $m_i \models \psi \wedge \neg\chi$.

Algorithm 2. CTL Model Checking

```
procedure CTL(φ: ctl formula, m: marking)
    if L(m)(φ) ≠ ⊥ then return
    end if
    if φ = ψ ∧ χ then ctl(ψ, m);                    ▷ similar for other Boolean operators
        if L(m)(ψ) = T then L(m)(φ) ← T; return
        end if
        ctl(χ, m); L(m)(φ) ← L(m)(χ); return
    end if
    if φ = EXψ then                                  ▷ similar for AX
        for all t: t enabled in m do m' ← m + t̲; ctl(ψ, m');
            if L(m')(ψ) = T then L(m)(φ) ← T; return
            end if
        end for
        L(m)(φ) ← F; return ;
    end if
    if φ = A(ψUχ) then searchAU(m, ψ, χ);
    end if
    if φ = E(ψUχ) then searchEU(m, ψ, χ);
    end if
end procedure                     ▷ AF, EF, AR, ER, AG, EG covered by tautologies
```

The search is restricted to markings m' that satisfy the following conditions:

- $L(m')(\psi) = T$ (or $\bot$);
- $L(m')(\chi) = F$ (or $\bot$);
- $L(m')(A(\psi U \chi)) = \bot$;

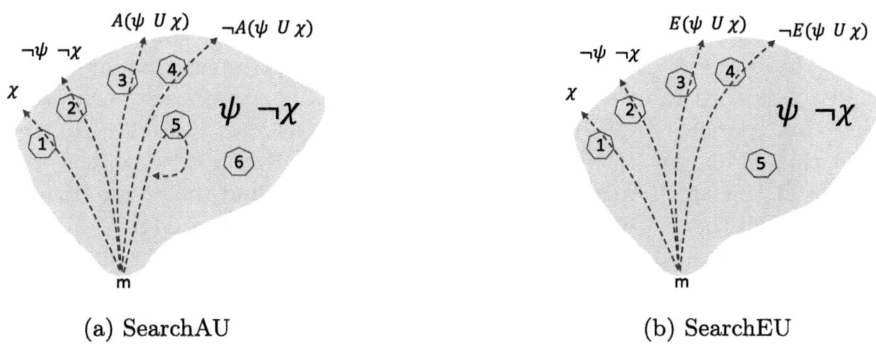

(a) SearchAU (b) SearchEU

Fig. 12. Explicit CTL model checking.

If any of these conditions is violated, we can either be sure that the path from m to m' cannot be extended to a counterexample, so we can backtrack from m', or we have found a counterexample and can terminate the whole search. To see

that, we can consider the following cases (illustrated in Fig. 12a).
Case 1: $L(m')(\chi) = T$ (after evaluation if $L(m)(\chi) = \bot$): Here, any extension of the path from m to m' satisfies $\psi U \chi$ since all elements between m and m' satisfy the above conditions, in particular ψ. So a counterexample cannot be found beyond m'. We can backtrack from m'.
Case 2: $L(m')(\chi) = F$ and $L(m')(\psi)$. Now, the path between m and m' is a finite counterexample since none of the states between m and m' satisfies χ and m' neither satisfies ψ nor χ. We can terminate the whole search and $m \not\models A(\psi U \chi)$.
Case 3: $L(m')(A(\psi U \chi)) = T$. We may backtrack since, if there would a counterexample that starts in m and runs through m', the suffix of the path starting in m' would be a counterexample proving that $m' \not\models A(\psi U \chi)$ which contradicts the case assumption. We may backtrack from m'.
Case 4: $L(m')(A(\psi U \chi)) = F$. According to the case assumption, there would be counterexample path π starting in m'. Then the path from m to m', extended by π, is a counterexample at m. We may terminate the search and $m \not\models A(\psi U \chi)$.

There are two more cases that can happen.
Case 5: There is a cycle in the search space: Since this cycle can be iterated forever, we have found an infinite path where all markings satisfy $\psi \wedge \neg\chi$. This is an infinite counterexample and we can terminate the whole search.
Case 6: The search finishes without early termination: It can be proven that no counterexample exists in this case, so $m \models A(\psi U \chi)$.

Including the condition $L(m')(A(\psi U \chi)) = \bot$ makes sense since there may have been a prior search involving m' and we do not want to do any work twice. Nevertheless, the runtime of CTL model checking would be $O(F \cdot R^2)$ where F is the length of ϕ and R is the size of the reachability graph: in worst case, we need to perform a depth first search in **searchAU** ($O(R)$) for every reachable marking (an additional $O(R)$), and for every subformula of ϕ ($O(F)$). Since the reachability graph is subject to state explosion, its quadratic influence of its size is unacceptable.

We can improve the run time using the following additional idea. So far, **searchAU** evaluates $A(\psi U \chi)$ just in m. In our improvement, that single depth first search is used to evaluate $A(\psi U \chi)$ in *all* markings that have been touched during that search, i.e. all markings that have status *visited* in the moment of termination. This way, thanks to condition $L(m')(A(\psi U \chi)) = \bot$, the search spaces of distinct calls to **searchAU** become disjoint, and the summarized run time for for all the searches amounts to only $O(R)$ instead of $O(R^2)$.

For setting the correct value for markings m' entered during **searchAU**(m, ψ, χ), consider the following cases.
Case Search terminated early and m' is open at termination: In this case, $m' \not\models A(\psi U \chi)$ since m' is a member of the counterexample path for m, and the suffix of that path starting and m' is a counterexample by itself.
Case Search terminated early and m' is processed at termination: This case cannot happen. If m' is processed, there must exist an open marking m'' that is strongly connected to m' since processed states are closed as soon as the last member of their SCC is processed (lines 19 to 23 of Algorithm 1). This SCC,

consisting of at least two distinct members m' and m'', would contain a cycle that would have led to earlier termination.
Case Search terminated early and m' is closed: No counterexample was found while m' was open. We may conclude $m' \models A(\psi U \chi)$.
Case Search did not terminate early: No counterexample has been found for m, so no counterexample can exist for any m' in the search space. We can set $m' \models A(\psi U \chi)$.

The implementation of **searchEU**(m, ψ, χ) is following the same ideas as considered for **searchAU**(m, ψ, χ). There are, however, few subtle differences. For this reason, we need to elaborate on **searchEU** separately.

The search space to be considered is similar. Elements of the search space have to satisfy:

- $L(m')(\psi) = T$ (or $\bot$);
- $L(m')(\chi) = F$ (or $\bot$);
- $L(m')(E(\psi U \chi)) = \bot$;

As before, if any of these conditions is violated, we may backtrack or terminate with a path that this time is a witness for $m \models E(\psi U \chi)$. In the situations where we leave that search space, we may draw the following conclusions (illustrated in Fig. 12b).
Case 1: $L(m')(\chi) = T$: The path from m to m' is a witness proving $m \models E(\psi U \chi)$ and we may terminate.
Case 2: $L(m')(\chi) = F$ and $L(m')(\psi) = F$: The path from m to m' violates $\psi U \chi$ and so does any extension of that path. We may backtrack from m'.
Case 3: $L(m')(E(\psi U \chi)) = T$: We may extend the path from m to m' with a witness proving $E(\psi U \chi)$ at m' and conclude $m \models E(\psi U \chi)$. We can terminate the search.
Case 4: $L(m')(E(\psi U \chi)) = F$: no witness can be found beyond m', so we may backtrack from m'.

In contrast to **searchAU**, a cycle in the search space does not provide any information, so there is only one remaining case.
Case 5: The search finishes without early termination: No witness has been found and $m \not\models E(\psi U \chi)$.

As for **searchAU**, we need to evaluate $E(\psi U \chi)$ for all markings entered during the search. This can be done by considering the following cases for markings m' entered during search.
Case Search terminated early and m' is open at termination: Then m' is a member of the witness path found for m and the suffix starting in m' is a witness by itself. So $m' \models E(\psi U \chi)$.
Case Search terminated early and m' is processed at termination: Then m' is strongly connected to some open m''. The path from m' to m'', extended with the witness path for m'' (see previous case), proves $m' \models E(\psi U \chi)$.
Case Search terminated early and m' is closed at termination: In this case, no witness has been found while m' was open or processed. We may conclude $m' \not\models E(\psi U \chi)$.

Case Search did not terminate early: No witness has been found for m, so no witness can exist for m'. We have $m' \not\models E(\psi U \chi)$.

In contrast to **searchAU**, there may be processed states at early termination of **searchEU** since the latter does not terminate if a cycle in the state space is found. For this reason, the cases to be considered for **searchEU** are slightly different. The difference also applies to the implementation of the two procedures. Since **searchAU** does not need to distinguish between processed and closed states, we can implement it by a simplified depth first search where we can skip the SCC stack and the updates to lowlink. In contrast, **searchEU** requires SCC detection since processed and closed states need to be treated differently.

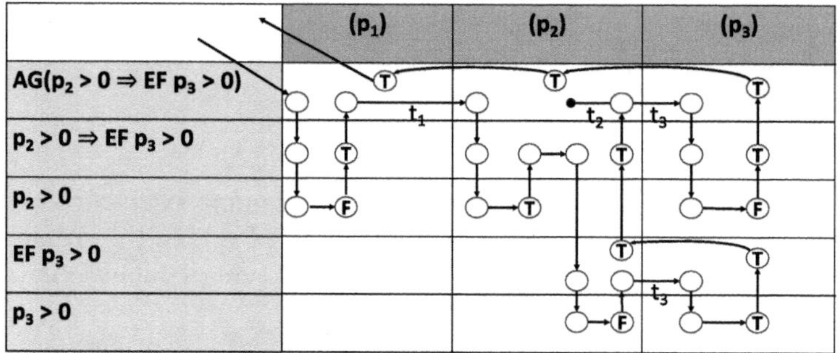

Fig. 13. Run of a CTL model checker

Figure 13 illustrates the run of a CTL model checker for the verification of $AG(p_1 > 0 \implies EF\ p3 > 0)$ on the net in Fig. 11a. Every entry in the matrix represents a call for some formula (row) and marking (column). Downward arrows represent recursive calls, upward arrows represent returns. T or F denotes the computed values $L(m)(\phi)$ for the respective arguments. A horizontal edge labeled with a transition is part of a search for the given subformula. The edge ending in a bullet stands for a transition to a marking that has been seen before. The bended edges symbolize the end of a search with final values for all visited markings. Thanks to the lazy evaluation of Boolean formulas, some matrix entries remain empty.

We may summarize that CTL model checking can be implemented in a run time that is linear both in the size of the formula and the size of the reachability graph.

5.3 Model Checking in Presence of Fairness Constraints

For most Petri nets, some of the modeled behavior is implausible. If the model contains, for instance, two independent components that both have nonterminating local behavior, one would expect that an infinite execution includes infinitely many transitions of both components. Nevertheless, the reachability graph contains paths where only one component changes its local states. As another example, if two transitions compete for a token on a shared pre-place, we would expect that none of transitions always wins that competition. Implausible behavior like this cannot be avoided by just modifying the Petri net model.

To rule out implausible executions, the concept of *fairness* has been introduced. A fairness specification is a property of infinite executions. It is part of the model and modifies the semantics of temporal logic formulas for this model. In presence of a fairness specification, a path quantifier of temporal logic considers only paths that satisfy the fairness specification (for all *fair* paths, there exists a *fair* path). An LTL formula ϕ is true in N in presence of a fairness specification if all *fair* paths starting in m_0 satisfy ϕ.

In the sequel, we attach fairness to transitions (it is also possible to attach it to states [78]). Furthermore, we use only weak and strong fairness while more complex approaches to fairness exist [38,70,122].

In our setting, a fairness specification for net N consists of two disjoint sets T_S and T_W of transitions. Transitions in T_S are to be treated *strongly fair* while transitions in T_W are to be treated weakly fair. There may be transitions for which neither weak nor strong fairness is required.

Definition 25 (Fairness). *Let* $\pi = m_1 \xrightarrow{t_1} m_2 \xrightarrow{t_2} m_3 \ldots$ *be an infinite execution in the extended reachability graph of a net* N. π *treats transition* t weakly fair *if, for every suffix* $m_k \xrightarrow{t_k} m_{k+1} \xrightarrow{t_{k+1}} m_{k+2} \ldots$ *of* π, t *is disabled in some* m_{k+i}, *or* $t = t_{k+i}$, *for some* i. π *treats transition* t strongly fair *if* t *is enabled in* m_i *for only finitely many* i, *or* $t_i = t$ *for infinitely many* i. π *is a* fair path *if it treats all transitions in* T_S *strongly fair and all transitions in* T_W *weakly fair.*

Weak fairness requires that a transition that is constantly enabled has to occur eventually. Weak fairness can rule out executions where one component transitions indefinitely while another independent component does nothing. Strong fairness states that a transition that recurrently (but not necessarily constantly) is enabled, eventually occurs. With strong fairness, we can specify that, if transitions compete for a token on a shared pre-place, each of them wins the competition from time to time.

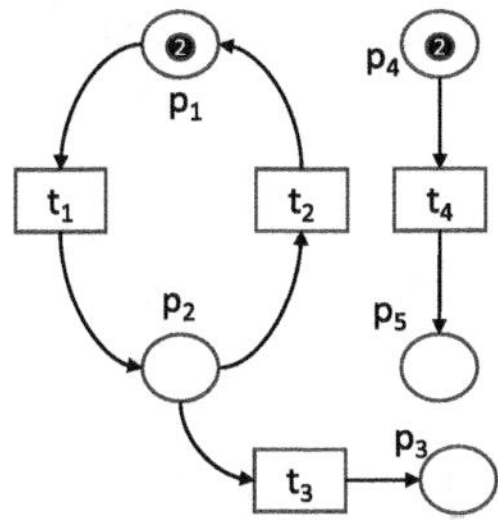

Fig. 14. Another simple Petri net

Consider the net in Fig. 14 and the run $(t_1t_2)^*$. This run treats t_4 weakly unfair. t_3 is treated weakly fair but strongly unfair. t_1 and t_2 are treated fair.

Fairness is inherently a property of infinite executions.

Lemma 4 (fair extension for finite paths). *Every finite execution can be extended to a fair infinite execution.*

Proof. The required execution can be obtained by the following simple strategy: among the enabled transitions, always take the transition that occurred furthest back in the past.

If that strategy brings us into a deadlock, all fairness requirements are satisfied since no transition is enabled and ever gets enabled again. Otherwise, all transitions are treated strongly fair (and hence weakly fair) since a transition can at most card(T) times be enabled while another enabled transition has its previous occurrence further back. □

Fairness can be translated into a property of a strongly subgraph of the reachability graph. This is based on the observation that an infinite sequence of markings in a finite reachability graph must have markings that occur infinitely often. Moreover, all the markings that occur infinitely often in a sequence are necessarily strongly connected.

Proposition 6 (fair execution induces strongly connected set). *Let* $\pi = m_1 \xrightarrow{t_1} m_2 \xrightarrow{t_2} m_3 \ldots$ *be an infinite execution, Let* $E_\pi = \{[m, t, m'] \mid$ *for infinitely many i:* $m = m_i, t = t_i, m' = m_{i+1}\}$. *Let* $M_\pi = \{m \mid$ *exists* $t, m' : [m, t, m'] \in E_\pi\}$.

π *treats transition* t *weakly fair if and only if* M_π *contains a marking* m *where* t *is disabled, or* E_π *contains an edge that is labeled with* t.

π *treats transition* t *strongly fair if and only if* t *is disabled in all markings* m *in* M_π, *or* E_π *contains an edge that is labeled with* t.

Since M_π is strongly connected, it is a subset of a strongly connected component of the reachability graph. At this point, let us revisit the witness and counterexample paths produced in LTL and CT model checking. We can incorporate fairness by making sure that we produce fair counterexamples and fair witnesses. In LTL model checking, our counterexample stems from an SCC C that intersects with all acceptance sets. With fairness, we need to investigate if some strongly connected subset of C meets the requirements of Proposition 6 and still intersects with all acceptance sets. In CTL model checking, we produce different types of paths. The witness path produced in **searchEU** is finite and can therefore be extended to a fair infinite execution by Lemma 4. Consequently, **searchEU** does not need any modification to handle fairness. In **searchAU**, we may produce two different types of counterexample path. First, we may find a finite path $m_1 \ldots m_k$ where all m_i $(i < k)$ satisfy ψ and m_k satisfies χ. Using Lemma 4 once more, this path does not require further consideration. The other type counterexample is an infinite path $m_1m_2 \ldots$ where all elements m_i satisfy $\psi \wedge \neg\chi$. It stems from a cycle in the inner of the search space of **searchAU**. If we

Algorithm 3. Find a fair subset

1: **procedure** FAIRSUBSET(S : set of markings, T_S, T_W set of transitions)
2: ▷ S expected to be strongly connected
3: ▷ T_S: transitions to be treated strongly fair
4: ▷ T_W: transitions to be treated weakly fair
5: **if** $\exists t \in T_W$: t enabled in all $m \in S$ and $\nexists m_1, m_2 \in S$: $m_1 \xrightarrow{t} m_2$ **then**
6: **return** $\emptyset$
7: **end if**
8: **if** LTL model checking and S is disjoint to some acceptance set **then**
9: **return** $\emptyset$
10: **end if**
11: **if** $\exists t \in T_S$: t enabled in some $m \in S$ and $\nexists m_1, m_2 \in S$: $m_1 \xrightarrow{t} m_2$ **then**
12: $S' \leftarrow S \setminus \{m \mid t \text{ enabled in } m\}$;
13: Partition S' into strongly connected components $S_1, \ldots, S_k$;
14: **for all** $i, 1 \leq i \leq k$ **do**
15: $F_i \leftarrow$ **fairSubset**(S_i, T_S, T_W);
16: **if** $F_i \neq \emptyset$ **then**
17: **return** F_i
18: **end if**
19: **end for**
20: **return** $\emptyset$
21: **end if**
22: **end procedure**

let **searchAU** look for an SCC of markings that satisfy $\psi \wedge \neg\chi$ instead of a simple cycle, we have the same situation as in LTL model checking: given a strongly connected set of markings, find a strongly connected subset that satisfies the conditions of Proposition 6. This task can be uniformly solved by Algorithm 3 proposed in [71].

The algorithm computes a fair subset of a given strongly connected set (initially an SCC detected in model checking) if one exists. It returns $\emptyset$ if no fair subset exists. In this case, LTL model checking and **searchAU** need to continue their search. The algorithm first checks for weak fairness in lines 5 to 7. If S violates the criteria for weak fairness in Proposition 6, all subsets of S violate the same criterion, too. Consequently, we immediately return $\emptyset$. Lines 8 to 10 take care of the acceptance set in LTL model checking. These lines can be left out in CTL model checking. If S violates the criteria for strong fairness of some transition t in line 11, only subsets where t is never enabled have the opportunity to treat t strongly fair. Every such subset in fact satisfies the criteria for strong fairness of t. Since we only search for strongly connected subsets, we partition S' into strongly connected components before recursively checking for other violations.

The run time of the algorithm is $(\text{card}(S) \cdot \mathrm{T_S})$ and therefore quite affordable. The complexity is justified as follows. Every transition to be treated strongly fair causes at most one level of recursion. Transitions to be treated weakly fair do not trigger recursive calls. On every level of recursion, we may need to partition a set of markings into strongly connected components which takes linear time.

5.4 Concluding Remarks

All explicit model checking algorithms are extremely lightweight and require linear runtime regarding the size of the reachability graph. The influence of the size of the formula is not restricting in practice even if that influence is exponential in the case of LTL model checking. In the model checking contest MCC, the percentage of solved LTL problems has always been higher than for CTL problems. This is in part due to state space reduction techniques (see Sect. 6) that perform better for LTL but it confirms that LTL model checking is competitive to CTL model checking.

6 State Space Reduction

The most important task in our fight against state explosion is to reduce the size of the reachability graph the model checking algorithms operate on. Instead of the actual reachability graph, we want to produce a smaller graph that, for a given temporal logic formula, produces the same result as the original formula. We present the two most powerful state space reduction method. The first method (Sect. 6.1) is the stubborn set method. It helps to reduce the number of permutations in which concurrently enabled transitions are executed and therefore the number of intermediate markings that are entered. The second method (Sect. 6.2) exploits symmetry in the Petri net. It does not explore a marking if a symmetric marking has already been explored. The sweep-line method (Sect. 6.3) does not reduce the number of markings to be explored but reduces the memory footprint of a search. In the end of this section, we briefly mention random walks (Sect. 6.4).

6.1 The Stubborn Set Method

The stubborn set method is the most powerful state space reduction method for Petri nets. Concurrently enabled transitions can be executed in any order and cause exponentially many intermediate markings. Using the stubborn set method, we try to explore concurrently enabled transitions in as few as possible of these orders, yet preserving the formula under verification. Doing so, we visit less intermediate markings. Stubborn sets are well-studied and there are numerous variations of the method [47,67,98,110,111,113,115] and closely related methods [49,92]. For LTL model checking, literature studies should always include [87] since that paper solves a subtle problem that may be present in earlier publications. In the sequel, we present just one of the available approaches, with emphasis on simplicity.

Using the stubborn set method, reduction is achieved by considering, in every marking m, only a subset stubborn(m) of T, called the stubborn set at marking m.

Definition 26 (Reduced Reachability Graph). *Let $N = [P, T, F, W, m_0]$ be a place/transition net and stubborn* : $\mathbb{N}^P \to 2^T$. *The* reduced reachability graph *$[V, E]$ for N and stubborn is inductively defined as follows.*

- $m_0 \in V$;
- *if $m \in V$, $t \in stubborn(m)$, and $m \xrightarrow{t} m'$ then $m' \in V$ and $[m, t, m'] \in E$.*

If we want to preserve a property in the reduced graph, we need to establish requirements that need to be satisfied in stubborn(m). Stubborn set theory is centered around conditions that regulate how transitions outside the set and transitions in the set can influence each other's activation. In the sequel, we use the following setting (called *strong stubbornness* in the literature).

Definition 27 (Stubborn set). *The set of transitions $T_S = stubborn(m)$ is* stubborn *in marking m if the following conditions hold for every transition $t \in T_S$ and every sequence w of transitions in $T \setminus T_S$:*

- *If there exist enabled transitions in m, then T_S contains at least one enabled transition;*
- *If t is enabled in m and $m \xrightarrow{w} m'$ then t is enabled in m';*
- *If $m \xrightarrow{wt} m'$ then $m \xrightarrow{tw} m'$.*

The conditions state that a stubborn set is not empty if possible, transitions outside the set cannot deactivate nor activate a transition in the set, and a transition in the set cannot deactivate transitions outside the set. A stubborn set T_S satisfying the conditions can be computed using the following observations. If an enabled transition T appears in T_S, we need to make sure that no transition in $T \setminus T_S$ can disable it. A simple way to achieve that is to add all transitions to T_S that compete for tokens with t. This is the case for transitions in $(\bullet t)\bullet$. As a side effect of this particular choice, transitions in $T \setminus T_S$ cannot be deactivated by transitions in T_S. If a disabled transition appears in T_S, we need to make sure that transitions in $T \setminus T_S$ cannot activate it. To this end, it is sufficient to pick an insufficiently marked pre-place p of t (i.e. $W([p, t]) > m(p)$) and to add $\bullet p$ to T_S. Such a place is called *scapegoat* for t in m. Having included $\bullet p$ to T_S, the occurrence of transitions in $T \setminus T_S$ cannot add tokens to p, so t remains disabled, regardless of the token game on its other pre-places. The different treatment of enabled and disabled transitions makes the computed stubborn set marking-specific.

The sketched idea for computing a stubborn set can be formalized as follows. We build a directed graph where the set of vertices is the set of transitions, and an edge $[t_1, t_2]$ has the semantics: if t_1 appears in the stubborn set, we want to include t_2 as well. To define the graph, we assume a fixed choice of scapegoats. That is, we assume a function scapegoat : $T \to P$ such that, for all transitions t, if t is disabled in m then $W(\text{scapegoat}(t)) > m(\text{scapegoat}(t))$. The set of edges is defined by

$$\bigcup_{t \text{ enabled in } m} \{t\} \times (\bullet t)\bullet \quad \cup \quad \bigcup_{t \text{ disabled in } m} \{t\} \times \bullet\text{scapegoat}(t)$$

In this graph, a set is stubborn if it is closed with respect to the edge relation. An efficient way to find such a set is to start with some enabled transition t and to perform depth-first search from t in the graph. We can terminate search as soon as we have found an SCC C where at least one enabled transition is contained. The set of transitions consisting of C and all SCC C' that are reachable from C is indeed closed with respect to the edge relation. SCC C' reachable from C have been closed by depth-first search before closing C and therefore they contain only disabled transitions. For this reason, it is sufficient to pick the enabled transitions of C since disabled transitions do not contribute to the reduced graph. The proposed procedure is linear in the size of the net which is preferable for a procedure that needs to be executed for every marking of the reduced graph. For other, partly more sophisticated approaches to stubborn set computation, we refer to [111,115].

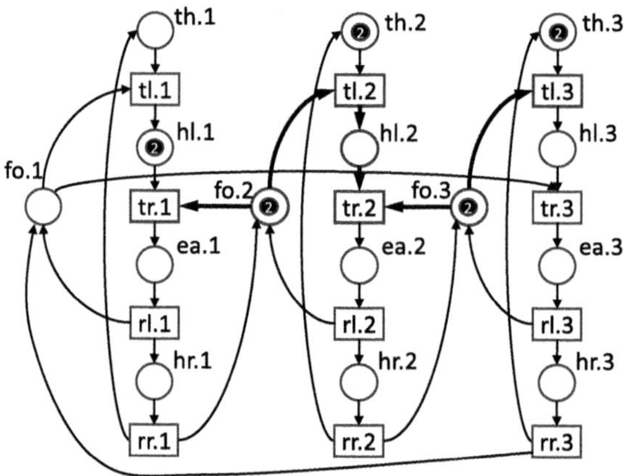

Fig. 15. Stubborn set calculation

Let us calculate a stubborn set for the three dining philosophers and the marking depicted in Fig. 15. We start with enabled transition $tl.3$. It is enabled, so we proceed to the conflicting transition $tr.2$. This transition is disabled, and $hl.2$ is the only possible scapegoat. We continue with $tl.2$, the pre-transition of $hl.2$. $tl.2$ is enabled, so we go to the conflicting transition $tr.1$. $tr.1$ is enabled, and $tl.2$ is conflicting. Consequently, $tr.1$ and $tl.2$ form a valid stubborn set, and the originally picked transition $tl.3$ does not need to be included.

The next two results demonstrate how the conditions for stubborn sets are typically applied to prove preservation of a property.

Lemma 5 (preservation of deadlocks). *Let N be a place/transition net and let, for all m, stubborn(m) be stubborn in m. Then, all reachable deadlocks m_d also appear in the reduced graph.*

Proof. Assume, m_d is a reachable deadlock and does not appear in the reduced graph. Since $m_0 \xrightarrow{*} m_d$ and m_0 appears in the reduced graph, there exists at least one path starting from a marking in the reduces graph and ends in m_d. We choose marking m^* in the reduced graph and sequence w such that $m^* \xrightarrow{w} m_d$ and the length of w is minimal. We consider T_S = stubborn(m) and consider two cases.
Case At least one transition of T_S occurs in w. Then w can be separated into $w = w_1 t w_2$ such that w_1 consists only of transitions in $T \setminus T_S$, and $t \in T_S$, so there exists m_2 such that $m^* \xrightarrow{w_1 t} m_2 \xrightarrow{w_2} m_d$. Using Definition 27, we may conclude that $m^* \xrightarrow{t} m_1 \xrightarrow{w_1} m_2 \xrightarrow{w_2} m_d$. Since $t \in T_S$, m_1 appears in the reduced graph and we can reach m_d from m_1 using path $w_1 w_2$ that is shorter than w. This contradicts the assumed minimality of w.
Case No transition of T_S appears in w. Since the length of w is at least one (otherwise, m_d would appear in the reduced graph anyway), there exist enabled transitions in m^*. That is, T_S contains at least one enabled transition t. Since all transitions of w are in $T \setminus T_S$, Definition 27 asserts that t remains enabled in m_d, contradicting the assumption that m_d is a deadlock. □

Lemma 6 (Preservation of infinite path). *Let N be a place/transition net and let, for all m, stubborn(m) be stubborn in m. Then there exists at least one executable infinite sequence in the reachability graph of N if and only if there exists such sequence in the reduced graph.*

Proof. We show that, whenever we have $m_0 \xrightarrow{w} m$ in the reduced graph and there is an infinite sequence in the original graph starting in m, we can find a transition t and a marking m' in the reduced graph such that $m_0 \xrightarrow{wt} m'$ in the reduced graph, and there is an infinite sequence in the original graph starting in m'. The claimed infinite sequence in the reduced graph can be obtained by repeating this argument forever. For m and T_S = stubborn(m), we consider the same cases as for Lemma 5.
Case Elements of T_S occur in the infinite sequence starting at m. Then, as in the proof of Lemma 5, we can swap the first occurrence of an element of T_S with the transitions in front of it and get t and m'. The remaining sequence is still infinite and enabled in m'
Case No element of T_S occurs in the infinite sequence at m.
Then T_S does contain an enabled transition t such that $m \xrightarrow{t} m'$ and the whole infinite sequence is still enabled in m'. □

The stubborn set approach for LTL can be seen as a refinement of Lemma 6. Instead of *any* infinite path, our new goal is to make sure that the reduced graph contains a *counterexample* to the given formula if and only if the original graph does. The proof of Lemma 6 can be seen as a stepwise transformation of the assumed infinite path from the original graph into an infinite path of the reduced system. The individual steps are to swap a transition in T_S with prior transitions in $T \setminus T_S$ (first case), and to insert a fresh transition at some stage (second case). For preserving a given LTL formula, we add conditions that make sure that the transformation preserves the validity of an LTL formula (where the negation of the given formula is the one we are actually interested in for preserving a counterexample).

To this end, we introduce the concept of visibility. Invisible transitions do not influence the value of atomic propositions of a formula.

Definition 28 (Visibility). *Transition t is* invisible *with respect to temporal logic formula ϕ if, for all atomic propositions $\alpha \in AP_\phi$ and all reachable markings m and m' where $m \xrightarrow{t} m'$, it holds $m \models \alpha$ if and only if $m' \models \alpha$. t is* visible *if it is not invisible.*

Transitions that do not consume or produce tokens on the places mentioned in α are certainly invisible. Transition t with $W([p_1, t]) + W([p_2, t]) = W([t, p_1]) + W([t, p_2])$ can also be considered invisible regarding atomic proposition $k_1 \cdot p_1 + k_1 \cdot p_2 \leq k$. With the following conditions, we force the transformation in the proof of Lemma 6 to respect the order of visible transitions.

Definition 29 (Visibility Respecting Stubborn Sets). *Let ϕ be a temporal logic formula with atomic propositions in AP_ϕ, let m be a marking and T_S be a set of transitions that is stubborn in m. T_S is* visibility respecting *if*

- *All visible transitions with respect to ϕ are contained either all in T_S or all in $T \setminus T_S$.*
- *If an invisible transition is enabled in m, T_S contains an enabled invisible transition.*

Both conditions can be easily integrated into stubborn set computation. With these conditions, we achieve the following effect for the transformation of Lemma in 6. In the first case, where a transition $t \in T_S$ is swapped with a sequence w of transitions in $T \setminus T_S$, t is invisible or all transitions in w are invisible. In the second case, if t is visible, all transitions in the infinite sequence to be transformed are invisible (which follows from that case's assumption). This means, however, that the stubborn set in that marking also contains an enabled invisible transition. Using that invisible transition for the transformation, we proceed our transformation in accordance with the original path. Consequently, those visible transitions that make it to the transformed path in the reduced graph, appear in the same order as they appeared in originally.

There are two catches with the sketched transformation of the visible transitions. First, visible transitions do indeed appear in the same order, but the number of invisible transitions between them may not be the same. This is a problem for formulas containing the X operator. A path that satisfies $X\phi$ may by transformed into a path violating $X\phi$ if an invisible transition is inserted at the beginning. For all other operators, the insertion or deletion of invisible transitions cannot alter the value of an LTL formula. The simple solution for this problem is to apply the stubborn set reduction only to formulas that do not contain the X operator: we preserve the logic LTL-X.

The second catch is that the transformation may apply the second case in the proof of Lemma 6 forever. In this case, we may insert an invisible transition even in the original infinite sequence contains visible transitions. That is, some visible transitions will not be shifted from the original sequence to the one in the reduced graph. To avoid this problem, we introduce another condition that is not a condition to the individual stubborn sets, but the reduced graph generation as a whole.

Definition 30 (Non-Ignorance). *The reduced graph is non-ignoring, if, for every visible transition t, every cycle of the reduced graph contains at least one marking m where $t \in stubborn(m)$.*

For implementing the condition, we may use the observation that, for every cycle, depth-first search will enter a situation where, while processing one marking m of the cycle, one of its successors m' is another member of the cycle and open in that moment (i.e. on the call stack). A simple implementation of the non-ignorance condition is to add all visible transitions to the stubborn set in m whenever we encounter such situation. This condition is indeed sufficient for making sure that all visible transitions of the original sequence eventually make it to the transformed sequence in the reduced graph. We may conclude.

Theorem 1 (preservation of LTL-X [87,92,119]**).** *Let ϕ be a formula in LTL-X. If a reduced graph is generated such that, for all m, stubborn(m) is stubborn, visibility respecting, and the reduced graph is non-ignoring, then ϕ holds in the reduced graph if and only if it holds in the original reachability graph.*

Unfortunately, the approach discussed so far is not sufficient for preserving CTL formulas. Thanks to the presence of path quantifiers, CTL is sensitive to the point where paths branch. A formula may be true if a visible transition occurs before a branch but false if it occurs after the branch. For this reason, stubborn sets in CTL need a condition that makes sure that the relative order between branches and visible transitions is not altered. The following condition is sufficient to solve that issue.

Definition 31 (All-Or-One Property). *A stubborn set T_S has the all-or-one property if $T_S = T$ or T_S contains at most one transition.*

Theorem 2 (Preservation of CTL-X, [47]**).** *Let ϕ be a formula in CTL-X. If a reduced graph is generated such that, for all m, stubborn(m) is stubborn, visibility respecting, has the all-or-one property, and the reduced graph is non-ignoring, then ϕ holds in the reduced graph if and only if it holds in the original reachability graph.*

Visibility respecting stubborn sets can only lead to substantial reduction if there exist sufficiently many invisible transitions. For this reason, a simplification of the formula as discussed in Sect. 3 may significantly improve the strength of the stubborn set method.

There exist stubborn set methods [98,112] that are capable of preserving some subclasses of CTL and LTL and do not need to respect visibility. With such a method, we may obtain reduction even in total absence of invisible transitions. For some subclasses of LTL and CTL, the non-ignorance criterion may be dropped. Today, stubborn set theory consists of a list of criteria that, in different combinations, preserve various classes of properties. Stubborn set methods for a subclass of CTL or LTL typically achieves better reduction than the application of the generic LTL preserving or CTL preserving methods. For some properties, there are even multiple stubborn set approaches with specific pros and cons [67]. For this reason, a Petri net model checker categorizes the given formula after simplification and selects suitable stubborn set approaches. Furthermore, strength reduction (Sect. 3.4) may employ formulas, for which a powerful stubborn set method exists, as a necessary or sufficient condition for the verification of a formula with weaker support by stubborn set methods.

6.2 The Symmetry Method

A Petri net with a symmetrical structure has symmetrical behavior. If we have explored some marking m, we do not need to explore marking m' if m' is symmetrical to m since all we can see is symmetrical to what we have already seen beyond m. The concept of a symmetry in the net can be formalized with the help of *automorphisms*, i.e. bijections σ on the set of places and transitions that preserve all the defining ingredients of a Petri net. For a marking m, its symmetric image is obtained by moving all tokens in place p to the place $\sigma(p)$.

Definition 32 (Symmetry). *Let* $N = [P, T, F, W, m_0]$ *be a place/transition net. A* symmetry *of* N *is a bijection* $\sigma : (P \cup T) \to (P \cup T)$ *such that, for all nodes* x, y*, and all places* p *of* N*,*

- $\sigma(x) \in P$ *if and only if* $x \in P$ *(*σ *preserves the node type);*
- $[x, y] \in F$ *if and only if* $[\sigma(x), \sigma(y)] \in F$ *(*σ *preserves the arc relation);*
- $W([x, y]) = W([\sigma(x), \sigma(y)])$*; (*$\sigma$ *preserves arc weights);*
- $m_0(\sigma(p)) = m_0(p)$ *(*σ *preserves the initial marking).*

For a marking m*, the marking* $\sigma(m)$ *is defined by* $\sigma(m)(\sigma(p)) = m(p)$*; for all* p*.*

In the sequel, let Σ_N be the set of all symmetries of N. Since a symmetry preserves everything that is relevant for activation and firing of transitions, the following observation is obvious.

Proposition 7 (Symmetrical behavior). *For all markings* m*,* m'*, and all transitions* $t_1, \ldots, t_n$*,* $m \xrightarrow{t_1 \ldots t_n} m'$ *implies* $\sigma(m) \xrightarrow{\sigma(t_1) \ldots \sigma(t_n)} \sigma(m')$*.*

The identity id holding $\mathrm{id}(x) = x$ for all x, is always a symmetry. If σ_1 and σ_2 are symmetries, so are σ_1^{-1} and $\sigma_1 \circ \sigma_2$. Consequently, $[\Sigma_N, \circ]$ is a group. The following concepts are defined with respect to an arbitrary subgroup $[\Sigma, \circ]$ since we may need to leave some symmetries out in order to preserve the property under verification. Subgroup Σ induces an equivalence relation on the set of markings.

Definition 33 (Equivalence Of Markings). *Markings m_1 and m_2 are equivalent with respect to Σ ($m_1 \equiv_\Sigma m_2$) if there exists a $\sigma \in \Sigma$ such that $m_2 = \sigma(m_1)$.*

For all subgroups Σ of Σ_N, $\equiv_\Sigma$ is indeed an equivalence relation. It is reflexive since always id $\in \Sigma$, it is symmetric since $\sigma \in \Sigma$ implies $\sigma^{-1} \in \Sigma$, and it is transitive since $\sigma_1, \sigma_2 \in \Sigma$ implies $\sigma_1 \circ \sigma_2 \in \Sigma$. Since we have $\sigma(m_0) = m_0$, for all $\sigma \in \Sigma_N$, Proposition 7 proves that the equivalence class of a reachable marking contains only reachable markings. This observation justifies the construction of the *quotient reachability graph.*

Definition 34 (Quotient Reachability Graph). *The set of vertices of the* quotient reachability graph *is $\{[m]_{\equiv_\Sigma} \mid m_0 \xrightarrow{*} m\}$. $[\,[m]_{\equiv_\Sigma}, [m']_{\equiv_\Sigma}\,]$ is an edge of the quotient reachability graph if there exist $m_1 \in [m]_{\equiv_\Sigma}$, $m_2 \in [m']_{\equiv_\Sigma}$, and a transition t such that $m_1 \xrightarrow{t} m_2$. $[m_0]_{\equiv_\Sigma}$ is the initial vertex.*

The size of Σ may be exponential in the size of the net but there exist generating sets for Σ with polynomially many elements. We introduce one particular generating set since that one is useful in the construction of the quotient reachability graph. To this end, we assume that $P \cup T = \{x_1, \ldots x_n\}$ and consider the following subsets of Σ. In the sequel, let card(M) be the cardinality of the M.

Definition 35 (Stabilizer, Orbit). *For a subgroup Σ of Σ_N and numbers i and k ($1 \leq i \leq card(P \cup T), i \leq k \leq card(P \cup T)$) the set Σ_i^k is defined by $\Sigma_i^k = \{\sigma \mid \sigma \in \Sigma, \sigma(j) = j \text{ (for } 1 \leq j < i), \sigma(i) = k\}$.*

Σ_i^i is a subgroup of Σ, called *stabilizer* subgroup for the first i elements. If $\Sigma_i^k \neq \emptyset$, we can fix an arbitrary element $\sigma_i^k \in \Sigma_i^k$ and it holds $\Sigma_i^k = \Sigma_i^i \circ \sigma_i^k = \{\sigma \circ \sigma_i^k \mid \sigma \in \Sigma_i^i\}$. For this reason, Σ_i^k is the *orbit* of σ_i^k with respect to Σ_i^i in the surrounding subgroupΣ_{i-1}^{i-1}. For convenience, let σ_i^i always be the identity id. Moreover, the following results can be immediately derived from Definition 35.

- If $k_1 \neq k_2$, $\Sigma_i^{k_1} \cap \Sigma_i^{k_2} = \emptyset$;
- $\Sigma_{i-1}^{i-1} = \bigcup_{k=i}^{n} \Sigma_i^k$;
- $\Sigma_n^n = \{\text{id}\}$.

From these observations, we can derive a generating set for Σ as follows. For all i, let $\Gamma_i = \{\sigma_i^k \mid \Sigma_i^k \neq \emptyset, i \leq k \leq n\}$.

Theorem 3 (generating set, [17]**).** *The set $\Gamma = \bigcup_{i=1}^{n} \Gamma_i$ generates Σ.*

Proof. We proceed inductively, starting at n and then proceeding from i to $i-1$.
Basis: Σ_n^n can be generated since $\Sigma_n^n = \{\text{id}\} = \sigma_n^n \in \Gamma_n$.
Step: Assume, Σ_i^i can be generated from Γ. Then, for all k ($i \leq k \leq n$), every nonempty Σ_i^k can be generated as $\sigma_i^k \circ \Sigma_i^i$ with $\sigma_i^k \in \Gamma_i \subseteq \Gamma$. As already stated, $\Sigma_{i-1}^{i-1} = \bigcup_{k=i}^{n} \Sigma_i^k$, so Σ_{i-1}^{i-1} can be generated as well.
Finally, we can generate $\Sigma = \bigcup_{k=1}^{n} \Sigma_1^k = \bigcup_{k=1}^{n} \sigma_1^k \circ \Sigma_1^1$. □

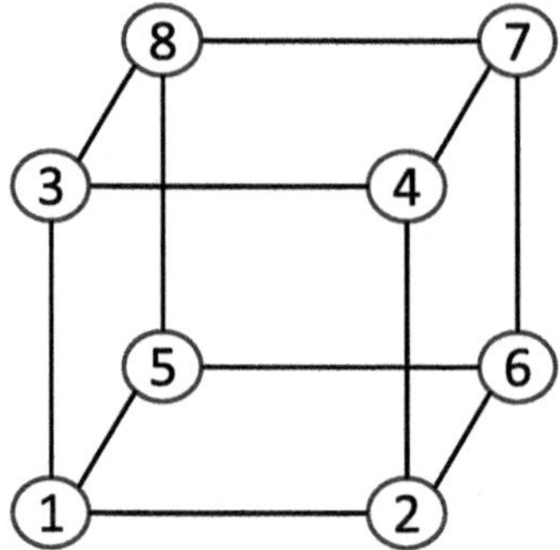

Fig. 16. An undirected graph with symmetries

Since we include only one element σ_i^k for every i and k, Γ has at most $\frac{n(n+1)}{2}$ elements.

For simplicity, we demonstrate the concept using just a plain undirected graph instead of a Petri net. Consider Fig. 16. Table 1 lists the generating set for the automorphisms of this graph. We did not include σ_1^1, σ_2^2, and σ_3^3, as these are by default the identity. So we have $7+2+1=10$ generators for $8 \cdot 3 \cdot 2 = 48$ distinct automorphisms.

Table 1. Generating set for the graph in Fig. 16.

		$\sigma(1)$	$\sigma(2)$	$\sigma(3)$	$\sigma(4)$	$\sigma(5)$	$\sigma(6)$	$\sigma(7)$	$\sigma(8)$	Geometrical illustration
Γ_1	σ_1^2	**2**	6	4	7	1	5	8	3	rotate left around y axis
	σ_1^3	**3**	1	4	2	8	5	6	7	rotate right around z axis
	σ_1^4	**4**	3	2	1	7	8	5	6	rotate twice around z axis
	σ_1^5	**5**	1	8	3	5	2	4	7	rotate left around y axis
	σ_1^6	**6**	5	7	8	2	1	3	4	rotate twice around y axis
	σ_1^7	**7**	8	6	5	4	3	1	2	mirror at central point
	σ_1^8	**8**	7	5	6	3	4	2	1	rotate twice around x axis
Γ_2	σ_2^3	1	**3**	5	8	2	4	7	6	rotate left at diagonal 1,7
	σ_2^5	1	**5**	2	6	3	8	7	4	rotate right at diagonal 1,7
Γ_3	σ_3^5	1	2	**5**	6	3	4	7	8	mirror at plane through 1,2,7,8

When we construct the quotient reachability graph, we represent vertex $[m]_{\equiv_\Sigma}$ by a representative of that equivalence class. The most popular representative is the lexicographically smallest element of the class.

Definition 36 (lexicographical order on markings). *Let N be a Petri net with a set $P = \{p_1, \ldots, p_m\}$ of places. Marking m_1 is* lexicographically smaller *than m_2 ($m_1 \sqsubset m_2$) if there is an i such that $m_1(p_i) < m_2(p_i)$ and, for all*

Algorithm 4. Transformation of a marking into a small equivalent one.

procedure CANONIZE(m: marking)
    for $i := 1$ to n **do**
        $m \leftarrow \min_{\sqsubset}(\{\sigma(m) \mid \sigma \in \Gamma_i\})$
    end for
    return m
end procedure

$j < i$, $m_1(p_j) = m_2(p_j)$. *Marking* m *is the* canonical representative *of a set* M *of markings if, for all* $m' \in M$, $m \neq m'$ *implies* $m \sqsubset m'$.

Transforming a marking into its canonical representative is most likely not solvable in polynomial time. This is due to the observation that the graph isomorphism problem can be reduced in polynomial time to the decision problem "Given a net and two markings m_1, m_2, decide whether $m_1 \equiv_{\Sigma_N} m_2$!" [62]. Graph isomorphism is in NP and despite focused research, no polynomial time algorithm has been found. We therefore propose an algorithm that transforms a marking into a small representative of its equivalence class, but not always into the smallest one. The procedure runs in polynomial time which is desirable, and causes the quotient graph to grow a little bit, compared to the use of a perfect canonization (in our experience, the graph never grows by more than 10%). The growth is caused by the fact that, due to our approximation, we may need to store more than one small representative of one and the same class. Correctness results are not affected.

We transform a given marking m by systematically applying elements of the generating set Γ to it. Our transformation exploits the special structure of our generating set Γ. Elements of Γ_i are contained in Σ_{i-1}^{i-1}, so they do not alter the first $i-1$ entries of the marking. So the idea is to first use Γ_1 to minimize $m(p_1)$, then Γ_2 to minimize $m(p_2)$ without destroying $m(p_1)$, then Γ_3 to minimize $m(p_3)$ without destroying $m(p_1)$ and $m(p_2)$, and so on. Moreover, the elements in Γ_i assign different values to i. By applying the inverse of the generators, we have card(Γ_i) different positions from which values can be shifted to position i. The resulting procedure is shown in Algorithm 4.

Suppose that the generators in Table 1 represent the automorphisms of a net with places $p_1, \dots, p_8$ and consider marking $m = (4, 2, 0, 2, 3, 1, 0, 1)$. We use Γ_1 to shift one of the zeros in $m(p_3)$ or $m(p_7)$ to the front. We have ${\sigma_1^3}^{-1}(m) = (0, 4, 2, 2, 1, 3, 1, 0)$ and ${\sigma_1^7}^{-1}(m) = (0, 1, 1, 3, 2, 0, 4, 2)$. So we proceed with $m_1 = {\sigma_1^7}^{-1}(m)$. With Γ_2, the best choice is to use σ_2^3 to shift $m_1(p_3) = 1$ to the second position in the vector. σ_2^5 will bring $m_1(p_5) = 2$ to that position and is clearly inferior. We obtain ${\sigma_2^3}^{-1} = (0, 1, 2, 2, 1, 3, 4, 0)$. This marking is, however, larger than $\sigma_2^2(m_1) = m_1$, so we proceed with m_1. In the last round of the algorithm, we use σ_3^5 to transform m_1 into the resulting representative ${\sigma_3^5}^{-1}(m_1) = (0, 1, 1, 3, 2, 2, 4, 0)$.

The quotient reachability graph can be computed by instrumenting the usual depth first search with our canonization procedure. Whenever we compute a new marking, we canonize it before searching and inserting it.

With the symmetry method, we can preserve every CTL* formula ϕ. All we need to do is to use a symmetry group Σ such that all subformulas of ϕ are insensitive to Σ [24].

Definition 37 (Insensitive formula). *State formula ϕ is insensitive to symmetry group Σ if, for all markings m and all $\sigma \in \Sigma$, $m \models \phi$ implies $\sigma(m) \models \phi$. Path formula ϕ is insensitive to Σ if, for all infinite paths $m_1 m_2 \ldots$. and all $\sigma \in \Sigma$, $m_1 m_2 \ldots \models \phi$ implies $\sigma(m_1)\sigma(m_2) \ldots \models \phi$.*

An atomic proposition $\alpha = k_1 \cdot p_1 + \cdots + k_m \cdot p_m \leq k$ is insensitive to Σ if, for all $\sigma \in \Sigma$, $\sigma(p_i) = p_j$ implies $k_i = k_j$. We can get additional insensitivity by exploiting commutativity and associativity of $\wedge$ and $\vee$. If all "atomic" propositions of ϕ (actual atomic propositions or Boolean combinations of atomic propositions) are insensitive to Σ, so is ϕ. We can systematically find symmetries that make ϕ insensitive by computing the automorphisms in the syntax tree of Boolean combinations of atomic propositions of ϕ.

This section was based on [99,100]. A systematic comparison of various ways to compute the quotient reachability graph can be found in [63]. For high-level nets, a limited set of symmetry groups can be detected by investigating the color sets and arc inscriptions [18,58].

6.3 The Sweep-Line Method

There are some reduction techniques that aim at reducing the memory footprint of the search by not storing all visited markings [68,101], or by removing visited markings from the prefix tree while the search is still running. We present the sweep-line method, that accords to the latter scenario.

Suppose first that we have a progress measure p that assigns a progress value $p(m)$ to every reachable marking such that $m \xrightarrow{t} m'$ implies $p(m) \leq p(m')$. Let, at any point during search, $B = \min p(m) \mid m \text{ is open } \}$. In this situation, all future queries to $m' \in Visited?$ in Algorithm 1 (page 23) will have $p(m') \geq B$. This means that all markings with a progress value less than B can be removed without altering the search. It should be mentioned that the method does not work well with depth-first search since m_0 has the smallest progress value of all reachable markings and remains open until the search terminates. With other search strategies, however, the method makes sense.

In its original form [19], the method has a limited scope. Whenever the reachability graph has a cycle (which is the case for most reasonable Petri nets), either all markings on the cycle have the same progress value, or there is a regress transition, i.e. a transition that decreases the progress value. The sweep-line method has thus be extended such that it can tolerate a few regress transitions [66]. Whenever a regress transition fires and reaches marking m^*, m^* is called *persistent* and stored permanently. Moreover, after having finished a run of the sweep-line method, another run is launched, starting with the persistent markings added in the previous round. Using this strategy, it can be proven that all reachable markings will eventually be visited. There exist algorithms for CTL and LTL model checking [34,75] that use the sweep-line method.

A progress measure can either be provided manually, or it can be computed automatically. The automatic approach [102] is based on linear algebra. It computes a value $p(t)$ for every transition t such that $m \xrightarrow{t} m'$ implies $p(m') = p(m) + p(t)$. It is computed such that the progress value of a marking m is independent from the path that leads from the initial marking m_0 to m. To this end, we select a maximal set of linearly independent transitions U among the effect vectors $\underline{t}$, for all transitions t. For transitions $t \in U$, we set $p(t) = 1$. For a transition $t \in T \setminus U$, the value is uniquely determined through the linear combination of $\underline{t}$ with transitions in U. If $U = \{\underline{u_1}, \ldots, \underline{u_\ell}\}$ and $\underline{t} = k_1\underline{u_1} + \cdots + k_\ell\underline{u_\ell}$, then $p(t) = k_1 + \ldots k_\ell$. This way, the progress value of all paths leading to m sum up to the same progress value for m since those paths all correspond to linear combinations of $m - m_0$. For acyclic nets, the approach leads to a monotonous measure that enables the basic sweep-line method. For other nets, transitions in $T \setminus U$ may have a value (t) that is greater than zero, equal to zero, or less than zero. In the three dining philosophers net (Fig. 8 on page 27), the method would assign 1 to three of the four transitions that model a philosopher i. The remaining transition t has $p(t) = -3$ since every local iteration of just one philosopher returns to the initial marking. This is basically what we would have used as a manually provided measure.

It is strongly recommended to use the sweep-line method together with the stubborn set method. Suppose that, in the three dining philosophers model, the regress transitions are $rr.i$, for all i. Then 15 of 26 reachable markings in the full reachability graph are reached by a regress transition while only 6 of 20 markings in the reduced graph are reached by a regress transition (see Fig. 17). The stubborn set method decouples the local cycles of the individual philosophers and thus improves the ratio between persistent and non-persistent markings.

6.4 Random Walks

In the temporal logic LTL, some formulas represent *safety properties*. Informally, ϕ is a safety property if its violation can be recognized on some finite prefix of a trace. Formally, for a safety property ϕ, $\pi \not\models \phi$ implies that there exists a finite prefix π^0 of π such that for every path π' that starts with π^0, $\pi' \not\models \phi$. For safety properties, counterexamples can be recognized using a normal finite acceptor instead of a Büchi automaton.

Given an LTL safety property, we can repeatedly generate transition sequences and feed the corresponding traces to the finite acceptor. If one of the traces happens to be accepted, we know that $N \not\models \phi$. If none of the traces is accepted, we known nothing. Consequently, the method is not very useful in isolation. It is, however, a valuable member of a verification portfolio where several methods are applied concurrently. It is valuable since it does not suffer from state explosion. For a random walk, we do not need to record visited markings. In addition, the overhead for managing the visited markings vanishes. We already mentioned that this amounts to about 90% of the total run time of depth-first search. Random transition sequences can therefore be generated much faster than paths in the reachability graph.

We do not need to generate the sequences completely random. In particular, it makes a lot of sense to apply the stubborn set method to every marking. When we additionally take care of not ignoring transitions too long, we increase the probability to find an accepting run. The respective state of the acceptor can be used to further attract the execution towards an accepting state [60, 72].

6.5 Concluding Remarks

The stubborn set method and the symmetry method are the most powerful state space reduction techniques. The stubborn set method does not require preprocessing but causes some overhead for computing a stubborn set at every marking. Computation of a reduced graph is nevertheless faster than the generation of a full graph in almost all cases, since fewer markings need to be explored. The symmetry method requires preprocessing for computing the generating set of the symmetry group. In addition, every marking needs to be transformed into its small representative. The size of a quotient graph cannot be smaller than the size of the original graph, divided by the size of the symmetry group since an equivalence class of markings cannot contain more elements than the size of the symmetry group. Since we can have up to exponentially many symmetries, the reduction can nevertheless be impressive.

We can apply the stubborn set method and the symmetry method in combination and get additional reduction.

Figure 17 shows reachability graphs for the three dining philosophers system (Fig. 8, page 27) using different reduction methods. For n philosophers, the full state space has 3^{n-1} markings while the fully reduced graph has $3n-1$ markings.

Figure 18 shows the principal design of an explicit model checking procedure. Assuming both the net and the formula to be simplified, we first do preprocessing, if necessary. Preprocessing may include the generation of a Büchi automaton (mentioned in Sect. 5.1) for the (negated) formula and the calculation of a generating set for the symmetries (Sect. 6.2). For the actual verification of the formula, we apply the procedures sketched in Sects. 5.1 and 5.2 which are centered around depth-first search (Sect. 4.1). Alternatively, we can use an LTL or CTL model checker that explores the state space with the sweep-line method (Sect. 6.3), or we compute a modular state space (Sect. 4.3), or we can try to run into a counterexample with a random walk (Sect. 6.4). In every iteration of the search, we determine which transitions we want to explore. This can be all enabled transitions, or a stubborn set (Sect. 6.1). Whenever the search encounters a marking m, we check whether m is already visited. To this end, we encode the marking to a vector of bits or bytes. We skip the encoding of places that functionally depend on other places through a place invariant (Sect. 4.2). If the symmetry method is applied (Sect. 6.2), we transform the marking into a small representative of its

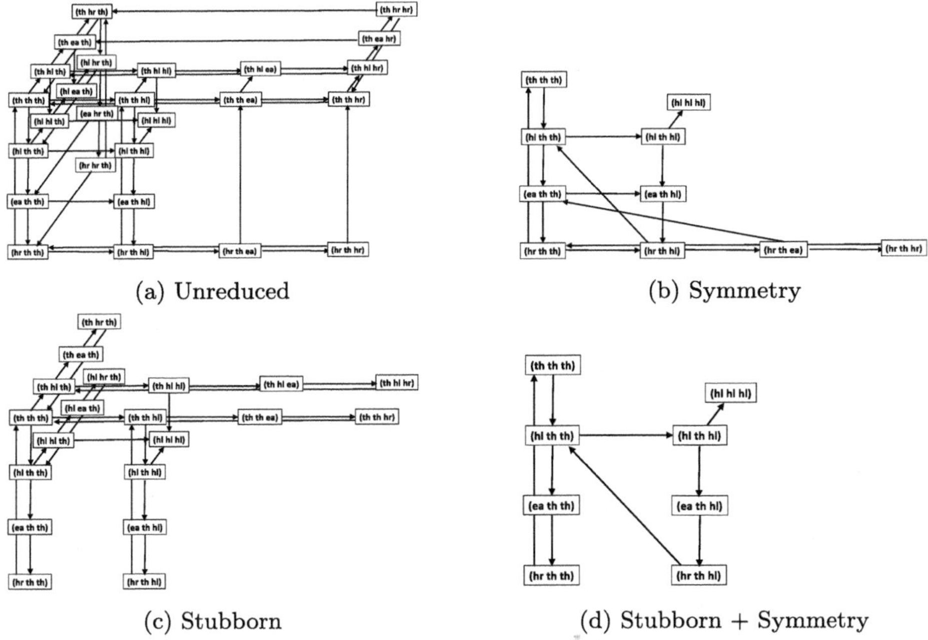

(a) Unreduced

(b) Symmetry

(c) Stubborn

(d) Stubborn + Symmetry

Fig. 17. Reachability graphs for the three dining philosophers

equivalence class. The resulting vector is then looked up (and inserted, if necessary) in the prefix tree for the visited markings (Sect. 4.2). In the end, we report the computed result. If possible, we also provide a witness or counterexample path that we mainly obtain from the call stack at the moment of termination. In addition, we may provide statistical information such as the size of the explored graph as well as memory and time consumption.

7 Symbolic Model Checking

Instead of reducing the *number* of represented markings, symbolic model checking tries to reduce the *size of the data structure* that represents a set of markings or a set of paths. Operations are performed on the data structure and effect *all* represented markings or paths at once.

We survey four approaches to symbolic model checking. In Sect. 7.1, we use binary decision diagrams to store sets of markings. In Sect. 7.2, formulas of propositional logic represent sets of paths. In Sect. 7.3, paths and markings are recorded in a data structure where transition occurrences are only partially ordered. In Sect. 7.4, we employ the state equation (already introduced in Sect. 3.2) for model checking. In the first three sections, we present approaches for safe Petri nets, i.e. nets where all reachable markings carry at most one token per place. Extensions to non-safe Petri nets are only briefly mentioned.

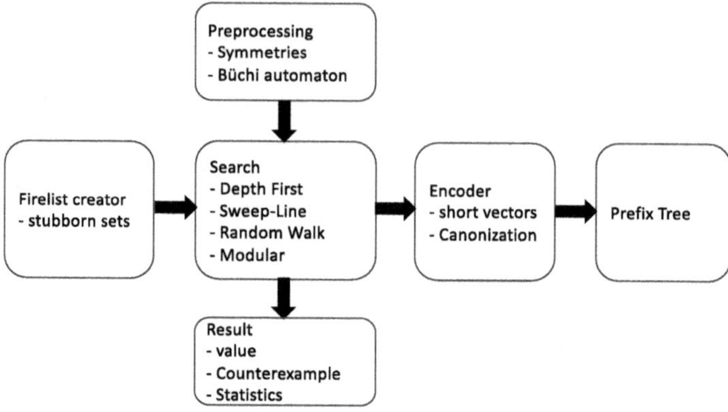

Fig. 18. Explicit model checking

7.1 Binary Decision Diagrams

A binary decision diagram (BDD, [12]) is a data structure that is able to store a set of bit vectors. In a safe Petri net, a marking can be such a bit vector. A BDD can be seen as a compact representation of a decision tree. Given an ordering of variables (indices in the vector), a vertex in the tree at depth i represents a decision to go left for vectors v with $v[i] = 0$, and to go right if $v[i] = 1$. Consequently, a bit vector is represented as path in the decision tree. A leaf of the tree carries a Boolean value indicating whether the unique vector that leads there is in the represented set. Figure 19 shows a decision tree and the corresponding BDD. It represents the set $\{(0,0,1),(0,1,0),(0,1,1),(1,0,0),(1,0,0)\}$.

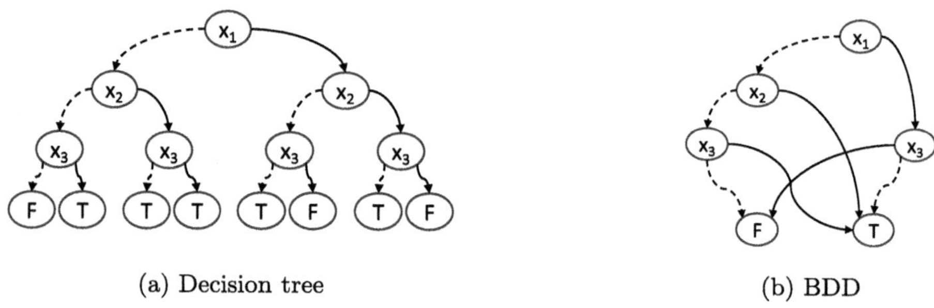

Fig. 19. Representations of Boolean functions

For compact representation, equivalent subtrees are folded and redundant vertices (vertices where both outgoing edges lead to the same successor) are left out. For a given ordering of the variables, the resulting BDD is unique for every represented set. The variable ordering may have significant impact on the size, so occasional reordering of variables is used to avoid memory overflow during computations. Some BDD libraries can even fold dual subtrees (equivalent but with opposite labels).

Many operations can be performed directly on BDDs, i.e. without unfolding the compact representation. For instance, basic set operations like union and intersection can be implemented in $O(\text{card}(BDD_1), \text{card}(BDD_2))$.

A BDD can alternatively be viewed as the representation of a propositional formula ϕ where the stored bit vectors represent the assignments where ϕ gets true. From a BDD that represents ϕ, we can compute a BDD that represents $\exists x\phi$, a formula that has one argument less than ϕ, so the BDD for $\exists x\phi$ is a bit shallower than the one for ϕ.

There exist highly optimized libraries that implement BDDs, so we may view a BDD library as an abstract data type for representing sets of bit vectors and propositional formulas that offers operations including set operations and existential quantification.

As BDDs can represent sets of markings, they are particularly well suited for CTL model checking where all subformulas are state formulas [16]. Starting with the atomic propositions, we compute, for every subformula ϕ' of ϕ, a BDD $BDD_{\phi'}$ that represents all markings m where $m \models \phi'$. Atomic propositions are directly translated into a BDD. Boolean operators conjunction, disjunction, and negation can be implemented using the capability of a BDD library to handle union, intersection, and complement.

For the temporal operators, we build another BDD BDD_T that represents the transition relation. It stores all pairs $[m_1, m_2]$ such that there is a transition t where $m_1 \xrightarrow{t} m_2$. A pair of markings is just a bitvector twice as long as a marking, so there is no principal problem for representing BDD_T. We can obtain BDD_T as a propositional formula θ that uses variable p for representing $m_1(p)$ and p' for representing $m_2(p)$, for all $p \in P$. In this setting (and remembering that we are talking about a safe net), BDD_T represents the formula

$$\theta = \bigvee_{t\in T} \left(\bigwedge_{p\in \bullet t} p \wedge \bigwedge_{p\in \bullet t \setminus t\bullet} \neg p' \wedge \bigwedge_{p\in t\bullet} p' \wedge \bigwedge_{p\notin t\bullet \cup \bullet t} p \iff p' \right)$$

The first part requires that t is enabled in m_1 while the remaining parts specify that m_2 is obtained from m_1 by firing t. For simplicity, we ignored the τ-transitions of the extended reachability graph.

Using BDD_T, we can compute $BDD_{EX\phi}$ from BDD_ϕ as

$$\exists p_1' \dots p_n' \; BDD_T(p_1, \dots, p_n, p_1', \dots, p_n') \wedge BDD_\phi(p_1', \dots, p_n')$$

Algorithms for $E(\psi U \chi)$ and $EG\phi$ can be derived from the tautologies

$$E(\psi U \chi) \iff \chi \vee (\psi \wedge EX\; E(\psi U \chi))$$

and

$$EG\phi \iff \phi \wedge EX\; EG\phi$$

The result is shown in Algorithm 5 and Algorithm 6.

Algorithm 5. BDD implementation for $E(\psi U \chi)$

```
BDD_{E(ψUχ)} ← BDD_χ;
repeat
    BDD_{E(ψUχ)} ← BDD_{E(ψUχ)} ∪ (BDD_ψ ∩ ∃p'_1 ... p'_n (BDD_T(p_1, ..., p'_n) ∩
    BDD_{E(ψUχ)}(p'_1, ..., p'_n)));
until nothing changes
```

$BDD_{E(\psi U \chi)} \leftarrow BDD_\chi$;
repeat
$\quad BDD_{E(\psi U \chi)} \leftarrow BDD_{E(\psi U \chi)} \cup (BDD_\psi \cap \exists p'_1 \dots p'_n \ (BDD_T(p_1, \dots, p'_n) \cap BDD_{E(\psi U \chi)}(p'_1, \dots, p'_n)))$;
until nothing changes

Algorithm 6. BDD implementation for $EG\phi$

$BDD_{EG\phi} \leftarrow BDD_\phi$;
repeat
$\quad BDD_{EG\phi} \leftarrow BDD_{EG\phi} \cap \exists p'_1 \dots p'_n \ (BDD_T(p_1, \dots, p'_n) \cap BDD_{EG\phi}(p'_1, \dots, p'_n))$;
until nothing changes

The remaining CTL operators can be handled via tautologies. Here, the tautology

$$A(\psi U \chi) \iff \neg(EG(\psi \wedge \neg\chi) \vee E(\neg\chi U(\neg\psi \wedge \neg\chi)))$$

is worth being mentioned as it reflects the two types of counterexample for $A(\psi U \chi)$ that we already discussed in Sect. 5.2.

For operating with the usually large BDD_T, it was proposed to partition it into a Boolean combination of individual BDDs and to apply them gradually [56]. This approach helps to avoid memory overflow during the computations.

Petri net structure theory can help to accelerate BDD based model checking. To name just one example [103], we can benefit from place invariants. Suppose we have a place invariant i where all weights are zero or one, and exactly one of the places in supp(i) is initially marked. Then, by Lemma 2 on page 17, exactly one of the places in supp(i) is marked in every reachable marking. If we consecutively number the places in supp(i), we can code the marking of these places by listing the number of the unique marked places. This way, we can code n places with just $\log n$ bits instead of n bits. The resulting BDD is more shallow than the original BDD. Shallower BDDs also tend to be smaller (there are less opportunities to branch).

The ideas of BDD based model checking can be transferred to Petri nets that are not safe. In principle, the marking of a non-safe Petri net can be represented as a bit vector as well. Since bit vectors in a BDD have uniform length, we need an a priori known bound for the marking of a place, so that a fixed number of bits can represent arbitrary markings. Since propositional formulas working on binary coded natural numbers are more complex than the formulas shown above, and since a bound for the number of tokens on places is not always known a priori, BDD technology has been adapted to cope with vectors of natural numbers rather than vectors of Booleans. In the adapted data structures [82,107], a vertex in the decision tree represents a place p and has multiple outgoing edges that stand for the possible values of $m(p)$. The various proposals differ in the details of implementing that idea.

7.2 SAT Based Model Checking

In SAT based model checking [9], we represent a set of paths by a propositional formula. The formula can be instrumented such that the formula is satisfied if and only if there is an LTL counterexample among the represented paths.

In Sect. 5.1 we learned that, for every violated LTL formula, there exists a counterexample where we proceed from m_0 to a marking m^* in some SCC C that contains sufficiently many acceptance states. Then we travel from m^* through all elements in C and return to m^*. In total, the path consists of n markings $m_1 \dots m_\ell$ such that $m_1 = m_0$ and m_ℓ has a successor m_r for $1 \leq r \leq \ell$. m_r is the marking m^* mentioned above. We can build a propositional formula that represents all such paths for fixed values of ℓ (length) and r (reentry). SAT based model checking repeatedly constructs such formulas for all combinations of ℓ and r until either a counterexample has been found, or we exceed some time or memory limit. The method is therefore inherently incomplete but may be a valuable member of a verification portfolio where we run complete and incomplete methods concurrently.

For a safe net with places $p_1, \dots, p_n$, the propositional formula ξ_ℓ^r for representing a path with ℓ markings and reentry point r works on variables p_i^j where i ranges between 1 and n while j ranges between 1 and ℓ. The idea is that a satsifying assignment of ξ_ℓ^r represents a path where p_i^j is true if and only if $m_j(p_i)$ is marked. To this end, we employ the formula θ that we used in Sect. 7.1 for creating the transition relation BDD_T. We get

$$\xi_\ell^r = \bigwedge_{m_0(p_i)=1} p_i^1 \wedge \theta(p_1^1, \dots, p_n^1, p_1^2, \dots, p_n^2) \wedge \theta(p_1^2, \dots, p_n^2, p_1^3, \dots, p_n^3) \wedge$$

$$\dots \wedge \theta(p_1^{\ell-1}, \dots, p_n^{\ell-1}, p_1^\ell, \dots, p_n^\ell) \wedge \theta(p_1^\ell, \dots, p_n^\ell, p_1^r, \dots, p_n^r)$$

For LTL model checking, we combine ξ_ℓ^r with a formula that corresponds to some LTL formula ϕ . Temporal operators in LTL talk about suffixes of a given path. To this end, we introduce another index s. The meaning of propositional formula $\lambda_\ell^r(\phi, s)$ is that LTL formula ϕ is valid in the suffix starting at marking m_s of a path with length ℓ and reentry point r. To demonstrate the principle, we just show the propositional formula $\lambda_\ell^r(\psi U \chi, s)$. It says that there must be a suffix starting at m_a beyond s that satisfies χ, and all suffixes starting at m_b between m_s and m_a satisfy ψ. The trick is that, if $s > r$, a can also be between r and s since we return to that part when entering the next round of the cycle.

$$\lambda_\ell^r(\psi U \chi, s) = \bigvee_{\min(s,r) \leq a \leq \ell} \left(\lambda_\ell^r(\chi, a) \wedge \bigwedge_{\substack{\text{if } s <= a \text{ then } s \leq b < a \\ \text{else } (s \leq b \leq \ell \text{or } r \leq b < a)}} \lambda_\ell^r(\psi, b) \right)$$

For other operators, similar formulas can be derived accordingly. We finally get:

Theorem 4 (SAT based model checking). *If, for some value ℓ and some value r $(r \leq l)$, the formula $\xi_\ell^r \wedge \lambda_\ell^r(\neg\phi, 1)$ is satisfiable then ϕ does not hold in the given Petri net.*

The formulas that are generated during SAT based model checking can easily grow big but contemporary SAT checkers [50] can handle quite big formulas.

The paper [90] uses an interesting alternative formula to represent the transition relation.

For Petri nets that are not safe, we can again use the binary encoding of numbers for representing the $m_i(p_j)$ with more than one Boolean variable. However, we run into similar problems as for BDD based model checking, concerning the arithmetics that is inherent to adding or removing tokens, and to compare a marking with a number. To solve this problem, [127] successfully represented the marking of a place using a unary encoding. If a place can carry up to b tokens, we use variables $x_0, \ldots, x_b$ for representing the marking such that $x_0, \ldots, x_k$ are supposed to be true to represent $m(p) = k$ while $x_{k+1}, \ldots, x_b$ are false. When we formulate activation of a transition t, we only need to refer to $x_{W([p,t])}$ to see whether p is sufficiently marked. If the occurrence of t adds k tokens to p, we can relate the current marking of p (using Boolean variables $x_1, \ldots, x_b$) and the successor marking of p (using variables $x'_1, \ldots, x'_n$) using the formula

$$\bigwedge_{0 \leq i \leq k} x'_i \wedge \bigwedge_{k+1 \leq i \leq b} x'_i \iff x_{i-k}$$

Removal of k tokens works similarly. If no bounds for a place p are known, we can gradually increase b since we can deduce a maximum number of tokens from the initial marking and the index of the marking in the path. The resulting formulas can be better digested by a SAT checker than formulas where the marking of places is represented based on binary encoding.

7.3 The Branching Prefix

A transition sequence $t_1 \ldots t_n$ of a safe Petri net an be represented in an occurrence net [88]. An occurrence net is an acyclic net where places (called *condition* in the occurrence net) correspond to tokens and transitions (called *events*) correspond to particular occurrences of a transition of the original net. Conditions are labeled with places of the original net and events are labeled with transitions of the original net.

To translate $m_0 \xrightarrow{t_1} m_1 \ldots m_{n-1} \xrightarrow{t_n} m_n$ into an occurrence net, we first add one condition with label p for every place p with $m_0(p) = 1$. We turn that into an inductive assumption saying that, before processing t_i, there is a condition c such that c is labeled with p and has no outgoing arc if and only if $m_{i-1}(p) = 1$. Moreover, there is never more than one condition with label p and no outgoing arcs. To add t_i in that situation, we add a distinct event e and label it with t_i. For every $p \in \bullet t_i$, we draw an arc to e from the unique condition c that is labeled with p and has no outgoing arc yet. For every place p in $t\bullet$, we add a new condition c' with label p and draw an arc from e to c. This way, the inductive assumption is re-established.

There is a net morphism (see Sect. 2.2) from the resulting occurrence net into the original net. Moreover, an occurrence net defines a partial order $\preceq$ on the contained events: $e_1 \preceq e_2$ if there is a path from e_1 to e_2 in the occurrence net. Several total orders can be compatible with this partial order. For one of these total orders, replacing the events with their labels, yields the original transition sequence $t_1 \ldots t_n$. Other total orders correspond to transition sequences that can be obtain by swapping concurrently enabled transitions. That is, a single occurrence net represents a set of transitions sequences.

It is easy to adapt the concept of occurrence nets to infinite transition sequences. If two occurrence nets share a common prefix, these prefixes can be merged. If we merge *all* occurrence nets that can be created for a given safe Petri net, we end up in the unique *branching process* [31]. It has been observed that we can identify *cutoffs* in the branching process. A cutoff represents a situation that is equivalent to a situation that we have seen earlier in the process. If we terminate the construction of a branch of the branching process whenever we detect a cutoff, we obtain a finite data structure, the *branching prefix* [80] that contains sufficient information to perform model checking on it. We skip the details and refer to the textbook [32]. Figure 20 shows the branching prefix of the three dinging philosophers net (Fig. 8, page 27). One of the contained occurrence nets is highlighted. It corresponds to the transition sequence tl.2 tr.2 rl.2 rr.2 tl.1 tr.1rl.1 rr.1 but also to other sequences, e.g. tl.1 tl.2 tr.2 rl.2 tr.1 rl.1 rr.1 rr.2.

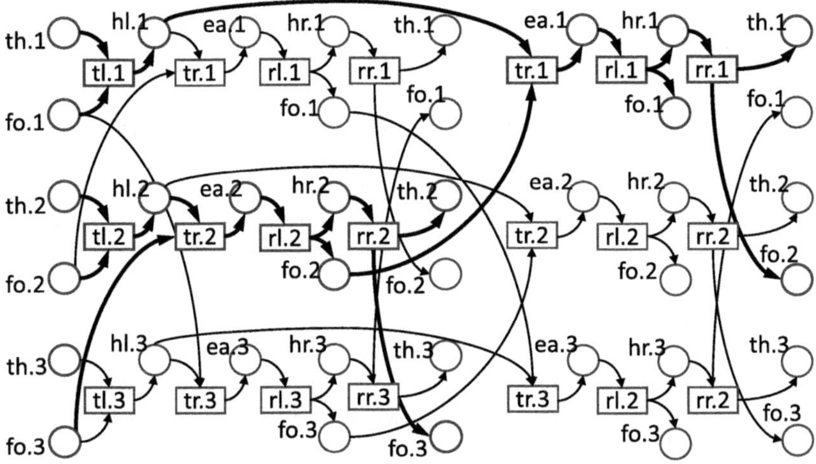

Fig. 20. A branching prefix.

An occurrence net can be constructed for non-safe Petri nets as well. In the simplest version, we have $m_i(p)$ conditions with label p and no outgoing arc at stage i of the construction. In this version, a branching process distinguishes a run where t consumes a token that has been produced by t_1 from a run that consumes a token produced by t_2 instead, so a single transition sequence my correspond to several occurrence nets. This may or may not be desired. There are attempts to create occurrence nets that are unique for a given transition sequence [117]. These approaches have some pros and cons that are outside the scope of this paper.

7.4 Using the State Equation

We already used the state equation in Sect. 3.2 for the static analysis of atomic propositions α. The techniques studied there are already sufficient for proving $AG\alpha$ to be true if α could be shown to be invariantly true. Likewise, $EF\alpha$ is false if α is invariantly false. The approach can be slightly extended. For instance, formula $EF(\alpha \wedge EF\beta)$ is false if the following integer linear program (ILP) is infeasible.

$$m_0 + C \cdot \underline{x} = \underline{y}, \alpha(\underline{y}), \underline{y} + C \cdot \underline{z} = \underline{u}, \beta(\underline{u}), \underline{x} \geq \underline{0}, \underline{y} \geq \underline{0}, \underline{z} \geq \underline{0}, \underline{u} \geq \underline{0}$$

In [73], the state equation approach is studied for a few more formulas.

We can squeeze more information out of the state equation. If the ILP is feasible, we obtain the Parikh vector of a transition sequence. If that transition sequence can be arranged into an executable firing sequence, we obtain a witness if the formula is existentially quantified, and we can assert that the formula is true. If the formula is universally quantified, the sequence is a counterexample and we can state that the formula is false. For finding a sequence, we do not need to try all permutations of transitions in the support of the Parikh vector. The number of permutations can be drastically reduced by employing the stubborn set method.

It may occur that the Parikh vector returned by the state equation cannot be transformed into an executable transition sequence. For such a case, [52,53,124] propose to add constraints to the ILP such that the spurious solution is excluded. This way, the process of solving an ILP and trying to realize the solution can be iterated, increasing the probability to terminate with a result.

7.5 Concluding Remarks

Symbolic model checking enhances the portfolio of available methods for model checking. There are problems where explicit model checking performs better, and there are problems where some symbolic approach performs better. It is not easy to predict the best method beforehand, so model checking is in the end a process of trial and error. Fortunately, model checking typically does not suffer from strict time restrictions (with the exception of contests). Being able to prove correctness of a system, or finding a severe error, is such a great achievement that we can easily invest several days for getting an answer. It is unlikely that model checking runs longer than that since all methods are extremely memory consuming, so an unsuccessful run will ultimately be aborted due to memory overflow.

8 Conclusion

We have seen that model checking for Petri nets is a complex endeavor. We are given net and a formula. Both inputs can be simplified by several approaches. Then, there is a rich portfolio of methods for solving the model checking problem. Model checking tools may have a sophisticated portfolio manager to keep track of the subproblems to be solved and the methods to be used, and handle the assigned memory and time ressources [53]. Figure 21 illustrates the complete story.

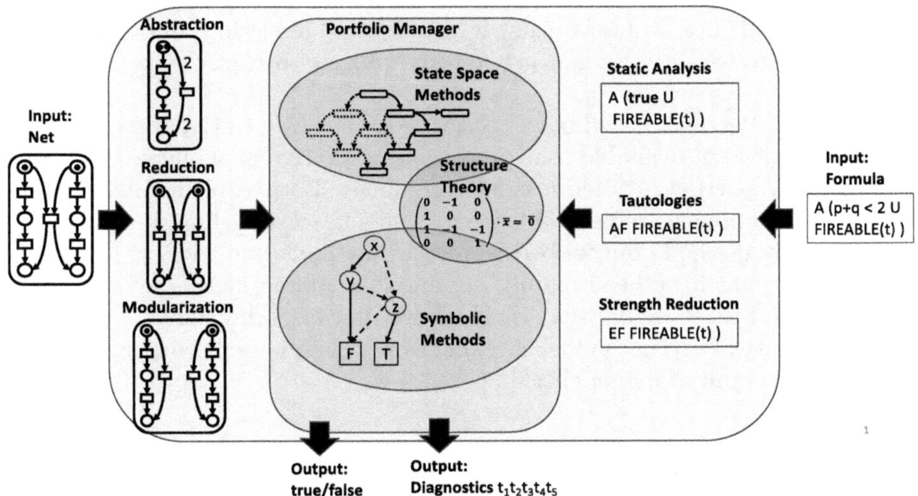

Fig. 21. The big picture of a Petri net model checker.

Several techniques such as the stubborn set method, the symmetry method, BDD based model checking, or SAT based model checking, are not limited to the use of Petri nets (some of them have even been invented for other formalisms and were then adapted to Petri nets). However, we can apply Petri net specific technology (the state equation, invariants, siphons, traps) everywhere in the process of model checking. In addition, Petri net specific features lead to implementations that tend to be easier than for other formalisms. There are three Petri net specific features that we would like to mention.

First, Petri nets have the property of *monotonicity*. If a transition sequence w is fireable in marking m, and we have $m' > m$, then w is executable in m' as well. Monotonicity is relevant for the concepts of siphons and traps, and simplifies the computation of stubborn sets, compared to other modeling formalisms. Monotonicity is also crucial for *coverability graphs.* A coverability graph [36,64,114] is a finite abstraction of the infinite reachability graph of an unbounded net and has some capabilities for model checking [97].

Second, *linearity* is a defining feature of Petri nets. Linearity means that the effect of a transition occurrence can be represented as the addition of the transition's effect vector. This way, linearity is crucial for the state equation and place invariants. It helps us to shorten the representation of markings, and it permits easy backtracking in depth-first search. With the help of linearity, we can determine a progress measure for the sweep-line method. Linearity is also beneficial for the stubborn set method. When we re-arrange the order of transitions, the final marking is not altered. For other formalisms, this is not guaranteed, so the stubborn set method needs to take additional precautions.

Third, Petri nets enjoy an explicit representation of *locality*. Every transition depends on, and effects, only the places in its immediate neighborhood. Locality helps us to find nice stubborn sets, it enables net reduction and modularization. Thanks to locality, we can use automorphisms to capture the concept of symmetry.

The yearly Petri net based *model checking contest* (MCC, [1]) gives a comprehensive overview on available tools and their respective capabilities. The tools differ in their portfolio of verification techniques. Both explicit and symbolic verification techniques are used. There exist nets in the benchmark of the MCC where explicit methods outperform symbolic methods and vice versa. Recent performance gains have been mainly obtained by adding methods for simplifying the net and the formula, that is, Petri net specific technology.

Consequently, Petri net model checking is more and more becoming a distinct dialect in the realm of model checking.

References

1. Amat, N., et al.: Behind the scene of the model checking contest, analysis of results from 2018 to 2023. In: Beyer, D., Hartmanns, A., Kordon, F. (eds.) TOOLympics Challenge 2023, pp. 52–89. Springer, Cham (2025). https://doi.org/10.1007/978-3-031-67695-6_3
2. Amparore, E.G., Donatelli, S., Gallà, F.: A CTL* model checker for petri nets. In: Janicki, R., Sidorova, N., Chatain, T. (eds.) PETRI NETS 2020. LNCS, vol. 12152, pp. 403–413. Springer, Cham (2020). https://doi.org/10.1007/978-3-030-51831-8_21
3. Barnat, J., Brim, L., Černá, I.: Cluster-based LTL model checking of large systems. In: de Boer, F.S., Bonsangue, M.M., Graf, S., de Roever, W.-P. (eds.) FMCO 2005. LNCS, vol. 4111, pp. 259–279. Springer, Heidelberg (2006). https://doi.org/10.1007/11804192_13
4. Barnat, J., Chaloupka, J., van de Pol, J.: Improved distributed algorithms for SCC decomposition. In: Cerná, I., Haverkort, B.R. (eds.) Proceedings of the 6th International Workshop on Parallel and Distributed Methods in VerifiCation, PDMC@CAV 2007, Berlin, Germany, 8 July 2007. Electronic Notes in Theoretical Computer Science, vol. 198, pp. 63–77. Elsevier (2007)
5. Barnat, J., Moravec, P.: Parallel algorithms for finding SCCs in implicitly given graphs. In: Brim, L., Haverkort, B., Leucker, M., van de Pol, J. (eds.) FMICS 2006. LNCS, vol. 4346, pp. 316–330. Springer, Heidelberg (2007). https://doi.org/10.1007/978-3-540-70952-7_22

6. Berthelot, G., Roucairol, G.: Reduction of petri-nets. In: Mazurkiewicz, A. (ed.) MFCS 1976. LNCS, vol. 45, pp. 202–209. Springer, Heidelberg (1976). https://doi.org/10.1007/3-540-07854-1_175
7. Best, E., Devillers, R., Hall, J.G.: The box calculus: a new causal algebra with multi-label communication. In: Rozenberg, G. (ed.) Advances in Petri Nets 1992. LNCS, vol. 609, pp. 21–69. Springer, Heidelberg (1992). https://doi.org/10.1007/3-540-55610-9_167
8. Beyer, D., Huisman, M., Kordon, F., Steffen, B.: Toolympics II: competitions on formal methods. Int. J. Softw. Tools Technol. Transf. **23**(6), 879–881 (2021)
9. Biere, A., Cimatti, A., Clarke, E.M., Fujita, M., Zhu, Y.: Symbolic model checking using SAT procedures instead of BDDs. In: Irwin, M.J. (ed.) Proceedings of the 36th Conference on Design Automation, New Orleans, LA, USA, 21–25 June 1999, pp. 317–320. ACM Press (1999)
10. Bønneland, F., Dyhr, J., Jensen, P.G., Johannsen, M., Srba, J.: Simplification of CTL formulae for efficient model checking of petri nets. In: Khomenko, V., Roux, O.H. (eds.) PETRI NETS 2018. LNCS, vol. 10877, pp. 143–163. Springer, Cham (2018). https://doi.org/10.1007/978-3-319-91268-4_8
11. Bønneland, F.M., Dyhr, J., Jensen, P.G., Johannsen, M., Srba, J.: Stubborn versus structural reductions for Petri nets. J. Log. Algebraic Methods Program. **102**, 46–63 (2019)
12. Bryant, R.E.: Symbolic Boolean manipulation with ordered binary-decision diagrams. ACM Comput. Surv. **24**(3), 293–318 (1992)
13. Buchholz, P.: An adaptive decomposition approach for the analysis of stochastic Petri nets. In: 2002 International Conference on Dependable Systems and Networks (DSN 2002), June 23–26 2002, Bethesda, MD, USA, Proceedings, pp. 647–656. IEEE Computer Society (2002)
14. Buchholz, P., Kemper, P.: Efficient computation and representation of large reachability sets for composed automata. Discret. Event Dyn. Syst. **12**(3), 265–286 (2002)
15. Büchi, J.R.: On a decision method in restricted second order arithmetic, pp. 425–435. Springer, New York, NY (1990)
16. Burch, J.R., Clarke, E.M., McMillan, K.L., Dill, D.L., Hwang, L.J.: Symbolic model checking: 10^20 states and beyond. In: Proceedings of the Fifth Annual Symposium on Logic in Computer Science (LICS '90), Philadelphia, Pennsylvania, USA, 4–7 June 1990, pp. 428–439. IEEE Computer Society (1990)
17. Butler, G. (ed.): Fundamental Algorithms for Permutation Groups. LNCS, vol. 559. Springer, Heidelberg (1991). https://doi.org/10.1007/3-540-54955-2
18. Chiola, G., Dutheillet, C., Franceschinis, G., Haddad, S.: A symbolic reachability graph for coloured Petri nets. Theor. Comput. Sci. **176**(1–2), 39–65 (1997)
19. Christensen, S., Kristensen, L.M., Mailund, T.: A sweep-line method for state space exploration. In: Margaria, T., Yi, W. (eds.) TACAS 2001. LNCS, vol. 2031, pp. 450–464. Springer, Heidelberg (2001). https://doi.org/10.1007/3-540-45319-9_31
20. Christensen, S., Petrucci, L.: Modular analysis of Petri nets. Comput. J. **43**(3), 224–242 (2000)
21. Clarke, E.M. Allen Emerson, E., Prasad Sistla, A.: Automatic verification of finite-state concurrent systems using temporal logic specifications. ACM Trans. Program. Lang. Syst. **8**(2), 244–263 (1986)
22. Clarke, E.M., Grumberg, O., Kroening, D., Peled, D.A., Veith, H.: Model Checking, 2nd edn. MIT Press (2018)

23. Clarke, E.M., Henzinger, T.A., Veith, H., Bloem, R. (eds.): Handbook of Model Checking. Springer (2018)
24. Clarke, E.M., Jha, S., Enders, R., Filkorn, T.: Exploiting symmetry in temporal logic model checking. Formal Methods Syst. Des. **9**(1/2), 77–104 (1996)
25. Clarke, E.M., Long, D.E., McMillan, K.L.: Compositional model checking. In: Proceedings of the Fourth Annual Symposium on Logic in Computer Science (LICS 1989), Pacific Grove, California, USA, 5–8 June 1989, pp. 353–362. IEEE Computer Society (1989)
26. de Putter, S., Wijs, A.: Compositional model checking is lively. In: Proença, J., Lumpe, M. (eds.) FACS 2017. LNCS, vol. 10487, pp. 117–136. Springer, Cham (2017). https://doi.org/10.1007/978-3-319-68034-7_7
27. Desel, J.: On abstractions of nets. In: Rozenberg, G. (ed.) ICATPN 1990. LNCS, vol. 524, pp. 78–92. Springer, Heidelberg (1991). https://doi.org/10.1007/BFb0019970
28. Desel, J., Esparza, J.: Free Choice Petri Nets. Cambridge Tracts in Theoretical Computer Science. Cambridge University Press (1995)
29. Duret-Lutz, A., Poitrenaud, D.: SPOT: an extensible model checking library using transition-based generalized büchi automata. In: DeGroot, D., Harrison, P.G., Wijshoff, H.A.G., Segall, Z. (eds.) 12th International Workshop on Modeling, Analysis, and Simulation of Computer and Telecommunication Systems (MASCOTS 2004), 4–8 October 2004, Vollendam, The Netherlands, pp. 76–83. IEEE Computer Society (2004)
30. Enevoldsen, S., Larsen, K.G., Mariegaard, A., Srba, J.: Dependency graphs with applications to verification. Int. J. Softw. Tools Technol. Transfer **22**(5), 635–654 (2020). https://doi.org/10.1007/s10009-020-00578-9
31. Engelfriet, J.: Branching processes of Petri nets. Acta Informatica **28**(6), 575–591 (1991)
32. Esparza, J., Heljanko, K.: Unfoldings - A Partial-Order Approach to Model Checking. Monographs in Theoretical Computer Science. An EATCS Series. Springer (2008)
33. Esparza, J., Melzer, S.: Verification of safety properties using integer programming: beyond the state equation. Formal Methods Syst. Des. **16**(2), 159–189 (2000)
34. Evangelista, S., Kristensen, L.M.: A sweep-line method for büchi automata-based model checking. Fundam. Informaticae **131**(1), 27–53 (2014)
35. Findlow, G.: Obtaining deadlock-preserving skeletons for coloured nets. In: Jensen, K. (ed.) ICATPN 1992. LNCS, vol. 616, pp. 173–192. Springer, Heidelberg (1992). https://doi.org/10.1007/3-540-55676-1_10
36. Finkel, A.: The minimal coverability graph for Petri nets. In: Rozenberg, G. (ed.) ICATPN 1991. LNCS, vol. 674, pp. 210–243. Springer, Heidelberg (1993). https://doi.org/10.1007/3-540-56689-9_45
37. Fleischer, L.K., Hendrickson, B., Pınar, A.: On identifying strongly connected components in parallel. In: Rolim, J. (ed.) IPDPS 2000. LNCS, vol. 1800, pp. 505–511. Springer, Heidelberg (2000). https://doi.org/10.1007/3-540-45591-4_68
38. Francez, N.: Fairness. Texts and Monographs in Computer Science. Springer (1986)
39. Furht, B. (ed.): Huffman Coding, pp. 278–280. Springer US, Boston, MA (2006)
40. Gaede, J., Wallner, S., Wolf, K.: Modular state spaces – a new perspective. In: Kristensen, L.M., van der Werf, J.M. (eds.) Application and Theory of Petri Nets and Concurrency - 45th International Conference, PETRI NETS 2024,

Geneva, Switzerland, 26–28 June 2024, Proceedings. LNCS, vol. 14628, pp. 312–332. Springer (2024)

41. Gaedei, J., Overath, J.-H., Wallner, S.: Automatic modularization of place/transition nets. In: Proceedings of the 2024 International Workshop on Petri Nets and Software Engineering (PNSE 2024) co-located with the 45th International Conference on Application and Theory of Petri Nets and Concurrency (PETRI NETS 2024), 24 June 2024, Geneva, Switzerland, CEUR Workshop Proceedings. CEUR-WS.org (2024)
42. Garavel, H., Lang, F., Mounier, L.: Compositional verification in action. In: Howar, F., Barnat, J. (eds.) FMICS 2018. LNCS, vol. 11119, pp. 189–210. Springer, Cham (2018). https://doi.org/10.1007/978-3-030-00244-2_13
43. Garavel, H., Mateescu, R., Smarandache, I.: Parallel state space construction for model-checking. In: Dwyer, M. (ed.) SPIN 2001. LNCS, vol. 2057, pp. 217–234. Springer, Heidelberg (2001). https://doi.org/10.1007/3-540-45139-0_14
44. Gastin, P., Oddoux, D.: Fast LTL to Büchi automata translation. In: Berry, G., Comon, H., Finkel, A. (eds.) CAV 2001. LNCS, vol. 2102, pp. 53–65. Springer, Heidelberg (2001). https://doi.org/10.1007/3-540-44585-4_6
45. Geldenhuys, J., Valmari, A.: More efficient on-the-fly LTL verification with Tarjan's algorithm. Theor. Comput. Sci. **345**(1), 60–82 (2005)
46. Genrich, H.J.: Predicate/transition nets. In: Brauer, W., Reisig, W., Rozenberg, G. (eds.) Petri Nets: Central Models and Their Properties, Advances in Petri Nets 1986, Part I, Proceedings of an Advanced Course, Bad Honnef, Germany, 8–19 September 1986. LNCS, pp. 207–247. Springer (1986)
47. Gerth, R., Kuiper, R., Peled, D.A., Penczek, W.: A partial order approach to branching time logic model checking. In: Third Israel Symposium on Theory of Computing and Systems, ISTCS 1995, Tel Aviv, Israel, January 4–6, 1995, Proceedings, pp. 130–139. IEEE Computer Society (1995)
48. Gerth, R., Peled, D.A., Vardi, M.Y., Wolper, P.: Simple on-the-fly automatic verification of linear temporal logic. In: Dembinski, P., Sredniawa, M. (eds.) Protocol Specification, Testing and Verification XV, Proceedings of the Fifteenth IFIP WG6.1 International Symposium on Protocol Specification, Testing and Verification, Warsaw, Poland, June 1995. IFIP Conference Proceedings, vol. 38, pp. 3–18. Chapman & Hall (1995)
49. Godefroid, P., Wolper, P.: A partial approach to model checking. Inf. Comput. **110**(2), 305–326 (1994)
50. Gong, W., Zhou, X.: A survey of sat solver, vol. 1836, p. 020059 (2017)
51. Graf, S., Steffen, B.: Compositional minimization of finite state systems. In: Clarke, E.M., Kurshan, R.P. (eds.) CAV 1990. LNCS, vol. 531, pp. 186–196. Springer, Heidelberg (1991). https://doi.org/10.1007/BFb0023732
52. Hajdu, Á., Vörös, A., Bartha, T.: New search strategies for the petri net CEGAR approach. In: Devillers, R., Valmari, A. (eds.) PETRI NETS 2015. LNCS, vol. 9115, pp. 309–328. Springer, Cham (2015). https://doi.org/10.1007/978-3-319-19488-2_16
53. Hajdu, Á., Vörös, A., Bartha, T., Mártonka, Z.: Extensions to the CEGAR approach on Petri nets. Acta Cybern. **21**(3), 401–417 (2014)
54. Harel, D.: Statecharts: a visual formalism for complex systems. Sci. Comput. Program. **8**(3), 231–274 (1987)
55. Hoare, C.A.R.: Communicating sequential processes. Commun. ACM **21**(8), 666–677 (1978)

56. Hojati, R., Krishnan, S.C., Brayton, R.K.: Early quantification and partitioned transition relations. In: 1996 International Conference on Computer Design (ICCD '96), VLSI in Computers and Processors, 7–9 October 1996, Austin, TX, USA, Proceedings, pp. 12–19. IEEE Computer Society (1996)
57. Holzmann, G.J., Bosnacki, D.: Multi-core model checking with SPIN. In: 21th International Parallel and Distributed Processing Symposium (IPDPS 2007), Proceedings, 26–30 March 2007, Long Beach, California, USA, pp. 1–8. IEEE (2007)
58. Huber, P., Jensen, A.M., Jepsen, L.O., Jensen, K.: Towards reachability trees for high-level petri nets. In: Rozenberg, G. (ed.) Advances in Petri Nets 1984. LNCS, vol. 188, pp. 215–233. Springer, Heidelberg (1985). https://doi.org/10.1007/3-540-15204-0_13
59. Jensen, K.: High-level petri nets. In: Pagnoni, A., Rozenberg, G. (eds.) Applications and Theory of Petri Nets, Selected Papers from the 3rd European Workshop on Applications and Theory of Petri Nets, Varenna, Italy, 27–30 September 1982. Informatik-Fachberichte, vol. 66, pp. 166–180. Springer (1982)
60. Jensen, P., Srba, J., Ulrik, N., Virenfeldt, S.: Automata-Driven Partial Order Reduction and Guided Search for LTL Model Checking, pp. 151–173 (2022)
61. Jensen, P.G., Larsen, K.G., Srba, J.: Ptrie: data structure for compressing and storing sets via prefix sharing. In: Van Hung, D., Kapur, D. (eds.) Theoretical Aspects of Computing - ICTAC 2017 - 14th International Colloquium, Hanoi, Vietnam, 23–27 October 2017, Proceedings. LNCS, vol. 10580, pp. 248–265. Springer (2017)
62. Junttila, T.A.: Computational complexity of the place/transition-net symmetry reduction method. J. Univers. Comput. Sci. **7**(4), 307–326 (2001)
63. Junttila, T.A.: New canonical representative marking algorithms for place/transition-nets. In: Cortadella, J., Reisig, W. (eds.) ICATPN 2004. LNCS, vol. 3099, pp. 258–277. Springer, Heidelberg (2004). https://doi.org/10.1007/978-3-540-27793-4_15
64. Karp, R.M., Miller, R.E.: Parallel program schemata. J. Comput. Syst. Sci. **3**(2), 147–195 (1969)
65. Rao Kosaraju, S.: Decidability of reachability in vector addition systems (preliminary version). In: Lewis, H.R., Simons, B.B., Burkhard, W.A., Landweber, L.H. (eds.) Proceedings of the 14th Annual ACM Symposium on Theory of Computing, 5–7 May 1982, San Francisco, California, USA, pp. 267–281. ACM (1982)
66. Kristensen, L.M., Mailund, T.: A generalised sweep-line method for safety properties. In: Eriksson, L.-H., Lindsay, P.A. (eds.) FME 2002. LNCS, vol. 2391, pp. 549–567. Springer, Heidelberg (2002). https://doi.org/10.1007/3-540-45614-7_31
67. Kristensen, L.M., Schmidt, K., Valmari, A.: Question-guided stubborn set methods for state properties. Formal Methods Syst. Des. **29**(3), 215–251 (2006)
68. Larsen, K.G., Larsson, F., Pettersson, P., Yi, W.: Efficient verification of real-time systems: compact data structure and state-space reduction. In: Proceedings of the 18th IEEE Real-Time Systems Symposium (RTSS '97), 3–5 December 1997, San Francisco, CA, USA, pp. 14–24. IEEE Computer Society (1997)
69. Latvala, T., Mäkelä, M.: LTL model checking for modular petri nets. In: Cortadella, J., Reisig, W. (eds.) ICATPN 2004. LNCS, vol. 3099, pp. 298–311. Springer, Heidelberg (2004). https://doi.org/10.1007/978-3-540-27793-4_17
70. Lehmann, D., Pnueli, A., Stavi, J.: Impartiality, justice and fairness: The ethics of concurrent termination. In: Even, S., Kariv, O. (eds.) ICALP 1981. LNCS, vol. 115, pp. 264–277. Springer, Heidelberg (1981). https://doi.org/10.1007/3-540-10843-2_22

71. Lichtenstein, O., Pnueli, A.: Checking that finite state concurrent programs satisfy their linear specification. In: Van Deusen, M.S., Galil, Z., Reid, B.K. (eds.) Conference Record of the Twelfth Annual ACM Symposium on Principles of Programming Languages, New Orleans, Louisiana, USA, January 1985, pp. 97–107. ACM Press (1985)
72. Liebke, T.: Büchi-automata guided partial order reduction for LTL. In: Köhler-Bußmeier, M., Kindler, E., Rölke, H. (eds.) Proceedings of the International Workshop on Petri Nets and Software Engineering co-located with 41st International Conference on Application and Theory of Petri Nets and Concurrency (PETRI NETS 2020), Paris, France, June 24, 2020 (due to COVID-19: virtual conference). CEUR Workshop Proceedings, vol. 2651, pp. 147–166. CEUR-WS.org (2020)
73. Liebke, T., Wolf, K.: Solving E (φuψ) using the CEGAR approach. In: Moldt, D., Kindler, E., Wimmer, M. (eds.) Proceedings of the International Workshop on Petri Nets and Software Engineering (PNSE 2019), co-located with the 40th International Conference on Application and Theory of Petri Nets and Concurrency Petri Nets 2019 and the 19th International Conference on Application of Concurrency to System Design ACSD 2019 and the 1st IEEE International Conference on Process Mining Process Mining 2019, Aachen, Germany, 23–28 June 2019. CEUR Workshop Proceedings, vol. 2424, pp. 47–56. CEUR-WS.org (2019)
74. Liebke, T., Wolf, K.: Taking some burden off an explicit CTL model checker. In: Donatelli, S., Haar, S. (eds.) PETRI NETS 2019. LNCS, vol. 11522, pp. 321–341. Springer, Cham (2019). https://doi.org/10.1007/978-3-030-21571-2_18
75. Lilleskare, A., Kristensen, L.M., Høyland, S.-O.: CTL model checking with the sweep-line state space exploration method. In: 30th Norsk Informatikkonferanse, NIK 2017, Westerdals Oslo ACT, Oslo, Norway, 27–29 November 2017. Bibsys Open Journal Systems, Norway (2017)
76. Liu, X., Smolka, S.A.: Simple linear-time algorithms for minimal fixed points. In: Larsen, K.G., Skyum, S., Winskel, G. (eds.) ICALP 1998. LNCS, vol. 1443, pp. 53–66. Springer, Heidelberg (1998). https://doi.org/10.1007/BFb0055040
77. Lohmann, N.: A feature-complete Petri net semantics for WS-BPEL 2.0. In: Dumas, M., Heckel, R. (eds.) Web Services and Formal Methods, 4th International Workshop, WS-FM 2007, Brisbane, Australia, 28–29 September 2007. Proceedings. LNCS, vol. 4937, pp. 77–91. Springer (2007)
78. Manna, Z., Pnueli, A.: The Temporal Logic of Reactive and Concurrent Systems - Specification. Springer (1992)
79. Mayr, E.W.: An algorithm for the general Petri net reachability problem. SIAM J. Comput. **13**(3), 441–460 (1984)
80. McMillan, K.L.: Using unfoldings to avoid the state explosion problem in the verification of asynchronous circuits. In: von Bochmann, G., Probst, D.K. (eds.) Computer Aided Verification, Fourth International Workshop, CAV '92, Montreal, Canada, 29 June–1 July 1992, Proceedings. LNCS, vol. 663, pp. 164–177. Springer (1992)
81. Meyer, T.: Parallele Zustandsraumsuche, Bachelor's thesis. Universität Rostock (2018)
82. Michael Miller, D., Drechsler, R.: On the construction of multiple-valued decision diagrams. In: 32nd IEEE International Symposium on Multiple-Valued Logic (ISMVL 2002), 15–18 May 2002, Boston, Massachusetts, USA, pp. 245–253. IEEE Computer Society (2002)
83. Milner, R. (ed.): A Calculus of Communicating Systems. LNCS, vol. 92. Springer, Heidelberg (1980). https://doi.org/10.1007/3-540-10235-3

84. Mostowski, A.W.: Regular expressions for infinite trees and a standard form of automata. In: Skowron, A. (ed.) Computation Theory - Fifth Symposium, Zaborów, Poland, 3–8 December 1984, Proceedings. LNCS, vol. 208, p. 157–168. Springer (1984)
85. Muller, D.E.: Infinite sequences and finite machines. In: 4th Annual Symposium on Switching Circuit Theory and Logical Design, Chicago, Illinois, USA, 28–30 October 1963, pp. 3–16. IEEE Computer Society (1963)
86. Murata, T.: Petri nets: properties, analysis and applications. Proc. IEEE **77**(4), 541–580 (1989)
87. Neele, T., Valmari, A., Willemse, T.A.C.: A detailed account of the inconsistent labelling problem of stutter-preserving partial-order reduction. Log. Methods Comput. Sci. **17**(3) (2021)
88. Nielsen, M., Plotkin, G.D., Winskel, G.: Petri nets, event structures and domains, part I. Theor. Comput. Sci. **13**, 85–108 (1981)
89. Oanea, O., Wimmel, H., Wolf, K.: New algorithms for deciding the siphon-trap property. In: Lilius, J., Penczek, W. (eds.) PETRI NETS 2010. LNCS, vol. 6128, pp. 267–286. Springer, Heidelberg (2010). https://doi.org/10.1007/978-3-642-13675-7_16
90. Ogata, S., Tsuchiya, T., Kikuno, T.: SAT-based verification of safe petri nets. In: Wang, F. (ed.) ATVA 2004. LNCS, vol. 3299, pp. 79–92. Springer, Heidelberg (2004). https://doi.org/10.1007/978-3-540-30476-0_11
91. Padberg, J., Gajewsky, M., Ermel, C.: Rule-based refinement of high-level nets preserving safety properties. In: Astesiano, E. (ed.) FASE 1998. LNCS, vol. 1382, pp. 221–238. Springer, Heidelberg (1998). https://doi.org/10.1007/BFb0053593
92. Peled, D.: All from one, one for all: on model checking using representatives. In: Courcoubetis, C. (ed.) CAV 1993. LNCS, vol. 697, pp. 409–423. Springer, Heidelberg (1993). https://doi.org/10.1007/3-540-56922-7_34
93. Pnueli, A.: The temporal semantics of concurrent programs. In: Kahn, G. (ed.) Semantics of Concurrent Computation. LNCS, vol. 70, pp. 1–20. Springer, Heidelberg (1979). https://doi.org/10.1007/BFb0022460
94. Queille, J.P., Sifakis, J.: Specification and verification of concurrent systems in CESAR. In: Dezani-Ciancaglini, M., Montanari, U. (eds.) Programming 1982. LNCS, vol. 137, pp. 337–351. Springer, Heidelberg (1982). https://doi.org/10.1007/3-540-11494-7_22
95. Rabin, M.O.: Decidability of second-order theories and automata on infinite trees. Trans. Am. Math. Soc. **141**, 1–35 (1969)
96. Ratzer, A.V., et al.: CPN tools for editing, simulating, and analysing coloured petri nets. In: van der Aalst, W.M.P., Best, E. (eds.) ICATPN 2003. LNCS, vol. 2679, pp. 450–462. Springer, Heidelberg (2003). https://doi.org/10.1007/3-540-44919-1_28
97. Schmidt, K.: Model-checking with coverability graphs. Formal Methods Syst. Des. **15**(3), 239–254 (1999)
98. Schmidt, K.: Stubborn sets for standard properties. In: Donatelli, S., Kleijn, J. (eds.) ICATPN 1999. LNCS, vol. 1639, pp. 46–65. Springer, Heidelberg (1999). https://doi.org/10.1007/3-540-48745-X_4
99. Schmidt, K.: How to calculate symmetries of Petri nets. Acta Informatica **36**(7), 545–590 (2000)
100. Schmidt, K.: Integrating low level symmetries into reachability analysis. In: Graf, S., Schwartzbach, M. (eds.) TACAS 2000. LNCS, vol. 1785, pp. 315–330. Springer, Heidelberg (2000). https://doi.org/10.1007/3-540-46419-0_22

101. Schmidt, K.: Using petri net invariants in state space construction. In: Garavel, H., Hatcliff, J. (eds.) TACAS 2003. LNCS, vol. 2619, pp. 473–488. Springer, Heidelberg (2003). https://doi.org/10.1007/3-540-36577-X_35
102. Schmidt, K.: Automated generation of a progress measure for the sweep-line method. In: Jensen, K., Podelski, A. (eds.) TACAS 2004. LNCS, vol. 2988, pp. 192–204. Springer, Heidelberg (2004). https://doi.org/10.1007/978-3-540-24730-2_17
103. Spranger, J.: Combining structural properties and symbolic representation for efficient analysis of Petri nets. In: Proceedings Workshop on Concurrency, Specification, and Programming 1998, Berlin, September 1998). Informatik-Bericht, vol. 110, pp. 236–244. Humboldt University at Berlin (1998)
104. Starke, P.H.: Analyse von Petri-Netz-Modellen. Leitfäden und Monographien der Informatik, Teubner (1990)
105. Stern, U., Dill, D.L.: Parallelizing the mur*phi* verifier. In: Grumberg, O. (ed.) Computer Aided Verification, 9th International Conference, CAV 1997, Haifa, Israel, 22–25 June 1997, Proceedings. LNCS, vol. 1254, pp. 256–278. Springer (1997)
106. Streett, R.S.: Propositional dynamic logic of looping and converse. In: Proceedings of the 13th Annual ACM Symposium on Theory of Computing, 11–13 May 1981, Milwaukee, Wisconsin, USA, pp. 375–383. ACM (1981)
107. Strehl, K., Thiele, L.: Interval diagram techniques for symbolic model checking of Petri nets. In: 1999 Design, Automation and Test in Europe (DATE '99), 9–12 March 1999, Munich, Germany, pp. 756–757. IEEE Computer Society / ACM (1999)
108. Tarjan, R.E.: Depth-first search and linear graph algorithms. SIAM J. Comput. **1**(2), 146–160 (1972)
109. Thierry-Mieg, Y.: Structural reductions revisited. In: Janicki, R., Sidorova, N., Chatain, T. (eds.) PETRI NETS 2020. LNCS, vol. 12152, pp. 303–323. Springer, Cham (2020). https://doi.org/10.1007/978-3-030-51831-8_15
110. Valmari, A.: Stubborn sets for reduced state space generation. In: Rozenberg, G. (ed.) ICATPN 1989. LNCS, vol. 483, pp. 491–515. Springer, Heidelberg (1991). https://doi.org/10.1007/3-540-53863-1_36
111. Valmari, A.: The state explosion problem. In: Reisig, W., Rozenberg, G. (eds.) ACPN 1996. LNCS, vol. 1491, pp. 429–528. Springer, Heidelberg (1998). https://doi.org/10.1007/3-540-65306-6_21
112. Valmari, A.: Stubborn set methods for process algebras. In: Peled, D.A., Pratt, V.R., Holzmann, G.J. (eds.) Partial Order Methods in Verification, Proceedings of a DIMACS Workshop, Princeton, New Jersey, USA, 24–26 July 1996. DIMACS Series in Discrete Mathematics and Theoretical Computer Science, vol. 29, pp. 213–231. DIMACS/AMS (1996)
113. Valmari, A.: Stop it, and be stubborn! ACM Trans. Embed. Comput. Syst. **16**(2), 46:1–46:26 (2017)
114. Valmari, A., Hansen, H.: Old and new algorithms for minimal coverability sets. In: Haddad, S., Pomello, L. (eds.) PETRI NETS 2012. LNCS, vol. 7347, pp. 208–227. Springer, Heidelberg (2012). https://doi.org/10.1007/978-3-642-31131-4_12
115. Valmari, A., Hansen, H.: Stubborn set intuition explained. Trans. Petri Nets Other Model. Concurr. **12**, 140–165 (2017)
116. van Eijk, P., Belinfante, A., Eertink, H., Alblas, H.: The term processor generator *Kimwitu*. In: Brinksma, E. (ed.) TACAS 1997. LNCS, vol. 1217, pp. 96–111. Springer, Heidelberg (1997). https://doi.org/10.1007/BFb0035383

117. van Glabbeek, R.J., Plotkin, G.D.: Configuration structures. In: Proceedings, 10th Annual IEEE Symposium on Logic in Computer Science, San Diego, California, USA, 26–29 June 1995, pp. 199–209. IEEE Computer Society (1995)
118. Vardi, M.Y., Wolper, P.: An automata-theoretic approach to automatic program verification (preliminary report). In: Proceedings of the Symposium on Logic in Computer Science (LICS '86), Cambridge, Massachusetts, USA, 16–18 June 1986, pp. 332–344. IEEE Computer Society (1986)
119. Varpaaniemi, K.: On stubborn sets in the verification of linear time temporal properties. In: Desel, J., Silva, M. (eds.) ICATPN 1998. LNCS, vol. 1420, pp. 124–143. Springer, Heidelberg (1998). https://doi.org/10.1007/3-540-69108-1_8
120. Vautherin, J.: Parallel systems specifications with coloured Petri nets and algebraic specifications. In: Rozenberg, G. (ed.) APN 1986. LNCS, vol. 266, pp. 293–308. Springer, Heidelberg (1987). https://doi.org/10.1007/3-540-18086-9_31
121. Vergauwen, B., Lewi, J.: A linear local model checking algorithm for CTL. In: Best, E. (ed.) CONCUR 1993. LNCS, vol. 715, pp. 447–461. Springer, Heidelberg (1993). https://doi.org/10.1007/3-540-57208-2_31
122. Völzer, H., Varacca, D., Kindler, E.: Defining fairness. In: Abadi, M., de Alfaro, L. (eds.) CONCUR 2005. LNCS, vol. 3653, pp. 458–472. Springer, Heidelberg (2005). https://doi.org/10.1007/11539452_35
123. Wallner, S., Wolf, K.: Skeleton abstraction for universal temporal properties. Fundam. Informaticae **187**(2–4), 245–272 (2022)
124. Wimmel, H., Wolf, K.: Applying CEGAR to the Petri net state equation. Log. Methods Comput. Sci. **8**(3) (2012)
125. Wolf, K.: Petri net model checking with LoLA 2. In: Khomenko, V., Roux, O.H. (eds.) PETRI NETS 2018. LNCS, vol. 10877, pp. 351–362. Springer, Cham (2018). https://doi.org/10.1007/978-3-319-91268-4_18
126. Zaitsev, D.: Composition of Functional Petri Nets, pp. 404–465 (2013)
127. Zech, L.: SAT-basierte Erreichbarkeitsanalyse von Petrinetzen, Bachelor's thesis. Universität Rostock (2021)
128. Zech, L., Wolf, K.: Verifying temporal logic properties in the modular state space. In: Kristensen, L.M., van der Werf, J.M. (eds.) Application and Theory of Petri nets and Concurrency - 45th International Conference, PETRI NETS 2024, Geneva, Switzerland, 26–28 June 2024, Proceedings. LNCS, vol. 14628, pp. 333–354. Springer (2024)

Author Index

F. Kordon et al. (Eds.): *Transactions on Petri Nets and Other Models of Concurrency XVIII*,
LNCTPN 16260, p. 381, 2026.
https://doi.org/10.1007/978-3-662-73305-9

GPSR Compliance

The European Union's (EU) General Product Safety Regulation (GPSR) is a set of rules that requires consumer products to be safe and our obligations to ensure this.

If you have any concerns about our products, you can contact us on ProductSafety@springernature.com

In case Publisher is established outside the EU, the EU authorized representative is:

Springer Nature Customer Service Center GmbH
Europaplatz 3
69115 Heidelberg, Germany

Batch number: 10437367

Printed by Printforce, the Netherlands